ACCA

STUDY TEXT

PAPER F8

AUDIT AND ASSURANCE

BPP Learning Media is an **ACCA Approved Content Provider**. This means we work closely with ACCA to ensure this Study Text contains the information you need to pass your exam.

In this Study Text, which has been reviewed by the **ACCA examination team**, we:

- Highlight the most important elements in the syllabus and the key skills you need
- Signpost how each chapter links to the syllabus and the study guide
- Provide lots of exam focus points demonstrating what is expected of you in the exam
- Emphasise key points in regular fast forward summaries
- Test your knowledge in quick quizzes
- Examine your understanding in our practice question bank
- Reference all the important topics in our full index

BPP's **Practice & Revision Kit** also supports this paper.

FOR EXAMS IN SEPTEMBER 2016, DECEMBER 2016, MARCH 2017 AND JUNE 2017

First edition 2007
Ninth edition February 2016

ISBN 9781 4727 4425 8
(Previous ISBN 9781 4727 2677 3)

e-ISBN 9781 4727 4667 2
(Previous e-ISBN 9781 4727 2755 8)

British Library Cataloguing-in-Publication Data

A catalogue record for this book
is available from the British Library

Published by

BPP Learning Media Ltd
BPP House, Aldine Place
London W12 8AA

www.bpp.com/learningmedia

Printed in the United Kingdom by

Polestar Wheatons
Hennock Road
Marsh Barton
Exeter
EX2 8RP

Your learning materials, published by BPP Learning Media Ltd,
are printed on paper obtained from traceable sustainable sources.

We are grateful to the Association of Chartered Certified Accountants
for permission to reproduce past examination questions. The
suggested solutions in the practice answer bank have been prepared
by BPP Learning Media Ltd, unless otherwise stated.

BPP Learning Media is grateful to the IASB for permission to
reproduce extracts from the International Financial Reporting
Standards including all International Accounting Standards, SIC and
IFRIC Interpretations (the Standards). The Standards together with
their accompanying documents are issued by:

The International Accounting Standards Board (IASB) 30 Cannon
Street, London, EC4M 6XH, United Kingdom. Email: info@ifrs.org
Web: www.ifrs.org

Disclaimer: The IASB, the International Financial Reporting
Standards (IFRS) Foundation, the authors and the publishers do not
accept responsibility for any loss caused by acting or refraining from
acting in reliance on the material in this publication, whether such
loss is caused by negligence or otherwise to the maximum extent
permitted by law.

BPP
LEARNING MEDIA

Contents

Helping you to pass

BPP Learning Media – ACCA Approved Content Provider

As an ACCA **Approved Content Provider**, BPP Learning Media gives you the **opportunity** to use study materials reviewed by the ACCA examination team. By incorporating the examination team's comments and suggestions regarding the depth and breadth of syllabus coverage, the BPP Learning Media Study Text provides excellent, **ACCA-approved** support for your studies.

The PER alert

Before you can qualify as an ACCA member, you have to not only pass all your exams but also fulfil a three year **practical experience requirement** (PER). To help you to recognise areas of the syllabus that you might be able to apply in the workplace to achieve different performance objectives, we have introduced the '**PER alert**' feature. You will find this feature throughout the Study Text to remind you that what you are **learning to pass** your ACCA exams is **equally useful to the fulfilment of the PER requirement**.

Your achievement of the PER should now be recorded in your online *My Experience* record.

Tackling studying

Studying can be a daunting prospect, particularly when you have lots of other commitments. The **different features** of the Study Text, the **purposes** of which are explained fully on the **Chapter features** page, will help you whilst studying and improve your chances of **exam success**.

Developing exam awareness

Our Study Texts are completely **focused** on helping you pass your exam.

Our advice on **Studying F8** outlines the **content** of the paper, the **necessary skills** you are expected to be able to demonstrate and any **brought forward knowledge** you are expected to have.

Exam focus points are included within the chapters to highlight when and how specific topics were examined, or how they might be examined in the future.

Using the syllabus and study guide

You can find the syllabus and study guide on page xii-xxiv of this Study Text.

Testing what you can do

Testing yourself helps you develop the skills you need to pass the exam and also confirms that you can recall what you have learnt.

We include **Questions** – lots of them – both within chapters and in the **Practice Question Bank**, as well as **Quick Quizzes** at the end of each chapter to test your knowledge of the chapter content.

Chapter features

Each chapter contains a number of helpful features to guide you through each topic.

Topic list

Topic list	Syllabus reference

What you will be studying in this chapter and the relevant section numbers, together with ACCA syllabus references.

Introduction

Puts the chapter content in the context of the syllabus as a whole.

Study Guide

Links the chapter content with ACCA guidance.

Exam Guide

Highlights how examinable the chapter content is likely to be and the ways in which it could be examined.

Knowledge brought forward from earlier studies

What you are assumed to know from previous studies/exams.

FAST FORWARD

Summarises the content of main chapter headings, allowing you to preview and review each section easily.

Examples

Demonstrate how to apply key knowledge and techniques.

Key terms

Definitions of important concepts that can often earn you easy marks in exams.

Exam focus points

When and how specific topics were examined, or how they may be examined in the future.

Formula to learn

Formulae that are not given in the exam but which have to be learnt.

PER alert

Gives you a useful indication of syllabus areas that closely relate to performance objectives in your Practical Experience Requirement (PER).

Question

Gives you essential practice of techniques covered in the chapter.

Case Study

Real world examples of theories and techniques.

Chapter Roundup

A full list of the Fast Forwards included in the chapter, providing an easy source of review.

Quick Quiz

A quick test of your knowledge of the main topics in the chapter.

Practice Question Bank

Found at the back of the Study Text with more comprehensive chapter questions. Cross referenced for easy navigation.

Studying F8

The F8 Audit and Assurance exam tests students' knowledge of auditing and assurance theory but also, very importantly, their ability to apply that knowledge to scenarios that they might well come across in their auditing careers.

The examination team's approach interview is available on the F8 area of the ACCA website, along with an examining team analysis interview looking at student performance in various exam sittings, which highlights how students can improve their performance.

All questions on this paper are **compulsory** so any topic from across the syllabus could be examined. As stated above, it is essential that students possess both **knowledge** of auditing and assurance and the ability to **apply that knowledge** to situations that could arise in real life.

1 What F8 is about

The purpose of the F8 syllabus is to develop **knowledge and understanding** of the process of carrying out the assurance engagement and its **application** in the context of the professional regulatory framework.

The syllabus is divided into **five** main sections:

(a) **Audit framework and regulation**

The syllabus introduces the concept of assurance engagements, such as the external audit and the different levels of assurance that can be provided. You need to understand the **purpose** of an external audit and the respective **roles** of auditors and management. This part of the syllabus also explains the importance of good **corporate governance** within an entity. The **regulatory framework** is also explained, as well as the key area of **professional ethics**.

Also in the context of the audit framework, we explain the nature of internal audit and describe its role as part of overall **performance management** and good **corporate governance** within an entity. It is essential that you understand the differences between internal and external audit at this stage.

(b) **Planning and risk assessment**

Planning and risk assessment are key stages of the external audit because it is the information and knowledge gained at this time that determine the audit approach to take. We also develop further the concept of **materiality** which was introduced briefly in the first part of the syllabus.

(c) **Internal control**

In this part of the syllabus you need to be able to describe and evaluate information systems and **internal controls** to identify and communicate **control risks** and their potential consequences to the entity's management, making appropriate recommendations to mitigate those risks. We cover key areas of purchases, sales, payroll, inventory, cash and non-current assets.

(d) **Audit evidence**

Audit conclusions need to be supported by **sufficient** and **appropriate** audit evidence. This area of the syllabus assesses the **reliability** of various types and sources of audit evidence and also examines in detail the audit of specific items (non-current assets, inventory, receivables, bank and cash and payables). We also look at the special considerations for the audit of not-for-profit organisations such as charities, which could come up in a scenario-based question.

(e) **Review and reporting**

Towards the end of an external audit, the auditor needs to consider the concept of **going concern** and **subsequent events** which could impact on the financial statements. We also look at the audit evidence provided by **written representations from management** and consider the impact of any **uncorrected misstatements** on the accounts.

This section concludes on the important topic of **audit reporting**. The outcome of the external audit is the **audit report** which sets out the **auditor's opinion** on the financial statements. This section of the syllabus looks at the various types of audit report that can be issued and what each of them means. It also looks at **reports to management**, which are a by-product of the audit but nevertheless very important for highlighting deficiencies in internal control to management.

2 What skills are required?

F8 builds on the knowledge and understanding gained from Paper F3 *Financial Accounting*.

You must possess good technical knowledge of audit and financial reporting but one of the key skills you will need is to be able to **apply** your knowledge to the question.

Section A of the exam will consist of multiple choice questions. These questions can cover any part of the syllabus, so it is important to gain a precise knowledge of each of the syllabus areas.

Section B of the exam will comprise four 10-mark written questions and two 20-mark questions. It is important to read the question requirements carefully and make sure that you **answer the question set**.

Another important skill you will need is to be able to **explain key ideas**, **techniques or approaches**. Explaining means providing simple definitions and including the reasons why these approaches have been developed. Your explanations need to be clearly focused on the particular scenario in the question.

3 How to improve your chances of passing

- There is no choice in this paper; all questions have to be answered. You must therefore study the **entire syllabus**; there are no shortcuts.

- The first section of the paper consists of 15 multiple choice questions which are worth 2 marks each. These will inevitably cover a wide range of areas within the syllabus.

- Practising questions under timed conditions is essential. BPP's **Practice & Revision Kit** contains questions on all areas of the syllabus.

- Questions will be based on simple scenarios, so answers must be **focused** and **specific** to the organisation.

- **Answer plans** will help you to focus on the requirements of the question and enable you to manage your time effectively.

- **Answer all parts** of the question. Even if you cannot do all of the calculation elements, you will still be able to gain marks in the discussion parts.

- Make sure your answers focus on **practical applications of management accounting**, common sense is essential!

- Keep an eye out for **articles**, as the **examination team** will use *Student Accountant* to communicate with students.

- Read journals etc to pick up on ways in which real organisations apply management accounting and think about your own organisation if that is relevant.

4 Brought forward knowledge

The F8 syllabus assumes knowledge brought forward from F3 *Financial Accounting*. It's important to be comfortable with your financial reporting studies because such aspects are likely to come up in scenario-based questions, such as subsequent events. ACCA therefore recommends that you sit papers in order so that you have the knowledge from Paper F7 *Financial Reporting* which will also be an advantage when taking Paper F8. However, please note that you do **not** have to have passed F7 in order to sit F8.

5 Answering questions

5.1 Analysing question requirements

It's particularly important to **consider the question requirements carefully** to make sure you understand exactly what the question is asking, and whether each question part has to be answered in the **context of the scenario** or is more general. You also need to be sure that you understand all the **tasks** that the question is asking you to perform.

Remember that every word will be important. If for example you are asked to:

'Explain the importance of carrying out a risk assessment at the planning stage of the statutory audit of Company X', then you would explain that:

- A risk assessment carried out under the ISAs helps the auditor to identify the areas that are susceptible to material misstatement.

- The risk assessment forms a basis for designing or performing further audit procedures.

You would **not** identify all the audit risks arising in Company X.

5.2 Understanding the question verbs

Important!

> The examination team will use the question verbs very deliberately to signal what they require.

Verbs that are likely to be frequently used in this exam are listed below, together with their intellectual levels and guidance on their meaning.

Intellectual level		
1	**Define**	Give the meaning of
1	**Explain**	Make clear
1	**Identify**	Recognise or select
1	**Describe**	Give the key features
2	**Distinguish**	Define two different terms, viewpoints or concepts on the basis of the differences between them
2	**Compare and contrast**	Explain the similarities and differences between two different terms, viewpoints or concepts
2	**Contrast**	Explain the differences between two different terms, viewpoints or concepts
2	**Analyse**	Give reasons for the current situation or what has happened
3	**Assess**	Determine the strengths/weaknesses/importance/ significance/ability to contribute
3	**Examine**	Critically review in detail
3	**Discuss**	Examine by using arguments for and against
3	**Explore**	Examine or discuss in a wide-ranging manner
3	**Criticise**	Present the weaknesses of/problems with the actions taken or viewpoint expressed, supported by evidence
3	**Evaluate/critically evaluate**	Determine the value of in the light of the arguments for and against (critically evaluate means weighting the answer towards criticisms/arguments against)
3	**Construct the case**	Present the arguments in favour or against, supported by evidence
3	**Recommend**	Advise the appropriate actions to pursue in terms the recipient will understand

A lower level verb such as define will require a more **descriptive answer**. A higher level verb such as evaluate will require a more **applied, critical answer**.

5.3 Analysing question scenarios

When reading through the scenario you need to think widely about how the scenario relates to the underlying themes of the syllabus, and also important content from whatever areas of the syllabus the question covers.

(a)   **Ethics**

In questions on **ethics**, you are likely to be looking out for **ethical threats** in the current arrangements, and trying to **recommend** appropriate responses (for example, ways to reduce the threats to an acceptable level) that are line with ethical codes.

(b)   **Internal control**

With **internal control** questions, you are most likely to be interested in the **deficiencies** in the internal control system, and the **implications** of the deficiencies. From here, you may need to either provide **recommendations** to management on how to eliminate the deficiencies, or consider the **audit risks** arising and suggest **audit procedures** in response to the deficiencies.

(c)   **Audit procedures**

If you are asked to suggest **tests of controls** or **substantive procedures** relating to a particular account balance, transaction or event, first identify the relevant financial statement **assertion**. Look in the scenario for potential sources of **audit evidence**. You should call on your knowledge of the standard audit procedures to apply, but always make sure that the procedures you suggest are **relevant** to the scenario.

(d)   **Financial analysis**

Where a question requires you to perform financial analysis and calculate **ratios**, read the scenario first for any **clues** as to the kind of overarching issue that is affecting the company. These clues may enable you to choose the **relevant ratios** to calculate. Always keep in mind what the ratios mean: remember what figures make up each ratio, so as to identify possible reasons for **fluctuations**/sources of **misstatement**.

(e)   **Modified audit opinions**

If you are presented with uncorrected misstatements or events which may have an impact on the auditor's report, first consider how **material** the misstatement or event is in the context of the financial statements as a whole. You will need to take into account the **nature of the company's business**, as well as any **quantitative measures** given (assets, revenue or profit) to make this assessment. It will not suffice to identify the appropriate audit opinion – you must **justify** it.

The exam paper

Format of the paper

From September 2016, the exam is 3 hours and 15 minutes long. The exam paper is divided into two sections.

Section A consists of 3 mini case scenario-based multiple choice questions of 10 marks each. 5 multiple choice questions worth 2 marks each will be related to each scenario. The questions in this section will be selected from the entire syllabus.

Section B consists of one constructive response question of 30 marks, and 2 constructive response questions of 20 marks. The questions in this section will focus on the following syllabus areas, but a minority of marks can be drawn from any other parts of the syllabus:

- Planning and risk assessment (syllabus area B)
- Internal control (syllabus area C)
- Audit evidence (syllabus area D)

All questions are compulsory.

Computer Based Examination

ACCA have announced that they intend to commence the launch of computer based exams (CBEs) for F5–F9 towards the end of 2016. At the time of going to print, the exact details had not been confirmed. Paper based examinations will be run in parallel while the CBEs are phased in and BPP materials have been designed to support you, whichever exam option you choose.

Syllabus and study guide

The F8 syllabus and Study Guide can be found below.

Audit and Assurance (F8) September 2016 to June 2017

This syllabus and study guide is designed to help with planning study and to provide detailed information on what could be assessed in any examination session.

THE STRUCTURE OF THE SYLLABUS AND STUDY GUIDE

Relational diagram of paper with other papers

This diagram shows direct and indirect links between this paper and other papers preceding or following it. Some papers are directly underpinned by other papers such as Advanced Performance Management by Performance Management. These links are shown as solid line arrows. Other papers only have indirect relationships with each other such as links existing between the accounting and auditing papers. The links between these are shown as dotted line arrows. This diagram indicates where you are expected to have underpinning knowledge and where it would be useful to review previous learning before undertaking study.

Overall aim of the syllabus

This explains briefly the overall objective of the paper and indicates in the broadest sense the capabilities to be developed within the paper.

Main capabilities

This paper's aim is broken down into several main capabilities which divide the syllabus and study guide into discrete sections.

Relational diagram of the main capabilities

This diagram illustrates the flows and links between the main capabilities (sections) of the syllabus and should be used as an aid to planning teaching and learning in a structured way.

Syllabus rationale

This is a narrative explaining how the syllabus is structured and how the main capabilities are linked. The rationale also explains in further detail what the examination intends to assess and why.

Detailed syllabus

This shows the breakdown of the main capabilities (sections) of the syllabus into subject areas. This is the blueprint for the detailed study guide.

Approach to examining the syllabus

This section briefly explains the structure of the examination and how it is assessed.

Study Guide

This is the main document that students, learning and content providers should use as the basis of their studies, instruction and materials. Examinations will be based on the detail of the study guide which comprehensively identifies what could be assessed in any examination session. The study guide is a precise reflection and breakdown of the syllabus. It is divided into sections based on the main capabilities identified in the syllabus. These sections are divided into subject areas which relate to the sub-capabilities included in the detailed syllabus. Subject areas are broken down into sub-headings which describe the detailed outcomes that could be assessed in examinations. These outcomes are described using verbs indicating what exams may require students to demonstrate, and the broad intellectual level at which these may need to be demonstrated (*see intellectual levels below).

INTELLECTUAL LEVELS

The syllabus is designed to progressively broaden and deepen the knowledge, skills and professional values demonstrated by the student on their way through the qualification.

The specific capabilities within the detailed syllabuses and study guides are assessed at one of three intellectual or cognitive levels:

Level 1: Knowledge and comprehension

Level 2: Application and analysis
Level 3: Synthesis and evaluation

Very broadly, these intellectual levels relate to the three cognitive levels at which the Knowledge module, the Skills module and the Professional level are assessed.

Each subject area in the detailed study guide included in this document is given a 1, 2, or 3 superscript, denoting intellectual level, marked at the end of each relevant line. This gives an indication of the intellectual depth at which an area could be assessed within the examination. However, while level 1 broadly equates with the Knowledge module, level 2 equates to the Skills module and level 3 to the Professional level, some lower level skills can continue to be assessed as the student progresses through each module and level. This reflects that at each stage of study there will be a requirement to broaden, as well as deepen capabilities. It is also possible that occasionally some higher level capabilities may be assessed at lower levels.

LEARNING HOURS AND EDUCATION RECOGNITION

The ACCA qualification does not prescribe or recommend any particular number of learning hours for examinations because study and learning patterns and styles vary greatly between people and organisations. This also recognises the wide diversity of personal, professional and educational circumstances in which ACCA students find themselves.

As a member of the International Federation of Accountants, ACCA seeks to enhance the education recognition of its qualification on both national and international education frameworks, and with educational authorities and partners globally. In doing so, ACCA aims to ensure that its qualifications are recognized and valued by governments, regulatory authorities and employers across all sectors. To this end, ACCA qualifications are currently recognized on the education frameworks in several countries. Please refer to your national education framework regulator for further information.

Each syllabus contains between 23 and 35 main subject area headings depending on the nature of the subject and how these areas have been broken down.

GUIDE TO EXAM STRUCTURE

The structure of examinations varies within and between modules and levels.

The Fundamentals level examinations contain 100% compulsory questions to encourage candidates to study across the breadth of each syllabus.

The Knowledge module is assessed by equivalent two-hour paper based and computer based examinations.

The Skills module examinations F5-F9 are paper based exams containing a mix of objective and longer type questions with a duration of three hours 15 minutes. From September 2016 these exams will also be available as computer-based exams. Further information will be released on these in April 2016. The *Corporate and Business Law* (F4) paper is a two- hour objective test examination which is also available as a computer based exams for English and Global variants, as well as paper based for all variants.

The Professional level papers are all of three hours 15 minutes duration and, all contain two sections. Section A is compulsory, but there will be some choice offered in Section B.

ACCA has removed the restriction relating to reading and planning time, so that while the time considered necessary to complete these exams remains at 3 hours, candidates may use the additional 15 minutes as they choose. ACCA encourages students to take time to read questions carefully and to plan answers but once the exam time has started, there are no additional restrictions as to when candidates may start writing in their answer books.

Time should be taken to ensure that all the information and exam requirements are properly read and understood.

The Essentials module papers all have a Section A containing a major case study question with all requirements totalling 50 marks relating to this case. Section B gives students a choice of two from three 25 mark questions.

Section A of both the P4 and P5 Options papers contain one 50 mark compulsory question, and Section B will offer a choice of two from three questions each worth 25 marks each.

Section A of each of the P6 and P7 Options papers contains 60 compulsory marks from two questions; question 1 attracting 35 marks, and question 2 attracting 25 marks. Section B of both these Options papers will offer a choice of two from three questions, with each question attracting 20 marks.

All Professional level exams contain four professional marks.

The pass mark for all ACCA Qualification examination papers is 50%.

GUIDE TO EXAMINATION ASSESSMENT

ACCA reserves the right to examine anything contained within the study guide at any examination session. This includes knowledge, techniques, principles, theories, and concepts as specified.

For the financial accounting, audit and assurance, law and tax papers except where indicated otherwise, ACCA will publish *examinable documents* once a year to indicate exactly what regulations and legislation could potentially be assessed within identified examination sessions..

For paper based examinations regulation *issued* or legislation *passed* on or before 31st August annually, will be examinable from 1st September of the following year to 31st August of the year after that. Please refer to the examinable documents for the paper (where relevant) for further information.

Regulation issued or legislation passed in accordance with the above dates may be examinable even if the *effective* date is in the future.

The term issued or passed relates to when regulation or legislation has been formally approved.

The term effective relates to when regulation or legislation must be applied to an entity transactions and business practices.

The study guide offers more detailed guidance on the depth and level at which the examinable documents will be examined. The study guide should therefore be read in conjunction with the examinable documents list.

Syllabus

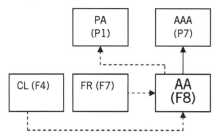

AIM

To develop knowledge and understanding of the process of carrying out the assurance engagement and its application in the context of the professional regulatory framework.

MAIN CAPABILITIES

On successful completion of this paper, candidates should be able to:

A   Explain the concept of audit and assurance and the functions of audit, corporate governance, including ethics and professional conduct, describing the scope and distinguishing between the functions of internal and external audit

B   Demonstrate how the auditor obtains and accepts audit engagements, obtains an understanding of the entity and its environment, assesses the risk of material misstatement (whether arising from fraud or other irregularities) and plans an audit of financial statements

C   Describe and evaluate internal controls, techniques and audit tests, including IT systems to identify and communicate control risks and their potential consequences, making appropriate recommendations

D   Identify and describe the work and evidence obtained by the auditor and others required to meet the objectives of audit engagements and the application of the International Standards on Auditing

E   Explain how consideration of subsequent events and the going concern principle can inform the conclusions from audit work and are reflected in different types of audit report, written representations and the final review and report.

RELATIONAL DIAGRAM OF MAIN CAPABILITIES

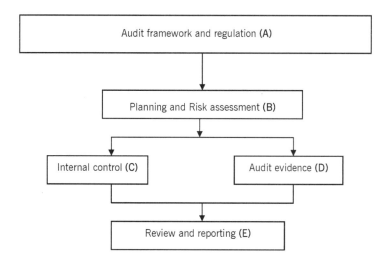

RATIONALE

The Audit and Assurance syllabus is essentially
divided into five areas. The syllabus starts with the
nature, purpose and scope of assurance
engagements both internal and external, including
the statutory audit, its regulatory environment, and
introduces governance and professional ethics
relating to audit and assurance. It then leads into
planning and risk assessment audit. The syllabus
then covers a range of areas relating to an audit of
financial statements including the scope of internal
control. These include, evaluating internal controls,
audit evidence, and a review of the financial
statements. In addition to final review procedures,
the final section concentrates on reporting, including
the form and content of the independent auditor's
report.

DETAILED SYLLABUS

A. Audit framework and regulation

1. The concept of audit and other assurance engagements

2. External audits

3. Corporate governance

4. Professional ethics and ACCA's Code of Ethics and Conduct

5. Internal audit and governance and the differences between external audit and internal audit

6. The scope of the internal audit function, outsourcing and internal audit assignments

B. Planning and risk assessment

1. Obtaining and accepting audit engagements

2. Objective and general principles

3. Assessing audit risks

4. Understanding the entity and its environment

5. Fraud, laws and regulations

6. Audit planning and documentation

C. Internal control

1. Internal control systems

2. The use and evaluation of internal control systems by auditors

3. Tests of control

4. Communication on internal control

D. Audit evidence

1. Financial statement assertions and audit evidence

2. Audit procedures

3. Audit sampling and other means of testing

4. The audit of specific items

5. Computer-assisted audit techniques

6. The work of others

7 Not-for-profit organisations

E. Review and reporting

1. Subsequent events

2. Going concern

3. Written representations

4. Audit finalisation and the final review

5. Audit reports

APPROACH TO EXAMINING THE SYLLABUS

The syllabus is assessed by a three-hour 15 minutes paper-based examination, All questions are compulsory.

Section A of the exam comprises three 10 mark case-based questions. Each case has five objective test questions worth 2 marks each.

Section B of the exam comprises one 30 mark question and two 20 mark questions.

Section B of the exam will predominantly examine one or more aspects of audit and assurance from planning and risk assessment, internal control or audit evidence, although topics from other syllabus areas may also be included

Study Guide

A AUDIT FRAMEWORK AND REGULATION

1. The concept of audit and other assurance engagements

a) Identify and describe the objective and general principles of external audit engagements.[2]

b) Explain the nature and development of audit and other assurance engagements.[1]

c) Discuss the concepts of accountability, stewardship and agency.[2]

d) Define and provide the objectives of an assurance engagement.[1]

e) Explain the five elements of an assurance engagement.[2]

f) Describe the types of assurance engagement[2]

g) Explain the level of assurance provided by an external audit and other review engagements and the concept of true and fair presentation.[1]

2. External audits

a) Describe the regulatory environment within which external audits take place.[1]

b) Discuss the reasons and mechanisms for the regulation of auditors.[1]

c) Explain the statutory regulations governing the appointment, rights, removal and resignation of auditors.[1]

d) Explain the regulations governing the rights and duties of auditors[1]

e) Describe the limitations of external audits.[1]

f) Explain the development and status of International Standards on Auditing (ISAs).[1]

g) Explain the relationship between International Standards on Auditing and national standards.[1]

3. Corporate governance

a) Discuss the objectives, relevance and importance of corporate governance.[2]

b) Discuss the provisions of international codes of corporate governance (such as OECD) that are most relevant to auditors.[2]

c) Describe good corporate governance requirements relating to directors' responsibilities (e.g. for risk management and internal control) and the reporting responsibilities of auditors.[2]

d) Evaluate corporate governance deficiencies and provide recommendations to allow compliance with international codes of corporate governance.[2]

e) Analyse the structure and roles of audit committees and discuss their benefits and limitations.[2]

f) Explain the importance of internal control and risk management.[1]

g) Discuss the need for auditors to communicate with those charged with governance.[2]

4. Professional ethics and ACCA's Code of Ethics and Conduct

a. Define and apply the fundamental principles of professional ethics of integrity, objectivity, professional competence and due care, confidentiality and professional behaviour.[2]

b) Define and apply the conceptual framework, including the threats to the fundamental principles of self-interest, self-review, advocacy, familiarity, and intimidation.[2]

c) Discuss the safeguards to offset the threats to the fundamental principles.[2]

d) Describe the auditor's responsibility with regard to auditor independence, conflicts of interest and confidentiality.[1]

5. Internal audit and governance, and the differences between external audit and internal audit

a) Discuss the factors to be taken into account when assessing the need for internal audit.[2]

b) Discuss the elements of best practice in the structure and operations of internal audit with reference to appropriate international codes of corporate governance.[2]

c) Compare and contrast the role of external and internal audit.[2]

6. The scope of the internal audit function, outsourcing and internal audit assignments

a) Discuss the scope of internal audit and the limitations of the internal audit function.[2]

b) Explain outsourcing and the associated advantages and disadvantages of outsourcing the internal audit function.[1]

c) Discuss the nature and purpose of internal audit assignments including value for money, IT, financial, regulatory compliance, fraud investigations and customer experience.[2]

d) Discuss the nature and purpose of operational internal audit assignments [2]

e) Describe the format and content of audit review reports and make appropriate recommendations to management and those charged with governance[2]

B PLANNING AND RISK ASSESSMENT

1. Obtaining, accepting and continuing audit engagements

a) Discuss the requirements of professional ethics and ISAs in relation to the acceptance / continuance of audit engagements [2]

b) Explain the preconditions for an audit [2]

c) Explain the process by which an auditor obtains an audit engagement [2]

d) Discuss the importance of engagement letters and their contents [1]

e) Explain the quality control procedures that should be in place over engagement performance, monitoring quality and compliance with ethical requirements [2]

2. Objective and general principles

a) Identify the overall objectives of the auditor and the need to conduct an audit in accordance with ISAs.[2]

b) Explain the need to plan and perform audits with an attitude of professional scepticism, and to exercise professional judgment.[2]

3. Assessing audit risks

a) Explain the components of audit risk.[1]

b) Explain the audit risks in the financial statements and explain the auditor's response to each risk.[2]

c) Define and explain the concepts of materiality and performance materiality.[2]

d) Explain and calculate materiality levels from financial information.[2]

4. Understanding the entity and its environment

a) Explain how auditors obtain an initial understanding of the entity and its environment.[2]

b) Describe and explain the nature, and purpose of, analytical procedures in planning.[2]

c) Compute and interpret key ratios used in analytical procedures.[2]

5. Fraud, laws and regulations

a) Discuss the effect of fraud and misstatements on the audit strategy and extent of audit work.[2]

b) Discuss the responsibilities of internal and external auditors for the prevention and detection of fraud and error.[2]

c) Explain the auditor's responsibility to consider laws and regulations.[2]

6. Audit planning and documentation

a) Identify and explain the need for and importance of planning an audit.[2]

b) Identify and describe the contents of the overall audit strategy and audit plan.[2]

c) Explain and describe the relationship between the overall audit strategy and the audit plan.[2]

d) Explain the difference between an interim and final audit.[1]

e) Describe the purpose of an interim audit, and the procedures likely to be adopted at this stage in the audit.[2]

f) Describe the impact of the work performed during the interim audit on the final audit.[2]

h) Explain the need for, and the importance of, audit documentation. [1]

i) Describe the form and contents of working papers and supporting documentation.[2]

j) Explain the procedures to ensure safe custody and retention of working papers.[1]

C   INTERNAL CONTROL

1. Internal control systems

a) Explain why an auditor needs to obtain an understanding of internal control relevant to the audit.[1]

b) Describe and explain the five components of internal control[2]

   i)   the control environment
   ii) the entity's risk assessment process,
   iii) the information system, including the related business processes, relevant to financial reporting and communication
   iv) control activities relevant to the audit
   v)   monitoring of controls

2. The use and evaluation of internal control systems by auditors

a) Explain how auditors record internal control systems including the use of, narrative notes, flowcharts, internal control questionnaires and internal control evaluation questionnaires. [2]

b) Evaluate internal control components, including deficiencies and significant deficiencies in internal control.[2]

c) Discuss the limitations of internal control components [2]

3. Tests of control

a) Describe computer systems controls including general IT controls and application controls {2}

b) Describe control objectives, control procedures, activities and tests of control in relation to:

   i)   The sales system;
   ii) The purchases system
   iii) The payroll system
   iv) The inventory system
   v)   The cash system
   vi) Non-current assets

4. Communication on internal control

a) Discuss the requirements and methods of how reporting significant deficiencies in internal control are provided to management and those charged with governance.[2]

b) Explain, in a format suitable for inclusion in a report to management significant deficiencies within an internal control system and provide recommendations for overcoming these deficiencies to management

D   AUDIT EVIDENCE

1. Financial statement assertions and audit evidence

a) Explain the assertions contained in the financial statements about:[2]
   (i) Classes of transactions and events and related disclosures;

(ii) Account balances and related disclosures at the period end;

b) Describe audit procedures to obtain audit evidence , including inspection , observation, external confirmation, recalculation, re-performance, analytical procedures and enquiry[2]

c) Discuss the quality and quantity of audit evidence[2]

d) Discuss the relevance and reliability of audit evidence [2]

2. Audit procedures

a) Discuss substantive procedures for obtaining audit evidence [2]

b) Discuss and provide examples of how analytical procedures are used as substantive procedures[2]

c) Discuss the problems associated with the audit and review of accounting estimates.[2]

d) Describe why smaller entities may have different control environments and describe the types of evidence likely to be available in smaller entities.[1]

e) Discuss the difference between tests of control and substantive procedures[2]

3. Audit sampling and other means of testing

a) Define audit sampling and explain the need for sampling.[1]

b) Identify and discuss the differences between statistical and non-statistical sampling.[2]

c) Discuss and provide relevant examples of, the application of the basic principles of statistical sampling and other selective testing procedures. [2]

d) Discuss the results of statistical sampling, including consideration of whether additional testing is required.[2]

4. The audit of specific items

For each of the account balances stated in this sub-capability:
Explain the audit objectives and the audit procedures to obtain sufficient, appropriate evidence in relation to:

a) Receivables: [2]
   i) direct confirmation of accounts receivable
   ii) other evidence in relation to receivables and prepayments, and
   iii) completeness and occurrence of revenue.

b) Inventory: [2]
   i) inventory counting procedures in relation to year-end and continuous inventory systems
   ii) cut-off testing
   iii) auditor's attendance at inventory counting
   iv) direct confirmation of inventory held by third parties,
   v) valuation
   vi) other evidence in relation to inventory.

c) Payables and accruals: [2]
   i) supplier statement reconciliations and direct confirmation of accounts payable,
   ii) obtain evidence in relation to payables and accruals, and
   iii) purchases and other expenses.

d) Bank and cash: [2]
   i) bank confirmation reports used in obtaining evidence in relation to bank and cash
   ii) other evidence in relation to bank and
   iii) other evidence in relation to cash.

e) Tangible and intangible non-current assets [2]
   i) evidence in relation to non-current assets and
   ii) depreciation
   iii) profit/loss on disposal

f) Non-current liabilities, provisions and contingencies[2]
   i) evidence in relation to non-current liabilities
   ii) provisions and contingencies

g) Share capital, reserves and directors' emoluments: [2]

i) evidence in relation to share capital, reserves and directors' emoluments

5. Computer-assisted audit techniques

a) Explain the use of computer-assisted audit techniques in the context of an audit.[1]

b) Discuss and provide relevant examples of the use of test data and audit software .[2]

6. The work of others

a) Discuss why auditors rely on the work of others.[2]

b) Discuss the extent to which external auditors are able to rely on the work of experts, including the work of internal audit.[2]

c) Explain the audit considerations relating to entities using service organisations [2]

d) Explain the extent to which reference to the work of others can be made in audit reports.[1]

7. Not-for-profit organisations

a) Apply audit techniques to not-for-profit organisations.[2]

E   REVIEW AND REPORTING

1. Subsequent events

a) Explain the purpose of a subsequent events review.[1]

b) Explain the responsibilities of auditors regarding subsequent events.[1]

c) Discuss the procedures to be undertaken in performing a subsequent events review.[2]

2. Going concern

a) Define and discuss the significance of the concept of going concern.[2]

b) Explain the importance of and the need for going concern reviews.[2]

c) Explain the respective responsibilities of auditors and management regarding going concern.[1]

d) Identify and explain potential indicators that an entity is not a going concern. [2]

e) Discuss the procedures to be applied in performing going concern reviews.[2]

f) Discuss the disclosure requirements in relation to going concern issues.[2]

g) Discuss the reporting implications of the findings of going concern reviews.[2]

3. Written representations

a) Explain the purpose of and procedure for obtaining written representations.[2]

b) Discuss the quality and reliability of written representations as audit evidence.[2]

c) Discuss the circumstances where written representations are necessary and the matters on which representations are commonly obtained. [2]

4. Audit finalisation and the final review

a) Discuss the importance of the overall review in ensuring that sufficient, appropriate evidence has been obtained.[2]

b) Describe procedures an auditor should perform in conducting their overall review of financial statements. [2]

c) Explain the significance of uncorrected misstatements.[1]

d) Evaluate the effect of dealing with uncorrected misstatements.[2]

5. Audit reports

a) Identify and describe the basic elements contained in the independent auditor's report[1]

b) Explain unmodified audit opinions in the auditor's report.[2]

c) Explain modified audit opinions in the audit report.[2]

d) Describe the format and content of emphasis of matter and other matter paragraphs.[2]

SUMMARY OF CHANGES TO F8

ACCA periodically reviews its qualification syllabuses so that they fully meet the needs of stakeholders such as employers, students, regulatory and advisory bodies and learning providers.

These syllabus changes are effective from September 2016 and will be updated with effect from 1st September each year, thereafter.

The main areas that have been changed in the syllabus are shown in the Table 1 below:

Table 1 – Amendments to F8

Section and subject area	Syllabus content
New A3d) New outcome covering evaluation of corporate governance practices and recommendations for improvements	A3d) Evaluate corporate governance deficiencies and provide recommendations to allow compliance with international codes of corporate governance.[2]
A6b) and A6c) Outcomes regarding outsourcing have been combined.	A6b) Explain outsourcing and the associated advantages and disadvantages of outsourcing the internal audit function.[1]
B1a) Outcome extended to specifically refer to continuance decisions	B1a) Discuss the requirements of professional ethics and ISAs in relation to the acceptance / continuance of audit engagements [2]
New B1e) New outcome covering quality control procedures as ISA 220 *Quality Control for an Audit of Financial Statements* will now be an examinable document for F8	B1e) Explain the quality control procedures that should be in place over engagement performance, monitoring quality and compliance with ethical requirements [2]
D1a) amended to reflect the new assertions as per ISA 315 (Revised) as detailed in IAASB's Addressing Disclosures in the Audit of Financial Statements – Revised ISAs and Related Conforming amendments	D1. Financial statement assertions and audit evidence a) Explain the assertions contained in the financial statements about:[2] (i) Classes of transactions and events and related disclosures; (ii) Account balances and related disclosures at the period end;
E4a) Outcome amended to refer to overall review to ensure sufficient appropriate evidence	E4a) Discuss the importance of the overall review in ensuring that sufficient, appropriate evidence has been obtained.[2]
E5a) Outcome amended to better reflect the new requirements of ISA 700 *Forming and Opinion and Reporting on Financial Statements* and ISA 701 *Communicating Key Audit Matters in the Independent Auditor's Report*	E5a) Identify and describe the basic elements contained in the independent auditor's report[1]

Audit framework and regulation

Audit and other assurance engagements

1

Topic list	Syllabus reference
1 The purpose of external audit engagements	A1
2 Accountability, stewardship and agency	A1
3 Types of assurance services	A1
4 Assurance and reports	A1, A2

Introduction

In the first section of this chapter we consider why there is a need for assurance in relation to financial and non-financial information. The main reason an assurance service such as an external audit is required is the fact that the ownership and management of a company are not necessarily one and the same.

In Section 2 we introduce the concepts of agency, accountability and stewardship and consider reporting as a means of communication to the different stakeholders who are interested in the financial statements of the company.

It is important to understand what other assurance services exist in addition to the external audit and these services are discussed in Section 3. The key assurance services which the F8 syllabus concentrates on are the external audit (statutory and non-statutory), review engagements and internal audit assignments.

The effect of audits and reviews is that the stakeholders of an entity are given a level of assurance as to the quality of the information in the accounts. The degrees of assurance provided by external audits and other engagements are discussed in Section 4.

The remainder of the Study Text builds on the themes introduced in this chapter.

Study guide

			Intellectual level
A1	**The concept of audit and other assurance engagements**		
(a)	Identify and describe the objective and general principles of external audit engagements.		2
(b)	Explain the nature and development of audit and other assurance engagements.		1
(c)	Discuss the concepts of accountability, stewardship and agency.		2
(d)	Define and provide the objectives of an assurance engagement.		1
(e)	Explain the five elements of an assurance engagement.		2
(f)	Describe the types of assurance engagement.		2
(g)	Explain the level of assurance provided by an external audit and other review engagements and the concept of true and fair presentation.		1
A2	**External audits**		
(e)	Describe the limitations of statutory audits.		1

Exam guide

This chapter explains the basis of auditing and the distinction between audit and other review assignments. The mechanics of these issues are expanded in more detail throughout the Text. Questions in the exam could draw on matters in this chapter, in conjunction with the knowledge you will obtain later in the Study Text. Therefore assurance could turn up in any of the questions in the F8 exam.

This topic can be examined in a written question, requiring you, for example, to explain the elements of an assurance engagement, to comment on the level of assurance in an assurance engagement to review a company's cash flow forecast, or to explain the meaning of true and fair presentation. All of these could equally be examined in Section A of the exam through OTQs.

1 The purpose of external audit engagements

FAST FORWARD

> An **external audit** is a type of **assurance engagement** that is carried out by an auditor to give an independent opinion on a set of financial statements.

1.1 Objective of external audit

Key term

> The objective of an **audit** of financial statements is to enable the auditor to express an opinion on whether the financial statements are prepared, in all material respects, in accordance with an applicable financial reporting framework. An audit of financial statements is an example of an assurance engagement.

The purpose of an external audit is to enable auditors to **give an opinion** on the financial statements. While an audit might produce by-products, such as advice to the directors on how to run the business, its objective is **solely to report to the shareholders**.

1.1.1 Statutory and non-statutory audits

In most countries, audits are required under national statute for many undertakings, including limited liability companies. Other organisations and entities requiring a statutory audit may include charities, investment businesses and trade unions. In the UK for example, under registered companies' legislation (currently the Companies Act 2006), most companies are required to have an audit.

The statutory audit can bring various advantages to the company and shareholders. The key benefit to shareholders is the impartial view provided by the auditors. However, the company also benefits from professional accountants reviewing the accounts and system as part of the audit. Advantages might include recommendations being made in relation to accounting and control systems and the possibility that auditors might detect fraud and error.

Non-statutory audits are performed by independent auditors because the company's owners, proprietors, members, trustees, professional and governing bodies or other interested parties want them, rather than because the law requires them. In consequence, **auditing may extend** to every type of undertaking which produces accounts, including clubs, charities (some of these may require statutory audits as well), sole traders and partnerships. Some of these organisations do not operate for profit, and this has a specific impact on the nature of their audit. The audit of not-for-profit organisations will be considered in more detail in Chapter 17.

1.1.2 Advantages of the non-statutory audit

In addition to the advantages common to all forms of audit, a non-statutory audit can bring other advantages. For example, the audit of the accounts of a **partnership** may have the following advantages.

(a)   It can provide a means of **settling accounts** between the partners.

(b)   Where audited accounts are available this may make the **accounts more acceptable** to the **taxation authorities** when it comes to agreeing an individual partner's liability to tax.

(c)   The **sale** of the business or the **negotiation of loan or overdraft facilities** may be facilitated if the firm is able to produce audited accounts.

(d)   An audit on behalf of a **'sleeping partner'** is useful since generally such a person will have few other means of checking the accounts of the business or confirming the share of profits due to them.

2 Accountability, stewardship and agency

An audit provides **assurance** to the shareholders and other stakeholders of a company on the financial statements because it is **independent and impartial**.

2.1 The nature and development of audit and other assurance engagements

The accounting and auditing professions have been under the public spotlight for many years now and, as a result of certain events, many changes have occurred in relation to audit and assurance engagements.

As a result of the stock market bubble of the late 1990s and speculation over the future of 'dotcom' companies, many countries experienced huge **corporate financial scandals and frauds**. The bubble burst in 2000, followed by a revelation that senior management at **Enron**, a US energy company, had been deceiving investors by fraudulently overstating profitability. Its auditor, **Arthur Andersen**, was shown to have lacked objectivity in evaluating Enron's accounting methods. This led to the demise of Arthur Andersen in 2002.

Other companies that were also involved in corporate frauds included WorldCom, Parmalat, Cable & Wireless and Xerox, to name but a few. The subsequent fallout of these frauds was a lack of confidence in the way companies were run and audited. In the US, this resulted in the **Sarbanes-Oxley Act 2002** which has not only radically changed the **regulation** of the accounting profession in the US but also influenced such issues worldwide.

In September 2008 Lehman Brothers, a global financial services firm, filed for bankruptcy in the US triggering a severe worldwide financial crisis. Lehman had expanded aggressively into property-related investments, including so-called sub-prime mortgages (loans to people on low incomes or with poor credit histories). In subsequent reports it was claimed that Lehman Brothers covered up the extent of its irrecoverable debts using an accounting manoeuvre known as 'Repo 105', which involves loaning 'bad'

assets to other firms in exchange for short-term financing. Lehman's auditors had issued a clean audit report on the accounts to 30 November 2007 and the Accountancy and Actuarial Discipline Board (AADB), an independent investigative and disciplinary body in the UK, commenced an investigation in 2010 into the conduct of the auditors of Lehman Brothers International Europe.

Following the collapse of Lehman Brothers, other banks failed worldwide and many needed government support to continue. There was a knock-on effect in the wider economy in many countries in 2008 and 2009, with many businesses struggling or failing altogether. The global economy has never really recovered from this and 2010 and 2011/2012 has seen nations in danger of defaulting on their debts, necessitating numerous restructurings of borrowing arrangements.

In light of this global financial crisis, regulators have again been considering the effectiveness of the audit and the auditor's role in helping to prevent, or at least provide warning of, corporate and financial institution collapses in the future.

One important area being focused on is the importance of professional scepticism for audit quality. Regulators have been trying to stimulate debate about what actions may be needed to ensure that the appropriate degree of scepticism is applied by auditors in practice. We look at professional scepticism in more detail in Chapter 6.

The above events illustrate how important it is to companies and their shareholders that auditing and other assurance engagements are carried out effectively. We will go on to illustrate this further below.

2.2 Accountability, stewardship and agency

The key reason for having an audit or review can be seen by working through the following case study.

 Case Study

Vera decides to set up a business selling flowers. She gets up early in the morning, visits the market and then sets up a stall by the side of the road. For the first year, all goes well. She sells all the flowers she is able to buy and she derives some income from the business.

However, Vera feels that she could sell more flowers if she was able to transport more to the place where she sells them, and she also knows that there are several other roads nearby where she could sell flowers, if she could be in two places at once. She could achieve these two things by buying a van and by employing people to sell flowers in other locations.

Vera needs more money to achieve this expansion of her business. She decides to ask her rich friend Peter to invest in the business.

Peter can see the potential of Vera's business and wants to invest, but he doesn't want to be involved in the management of the business. He also does not want to have ultimate liability for the debts of the business if it fails. He therefore suggests that they set up a limited company. He will own the majority of the shares and be entitled to dividends. Vera will be managing director and be paid a salary for her work.

At the end of the first year of trading as a limited company, Peter receives a copy of the financial statements. Profits are lower than expected, so his dividend will not be as large as he had hoped. He knows that Vera is paid a salary so does not care as much as him that profits are low.

Peter is concerned by the level of profits and feels that he wants further assurance on the accounts. He doesn't know whether they give a true reflection of the last year's trading, particularly as the profits do not seem as high as those Vera had predicted when he agreed to invest.

The solution is that the **assurance** Peter is seeking can be given by an independent **audit or review** of the financial statements.

An auditor can provide the two things that Peter requires:

- A **knowledgeable review** of the company's business and of the accounts
- An **impartial view**, since Vera's view might be biased

Other people will also view the company's accounts with interest, for example:

- Creditors of the company
- Taxation authorities

The various parties interested in the accounts of a company are sometimes referred to as **stakeholders**. Although they will each judge the accounts by different criteria, they will all **gain assurance** from learning that the accounts they are reading have been subject to an independent report.

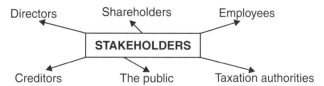

The example above is a simple one. In practice, companies may have thousands of shareholders and may not know the management personally. It is therefore important that directors are **accountable** to shareholders. Directors act as **stewards** of the shareholders' investments. They are **agents** of the shareholders.

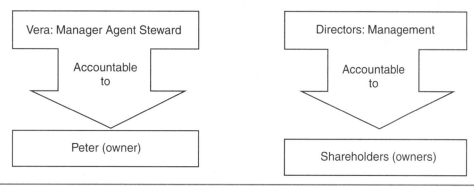

Key terms

Accountability is the quality or state of being accountable; that is, being required or expected to justify actions and decisions. It suggests an obligation or willingness to accept responsibility for one's actions.

Stewardship refers to the duties and obligations of a person who manages another person's property.

Agents are people employed or used to provide a particular service. In the case of a company, the people being used to provide the service of managing the business also have the second role of trying to maximise their personal wealth in their own right.

You may ask, 'what are the directors accountable for?' It is important to understand the answer to this question. The directors are accountable for the **shareholders' investment**. The shareholders have bought shares in that company (they have invested). They **expect a return** from their investment. As the **directors** manage the company, they are **in a position to affect that return**.

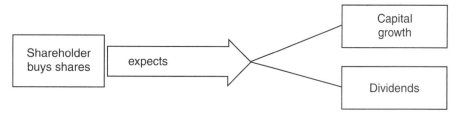

The exact nature of the return expected by the shareholder will depend on the type of company they have chosen to invest in: that is part of their investment risk analysis. However, certain issues are true of any such investment. For example, if the directors **mismanage** the company, and it goes **bankrupt**, it will not provide a source of future dividends, nor will it create capital growth in the investment – indeed, the opposite is true and the original investment may even be lost.

Accountability therefore covers a range of issues:

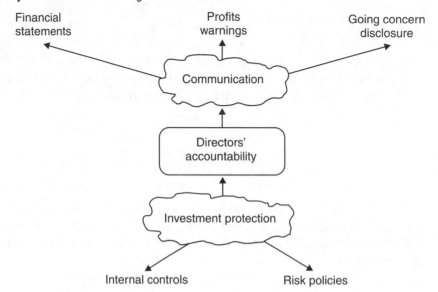

These issues are often discussed under the umbrella title '**corporate governance**', where 'governance' indicates the management (governing) role of the directors, and 'corporate' indicates that the issue relates to companies (bodies corporate). This is illustrated by our scenario, where we saw Vera taking up a corporate governance position in relation to Peter. We shall consider corporate governance further in Chapter 3.

2.3 Assurance provision   June 13

Many of the requirements in relation to corporate governance necessitate **communication** between the directors and the shareholders.

As discussed in Section 1, **directors** of all companies are usually **required to produce financial statements** annually which give a **true and fair view** of the affairs of the company and its profit or loss for the period. They are also **encouraged** to **communicate with shareholders** on matters relating to **directors' pay** and **benefits** (this is required by law in the case of public limited companies), **going concern** and **management of risks**.

But how will the shareholders know whether the directors' communications are **accurate**, or present a **fair picture?** We are back to the problem that Peter had in the scenario we presented at the beginning of this section. He knew that Vera's view might be **biased** in a different way to his own, and he sought **assurance** on the information he was presented with.

The International Auditing and Assurance Standards Board (IAASB) *International framework for assurance engagements* provides a frame of reference for professional accountants when performing assurance engagements. It provides the following definition of an assurance engagement.

Key term

> An **assurance engagement** is one in which a practitioner expresses a conclusion designed to enhance the degree of confidence of the intended users other than the responsible party about the subject matter information (that is, the outcome of the evaluation or measurement of a subject matter against criteria).

2.3.1 Elements of an assurance engagement   June 10

An assurance engagement performed by a practitioner will consist of the following elements:

(a) **A three party relationship**. The three parties are the intended user, the responsible party and the practitioner (each party is described in the Key terms box below).

(b) **A subject matter**. This is the data to be evaluated that has been prepared by the responsible party. It can take many forms, including financial performance (eg historical financial information), non-financial performance (eg key performance indicators), processes (eg internal control) and behaviour (eg compliance with laws and regulations).

(c) **Suitable criteria**. The subject matter is evaluated or measured against criteria in order to reach an opinion.

(d) **Evidence**. Sufficient appropriate evidence needs to be gathered to support the required level of assurance.

(e) **An assurance report**. A written report containing the practitioner's opinion is issued to the intended user, in the form appropriate to a reasonable assurance engagement or a limited assurance engagement.

Key terms

> **Intended users** are the person, persons or class of persons for whom the practitioner prepares the assurance report.
>
> The **responsible party** is the party responsible for the underlying subject matter (in a direct reporting engagement) or subject matter information of the assurance engagement.
>
> The **practitioner** is the individual providing professional services that will review the subject matter and provide the assurance.

One way to remember these five elements of an assurance engagement is using the mnemonic **CREST**.

- **C**riteria
- **R**eport
- **E**vidence
- **S**ubject matter
- **T**hree party relationship

In the following section, we look at different types of assurance engagements.

Exam focus point

> It is important that you understand, and are able to explain, the elements of an assurance engagement. This was an area which has been poorly answered when examined previously. Try to use the memory aid above to ensure that you are prepared for such a question.

2.3.2 Objectives of an assurance engagement

The objective of an assurance engagement will depend on the level of assurance given. First we will consider a **reasonable assurance** engagement, where a **high, but not absolute**, level of assurance is given.

ISAE 3000 (Revised) *Assurance engagements other than audits or reviews of historical financial information* was revised in September 2013 and applies to assurance reports dated on or after 15 December 2015. The revised ISAE distinguishes between two forms of assurance engagements:

- **Reasonable assurance** engagements
- **Limited assurance** engagements

The objective of a **reasonable assurance engagement** is a reduction in assurance engagement risk to an acceptably low level in the circumstances of the engagement as the basis for the assurance practitioner's conclusion. The conclusion would usually be expressed in a **positive form**.

In order to give reasonable assurance, a significant amount of testing and evaluation is required to support the conclusion. We look at reasonable assurance in the context of an audit in Section 4.1.

Limited assurance is a lower level of assurance. The nature, timing and extent of the procedures carried out by the practitioner in a limited assurance engagement would be limited compared with what is required in a reasonable assurance engagement. Nevertheless, the procedures performed should be planned to obtain a level of assurance which is meaningful, in the practitioner's professional judgement.

For a limited assurance engagement, the conclusion conveys whether, based on the procedures performed and evidence obtained, a matter(s) has come to the practitioner's attention to cause the practitioner to believe the subject matter information is materially misstated. This would usually be expressed in a **negative form of words**.

We look at the different levels of assurance in more detail in Section 4.3.

For both reasonable and assurance engagements, the revised ISAE requires the practitioner to provide a summary of the **procedures undertaken** within the **assurance report**.

3 Types of assurance services   Dec 09, June 12, June 15

Assurance services include a range of assignments, from **external audits** to **review engagements**.

3.1 Other assurance engagements

As discussed earlier in this chapter, an audit can be used to give assurance to a variety of stakeholders on many issues. However, an audit is an exercise designed to give a high level of assurance and involves a high degree of testing, and therefore a high level of cost. In some cases, stakeholders may find that they receive **sufficient assurance** about an issue from a less detailed engagement, for example, a **review**. A review can provide a cost-efficient alternative to an audit where an audit is not required by law, and would provide **limited assurance**.

Key term

> The objective of a **review engagement** is to obtain limited assurance about whether the subject matter information is free from material misstatement.

The major outcome for recipients of a review engagement is that the **level of assurance** they gain from it is not as high as would be expected from an audit, although the procedures carried out in a review engagement are similar to an audit.

Alternatively, if the engagement in question is not about the financial statements, then ISAE 3000 *Assurance engagements other than audits or reviews of historical financial information* states that this could be **either a reasonable assurance or a limited assurance** engagement, as appropriate in the circumstances.

3.1.1 Types of review engagements

There are two types of assurance engagements: **attestation engagements** and **direct engagements**. The main difference between the two lies in **who is measuring, or evaluating**, the underlying subject matter against the criteria.

(a)   **An attestation engagement**: This is where the underlying subject matter has not been measured or evaluated by the practitioner, and the practitioner concludes whether or not the subject matter information is free from material misstatement.

      A good example of an attestation engagement is the **review of a sustainability report**, which has been prepared by management. In this case, management measures and evaluates the extent to which the company has achieved its sustainability targets, and the practitioner provides a conclusion as to whether the measurement and evaluation is free from material misstatement.

(b)   **A direct engagement**: This is where the underlying subject matter has been measured and evaluated by the practitioner, and the practitioner then presents conclusions on the reported outcome in the assurance report.

      An example of this is when the practitioner is engaged to carry out a **review of the effectiveness of a company's system of internal controls**. The practitioner would evaluate the internal controls, and then issue an assurance report explaining the outcome of the review.

3.2 Internal audit reviews

Internal auditors are employed as part of an organisation's system of controls. Their responsibilities are determined by management and may be wide-ranging.

Key term

The **internal audit function** performs assurance and consulting activities designed to evaluate and improve the effectiveness of the entity's governance, risk management and internal control processes.

Up to now we have discussed assurance services where an independent outsider provides an opinion on financial information. Assurance can also be provided to management (and, by implication, to other parties) by **internal auditors**.

As we shall see in Chapter 3, as part of good corporate governance all directors are advised to review the effectiveness of the company's risk management and internal control systems. They should also consider the need for an **internal audit function to help them carry out their duties**.

Larger organisations may therefore appoint full-time staff whose **function is to monitor and report on the running of the company's operations**. Internal audit staff members are one type of control. Although some of the work carried out by internal auditors is similar to that performed by external auditors, there are **important distinctions** between the two functions in terms of their responsibilities, scope and relationship with the company, and we will examine these in more detail in Chapter 5.

There are a number of assignments that may be carried out by internal auditors and these include:

(a)   **Value for money (VFM) audits**. These examine the **economy**, **efficiency** and **effectiveness** of activities and processes.

(b)   An **information technology (IT) audit**. This is a test of controls in a specific area of the business.

(c)   **Best value audits**. 'Best value' is a performance framework introduced into local authorities by the UK Government. They are required to publish annual best value performance plans and review all of their functions over a five year period and internal audit can carry out this review.

(d)   **Financial, operational** and **procurement** audits

We will look at each of these assignments in more detail in Chapter 5 on internal audit.

4 Assurance and reports

The auditors' report on company financial statements is expressed in terms of **truth** and **fairness**. This is generally taken to mean that financial statements:

- Are factual
- Are free from bias
- Reflect the commercial substance of the business's transactions

4.1 Truth and fairness/ fair presentation   Dec 10

External auditors give an opinion on the **fair presentation**, or **truth and fairness**, of financial statements. Fair presentation, the term used in the IAASB's international ISAs, and truth and fairness, the term used in the ISAs (UK & Ireland), mean essentially the same thing.

The audit opinion is not an opinion of absolute correctness. 'True' and 'fair' are not defined in law or audit guidance, but the following definitions are generally accepted.

Key terms

True: Information is factual and conforms with reality. In addition, the information conforms with required standards and law. The financial statements have been correctly extracted from the books and records.

Fair: Information is free from discrimination and bias and in compliance with expected standards and rules. The accounts should reflect the commercial substance of the company's underlying transactions.

Below is an example of an auditor's report on an entity's financial statements. This is a report with an **unmodified** opinion (which means the financial statements are presented fairly, or true and fair and properly prepared).

INDEPENDENT AUDITOR'S REPORT

To the Shareholders of ABC Company [or Other Appropriate Addressee]

Report on the Audit of the Financial Statements

Opinion

We have audited the financial statements of ABC Company (the Company), which comprise the statement of financial position as at December 31, 20X1, and the statement of comprehensive income, statement of changes in equity and statement of cash flows for the year then ended, and notes to the financial statements, including a summary of significant accounting policies.

In our opinion, the accompanying financial statements present fairly, in all material respects, (or **give a true and fair view of**) the financial position of the Company as at December 31, 20X1, and (of) its financial performance and its cash flows for the year then ended in accordance with International Financial Reporting Standards (IFRSs).

Basis for Opinion

We conducted our audit in accordance with International Standards on Auditing (ISAs). Our responsibilities under those standards are further described in the *Auditor's Responsibilities for the Audit of the Financial Statements* section of our report. We are independent of the Company in accordance with the International Ethics Standards Board for Accountants' *Code of Ethics for Professional Accountants* (IESBA Code) together with the ethical requirements that are relevant to our audit of the financial statements in [jurisdiction], and we have fulfilled our other ethical responsibilities in accordance with these requirements and the IESBA Code. We believe that the audit evidence we have obtained is sufficient and appropriate to provide a basis for our opinion.

Key Audit Matters

Key audit matters are those matters that, in our professional judgment, were of most significance in our audit of the financial statements of the current period. These matters were addressed in the context of our audit of the financial statements as a whole, and in forming our opinion thereon, and we do not provide a separate opinion on these matters.

[Description of each key audit matter in accordance with ISA 701, which applies to audits of the financial statements of listed entities.]

Other Information

Management is responsible for the other information. The other information comprises the [information included in the X report, but does not include the financial statements and our auditor's report thereon.]

Our opinion on the financial statements does not cover the other information and we do not express any form of assurance conclusion thereon.

In connection with our audit of the financial statements, our responsibility is to read the other information and, in doing so, consider whether the other information is materially inconsistent with the financial statements or our knowledge obtained in the audit or otherwise appears to be materially misstated. If, based on the work we have performed, we conclude that there is a material misstatement of this other information, we are required to report that fact. We have nothing to report in this regard.

Responsibilities of Management and Those Charged with Governance for the Financial Statements

Management is responsible for the preparation and fair presentation of the financial statements in accordance with IFRSs and for such internal control as management determines is necessary to enable the preparation of financial statements that are free from material misstatement, whether due to fraud or error.

In preparing the financial statements, management is responsible for assessing the Company's ability to continue as a going concern, disclosing, as applicable, matters related to going concern and using the

---

going concern basis of accounting unless management either intends to liquidate the Company or to cease operations, or has no realistic alternative but to do so.

Those charged with governance are responsible for overseeing the Company's financial reporting process.

Auditor's Responsibilities for the Audit of the Financial Statements

Our objectives are to obtain reasonable assurance about whether the financial statements as a whole are free from material misstatement, whether due to fraud or error, and to issue an auditor's report that includes our opinion. Reasonable assurance is a high level of assurance, but is not a guarantee that an audit conducted in accordance with ISAs will always detect a material misstatement when it exists. Misstatements can arise from fraud or error and are considered material if, individually or in the aggregate, they could reasonably be expected to influence the economic decisions of users taken on the basis of these financial statements.

As part of an audit in accordance with ISAs, we exercise professional judgment and maintain professional scepticism throughout the audit. We also:

- Identify and assess the risks of material misstatement of the financial statements, whether due to fraud or error, design and perform audit procedures responsive to those risks, and obtain audit evidence that is sufficient and appropriate to provide a basis for our opinion. The risk of not detecting a material misstatement resulting from fraud is higher than for one resulting from error, as fraud may involve collusion, forgery, intentional omissions, misrepresentations, or the override of internal control.

- Obtain an understanding of internal control relevant to the audit in order to design audit procedures that are appropriate in the circumstances, but not for the purpose of expressing an opinion on the effectiveness of the Company's internal control.

- Evaluate the appropriateness of accounting policies used and the reasonableness of accounting estimates and related disclosures made by management.

- Conclude on the appropriateness of management's use of the going concern basis of accounting and, based on the audit evidence obtained, whether a material uncertainty exists related to events or conditions that may cast significant doubt on the Company's ability to continue as a going concern. If we conclude that a material uncertainty exists, we are required to draw attention in our auditor's report to the related disclosures in the financial statements or, if such disclosures are inadequate, to modify our opinion. Our conclusions are based on the audit evidence obtained up to the date of our auditor's report. However, future events or conditions may cause the Company to cease to continue as a going concern.

- Evaluate the overall presentation, structure and content of the financial statements, including the disclosures, and whether the financial statements represent the underlying transactions and events in a manner that achieves fair presentation.

We communicate with those charged with governance regarding, among other matters, the planned scope and timing of the audit and significant audit findings, including any significant deficiencies in internal control that we identify during our audit.

We also provide those charged with governance with a statement that we have complied with relevant ethical requirements regarding independence, and to communicate with them all relationships and other matters that may reasonably be thought to bear on our independence, and where applicable, related safeguards.

From the matters communicated with those charged with governance, we determine those matters that were of most significance in the audit of the financial statements of the current period and are therefore the key audit matters. We describe these matters in our auditor's report unless law or regulation precludes public disclosure about the matter or when, in extremely rare circumstances, we determine that a matter should not be communicated in our report because the adverse consequences of doing so would reasonably be expected to outweigh the public interest benefits of such communication.

Report on Other Legal and Regulatory Requirements

[*The form and content of this section of the auditor's report would vary depending on the nature of the auditor's other reporting responsibilities prescribed by local law, regulation, or national auditing standards. The matters addressed by other law, regulation or national auditing standards (referred to as "other reporting responsibilities") shall be addressed within this section unless the other reporting responsibilities address the same topics as those presented under the reporting responsibilities required by the ISAs as part of the Report on the Audit of the Financial Statements section. The reporting of other reporting responsibilities that address the same topics as those required by the ISAs may be combined (ie, included in the Report on the Audit of the Financial Statements section under the appropriate subheadings) provided that the wording in the auditor's report clearly differentiates the other reporting responsibilities from the reporting that is required by the ISAs where such a difference exists.*]

The engagement partner on the audit resulting in this independent auditor's report is [name].

[Signature in the name of the audit firm, the personal name of the auditor, or both, as appropriate for the particular jurisdiction]

[Auditor Address]

[Date]

Auditors' reports with **modified** opinions may arise because of a number of different reasons and are discussed in depth in Chapter 19.

The auditor's report refers to the fact that the audit is planned and performed to obtain 'reasonable assurance' as to whether the financial statements are free from material misstatement. This is because the auditor cannot check everything and therefore can only provide 'reasonable', not 'absolute', assurance.

Key term

An audit gives the reader **reasonable assurance** on the truth and fairness of the financial statements, which is a high, but not absolute, level of assurance. The auditor's report does not guarantee that the financial statements are correct, but that they are true and fair within a reasonable margin of error.

One of the reasons that an auditor does not give absolute assurance is because of the **inherent limitations** of audit. We discuss these limitations below.

4.2 Limitations of audit and materiality

FAST FORWARD

External audits give **reasonable assurance** that the financial statements are free from material misstatement.

The assurance given by auditors is governed by the fact that auditors use **judgement** in deciding what audit procedures to use and what conclusions to draw, and also by the **limitations** of every audit. These are illustrated in the following diagram.

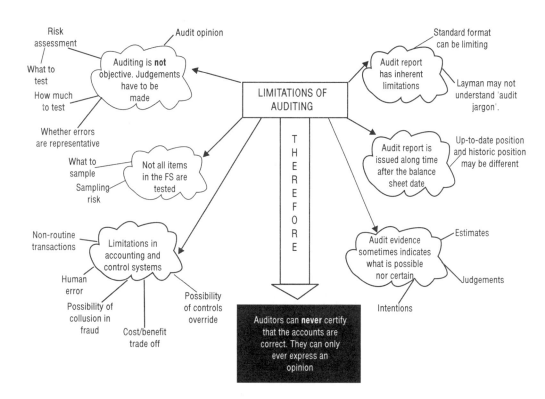

Misstatements which are significant to readers may exist in financial statements and auditors will plan their work on this basis; that is, with **professional scepticism**. The concept of '**significance to readers**' is the concept of **materiality** (which will be discussed in more detail in Chapter 6).

Key term

> **Materiality** is an expression of the relative significance or importance of a particular matter in the context of the financial statements as a whole. A matter is material if its omission or misstatement would reasonably be expected to influence the economic decisions of users taken on the basis of the financial statements. Materiality depends on the size of the item or error judged in the particular circumstances of its omission or misstatement.

The auditors' task is to decide whether the financial statements show a **true and fair view**. The auditors are not responsible for establishing whether the financial statements are correct in every particular. This is because it can take a great deal of time and trouble to check the accuracy of even a very small transaction and the resulting benefit may not justify the effort. Also, financial accounting inevitably involves a degree of estimation which means that financial statements can never be completely precise.

Although the definition of materiality refers to the decisions of the addressees of the auditor's report (the company's members), their decisions may well be influenced by other entities that use the financial statements, for example, the bank.

4.3 Levels of assurance

FAST FORWARD

> The **degree of assurance** given by the impartial professional will depend on the nature of the exercise being carried out.

'Assurance' here means **the auditors' satisfaction as to the reliability of the assertion made by one party for use by another party**.

Directors prepare financial statements for the benefit of members. They **assert** that the financial statements give a true and fair view. The auditors provide **assurance** on that assertion. To provide such assurance, the auditors must:

- Assess risk
- Plan audit procedures
- Conduct audit procedures

- Assess results
- Express an opinion

The degree of satisfaction achieved and, therefore, **the level of assurance which may be provided** is determined by the **nature** of **procedures performed** and their results.

Another type of assurance engagement where a lower level of assurance is given is a **review engagement**, which we looked at in Section 3.

<table>
<tr><td>Exam focus point</td><td>You must understand the levels of assurance provided by these different types of engagement, as you could be asked to explain this in the exam.</td></tr>
</table>

The following table summarises the different types of assurance engagements that can be carried out by practitioners.

Type of assurance provided	Typical form of conclusion provided	Example
Reasonable	Positive	– Statutory external audit
Limited	Negative	– Review of interim financial statements

Chapter Roundup

- An **external audit** is a type of **assurance engagement** that is carried out by an auditor to give an independent opinion on a set of financial statements.

- An audit provides **assurance** to the shareholders and other stakeholders of a company on the financial statements because it is **independent and impartial**.

- Assurance services include a range of assignments, from **external audits** to **review engagements**.

- **Internal auditors** are employed as part of an organisation's system of controls. Their responsibilities are determined by management and may be wide-ranging.

- The auditor's report on company financial statements is expressed in terms of **truth** and **fairness**. This is generally taken to mean that financial statements:

  - Are factual
  - Are free from bias
  - Reflect the commercial substance of the business's transactions

- External audits give **reasonable assurance** that the financial statements are free from material misstatement.

- The **degree of assurance** given by the impartial professional will depend on the nature of the engagement being performed and the procedures carried out.

Quick Quiz

1   Complete the IFAC definition of an audit:

The objective of an .... of .... is to enable the auditor to .... an .... on whether the financial statements are prepared, in all .... respects, in accordance with an identified financial reporting framework.

2   Link the correct definition to each term.

(i)	Accountable	(iv)	True
(ii)	Steward	(v)	Fair
(iii)	Agent	(vi)	Materiality

(a)   An expression of the relative significance or importance of a particular matter in the context of the financial statements as a whole

(b)   A person employed to provide a particular service

(c)   Factual and conforming with reality. In conformity with relevant standards and law and correctly extracted from accounting records

(d)   A person employed to manage other people's property

(e)   Free from discrimination and bias and in compliance with expected standards and rules. Reflecting the commercial substance of underlying transactions

(f)   Being required or expected to justify actions and decisions

3   What level of assurance is provided by a review engagement?

4   Which of the following assurance engagements provides the highest level of assurance?

- External audit
- Review engagement

5   What are the five elements of an assurance engagement?

1   Audit, financial statements, express, opinion, material

2   (i)   (f)   (iv)   (c)
     (ii)   (d)   (v)   (e)
     (iii) (b)   (vi)   (a)

3   Negative assurance

4   An external audit provides the higher level of assurance, since a positive opinion is used to provide reasonable assurance that the financial statements are not materially misstated. The negative assurance given in a review engagement is a lower level of assurance, since the practitioner only states that nothing has come to their attention that indicates that the financial information is materially misstated.

5   (a)   **A three party relationship**. The three parties are the intended user, the responsible party and the practitioner.

     (b)   **A subject matter**. This is the data to be evaluated that has been prepared by the responsible party. It can take many forms, including financial performance (eg historical financial information), non-financial performance (eg key performance indicators), processes (eg internal control) and behaviour (eg compliance with laws and regulations).

     (c)   **Suitable criteria**. The subject matter is evaluated or measured against criteria in order to reach an opinion.

     (d)   **Evidence**. Sufficient appropriate evidence needs to be gathered to support the required level of assurance.

     (e)   **An assurance report**. A written report containing the practitioner's opinion is issued to the intended user, in the form appropriate to a reasonable assurance engagement or a limited assurance engagement.

Now try the question below from the Practice Question Bank

Number	Level	Marks	Time
Q1	Introductory	n/a	n/a

Statutory audit and regulation

Topic list	Syllabus reference
1 Objective of statutory audits and the audit opinion	A2
2 Appointment, removal and resignation of auditors	A2
3 Regulation of auditors	A2
4 International Standards on Auditing	A2

Introduction

This chapter describes the aims and objectives of the statutory audit and the regulatory environment within which it takes place.

The regulatory framework for auditors discussed in this chapter and the regulation of auditors by bodies such as the ACCA are very important.

This chapter considers in detail the regulatory aspects of the appointment, removal and resignation of auditors.

It ends with an examination of International Standards on Auditing which auditors must comply with when carrying out an external audit.

Study guide

		Intellectual level
A2	**External audits**	
(a)	Describe the regulatory environment within which external audits take place.	1
(b)	Discuss the reasons and mechanisms for the regulation of auditors.	1
(c)	Explain the statutory regulations governing the appointment, rights, removal and resignation of auditors.	1
(f)	Explain the development and status of International Standards on Auditing.	1
(g)	Explain the relationship between International Standards on Auditing and national standards.	1

Exam guide

A knowledge of the overall regulatory regime is essential to an understanding of external audit and could be examined as part of a longer question on audit planning or in conjunction with a question on professional ethics. It is also a topic that is likely to be tested in the form of OTQs in Section A of the exam.

1 Objective of statutory audits and the audit opinion

FAST FORWARD

Most companies are required to have an external audit by law, but some small companies are exempt. The outcome of the audit is the **auditor's report**, which sets out the auditor's **opinion** on the financial statements.

1.1 The statutory audit opinion

As introduced in Chapter 1, the purpose of an audit is for the auditor to express an opinion on the financial statements.

The audit opinion may also **imply** certain things are true, because otherwise the audit report would have mentioned them. For example, in the UK, such implications include the following.

- **Adequate accounting records** have been kept.
- **Returns** adequate for the audit have been received from branches not visited.
- The **accounts agree** with the **accounting records** and **returns**.
- **All information and explanations** have been **received** that the auditor believes are necessary for the purposes of the audit.
- **Details** of **directors' emoluments** and **other benefits** have been correctly **disclosed** in the financial statements.
- Particulars of **loans** and **other transactions** in favour of **directors** and others have been correctly in the financial statements.

1.1.1 The value of the statutory audit

We have discussed already the principal aim of the external audit – to provide an independent opinion on the truth and fairness of the financial statements. However, an external audit can be invaluable to an entity because it may **enhance the credibility** of the financial statements, as they will have been examined independently.

The external audit can also highlight other issues as a result of work relating to the financial statements, such as **deficiencies in the internal control system** of the entity, which can be improved by the entity's management. We will look at this aspect later in this Study Text.

For these reasons, even where entities are not obliged to undergo an external audit, they may choose to do so, regardless of the costs involved (time and money) because the benefits outweigh those costs.

1.2 Small company audit exemption

The majority of companies are required by national law to have an audit. A key exception to this requirement is that given to small companies. Many European Commission (EC) countries have a small company exemption from audit that is based on the turnover and total assets at the year end.

Note that, unless otherwise stated, companies in the F8 paper will require an audit.

In most countries, the majority of companies are very small, employing few people (if any) and are often owner-managed. This is very different from a large business where the owners (the shareholders) devolve the day-to-day running of the business to a group of managers or directors. International auditing standards use the term 'smaller entities'.

Key term

> A **smaller entity** is an entity which typically possesses qualitative characteristics, such as:
>
> (a) Concentration of ownership and management in a small number of individuals (often a single individual); and
>
> (b) One or more of the following:
>
>   (i) Straightforward or uncomplicated transactions
>   (ii) Simple record-keeping
>   (iii) Few lines of business and few products within business lines
>   (iv) Few internal controls
>   (v) Few levels of management with responsibility for a broad range of controls
>   (vi) Few personnel, many having a wide range of duties

There has long been a debate over the benefits of audit to small entities. Where such entities are owned by the same people that manage them, there is significantly less value in an independent review of the stewardship of the managers than where management and ownership are separate.

The case for retaining the small company audit rests on the value of the statutory audit to those who have an interest in audited financial statements; that is, the users of the financial statements. From the viewpoint of each type of user, the arguments for and against abolition are summarised in the table below.

User	For abolition	Against abolition
Shareholders	Benefit may not be worth the cost	Provides reassurance to shareholders not involved in managing Assists in fair valuation of share in unquoted companies
Bank and other institutions or lenders	Doubt over whether banks rely on audited financial statements more than unaudited ones	Banks may rely on audited financial statements for making loans and reviewing value of security
Other payables	Limited reliance in practice, as financial statements are filed too late	Provides opportunity to assess strength of customers
Taxation authorities	Little evidence of whether reliance is placed on audited financial statements	Taxation authorities may rely on audited financial statements to calculate corporation tax and check returns
Employees	Little evidence that employees make assessments of financial statements for wage negotiations	Employees entitled to assess financial statements for wage negotiations and considering future viability of their employer
Management	System review and management consultancy review would be of greater benefit with less or similar cost to an audit	Useful independent check on accounting systems and recommendations for improving those systems

1.3 Auditor rights and duties

The law gives auditors both rights and duties. This allows auditors to have sufficient power to carry out an independent and effective audit.

The audit is primarily a statutory concept, and eligibility to conduct an audit is often set down in statute. Similarly, the rights and duties of auditors can be set down in law, to ensure that the auditors have sufficient power to carry out an effective audit. In this section we look at the rights and duties of auditors in the **UK as an example** (but bear in mind that these may be different in other jurisdictions). The relevant legislation in the UK is the **Companies Act 2006**.

1.3.1 Duties

The auditors are required to report on every statement of financial position (balance sheet) and statement of profit or loss and comprehensive income (profit and loss account) laid before the company in general meeting.

The auditors must consider the following.

Compliance with legislation	Whether the financial statements have been prepared in accordance with the relevant legislation
Truth and fairness of accounts	Whether the statement of financial position shows a true and fair view of the company's affairs at the end of the period and the statement of profit or loss and other comprehensive income (and statement of cash flows) show a true and fair view of the results for that period
Adequate accounting records and returns	Whether adequate accounting records have been kept and returns adequate for the audit received from branches not visited by the auditor
Agreement of accounts to records	Whether the accounts are in agreement with the accounting records and returns
Consistency of other information	Whether the information in the directors' report is consistent with the financial statements
Directors' benefits	Whether disclosure of directors' benefits has been made in accordance with the Companies Act 2006

1.3.2 Rights

The auditors must have certain rights to enable them to carry out their duties effectively.

The principal rights that auditors should have, excepting those dealing with resignation or removal, are set out in the table that follows.

Access to records	A right of access at all times to the books, accounts and vouchers of the company (in whatever form they are held)
Information and explanations	A right to require from the company's officers such information and explanations as they think necessary for the performance of their duties as auditors
Attendance at / notices of general meetings	A right to attend any general meetings of the company and to receive all notices of and other communications relating to such meetings which any member of the company is entitled to receive
Right to be heard at general meetings	A right to be heard at general meetings which they attend on any part of the business that concerns them as auditors
Rights in relation to written resolutions	A right to receive a copy of any written resolution proposed

If auditors have not received all the information and explanations they consider necessary, they should state this fact in their audit report.

The Companies Act 2006 makes it an offence for a company's officer to knowingly or recklessly make a statement in any form to an auditor which:

- Conveys or purports to convey any information or explanation required by the auditor
- Is misleading, false or deceptive in a material particular

2 Appointment, removal and resignation of auditors

FAST FORWARD

There are various legal and professional requirements on appointment, resignation and removal of auditors which must be followed.

2.1 Appointment

The auditors should be appointed by and therefore **answerable** to the **shareholders**. The table below shows what the position should ideally be, again using the **UK as an example**. The Companies Act 2006 sets out the rules for appointment of auditors. An auditor must be appointed for each financial year unless the directors reasonably resolve otherwise on the grounds that audited financial statements are unlikely to be required. The table summarises who can appoint auditors for UK public companies.

AUDITOR APPOINTMENT (UK)	
Directors	Can appoint auditor: (a) Before company's **first period for appointing auditors** (b) Following a period during which the company **did not have an** auditor (as exempt), at any time before the next period for appointing auditors (c) To fill a **casual vacancy**
Members	Can appoint auditor by ordinary resolution: (a) During a **period for appointing auditors** (b) If company **should have** appointed auditor during a period for appointing auditors **but failed to do so** (c) If directors **fail to do so**
Secretary of State	Can appoint auditors if **no auditors** are **appointed** per above

2.1.1 Remuneration

The remuneration of the auditors, which will include auditors' expenses, will be fixed by whoever made the appointment.

However the auditors' remuneration is fixed, in many countries it must be disclosed in the annual financial statements of the company.

2.2 Resignation and removal

The legal requirements for resignation and removal of auditors using the **UK as an example** are discussed below.

It is important that auditors know the procedures, because as part of their client acceptance, they have a duty to ensure the old auditors were properly removed from office.

RESIGNATION OF AUDITORS (UK)		
1	Resignation procedures	Auditors deposit **written notice** together with **statement of circumstances** relevant to members/creditors or statement that no such circumstances exist. A statement of circumstance must always be submitted for a quoted company, even if the auditor considers that there are no circumstances that should be brought to the attention of members or creditors.
2	Notice of resignation	Sent by **company** to regulatory authority.
3	Statement of circumstances	Sent by: (a) Auditors to regulatory authority (b) Company to everyone entitled to receive a copy of accounts
4	Convening of general meeting	**Auditors** can **require directors** to call an **extraordinary general meeting** to discuss circumstances of resignation. Directors must send out notice for meeting within **21 days** of having received requisition by auditors.
5	Statement prior to general meeting	**Auditors** may require company to circulate (different) **statement of circumstances** to everyone entitled to notice of meeting.
6	Other rights of auditors	Can **receive all notices** that relate to: (a) A general meeting at which their term of office would have expired (b) A general meeting where casual vacancy caused by their resignation is to be filled Can **speak** at these meetings on **any matter** which **concerns them as auditors.**

REMOVAL OF AUDITORS (UK)		
1	Notice of removal	**Either special notice** (28 days) with copy sent to auditor **Or** if elective resolution in place, **written resolution** to terminate auditors' appointment Directors must convene a meeting within a reasonable period of time.
2	Representations	**Auditors** can make **representations** on why they ought to stay in office. They may require company to state in notice that representations have been made and send copy to members.
3	If resolution passed	(a) Company must **notify** regulatory authority (b) Auditors must **deposit statement of circumstances** at company's registered office **within 14 days** of ceasing to hold office. Statement must be sent to regulatory authority
4	Auditor rights	Can **receive notice** of and **speak** at: (a) A general meeting at which their term of office would have expired (b) A general meeting where casual vacancy caused by their removal is to be filled

The UK's Companies Act 2006 places a requirement on auditors to notify the appropriate audit authority in certain circumstances on leaving office.

If it is a **major audit** (quoted company or major public interest company), the notification must be given **whenever** an auditor ceases to hold office.

If it is **not a major audit**, the notification is only required if the auditor is leaving **before** the end of their term of office.

The appropriate audit authority is:

• Secretary of State or delegated body (such as the UK Conduct Committee) if a major audit
• Recognised Supervisory Body (eg ACCA) for other audits

Notice must inform the appropriate audit authority that the auditor has ceased to hold office and be accompanied by a statement of circumstances or no circumstances.

3 Regulation of auditors

FAST FORWARD

Requirements for the **eligibility**, **registration** and **training** of auditors are extremely important, as they are designed to maintain standards in the auditing profession.

3.1 National level

The accounting and auditing profession varies in structure from country to country. In some countries accountants and auditors are subject to strict legislative regulation, while in others the profession is allowed to regulate itself. We cannot look at every country, but some of the examples below will show you the divergence of structure and we can make some general points.

3.1.1 United Kingdom

In the UK there are a number of different accountancy, or accountancy-related, institutes and associations, such as the Association of Chartered Certified Accountants (ACCA), the Institute of Chartered Accountants in England and Wales (ICAEW) and the Institute of Chartered Accountants of Scotland (ICAS). All these bodies vary from each other but they are all characterised by various attributes:

- Stringent entrance requirements (examinations and practical experience)
- Strict code of ethics
- Technical updating of members

3.1.2 France

In France, the accounting profession is split into two distinct organisations:

- Accountants (Ordre des Experts Comptables et des Comptables Agréés)
- Auditors (Compagnie Nationale des Commissaires aux Comptes)

Most members of the auditors' organisation are also members of the more important accountants' organisation. Examinations, work experience and articles are similar to those of the UK accountancy bodies. The profession's main influence is through the issue of non-mandatory opinions and recommendations of accounting principles relevant to the implementation of the National Plan.

3.1.3 Germany

The main professional body in Germany is the Institute of Certified Public Accountants (Institut der Wirtschaftsprüfer). Members of this institute carry out all the statutory audits, and are required to have very high educational qualifications and experience. The Institute issues a form of auditing standard but this is tied very closely to legislation. As well as auditing, members are mainly involved in tax and business management, with no obvious significant role in establishing financial accounting principles and practices. There is no independent accounting standard-setting body.

3.1.4 US

In the US, accountants are members of the American Institute of Certified Public Accountants (AICPA), a private sector body. Although the Securities and Exchange Commission in the US can prescribe accounting standards for listed companies, it relies on the Financial Accounting Standards Board (FASB), an independent body, to set such standards. In turn, FASB keeps in close contact with the AICPA, which issues guidance on US standards and is closely involved in their development.

3.1.5 Ghana

In Ghana, the Institute of Chartered Accountants (Ghana), established in 1963, is the sole body charged with the regulation of the accountancy profession. Its members are the only persons recognised under the country's companies' legislation to carry out the audit of company financial statements. The institute is governed by a council of 11 chartered accountants.

3.1.6 Singapore

The Institute of Certified Public Accountants of Singapore (ICPAS) is the national organisation of the accountancy profession in Singapore. It was established in 1963 and its objective is to develop, support and enhance the integrity, status and interests of the accountancy profession in Singapore. ICPAS has a Joint Scheme of Examination agreement in place with ACCA.

3.1.7 General points

It can be seen from the above paragraphs that the accounting and auditing profession in most Western countries is regulated by legislation to some extent. In the UK and the US the profession effectively regulates itself, ie regulation is devolved from statute to the private bodies involved in the accountancy profession. In many European countries, statutory control by governments is much more direct.

3.2 EU member states

Persons carrying out audits in EU member states must have the permission of the relevant authorities. New legislation to improve the quality of statutory audit across the EU was finalised in June 2014. Key measures include strengthening the independence of statutory auditors, making the auditor's report more informative, and improving audit supervision throughout the EU. The new legislation will become applicable in mid-2016.

In the UK, the relevant authorities are **Recognised Supervisory Bodies** (RSBs). As well as giving authority, RSBs in the UK supervise and monitor auditors. In other countries, however, supervising and monitoring is carried out by a state body or by the national government.

The Companies Act 2006 defines an RSB as a body established in the UK which maintains and enforces rules as to the:

*   Eligibility of persons for appointment as a statutory auditor
*   Conduct of statutory audit work

The following bodies are all RSBs:

*   ACCA
*   ICAEW
*   ICAS
*   Chartered Accountants Ireland
*   Association of Authorised Public Accountants (AAPA)

Professional qualifications, which will be prerequisites for membership of an RSB, are offered by **Recognised Qualifying Bodies** (RQBs) approved by the Government. RQBs include ACCA, ICAEW and ICAS among others.

3.3 International level

Regulations governing auditors will, in most countries, be most important at the national level. International regulation, however, can play a major part by:

(a)   Setting **minimum standards** and **requirements** for auditors
(b)   Providing **guidance** for those countries without a **well-developed national regulatory framework**
(c)   Aiding **intra-country recognition** of professional accountancy qualifications

3.3.1 International Federation of Accountants (IFAC)

IFAC, based in New York, is a non-profit, non-governmental, non-political international organisation of accountancy bodies. The ACCA is a member of IFAC.

IFAC came into being in the 1970s as a result of proposals put forward and eventually approved by the International Congress of Accountants. IFAC's mission is:

> 'To serve the public interest by: contributing to the development, adoption and implementation of high quality international standards and guidance; contributing to the development of strong professional accountancy organisations and accounting firms, and to high quality practices by professional accountants; promoting the value of professional accountants worldwide; speaking out on public interest issues where the accountancy profession's expertise is most relevant.'

IFAC co-operates with member bodies, regional organisations of accountancy bodies and other world organisations. Through such co-operation, IFAC initiates, co-ordinates and guides efforts to achieve international technical, ethical and educational pronouncements for the accountancy profession.

Any accountancy body may join IFAC if it is recognised by law or general consensus within its own country as a substantial national organisation of good standing within the accountancy profession. Members of IFAC automatically become members of the International Accounting Standards Committee Foundation, which is an independent not-for-profit, private sector organisation which sets international financial reporting standards through its standard-setting body, the International Accounting Standards Board.

3.4 Regulation, monitoring and supervision

Each country's regulation of external audits will differ. Most regimes do have certain common elements:

(a) **Education and work experience**: IFAC has issued guidance on this (see Section 3.5).

(b) **Eligibility**: There may well be statutory rules determining who can act as auditors. Membership of an appropriate body is likely to be one criterion.

(c) **Supervision and monitoring**: These activities initially came under particular scrutiny in a number of countries during the 1990s and these activities are again under the spotlight following the recent global economic crisis. Questions have been asked about why auditors have failed to identify impending corporate failures and whether they were being regulated strongly enough. The supervision regime has come under particular scrutiny in countries where regulation and supervision is done by the auditors' own professional body (self-regulation). Suggestions have been made in these countries that supervision ought to be by external government agencies.

3.5 Education, examinations and experience

IFAC issues guidance to tackle the problems of intra-country recognition of qualifications. It sets minimum standards for accountancy qualifications. The International Accounting Education Standards Board (IAESB) is part of IFAC and its *Framework for International Education Standards for Professional Accountants* is intended to assist IFAC member bodies, as they have direct or indirect responsibility for the education and development of their members and students. The IAESB also publishes International Education Standards (IESs) which aim to increase the competence of the global accountancy profession. These documents are not examinable for F8 but can provide useful supplementary information and are accessible on the IFAC website. Here we will consider three important areas in general below.

3.5.1 Education

The theoretical knowledge to be contained in the body of knowledge of accountants should include compulsory subjects (such as audit, consolidated accounts and general accounting) and relevant subjects (such as law and economics). Accountants should have covered these subjects in a breadth and depth sufficient to enable them to perform their duties to the expected standard.

3.5.2 Examinations

Accountants should demonstrate that they have passed an examination of professional competence. This examination must assess not only the necessary level of **theoretical** knowledge but also the ability to apply that knowledge competently in a **practical** situation. Objective evaluation of professional examinations is important.

3.5.3 Experience

It is crucial for any professional to not only have a sound theoretical knowledge, but also be able to apply that knowledge competently in the work place.

Individuals should have completed an appropriate period of approved and properly supervised practical experience primarily in the area of audit and accountancy and in a suitable professional environment.

3.6 Eligibility to act as auditor

Eligibility to act as an auditor is likely to arise from membership of some kind of regulatory body.

Bodies of this type will offer qualifications and set up rules to ensure compliance with any statutory requirements related to auditors. In this way national governments will control who may act as an auditor to limited liability companies, or to any other body requiring a statutory audit.

The regulatory body should have rules to ensure that those eligible for appointment as a company auditor are either:

- **Individuals** holding an **appropriate qualification**, or
- **Firms controlled** by **qualified persons**

Regulatory bodies should also have procedures to maintain the competence of members. The regulatory body's rules should ensure that only **fit and proper** persons are appointed as company auditors and that company audit work is conducted **properly** and with **professional integrity**.

The regulatory body should include rules as to the **technical standards** to be followed when carrying out company audit work (eg following International Standards on Auditing (ISAs)).

The regulatory body should also provide for adequate monitoring and enforcement of compliance with its rules.

Membership of a regulatory body is the main prerequisite for **eligibility** as an auditor.

A person should be **ineligible** for appointment as a company auditor if they are:

- An **officer or employee** of the company
- A **partner or employee** of such a person
- A **partnership** in which such a person is a partner

There may be further rules about connections between the company or its officers and the auditor, depending on local statutory rules.

3.7 Supervisory and monitoring roles

Some kind of supervision and monitoring regime should be implemented by the regulatory body. This should inspect auditors on a regular basis.

The frequency of inspection will depend on the number of partners, number of offices and number of listed company audits (these factors may also be reflected in the size of annual registration fees payable by approved audit firms).

The following features should be apparent in each practice visited by the monitoring regulatory body.

(a) A **properly structured audit approach**, suitable for the range of clients served and work undertaken by the practice

(b)   **Carefully instituted quality control procedures**, revised and updated constantly, to which the practice as a whole is committed

(c)   Commitment to **ethical guidelines**, with an emphasis on independence issues

(d)   An emphasis on **technical excellence**

(e)   Adherence to the **'fit and proper' criteria** by checking personnel records and references

(f)   Use of internal and, if necessary, external **peer reviews**, consultations etc

(g)   Charging **appropriate fee** per audit assignment

4 International Standards on Auditing   Dec 10

International Standards on Auditing are set by the **International Auditing and Assurance Standards Board.**

4.1 Rules governing audits

We discussed in Chapter 1 the various stakeholders in a company, and the various people who might read a company's financial statements. Consider also that some of these readers will not just be reading a single company's financial statements, but will also be looking at those of a large number of companies, and making comparisons between them.

Readers want **assurance** when making comparisons that the **reliability** of the financial statements **does not vary from company to company**. This assurance will be obtained not just from knowing that each set of financial statements has been audited, but also from knowing that this has been done to **common standards**.

Hence there is a need for audits to be **regulated** so that auditors follow the same standards. As we see in this chapter, auditors have to follow rules issued by a variety of bodies. Some obligations are imposed by governments in law or statute. Some obligations are imposed by the professional bodies to which auditors are required to belong, such as the ACCA.

ISAs are produced by the **International Auditing and Assurance Standards Board (IAASB)**, a technical standing committee of IFAC, which also issues standards relating to review engagements, other assurance engagements, quality control and related services.

An explanation of the workings of the IAASB, the authority of ISAs and so on are laid out in the *Preface to the International Standards on Quality Control, Auditing, Review, Other Assurance and Related Services*, and we will look at this in the next section. The IAASB also provide a *Glossary of Terms* which provides definitions for the key terms and criteria used throughout the ISAs.

4.2 Preface

The preface states that the IAASB's objective is the development of a set of international standards that are accepted worldwide. The IAASB's pronouncements relate to audit, other assurance and related services that are conducted in accordance with international standards.

Within each country, local laws and regulations govern, to a greater or lesser degree, the practices followed in the auditing of financial or other information. Such regulations may be either of a statutory nature or in the form of statements issued by the regulatory or professional bodies in the countries concerned. For example, in the UK, the Financial Reporting Council Board sets ISAs, and the Companies Act 2006 provides legislative regulations.

4.2.1 The authority attached to ISAs and other pronouncements

The preface also lays out the authority attached to international standards issued by the IAASB:

IAASB Pronouncements	
International Standards on Auditing (ISAs)	To be applied in the audit of historical financial information
International Standards on Review Engagements (ISREs)	To be applied in the review of historical financial information
International Standards on Assurance Engagements (ISAEs)	To be applied in assurance engagements dealing with subject matters other than historical financial information
International Standards on Related Services (ISRSs)	To be applied to compilation engagements, engagements to apply agreed-upon procedures to information and other related services engagements as specified by the IAASB
International Standards on Quality Control (ISQCs)	To be applied for all services falling under the IAASB's engagement standards (ISAs, ISREs, ISAEs, ISRSs)
International Auditing Practice Notes (IAPNs)	Provide practical assistance to auditors

Note that IAPNs are a new category of pronouncement for use in issuing non-authoritative material and at the time of writing this Text there is only one IAPN in issue relating to the auditing of financial instruments.

Any **limitation** of the applicability of a specific ISA is made very clear in the Preface.

4.2.2 Relationship between ISAs and national regulation

Exam focus point

> The relationship between ISAs and national regulation is not examinable under the current ACCA F8 syllabus. This section has been included for your reference only.

ISAs do **not** override the local regulations referred to above governing the audit of financial or other information in a particular country.

(a) To the extent that ISAs **conform** with local regulations on a particular subject, the audit of financial or other information in that country in accordance with local regulations will automatically comply with the ISA regarding that subject.

(b) In the event that the local regulations **differ from**, or conflict with, ISAs on a particular subject, member bodies should comply with the obligations of members set forth in the IFAC Constitution as regards these ISAs (ie **encourage changes** in local regulations to comply with ISAs).

The IAASB also publishes other papers, such as **Discussion Papers**, to promote discussion on auditing, review, other assurance and related services and quality control issues affecting the accounting profession, present findings, or describe matters of interest relating to these engagements.

4.2.3 Working procedures of the IAASB

A rigorous due process is followed by the IAASB to ensure that the views of all those affected by its guidance are taken into account. The following diagram summarises the process followed in the development of IAASB standards.

Research and consultation
A project task force is established to develop a draft standard or practice statement.

↓

Transparent debate
A proposed standard is discussed at a meeting, open to the public.

↓

Exposure for public comment
Exposure drafts are put on the IAASB's website and widely distributed for comment for a minimum of 120 days.

↓

Consideration of comments
Any comments as a result of the exposure draft are considered at an open meeting of the IAASB, and it is revised as necessary.

↓

Affirmative approval
Approval is made by the affirmative vote of at least $^2/_3$ of IAASB members.

4.3 Current ISAs and other standards

The following list sets out the clarified ISAs that this Study Text is based on and other documents expected to be examinable for F8.

No	Title
200	Overall objectives of the independent auditor and the conduct of an audit in accordance with International Standards on Auditing
210	Agreeing the terms of audit engagements
220	Quality control for an audit of financial statements
230	Audit documentation
240	The auditor's responsibilities relating to fraud in an audit of financial statements
250	Consideration of laws and regulations in an audit of financial statements
260 (Revised)	Communication with those charged with governance
265	Communicating deficiencies in internal control to those charged with governance and management
300	Planning an audit of financial statements
315 (Revised)	Identifying and assessing the risks of material misstatement through understanding the entity and its environment
320	Materiality in planning and performing an audit
330	The auditor's responses to assessed risks
402	Audit considerations relating to an entity using a service organisation
450	Evaluation of misstatements identified during the audit
500	Audit evidence
501	Audit evidence – specific considerations for selected items
505	External confirmations

No	Title
510	Initial audit engagements – opening balances
520	Analytical procedures
530	Audit sampling
540	Auditing accounting estimates, including fair value accounting estimates, and related disclosures
560	Subsequent events
570 (Revised)	Going concern
580	Written representations
610 (Revised)	Using the work of internal auditors
620	Using the work of an auditor's expert
700 (Revised)	Forming an opinion and reporting on financial statements
701	Communicating key audit matters in the independent auditor's report
705 (Revised)	Modifications to the opinion in the independent auditor's report
706	Emphasis of matter paragraphs and other matter paragraphs in the independent auditor's report
720 (Revised)	The auditor's responsibilities relating to other information
	Addressing Disclosures in the Audit of Financial Statements – Revised ISAs and Related Conforming Amendments

The **preface**, **glossary of terms** and *International framework for assurance engagements* are also examinable, along with the following IAASB pronouncement:

International Standards on Assurance Engagements	
ISAE 3000 (Revised)	Assurance engagements other than audits or reviews of historical financial information

Examinable documents other than the IAASB pronouncements are:

Other documents
ACCA's Code of Ethics and Conduct
FRC Guidance on Audit Committees (Revised September 2012) as an example of guidance on best practice in relation to audit committees
The UK Corporate Governance Code (Revised September 2014) as an example of a code of best practice

Exam focus point

> ISAs are quoted throughout this Text and you must understand how they are applied in practice. You do not therefore need to know ISA numbers, the names of the standards or the details off by heart – it's your ability to **apply** them in the exam that will be tested.

4.4 Application of ISAs to small and medium-sized entities

4.4.1 Introduction

The IAASB is strongly of the view that an 'audit is an audit' and that users who receive audit reports expressing an opinion have to have confidence in those opinions, whether they are in relation to large or small entity financial statements. However, the IAASB have recognised the importance of those who audit small and medium-sized entities (SMEs) and the ISAs include guidance where relevant on how certain requirements can be met when auditing **smaller entities**.

4.4.2 Qualitative characteristics of a smaller entity

These are identified by ISA 200 as follows:

(a)   Concentration of ownership and management in a small number of individuals; and
(b)   One or more of the following:

      (i)   Straightforward or uncomplicated transactions
      (ii)   Simple record-keeping
      (iii)   Few lines of business and few products within business lines
      (iv)   Few internal controls
      (v)   Few levels of management with responsibility for a broad range of controls; or
      (vi)   Few personnel, many having a wide range of duties

4.4.3 Considerations specific to SME entities

The structure of the ISAs means they are suitable for SMEs. Notably they include:

- A separate section for requirements to help readability and clarification of conditional requirements
- Requirements capable of being applied proportionately
- Additional guidance specific to SME audits

4.4.4 IAASB guidance

In August 2009 the IAASB issued a Question and Answer documents *Applying ISAs proportionately with the size and complexity of an entity*. This provides a good overview of the key messages in this area.

More detailed guidance can be found in the IAASB's *Guide to using international standards on auditing in the audits of small and medium-sized entities*, the second edition of which was released in October 2010.

Both of these publications can be downloaded from the IAASB website.

Chapter Roundup

- Most companies are required to have an audit by law, but some small companies are exempt. The outcome of the audit is the **auditor's report**, which sets out the auditor's **opinion** on the financial statements.

- The law gives auditors both rights and duties. This allows auditors to have sufficient power to carry out an independent and effective audit.

- There are various legal and professional requirements on appointment, resignation and removal of auditors which must be followed.

- Requirements for the **eligibility**, **registration** and **training** of auditors are extremely important, as they are designed to maintain standards in the auditing profession.

- **International Standards on Auditing** are set by the **International Auditing and Assurance Standards Board**.

Quick Quiz

1   What position would make a person ineligible for appointment as a company auditor?

2   A person does not have to satisfy membership criteria to become a member of an RSB.

    True ☐   False ☐

3   Using the UK as an example, who can appoint an auditor?

4   The ACCA has its own monitoring unit which inspects registered auditors on a regular basis.

    True ☐   False ☐

5   What is the function of IFAC?

6   Which of the following are not engagement standards issued by the IAASB?

- International Standards on Auditing
- International Standards on Quality Control
- International Auditing Practice Notes
- International Standards on Related Services
- International Standards on Assurance Engagements
- International Standards on Review Engagements

1   An officer or employee of the company
     A partner or employee of such a person
     A partnership in which such a person is a partner

2   False. All RSBs have stringent membership requirements.

3   Members can appoint the auditors (at each general meeting where accounts are laid).

     Directors can appoint the auditors (before the first general meeting where accounts are laid or to fill a casual vacancy).

     The Secretary of State can appoint the auditors (if no auditors are appointed/reappointed at the general meeting where accounts are laid).

4   True

5   The function of IFAC is to initiate, co-ordinate and guide efforts to achieve international technical, ethical and educational pronouncements for the accountancy profession.

6   International Standards on Quality Control and International Auditing Practice Notes are not engagement standards issued by the IAASB. The others are all classed as engagement standards.

Now try the questions below from the Practice Question Bank

Number	Level	Marks	Time
Q2	Examination	10	20 mins
Q3	Introductory	n/a	n/a

3

Corporate governance

Topic list	Syllabus reference
1 Codes of corporate governance	A3
2 Audit committees	A3
3 Internal control effectiveness	A3
4 Communication with those charged with governance	A3

Introduction

The concept of corporate governance was introduced in Chapter 1. In this chapter we will look at the codes of practice that have been put in place to ensure that companies are well managed and controlled. The UK Corporate Governance Code is an internationally recognised code which we will use as an example of a code of best practice. The audit carried out by the external auditors is a very important part of corporate governance, as it is an independent check on what the directors are reporting to the shareholders.

Auditors of all kinds have most contact with the audit committee, a sub-committee of the board of directors. External auditors liaise with the audit committee over the audit, and internal auditors will report their findings about internal control effectiveness to it. We shall look at audit committees in Section 2 and internal control effectiveness in Section 3.

We end this chapter with a consideration of the importance of auditors communicating with those charged with governance in an entity. ISA 260 *Communication with those charged with governance* provides guidance for auditors in this respect.

Study guide

		Intellectual level
A3	**Corporate governance**	
(a)	Discuss the objectives, relevance and importance of corporate governance.	2
(b)	Discuss the provisions of international codes of corporate governance (such as OECD) that are most relevant to auditors.	2
(c)	Describe good corporate governance requirements relating to directors' responsibilities (eg for risk management and internal control) and the reporting responsibilities of auditors.	2
(d)	Evaluate corporate governance deficiencies and provide recommendations to allow compliance with international codes of corporate governance.	2
(e)	Analyse the structure and roles of audit committees and discuss their benefits and limitations.	2
(f)	Explain the importance of internal control and risk management.	1
(g)	Discuss the need for auditors to communicate with those charged with governance.	2

Exam guide

Questions on corporate governance could be either knowledge-based or application-based and may be part of a scenario question on ethics. This topic can also be examined in the form of OTQs in Section A of the exam.

1 Codes of corporate governance   Dec 11, June 14

FAST FORWARD

> **Corporate governance** is the system by which companies are **directed and controlled**. Good corporate governance is important because the owners of a company and the people who manage the company are not always the same.

1.1 The importance of corporate governance

Key term

Corporate governance is the system by which companies are directed and controlled.

There are various stakeholders in companies, as we discussed in Chapter 1. The **Cadbury Report** on financial aspects of corporate governance commissioned by the UK Government identified the following.

- **Directors**: responsible for corporate governance
- **Shareholders**: linked to the directors by the financial statements
- **Other relevant parties**: such as employees, customers and suppliers (stakeholders)

In some companies, the **shareholders** are **fully informed about** the **management** of the business because they are directors themselves, whereas in other companies the **shareholders** only have an opportunity to find out about the management of the company at the **annual general meeting (AGM)**.

The **day to day running of a company is the responsibility of the directors** and other management staff to whom they delegate and, although the company's results are submitted for shareholders' approval at the AGM, there is often apathy and acquiescence to directors' recommendations.

AGMs are often very poorly attended. For these reasons, there is the **potential** for **conflicts of interest** between management and shareholders.

Corporate governance is important because it ensures that stakeholders with a relevant interest in the company's business are fully taken into account.

In other words, it is necessary for structures to be in place to ensure that every stakeholder in the company is not disadvantaged. As it is the directors that manage the company, the burden of good corporate governance falls on them. It is important that they manage the company in the best way for the shareholders, employees and other parties.

1.2 OECD Principles of Corporate Governance

FAST FORWARD

The **OECD Principles of Corporate Governance** set out the rights of shareholders, the importance of disclosure and transparency and the responsibilities of the board of directors.

An important question to consider is 'Will the same way of managing companies be the best method for all companies?' The answer is likely to be no. Companies are different from each other, and, globally, they operate in different legal systems with different institutions, frameworks and traditions. It would not be possible to construct one single way of operating companies that could be described as good practice for all.

The key issue in corporate governance is that 'a high degree of priority [is] placed on the interests of shareholders, who place their trust in corporations to use their investment funds wisely and effectively'. Shareholders in a company might be a family, they might be the general public or they might be institutional investors representing, in particular, people's future pensions. These shareholders will vary in their degree of interaction with the company and their directors.

In the context of this great variety in the basic element of these companies, the Organisation for Economic Co-operation and Development (OECD) has established a number of **Principles of Corporate Governance**, which were issued in 1999 and reviewed in 2004, and which serve as a **reference point** for countries (to develop corporate governance codes if they wish) and companies. They were developed in response to a mandate given to the OECD to develop a set of standards and guidelines on good corporate governance.

OECD Principles of Corporate Governance	
I	The corporate governance framework should promote transparent and efficient markets, be consistent with the rule of law and clearly articulate the division of responsibilities among different supervisory, regulatory and enforcement authorities.
II	The corporate governance framework should protect and facilitate the exercise of shareholders' rights.
III	The corporate governance framework should ensure the equitable treatment of all shareholders, including minority and foreign shareholders. All shareholders should have the opportunity to obtain effective redress for violation of their rights.
IV	The corporate governance framework should recognise the rights of stakeholders established by law or through mutual agreements and encourage active co-operation between corporations and stakeholders in creating wealth, jobs and the sustainability of financially sound enterprises.
V	The corporate governance framework should ensure that timely and accurate disclosure is made on all material matters regarding the corporation, including the financial situation, performance, ownership and governance of the company.
VI	The corporate governance framework should ensure the strategic guidance of the company, the effective monitoring of management by the board, and the board's accountability to the company and the shareholders.

The global financial crisis prompted the OECD to investigate the shortcomings in corporate governance highlighted by the crisis. This investigation started in 2008 and led to the publication of *Conclusions and emerging good practices to enhance implementation of the Principles* in February 2010. The guidance includes recommendations to help companies and governments to overcome corporate governance weaknesses and support a more effective implementation of the OECD principles described above. It concentrates on the following areas:

- Governance of **remuneration and incentives**
- Improving the governance of **risk management**
- Improving **board practices**
- The exercise of **shareholder rights**

This publication (and the OECD Principles) can be found on the OECD website at www.oecd.org.

When applying the OECD principles, in order to obtain the best advantages and avoid the worst disadvantages, countries may take a hybrid approach and make some elements of corporate governance mandatory and some voluntary. For instance, in the UK, companies are required to comply with **legislation** (such as the Companies Act) and there is also a **voluntary corporate governance code**, the UK Corporate Governance Code, which contains some **mandatory elements** for listed companies. We discuss the provisions of the UK Corporate Governance Code below.

1.3 The UK Corporate Governance Code

The **UK Corporate Governance Code** contains detailed guidance for UK companies on good corporate governance.

1.3.1 A history of corporate governance in the UK

Before we discuss the principles of the UK Corporate Governance Code (formerly known as The Combined Code on Corporate Governance) in detail, it is useful to provide a short history of corporate governance in the UK.

As a result of several accounting scandals in the 1980s and 1990s (Mirror Group, BCCI, PollyPeck), the **Cadbury** committee produced a report entitled *Financial aspects of corporate governance*.

In 1995, the **Greenbury** report added a set of principles on the remuneration of executive directors. The **Hampel** report in 1998 brought the Cadbury and Greenbury reports together to form the first **Combined Code**. In 1999, **Turnbull** produced a report relating to risk management and internal control which ultimately resulted in the Financial Reporting Council (FRC) providing guidance for directors on how to comply with internal control provisions in the Combined Code.

In 2002, the **Higgs** report (*Review of the role and effectiveness of non-executive directors*) was commissioned to produce a single comprehensive code, which was refined by the FRC to produce the Combined Code. At the same time, the **Smith** report was produced on the role of audit committees, and the recommendations of this were incorporated into the new Combined Code. The Smith guidance on audit committees, intended to help companies implement the audit committee related sections of the Combined Code, became the **FRC *Guidance on Audit Committees*** when a new edition of the guidance was published in 2008 (again updated in 2010 – see below).

The Combined Code was reviewed in 2005 and 2007 resulting in a small number of changes. However, the financial crisis in 2008 and 2009 prompted the FRC to undertake an extensive review in 2009 and a revised code, the ***UK Corporate Governance Code***, was published in May 2010 (subsequently updated in September 2012). This code incorporates recommendations made by **Sir David Walker** in a report on his review of the governance of banks and other financial institutions.

Having concluded during its 2009 review that a major reason for corporate governance failings was a lack of interaction between the boards of listed companies and shareholders, the FRC deemed it necessary to also publish a UK Stewardship Code in July 2010. This Stewardship Code provides guidance on good practice for investors and separates out the principles and provisions relevant to institutional shareholders, which used to be included in the Combined Code.

Later that year (December 2010) the FRC published its *Guidance on Audit Committees* which is designed to assist company boards in making suitable arrangements for their audit committees, and to assist directors serving on audit committees in carrying out their role. The guidance aims to help company boards to implement the relevant provisions of the UK Corporate Governance Code.

In March 2011 the FRC published its *Guidance on Board Effectiveness*, a guidance note issued by the FRC to assist companies in applying the principles of the UK Corporate Governance Code. It replaced the *Good Practice Suggestions from the Higgs Report*.

In September 2012, the FRC revised the *UK Corporate Governance Code*, *Stewardship Code* and *Guidance on Audit Committees* to introduce further guidance aimed at ensuring management, audit committees and auditors report material issues to investors completely and fairly.

Following a consultation in late 2013, the FRC published a revised *UK Corporate Governance Code* again in September 2014, this time targeting the going concern, executive remuneration and risk management reporting. The changes, made in response to the Sharman Inquiry in 2012, are controversial with companies and investors. The changes around the assessment of going concern by companies, in particular, have been criticised for failing to address the investors' concerns and placing a heavy risk management and reporting burden on the boards.

FRC publications can be found on the FRC website (www.frc.org.uk).

1.3.2 Principles of the UK Corporate Governance Code

The UK Corporate Governance Code, produced by the FRC, sets out standards of good practice regarding board leadership and effectiveness, accountability (including audit), remuneration and relations with shareholders.

All companies with a Premium Listing of equity shares in the UK are required under the Listing Rules to report on how they have applied the Code in their annual report and accounts (regardless of whether the company is incorporated in the UK or elsewhere).

The Code contains **broad principles** and more **specific provisions**. Listed companies have to report how they have applied the principles, and either confirm that they have applied the provisions or provide an explanation if they have not. There is a separate section of the Code devoted to the application of this '**comply or explain**' concept. It sets out that choosing not to follow a provision may be justified by the board if good governance is achieved by other means. However, the reasons for not complying should be clearly and fully explained to the shareholders. Any explanation must include details as to how actual practices are consistent with the overall principle to which a provision relates.

The broad principles of the Code are as follows.

Principles of the UK Corporate Governance Code (for listed UK companies)

Leadership

- Every company should be headed by an effective board, which is collectively responsible for the long-term success of the company.

- There should be a clear division of responsibilities at the head of the company between the running of the board and the executive responsibility for the running of the company's business. No one individual should have unfettered powers of decision.

- The chairman is responsible for leadership of the board and ensuring its effectiveness on all aspects of its role.

- As part of their role as members of a unitary board, non-executive directors should constructively challenge and help develop proposals on strategy.

Principles of the UK Corporate Governance Code (for listed UK companies)
Effectiveness
• The board and its committees should have the appropriate balance of skills, experience, independence and knowledge of the company to enable them to discharge their respective duties and responsibilities effectively.
• There should be a formal, rigorous and transparent procedure for the appointment of new directors to the board.
• All directors should be able to allocate sufficient time to the company to discharge their responsibilities effectively.
• All directors should receive induction on joining the board and should regularly update and refresh their skills and knowledge.
• The board should be supplied in a timely manner with information in a form and of a quality appropriate to enable it to discharge its duties.
• The board should undertake a formal and rigorous annual evaluation of its own performance and that of its committees and individual directors.
• All directors should be submitted for re-election at regular intervals, subject to continued satisfactory performance.
Accountability
• The board should present a balanced and understandable assessment of the company's position and prospects.
• The board is responsible for determining the nature and extent of the principal risks it is willing to take in achieving its strategic objectives. The board should maintain sound risk management and internal control systems.
• The board should establish formal and transparent arrangements for considering how it should apply the corporate reporting and risk management and internal control principles and for maintaining an appropriate relationship with the company's auditor.
Remuneration
• Executive directors' remuneration should be designed to promote the long-term success of the company. Performance-related elements should be transparent, stretching and rigorously applied.
• There should be a formal and transparent procedure for developing policy on executive remuneration and for fixing the remuneration packages of individual directors. No director should be involved in deciding their own remuneration.
Relations with shareholders
• There should be a dialogue with shareholders based on the mutual understanding of objectives. The board as a whole has responsibility for ensuring that a satisfactory dialogue with shareholders takes place.
• The board should use the AGM to communicate with investors and to encourage their participation.

Exam focus point

Make sure you learn the principles in the table above. You may be presented with a scenario in which you are asked to identify corporate governance deficiencies and make recommendations to improve corporate governance.

1.3.3 Auditors and the UK Corporate Governance Code

The principles and provisions in the 'Accountability' section of the UK Corporate Governance Code deal with the board's relationship with the auditor.

In the UK, companies affected by the UK Corporate Governance Code will need an annual, independent audit of the financial statements. As we have seen, one of the Code's main principles is:

'The board should establish formal and transparent arrangements for considering how it should apply the corporate reporting and risk management and internal control principles and for maintaining an appropriate relationship with the company's auditor.'

The Code goes on to suggest that, in order to maintain an appropriate relationship with the auditor, an **audit committee** (see Section 2) should be set up.

The auditor's suitability and performance for large UK listed entities should be periodically compared to those of other potential auditors, according to a provision that was added to the Code when it was updated in September 2012. This states that FTSE 350 companies (the top 350 listed companies in the UK) should put the external audit contract out to tender **at least every ten years**. We will revisit this provision when we look at audit committees in Section 2 of this chapter, since that committee is normally responsible for making recommendations on appointment and removal of external auditors.

Auditors have an important role to play in maintaining good corporate governance. If information is disclosed and audited according to a high quality, the reliability and comparability of reporting will be increased and investors will be able to make better investment decisions. Shareholders should benefit from auditors' checks on the disclosures made by the board in order to comply with corporate governance best practice.

So for example, auditors could be asked to review whether companies are applying certain aspects of corporate governance codes. What auditors need to report on will depend on the laws and regulations applicable in specific countries.

Auditors of listed companies in the UK are required to report on whether the companies comply with the provisions of the UK Corporate Governance Code. The Code sets out a list of specific disclosures which entities applying the Code must include in their annual reports.

In September 2012, the Code was revised to require directors to include a statement in the annual report that they consider the annual report and accounts as a whole to be fair, balanced and understandable and provides the information necessary for shareholders to assess the entity's performance, business model and strategy.

The 2014 revision of the Code adds another specific requirement, this time about going concern. The directors are required to state in annual and half-yearly financial statements whether they considered it appropriate to adopt the going concern basis of accounting, and identify any material uncertainties in relation to going concern over a period of at least 12 months from the date of approval of the financial statements.

Entities applying the Code also need to describe the work of the audit committee in discharging its responsibilities and should include the significant issues the committee considered relating to the financial statements, including matters communicated to it by the auditor and what action was taken in response.

These provisions in the Code have given rise to additional reporting responsibilities in the UK, since auditors now have to report by exception if these areas of the annual report are inconsistent with the auditor's knowledge acquired during the audit.

1.3.4 Directors

The directors of a company should set company policy, including risk policy, and are responsible for the company's systems and controls. They should make sure they set enough time aside, and that they have the necessary experience and skill, to do this effectively.

Policy

Directors are ultimately responsible for managing the company, and this includes setting strategy, budgets, managing the company's people, maintaining company assets and ensuring corporate governance rules are kept. An important element of setting strategies is determining and managing risks. We shall outline in Chapter 5 how internal audit may have a role in this area.

The UK Corporate Governance Code requires that there is clear division of responsibility at the head of a company between the chairman and the chief executive. It requires that no one individual has unfettered powers of decision. The chairman also has to meet the same independence criteria as non-executive

directors and should not be a former chief executive of the same company except in exceptional circumstances.

The board should be supplied with information in a timely manner to enable it to carry out its duties and directors should receive induction on joining the board and should regularly update and refresh their skills.

Systems, controls and monitoring

Directors are responsible for the systems put in place to achieve the company policies and the controls put in place to mitigate risks. These issues will be considered further later in this chapter. Under the Code, UK boards (through the audit committee) are required to consider annually whether an internal audit department is required. If there is no internal audit function, the reasons for not having one need to be explained in the annual report.

The directors are also responsible for **monitoring** the effectiveness of systems and controls. **Internal auditors** have an important role in this area, as we shall discuss in Chapter 5, but remember it is the directors that are responsible for determining whether to have an internal audit department to assist them in monitoring in the first place.

In the UK, the Turnbull report on internal control made the following recommendations which formed the basis of guidance on internal control issued by the FRC (*Internal Control: Guidance for Directors*) aimed at assisting companies in applying the UK Corporate Governance Code internal control provisions.

Turnbull Guidelines
Have a **defined process** for the effectiveness of internal control
Review **regular reports** on internal control
Consider **key risks** and how they have been managed
Check the **adequacy** of **action taken** to remedy weaknesses and incidents
Consider the **adequacy** of **monitoring**
Conduct an **annual assessment** of risks and the effectiveness of internal control
Make a **statement** on this process in the **annual report**

Key term

> **Non-executive directors** are directors who do not have day to day operational responsibility for the company. They are not employees of the company or affiliated with it in any other way.

An important recommendation of the principles of the UK Corporate Governance Code is that the board contains some non-executive directors to ensure that it exercises **objective judgement**. The UK Corporate Governance Code requires 'an appropriate combination' of executive and non-executive directors on the board and recommends that at least half the board should comprise non-executive directors.

Such non-executive directors may have a particular role in some sensitive areas, such as company reporting, nomination of directors and remuneration of executive directors. It is important, therefore, that they have the appropriate mix of skills, commitment, experience and independence to carry out their roles effectively. One of the non-executives should be appointed as the senior independent director who will be available to shareholders if they have concerns.

Because the composition and effectiveness of the board is so important, it is recommended that board evaluation reviews are externally facilitated at least every three years for boards of FTSE 350 companies. The directors of these companies should also be subject to **annual re-election** by shareholders. For other companies, the directors should be subject to re-election at regular intervals of no more than three years.

Often, companies will set up sub-committees of the board to deal with specific issues highlighted by the Code. We are now going on to consider one such sub-committee, the **audit committee**, in more detail.

Exam focus point

> A question on corporate governance could come up in a scenario-based question, perhaps in conjunction with internal audit (which we cover in Chapter 5), as the two are linked.

2 Audit committees

June 2009, Dec 14

An **audit committee** can help a company maintain objectivity with regard to financial reporting and the audit of financial statements.

2.1 Role and function of audit committees

An **audit committee** is a sub-committee of the board of directors, usually containing a number of non-executive directors. The role and function of the audit committee should be set out in written terms of reference and the extract from the UK Corporate Governance Code on the next page details what the roles and responsibilities of the audit committee should include.

First, though, we will consider the **advantages** of having an audit committee. An audit committee can:

(a) Improve the quality of financial reporting, by reviewing the financial statements on behalf of the board

(b) Create a climate of discipline and control which will reduce the opportunity for fraud

(c) Enable the non-executive directors to contribute an independent judgement and play a positive role

(d) Help the finance director, by providing a forum in which they can raise issues of concern and which they can use to get things done which might otherwise be difficult

(e) Strengthen the position of the external auditor by providing a channel of communication and forum for issues of concern

(f) Provide a framework within which the external auditor can assert their independence in the event of a dispute with management

(g) Strengthen the position of the internal audit function, by providing a greater degree of independence from management

(h) Increase public confidence in the credibility and objectivity of financial statements

One of the principles of the UK Corporate Governance Code is that 'the board should establish formal and transparent arrangements for considering how they should apply the corporate reporting and risk management and internal control principles and for maintaining an appropriate relationship with the company's auditors'. The provisions relating to this principle are set out in the following table.

UK Corporate Governance Code provisions relating to the audit committee

The board should establish an audit committee of at least three or, in the case of smaller companies, two **independent non-executive directors**.

In smaller companies the company chairman may be a member of, but not chair, the committee in addition to the independent non-executive directors, provided they were considered independent on appointment as chairman. The board should satisfy itself that at least one member of the audit committee has recent and relevant financial experience.

The main role and responsibilities should be set out in **written terms of reference** and should include:

(a) To monitor the integrity of the financial statements of the company and any formal announcements relating to the company's financial performance, reviewing significant financial reporting issues and judgements contained in them

(b) To review the company's internal financial controls and, unless expressly addressed by a separate board risk committee composed of independent directors, or by the board itself, the company's control and risk management systems

(c) To monitor and review the effectiveness of the company's internal audit function

(d) To make recommendations to the board, for it to put to the shareholders for their approval in general meeting, in relation to the appointment, reappointment and removal of the external auditor and to approve the remuneration and terms of engagement of the external auditors

(e) To review and monitor the external auditor's independence and objectivity and the effectiveness of the audit process, taking into consideration relevant UK professional and regulatory requirements

BPP
LEARNING MEDIA

Part A Audit framework and regulation | **3: Corporate governance**   45

(f)   To develop and implement policy on the engagement of the external auditor to supply non-audit services, taking into account relevant ethical guidance regarding the provision of non-audit services by the external audit firm, and to report to the board, identifying any matters in respect of which it considers that action or improvement is needed and making recommendations as to the steps to be taken

(g)   To report to the board on how it has discharged its responsibilities

The terms of reference of the audit committee, including its role and the authority delegated to it by the board, should be made available.

Where requested by the board, the audit committee should provide advice on whether the annual report and accounts, taken as a whole, is fair, balanced and understandable and provides the information necessary for shareholders to assess the company's performance, business model and strategy.

The audit committee should review arrangements by which staff of the company may, in confidence, raise concerns about possible improprieties in matters of financial reporting or other matters. The audit committee's objective should be to ensure that arrangements are in place for the proportionate and independent investigation of such matters and for appropriate follow-up action.

The audit committee should monitor and review the effectiveness of the internal audit activities. Where there is no internal audit function, the audit committee should consider annually whether there is a need for an internal audit function and make a recommendation to the board, and the reasons for the absence of such a function should be explained in the relevant section of the annual report.

The audit committee should have primary responsibility for making a recommendation on the appointment, reappointment and removal of the external auditors. FTSE 350 companies should put the external audit contract out to tender at least every ten years. If the board does not accept the audit committee's recommendation, it should include it in the annual report and, in any papers recommending appointment or reappointment, a statement from the audit committee explaining the recommendation and should set out reasons why the board has taken a different position.

A separate section of the annual report should describe the work of the committee in discharging its responsibilities. The report should include:

(a)   The significant issues that the committee considered in relation to the financial statements, and how these issues were addressed

(b)   An explanation of how it has assessed the effectiveness of the external audit process and the approach taken to the appointment or reappointment of the external auditor and information on the length of tenure of the current audit firm and when a tender was last conducted

(c)   If the external auditor provides non-audit services, an explanation of how auditor objectivity and independence is safeguarded

2.2 Relationship with the board

The UK FRC published its latest *Guidance on audit committees* in September 2012. This guidance, which largely echoes the UK Corporate Governance Code, points out that audit committee arrangements will vary from company to company. It is the responsibility of every board to consider what arrangements are most suitable to the organisation's particular circumstances: 'Audit committee arrangements need to be proportionate to the task, and will vary according to the size, complexity and risk profile of the company.'

As we have seen in the summary of the UK Corporate Governance Code requirements above, the board should set out the roles and responsibilities of the audit committee in written terms of reference. The FRC guidance suggests that the audit committee should review its terms of reference annually. Both the board and the audit committee should review the audit committee's effectiveness on an annual basis.

As the audit committee undertakes tasks on behalf of the board, it is to the board that the audit committee reports the results of its work. It is important to remember, as FRC's guidance states, 'many of the core functions of the audit committees [...] are expressed in terms of '**oversight**', '**assessment**' and '**review**' of a particular function.' Although its oversight function may require it to do detailed work at times, it is not the audit committee's duty to carry out work which properly belongs to others. For example, it would be inappropriate for the audit committee to prepare the financial statements on behalf of management.

2.3 Drawbacks of audit committees

We discussed the possible benefits of the audit committee above.

Opponents of audit committees argue that:

(a)   The executive directors may **not understand** the purpose of an audit committee and may perceive that it detracts from their authority.

(b)   There may be **difficulty selecting** sufficient non-executive directors with the necessary competence in auditing matters for the committee to be really effective.

(c)   The establishment of such a **formalised reporting procedure** may **dissuade** the **auditors** from raising matters of judgement and limit them to reporting only on matters of fact.

(d)   **Costs** may be **increased**.

3 Internal control effectiveness

FAST FORWARD

> The **directors** of a company are **responsible** for ensuring that a company's **risk management and internal controls systems** are **effective**.

3.1 Importance of internal control and risk management

Internal controls are essential to management, as they contribute to:

*   Safeguarding the company's **assets**
*   Helping to prevent and detect **fraud**
*   Safeguarding the shareholders' **investment**

Good internal control helps the business to run efficiently. A control system reduces identified risks to the business. It also helps to ensure reliability of reporting and compliance with laws.

3.2 Directors' responsibilities for internal control

The **ultimate responsibility** for a company's system of internal controls lies with the **board of directors**. It should set procedures of internal control and regularly monitor that the system operates as it should.

Part of setting up an internal control system will involve **assessing the risks** facing the business, so that the **system** can be **designed** to ensure those **risks are avoided**.

Internal control systems will always have **inherent limitations**, the most important being that a system of internal control cannot eliminate the possibility of human error, or the chance that staff will collude in fraud.

Once the directors have set up a system of internal control, they are responsible for **reviewing** it regularly to ensure that it **still meets its objectives**.

The board may decide that in order to carry out its review function properly it has to employ an **internal audit function** to undertake this task. When deciding whether an internal audit function is required, directors will need to consider the extent of systems and controls, and the relative expense of obtaining checks from other parties, such as the external auditors. These issues will be considered in more detail in Chapter 5.

If the board does not see the need for an internal audit function, in the UK, the UK Corporate Governance Code requires companies to consider the need for one annually, so that the **need for internal audit is regularly reviewed**.

The Code also recommends that the board of directors **reports** on its **review of** the company's **risk management** and **internal controls** systems as part of the annual report.

The statement should be based on an **annual assessment** of internal control which should confirm that the board has considered **all significant aspects** of internal control. In particular the assessment should cover:

(a)   The **changes** since the last **assessment** in **risks** faced, and the company's **ability** to **respond** to **changes** in its business environment

(b)   The **scope** and **quality** of management's monitoring of risk and internal control, and of the work of internal audit, or consideration of the need for an internal audit function if the company does not have one

(c)   The **extent** and **frequency** of reports to the board

(d)   **Significant controls**, **failings** and **weaknesses** (deficiencies) which have or might have material impacts on the accounts

(e)   The **effectiveness** of the **public reporting** processes

3.3 Auditors' responsibilities for internal control

The auditors' detailed responsibilities with regard to reporting on the requirements of the UK Corporate Governance Code are set out in bulletins issued by the UK's FRC, which are not examinable.

However, in summary, the auditors should **review the statements** made concerning internal control in the annual report to ensure that they appear **true** and are **not in conflict** with the audited financial statements.

4 Communication with those charged with governance
Dec 09, June 13

FAST FORWARD

Auditors shall **communicate** specific matters to **those charged with governance** and ISA 260 provides guidance for auditors in this area.

4.1 The importance of communicating with those charged with governance

ISA 260 *Communication with those charged with governance* sets out guidance for auditors on the communication of audit matters arising from the audit of the financial statements of an entity with those charged with governance.

'Those charged with governance' is defined by ISA 260 as 'the person(s) or organisation(s) with responsibility for **overseeing the strategic direction** of the entity and obligations related to the **accountability** of the entity'.

'Management' is defined by ISA 260 as 'the person(s) with executive responsibility for the conduct of the entity's operations'.

Communication with those charged with governance is important because:

•   It assists the auditor and those charged with governance to **understand** audit-related matters in context and allows them to **develop a constructive working relationship**.

•   It allows the auditor to **obtain information** relevant to the audit.

•   It assists those charged with governance to fulfil their **responsibility** to oversee the financial reporting process, thus reducing the risks of material misstatement in the financial statements.

4.2 Matters to be communicated by auditors to those charged with governance

The following matters shall be communicated to those charged with governance.

The auditor's responsibilities in relation to the financial statement audit

Including that the auditor is responsible for forming and expressing an opinion on the financial statements and that the audit does not relieve management or those charged with governance of their responsibilities.

Planned scope and timing of the audit

An overview of the planned scope and timing of the audit – this also includes communicating about the significant risks identified by the auditor.

Significant findings from the audit

The auditor shall communicate the following:

- The auditor's views about significant qualitative aspects of the entity's accounting practices, including accounting policies, accounting estimates and financial statement disclosures

- Significant difficulties encountered during the audit

- Significant matters arising from the audit that were discussed or subject to correspondence with management

- Written representations requested by the auditor

- Any circumstances that affect the form and content of the auditor's report, including

    - Modifications to the auditor's report
    - Material uncertainty related going concern
    - Key audit matters
    - The inclusion of an Emphasis of Matter or Other Matter paragraph

- Any other significant matters that, in the auditor's professional judgement, are relevant to the oversight of the financial reporting process

Auditor independence

The auditor shall communicate the following for **listed** entities:

- A statement that the engagement team and others in the firm, the firm, and network firms have complied with relevant ethical requirements regarding independence

- All relationships between the firm and entity that may reasonably be thought to bear on independence

- Related safeguards that have been applied to eliminate identified threats to independence or reduce them to an acceptable level

4.3 The communication process

The auditor shall communicate with those charged with governance the **form, timing and expected general content** of communications. The auditor shall communicate with those charged with governance on a **timely basis**.

As we saw above, the auditor is required to communicate with those charged with governance in respect of the auditor's responsibilities, the planned scope and timing of the audit, significant findings and auditor independence.

The auditor's responsibilities will initially be set out in the **engagement letter**, which is a written agreement of the terms of the audit engagement. The letter will detail the respective responsibilities of the auditor and management at the client. We cover the engagement letter in detail in Chapter 4.

The engagement letter will also set out the scope and objective of the audit, but there will often be a separate **planning letter** dealing with timings, fees and other matters which may change on an annual basis.

In addition, an initial **planning meeting** may be set up to discuss and plan the scope and timing of detailed audit work. Commonly the auditors will provide a list of records and documents they require and agree with management when they will be made available. Any issues relating to auditor independence may also be discussed along with trading performance and significant events occurring in the year under review.

During the audit itself there is ongoing communication between the audit team and management as issues arise. This includes having open and constructive communication about significant qualitative aspects of the entity's accounting practices and the quality of the related disclosures. For example, those charged with governance may be interested to know the auditor's evaluation of whether disclosures of the estimation uncertainty relating to provisions are adequate.

However, the significant findings referred to in Section 4.2 are commonly presented and discussed in a meeting with those charged with governance following the detailed audit work. There will be a written form of communication from the auditors present at the meeting setting out all the significant matters. This written communication of key issues will usually be accompanied by (or include) a **report to management** setting out significant deficiencies encountered in internal control discovered during the audit, the implications of the deficiencies and related recommendations. We look at the report to management in detail in Chapter 19.

Chapter Roundup

- **Corporate governance** is the system by which companies are **directed and controlled**.
- The **OECD Principles of Corporate Governance** set out the rights of shareholders, the importance of disclosure and transparency and the responsibilities of the board of directors.
- The **UK Corporate Governance Code** contains detailed guidance for UK companies on good corporate governance.
- An **audit committee** can help a company maintain objectivity with regard to financial reporting and the audit of financial statements.
- The **directors** of a company are **responsible** for ensuring that a company's **risk management and internal control systems** are **effective**.
- Auditors shall **communicate** specific matters to **those charged with governance** and ISA 260 provides guidance for auditors in this area.

Quick Quiz

1   Briefly explain the meaning of the term 'corporate governance'.

2   The OECD principles strongly recommend:

    A   An annual audit
    B   Internal audit
    C   Directors should not receive pay
    D   Directors should be non-executive

3   Complete the blanks.

    An audit.............is a sub-committee of the............. ...., usually containing a number of.........................directors.

4   When a company cannot easily find non-executive directors it should not have an audit committee.

    True   ☐

    False   ☐

5   Why are internal controls important in a company?

Answers to Quick Quiz

1   'Corporate governance' is the system by which companies are directed and controlled.

2   A

3   An audit **committee** is a sub-committee of the **board of directors**, usually containing a number of **non-executive** directors.

4   False. It should have an audit committee if required, or if the directors feel it is in the best interests of the shareholders, even if it is difficult to find non-executive directors.

5   Internal controls contribute to:

- Safeguarding company assets
- Preventing and detecting fraud
- Safeguarding the shareholder's investment

Now try the question below from the Practice Question Bank

Number	Level	Marks	Time
Q4	Introductory	n/a	n/a

Professional ethics and quality control procedures

4

Topic list	Syllabus reference
1 Fundamental principles of professional ethics	A4, B1
2 Accepting audit appointments	B1
3 Agreeing the terms of the engagement	B1
4 Quality control at a firm level	B1
5 Quality control on an individual audit	B1

Introduction

In Chapter 2 we looked at some of the regulations surrounding the external audit. Here we look at the ethical requirements of the RSBs, specifically the ACCA's *Code of ethics and conduct*, which is based on the IESBA's *Code of ethics for professional accountants*.

The ethical matters covered in this chapter are very important. They could arise in almost every type of exam question and you must be able to apply the ACCA's guidance on ethical matters to any given situation, but remember that common sense is usually a good guide.

First we examine the five fundamental principles of professional ethics as defined in the ACCA's *Code of ethics and conduct*. We then look at the five main threats to compliance with these principles and the sorts of safeguards that can be put in place to mitigate these threats.

Sections 2 and 3 of this chapter are concerned with obtaining audit engagements and agreeing the terms of the engagement.

Study guide

		Intellectual level
A4	**Professional ethics and ACCA's Code of Ethics and Conduct**	
(a)	Define and apply the fundamental principles of professional ethics of integrity, objectivity, professional competence and due care, confidentiality and professional behaviour.	2
(b)	Define and apply the conceptual framework, including the threats to the fundamental principles of self-interest, self-review, advocacy, familiarity and intimidation.	2
(c)	Discuss the safeguards to offset the threats to the fundamental principles.	2
(d)	Describe the auditor's responsibility with regard to auditor independence, conflicts of interest and confidentiality.	1
B1	**Obtaining and accepting audit engagements**	
(a)	Discuss the requirements of professional ethics and ISAs in relation to the acceptance/continuance of audit engagements.	2
(b)	Explain the preconditions for an audit.	2
(c)	Explain the process by which an auditor obtains an audit engagement.	2
(d)	Discuss the importance of engagement letters and their contents.	1
(e)	Explain the quality control procedures that should be in place over engagement performance, monitoring quality and compliance with ethical requirements.	2

Exam guide

Questions about auditor independence and objectivity may involve discussion of topical or controversial issues in a scenario-based question, such as the provision of services other than the audit to audit clients. Exam questions will generally require you to consider the possible threats and to suggest appropriate safeguards to mitigate those threats. Other questions may include knowledge-based questions on topics such as the audit engagement letter. You are equally likely to encounter a scenario-based question on ethical threats and threats to auditor independence, asking you to recommend safeguards to mitigate those threats.

Remember to be realistic when suggesting safeguards. In past exams, it was noted that candidates suggested resignation where this may have been too extreme for the situation in question. The same question also asked students to describe the steps an audit firm should take prior to accepting a new audit engagement.

Other possible topics to be examined include:

(a) Assessing whether the preconditions for an audit are present. Assessing 'preconditions' is a topic of F8 which has arisen from the International Auditing and Assurance Standards Board (IAASB) Clarity project.

(b) Explaining the purpose of the engagement letter and detailing the matters contained in an engagement letter.

(c) Discussing voluntary and obligatory disclosure in accordance with auditors' responsibilities in relation to client confidentiality.

ISA 220 *Quality control for an audit of financial statements* has become examinable for exams from September 2016. As this is a new syllabus area, make sure that you are well prepared to answer questions on this topic.

1 Fundamental principles of professional ethics

The ACCA's *Code of ethics and conduct* sets out the five **fundamental principles** of professional ethics and provides a **conceptual framework** for applying them.

The ACCA's *Code of ethics and conduct* sets out five fundamental principles of professional ethics and provides a conceptual framework for applying those principles. Members must apply this conceptual framework to identify threats to compliance with the principles, evaluate their significance and apply appropriate safeguards to eliminate or reduce them so that compliance is not compromised.

One of the PER performance objectives is to demonstrate the application of professional ethics, values and judgement (objective 1). Applying the knowledge you gain from this chapter will help you to achieve that objective.

1.1 The fundamental principles

Members of the ACCA must comply with the fundamental principles set out in the *Code of ethics and conduct* (**integrity, objectivity, professional competence and due care, confidentiality and professional behaviour**).

The five fundamental principles are summarised in the table below.

The ACCA's fundamental principles of professional ethics	
Integrity	Members shall be straightforward and honest in all professional and business relationships.
Objectivity	Members shall not allow bias, conflicts of interest or undue influence of others to override professional or business judgements.
Professional competence and due care	Members have a continuing duty to maintain professional knowledge and skill at the level required to ensure that a client or employer receives competent professional services based on current developments in practice, legislation and techniques. Members shall act diligently and in accordance with applicable technical and professional standards.
Confidentiality	Members shall respect the confidentiality of information acquired as a result of professional and business relationships and, therefore, not disclose any such information to third parties without proper and specific authority, or unless there is a legal or professional right or duty to disclose. Confidential information acquired as a result of professional and business relationships must not be used for the personal advantage of members or third parties.
Professional behaviour	Members shall comply with relevant laws and regulations and avoid any action that discredits the profession.

1.2 Confidentiality

Although auditors have a professional duty of **confidentiality**, they may be compelled by **law** or consider it necessary in the **public interest** to disclose details of clients' affairs to third parties.

Confidentiality requires members to refrain from disclosing information acquired in the course of professional work except where:

(a)   Disclosure is permitted by law and is **authorised by the client** or the employer;

(b)   Disclosure is **required by law**, for example:

   (i)   Production of documents or other provision of evidence in the course of legal proceedings; or

   (ii)   Disclosure to the appropriate public authorities of infringements of the law that come to light; and

(c)   There is **a professional duty or right to disclose**, when not prohibited by law:

   (i)   To comply with the quality review of ACCA or another professional body;
   (ii)   To respond to an inquiry or investigation by ACCA or a regulatory body;
   (iii)   To protect the professional interests of a professional accountant in legal proceedings; or
   (iv)   To comply with technical standards and ethics requirements.

There are a number of factors to consider when deciding whether to disclose confidential information and the following factors are identified in the ACCA Code:

- Whether the interests of all parties (including affected third parties) could be harmed if the client or employer consents to the disclosure of information by the professional accountant

- Whether all the relevant information is known and substantiated, to the extent it is practicable

- The type of communication that is expected and to whom it is addressed

- Whether the parties to whom the communication is addressed are appropriate recipients.

Members acquiring information in the course of professional work should neither use nor appear to use that information for their **personal advantage** or for the **advantage of a third party**.

In general, where there is a right (as opposed to a duty) to disclose information, members should only make disclosure in pursuit of a public duty or professional obligation.

Members must make clear to a client that they may only act for them if the client agrees to disclose in full to all information relevant to the engagement.

Where a member agrees to serve a client in a professional capacity both the member and the client should be aware that it is an **implied term** of that agreement that the **member will not disclose** the client's affairs to any other person except with the client's consent or within the terms of certain **recognised exceptions**, which fall under **obligatory** and **voluntary** disclosures.

1.2.1 Obligatory disclosure

If members know or suspect their client to have committed **money-laundering**, **treason**, **drug-trafficking** or **terrorist** offences, they are obliged to disclose all the information at their disposal to a competent authority.

Auditing standards require auditors to consider whether **non-compliance** with laws and regulations affects the accounts.

1.2.2 Voluntary disclosure

Voluntary disclosure may be applicable in the following situations.

- Disclosure is reasonably necessary to **protect** the **member's interests**, for example to enable them to sue for fees or defend an action for, say, negligence.

- Disclosure is **authorised by statute**.

- Where it is in the **public interest to disclose**, say, where an offence has been committed which is contrary to the public interest.

- **Disclosure** is to **non-governmental bodies** which have statutory powers to compel disclosure.

If ACCA members are requested to assist the police, the taxation or other authorities by providing information about a client's affairs in connection with enquiries being made, they should first enquire under what **statutory authority** the information is demanded.

Unless they are satisfied that such statutory authority exists they should decline to give any information until they have obtained their client's authority. If the client's authority is not forthcoming and the demand for information is pressed the member should not accede unless advised by their legal adviser.

If members know or suspect that a client has committed a wrongful act they must give careful thought to their own position. They must ensure that they have not prejudiced themselves by, for example, relying on information given by the client which subsequently proves to be incorrect.

However, it would be a **criminal offence** for **members to act positively**, without lawful authority or reasonable excuse, in such a manner as **to impede with intent** the arrest or prosecution of a client whom they know or believe to have committed an arrestable offence.

1.2.3 Disclosure in the public interest

The courts have never given a definition of 'the public interest'. This means that, again, the issue is left to the judgement of the auditor. It is often therefore appropriate for the member to seek legal advice.

It is only appropriate for information to be disclosed to certain authorities; for example, the police.

The ACCA guidance states that there are several factors that the member should take into account when deciding whether to make disclosure. These are:

- The size of the amounts involved and the extent of likely financial damage
- Whether members of the public are likely to be affected
- The possibility or likelihood of repetition
- The reasons for the client's unwillingness to make disclosures to the authority
- The gravity of the matter
- Relevant legislation, accounting and auditing standards
- Any legal advice obtained

Under ISA 250 *Consideration of laws and regulations in an audit of financial statements*, if auditors become aware of a suspected or actual instance of non-compliance with law and regulation which gives rise to a statutory duty to report, they should report it to the proper authority immediately. They should also seek legal advice.

1.3 Integrity, objectivity and independence

The fundamental principles require that members behave with integrity in all professional and business relationships and strive for objectivity in all their professional and business judgements. Objectivity is a state of mind but in certain roles the preservation of objectivity has to be shown by the maintenance of **independence** from those influences which could impair objectivity.

What is required in order to be, and be seen to be, independent?

Key terms

> **Independence of mind:** The state of mind that permits the provision of an opinion without being affected by influences that compromise professional judgement, allowing an individual to act with integrity, and exercise objectivity and professional scepticism.
>
> **Independence in appearance:** The avoidance of facts and circumstances that are so significant that a reasonable and informed third party, having knowledge of all relevant information, including safeguards applied, would reasonably conclude a firm's, or a member of the assurance team's, integrity, objectivity or professional scepticism had been compromised.

It is very important that auditors are **impartial** and **independent** of management, so that they can give an **objective** view on the financial statements of an entity. The onus is always on the auditor not only to be ethical but also to be **seen** to be ethical.

Independence and objectivity matter because of:

(a)   The **expectations** of those directly affected, particularly the members of the company. The audit should be able to provide **objective** assurance on the truth and fairness of the financial statements that the directors can never provide.

(b)   The **public interest**. Companies are public entities, governed by rules requiring the disclosure of information.

What can the auditor do to preserve objectivity? The simple answer would be to **withdraw from any engagement** where there is the **slightest threat** to objectivity. However, there are disadvantages in this strict approach.

*   Clients may lose an auditor who knows their business.
*   It denies clients the freedom to be advised by the accountant of their choice.

A better approach would be to **consider** whether the **auditors' own objectivity** and the **general safeguards** operating in the professional environment are **sufficient** to offset the threat and to **consider** whether **safeguards over and above** the general safeguards are required, for example specified partners or staff not working on an assignment.

Having said that, it may not be desirable to withdraw from an engagement or to refuse to act for a client; in some cases this may be the only option if the threat to independence is too great.

1.4 Threats to independence and objectivity   Specimen Exam, June 15

FAST FORWARD

> Threats to independence and objectivity may arise in the form of **self-review, self-interest, advocacy, familiarity and intimidation threats**. Appropriate **safeguards** must be put in place to eliminate or reduce such threats to acceptable levels.

Compliance with the fundamental principles of professional ethics may potentially be threatened by a wide range of different circumstances. These generally fall into five categories:

*   Self-interest (discussed in Section 1.4.1)
*   Self-review (discussed in Section 1.4.2)
*   Advocacy (discussed in Section 1.4.3)
*   Familiarity (discussed in Section 1.4.4)
*   Intimidation (discussed in Section 1.4.5)

Although we may talk about circumstances resulting in threats under a particular threat heading (such as self-interest), it is important to note that certain situations give rise to more than one type of threat.

As we progress through the rest of the chapter you will see there are some ethical requirements relating purely to **public interest entities**.

Key term

> **Public interest entities** are defined in the ACCA Code as:
>
> (a)   All listed entities; and
>
> (b)   Any entity:
>   (i)   Defined by regulation or legislation as a public interest entity; or
>   (ii)   For which the audit is required by regulation or legislation to be conducted in compliance with the same independence requirements that apply to the audit of listed entities. Such regulation may be promulgated by any relevant regulator, including an audit regulator; and
>
> (c)   Entities that are of significant public interest because of their business, their size or their number of employees or their corporate status is such that they have a wide range of stakeholders. Examples of such entities may include credit institutions (for example, banks), insurance companies, investment firms and pension firms.

1.4.1 Self-interest

The ACCA *Code of ethics and conduct* highlights a number of areas in which a self-interest threat might arise. A self-interest threat is the threat that a financial or other interest will inappropriately influence the professional accountant's judgement or behaviour.

Self-interest threats may arise as a result of the financial or other interests of members or of immediate or close family and are summarised in the diagram below.

We will look at each of these areas in turn.

(a) **Financial interests**

A **financial interest** exists where an audit firm has a financial interest in a client's affairs, for example, the audit firm owns shares in the client, or is a trustee of a trust that holds shares in the client.

The ACCA does not allow the following to own a direct financial interest or an indirect material financial interest in a client:

- The **audit** firm
- A **member** of the audit team
- An **immediate family member of a member** of the audit team

The following safeguards will therefore be relevant:

- Disposing of the interest
- Removing the individual from the team if required
- Keeping the client's audit committee informed of the situation
- Using an independent partner to review work carried out if necessary

Audit firms should have quality control procedures requiring staff to disclose relevant financial interests for themselves and close family members. They should also foster a culture of voluntary disclosure on an ongoing basis so that any potential problems are identified in a timely manner.

(b) **Close business relationships**

Close business relationships between a firm, or an audit team member, or a member of that individual's immediate family, and the audit client (or its management) arise from commercial relationships or common financial interests.

Examples of when an audit firm and an audit client have a close business relationship include:

(i) Having a financial interest in a joint venture with either the client or a controlling owner, director, officer or other individual who performs senior managerial activities for that client

(ii) Arrangements to combine one or more services or products of the firm with one or more services or products of the audit client and to market the package with reference to both parties

(iii) Distribution or marketing arrangements under which the firm acts as distributor or marketer of the audit client's products or services or vice versa

It will be necessary for the partners to judge the materiality of the interest and therefore its significance. However, **unless the interest is clearly insignificant, an audit provider should not**

participate in such a venture with an audit client. Appropriate safeguards are therefore to end the assurance provision or to terminate the (other) business relationship.

If an individual member of an audit team has such an interest, they should be removed from the audit team.

If the business relationship is between an immediate family member of a member of the audit team and the audit client or its management, the significance of any threat must be evaluated and safeguards applied when necessary to eliminate the threat or reduce it to an acceptable level.

Generally speaking, **purchasing goods and services from an audit client on an arm's length basis does not constitute a threat to independence**. However, the transactions may be of such a nature or magnitude that they create a self-interest threat. If this results in a threat to independence then safeguards may be necessary.

(c) **Employment with an audit client**

It is possible that staff might transfer between an audit firm and a client, or that negotiations or interviews to facilitate such movement might take place. Both situations are a threat to independence:

(i)   An audit staff member might be motivated by a desire to impress a future possible employer (objectivity is therefore affected – self-interest threat).

(ii)   A former audit partner turned Finance Director has too much knowledge of the audit firm's systems and procedures.

In general, there may be **familiarity** and **intimidation threats** when a member of the audit team joins an audit client. If a **'significant connection'** still **remains** between the audit firm and the former employee/partner, **then no safeguards could reduce the threat to an acceptable level**. This would be the case where:

(i)   The individual is entitled to benefits from the audit firm (unless fixed and predetermined, and not material to the firm).

(ii)   The individual continues to participate in the audit firm's business or professional activities.

If there is no significant connection, then the threat depends on:

(i)   The **position** the individual has taken at the client

(ii)   Any **involvement** the individual will have **with the audit team**

(iii) The **length of time** since the individual was a member of the audit team or partner of the firm

(iv)   The **former position** of the individual **within the audit team or firm**; for example, whether the individual was responsible for maintaining regular contact with the client's management or those charged with governance

Safeguards could include:

(i)   **Modifying** the **audit plan**

(ii)   **Assigning individuals** to the audit team **who have sufficient experience** in relation to the individual who has joined the client

(iii) Having an independent professional accountant **review** the work of the former member of the audit team

If the **audit client** is a **public interest entity**, 'cooling off' periods are required. The ACCA Code states that **when a key audit partner (defined below) joins such a client**, either as a director or as an employee with significant influence on the financial statements, independence would be deemed to be compromised unless:

(i)   Subsequent to the partner ceasing to be a key audit partner, the public interest entity had issued audited financial statements covering a period of not less than twelve months.

(ii)   The partner was not a member of the audit team with respect to the audit of those financial statements.

In the case of a **senior or managing partner joining an audit client**, 12 months must have passed since the individual was senior or managing partner (ie there is no requirement for audited financial statements to have been issued).

The **key audit partner** is the:

- Engagement partner;
- Individual responsible for the engagement quality control review; or
- One of the other audit partners on the engagement team.

The key audit partner makes key decisions or judgements on significant matters with respect to the audit of the financial statements on which the firm will express an opinion. Depending on the circumstances and the role of the individuals on the audit, 'other audit partners' may include, for example, audit partners responsible for significant subsidiaries or divisions.

(d)   **Temporary staff assignments**

Staff may be loaned to an audit client, but only **for a short period of time. Staff must not assume management responsibilities**, or undertake any audit work that is prohibited elsewhere in the Code.

The audit client must be responsible for directing and supervising the activities of the loaned staff. Possible safeguards include:

- Conducting an additional review of the work performed by the loaned staff

- Not giving the loaned staff audit responsibility for any function or activity on the audit that they performed during the temporary staff assignment

- Not including the loaned staff in the audit team

(e)   **Partner on client board**

A partner or employee of an audit firm should not serve on the board of an audit client.

It may be acceptable for a partner or an employee of an audit firm to perform the role of company secretary for an audit client, if the role is essentially administrative.

(f)   **Family and personal relationships**

Family or close personal relationships between audit firm and client staff could seriously threaten independence. Each situation has to be evaluated individually. Factors to consider are:

- The individual's responsibilities on the audit engagement
- The closeness of the relationship
- The role of the other party at the audit client

When an immediate family member of a member of the audit team is a director, an officer or an employee of the audit client in a position to exert direct and significant influence over the subject matter information of the audit engagement, the individual should be removed from the audit team.

The audit firm should also consider whether there is any threat to independence if an employee who is not a member of the audit team has a close family or personal relationship with a director, an officer or an employee of an audit client.

A firm should have quality control policies and procedures under which staff should disclose if a close family member employed by the client is promoted within the client.

If a firm inadvertently violates the rules concerning family and personal relationships they must apply additional safeguards, such as undertaking a quality control review of the audit and discussing the matter with the audit committee of the client, if there is one.

(g) **Compensation and evaluation policies**

There is a self-interest threat when a member of the audit team is evaluated on selling non-assurance services to the client. The significance of the threat depends on:

- The proportion of the individual's compensation or performance evaluation that is based on the sale of such services

- The role of the individual on the audit team

- Whether promotion decisions are influenced by the sale of such services

The firm should either revise the compensation plan or evaluation process, or put in place appropriate safeguards. Safeguards include:

- Removing the member from the audit team
- Having the team member's work reviewed by a professional accountant

A **key audit partner shall not be evaluated or compensated based on their success in selling non-assurance services** to their audit client.

(h) **Gifts and hospitality**

Unless the value of the gift/hospitality is **trivial and inconsequential**, a firm or a member of an audit team should not accept.

(i) **Loans and guarantees**

The advice on loans and guarantees falls into two categories:

- The client is a bank or other similar institution
- Other situations

If a lending institution client (eg a bank) lends an immaterial amount to an audit firm or member of assurance team on normal commercial terms, there is no threat to independence. If the loan is material it will be necessary to apply appropriate safeguards to bring the risk to an acceptable level. A suitable safeguard is likely to be an independent review (by a partner from another office in the firm).

Loans to members of the audit team from a bank or other lending institution client are likely to be material to the individual, but, provided that they are on normal commercial terms, these do not constitute a threat to independence.

An audit firm or individual on the audit engagement should not enter into any loan or guarantee arrangement with a client that is not a bank or similar institution (unless immaterial to both parties which is unlikely). The self-interest threat created by entering into such an arrangement would be so significant that no safeguard would be able to reduce the threat to an acceptable level. In addition, loans should not be made by an audit firm or an audit team member to an audit client.

(j) **Overdue fees**

A self-interest threat arises if fees due from an audit client remain unpaid for a long time, especially if a significant part is not paid before the issue of the audit report for the following year. Generally the firm will require payment of such fees before such an audit report is issued.

However, if fees remain unpaid after the report has been issued, the existence and significance of any threat must be evaluated and safeguards applied when necessary. One safeguard might be to arrange for an additional professional accountant who did not take part in the audit engagement to review the work performed.

Also, in a situation where there are overdue fees, the auditor runs the risk of, in effect, making a loan to a client, whereupon the guidance above becomes relevant.

Audit firms should guard against significant fees building up by discussing the issues with those charged with governance and, if necessary, the possibility of resigning if overdue fees are not paid.

(k)   **Contingent fees**

Contingent fees are fees calculated on a predetermined basis relating to the outcome or result of a transaction or the result of the work performed.

A firm is not permitted to enter into any fee arrangement for an audit or assurance engagement under which the amount of the fee is contingent on the result of the assurance work or on items that are the subject matter of the assurance engagement.

It would also usually be inappropriate to accept a contingent fee for non-assurance work from an audit client, as it will create a self-interest threat. The engagement should not be accepted if:

- The fee is charged by the firm expressing the opinion on the financial statements and the fee is material or expected to be material to that firm;

- The fee is charged by a network firm that participates in a significant part of the audit and the fee is material or expected to be material to that firm; or

- The outcome of the non-assurance service, and therefore the amount of the fee, is dependent on a future or contemporary judgement related to the audit of a material amount in the financial statements.

Where contingent fees on non-assurance services are not prohibited by the rules above, the following factors must be considered in deciding whether a contingent fee is acceptable or not.

- The range of possible fee outcomes
- Whether an appropriate authority determines the outcome of the matter on which the fee depends
- The nature of the service
- The effect of the transaction on the financial statements

In other circumstances it may be appropriate to accept a contingent fee for non-assurance work if suitable safeguards are in place. Examples include:

- Using professionals who are not part of the audit team for the non-assurance service
- Having the relevant audit work reviewed by an independent professional accountant

(l)   **High percentage of fees**

When a firm receives a high proportion of its fee income from just one audit client there is **a self-interest** or **intimidation threat**, as the firm will be concerned about losing the client. This depends on:

- The operating **structure** of the **firm**
- Whether the **firm** is established or **new**
- The **significance of the client** to the firm (both quantitatively and qualitatively)

It is important not to overlook these caveats: a high percentage fee income from a client does not by itself create an insurmountable threat. The threat from the percentage fee income might be mitigated by the structure of the firm, or by the fact that the audit firm is new (so the fee dependence is likely to be temporary).

Possible safeguards include:

- **Reducing** the **dependency** on the client

- **External** quality control **reviews**

- **Consulting a third party**, such as a professional regulatory body or a professional accountant, **on key audit judgements.**

It is not just a matter of the audit firm actually **being** independent in terms of fees, but also of it being **seen to be independent by the public**. It is as much about public perception as reality.

The Code also states that a threat may be created where an individual partner or office's percentage fees from one client is high. The safeguards are as above, except that internal quality control reviews are also relevant.

For audit clients that are **public interest entities**, the Code states that where **total fees** from the client represent **more than 15% of the firm's total fees for two consecutive years**, the firm shall:

- **Disclose** this to **those charged with governance**, and

- **Arrange for a review to be conducted**, either by an external professional accountant or by a regulatory body; this review can be either before the audit opinion on the second year's financial statements is issued (a '**pre-issuance review**') or after it is issued (a '**post-issuance review**')

If total fees significantly exceed 15%, then a post-issuance review may not be sufficient, and a pre-issuance review will be required.

If fees continue to exceed 15% each year the disclosure to and discussion with those charged with governance shall occur and a pre-issuance or post-issuance review must be carried out each year, depending on the extent of the threat.

(m) **Lowballing**

When a firm quotes a significantly lower fee level for an audit service than would have been charged by the predecessor firm, there is a significant self-interest threat. If the firm's tender is successful, the firm must apply safeguards, such as:

- Maintaining records such that the firm is able to demonstrate that appropriate staff and time are allocated to the engagement

- Complying with all applicable auditing standards, guidelines and quality control procedures

(n) **Recruitment**

Recruiting senior management for an audit client, particularly those able to affect the subject matter of an audit engagement, creates a self-interest threat for the audit firm.

Audit providers must not make management decisions for the client. Their involvement could be limited to reviewing a shortlist of candidates, providing that the client has drawn up the criteria by which they are to be selected.

In addition to the self-interest threats discussed above, the **holding of client assets** also creates a self-interest threat to professional behaviour and may also create a self-interest threat to objectivity. A professional accountant in public practice must not assume custody of client monies or other assets unless permitted to do so by law. If permitted by law the assets are kept separately and closely controlled and accounted for.

1.4.2 Self-review threat

Self-review threats arise when members review their own work or advice as part of an assurance engagement. Circumstances that may give rise to such threats include the following.

The key area in which there is likely to be a self-review threat is where a firm provides services other than assurance services for an audit client (providing multiple services). There is a great deal of guidance in the ACCA and International Ethics Standards Board for Accountants (IESBA) rules about the other services accountancy firms could provide. These are discussed below.

(a) **Recent service with an audit client**

Individuals who have been a **director or officer of the audit client, or an employee in a position to exert direct and significant influence** over the preparation of the accounting records or financial statements in the period covered by the audit report, should not be assigned to the audit team.

If an individual had been closely involved with the client before the period covered by the audit report, the audit firm should consider the threat to independence arising and apply appropriate safeguards, such as:

- Obtaining a quality control review of the individual's work on the assignment
- Discussing the issue with the audit committee

(b) **Provision of non-audit services in general**

Providing non-assurance services for audit clients may create threats to the independence of the firm or members of the audit team. Audit firms must evaluate any threat arising and decline to provide a non-audit service if the application of safeguards will not reduce the threat to an acceptable level.

Provision of some non-audit services for audit clients will not create an insurmountable threat and can be provided when certain safeguards are in place. Depending on the nature of the other service, safeguards may not even be necessary.

An important question to ask when deciding whether provision of non-audit services for an audit client is acceptable is 'does providing the service result in the audit firm carrying out activities that would generally be considered a **management responsibility**?'

This is because according to the ACCA Code **a firm is not permitted to assume a management responsibility for an audit client**.

Whether an activity is a management responsibility depends on the circumstances and requires the relevant partners at the audit firm to use judgement. The following activities listed in the ACCA Code are generally considered to be a management responsibility.

- Setting policies and strategic direction
- Directing and taking responsibility for the actions of the entity's employees
- Authorising transactions
- Deciding which recommendations of the firm or other third parties to implement

- Taking responsibility for the preparation and fair presentation of the financial statements
- Taking responsibility for designing, implementing and maintaining internal control

Activities that are **routine and administrative**, or involve matters that are insignificant, are generally deemed **not** to be a management responsibility and are permitted by the ACCA Code.

(c) **Preparing accounting records and financial statements**

There is clearly a significant risk of self-review if a firm prepares accounting records and financial statements and then audits them. However, in practice, auditors routinely assist management with the preparation of financial statements and give advice about accounting treatments and journal entries.

Audit firms must therefore analyse the risks arising and put safeguards in place to ensure that the risk is at an acceptable level. Safeguards include:

- Using staff members other than audit team members to carry out work

- If non-audit services are performed by a member of the audit team, using an independent partner or senior staff member (not part of the audit team) to review the work performed

- Obtaining client approval for work undertaken

The rules are more stringent when the client is listed or public interest. Except in emergency situations, **a firm must not provide for an public interest audit client accounting and bookkeeping services, including payroll services, or prepare financial statements on which the firm will express an opinion**. The same rule applies to financial information which forms the basis of the financial statements.

Note that an 'emergency situation' as stated above is where it is impractical for the audit client to make other arrangements. However, in this situation the accountancy services must be provided by a separate team to that performing the audit and it should not be a long or recurring service. Those charged with governance should be kept informed of the situation.

(d) **Valuation services**

Key term

> A **valuation** comprises the making of assumptions with regard to future developments, the application of certain methodologies and techniques, and the combination of both in order to compute a certain value, or range of values, for an asset, a liability or for a business as a whole.

If an audit firm performs a valuation which will be included in financial statements audited by the firm, a self-review threat arises.

Audit firms should not carry out valuations on matters which will be material to the financial statements which involve a significant degree of subjectivity.

It the audit client is a public interest entity, **the audit firm is not permitted to provide valuation services if the valuations would have a material effect, separately or in the aggregate**, on the financial statements on which the firm will express an opinion. Note that for a public interest client the degree of subjectivity is irrelevant.

If the valuation is for an immaterial matter, the audit firm should apply safeguards to ensure that the risk is reduced to an acceptable level. Matters to consider when applying safeguards are the extent of the audit client's knowledge of the relevant matters in making the valuation and the degree of judgement involved, how much use is made of established methodologies and the degree of uncertainty in the valuation. Safeguards include:

- Second partner review
- Confirming that the client understands the valuation and the assumptions used
- Ensuring that the client acknowledges responsibility for the valuation
- Using separate personnel for the valuation and the audit

(e) **Taxation services**

The Code divides taxation services into four categories.

(i) Tax return preparation
(ii) Tax calculations for the purpose of preparing the accounting entries
(iii) Tax planning and other tax advisory services
(iv) Assistance in the resolution of tax disputes

Guidance in respect of each of these categories is as follows.

(i) **Tax return preparation generally does not threaten independence**, as long as management takes responsibility for the returns.

(ii) **Tax calculations for the purpose of preparing the accounting entities may not be prepared for public interest entities**, except in emergency situations. For non public interest entities, it is acceptable to do so provided that safeguards are applied.

(iii) **Tax planning may be acceptable in certain circumstances**, eg where the advice is clearly supported by tax authority or other precedent. However, if the effectiveness of the tax advice depends on a particular accounting treatment or presentation in the financial statements, the audit team has reasonable doubt about the accounting treatment, and the consequences of the tax advice would be material, then the service should not be provided.

(iv) **Assistance in the resolution of tax disputes may be provided** in some cases. However, if the firm is acting as an advocate of the client and the effect of the matter is material to the financial statements to be audited the firm is not permitted to act. Also to be taken into consideration is whether the firm itself provided the service which is the subject of the dispute, as this will increase the threat. If it is appropriate to provide the service, the safeguards include using professionals who are not members of the audit team to perform the service, and obtaining advice on the service from an external tax professional.

(f) **Internal audit services**

A firm may provide certain internal audit services for an audit client depending on the nature of the services and the type of entity being audited.

An audit firm's personnel **must not assume a management responsibility** as a result of providing internal audit services. Internal audit services where management responsibilities would be assumed include:

(i) Setting internal audit policies or the strategic direction of the internal audit department

(ii) Directing and taking responsibility for the actions of the entity's internal audit employees

(iii) Deciding which recommendations resulting from internal audit activities are implemented

(iv) Reporting the results of the internal audit activities to those charged with governance on behalf of management

(v) Performing procedures that form part of the internal control

(vi) Taking responsibility for designing, implementing and maintaining internal control

(vii) Performing outsourced internal audit services, comprising all or a substantial portion of the internal audit function, where the firm is responsible for determining the scope of the internal audit work and may have management responsibilities

To avoid inadvertently assuming a management responsibility the audit firm must make sure senior management at the client accepts responsibility for designing, implementing and maintaining internal control and continues to approve the scope, risk and frequency of internal audit services.

Client management should also remain responsible for evaluating and acting on internal audit findings and for reporting significant findings to those charged with governance.

BPP
LEARNING MEDIA

Recurring internal audit services must not be provided for **public interest entities** if they relate to:

(i)   A **significant** part of **the internal controls** over **financial reporting**;

(ii)   Financial accounting systems generating information which is significant to the financial statements; or

(iii) Amounts or disclosures which are **material** to the financial statements.

For internal audit services that are permitted but still create a threat it may be appropriate to use safeguards, such as using personnel not involved in the audit, ensuring that an employee of the client is designated responsible for internal audit activities and ensuring that the client approves all the work that internal audit does.

(g)   **Corporate finance**

Certain aspects of corporate finance will create self-review threats that cannot be reduced to an acceptable level by safeguards.

Where the effectiveness of corporate finance advice depends on a particular accounting treatment or presentation in the financial statements and the audit team has reasonable doubt as to the appropriateness of that treatment and the consequences of the corporate finance advice will have a material effect on the financial statements, the corporate finance advice must not be provided.

In addition, **assurance firms are not allowed to promote, deal in or underwrite an assurance client's shares**. They are also not allowed to commit an assurance client to the terms of a transaction or consummate a transaction on the client's behalf.

Other corporate finance services, such as assisting a client in defining corporate strategies, assisting in identifying possible sources of capital and providing structuring advice, may be acceptable providing that safeguards are used, such as using different teams of staff and ensuring that no management decisions are taken on behalf of the client.

(h)   **IT systems services**

In general, IT system work for audit clients not related to internal control over financial reporting is not deemed to create a threat as long as no management responsibility is assumed by the audit firm's personnel. The implementation of 'off the shelf' accounting or financial information reporting software and making recommendations in relation to a system not designed, implemented or operated by the audit firm is also permitted.

However, significant threats arise when the audit firm provides **services for an audit client involving the design or implementation of IT systems** that do either of the following.

(i)   Form a **significant part of the internal control** over financial reporting

(ii)   Generate **information that is significant to** the client's **accounting records or financial statements**

If the client is a public interest entity the audit firm must not provide such a service.

If the client is not a public interest entity, services relating to design and implementation of IT systems of the nature discussed above may be provided, but only if the client acknowledges its responsibility for establishing and monitoring a system of internal controls and management (or a competent employee at the client) maintains responsibility for making all relevant management decisions, evaluation of the system and the operation of the system.

(i)   **Other services**

The audit firm might sell a variety of other services to audit clients, such as:

- Litigation support
- Legal services

The audit firm should consider whether there are any barriers to independence and consider whether the threat to independence could be reduced to an acceptable level by appropriate safeguards.

On 31 July 2009, a listed firm, Rentokil, announced that its new auditor would be KPMG, one of the 'Big Four' accountancy firms. However, the appointment was a controversial one because the package offered by KPMG was an 'extended assurance' package. This meant that KPMG would fulfil all the functions of external audit, but would also perform some tasks that would normally be carried out by internal audit. As a result, Rentokil's audit costs were cut by 30%. This sparked a debate that still rages on about whether this sort of arrangement is acceptable in the context of ethical guidance. In particular, there is a self-review threat that the external auditor may rely too heavily on its own internal audit work and a management threat that, in performing the internal audit tasks, the external auditor could assume the role of management.

1.4.3 Advocacy threat

Advocacy threats arise in those situations where the audit firm promotes a position or opinion to the point that subsequent objectivity is compromised. Examples include commenting publicly on future events in particular circumstances, having made assertions without detailing the assumptions, or acting as an advocate on behalf of an audit client in litigation or disputes with third parties. Advocacy threats might also arise if the firm promoted shares in a listed audit client.

Acting in an advocacy role for an audit client in resolving a dispute or litigation when the amounts involved are material to the financial statements on which the firm will express an opinion is not permitted by the ACCA Code. In addition, the Code does not allow the appointment of a partner or an employee of the firm as General Counsel for legal affairs of an audit client.

Where advocacy threats arise and the work or actions are permitted by the Code then relevant safeguards might include using different departments to carry out the work and making disclosures to the audit committee. Remember, the audit firm has the option to withdraw from an engagement if the risk to independence is too high.

1.4.4 Familiarity threat

Having an audit client for a **long period of time may create a familiarity threat** to independence. The severity of the threat depends on such factors as how long the individual has been on the audit team, how senior the person is, whether the client's management has changed and whether the client's accounting issues have changed in nature or complexity.

Possible **safeguards** include:

- **Rotating** the **senior personnel** off the **audit team**

- Having a **professional accountant** who was not a member of the audit team **review** the work of the senior personnel

- **Regular** independent **internal or external quality reviews** of the engagement

The rules for **public interest entities** are stricter. If an individual is a **key audit partner** for **seven years**, they must be rotated off the audit for **two years**. During this time, they cannot be on the audit team and cannot consult with the audit team or the client on any issues that may affect the engagement (including giving just general industry advice).

The Code does allow some flexibility here. **If** key partner **continuity** is particularly beneficial to **audit quality**, and there is some **unforeseen circumstance** (such as the intended engagement partner becoming seriously ill), then the key audit partner **can remain on the audit for an additional year**, making eight years in total.

If a client that was not a public interest entity becomes one, then the seven-year limit still applies, starting from the date when the key audit partner originally became the key partner for that audit client. However, if the individual has served the audit client as a key audit partner for six or more years when the client

becomes a public interest entity, the partner may continue to serve in that capacity for a maximum of two additional years before rotating off the engagement.

Finally, if the firm has only a few people capable of being a key audit partner for a public interest client, it is possible for an independent regulator to give permission for an audit partner to remain a key audit partner indefinitely, provided that alternative safeguards specified by that regulator are applied (eg external review).

1.4.5 Intimidation threat

An intimidation threat arises when members of the audit team may be deterred from acting objectively by threats, actual or perceived. These could arise from family and personal relationships, litigation, or close business relationships. These are also examples of self-interest threats, largely because intimidation may only arise significantly when the audit firm has something to lose.

The most obvious example is when the client threatens to sue, or does sue, the audit firm for work that has been done previously. The firm is then faced with the risk of losing the client, bad publicity and the possibility that it will be found to have been negligent. This could lead to the firm being under pressure to produce an unmodified audit opinion in the auditor's report.

Generally, audit firms should seek to avoid such situations arising. If they do arise, factors to consider are:

- The materiality of the litigation
- The nature of the audit engagement
- Whether the litigation relates to a prior audit engagement

The following safeguards could be considered:

- Disclosing to the audit committee the nature and extent of the litigation
- Removing specific affected individuals from the engagement team
- Involving an additional professional accountant on the team to review work

However, if the litigation is at all serious, it may be necessary to resign from the engagement, as the threat to independence may be too great.

1.5 Conflicts of interest   June 14

In some ways, conflict of interest issues are similar to the difficulties firms have in maintaining independence. They can arise in a variety of circumstances and each problem has to be dealt with on its own merits.

A professional accountant must take reasonable steps to identify circumstances that could pose a conflict of interest because such circumstances may create threats to compliance with the fundamental principles.

When considering whether to accept a client or when there is a change in a client's circumstances, audit firms must take reasonable steps to ascertain whether there is a conflict of interest or if there is likely to be one in the future.

1.5.1 Conflicts between members' and clients' interests

A conflict between members' and clients' interests might arise if members compete directly with a client, or have a joint venture or similar with a company that is in competition with the client. This may threaten the member's objectivity.

The rules state that **members and firms should not accept or continue engagements in which there are, or are likely to be, significant conflicts of interest between members, firms and clients**. Any form of financial gain which accrues or is likely to accrue to the member as a result of an engagement, or as a result of using information known to them about a client, will usually always amount to a significant conflict of interest between the member and client.

Members should evaluate the threats arising from a conflict of interest that are not significant and apply safeguards where necessary to reduce them to an acceptable level. One applicable safeguard is notifying the client of the conflict of interest and obtaining their consent to act.

1.5.2 Conflicts between the interests of different clients

Conflicts of interest can arise when a firm has two (or more) audit clients, both of which have reason to be unhappy that their auditors are also auditors of the other company. This situation frequently arises when the companies are in **direct competition** with each other, and particularly when the **auditors have access to** particularly **sensitive information**. In such circumstances, objectivity and confidentiality may be threatened.

Audit firms are at liberty to have clients who are in competition with each other. However, the firm should ensure that it is not the subject of a dispute between the clients. It must also manage its work so that the interests of one client do not adversely affect another client.

However, **where acceptance or continuance of an engagement would, even with safeguards, materially prejudice the interests of any client, the appointment should not be accepted or continued**.

Where interests are **not** materially prejudiced but threats to objectivity or confidentiality arise due to the auditor acting for two clients whose interests are in conflict then the firm must:

(a)   Evaluate the significance of any threats

(b)   Apply safeguards when necessary to eliminate the threats or reduce them to an acceptable level

Conflicts can of course be avoided by not accepting any appointment or assignment in which they seem likely to occur but this may not be practicable.

Where threats may arise as a result of a conflict of interests, the primary safeguard will always be to notify all known relevant parties that the member or firm is acting (or plans to act) for two or more parties in respect of a matter where their respective interests are in conflict and **obtaining their consent to act**.

As well as obtaining consent, additional safeguards include:

(a)   The use of separate engagement teams

(b)   Procedures to prevent access to information (eg strict physical separation of such teams, confidential and secure data filing, password protection)

(c)   Clear guidelines for members of the engagement team on issues of security and confidentiality

(d)   The use of confidentiality agreements signed by employees and partners of the firm

(e)   Regular review of the application of safeguards by a senior individual not involved with relevant client engagements

(f)   Advising one or more clients to seek additional independent advice

Larger firms can often apply the safeguards (a) to (d) above by building a **'Chinese wall'** within the firm. This would mean that the respective audits are undertaken by different audit 'groups', the engagement partners are different and all the other audit staff are allowed to work on one of the clients. In addition, records are only accessible to the teams working on their particular client.

Small firms, on the other hand, may struggle to implement such procedures.

A final point to note is that if consent to act for another party has not been obtained from an existing client then the firm should not act for one of the parties.

1.6 Enforcement mechanisms

In this section we briefly consider how ACCA enforces the *Code of ethics and conduct*. Members are liable to disciplinary action if they breach the ethical guidance.

The professional conduct department first investigates the potential breach and if liability is indicated, it prepares a report for consideration by an external assessor. If the assessor concludes there is a case to answer, they may refer the matter to the ACCA's Disciplinary Committee.

The Disciplinary Committee hears the case and if the complaint is proved wholly or in part, the member concerned could be excluded from membership of the ACCA, severely reprimanded or fined.

Members can appeal to the Appeal Committee which will consider the appeal at a hearing.

Members have to confirm in their annual Continuing Professional Development (CPD) returns that they have kept their professional ethics knowledge up to date. ACCA does monitor CPD returns by checking a sample on an annual basis.

1.7 Ethical requirements and quality control

Compliance with ethical requirements form a crucial part of the auditor's responsibility in ensuring the quality of individual audits. ISA 220 makes this clear.

ISA 220.9

Throughout the audit engagement, the engagement partner shall remain alert, through observation and making enquiries as necessary, for evidence of non-compliance with relevant ethical requirements by members of the engagement team.

This includes the ACCA *Code of Ethics and Conduct*, with its fundamental principles and all the other detailed requirements.

It is also the engagement partner's responsibility to form a conclusion on the audit team's compliance with independence requirements. The engagement partner must:

ISA 220.11

(a) Obtain relevant information from the firm and, where applicable, network firms, to identify and evaluate circumstances and relationships that create threats to independence

(b) Evaluate information on identified breaches, if any, of the firm's independence policies and procedures to determine whether they create a threat to independence for the audit engagement

(c) Take appropriate action to eliminate such threats or reduce them to an acceptable level by applying safeguards, or, if considered appropriate, to withdraw from the audit engagement, where withdrawal is possible under applicable law and regulation. The engagement partner shall promptly report to the firm any inability to resolve the matter for appropriate action.

Finally, the audit team must document the conclusions on compliance with independence requirements that apply to the audit engagement, including any relevant discussions with the firm.

1.8 Country-specific ethical guidance

Although the ACCA and the IESBA have produced detailed ethical guidance for professional accountants, countries may have their own additional ethical guidance.

For example, in the UK, the Auditing Practices Board of the Financial Reporting Council has issued five ethical standards, an ethical standard specific to small entities and an ethical standard for reporting accountants, which provide an additional source of guidance. These are not examinable under your syllabus, but are simply mentioned here as an example.

2 Accepting audit appointments

FAST FORWARD

> The present and proposed auditors must **communicate** with each other prior to the audit being accepted; however, if the client refuses to give **permission** to the proposed auditors to make contact, the proposed auditors must **decline nomination**.

2.1 Tendering and obtaining work

Members are entitled to advertise their services and products. The advertising medium should not reflect adversely on the member, ACCA or the accountancy profession. Adverts should not:

- Bring ACCA into disrepute or bring discredit to the member, firm or accountancy profession
- Discredit the services of others
- Be misleading
- Fall short of local regulatory or legislative requirements

2.1.1 Fee negotiation and lowballing

The audit fee is a sensitive subject for most companies. It represents a cost for something the company often does not really want and the fees may be perceived as too high just for this reason. The auditors must ensure that they can provide a quality audit for the price.

Many large companies invite **tenders** for their audit work. The directors then have the opportunity to directly compare a range of offers.

Generally, a tender will take the form of detailed written proposals and a presentation. Factors include:

- The **level** of **expertise** each firm has in the industry
- **Similar companies** audited by each firm (good for expertise, bad for confidentiality?)
- **National** and **international presence**
- The proposed **fee**

Audit firms which tender for such audits will usually give at least an indication of the level of fees in the next few years, including likely overall rate rises. Fee levels are very important to most companies and are often the determining factor.

In all situations, the auditors should quote a fee based on the estimated hours worked by each member of staff required on the audit, multiplied by the hourly rate plus any travel and other expenses to be incurred during the audit. They may also charge a premium for more complex audits.

Sometimes it appears that firms are charging less than 'market rate' for an audit, especially when tendering for new clients. This practice is known as **lowballing**, and we discussed it in Section 1.4.1.

It is not considered ethically wrong to charge a low price for an audit in itself. However, the auditors must ensure that they carry out an audit of the quality demanded by auditing standards and that the 'cut-price' audit fee does not call their independence into question.

This is always going to be a topical debate, but in terms of negotiating the audit fee the following factors need to be taken into account.

(a) The audit is perceived to have a **fluctuating 'market price'** as any other commodity or service.

(b) Companies can reduce external audit costs through various **legitimate measures**:

- Extending the size and function of internal audit
- Reducing the number of different audit firms used worldwide
- Selling off subsidiary companies leaving a simplified group structure to audit
- The tender process itself simply makes auditors more competitive
- Exchange rate fluctuations in audit fees

(c)   Auditing firms have **increased productivity**, partly through the use of more sophisticated information technology techniques in auditing.

In any case, an auditing firm lays itself open to accusations of loss of independence if it reduces its fees below a certain level, particularly if it is difficult to see how such fees will cover direct labour costs. This is also true of firms which use the audit as a 'loss leader' to obtain profitable consultancy work from audit clients. When such non-audit services are offered to a client by the auditors, there can, of course, be an apparent loss of independence. The allegation may arise that the price of an 'acceptable' audit opinion is lucrative taxation or consulting work.

2.2 Appointment ethics

This section covers the procedures that the auditors must undertake to ensure that their appointment is valid and that they are clear to act.

2.2.1 Before accepting nomination

Before a new audit client is accepted, the auditors must ensure that there are no **independence** or **other ethical problems** likely to cause conflict with the ethical code. Furthermore, new auditors should ensure that they have been appointed in a proper and legal manner.

The nominee auditors must carry out the following procedures.

ACCEPTANCE PROCEDURES	
Ensure **professionally qualified** to act	Consider whether they could be disqualified on legal or ethical grounds
Ensure **existing resources adequate**	Consider available time, staff and technical expertise
Obtain references	Make independent enquiries if directors are not personally known
Communicate with present auditors	Enquire whether there are reasons/circumstances behind the change which the new auditors ought to know, also as a courtesy

You should note that communication with the existing auditor is not just a matter of professional courtesy. Its main purpose is to enable a professional accountant to ensure that there has been no action by the client which would on ethical grounds preclude the professional accountant from accepting the appointment. The current auditor, after considering all the facts, needs to decide if the client is someone for whom the auditor would wish to act. That is why there **must** be communication with the existing auditor on being asked to accept appointment.

An appointment decision chart is shown below.

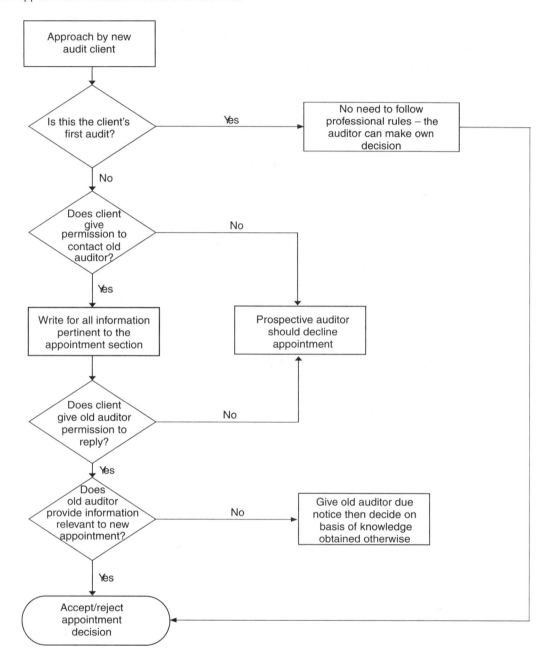

2.2.2 Example nomination letter

This is an example of an initial communication with the previous auditor.

To: Retiring & Co
                  Certified Accountants

Dear Sirs

Re: New Client Co Ltd

We have been asked to allow our name to go forward for nomination as auditors of the above company, and we should therefore be grateful if you would let us know whether there are any professional reasons why we should not accept nomination ....

Acquiring & Co

Certified Accountants

Having negotiated these steps, the auditors will be in a position to accept the nomination, or not, as the case may be. These procedures are demonstrated in the appointment decision chart.

2.2.3 Procedures after accepting nomination

The following procedures should be carried out after accepting nomination. (Note that these should not be carried out until the client screening procedures discussed in Section 2.3 have been carried out.)

(a)   **Ensure** that the **outgoing auditors' removal** or **resignation** has been **properly conducted** in accordance with national legislation. The new auditors should see a valid notice of the outgoing auditors' resignation, or confirm that the outgoing auditors were properly removed.

(b)   **Ensure** that the **new auditors' appointment is valid**. The new auditors should obtain a copy of the resolution passed at the general meeting appointing them as the company's auditors.

(c)   Set up and **submit a letter of engagement** to the directors of the company. Letters of engagement are discussed in the next section.

2.2.4 Other matters

Where the previous auditors have fees still owing to them by the client, the new auditors need not decline appointment solely for this reason. They should decide how far they may go in aiding the former auditors to obtain their fees, as well as whether they should accept the appointment.

Once a new appointment has taken place, the **new auditors should obtain all books and papers which belong to the client from the old auditors**. The former auditors should ensure that all such documents are transferred, **unless** they have a **lien** (a legal right to hold on to them) over the books because of unpaid fees. They should also pass any useful information on to the new auditors if it will be of help, without charge, unless a lot of work is involved.

2.3 Client screening

As well as contacting the previous auditors many firms, particularly larger ones, carry out **stringent checks** on potential client companies and their management. Some of the basic factors for consideration are given below.

2.3.1 Management integrity

The integrity of those managing a company will be of great importance, particularly if the company is controlled by one or a few dominant personalities.

2.3.2 Risk

The following table contrasts low and high risk clients.

LOW RISK	HIGH RISK
Good long-term prospects	Poor recent or forecast performance
Well-financed	Likely lack of finance
Strong internal controls	Significant control deficiencies
Conservative, prudent accounting policies	Evidence of questionable integrity, doubtful accounting policies
Competent, honest management	Lack of finance director
Few unusual transactions	Significant related party or unexplained transactions

Where the risk level of a company's audit is determined as anything other than low, then the specific risks should be identified and documented. It might be necessary to assign specialists in response to these risks, particularly industry specialists, as independent reviewers. Some audit firms have procedures for closely monitoring audits which have been accepted, but which are considered high risk.

2.3.3 Engagement economics

Generally, the expected fees from a new client should reflect the **level of risk** expected. They should also offer the same sort of return expected of clients of this nature and reflect the overall financial strategy of the audit firm. Occasionally, the audit firm will want the work to gain entry into the client's particular industry, or to establish better contacts within that industry. These factors will all contribute to a total expected economic return.

2.3.4 Relationship with client

The audit firm will generally want the relationship with a client to be **long term**. This is not only to enjoy receiving fees year after year but also to allow the audit work to be enhanced by better knowledge of the client, thereby offering a better service.

Conflict of interest problems are significant here; the firm should establish that no existing clients will cause difficulties as competitors of the new client. Other services to other clients may have an impact here, not just audit.

2.3.5 Ability to perform the work

The audit firm must have the **resources** to perform the work properly, as well as any **specialist knowledge or skills**. The impact on existing engagements must be estimated, in terms of staff time and the timing of the audit.

2.4 Approval

Once all the relevant procedures and information gathering has taken place, the company can be put forward for approval. The engagement partner will have completed a **client acceptance form** and this, along with any other relevant documentation, will be submitted to the partner who is in overall charge of accepting clients.

Exam focus point

> In the exam you may be given a 'real-life' client situation and asked what factors you would consider in deciding whether to accept appointment.

2.5 Continuance assessments

Once a client has been approved as an audit client, the auditor should perform assessments of whether the recurring audit engagement should continue from year on year. Many large audit firms require such continuance assessments to be made on an annual basis.

The underlying considerations for determining client continuance are similar to those which apply to the acceptance of new clients. Essentially, the auditor has to evaluate the risks of being associated with the client: what new potential risks may arise, and how might the existing, previously assessed risks change?

The auditor should consider changes associated with:

- Main decision-makers, directors, officers or owners

- The financial condition of the entity

- The industry and business environment (eg economic trends, inflation/deflation, industry consolidation, litigation, regulatory environment, expansion into new areas of business)

- The auditor-client relationship (eg any disagreements with the entity, overdue fees, issues relating to the imposed scope limitation)

- The business reputation of the client

3 Agreeing the terms of the engagement
Dec 10, June 11, Dec 13

FAST FORWARD

The **terms** of the audit engagement shall be **agreed** with management and **recorded** in an audit engagement letter.

3.1 Preconditions for an audit

ISA 210 *Agreeing the terms of audit engagements* states that the objective of the auditor is to accept or continue an audit engagement only when the basis on which it is to be carried out has been agreed by establishing whether the **preconditions for an audit** are present and confirming that there is a common understanding between the auditor and management of the terms of the engagement.

Key term

The **preconditions for an audit** are the use by management of an acceptable financial reporting framework in the preparation of the financial statements and the agreement of management and, where appropriate, those charged with governance to the premise on which an audit is conducted.

To determine whether the preconditions for an audit are present, the auditor shall do the following:

(a) Determine whether the **financial reporting framework is acceptable**. Factors to consider include the nature of the entity, the purpose of the financial statements, the nature of the financial statements, and whether law or regulation prescribes the applicable financial reporting framework.

(b) Obtain management's agreement that it **acknowledges and understands** its **responsibilities** for the following.

    (i) **Preparing the financial statements** in accordance with the applicable financial reporting framework

    (ii) **Internal control** that is necessary to enable the preparation of financial statements which are free from material misstatement

    (iii) **Providing the auditor with access to all information** of which management is aware that is relevant to the preparation of the financial statements, with **additional information** that the auditor may request, and with **unrestricted access** to entity staff from whom the auditor determines it necessary to obtain audit evidence

If these preconditions are not present, the auditor shall **discuss** the matter with management. The auditor **shall not accept** the audit engagement if:

- The auditor has determined that the **financial reporting framework** to be applied is **not acceptable**.
- **Management's agreement** referred to above has **not been obtained**.

3.2 The audit engagement letter

Key term

> The **engagement letter** is the written terms of an engagement in the form of a letter.

The auditor shall agree the terms of the engagement with management or those charged with governance and these shall be recorded in an **audit engagement letter** or other suitable form of written agreement. This has to be done before the audit engagement begins so as to **avoid misunderstandings** regarding the audit.

3.2.1 Form and content of the audit engagement letter

The audit engagement letter shall include the following:

- The **objective and scope** of the audit
- The **auditor's responsibilities**
- **Management's responsibilities**
- Identification of the **applicable financial reporting framework** for the preparation of the financial statements
- Reference to the **expected form and content of any reports** to be issued by the auditor and a statement that there may be circumstances in which a report may differ from its expected form and content

3.2.2 Additional matters that may be included

The audit engagement letter may also make reference to the following:

- **Elaboration of scope of audit**, including reference to legislation, regulations, ISAs, ethical and other pronouncements
- Form of **any other communication** of results of the engagement
- The fact that due to the inherent limitations of an audit and those of internal control, there is an **unavoidable risk that some material misstatements may not be detected**, even though the audit is properly planned and performed in accordance with ISAs
- **Arrangements regarding planning and performance**, including audit team composition
- Expectation that management will provide **written representations**
- **Agreement** of management to provide **draft financial statements** and other information in time to allow auditor to complete the audit in accordance with proposed timetable
- **Agreement** of management to inform auditor of **facts** that may affect the financial statements, of which management may become aware from the date of the auditor's report to the date of issue of the financial statements
- **Fees and billing arrangements**
- Request for management to **acknowledge receipt** of the letter and agree to the terms outlined in it
- Involvement of **other auditors and experts**
- Involvement of **internal auditors and other staff**
- Arrangements to be made with **predecessor auditor**

- Any **restriction of auditor's liability**
- Reference to **any further agreements** between auditor and entity
- Any **obligations to provide audit working papers** to other parties

Appendix 1 of ISA 210 includes an example of an audit engagement letter.

3.3 Recurring audits

On recurring audits, the auditor shall assess whether the terms of the engagement need to be revised and whether there is a need to remind the entity of the existing terms. The following factors may indicate that it would be appropriate to revise the terms of the engagement or remind the entity of the existing terms. As you may expect, these are likely to be identified in the course of a continuance assessment, discussed in Section 2.5 above.

- Any indication that the entity **misunderstands** the objective and scope of the audit
- Any **revised or special terms** of the audit engagement
- A recent change of **senior management**
- A significant change in **ownership**
- A significant change in **nature or size** of the entity's business
- A change in **legal or regulatory requirements**
- A change in the **financial reporting framework**
- A change in **other reporting requirements**

3.4 Acceptance of a change in terms

A change in the terms of audit engagement prior to completion may result from:

(a) A **change in circumstances** affecting the need for the service

(b) A **misunderstanding** as to the nature of an audit or of the related service originally requested

(c) A **restriction on the scope** of the audit engagement, whether imposed by management or caused by circumstances

The auditor shall not agree to a change in the terms of the audit engagement where there is no **reasonable justification** for doing so. In the case of (a) and (b) above, these might be acceptable reasons for requesting a change in the engagement. However, a change may not be considered reasonable if it seems to relate to information that is incorrect, incomplete or otherwise unsatisfactory. An example would be if the auditor could not obtain sufficient appropriate audit evidence for receivables and is then asked to change the engagement from an audit to a review so as to avoid a modification of the auditor's opinion.

If the auditor is asked to **change** the audit engagement before it is completed to an engagement providing a **lower level of assurance**, such as a review or a related service, the auditor shall determine whether there is **reasonable justification** for doing so because there may be legal or contractual implications.

If the terms are **changed**, the auditor and management shall **agree and record** the new terms in an engagement letter. However, to avoid confusing users, the report on the related service will not include reference to the original audit engagement or any procedures performed in the original audit engagement (unless the engagement is changed to an agreed-upon procedures engagement, where reference to procedures performed is included in the report).

However, if the auditor **cannot agree** to a change of terms and management does not allow the auditor to carry on with the original audit engagement, the auditor shall **withdraw** from the engagement and determine whether there is an **obligation to report** this to other parties (eg those charged with governance, owners, regulators).

Question
New auditors

You are a partner in Messrs Borg, Connors & Co, Certified Accountants. You are approached by Mr Nastase, the managing director of Navratilova Enterprises Ltd, who asks your firm to become auditors of his company. In return for giving you this appointment Mr Nastase says that he will expect your firm to waive 50% of your normal fee for the first year's audit. The existing auditors, Messrs Wade, Austin & Co, have not resigned but Mr Nastase informs you that they will not be reappointed in the future.

Required

(a) What action should Messrs Borg, Connors & Co take in response to the request from Mr Nastase to reduce their first year's fee by 50%?

(b) Are Messrs Wade, Austin & Co within their rights in not resigning when they know Mr Nastase wishes to replace them? Give reasons for your answer.

Answer

(a) The request by Mr Nastase that half of the first year's audit fee should be waived is quite improper. If this proposal were to be accepted it could be held that Borg, Connors & Co had sought to procure work through the quoting of lower fees. This would be unethical and could result in disciplinary proceedings being taken against the firm.

Mr Nastase should be informed that the audit fee will be determined by reference to the work involved in completion of a satisfactory audit, taking into account the nature of the audit tasks involved and the resources required to carry out those tasks in an efficient manner. He should also be told that if he is not prepared to accept an audit fee arrived at in this way and insists on there being a reduction then regrettably the nomination to act as auditor will have to be declined.

(b) Wade, Austin & Co have every right not to resign even though they may be aware that Mr Nastase wishes to replace them. The auditors of a company are appointed by, and report to, the members of a company and the directors are not empowered to remove the auditors. If the reason for the proposed change arises out of a dispute between management and the auditors then the auditors have a right to put forward their views as seen above and to insist that any decision should be made by the members, but only once they have been made aware of all pertinent facts concerning the directors' wishes to have them removed from office.

4 Quality control at a firm level

FAST FORWARD

The International Standard on Quality Control (ISQC 1) helps audit firms to establish quality standards for their business.

The fact that auditors follow international auditing standards provides a general quality control framework within which audits should be conducted.

Quality control at the firm level encompasses the following areas.

- **Firm and leadership responsibilities for quality within the firm**: promoting a culture where quality is regarded as essential, and providing training to ensure all staff understand quality objectives and procedures
- **Human resources**: recruiting and retaining staff with the right capabilities, competence, and commitment to ethical principles to perform engagements in accordance with professional standards and regulatory requirements

- **Engagement performance**: implementing policies and procedures to ensure quality control at the individual engagement level
- **Monitoring**: evaluating quality control procedures to ensure that they remain relevant, adequate and effective and are complied with.

Exam focus point

ISQC 1 *Quality Controls for firms that perform audits and reviews of financial statements, and other assurance and related services engagements*, which provides guidance on quality control at a firm level, is not examinable for F8. However, you will need to demonstrate an understanding the firm wide controls that ensures audit quality.

We will briefly discuss this below.

4.1 Engagement performance

The firm should take steps to ensure that engagements are performed correctly, that is, in accordance with standards and guidance. Firms often produce a **manual of standard engagement procedures** to give to all staff so that they know the standards they are working towards.

Ensuring good engagement performance involves a number of issues:

- Direction
- Supervision
- Review
- Consultation
- Resolution of disputes

Many of these issues will be discussed in the context of an individual audit assignment (see Section 5 below).

When there are differences of opinion on an engagement team, a report should not be issued until the dispute has been resolved. This may involve the intervention of the quality control reviewer.

Key terms

A **peer review** is a review of an audit file carried out by another partner in the assurance firm.

A **hot review** (also known as a pre-issuance review) is a peer review carried out before the auditor's report is signed.

A **cold review** (also known as a post-issuance review) is a peer review carried out after the auditor's report is signed.

The firm should have policies and procedures to determine when an engagement quality control reviewer will be necessary for an engagement.

Engagement quality control reviewers (also known as independent review partners) are required to be appointed for the audit of listed entities, and other entities which the meet audit firm's criteria for engagement quality control reviews. Engagement quality control reviews are likely to be carried out on audits which are assessed to be high risk, as a safeguard against a potential ethical threat.

The firm must also have standards as to what constitutes a suitable engagement quality control review (the nature, timing and extent of such a review, the criteria for eligibility of reviewers and documentation requirements).

The engagement quality control review is covered further in Section 5.5.5.

4.2 Monitoring

The monitoring of the firm's quality control system and procedures involves:

- Ongoing evaluation: including considering whether the firm has kept up to date with regulatory requirements

- Periodic inspection: inspecting the audit engagements of each engagement partner over an inspection cycle

The people monitoring the system are required to evaluate the effect of any **deficiencies** found. These deficiencies might be one-offs. Monitors will be more concerned with **systematic or repetitive deficiencies that require corrective action**. When evidence is gathered that an inappropriate report might have been issued, the audit firm may want to take legal advice.

Corrective action

- Remedial action with an individual
- Communication of findings with the training department
- Changes in the quality control policies and procedures
- Disciplinary action, if necessary

5 Quality control on an individual audit

FAST FORWARD

ISA 220 requires firms to implement quality control procedures over individual audit engagements.

The requirements concerning quality control on individual audits are found in ISA 220 *Quality control for an audit of financial statements*.

ISA 220.6

The objective of the auditor is to implement quality control procedures at the engagement level that provide the auditor with reasonable assurance that:

(a)   The audit complies with professional standards and applicable legal and regulatory requirements; and

(b)   The auditor's report issued is appropriate in the circumstances

---

The responsibility for this falls largely on the audit engagement partner, who is responsible for the audit and the ultimate conclusion.

5.1 Leadership responsibilities

The engagement partner is required to set an example with regard to the importance of quality.

5.2 Ethical requirements

The engagement partner must ensure that the audit team complies with applicable ethical requirements, including independence, throughout the course of the audit. The ethical requirements are discussed in Section 1.3 above.

5.3 Acceptance/continuance of client relationships and specific audit engagements

The partner is required to ensure that appropriate procedures in respect of accepting and continuing with the audit are followed. If the engagement partner obtains information that would have caused them to decline the audit in the first place they should communicate that information to the firm so that swift action may be taken. They must document conclusions reached about accepting and continuing the audit.

5.4 Assignment of engagement teams

The engagement partner must ensure that the audit team as a whole, as well as any auditor's experts, has the appropriate competence to:

- Perform the audit in accordance with professional standards, laws and regulations; and
- Ensure that the auditor's report issued is appropriate to the circumstances.

5.5 Engagement performance

Ensuring good engagement performance involves:

- Direction
- Supervision
- Review

- Consultation
- Resolution of disputes

5.5.1 Direction

The partner directs the audit. They are required by other auditing standards to hold a meeting with the audit team to discuss the audit, in particular the risks associated with the audit.

ISA 220 states that direction includes 'informing members of the engagement team of:

(a)   Their responsibilities (including objectivity of mind and professional scepticism)

(b)   Responsibilities of respective partners where more than one partner is involved in the conduct of the audit engagement

(c)   The objectives of the work to be performed

(d)   The nature of the entity's business

(e)   Risk-related issues

(f)   Problems that may arise

(g)   The detailed approach to the performance of the engagement'

5.5.2 Supervision

The audit is supervised overall by the engagement partner, but more practical supervision is given within the audit team by senior staff to more junior staff, as is also the case with review. It includes:

- Tracking the progress of the audit engagement
- Considering the capabilities and competence of individual members of the team, and whether they have sufficient time and understanding to carry out their work
- Addressing significant issues arising during the audit engagement and modifying the planned approach appropriately
- Identifying matters for consultation or consideration by more experienced engagement team members during the audit engagement

5.5.3 Review

Review includes consideration of whether:

- The work has been performed in accordance with professional standards and regulatory and legal requirements

- Significant matters have been raised for further consideration

- Appropriate consultations have taken place and the resulting conclusions have been documented and implemented

- There is a need to revise the nature, timing and extent of work performed

- The work performed supports the conclusions reached and is appropriately documented

- The evidence obtained is sufficient and appropriate to support the auditor's report

- The objectives of the engagement procedures have been achieved

Before the auditor's report is issued, the engagement partner must be sure that sufficient and appropriate audit evidence has been obtained to support the audit opinion. Reviews should be carried out at the appropriate stage of the audit, in order to ensure that any significant matters are resolved on a timely basis.

The audit engagement partner need not review all audit documentation, but may do so. They should review critical areas of judgement, significant risks and other important matters.

5.5.4 Consultation

The partner is also responsible for ensuring that if difficult or contentious matters arise the team takes appropriate consultation on the matter and that such matters and conclusions are properly recorded.

If differences of opinion arise between the engagement partner and the team, or between the engagement partner and the quality control reviewer, these differences should be resolved according to the firm's policy for such differences of opinion.

5.5.5 Engagement quality control review

The audit engagement partner is responsible for **appointing** a reviewer, if one is required. They are then responsible for discussing significant matters that arise with the reviewer and for not issuing the audit report until the engagement quality control review has been completed.

Engagement quality control reviewers (also known as independent review partners) are appointed for the audit of listed entities, or other entities which meet audit firm's criteria for engagement quality control reviews. Engagement quality control reviews are likely to be carried out on audits which are assessed to be high risk, as a safeguard against a potential ethical threat.

An engagement quality control review should include:

- An evaluation of the **significant judgements** made by the engagement team
- An evaluation of the **conclusions** reached in formulating the auditor's report

> **ISA 220.25**
>
> The engagement quality control reviewer shall document, for the audit engagement reviewed, that:
>
> (a) The procedures required by the firm's policies on engagement quality control review have been performed;
>
> (b) The engagement quality control review has been completed on or before the date of the auditor's report; and
>
> (c) The reviewer is not aware of any unresolved matters that would cause the reviewer to believe that the significant judgements the engagement team made and the conclusions it reached were not appropriate.

A quality control review for a listed entity will include a review of:

- Discussion of significant matters with the engagement partner

- Review of financial statements and the proposed report

- Review of selected audit documentation relating to significant audit judgements made by the audit team and the conclusions reached

- Evaluation of the conclusions reached in formulating the auditor's report and consideration of whether the auditor's report is appropriate

- The engagement team's evaluation of the firm's independence towards the audit

- Whether appropriate consultations have taken place on differences of opinion/contentious matters and the conclusions drawn

- Whether the audit documentation selected for review reflects the work performed in relation to significant judgements/supports the conclusions reached

Other matters relevant to evaluating significant judgements made by the audit team are likely to be:

- The significant risks identified during the engagement and the responses to those risks (including assessment of, and response to, fraud)

- Judgements made, particularly with respect to materiality and significant risks

- Significance of corrected and uncorrected misstatements identified during the audit
- Matters to be communicated with management/those charged with governance

5.6 Monitoring

The audit engagement partner is required to consider the results of monitoring of the firm's (or network firm's) quality control systems and consider whether they have any impact on the specific audit they are conducting.

Question	Quality control issues

You are an audit senior working for the firm Addystone Fish. You are currently carrying out the audit of Wicker Co, a manufacturer of waste paper bins. You are unhappy with Wicker's inventory valuation policy and have raised the issue several times with the audit manager. The audit manager has dealt with the client for a number of years and does not see what you are making a fuss about. He has refused to meet you on site to discuss these issues.

The former engagement partner to Wicker retired two months ago. As the audit manager had dealt with Wicker for so many years, the other partners have decided to leave the audit of Wicker in their capable hands.

Required

Comment on the situation outlined above.

Answer

Several quality control issues are raised in the above scenario:

Engagement partner

An engagement **partner** is usually appointed to each audit engagement undertaken by the firm, to take responsibility for the engagement on behalf of the firm. Assigning the audit to the experienced audit manager is not sufficient.

The lack of an audit engagement partner also means that several of the requirements of ISA 220 about ensuring that arrangements in relation to independence and directing, supervising and reviewing the audit are not in place.

Conflicting views

In this scenario the audit manager and senior have conflicting views about the valuation of inventory. This does not appear to have been handled well, with the manager refusing to discuss the issue with the senior.

ISA 220 requires that the audit engagement partner takes responsibility for settling disputes in accordance with the firm's policy in respect of resolution of disputes as required by ISQC 1. In this case, the lack of engagement partner may have contributed to this failure to resolve the disputes. In any event, at best, the failure to resolve the dispute is a breach of the firm's policy under ISQC 1. At worst, it indicates that the firm does not have a suitable policy concerning such disputes as required by ISQC 1.

Chapter Roundup

- The ACCA's *Code of ethics and conduct* sets out the five **fundamental principles** of professional ethics and provides a **conceptual framework** for applying them.

- Members of the ACCA must comply with the fundamental principles set out in the *Code of ethics and conduct* (**integrity, objectivity, professional competence and due care, confidentiality and professional behaviour**).

- Although auditors have a professional duty of **confidentiality**, they may be compelled by **law** or consider it necessary in the **public interest** to disclose details of clients' affairs to third parties.

- Threats to independence and objectivity may arise in the form of **self-review, self-interest, advocacy, familiarity and intimidation threats**. Appropriate **safeguards** must be put in place to eliminate or reduce such threats to acceptable levels.

- The present and proposed auditors must **communicate** with each other prior to the audit being accepted; however, if the client refuses to give **permission** to the proposed auditors to make contact, the proposed auditors must **decline nomination**.

- The **terms** of the audit engagement shall be **agreed** with management and **recorded** in an audit engagement letter.

- The International Standard on Quality Control (ISQC 1) helps audit firms to establish quality standards for their business.

- ISA 220 requires firms to implement quality control procedures over individual audit engagements.

1   Match each ethical principle to the correct definition.

    (a)   Integrity
    (b)   Objectivity
    (c)   Professional competence and due care
    (d)   Confidentiality
    (e)   Professional behaviour

    (i)   Not allow bias, conflicts of interest or undue influence of others to override professional or business judgements.

    (ii)   Have a continuing duty to maintain professional knowledge and skill at a level required to ensure that a client or employer receives competent professional service based on current developments in practice, legislation and techniques. Act diligently and in accordance with applicable technical and professional standards when providing professional services.

    (iii)   Be straightforward and honest in all business and professional relationships.

    (iv)   Comply with relevant laws and regulations and avoid any action that discredits the profession.

    (v)   Respect the confidentiality of information acquired as a result of professional and business relationships and should not disclose any such information to third parties without proper or specific authority or unless there is a legal or professional right or duty to disclose. Confidential information acquired as a result of professional and business relationships should not be used for the personal advantage of members or third parties.

2   ACCA's *Code of ethics and conduct* applies only to statutory audits.

    True   ☐   False   ☐

3   Fill in the blanks.

    A post-issuance or pre-issuance review is required for audits of clients that are ………… ………… ………… and where total fees from the client represent more than ……..% of the firm's total fees for …… consecutive years.

4   (a)   Which of the following are legitimate reasons for breach of client confidentiality?

        (i)   Auditor **suspects** client has committed treason
        (ii)   Disclosure **needed** to protect auditor's own interests
        (iii)   Information is **required** for the auditor of another client
        (iv)   Auditor **knows** client has committed terrorist offence
        (v)   It is in the **public interest** to disclose
        (vi)   Auditor **considers** there to be non-compliance with law and regulations
        (vii)   Auditor **suspects** client has committed fraud

    (b)   Of the above reasons, which are voluntary disclosures and which are obligatory disclosures?

5   An engagement letter is only ever sent to a client before the first audit.

    True   ☐   False   ☐

1   (a)   (iii)
    (b)   (i)
    (c)   (ii)
    (d)   (v)
    (e)   (iv)

2   False. The spirit of the guidance applies to professional situations in which ACCA members may find themselves – be it as an auditor or as an accountant in business.

3   Public interest entities, 15, two

4   (a)   (i), (ii), (iv), (v), (vi)

    (b)   (i)   Obligatory
          (ii)   Voluntary
          (iv)   Obligatory
          (v)   Voluntary
          (vi)   Obligatory

    (**Note**. In the case of (vii), the auditor should not take action outside the company until they are certain. When they are certain, they should seek legal advice.)

5   False. It should be re-issued if there is a change in circumstances.

Now try the questions below from the Practice Question Bank

Number	Level	Marks	Time
Q5	Introductory	n/a	n/a
Q6	Examination	20	39 mins

Internal audit

Topic list	Syllabus reference
1 Internal audit and corporate governance	A5, B5
2 Distinction between internal and external audit	A5
3 Scope of the internal audit function	A6
4 Internal audit assignments	A6
5 Internal audit reports	A6
6 Outsourcing the internal audit function	A6

Introduction

Internal audit is a function established by management to assist in corporate governance by assessing internal controls and helping in risk management. It can be a department of employees or can be outsourced to expert service providers.

Internal auditing is different from external auditing, although the techniques used by both are very similar. While the techniques used may be similar, the focus and reasons behind the audit are different.

Various assurance assignments may be undertaken by internal auditors and these are outlined in Section 4. The role of internal audit with regard to fraud is also discussed briefly.

The chapter ends with a consideration of outsourcing the internal audit function – this is very common in the real world and we discuss the potential benefits and drawbacks of doing so.

Study guide

		Intellectual level
A5	**Internal audit and corporate governance**	
(a)	Discuss the factors to be taken into account when assessing the need for internal audit.	2
(b)	Discuss the elements of best practice in the structure and operations of internal audit with reference to appropriate international codes of corporate governance.	2
(c)	Compare and contrast the role of external and internal audit.	2
A6	**The scope of the internal audit function**	
(a)	Discuss the scope of internal audit and the limitations of the internal audit function.	2
(b)	Explain outsourcing and the advantages and disadvantages of outsourcing the internal audit function.	1
(c)	Discuss the nature and purpose of internal audit assignments including value for money, IT, financial, regulatory compliance, fraud investigations and customer experience.	2
(d)	Discuss the nature and purpose of operational internal audit assignments.	2
(e)	Describe and explain the format and content of audit review reports and make appropriate recommendations to management and those charged with governance.	2
B5	**Fraud, laws and regulations**	
(b)	Discuss the responsibilities of internal and external auditors for the prevention and detection of fraud and error.	2

Exam guide

Internal audit has featured in most of the F8 papers to date. It is therefore very important that you understand what internal auditing is and how it differs from external auditing, as there is a good chance it could come up again.

This topic can be tested from a variety of angles. The Specimen Exam published in 2015 included a question on the differences between internal and external audit, integrated into a mini-case scenario focusing on the implications of outsourcing internal audit to the external auditor on auditor independence. Other topics that could be examined include:

- Explaining the role of the internal audit function, and the purpose of the different types of assignments performed by the internal audit function
- Discussing the advantages and disadvantages of outsourcing the internal audit function

All of these can also be examined in Section A as well as Section B.

1 Internal audit and corporate governance

Internal audit assists management in achieving the entity's corporate objectives, particularly in establishing good corporate governance.

1.1 Introduction

The following definition of internal auditing was given in Chapter 1, for comparison with other forms of assurance service and providers.

Key term

> **Internal auditing** is an appraisal or monitoring activity established within an entity as a service to the entity. It functions by, among other things, examining, evaluating and reporting to management and the directors on the adequacy and effectiveness of components of the accounting and internal control systems.

Internal audit is generally a feature of large companies. It is a function, provided either by employees of the entity or sourced from an external organisation, to assist management in **achieving corporate objectives**. An entity's corporate objectives will vary from company to company, and will be found in a company's mission statement and strategic plan. However, other corporate objectives will not vary so much between companies, and are linked to a key issue we have already discussed in Chapter 3 on **good corporate governance**.

1.2 Internal audit and corporate governance

Established codes of corporate governance such as the UK Corporate Governance Code highlight the need for businesses to maintain **good systems of internal control** to manage the risks the company faces. **Internal audit** can play a key role in assessing and monitoring internal control policies and procedures.

The internal audit function can assist the board in other ways as well:

- By, in effect, acting as auditors for board reports not audited by the external auditors

- By being the experts in fields such as auditing and accounting standards in the company and assisting in implementation of new standards

- By liaising with external auditors, particularly where external auditors can use internal audit work and reduce the time and therefore cost of the external audit

One of the principles of the UK Corporate Governance Code that was set out in Chapter 3 is that:

> The board should establish formal and transparent arrangements for considering how it should apply the corporate reporting and risk management and internal control principles, and for maintaining an appropriate relationship with the company's auditors.

Part of achieving this principle requires the audit committee to:

- Monitor and review the effectiveness of internal audit activities

- Where there is no internal audit function, to consider annually whether there is a need for this function and make a recommendation to the board

- Where there is no internal audit function, to explain in the annual report the absence of such a function

1.3 Assessing the need for internal audit

We have seen that internal audit can assist an entity in providing effective corporate governance and this may be enough to prompt an entity to establish an internal audit department. Other factors an entity might consider when assessing the need for an internal audit function include:

- The cost of setting up an internal audit department versus the predicted benefit
- Predicted savings in external fees where work carried out by consultants will be carried out by the new internal audit department
- The complexity and scale of the organisation's activities and the systems supporting those activities
- The ability of existing managers and employees to carry out assignments that internal audit may be asked to carry out
- Management's perceived need for assessing risk and internal control
- Whether it is more cost effective or desirable to outsource the work
- The pressure from external stakeholders to establish an internal audit department

It may be that a company will benefit from some internal audit work but not enough to warrant the cost of full-time employees. If existing staff do not have the time or experience to carry out this work, it may be more cost effective to ask an external accounting firm to carry out just those projects that may be of most benefit, rather than setting up an internal audit function. We look at outsourcing internal audit work later in the chapter.

If the volume of internal audit work required is such that the price differential between employing an internal audit team and outsourcing the work is small, the company will need to consider whether there are longer-term benefits, such as:

- Establishing an internal audit department will help maintain a group of highly skilled people which may help the business develop faster that it would otherwise have done
- Working in internal audit can be a route to providing training for future senior executives because internal auditors are likely to obtain knowledge of many aspects of the business and liaise with personnel at all levels.

2 Distinction between internal and external audit
June 09, June 12, Specimen Exam

FAST FORWARD

Although many of the techniques internal and external auditors use may be similar, the basis and reasoning of their work is different.

The **external audit** is focused on the **financial statements**, whereas the **internal audit** is focused on the **operations of the entire business**.

The following table highlights the key differences between internal and external audit.

	Internal audit	External audit
Objective	Designed to add value to and improve an organisation's operations.	An exercise to enable auditors to express an opinion on the financial statements.
Reporting	Reports to the board of directors, or other people charged with governance, such as the audit committee. Reports are private and for the directors and management of the company.	Reports to the shareholders or members of a company on the truth and fairness of the accounts. Audit report is publicly available to the shareholders and other interested parties.
Scope	Work relates to the operations of the organisation.	Work relates to the financial statements.

	Internal audit	External audit
Relationship	Often employees of the organisation, although sometimes the function is outsourced.	Independent of the company and its management. Usually appointed by the shareholders.
Planning and collection of evidence	Strategic long-term planning carried out to achieve objective of assignments, with no materiality level being set.	Planning carried out to achieve objective regarding truth and fairness of financial statements.
	Some audits may be procedural, rather than risk-based.	Materiality level set during planning (may be amended during course of audit).
	Evidence mainly from interviewing staff and inspecting documents (ie not external).	External audit work is risk-based.
		Evidence collected using a variety of procedures per ISAs to obtain sufficient appropriate audit evidence.

The table demonstrates that the **whole basis and reasoning** of internal audit work is **fundamentally different** to that of external audit work.

2.1 Regulation of internal auditors

Internal auditing is not regulated in the same way as statutory external auditing (which we covered in Chapter 2). There are **no legal requirements** associated with becoming an internal auditor. The **scope** and **nature** of **internal audit's work** is more likely to be set by **company policy** than by any external guidelines.

In contrast to external auditors, internal auditors are not required to be members of a professional body such as the ACCA. However, this does not mean they cannot be, and many are. There is also a global Institute of Internal Auditors (IIA) which internal auditors may become members of. It issues 'Standards for the Professional Practice of Internal Auditing'. These are not examinable, so are not detailed in this Study Text, but you should be aware of the them as being another Code of Good Practice that internal auditors can follow, providing a framework for a wide range of internal audit services.

3 Scope of the internal audit function   Dec 07, June 13

FAST FORWARD

Internal audit has two key roles to play in relation to organisational risk management:
- Ensuring the company's risk management system operates effectively
- Ensuring that strategies implemented in respect of business risks operate effectively

Being able to explain the overall role and process of internal audit, review and control is identified in the performance objectives booklet as being part of the key knowledge and understanding required for Performance Objective 17 (PO 17). This section will help you to gain that knowledge and understanding and ultimately help you to achieve PO 17.

3.1 Business risk

In the UK, the Financial Reporting Council (FRC) issued a publication 'Internal Control: Guidance to directors' (formerly known as the Turnbull Guidance) to assist companies in applying the principles and provisions of the UK Corporate Governance Code relating to internal control. The UK Corporate Governance Code was formerly known as the Combined Code and the latest version of the FRC guidance on internal control in issue at the date of updating this Study Text still refers to the Combined Code.

However, the guidance can still be applied to the equivalent sections of the UK Corporate Governance Code.

The FRC guidance on internal control refers to the management of risks that are significant to the fulfilment of the company's objectives which is known as **business risk**. You do not need to be able to discuss business risks in detail in the F8 exam, but you should understand it in the context of the internal audit function's responsibilities.

> **Business risk** is a risk resulting from significant conditions, events, circumstances, actions or inactions that could adversely affect an entity's ability to achieve its objectives and execute its strategies, or from the setting of inappropriate objectives and strategies.

Business risk cannot be eliminated, but it must be **managed** by the company.

Designing and operating internal control systems is a key part of a company's risk management. This will often be done by employees in their various departments, although sometimes (particularly in the case of specialised computer systems) the company will hire external expertise to design systems.

3.2 The role of internal audit

The internal audit department has a twofold role in relation to risk management.

- It monitors the company's overall risk management policy to ensure it operates effectively.
- It monitors the strategies implemented to ensure that they continue to operate effectively.

As a significant risk management policy in companies is to implement internal controls, internal audit has a key role in assessing systems and testing controls.

Internal audit may assist in the development of systems. However, its key role will be in **monitoring the overall process** and in **providing assurance** that the **systems** which the departments have designed **meet objectives** and **operate effectively**.

It is important that the internal audit department retains its **objectivity** towards these aspects of its role, which is another reason why internal audit would generally not be involved in the assessment of risks and the design of the system.

3.3 Responsibility for fraud and error   June 13

> It is the responsibility of management and those charged with governance to prevent and detect fraud, and, in this respect, internal auditors may have a role to play.

Fraud is a **key business risk**. It is the responsibility of the **directors** to prevent and detect fraud. As the internal auditors have a role in risk management, they are involved in the process of managing the risk of fraud. It is not the responsibility of the external auditors to prevent and detect fraud, although they may unearth fraud as part of their audit of the financial statements, and they shall be aware of the risks of fraud while carrying out the audit. (We look at the external auditor's responsibilities for fraud and error in more detail in Chapter 6.)

Internal auditors can help to **prevent** fraud by carrying out work on **assessing the adequacy and effectiveness of control systems**. They can help to **detect** fraud by **being mindful** when carrying out their work and **reporting any suspicions**.

The very **existence of an internal audit** department may act as a **deterrent** to fraud. The internal auditors might also be called upon to undertake **special projects** to investigate a suspected fraud.

3.4 Limitations of the internal audit function   June 13

Although the presence of an internal audit department within an organisation is indicative of good internal control, by its very nature, there are some **limitations** of the internal audit function.

Internal auditors are employed by the organisation and this can **impair their independence and objectivity** and ability to report fraud/error to senior management because of perceived threats to their continued employment within the company.

To ensure transparency, best practice indicates that the internal audit function should have a **dual reporting relationship**, ie report both to management and those charged with governance (the audit committee). If this reporting structure is not in place, management may be able to unduly influence the internal audit plan, scope, and whether issues are reported appropriately. This results in a serious conflict, limits the scope and compromises the effectiveness of the internal audit function.

Internal auditors are not required to be **professionally qualified** (as accountants are) and so there may be limitations in their knowledge and technical expertise.

Even if they are professionally qualified, due to the perceived lack of independence compared with external professionals, internal audit work would not be accepted on many assignments where the interested party is an external stakeholder. For example, where finance is sought and the lender requires assurance on cash flow projections, that lender will usually require that the assurance is from a firm of independent professional accountants.

Question   Internal control procedures

The growing recognition by management of the benefits of good internal control and the complexities of an adequate system of internal control have led to the development of internal auditing as a form of control over all other internal controls. The emergence of internal auditors as experts in internal control is the result of an evolutionary process similar in many ways to the evolution of external auditing.

Required

(a)   Explain why the internal and independent external auditors' review of internal control procedures differ in purpose.

(b)   Explain the reasons why internal auditors should or should not report their findings on internal control to the following company officials:

(i)   The board of directors
(ii)   The chief accountant

Answer

(a)   Internal auditors review and test the system of internal control and report to management in order to improve the information received by managers and to help in their task of running the company. They will recommend changes to the system to ensure that management receives objective information which is efficiently produced. They also have a duty to search for and discover fraud. The external auditors review the system of internal control in order to determine the extent of the substantive work required on the year-end accounts.

The external auditors report to the shareholders rather than the managers or directors. They report on the truth and fairness of the financial statements, not directly on the system of internal control. However, external auditors usually issue a report to management, laying out any areas of weakness (deficiency) and recommendations for improvement in the system of internal control. They do not have a specific duty to detect fraud, although they should plan their audit procedures so as to detect any material misstatements in the accounts on which they give an opinion.

(b)　(i)　*Board of directors*

A high level of independence is achieved by the internal auditors if they report directly to the board. There may be problems with this approach.

(1)　The members of the board may not understand all the implications of the internal audit reports when accounting or technical information is required.

(2)　The board may not have enough time to spend considering the reports in sufficient depth. Important recommendations might therefore remain unimplemented.

A way around these problems might be to delegate the review of internal audit reports to an audit committee, which would act as a sub-committee to the main board. The audit committee should be made up largely of non-executive directors who have more time and independence from the day-to-day running of the company.

(ii)　*Chief accountant*

It would be inappropriate for internal audit to report to the chief accountant, who is in charge of running the system of internal control. It may be feasible for the chief accountant to receive the report as well as the board. Otherwise, the internal audit function cannot be effectively independent, as the chief accountant may suppress unfavourable reports or may just not act on the recommendations of such reports.

4 Internal audit assignments　　　　Dec 10, Dec 13, June 14

FAST FORWARD

Internal audit can be involved in many different assignments as directed by management. These can range from **value for money** projects to **operational** assignments looking at specific parts of the business.

In the next section we will consider a number of the detailed assignments which an internal auditor could get involved in.

4.1 Value for money audits

Value for money (VFM) audits examine the **economy**, **efficiency** and **effectiveness** of activities and processes. These are known as the **three Es** of VFM audits.

The three Es which form the basis of the VFM audit are very important for assessing the performance of not-for-profit organisations, because their performance cannot be properly assessed using conventional accounting ratios. As a result, most not-for-profit organisations rely on measures that estimate the performance of the organisation in relation to the three Es. For example, in Singapore, the Auditor-General's Office carries out VFM audits on the economic, efficient and effective use of public resources. We look at not-for-profit entities in detail in Chapter 17.

The three Es can be defined as follows.

(a)　**Economy**: Attaining the appropriate quantity and quality of physical, human and financial resources (**inputs**) at lowest cost. An activity would not be economical if, for example, there was overstaffing or failure to purchase materials of requisite quality at the lowest available price.

(b)　**Efficiency**: This is the relationship between goods or services produced (**outputs**) and the resources used to produce them. An efficient operation produces the maximum output for any given set of resource inputs, or it has minimum inputs for any given quantity and quality of product or service provided.

(c)　**Effectiveness**: This is concerned with how well an activity is achieving its policy objectives or other intended effects.

The internal auditors will **evaluate** these three factors for any given business system or operation in the company. Value for money can often only be judged by **comparison.** In searching for value for money, present methods of operation and uses of resources must be **compared with alternatives**.

The following list identifies areas of an organisation, process or activity where there might be scope for significant value for money improvements. Each of these should be reviewed within individual organisations.

- Service delivery (the actual provision of a public service)
- Management process
- Environment

An alternative approach is to look at areas of spending. A value for money assessment of economy, efficiency and effectiveness would look at whether:

- Too much money is being spent on certain items or activities, to achieve the targets or objectives of the overall operation.
- Money is being spent to no purpose, because the spending is not helping to achieve objectives.
- Changes could be made to improve performance.

An illustrative list is shown below of the sort of spending areas that might be looked at, and the aspects of spending where value for money might be improved.

- Employee expenses
- Premises expenses
- Suppliers and services
- Establishment expenses
- Capital expenditure

Problems with VFM auditing	
Measuring outputs	For example, the outputs of a fire brigade can be measured by the number of call-outs, but it is not satisfactory to compare a call-out to individuals stuck in a lift with a call-out to a small house fire or a major industrial fire or a road accident etc.
Defining objectives	In not-for-profit organisations the quality of the service provided will be a significant feature of their service. For example, a local authority has, among its various different objectives, the objective of providing a rubbish collection service. The effectiveness of this service can only be judged by establishing what standard or quality of service is required.
Sacrifice of quality	Economy and efficiency can be achieved by sacrificing quality. Neither outputs nor impacts are necessarily measured in terms of quality. For example, the cost of teaching can be reduced by increasing the pupil:teacher ratio in schools, but it is difficult to judge the consequences of such a change on teaching standards and quality.
Measuring effectiveness	For example, the effectiveness of the health service could be said to have improved if hospitals have greater success in treating various illnesses and other conditions, or if the life expectancy of the population has increased, but a consequence of these changes will be overcrowded hospitals and longer waiting lists.
Over-emphasis on cost control	There can be an emphasis with VFM audits on costs and cost control rather than on achieving more benefits and value, so that management might be pressurised into 'short-term' decisions, such as abandoning capital expenditure plans which would create future benefits in order to keep current spending levels within limits.

Problems with VFM auditing	
Measuring efficiency	In profit-making organisations, the efficiency of the organisation as a whole can be measured in terms of return on capital employed. Individual profit centres or operating units can also have efficiency measured by relating the quantity of output produced, which has a market value and therefore a quantifiable financial value, to the inputs (and their cost) required to make the output.
	In not-for-profit organisations, output does not usually have a market value, and it is therefore more difficult to measure efficiency. This difficulty is compounded by the fact that, since such organisations often have many different activities or operations, it is difficult to compare the efficiency of one operation with the efficiency of another. For example, with the police force, it might be difficult to compare the efficiency of a serious crime squad with the efficiency of the traffic police.

4.2 Information technology audits

An information technology (IT) audit is a test of controls in a specific area of the business, the computer systems. Increasingly in modern business, computers are vital to the functioning of the business, and therefore the controls over them are key to the business.

It is likely to be necessary to have an IT specialist in the internal audit team to undertake an audit of the controls, as some of them will be programmed into the computer system.

The diagram below shows the various areas of IT in the business which might be subject to a test of controls by the auditors.

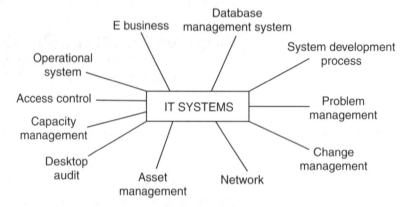

4.3 Best value audits

'Best value' is a performance framework introduced into local authorities by the UK Government. They are required to publish annual best value performance plans and review all their functions over a five-year period.

As part of best value, authorities are required to strive for continuous improvement by implementing the '4 Cs':

- **Challenge**. How and why is a service provided?
- **Compare**. Make comparisons with other local authorities and the private sector.
- **Consult**. Talk to local taxpayers and services users and the wider business community in setting performance targets.
- **Compete**. Embrace fair competition as a means of securing efficient and effective services.

One of internal audit's standard roles in a company is to provide assurance that internal control systems are adequate to promote the effective use of resources and that risks are being managed properly.

This role can be extended to ensure that the local authority has arrangements in place to achieve best value, that the risks and impacts of best value are incorporated into normal audit testing and that the authority keeps abreast of best value developments.

As best value depends on assessing current services and setting strategies for development, internal audit can take part in the 'position audit', as they should have a good understanding of how services are currently organised and relate to each other.

As assurance providers, internal audit will play a key part in giving management assurance that its objectives and strategies in relation to best value are being met.

4.4 Financial audits

The financial audit is internal audit's traditional role. It involves reviewing all the available evidence to substantiate information in management and financial reporting. The substantive procedures and tests of controls employed by external audit are also used by internal audit.

The importance of controls in preventing financial reporting errors means that it is necessary to review certain areas regularly to ensure the relevant controls continue to be in place. Many internal audit functions will therefore adopt a **cycle approach** to financial internal audit engagements to ensure each area is reviewed on a regular basis.

The below diagram shows a cycle that could be followed, along with some examples of areas that may be considered as part of the reviews of those areas.

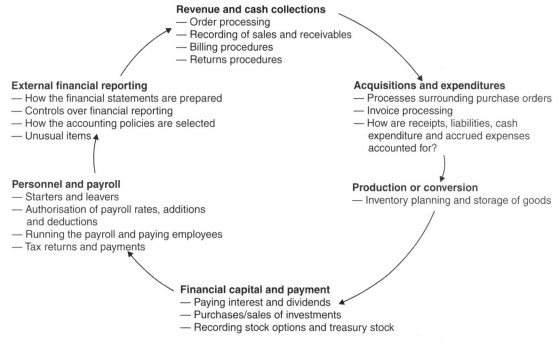

Revenue and cash collections
— Order processing
— Recording of sales and receivables
— Billing procedures
— Returns procedures

Acquisitions and expenditures
— Processes surrounding purchase orders
— Invoice processing
— How are receipts, liabilities, cash expenditure and accrued expenses accounted for?

Production or conversion
— Inventory planning and storage of goods

Financial capital and payment
— Paying interest and dividends
— Purchases/sales of investments
— Recording stock options and treasury stock

Personnel and payroll
— Starters and leavers
— Authorisation of payroll rates, additions and deductions
— Running the payroll and paying employees
— Tax returns and payments

External financial reporting
— How the financial statements are prepared
— Controls over financial reporting
— How the accounting policies are selected
— Unusual items

This role in many ways echoes that of the external auditor, and is one in which the value the internal auditors can add to the business is limited. Therefore, the range of assignments internal auditors have undertaken has increased, as organisations seek to apply their skills in areas which will add most value to the business.

4.5 Operational audits

Key term

> **Operational audits** are audits of the operational processes of the organisation. They are also known as management or efficiency audits. Their prime objective is the monitoring of management's performance, ensuring that company policy is adhered to.

4.5.1 Approaching operational internal audit assignments

There are two aspects of an operational assignment:

- Ensure policies are adequate
- Ensure policies work effectively

In terms of adequacy, the internal auditor will have to review the policies of a particular department by:

- Reading them
- Discussion with members of the department

Then the auditor will have to assess whether the policies are adequate, and possibly advise the board of improvement.

The auditor will then have to examine the effectiveness of the controls by:

- Observing them in operation
- Testing them

This will be done on similar lines to the testing of controls by external auditors which is discussed in Section D of this Study Text, even though the controls being tested may differ.

4.5.2 Procurement audits

Procurement is the process of **purchasing** for the business. A procurement audit will therefore concentrate on the **systems** of the purchasing department(s). The internal auditor will be checking that the system achieves key objectives and that it operates according to company guidelines.

4.6 Examples of internal audit assignments

The assignments internal auditors will carry out will depend on the particular circumstances of the company involved and its objectives. However, the following are examples of the sorts of assignment internal auditors may be asked to carry out by management.

(a) **Testing operational or financial controls**: This may include testing controls operating centrally (at head office) or at branches. One example is the testing of controls over inventory counting or cash counting. This would include observation of controls in operation at warehouses or retail stores during attendance at counts.

(b) **IT system reviews**: We mentioned IT audits earlier. Internal auditors may be asked to look specifically at controls over the accounting system, or, instead, over other computer systems that supply data to the accounting system. For example, a travel company's reservation system will usually link to the accounting system and is an important element in determining when the revenue on a flight or holiday is recorded. Or for companies with retail stores, assignments may include reviewing controls over computer systems linking tills to head office.

(c) **Value for money reviews**: As stated earlier, these are often common in not-for-profit entities. However, they are carried out by internal auditors in profit-making entities too. This could be in the context of whether the company is obtaining from its assets or its suppliers, as well as whether the company is providing value for money for its customers.

(d) **Fraud investigations**: Fraud can range from theft of assets to fraudulent financial reporting. Internal audit may be asked to investigate specific instances of suspected fraud or, more generally, to review and test controls to prevent or detect fraud.

(e) **Review of compliance with laws and regulations**: There will be a number of regulations a company will need to comply with. Some will be specific to the industry the client operates in (eg regulations over disposing of hazardous waste in the nuclear industry) and some will apply to all companies operating in a region or country (eg tax laws and employee-related laws). Internal auditors may assist with or review compliance with these laws and regulations. For example, if a company has an overseas branch, the internal audit department may review compliance with laws/regulations specific to that country (such as filing adequate financial or non-financial returns).

(f) **Customer service reviews**: Internal auditors may be asked to assess the level of customer service. They could do this by phoning in or visiting stores/outlets and pretending to be customers. Alternatively they could review and analyse the results of customer surveys.

The list of examples above is not exhaustive and those charged with governance could ask internal audit to review and report on any business area where feedback could be useful in improving the company's position and performance.

5 Internal audit reports

FAST FORWARD »

The internal auditors' report may take any form, as there are no formal reporting requirements for these reports as there are for the external auditor's report.

5.1 Reporting on internal audit assignments

Internal auditors produce reports for directors and management as a result of work performed. These reports are internal to the business and are unlikely to be shared with third parties other than the external auditors.

We have looked in detail at the types of assignment that internal audit will carry out. These may be summarised as '**risk-based**', where the internal auditors consider internal and external risks and discuss company operations and systems in place in respect of them or '**performance enhancement**' where internal auditors consider risk and strategy on a higher level. For the most part, work is likely to be **risk-based**. Regardless of the nature of the assignment, however, all internal audits are likely to result in a formal report.

At the end of the audit engagement, the results have to be communicated to relevant staff. The results will be made up of a number **of findings and recommendations** and their aim is to get management to implement measures to solve the problems identified.

Exam focus point

Internal auditors could report their findings in a similar format to that used in the 'report to management' by the external auditor when reporting significant deficiencies. The report to management is covered in detail in Chapter 19 and it sets out each deficiency identified, the implication of each deficiency and a recommendation to overcome the deficiency.

An internal auditor may, for example, present findings from an operational audit in the same way. The internal auditor's report could state deficiencies found during the operational audit, along with the related implications and recommendations.

As a result, in the exam you may need to consider details in a scenario from an internal auditor's point of view before being asked to identify and report deficiencies, implications and recommendations.

Internal audit reports are most likely to be received favourably if there are 'no surprises' ie the findings should already have been discussed with key personnel and their views incorporated to ensure that the recommendations in the report are suitable, feasible, likely to work and likely to be accepted by management.

Usually at the end of the fieldwork, the internal auditors produce a draft report which is sent out for consideration by the relevant management. The internal auditors will meet with management to discuss the work and the findings and recommendations. This is known as the exit meeting and is discussed in Section 5.2.

After the meeting, the internal auditors then produce a formal report which, once approved by the relevant people, is used to produce the final report for distribution. We look in detail at the processes around finalising and distributing the report, and the contents of internal audit reports in the sub-sections that follow.

5.2 Exit meetings

An **exit meeting** is held at the end of the internal audit engagement after a **draft report** has been produced. The people at this meeting are likely to include both operational staff who understand the workings of the operation that has been reviewed, and staff with suitable levels of authorisation to authorise the implementation of the corrective actions identified.

The objectives of this meeting are to:

- Discuss the findings and associated recommendations

- Provide management with the opportunity to give their views on, and ask for clarification of, the observations and recommendations allowing any misunderstandings to be resolved

- Agree on possible solutions to the problems the internal audit assignment has identified

5.3 Final report

Depending on the organisation in question, the final report may take the form of a written report or take a different format, such as a powerpoint presentation.

One format for formal written reports in business is laid out below. This format makes reports useful to readers, as it highlights the conclusions drawn and gives easy reference to the user.

Standard report format
TERMS OF REFERENCE
EXECUTIVE SUMMARY
BODY OF THE REPORT
APPENDICES FOR ANY ADDITIONAL INFORMATION

The **executive summary** is like a condensed version of the full report and an executive summary in an internal audit report will usually include:

- Background to the assignment
- Objectives of the assignment
- Major outcomes of the work
- Key risks identified
- Key action points
- Summary of the work left to do

Although the content and format of the final internal audit report will vary, somewhere the report should, as a minimum, describe the **purpose**, **scope** and **results** of the engagement.

Minimum contents	
Purpose	The objective of the audit engagement should be clearly stated. This makes the report easier to read and helps the reader to interpret it. Findings should be linked back to this objective.
Scope	The scope defines what specifically is audited. It identifies which activities are audited and also highlights any activities that are excluded from the audit.
Results	This should include: • Observations • Conclusions • Opinions • Recommendations • Action plans

In addition, the final internal audit report may include the following, optional, sections.

Additional contents	
Background information	This could include such information as details of the organisation and the activities reviewed, and the outcome of previous audits of the same areas.
Summaries	An executive summary (as described earlier) may be included to present the main findings of the report for those who do not have time to read the entire report.
Accomplishments	Improvements in relation to the past audit of the area may be acknowledged.
Opinions	The opinions of management or other staff on the findings and recommendations may be incorporated into either the main body of the report, an appendix or as a covering letter. Executives may need to intervene if there is a disagreement between management and internal audit.

High-quality internal audit reports will have the following attributes.

Attributes	
Accurate	The report should be free from error.
Objective	It should be fair, impartial and unbiased. It should be based on facts.
Clear	The report should be logical, easily understood and free from jargon.
Concise	It should be to the point and free from unnecessary detail.
Complete	No information essential to the intended audience should be omitted.
Timely	The report should convey a sense of urgency.

5.4 Distribution of the final report

The full report should be provided to those people who can take corrective action on the issues raised in the report. Summary reports should be provided to more senior managers.

Communication may also go to:

- External auditors
- The board
- Others who are affected by, or interested in, the results

5.4.1 Amendments

If any amendments are made to the report after it has been issued, a new report should be issued which highlights any changes. This should be distributed to everyone who received the original report.

5.4.2 Releasing the report

If the report is to be released to parties outside the organisation, the risks to the organisation of doing so should be assessed. Approval to release should be gained from senior management, legal counsel or both.

5.5 Management response

After the issue of the final report, management will be given the opportunity to provide their formal response to the report. This formally communicates back what is going to be done about the recommendations raised.

6 Outsourcing the internal audit function

June 08, June 11, June 14

FAST FORWARD

Internal audit departments may consist of employees of the company, or may be **outsourced** to external service providers. The **advantages** of outsourcing the internal audit function include speed, cost and a tailored answer to internal audit requirements. One of the main **disadvantages** may include threats to independence and objectivity if the external audit service is provided by the same firm.

6.1 What is outsourcing?

Key term

Outsourcing is the use of external suppliers as a source of finished products, components or services. It is also known as sub-contracting.

While the scope of the internal auditor's work is different to that of the external auditor, there are many features that can link them. One of the key factors is that the **techniques** used to carry out audits are the same for internal and external auditors.

It can be expensive to maintain an internal audit function consisting of employees of the company. It is possible that the monitoring and review required by a certain company could be done in a small amount of time and full-time employees cannot be justified.

It is also possible that a number of internal audit staff are required, but the cost of recruitment is prohibitive, or the directors are aware that the need for internal audit is only short-term.

In such circumstances, it is possible to **outsource** the internal audit function; that is, purchase the service from outside.

In this respect, many of the larger accountancy firms offer internal audit services. It is likely that the same firm might offer one client both internal and external audit services. In such circumstances the firm would have to be aware of the **independence issues** this would raise for the external audit team and **implement safeguards** to ensure that its independence and objectivity were not impaired. We discussed such issues in Chapter 4 when we looked at professional ethics.

6.2 Advantages and disadvantages of outsourcing

The advantages and disadvantages of outsourcing the internal audit function are set out in the following table.

Advantages of outsourcing	Disadvantages of outsourcing
• Staff do not need to be recruited, as the **service provider has good quality staff**. • The service provider has different **specialist skills** and can assess what management require them to do. • Outsourcing can provide an **immediate** internal audit department. • **Associated costs**, such as staff training, are **eliminated**. • The service contract can be for the **appropriate timescale**. • Because the timescale is **flexible**, a **team of staff** can be provided if required. • It can be used on a **short-term basis**.	• There will be **independence** and **objectivity** issues if the company uses the same firm to provide both internal and external audit services. • The **cost** of outsourcing the internal audit function might be high enough to make the directors choose not to have an internal audit function at all. • Company staff may oppose outsourcing if it results in **redundancies**. • There may be a **high staff turnover** of internal audit staff. • The outsourced staff may only have a **limited knowledge** of the company. • The company will **lose** in-house skills.

6.3 Managing an outsourced department

A company will need to establish **controls** over the outsourced internal audit department. These would include:

(a)   Setting **performance measures** in terms of cost and areas of the business reviewed and investigating any variances

(b)   Ensuring appropriate **audit methodology** (working papers/reviews) is maintained

(c)   **Reviewing** working papers on a sample basis to ensure they meet internal standards/guidelines

(d)   **Agreeing** internal audit work plans in advance of work being performed

(e)   If an external auditor is used, ensuring the firm has suitable controls to keep the two functions separate so that **independence and objectivity** is not impaired

Chapter Roundup

- Internal audit assists management in achieving the entity's corporate objectives, particularly in establishing good corporate governance.

- Although many of the techniques internal and external auditors use may be similar, the basis and reasoning of their work is different.

- Internal audit has two key roles to play in relation to organisational risk management:
  - Ensuring the company's risk management system operates effectively
  - Ensuring that strategies implemented in respect of business risks operate effectively

- It is the responsibility of management and those charged with governance to prevent and detect fraud, and, in this respect, internal auditors may have a role to play.

- Internal audit can be involved in many different assignments as directed by management. These can range from **value for money** projects to **operational** assignments looking at specific parts of the business.

- The internal auditors' report may take any form, as there are no formal reporting requirements for these reports as there are for the external auditor's report.

- Internal audit departments may consist of employees of the company, or may be **outsourced** to external service providers. The **advantages** of outsourcing the internal audit function include speed, cost and a tailored answer to internal audit requirements. One of the main **disadvantages** may include threats to independence and objectivity if the external audit service is provided by the same firm.

1   What is an internal audit?

2   Name three key differences between internal and external audit.

(1)   ....

(2)   ....

(3)   ....

3   Link the value for money 'E' with its definition.

(a)   Economy

(b)   Efficiency

(c)   Effectiveness

(i)   The relationships between the goods and services produced (outputs) and the resources used to produce them.

(ii)   The concern with how well an activity is achieving its policy objectives or other intended effects.

(iii)   Attaining the appropriate quantity and quality of physical, human and financial resources (inputs) at lowest cost.

4   Name five areas of the computer system which might benefit from an IT audit.

(1)   ....

(2)   ....

(3)   ....

(4)   ....

(5)   ....

5   There are formal statutory rules governing the format of internal audit reports.

True   ☐

False   ☐

6   It is possible to buy in an internal audit service from an external organisation.

True   ☐

False   ☐

Answers to Quick Quiz

1   Internal audit is an appraisal or monitoring activity established by the entity as a service to the entity.

2   (1)   External auditors report to members, internal auditors report to directors.

           (2)   External auditors report on financial statements, internal auditors report on systems, controls and risks.

           (3)   External auditors are independent of the company, internal auditors are often employed by it.

3   (a) (iii), (b) (i), (c) (ii)

4   Five from e-business, operational system, access control, capacity management, desktop audit, asset management, networks, change management, problem management, system development process, database management system

5   False

6   True – this is known as outsourcing.

Now try the question below from the Practice Question Bank

Number	Level	Marks	Time
Q7	Examination	20	39 mins

Note. Further questions containing requirements relating to internal audit include questions 9 and 20.

Planning and
risk assessment

Risk assessment

Topic list	Syllabus reference
1 Introduction to risk	B2, B3
2 Materiality	B3
3 Understanding the entity and its environment	B4
4 Assessing the risks of material misstatement	B3
5 Responding to the risk assessment	B3, B4
6 Fraud, law and regulations	B5
7 Documentation of risk assessment	B2, B3, B4

Introduction

This chapter covers the aspects of the external audit which will be considered at the earliest stages, during planning.

Firstly we introduce the concept of risk and look in detail at audit risk and its components (control risk, inherent risk and detection risk) and at how audit risk is managed by the auditor. The distinction between audit risk and business risk is also made.

We discuss the concept of materiality for the financial statements as a whole and performance materiality and the methods used for calculating them. It is important to understand that the calculation of materiality is a matter of judgement and that materiality must be reviewed during the course of the audit and revised if necessary.

The importance of understanding the entity being audited and its environment is a key aspect of audit planning and helps the auditor to identify potential risk areas to focus on. Various techniques can be used here, such as enquiry, analytical procedures, observation and inspection. The risk assessment stage allows the auditor to respond with a proposed audit approach which may be controls based or totally substantive.

The auditor also needs to consider the risks of fraud and non-compliance with laws and regulations in the audit and this is examined towards the end of this chapter.

Study guide

		Intellectual level
B2	**Objective and general principles**	
(a)	Identify the overall objectives of the auditor and the need to conduct an audit in accordance with ISAs.	2
(b)	Identify the need to plan and perform audits with an attitude of professional scepticism, and to exercise professional judgement.	2
B3	**Assessing audit risks**	
(a)	Explain the components of audit risk.	1
(b)	Explain the audit risks in the financial statements and explain the auditor's response to each risk.	2
(c)	Define and explain the concepts of materiality and performance materiality.	2
(d)	Explain and calculate materiality levels from financial information.	2
B4	**Understanding the entity and its environment**	
(a)	Explain how auditors obtain an initial understanding of the entity and its environment.	2
(b)	Describe and explain the nature, and purpose, of analytical procedures in planning.	2
(c)	Compute and interpret key ratios used in analytical procedures.	2
B5	**Fraud, laws and regulations**	
(a)	Discuss the effect of fraud and misstatements on the audit strategy and extent of audit work.	2
(b)	Discuss the responsibilities of internal and external auditors for the prevention and detection of fraud and error.	2
(c)	Explain the auditor's responsibility to consider laws and regulations.	2

Exam guide

Audit planning is a very important stage of the audit because it helps direct the focus of the audit. Within planning, risk is a key topic area. You may be asked in the exam to explain various terms, such as risk and materiality. This involves not merely learning the definitions but also being able to show how the auditor uses these techniques in practice when planning an audit. You might also have to identify the risks from a given scenario – in such a question it's important to explain fully why any factors you have identified are risks, otherwise you will not attain the maximum marks available.

Examples of the ways the topic may be examined in a written question include:

- Describing analytical procedures used during planning (may require the application of analytical procedures to financial statement extracts)

- Defining audit risk and identifying inherent risk areas in different types of organisation

- Explaining the external auditor's responsibilities for the detection of fraud

- Explaining the risks relating to the audit of a new audit client

- Explaining the importance of understanding the entity and its environment

- Defining materiality and performance materiality

- Identifying and explaining the risks of fraud in a scenario, and recommending ways to mitigate the fraud risks

- Explaining the responsibilities of management and auditors in relation to compliance with laws and regulations

All the above may also be examined in the form of mini-case scenarios in Section A.

1 Introduction to risk

A **risk assessment** carried out under the ISAs helps the auditor to identify financial statement areas susceptible to material misstatement and provides a basis for designing and performing further audit procedures.

1.1 The overall objectives of the auditor

At all stages of the audit, including during risk assessment, the auditor must bear in mind what the **overall objectives** are. We touched on this in Chapters 1 and 2, but the full description of the auditor's objectives are given in ISA 200 *Overall objectives of the independent auditor and the conduct of an audit in accordance with International Standards on Auditing*. This ISA states that, in conducting an audit of financial statements, the overall objectives are:

'To obtain reasonable assurance about whether the financial statements as a whole are free from material misstatement, whether due to fraud or error, thereby enabling the auditor to express an opinion on whether the financial statements are prepared, in all material respects, in accordance with an applicable financial reporting framework; and to report on the financial statements, and communicate as required by the ISAs, in accordance with the auditor's findings.'

In order to obtain assurance about whether the financial statements are free from material misstatement, the auditor needs to consider how and where misstatements are most likely to arise. A **risk assessment** under the ISAs helps the auditor to ensure the key areas more susceptible to material misstatement are adequately investigated and tested during the audit. It also helps the auditor identify low risk areas where reduced testing may be appropriate, ensuring time is not wasted by over-testing these areas.

As we discussed in Chapter 2, each ISA has its own individual objective followed by requirements and explanatory material.

1.1.1 Conducting the audit in accordance with ISAs

Conducting the audit in accordance with ISAs and achieving each **individual objective** will allow the auditor to achieve the **overall objective** stated above. Consequently, ISA 200 requires that the auditor must **fully understand and comply** with **all** the ISAs relevant to the audit. Furthermore, the auditor must go beyond the requirements in the ISA if they consider it necessary in order to achieve an ISA's objective.

In order to achieve the overall objective, auditors also need to plan and perform the audit with **professional scepticism** and apply **professional judgement**, which we look at in detail in the following section.

The ISAs also deal with the general responsibilities of the auditor, as well as the auditor's further considerations relevant to the application of those responsibilities to specific topics. If the auditor does not conduct an audit in accordance with a recognised set of auditing standards (such as the ISAs), important responsibilities may not be fulfilled.

Furthermore, the auditor needs to be able to refer to globally recognised standards in the audit report. If all audits are conducted in accordance with standards setting out what is expected of auditors, this means that users of the financial statements should be able to be as confident in one auditor's opinion as another's.

The fact that audits are conducted in accordance with ISAs also gives regulators of the audit profession a framework against which to judge auditors. If auditors are not carrying out audits in accordance with ISAs, they will be prohibited from undertaking audit assignments. The overall effect is that the quality of audit assignments is maintained at a high standard.

1.2 Professional scepticism, professional judgement and ethical requirements

FAST FORWARD

Auditors are required to carry out the audit with an attitude of **professional scepticism**, exercise **professional judgement** and comply with **ethical requirements**.

Key terms

Professional scepticism is an attitude that includes a questioning mind, being alert to conditions which may indicate possible misstatement due to error or fraud, and a critical assessment of audit evidence.

Professional judgement is the application of relevant training, knowledge and experience in making informed decisions about the courses of action that are appropriate in the circumstances of the audit engagement.

1.2.1 Professional scepticism

ISA 200 states that auditors must plan and perform an audit with an attitude of **professional scepticism** recognising that circumstances may exist that cause the financial statements to be materially misstated.

This requires the auditor to be alert to:

- Audit evidence that **contradicts** other audit evidence obtained

- Information that brings into question the **reliability** of documents and responses to enquiries to be used as audit evidence

- Conditions that may indicate **possible fraud**

- Circumstances that suggest the need for **audit procedures in addition** to those required by ISAs

Professional scepticism needs to be maintained throughout the audit to reduce the risks of overlooking unusual transactions, over-generalising when drawing conclusions, and using inappropriate assumptions in determining the nature, timing and extent of audit procedures and evaluating the results of them.

Professional scepticism is also necessary to the critical assessment of audit evidence. This includes questioning contradictory audit evidence and the reliability of documents and responses from management and those charged with governance.

1.2.2 Professional judgement

ISA 200 also requires the auditor to exercise **professional judgement** in planning and performing an audit of financial statements. Professional judgement is required in the following areas:

- Materiality and audit risk
- Nature, timing and extent of audit procedures
- Evaluation of whether sufficient appropriate audit evidence has been obtained
- Evaluating management's judgements in applying the applicable financial reporting framework
- Drawing conclusions based on the audit evidence obtained

1.2.3 Ethical requirements

ISA 200 states that the auditor must comply with the relevant ethical requirements, including those relating to independence, that are relevant to financial statement audit engagements. We discussed professional ethics in Chapter 4 of this Study Text.

1.3 Audit risks   Dec 08, June 10, June 11, Dec 11, Dec 13, June 14, Dec 2014, June 2015, Specimen Paper

Auditors usually follow a **risk-based approach** to auditing as required by ISAs. In this approach, auditors analyse the risks associated with the client's business, transactions and systems which could lead to misstatements in the financial statements, and direct their testing to risky areas.

Exam focus point

In the examination, you could be asked to identify and explain audit risks based on a scenario. In order to score well in such questions, you should state the assertion or financial statement area which is at risk. Just explaining the fact from the scenario without stating which element of the financial statements is impacted (and which assertion is affected) will significantly limit the number of marks you can obtain. This issue was identified again in the June 2014 exam.

This is one of many issues highlighted for such questions in an article written by the F8 examining team entitled 'Answering audit risk questions'. The article identifies the common mistakes made by candidates on audit risk questions in previous exam sittings, and suggests how these questions should be approached in order to obtain as many marks as possible. It is very important you read the article in advance of attempting audit risk questions.

Another article, entitled 'Audit risk', discusses the concept of audit risk. Both articles can be found via the Technical Articles link on the ACCA website: www.accaglobal.com/gb/en/student/acca-qual-student-journey/qual-resource/acca-qualification/f8/technical-articles.html.

In addition, a video lecture on audit risks has been recorded by John Glover from Kaplan for ACCA. This video is available on the Technical Articles page on the ACCA website (link provided above), or via YouTube, here: www.youtube.com/watch?v=4anGILgLzN4.

1.3.1 How to identify audit risks

A competent auditor needs to be able to identify those risks that may lead to a misstatement in the financial statements. This is why audit risk questions commonly come up in the F8 examination. One of the most important things to realise is what makes a risk an **audit** risk (as opposed to a general operational or business risk) is the **link to the financial statements**. If an auditor does not maintain a focus on those risks that may lead to a misstatement in the financial statements, the audit will be a very long process and not at all efficient.

Imagine you are auditing a manufacturing company (XYZ Co with a profit before tax of $60 million) and the following information comes to light about your client.

'XYZ Co has significant plant and machinery which it uses to make its products. During the year the efficiency of the company's machinery was improved significantly. This was because a comprehensive review of each piece of machinery was undertaken and an assessment was made as to whether a minor repair, extensive refurbishment or a complete replacement was needed. XYZ then took the appropriate action in each case and spent a total of $15 million in doing so.'

From the above you can see management had identified a general risk from their point of view – that the plant and machinery was not efficient enough for the needs of the business. Management has taken what they consider to be the appropriate action by replacing, overhauling or repairing the machinery. There may also be further operational risks arising as a result, such as staff not being used to the new machinery and taking some time to get up to speed.

However, auditors need to look past these and ask themselves how the issues above could ultimately lead to a misstatement in the financial statements. This will bring out the **audit risks**. Where will the repairs, refurbishment and new machinery end up in the financial statements and what could go wrong? Where should it end up?

Your knowledge of IAS 16 from your earlier studies tells you that the expenditure must generate future economic benefit in order to be included in non-current assets. Other costs that do not meet this criterion should be included as repairs in the statement of profit or loss. In our scenario we appear to have some expenditure on replacement assets, some on extensive refurbishment and some on general repairs.

There is judgement involved here as to whether some of the expenditure is capital or revenue expenditure and the situation is unlikely to be clear-cut. Therefore, there is a risk that the $15 million has not been correctly accounted for. In addition:

(a)   Amounts included in non-current assets might not actually **exist**, as they are really repairs (related assertion is existence of non-current assets).

(b)   The repairs expense may be **incomplete** (or indeed the non-current assets may be incomplete if expenditure of a capital nature has also been included in repairs).

So, if the above scenario came up in the exam, one of the audit risks arising is 'Expenditure on repairs is incorrectly recorded as non-current assets, resulting in assets that do not exist being included in the statement of financial position'.

Exam focus point

> As pointed out in an earlier Exam focus point, when asked to describe audit risks **make sure you relate your risk to the financial statements being audited.** Follow the thought process above to make sure you can gain a full mark for each audit risk you identify in an audit risk question. Question practice is essential so make sure you have a go at the audit risk questions in the exam question bank at the back of this Study Text.

Once the auditor has identified the audit risks, procedures can be put in place in response to that risk. We look again at identifying and assessing risks in the context of the guidance in the relevant ISAs in Section 4 of this chapter. We also look in detail at responding to risks in Section 5.

1.3.2 The procedural approach

This is in contrast to a procedural approach which is **not in accordance with ISAs**. In a procedural approach, the auditor would perform a set of standard tests regardless of the client and its business. The risk of the auditor providing an incorrect opinion on the truth and fairness of the financial statements might be higher if a procedural approach was adopted.

1.4 Overall audit risk   Dec 11

FAST FORWARD

> **Audit risk** is the risk that the auditor expresses an inappropriate audit opinion when the financial statements are materially misstated. It is a function of the risk of material misstatement (**inherent risk** and **control risk**) and the risk that the auditor will not detect such misstatement (**detection risk**).

In the previous section we looked at identifying individual risks that could lead to misstatements in the financial statements and we referred to these risks as audit risks (this is also the term used in the F8 exams). The ISAs refer to the individual risks as the risks of material misstatement.

Each of these individual risks can contribute to the **overall audit risk** that the auditor expresses an inappropriate audit opinion when the financial statements are materially misstated.

Now we will consider the concept of the overall audit risk and in particular the **audit risk model**. Understanding this model helps the auditor to take action to reduce overall audit risk to an acceptable level. Where we refer to audit risk below we are referring to the overall risk that an inappropriate audit opinion is expressed.

Key term

> **Audit risk** is the risk that the auditor expresses an inappropriate audit opinion when the financial statements are materially misstated.

Audit risk has **two** major components. One is dependent on the entity, and is the risk of material misstatement arising in the financial statements (**inherent risk** and **control risk**). The other is dependent on the auditor, and is the risk that the auditor will not detect material misstatements in the financial statements (**detection risk**). We shall look in detail at the concept of materiality in the next section of this chapter. Audit risk can be represented by the **audit risk model**:

> **Audit risk = Inherent risk × control risk × detection risk**

1.4.1 Inherent risk

> **Inherent risk** is the susceptibility of an assertion to a misstatement that could be material individually or when aggregated with other misstatements, assuming there were no related internal controls.

Inherent risk is the risk that items will be misstated due to the characteristics of those items, such as the fact they are estimates or that they are important items in the accounts. The auditors must use their professional judgement and all available knowledge to assess inherent risk. If no such information or knowledge is available then the inherent risk is **high**.

Inherent risk is affected by the nature of the entity; for example, the industry it is in and the regulations it falls under, and also the nature of the strategies it adopts. We shall look at more examples of inherent risks later in this chapter.

1.4.2 Control risk

The other element of the risk of material misstatements in the financial statements is control risk.

> **Control risk** is the risk that a material misstatement, that could occur in an assertion and that could be material, individually or when aggregated with other misstatements, will not be prevented or detected and corrected on a timely basis by the entity's internal control.

We shall look at control risk in more detail in Chapter 9 when we discuss internal controls.

1.4.3 Detection risk

> **Detection risk** is the risk that the procedures performed by the auditor to reduce audit risk to an acceptably low level will not detect a misstatement that exists and that could be material, either individually or when aggregated with other misstatements.

The third element of audit risk is detection risk. This is the component of audit risk that the auditors have a degree of control over, because if risk is too high to be tolerated, the auditors can carry out more work to reduce this aspect of audit risk and, therefore, audit risk as a whole.

One way to decrease detection risk is to increase sample sizes. **Sampling risk** and **non-sampling risk** are components of detection risk, and will be examined further in Chapter 11.

However, increasing sample sizes and carrying out more work is not the only way to manage detection risk. This is because **detection risk is a function of the effectiveness of an audit procedure and of its application** by the auditor.

Although increasing sample sizes or doing more work can help to reduce detection risk, the following actions can also improve the effectiveness and application of procedures and therefore help to reduce detection risk:

- Adequate planning
- Assignment of more experienced personnel to the engagement team
- The application of professional scepticism
- Increased supervision and review of the audit work performed

All the above reduce the possibility that an auditor might select an inappropriate audit procedure, misapply an appropriate audit procedure or misinterpret the audit results.

1.5 Management of audit risk

ISA 200 states that 'to obtain reasonable assurance, the auditor shall obtain sufficient appropriate audit evidence to reduce audit risk to an acceptably low level and thereby enable the auditor to draw reasonable conclusions on which to base the auditor's opinion.'

Auditors will want their overall audit risk to be at an acceptable level, or it will not be worth them carrying out the audit. In other words, if the chance of them giving an inappropriate opinion and being sued is high, it might be better not to do the audit at all.

The auditors will obviously consider how risky a new audit client is during the acceptance process and may decide not to go ahead with the relationship. However, they will also consider audit risk for each individual audit and will seek to manage the risk.

As we have seen above, it is not in the auditors' power to affect inherent or control risk. These are risks integral to the client, and the auditor cannot change the level of these risks. The auditors therefore manage overall audit risk by manipulating detection risk, the only element of audit risk they have control over. This is because the more audit work the auditors carry out, the lower detection risk becomes, although it can never be entirely eliminated due to the inherent limitations of audit. The auditors will decide what level of overall risk is acceptable and then determine a level of audit work so that detection risk is as low as possible.

It is important to understand that there is not a standard level of audit risk which is generally considered by auditors to be acceptable. This is a matter of **audit judgement** and so will vary from firm to firm and audit to audit. Audit firms are likely to charge higher fees for higher risk clients. Regardless of the risk level of the audit, however, it is vital that audit firms always carry out an audit of **sufficient quality**.

Question

Hippo Co is a long-established client of your firm. It manufactures bathroom fittings and fixtures, which it sells to a range of wholesalers, on credit. You are the audit senior and have recently been sent the following extract from the draft statement of financial position by the finance director.

	Budget		Actual	
	$'000	$'000	$'000	$'000
Non-current assets		453		367
Current assets				
Trade accounts receivable	1,134		976	
Bank	–		54	
Current liabilities				
Trade accounts payable	967		944	
Bank overdraft	9		–	

During the course of your conversation with the finance director, you establish that a major new customer the company had included in its budget went bankrupt during the year.

Required

Identify any potential risks for the audit of Hippo and explain why you believe they are risks.

Answer

Potential risks relevant to the audit of Hippo

(1) **Credit sales**. Hippo makes sales on credit. This increases the risk that Hippo's sales will not be converted into cash. Trade receivables is likely to be a risky area and the auditors will have to consider what the best evidence that customers are going to pay is likely to be.

(2) **Related industry**. Hippo manufactures bathroom fixtures and fittings. These are sold to wholesalers, but it is possible that Hippo's ultimate market is the building industry. This is a notoriously volatile industry, and Hippo may find that its results fluctuate too, as demand rises and

falls. This suspicion is added to by the bankruptcy of the wholesaler in the year. The auditors must be sure that accounts which present Hippo as a viable company are in fact correct.

(3) **Controls**. The fact that a major new customer went bankrupt suggests that Hippo did not undertake a very thorough credit check on that customer before agreeing to supply them. This implies that the controls at Hippo may not be very strong.

(4) **Variance**. The actual results are different from budget. This may be explained by the fact that the major customer went bankrupt, or it may reveal that there are other errors and problems in the reported results, or in the original budget.

(5) **Bankrupt wholesaler**. There is a risk that the result reported contains balances due from the bankrupt wholesaler, which are likely to be irrecoverable.

1.6 Business risk

The other major category of risk which the auditor should be aware of is **business risk** and this came up earlier when we talked about focusing on risks that impact on the financial statements. Although business risk from an external audit point of view is outside the scope of the F8 syllabus, it is useful to consider it briefly so you do not confuse it with audit risk (which is a key element of the Audit and Assurance syllabus).

We briefly introduced the concept of business risk in Chapter 5 in the context of internal audit's role in risk management and organisational control. Remember, business risk is the risk inherent to the company in its operations.

Exam focus point

It is important that you do not confuse the concepts of audit and business risks. Remember – **audit risk is focused on the financial statements** of a company, whereas business risk is related to the company as a whole. If an exam question asks you to identify audit risks, make sure you explain them in relation to the financial statements. The examining team noted that in all the recent exam sittings a number of candidates lost marks on an audit risk scenario-based question because they did not understand what audit risk relates to. Instead they provided answers considering business risks.

2 Materiality

June 10, June 13

FAST FORWARD

Materiality for the financial statements as a whole and **performance materiality** must be calculated at the planning stages of all audits. The calculation or estimation of materiality should be based on experience and judgement. Materiality for the financial statements as a whole must be **reviewed throughout** the audit and **revised if necessary**.

ISA 320 *Materiality in planning and performing an audit* provides guidance for auditors in this area and states that the objective of the auditor is to apply the concept of materiality appropriately in planning and performing the audit.

ISA 320 does not define materiality (in relation to the financial statements as a whole) but notes that while it may be discussed in different terms by different financial reporting frameworks the following are generally the case:

(a) Misstatements are considered to be material if they, individually or in aggregate, could reasonably be expected to influence the economic decisions of users.

(b) Judgements about materiality are made in the light of surrounding circumstances, and are affected by the size and nature of a misstatement or a combination of both.

(c) Judgements about matters that are material to users of financial statements are based on a consideration of the common financial information needs of users as a group.

The practical implication of this is that the auditor must be concerned with identifying 'material' errors, omissions and misstatements. Both the amount (quantity) and nature (quality) of misstatements need to be considered, eg lack of disclosure regarding ongoing litigation is likely to be considered material.

To implement this, the auditor therefore has to set their own materiality levels – this will always be a matter of judgement and will depend on the level of audit risk. The higher the anticipated risk, the lower the value of materiality will be.

The materiality level will impact on the auditor's decisions relating to:

- How many items to examine
- Which items to examine
- Whether to use sampling techniques
- What level of misstatement is likely to result in a modified audit opinion

Conforming amendments to ISA 320 published in 2015 make it clear that auditors must consider the risks of material misstatement in **qualitative disclosures**. In doing so, the auditor should consider:

- The circumstances of the entity (eg any business acquisitions or disposals during the period)

- The applicable financial reporting framework (eg new qualitative disclosures may be required by a new financial reporting standard)

- Qualitative disclosures that are important to the users of the financial statements because of the nature of the entity (eg liquidity risk disclosures for a financial institution)

2.1 Determining and calculating materiality and performance materiality when planning the audit

During planning, the auditor must establish materiality for the **financial statements as a whole**, but must also set **performance materiality** levels.

Determining **materiality for the financial statements as a whole** involves the exercise of professional judgement (which we covered in Section 1 of this chapter). Generally, a percentage is applied to a chosen benchmark as a starting point for determining materiality for the financial statements as a whole. The following factors may affect the identification of an appropriate benchmark:

- **Elements** of the financial statements (eg assets, liabilities, equity, revenue, expenses)
- Whether there are items on which **users tend to focus**
- **Nature of the entity, industry** and **economic environment**
- Entity's **ownership structure and financing**
- Relative **volatility** of the benchmark

The following **benchmarks and percentages** may be appropriate in the calculation of materiality for the financial statements as a whole.

Value	%
Profit before tax	5
Gross profit	½-1
Revenue	½-1
Total assets	1-2
Net assets	2-5
Profit after tax	5-10

Consider what would happen if this materiality for the financial statements as a whole was applied directly to, for example, different account balances (such as receivables and inventory). It could be that a number of balances (or elements making up those balances) are untested or dismissed on the grounds that they are immaterial. However, a number of errors or misstatements could exist in those untested balances, and these could aggregate to a material misstatement.

For this reason the auditor is required to set **performance materiality** levels which are lower than the materiality for the financial statements as a whole. This means a lower threshold is applied during testing. The risk of misstatements which could add up to a material misstatement is therefore reduced.

As we can see in the Key term box below, performance materiality really has two definitions (taken from ISA 320).

Key term

Performance materiality is the amount or amounts set by the auditor at less than materiality for the financial statements as a whole to reduce to an appropriately low level the probability that the aggregate of uncorrected and undetected misstatements exceeds materiality for the financial statements as a whole.

Performance materiality also refers to the amount or amounts set by the auditor at less than the materiality level or levels for particular classes of transactions, account balances or disclosures.

This indicates that the auditor sets a level or levels of materiality lower than overall materiality for the purposes of performing procedures in general (for example on a low risk area) and this is just to account for aggregation. However, an even lower level is set for certain balances, transactions or disclosures where there is an increased risk or if qualitative considerations (discussed below) necessitate it.

As you can see, determining performance materiality is very much dependent on the auditor's professional judgement. In summary, it is affected by:

- The nature and extent of misstatements identified in prior audits
- The auditor's understanding of the entity
- Result of risk assessment procedures

Exam focus point

Bear in mind that materiality has qualitative, as well as quantitative, aspects. You must not simply think of materiality as being a percentage of items in the financial statements. The expected degree of accuracy of disclosures such as directors' emoluments may make normal materiality considerations irrelevant.

Materiality has **qualitative** aspects. Some misstatements may fall under specified benchmarks, but are still considered material overall due to their qualitative effects.

Magnitude by itself, without regard to the nature of the item and the circumstances in which the judgement has to be made, may not be a sufficient basis for a materiality judgement. As a result, qualitative factors may cause misstatements of quantitatively small amounts to be material.

Examples of this are given in ISA 320:

- Law, regulation or the applicable financial reporting framework affect users' expectations regarding the measurement or disclosure of certain items (for example, related party transactions, and the remuneration of management and those charged with governance).

- Some disclosures are key disclosures in relation to the industry in which the entity operates (for example, research and development costs for a pharmaceutical company).

- Attention is sometimes focused on a particular aspect of the entity's business that is separately disclosed in the financial statements (for example, a newly acquired business).

2.2 Revision of materiality

The level of materiality must be revised for the financial statements as a whole if the auditor becomes aware of information during the audit that would have caused the auditor to have determined a different amount during planning.

If the auditor concludes that a lower amount of materiality for the financial statements as a whole is appropriate, the auditor must determine whether performance materiality also needs to be revised, and whether the nature, timing and extent of further audit procedures are still appropriate. A revision to materiality might be required for example if during the audit it appears that actual results are going to be significantly different from the expected results, which were used to calculate materiality for the financial statements as a whole during planning.

2.3 Documentation of materiality

ISA 320 requires the following to be documented:

- Materiality for the financial statements as a whole
- Materiality level or levels for particular classes of transactions, account balances or disclosures if applicable
- Performance materiality
- Any revision of the above as the audit progresses

3 Understanding the entity and its environment
June 08, Dec 09, Dec 10, June 15

FAST FORWARD

The auditor is required to obtain an **understanding** of the entity and its environment in order to be able to assess the risks of material misstatements.

PER alert

Objective 17 of the PER performance objectives is to prepare for and collect evidence for audit. An important aspect of preparing for an audit is understanding the nature of the client's organisation. The knowledge you gain in this section will assist you in demonstrating the achievement of this element of PO 17 in practice. An article published in the May 2010 edition of *Student Accountant* provides more detail on how you can achieve PO 17.

3.1 Why do we need an understanding?

ISA 315 (Revised) *Identifying and assessing the risks of material misstatement through understanding the entity and its environment* states that the objective of the auditor is to identify and assess the risks of material misstatement, whether due to fraud or error, through understanding the entity and its environment, including the entity's internal control, thereby providing a basis for designing and implementing responses to the assessed risks of material misstatement.

The following table summarises this simply.

OBTAINING AN UNDERSTANDING OF THE ENTITY AND ITS ENVIRONMENT	
Why?	– To identify and assess the risks of material misstatement in the financial statements
	– To enable the auditor to design and perform further audit procedures
	– To provide a frame of reference for exercising audit judgement, for example, when setting audit materiality
What?	– Industry, regulatory and other external factors, including the applicable financial reporting framework
	– Nature of the entity, including operations, ownership and governance, investments, structure and financing
	– Entity's selection and application of accounting policies
	– Objectives and strategies and related business risks that might cause material misstatement in the financial statements
	– Measurement and review of the entity's financial performance
	– Internal control (which we shall look at in detail in Chapter 9)
How?	– Enquiries of management, appropriate individuals within the internal audit function and others within the entity
	– Analytical procedures
	– Observation and inspection
	– Prior period knowledge

BPP LEARNING MEDIA

–	Client acceptance or continuance process
–	Discussion by the audit team of the susceptibility of the financial statements to material misstatement
–	Information from other engagements undertaken for the entity

As can be seen in the table, the reasons the auditor has to obtain an understanding of the entity and its environment are very much bound up with assessing risks and exercising audit judgement. We shall look at these aspects more in the next two sections of this chapter.

3.2 What do we need an understanding of?

The ISA sets out a number of requirements about what the auditors shall consider in relation to obtaining an understanding of the business. The general areas are shown in the following diagram.

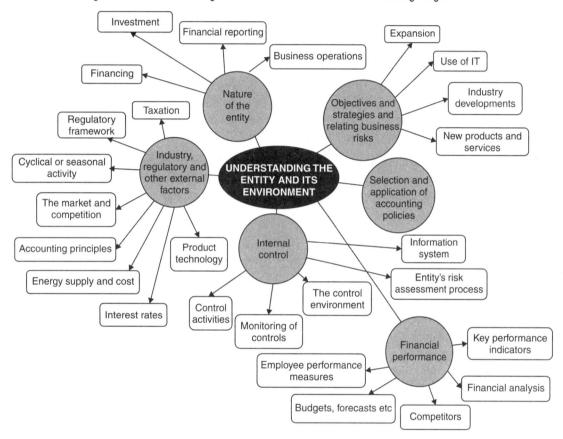

3.3 How do we gain an understanding?

ISA 315 sets out the methods that the auditor shall use to obtain the understanding; these were shown in the table in Section 3.1. In addition to the sources shown in the diagram above, the auditor will refer to the following to help in obtaining an understanding of the entity and its environment.

- The **permanent audit file** where information of continuing importance to the audit is kept (we cover the permanent audit file in more detail in Chapter 7)

- Audit working papers from the **previous year's audit file**

- Information from the **client's website**

- **Publications or websites related to the industry** the client operates in

A combination of the following procedures should be used to obtain an understanding.

- **Enquiries** of management, internal auditors and others within the entity
- **Analytical procedures**
- **Observation** and **inspection**

ISA 315 also states that the auditor shall consider whether information obtained from client acceptance or continuance processes is relevant.

If the engagement partner has performed other engagements for the entity, (s)he shall consider whether information from these is relevant to identifying risks of material misstatement.

ISA 315 states that if the auditor is going to use information from prior year audits, the auditor shall determine whether changes have occurred that could affect the relevance to the current year's audit.

ISA 315 also requires the engagement partner and other key team members to discuss the susceptibility of the financial statements to material misstatement, and the application of the applicable financial reporting framework to the entity's facts and circumstances. The engagement partner shall determine what matters are to be communicated to team members not involved in the discussion.

3.3.1 Enquiry

The auditors will usually obtain most of the information they require from staff in the accounts department, but may also need to make enquiries of other personnel: for example, production staff and those charged with governance.

Those charged with governance may give insight into the environment in which the financial statements are prepared. In-house legal counsel may help with understanding such matters as outstanding litigation and compliance with laws and regulations. Sales and marketing personnel may give information about marketing strategies and sales trends.

If the client has an internal audit function, enquiries should be made of internal auditors as appropriate as part of risk assessment procedures. ISA 315 was revised in March 2012 and one of the key revisions made was to require the auditor to make enquiries of appropriate individuals within the internal audit function.

3.3.2 Analytical procedures   Dec 10, June 13, June 14

Key term

> **Analytical procedures** consist of evaluations of financial information through analysis of plausible relationships among both financial and non-financial data. Analytical procedures also encompass investigation of identified fluctuations or relationships that are inconsistent with other relevant information or that differ from expected values by a significant amount.

Analytical procedures can be used at all stages of the audit. ISA 315 requires their use during the risk assessment stage of the audit. Their use during other stages of the audit is considered in Chapters 11 and 18.

Analytical procedures include:

(a) The consideration of comparisons with:

- **Similar information** for prior periods
- **Anticipated results** of the entity, from budgets or forecasts
- **Predictions** prepared by the auditors
- **Industry information**

(b) The consideration of the relationship between elements of **financial information** that are expected to conform to a predicted pattern based on the entity's experience, such as the relationship of gross profit to sales.

(c) The consideration of the relationship between financial information and **relevant non-financial information**, such as the relationship of payroll costs to number of employees.

A variety of methods can be used to perform the procedures discussed above, ranging from **simple comparisons** to **complex analysis** using statistics, on a company level, branch level or individual account level. **Ratio analysis** can be a useful technique when carrying out analytical procedures. We consider ratio analysis in Chapter 11 which considers analytical procedures as a form of substantive procedures when collecting audit evidence. Ratio analysis can also be used when applying analytical procedures at the risk assessment stage.

The choice of procedures is a matter for the auditors' professional judgement. The use of information technology may be extensive when carrying out analytical procedures during risk assessment.

Auditors may also use specific industry information or general knowledge of current industry conditions to assess the client's performance.

As well as helping to determine the nature, timing and extent of other audit procedures, such analytical procedures may also indicate aspects of the business of which the auditors were previously unaware. Auditors are looking to see if developments in the client's business have had the expected effects. They will be particularly interested in changes in audit areas where problems have occurred in the past.

Analytical procedures at the risk assessment stage of the audit are usually based on interim financial information, budgets or management accounts.

3.3.3 Observation and inspection

These techniques are likely to confirm the answers given to enquiries made of management. They will include observing the normal operations of a company, reading documents or manuals relating to the client's operations and visiting premises and meeting staff.

3.3.4 Companies that use e-business

When considering the effect on the financial statements of a company using e-commerce, the auditor needs to consider whether the **skills and knowledge** of team members are appropriate to perform the audit, and also whether an **expert** is required.

The auditor also needs to have a good **understanding of the business** to assess the significance of e-commerce and its effect on audit risk. The auditor should consider the following.

- The entity's **business activities and industry**
- The entity's **e-commerce strategy**
- The **extent** of e-commerce activities
- **Outsourcing** arrangements

Specific risks affecting entities that engage in e-commerce include:

- Loss of transaction integrity

- Security risks

- Improper accounting policies (eg capitalisation of expenditure, translation of foreign currency, allowances for warranties and returns, revenue recognition)

- Non-compliance with taxation and other laws and regulations

- Failure to ensure that contracts are binding

- Overreliance on e-commerce

- Systems and infrastructure failures or crashes

The auditor uses the knowledge of the business gained to identify events, transactions and practices related to business risks arising from e-commerce activities that may result in material misstatements in the financial statements.

The auditor also considers the control environment and control procedures that are relevant to the financial statement assertions, in accordance with ISA 315, in particular those relating to **security, transaction integrity** and **process alignment**.

You are auditing the financial statements of Pumpkin Co for the year ended 31 March 20X9. Pumpkin Co is a chain of bakeries operating in five locations. The bakeries sell a range of cakes, pastries, bread, sandwiches, pasties and drinks which customers purchase in cash. The company has had a 'challenging' year, according to its directors, and is renegotiating its bank overdraft facility with its bank. The statement of profit or loss for the year ended 31 March 20X8 is shown below together with the draft statement of profit or loss for the year ended 31 March 20X9.

Pumpkin Co: Statements of profit or loss

	31 March 20X9	31 March 20X8
	$'000	$'000
Revenue	4,205	3,764
Cost of sales	(1,376)	(1,555)
Gross profit	2,829	2,209
Operating expenses		
Administration	(667)	(798)
Selling and distribution	(423)	(460)
Interest payable	(50)	(49)
Profit/(loss) before tax	1,689	902

Required

As part of your risk assessment procedures for the audit of Pumpkin Co, perform analytical procedures on the draft statement of profit or loss to identify possible risk areas requiring further audit work.

Answer

In total, Pumpkin's profit for the year has increased by 87% which appears at odds with the revenue figure, which has only increased by 12% in comparison to the previous year. This may indicate that revenue has been inflated or incorrect cut-off applied, especially given the fact that the directors of Pumpkin have described the year as 'challenging'.

Revenue has increased overall by 12% but cost of sales has fallen by 12% – we would expect an increase in revenue to be matched by a corresponding increase in cost of sales. Again this may indicate incorrect allocation of revenue in order for the bank to look favourably on the company and increase its overdraft facility. It could also indicate an error in the valuation of closing inventory.

The gross profit has increased by 28% compared to the previous period. The audit will need to focus on this change which is significant, focusing on the revenue and costs of sales figures to establish the reasons for the increase.

Administration expenses have fallen in comparison to the previous year (decrease of 16%) which is unusual given that revenue has increased by 12%. We would expect an increase in costs to be in line with the increase in the revenue figure. This could indicate that expenses may be understated through incorrect cut-off or incorrectly capitalising expenditure which should be written off to the statement of profit or loss for the year.

A similar issue applies to selling and distribution costs which have fallen by 8% – they have not increased as expected in line with revenue. There could be legitimate reasons for the change but this area needs to be investigated further during the audit fieldwork stage.

Interest payable has stayed in line with the previous year (increase of 2%). This figure can be verified easily during the audit fieldwork by inspecting bank statements and other relevant documentation from the bank.

4 Assessing the risks of material misstatement

FAST FORWARD

When the auditor has obtained an understanding of the entity, (s)he shall assess the risks of material misstatement in the financial statements, also identifying significant risks.

Exam focus point

Assessing and responding to risk is a fundamental part of the audit process. In the exam you could be asked to identify risks related to a client in a scenario. An article was published in the November 2009 edition of *Student Accountant* which specifically considers the requirements of ISA 315. You should read this to supplement your knowledge and understanding of undertaking a risk assessment.

4.1 Identifying and assessing the risks of material misstatement

ISA 315 says that the auditor shall identify and assess the risks of material misstatement at the financial statement level and at the assertion level for classes of transactions, account balances and disclosures.

It requires the auditor to take the following steps:

- Identify risks throughout the process of obtaining an understanding of the entity and its environment
- Assess the identified risks and evaluate whether they relate more pervasively to the financial statements as a whole
- Relate the risks to what can go wrong at the assertion level
- Consider the likelihood of the risks causing a material misstatement

Key term

Assertions are representations by management, explicit or otherwise, that are embodied in the financial statements, as used by the auditor to consider the different types of potential misstatements that may occur. We look at these in detail in Chapter 8.

4.2 Significant risks

FAST FORWARD

Significant risks are complex or unusual transactions that may indicate fraud, or other special risks.

Key term

Significant risks are those that require special audit consideration.

As part of the risk assessment described above, the auditor shall determine whether any of the risks are **significant risks**.

The following factors indicate that a risk might be significant.

- Risk of fraud (see Section 6)
- Its relationship with recent economic, accounting or other developments
- The degree of subjectivity in the financial information
- It is an unusual transaction
- It is a significant transaction with a related party
- The complexity of the transaction

Routine, non-complex transactions are less likely to give rise to significant risk than unusual transactions or matters of management judgement. This is because unusual transactions are likely to have more:

- Management intervention
- Complex accounting principles or calculations
- Manual intervention
- Opportunity for control procedures not to be followed

When the auditor identifies a significant risk, if they have not done so already, they shall obtain an understanding of the entity's controls relevant to that risk.

You are involved with the audit of Tantpro Co, a small company. You have been carrying out procedures to gain an understanding of the entity. The following matters have come to your attention:

The company offers standard credit terms to its customers of 60 days from the date of invoice. Statements are sent to customers on a monthly basis. However, Tantpro does not employ a credit controller and, other than sending the statements on a monthly basis, it does not otherwise communicate with its customers on a systematic basis. On occasion, the sales ledger clerk may telephone a customer if the company has not received a payment for some time. Some customers pay regularly according to the credit terms offered to them, but others pay on a very haphazard basis and do not provide a remittance advice. Sales ledger receipts are entered onto the sales ledger but not matched to invoices remitted. The company does not produce an aged list of balances.

Required

From the above information, assess the risks of material misstatement arising in the financial statements. Outline the potential materiality of the risks and discuss factors in the likelihood of the risks arising.

Answer

The key risk arising from the above information is that trade receivables will not be carried at the appropriate **value** in the financial statements, as some may be irrecoverable. Where receipts are not matched against invoices in the ledger, the balance on the ledger may include old invoices that the customer has no intention of paying.

It is difficult to assess at this stage whether this will be material. Trade receivables is likely to be a material balance in the financial statements, but the number of irrecoverable balances may not be material. Analytical procedures, for example, to see if the level of receivables has risen year-on-year in a manner that is not explained by price rises or levels of production, might help to assess this.

A key factor that affects the likelihood of the material misstatement arising is the poor controls over the sales ledger. The fact that invoices are not matched against receipts increases the chance of old invoices not having been paid and not noticed by Tantpro. It appears reasonably likely that the trade receivables balance is overstated in this instance.

5 Responding to the risk assessment
Dec 10, June 11, Dec 11, June 13, Dec 13, June 14

FAST FORWARD

The auditor shall **formulate an approach** to the assessed risks of material misstatement.

The main objective of ISA 330 *The auditor's responses to assessed risks* is to obtain sufficient appropriate audit evidence regarding the assessed risks of material misstatement, through designing and implementing appropriate responses to those risks.

Exam focus point

Once the auditor has assessed the risks of material misstatement, there must be a suitable response. In the exam you could be asked to suggest procedures in response to identified risks. In June 2014, the examining team noted that this was an area of weakness among candidates:

'Many candidates gave business advice [...], or provided vague responses such as perform detailed substantive testing or maintain professional scepticism. Responses which start with "ensure that ..." are unlikely to score marks as they usually fail to explain exactly how the auditor will address the audit risk. Audit responses need to be practical and should relate to the approach (ie what testing) the auditor will adopt to assess whether the balance is materially misstated or not.'

An article titled 'ISA 330 and responses to assessed risks' was published in the August 2010 edition of *Student Accountant* which considers the requirements of ISA 330. It is available in the Technical Articles section of the ACCA website (www.accaglobal.com/uk/en/student/acca-qual-student-journey/qual-resource/acca-qualification/f8/technical-articles.html). You should read this to supplement your knowledge and understanding of responding to assessed risk during the audit process. You should also read the article from November 2011 mentioned in an earlier Exam focus point.

5.1 Overall responses

Overall responses include such issues as emphasising to the team the importance of professional scepticism, allocating more staff, using experts or providing more supervision.

Overall responses to address the risks of material misstatement at the financial statement level will be changes to the general audit strategy or re-affirmations to staff of the general audit strategy. For example:

- Emphasising to audit staff the need to maintain professional scepticism
- Assigning additional or more experienced staff to the audit team
- Providing more supervision on the audit
- Incorporating more unpredictability into the audit procedures
- Making general changes to the nature, timing or extent of audit procedures

The evaluation of the control environment that will have taken place as part of the assessment of the client's internal control systems will help the auditor determine what type of audit approach to take.

5.2 Responses to the risks of material misstatement at the assertion level
Dec 07

The ISA says that the auditor shall design and perform further audit procedures whose **nature**, **timing** and **extent** are based on and are responsive to the assessed risks of material misstatement at the assertion level. 'Nature' refers to the purpose and the type of test that is carried out, which include **tests of controls** and **substantive tests**.

5.2.1 Tests of controls

When the auditor's risk assessment includes an expectation that controls are operating effectively, the auditor shall design and perform tests of controls to obtain sufficient appropriate audit evidence that the controls were operating.

The auditor shall also undertake tests of controls when it will not be possible to obtain sufficient appropriate audit evidence simply from substantive procedures. This might be the case if the entity conducts its business using IT systems which do not produce documentation of transactions.

In carrying out tests of control, auditors shall use **enquiry**, but shall also use other procedures. **Reperformance** and **inspection** will often be helpful procedures.

When considering timing in relation to tests of controls, the purpose of the test will be important. For example, if the company carries out a year-end inventory count, controls over the inventory count can only be tested at the year end. Other controls will operate all year round, and the auditor may need to test that those controls have been effective throughout the period.

Some controls may have been tested in prior audits and the auditor may choose to rely on that evidence of their effectiveness. If this is the case, the auditor shall obtain evidence about any changes since the controls were last tested and shall test the controls if they have changed. In any case, controls shall be tested for effectiveness at least once in every three audits.

If the related risk has been designated a significant risk, the auditor shall not rely on testing done in prior years, but shall perform testing in the current year.

5.2.2 Substantive procedures

Key term

> **Substantive procedures** are audit procedures designed to detect material misstatements at the assertion level. They consist of tests of details (of classes of transactions, account balances and disclosures) and substantive analytical procedures.

The auditor shall always carry out substantive procedures on material items. The ISA says that, irrespective of the assessed risk of material misstatement, the auditor shall design and perform substantive procedures for each material class of transactions, account balance and disclosure.

In addition, the auditor shall carry out the following substantive procedures:

- Agreeing or reconciling the financial statements to the underlying accounting records
- Examining material journal entries
- Examining other adjustments made in preparing the financial statements

Substantive procedures fall into two categories: analytical procedures and tests of details. The auditor must determine when it is appropriate to use which type of substantive procedure. We discuss these in more detail in Chapter 11 but they are introduced below.

Analytical procedures as substantive procedures tend to be appropriate for large volumes of predictable transactions (for example, wages and salaries). **Tests of detail** may be appropriate to gain information about account balances; for example, inventory and trade receivables.

Tests of detail rather than analytical procedures are likely to be more appropriate with regard to matters which have been identified as **significant risks**, but the auditor must develop procedures that are specifically responsive to that risk, which may include analytical procedures. Significant risks are likely to be the most difficult to obtain sufficient appropriate audit evidence about.

5.3 Examples of responses to audit risks

The best way to understand how the auditor can respond to the risks identified during audit planning is to consider some examples of audit risks along with an adequate response to each risk. (**Note**. We will look at auditing specific financial statement balances, such as non-current assets, receivables and payables, in later chapters. Therefore you may want to revisit the responses in this section once you have covered Chapters 12 to 16.)

Examples of risks	Possible responses
Risk that inventory has a lower net realisable value than cost and is therefore overstated (eg NRV falls due to the client being in an industry where tastes/fashions change quickly).	Examine the instructions to identify slow moving inventory lines when attending the inventory count.
	Increase the emphasis on reviewing the year end aged inventory analysis for evidence of slow moving inventory.
	Ascertain sales values for items sold post year end that were in inventory at the year end to ensure their NRV was higher than the cost recorded as part of the inventory value in the financial statements.

Examples of risks	Possible responses
Assets are desirable / more susceptible to theft leading to a risk that recorded assets do not exist (eg inventory/non-current assets).	Focus on testing internal controls over those assets (including physical controls to prevent theft).
	Increase sample sizes for inspecting recorded assets, ensuring any material assets are verified (in the context of performance materiality).
Increased risk of revenue expenditure being incorrectly classified as capital (or vice versa), leading to misstatement of assets/expenses (eg extensive refurbishment of non-current assets where judgement is needed to establish whether the nature of the work is to enhance the asset or repair/replace it).	Obtain a breakdown of related costs and review accounting entries against invoices/details of work done to ensure expenditure is correctly treated as capital/revenue.
	Perform a detailed review of repairs accounts for any items which should be included in non-current assets.
	Review the asset register to ensure only capital items have been included.
Increased risk of incomplete or unrecorded income due to fraud or theft (eg large amounts of cash collected and held prior to banking).	Perform analytical procedures focusing on comparing revenue with expected seasonal/monthly patterns.
	If a retail client, perform/reperform a reconciliation of a sample of till records to actual bankings.
Receipts/invoicing significantly in advance/arrears of providing services or goods, therefore leading to an increased risk of revenue being in the wrong period (eg deposits received in advance, reservation fees, contracts spanning the year end).	For a sample of revenue entries recorded prior to the year end, agree the transactions as relating to pre year end sales by inspecting the contract / other supporting documentation.
	Trace post year end transactions back to a supporting contract/documentation to test that revenue was recorded in the proper period.
	For a sample of contracts or GDNs, verify the revenue was recognised according to the provision of services/goods.
	Perform analytical procedures where monthly revenue is compared to expectations and budgeted revenue. Unexpected deviations should be investigated.
Invoices received (or payments made) in advance/arrears of goods or services delivery date leading to overstatement or understatement of costs and/or liabilities.	Review post year end bank statements / cash book payments for evidence of amounts relating to the financial year but not included in liabilities.
	For a sample of documents pre and post year end indicating date of delivery of goods/services (eg GRNs), verify the cost and liability were recorded in the appropriate period.
There is an increased risk of irrecoverable debts (eg due to the nature of the client's industry or customers), resulting in assets being potentially overstated.	Identify year end receivable balances still outstanding at the date of the audit by reviewing post year end receipts from customers. For amounts still outstanding establish whether these are provided for.
	Review aged receivables analysis and customer correspondence files for evidence of disputes with receivables and consider the adequacy of any related receivables allowance.

Examples of risks	Possible responses
Significant client borrowing and/or overdraft with cash flow problems which may indicate going concern problems.	Review correspondence with the bank/lender for any evidence of withdrawal or extension of facilities. If there are bank covenants linked to performance on which facilities depend, review compliance with these, and increase testing on areas where management could manipulate performance indicators (such as provisions). Review post year end results and cash flow forecasts (if prepared) for evidence the company can continue as a going concern.
New client systems/controls/staff impacting on amounts recorded in the financial statements, increasing the risk of errors and the risk of internal controls not operating effectively.	Undertake additional visits (eg interim audit) to assess the effectiveness of controls operating over areas affected. Perform extra work to document and evaluate new systems/controls, performing tests of controls where necessary. Increase sample sizes for substantive testing over financial statement areas impacted.
Management has an incentive to manipulate performance, increasing the risk of profits being overstated (eg remuneration or bank funding is reliant on performance).	Focus on and increase testing on judgemental areas in the financial statements (eg provisions, revenue recognition accounting policies).

Above are just **some examples** of risks you may encounter in an exam question on audit risks and responses. The best response to each risk will depend on the particular circumstances of the client and the environment in which it operates.

Your approach should not be to simply learn a list of responses. Instead, your focus should be on understanding the link between audit risks and responses, and being able to identify and explain risks and suitable responses when presented with different scenarios.

6 Fraud, law and regulations

June 09, June 11, Dec 11, June 12, June 15

> When carrying out risk assessment procedures, the auditor shall also consider the risk of fraud or non-compliance with law and regulations causing a misstatement in the financial statements.

6.1 What is fraud?

Key terms

> **Fraud** is an intentional act by one or more individuals among management, those charged with governance, employees, or third parties, involving the use of deception to obtain an unjust or illegal advantage. Fraud may be perpetrated by an individual, or colluded in, with people internal or external to the business.
>
> **Fraud risk factors** are events or conditions that indicate an incentive or pressure to commit fraud or provide an opportunity to commit fraud.

Fraud is a wide legal concept, but the auditor's main concern is with fraud that causes a material misstatement in financial statements. It is distinguished from error, which is when a material misstatement is caused by mistake, for example, in the misapplication of an accounting policy.

Specifically, there are two types of fraud causing material misstatement in financial statements:

- Fraudulent financial reporting
- Misappropriation of assets

6.1.1 Fraudulent financial reporting

> **Fraudulent financial reporting** involves intentional misstatements, including omissions of amounts or disclosures in financial statements, to deceive financial statement users.

This may include:

- Manipulation, falsification or alteration of accounting records / supporting documents
- Misrepresentation (or omission) of events or transactions in the financial statements
- Intentional misapplication of accounting principles

Such fraud may be carried out by overriding controls that would otherwise appear to be operating effectively, for example by recording fictitious journal entries and improperly adjusting assumptions or estimates used in financial reporting.

6.1.2 Misappropriation of assets

> **Misappropriation of assets** involves the theft of an entity's assets and is often perpetrated by employees in relatively small and immaterial amounts. However, it can also involve management who are usually more capable of disguising or concealing misappropriations in ways that are difficult to detect.

This is the theft of the entity's assets (for example, cash, inventory). Employees may be involved in such fraud in small and immaterial amounts, but it can also be carried out on a larger scale by management who may then conceal the misappropriation, for example, by:

- Embezzling receipts (for example, diverting them to private bank accounts)
- Stealing physical assets or intellectual property (inventory, selling data)
- Causing an entity to pay for goods not received (payments to fictitious vendors)
- Using assets for personal use

6.2 Fraud and the auditor

ISA 240 *The auditor's responsibilities relating to fraud in an audit of financial statements* provides guidance for auditors in this area.

6.2.1 Responsibilities of management compared with responsibilities of auditors

> This is an important area and you should be able to distinguish the auditors' responsibilities from those of management. It is important you read questions on this area carefully. You may be asked to contrast the responsibilities of the auditor and management, or to identify the responsibilities of one of the parties. In the June 2012 exam, question 3(a) asked for the auditors' responsibilities only (in relation to prevention and detection of fraud and error), and the F8 examining team noted that many candidates also included management's responsibilities when there were no marks available for these.
>
> This principle of reading the question carefully and focusing your answer can be applied to questions on all areas of the F8 syllabus.

The primary responsibility for the prevention and detection of fraud is with those charged with governance and the management of an entity. This is effected by having a commitment to creating a **culture of honesty and ethical behaviour** and **active oversight** by those charged with governance.

The auditor is responsible for obtaining reasonable assurance that the financial statements are free from material misstatement, whether caused by fraud or error. The risk of not detecting a material misstatement from fraud is higher than from error because of the following reasons :

- Fraud may involve **sophisticated schemes** designed to conceal it.

- Fraud may be perpetrated by individuals in **collusion**.

- Management fraud is harder to detect because management is in a position to **manipulate accounting records** or **override control procedures**.

The auditor is responsible for maintaining **professional scepticism** throughout the audit, considering the possibility of management override of controls, and recognising that audit procedures effective for detecting errors may not be effective for detecting fraud.

6.2.2 Risk assessment

ISA 315 requires a **discussion** among team members that places particular emphasis on how and where the financial statements may be susceptible to fraud.

Risk assessment procedures to obtain information in identifying the risks of material misstatement due to fraud shall include the following:

- **Enquiries of management** regarding:
    - **Management's assessment** of the risk that the financial statements may be misstated due to fraud
    - **Management's process** for identifying and responding to the risk of fraud
    - **Management's communication to those charged with governance** in respect of its process for identifying and responding to the risk of fraud
    - **Management's communication to employees** regarding its views on business practices and ethical behaviour
    - **Knowledge** of any actual, suspected or alleged fraud
- **Enquiries of internal audit** for knowledge of any actual, suspected or alleged fraud, and its views on the risks of fraud
- Obtaining an **understanding** of how those charged with governance **oversee** management's processes for identifying and responding to the risk of fraud and the internal control established to mitigate these risks
- **Enquiries of those charged with governance** for knowledge of any actual, suspected or alleged fraud
- Evaluating whether any unusual relationships have been identified in performing **analytical procedures** that may indicate risk of material misstatement due to fraud
- Considering whether any **other information** may indicate risk of material misstatement due to fraud
- Evaluating whether any **fraud risk factors** are present

In accordance with ISA 315, the auditor shall identify and assess the risks of material misstatement due to fraud at the financial statement level and at the assertion level for classes of transactions, account balances and disclosures. These risks shall be treated as **significant risks**.

In accordance with ISA 330, the auditor shall determine **overall responses** to address the assessed risks of material misstatement due to fraud at the financial statement level. In this regard, the auditor shall:

- **Assign and supervise** staff responsible taking into account their knowledge, skill and ability
- Evaluate whether the **accounting policies** may be indicative of fraudulent financial reporting
- Incorporate **unpredictability** in the selection of the nature, timing and extent of audit procedures

As we mentioned above, management fraud is more difficult to detect than employee fraud because of management's ability to override controls and therefore manipulate accounting records. ISA 240 states that irrespective of the auditor's assessment of the risks of management override of controls, the auditor shall design and perform audit procedures to:

- Test the appropriateness of **journal entries and other adjustments**
- Review **accounting estimates for bias**
- For **significant transactions** outside the normal course of business, evaluate whether they have been entered into to engage in fraudulent financial reporting or to conceal misappropriation of assets

BPP
LEARNING MEDIA

6.2.3 Written representations

ISA 240 requires the auditor to obtain **written representations** from management and those charged with governance that:

(a) They acknowledge their **responsibility** for the design, implementation and maintenance of internal control to prevent and detect fraud.

(b) They have disclosed to the auditor **management's assessment** of the risk of fraud in the financial statements.

(c) They have disclosed to the auditor their **knowledge of fraud / suspected fraud** involving management, employees with significant roles in internal control, and others where fraud could have a material effect on the financial statements.

(d) They have disclosed to the auditor their **knowledge of any allegations of fraud / suspected fraud** communicated by employees, former employees, analysts, regulators or others.

We shall look at written representations from management in more detail in Chapter 18 of this Study Text.

6.2.4 Communication to management and those charged with governance

If the auditor identifies fraud or receives information that a fraud may exist, the auditor shall report this on a **timely basis** to the **appropriate level of management**.

If the auditor identifies or suspects fraud involving management, employees with significant roles in internal control, and others where fraud could have a material effect on the financial statements, they shall communicate this on a **timely basis** to **those charged with governance**.

The auditor also needs to consider whether there is a responsibility to report to the **regulatory or enforcement authorities** – the auditor's professional duty of **confidentiality** may be **overridden** by **laws and statutes** in certain jurisdictions.

6.3 Law and regulations

The auditor is also required to consider the issue of law and regulations in the audit. Auditors are given guidance in ISA 250 *Consideration of laws and regulations in an audit of financial statements*. The objectives of the auditor are:

(a) To obtain sufficient appropriate audit evidence regarding compliance with the provisions of those laws and regulations that have a **direct effect** on the determination of material amounts and disclosures in the financial statements

(b) To perform specified audit procedures to help identify non-compliance with other laws and regulations that may have a **material effect** on the financial statements

(c) To respond appropriately to **non-compliance / suspected non-compliance** identified during the audit

6.3.1 Responsibilities of management compared with auditors

Exam focus point

> As explained in the earlier Exam focus point, you must read any exam question on this area carefully. You need to know these respective responsibilities in relation to laws and regulations, and must be able to select the right ones for use in your answer depending on the question set. The examiner's report on the December 2011 exam highlighted that candidates' answers were weak when trying to explain the auditors' responsibilities in relation to compliance with laws and regulations, with most candidates instead focusing on management's responsibilities. Don't fall into the same trap – learn the responsibilities, understand them and make sure you read any related question carefully.

It is management's responsibility to ensure that the entity complies with the relevant laws and regulations. It is not the auditor's responsibility to prevent or detect non-compliance with laws and regulations.

The auditor's responsibility is to obtain reasonable assurance that the financial statements are free from material misstatement and, in this respect, the auditor must take into account the legal and regulatory framework within which the entity operates.

ISA 250 distinguishes the auditor's responsibilities in relation to compliance with two different categories of laws and regulations:

(a) Those that have a **direct effect** on the determination of **material amounts** and disclosures in the financial statements

(b) Those that **do not have a direct effect** on the determination of material amounts and disclosures in the financial statements but where compliance may be fundamental to the **operating aspects**, ability to **continue in business**, or to avoid **material penalties**

For the first category, the auditor's responsibility is to obtain sufficient appropriate audit evidence about **compliance** with those laws and regulations.

For the second category, the auditor's responsibility is to undertake specified audit procedures to help **identify non-compliance** with laws and regulations that may have a **material effect** on the financial statements. These include enquiries of management and inspecting correspondence with the relevant licensing or regulatory authorities.

6.3.2 Audit procedures

In accordance with ISA 315, the auditor shall obtain a general understanding of:

- The applicable legal and regulatory framework
- How the entity complies with that framework

The auditor can achieve this understanding by using their **existing understanding** and updating it, and making **enquiries of management** about other laws and regulations that may affect the entity, and about its policies and procedures for ensuring compliance and about its policies and procedures for identifying, evaluating and accounting for litigation claims.

The auditor shall remain alert throughout the audit to the possibility that **other audit procedures** may bring instances of non-compliance or suspected non-compliance to the auditor's attention. These audit procedures could include:

- Reading minutes
- Making enquiries of management and in-house/external legal advisers regarding litigation, claims and assessments
- Performing substantive tests of details of classes of transactions, account balances or disclosures

The auditor shall request **written representations** from management that all known instances of non-compliance or suspected non-compliance with laws and regulations whose effects should be considered when preparing the financial statements have been disclosed to the auditor.

6.3.3 Audit procedures when non-compliance is identified or suspected

The following factors may indicate non-compliance with laws and regulations:

- Investigations by regulatory authorities and government departments
- Payment of fines or penalties
- Payments for unspecified services or loans to consultants, related parties, employees or government employees
- Sales commissions or agents' fees that appear excessive
- Purchasing at prices significantly above/below market price
- Unusual payments in cash

- Unusual transactions with companies registered in tax havens
- Payment for goods and services made to a country different to the one in which the goods and services originated
- Payments without proper exchange control documentation
- Existence of an information system that fails to provide an adequate audit trail or sufficient evidence
- Unauthorised transactions or improperly recorded transactions
- Adverse media comment

The following table summarises audit procedures to be performed when non-compliance is identified or suspected.

Non-compliance: audit procedures
Obtain understanding of nature of act and circumstances
Obtain further information to evaluate possible effect on financial statements
Discuss with management and those charged with governance
Consider need to obtain legal advice if sufficient information not provided and matter is material
Evaluate effect on auditor's opinion if sufficient information not obtained
Evaluate implications on risk assessment and reliability of written representations

6.3.4 Reporting identified or suspected non-compliance

The auditor shall communicate with **those charged with governance**, but, if the auditor suspects that those charged with governance are involved, the auditor shall communicate with the next highest level of authority, such as the **audit committee or supervisory board**. If this does not exist, the auditor shall consider the need to obtain **legal advice**.

The auditor shall consider the impact on the **auditor's report** if they conclude that the non-compliance has a material effect on the financial statements and has not been adequately reflected or is prevented by management and those charged with governance from obtaining sufficient appropriate audit evidence to evaluate whether non-compliance is material to the financial statements.

The auditor shall determine whether identified or suspected non-compliance has to be reported to the **regulatory and enforcement authorities**. Although the auditor must maintain the fundamental principle of **confidentiality**, in some jurisdictions the duty of confidentiality may be **overridden** by law or statute.

7 Documentation of risk assessment

FAST FORWARD

Auditors must ensure they have **documented** the work done at the risk assessment stage, such as the discussion among the audit team of the susceptibility of the financial statements to material misstatements, significant risks, and overall responses.

The need for auditors to document their audit work is discussed in the next chapter where we will look in particular at the **audit plan** and the **audit strategy**, two documents for planning. ISAs 315 and 330 contain a number of general requirements about documentation, and we shall briefly run through those here.

The following matters shall be documented during planning.

- The discussion among the audit team concerning the susceptibility of the financial statements to material misstatements, including any significant decisions reached
- Key elements of the understanding gained of the entity regarding the elements of the entity and its internal control components specified in ISA 315, the sources of the information gained and the risk assessment procedures carried out

- The identified and assessed risks of material misstatement at the financial statement level and at the assertion level

- Risks identified and related controls evaluated

- The overall responses to address the risks of material misstatement at the financial statement level

- Nature, extent and timing of further audit procedures linked to the assessed risks at the assertion level

- Results of audit procedures

- If the auditors have relied on evidence about the effectiveness of controls from previous audits, conclusions about how this is appropriate

- Demonstration that the financial statements agree or reconcile with the underlying accounting records

Chapter Roundup

- A **risk assessment** carried out under the ISAs helps the auditor to identify financial statement areas susceptible to material misstatement and provides a basis for designing and performing further audit procedures.

- Auditors are required to carry out the audit with an attitude of **professional scepticism**, exercise **professional judgement** and comply with **ethical requirements**.

- **Audit risk** is the risk that the auditor expresses an inappropriate audit opinion when the financial statements are materially misstated. It is a function of the risk of material misstatement (**inherent risk** and **control risk**) and the risk that the auditors will not detect such misstatement (**detection risk**).

- **Materiality for the financial statements as a whole** and **performance materiality** must be calculated at the planning stages of all audits. The calculation or estimation of materiality should be based on experience and judgement. Materiality for the financial statements as a whole must be **reviewed throughout** the audit and **revised if necessary**.

- The auditor is required to obtain an **understanding** of the entity and its environment in order to be able to assess the risks of material misstatements.

- When the auditor has obtained an understanding of the entity, they shall assess the risks of material misstatement in the financial statements, also identifying significant risks.

- **Significant risks** are complex or unusual transactions that may indicate fraud, or other special risks.

- The auditor shall **formulate an approach** to the assessed risks of material misstatement.

- When carrying out risk assessment procedures, the auditor shall also consider the risk of fraud or non-compliance with law and regulations causing a misstatement in the financial statements.

- Auditors must ensure they have **documented** the work done at the risk assessment stage, such as the discussion among the audit team of the susceptibility of the financial statements to material misstatements, significant risks, and overall responses.

Quick Quiz

1   Complete the definitions.

   .... risk is the risk that .... may give an ....opinion on the financial statements.

   .... risk is the .... of an assertion to a .... that could be material, assuming there were no related ....

2   If control risk and inherent risk are assessed as sufficiently low, substantive procedures can be abandoned completely.

   True ☐   False ☐

3   Which procedures might an auditor use in gaining an understanding of the entity?

4   The audit team is required to discuss the susceptibility of the financial statements to material misstatements.

   True ☐   False ☐

5   Auditors have a duty to detect fraud.

   True ☐   False ☐

Answers to Quick Quiz

1   Audit, auditors, inappropriate

       Inherent, susceptibility, misstatement, internal controls

2   False

3   Enquiry, analytical procedures, observation and inspection

4   True

5   False

Now try the questions below from the Practice Question Bank

Number	Level	Marks	Time
Q8	Examination	20	39 mins
Q9	Examination	20	39 mins
Q10 parts (a) and (b)(i)	Examination	20	39 mins
Q11 parts (a) to (c)	Examination	30	59 mins
Q12	Examination	30	59 mins

Audit planning and documentation

Topic list	Syllabus reference
1 Audit planning	B6
2 Audit documentation	B6

Introduction

In the chapter we look at the contents of the overall audit strategy and the detailed audit plan.

We also look at how auditors document their work in general. Audit documentation is important because it provides the evidence of the work performed by the auditors in carrying out the audit.

Study guide

		Intellectual level
B6	**Audit planning and documentation**	
(a)	Identify and explain the need for, and importance of, planning an audit.	2
(b)	Identify and describe the contents of the overall audit strategy and audit plan.	2
(c)	Explain and describe the relationship between the overall audit strategy and the audit plan.	2
(d)	Explain the difference between interim and final audit.	1
(e)	Describe the purpose of an interim audit, and the procedures likely to be adopted at this stage in the audit.	2
(f)	Describe the impact of the work performed during the interim audit on the final audit.	2
(g)	Explain the need for, and the importance of, audit documentation.	1
(h)	Describe the form and contents of working papers and supporting documentation.	2
(i)	Explain the procedures to ensure safe custody and retention of working papers.	1

Exam guide

Audit planning is a very important part of the audit process because it sets the direction for the audit, based on an assessment of the risks relevant to the entity. Questions on planning could come up in a variety of ways, both in Section A and Section B of the exam:

- Identifying audit risks in a scenario-based setting
- Explaining the matters covered in the overall audit strategy document and the audit plan
- Explaining the importance of audit planning
- Distinguishing between the interim and final audit

1 Audit planning   June 09, Dec 09, June 12, Dec 14

FAST FORWARD

The auditor formulates an **overall audit strategy** which is translated into a **detailed audit plan** for audit staff to follow.

1.1 The importance of planning

An effective and efficient audit relies on proper planning procedures. The planning process is covered in general terms by ISA 300 *Planning an audit of financial statements* which states that the auditor shall plan the audit so that the engagement is performed in an effective manner.

Audits are planned to:

- Help the auditor devote appropriate attention to important areas of the audit
- Help the auditor identify and resolve potential problems on a timely basis
- Help the auditor properly organise and manage the audit so it is performed in an effective manner
- Assist in the selection of appropriate team members and assignment of work to them
- Facilitate the direction, supervision and review of work
- Assist in co-ordination of work done by auditors of components and experts

Audit procedures should be discussed with the client's management, staff and/or audit committee in order to co-ordinate audit work, including that of internal audit. However, all audit procedures remain the responsibility of the external auditors.

A structured approach to planning will include:

Step 1 Ensuring that ethical requirements are met, including independence

Step 2 Ensuring the terms of the engagement are understood

Step 3 Establishing the overall audit strategy that sets the scope, timing and direction of the audit and guides the development of the audit plan

- Identify the characteristics of the engagement that define its scope.

- Ascertain the reporting objectives to plan the timing of the audit and nature of communications required.

- Consider significant factors in directing the team's efforts.

- Consider results of preliminary engagement activities.

- Ascertain nature, timing and extent of resources necessary to perform the engagement.

Step 4 Developing an audit plan that includes the nature, timing and extent of planned risk assessment procedures and further audit procedures

1.2 The overall audit strategy and the audit plan

FAST FORWARD The overall audit strategy and audit plan shall be updated and changed as necessary during the course of the audit.

1.2.1 The audit strategy

Key term

The overall **audit strategy** sets the scope, timing and direction of the audit, and guides the development of the more detailed audit plan.

The matters the auditor may consider in establishing an overall audit strategy are set out in the table below.

THE OVERALL AUDIT STRATEGY: MATTERS TO CONSIDER	
Characteristics of the engagement	<ul><li>Financial reporting framework</li><li>Industry-specific reporting requirements</li><li>Expected audit coverage</li><li>Nature of business segments</li><li>Availability of internal audit work</li><li>Use of service organisations</li><li>Effect of information technology on audit procedures</li><li>Availability of client personnel and data</li></ul>
Reporting objectives, timing of the audit and nature of communications	<ul><li>Entity's timetable for reporting</li><li>Organisation of meetings with management and those charged with governance</li><li>Discussions with management and those charged with governance</li><li>Expected communications with third parties</li></ul>

THE OVERALL AUDIT STRATEGY: MATTERS TO CONSIDER	
Significant factors, preliminary engagement activities, and knowledge gained on other engagements	• Determination of materiality • Areas identified with higher risk of material misstatement • Results of previous audits • Need to maintain professional scepticism • Evidence of management's commitment to design, implementation and maintenance of sound internal control • Volume of transactions • Significant business developments • Significant industry developments • Significant changes in financial reporting framework • Other significant recent developments
Nature, timing and extent of resources	• Selection of engagement team • Assignment of work to team members • Engagement budgeting

Examples of items to include in the overall audit strategy could be:

- Industry-specific financial reporting requirements
- Number of locations to be visited
- Audit client's timetable for reporting to its members
- Communication between the audit team and the client

1.2.2 The audit plan

Key term

> The **audit plan** converts the audit strategy into a more detailed plan and includes the nature, timing and extent of audit procedures to be performed by engagement team members in order to obtain sufficient appropriate audit evidence to reduce audit risk to an acceptably low level.

The audit plan shall include the following:

- A description of the nature, timing and extent of planned risk assessment procedures

- A description of the nature, timing and extent of planned further audit procedures at the assertion level

- Other planned audit procedures required to be carried out for the engagement to comply with ISAs

The planning for these procedures occurs over the course of the audit as the audit plan develops.

Examples of items included in the audit plan could be:

- Timetable of planned audit work
- Allocation of work to audit team members
- Audit procedures for each major account area (eg inventory, receivables, cash)
- Materiality for the financial statements as a whole and performance materiality

Further application guidance was added to ISA 300 in 2015, to highlight the need for auditors **to consider** financial statement **disclosures at the planning stage**. Considering disclosures early in the audit helps auditors to identify:

- Changes in the entity's environment, financial condition or activities

- Changes in the applicable financial reporting framework

- The need to involve an auditor's expert (eg for disclosures related to pension)

- The need to discuss matters with those charged with management (eg changes in the entity's environment or issues regarding the quality of the disclosures, as covered under ISA 260).

Any changes made during the audit engagement to the overall audit strategy or audit plan, and the reasons for such changes, shall be included in the audit documentation.

You must understand the difference between the audit strategy and the audit plan.

1.3 Interim and final audits   Dec 09, June 12, June 14

Auditors usually carry out their audit work for a financial year in one or more sittings. These are referred to as the **interim audit(s)** and the **final audit**.

The interim audit visit is carried out during the period of review and the final audit visit will take place after the year end.

We look at the different types of procedures in detail in Chapters 8, 9 and 10, but because we refer to **substantive procedures** and **tests of control** during our explanation of the interim and final audit, we will define those terms here.

Key terms

Tests of controls are designed to evaluate the operating effectiveness of controls in preventing, or detecting and correcting, material misstatements at the assertion level.

Substantive procedures are designed to detect material misstatements at the assertion level. Substantive procedures comprise:

- Tests of details (of classes of transactions, account balances, and disclosures);
- Substantive analytical procedures

1.3.1 The purpose of the interim audit and procedures likely to be adopted

The purpose of the interim audit is to carry out procedures that would be difficult to perform at the year end because of time constraints. Work at this visit tends to focus on risk assessment and on documenting and testing internal controls. Some substantive procedures can also be carried out but these are limited because statement of financial position figures will not be the ones to be reported on.

The final audit will focus on the audit of the financial statements. It concludes with the auditor issuing a report which contains the opinion expressed on the financial statements covering the entire year being audited. The final audit opinion will take account of conclusions reached at both (or all) audit visits.

ISA 330 *The auditor's responses to assessed risks* states that the higher the risk of material misstatement, the more likely it is that the auditor will decide that it is more effective to undertake substantive procedures nearer to, or at, the period end rather than earlier.

Some audit procedures can only be performed at the final audit visit, such as agreeing the financial statements to the accounting records and examining adjustments made during the process of preparing the financial statements.

The following table summarises some of the typical procedures carried out during the interim and final audits.

Interim audit procedures may include:	Final audit procedures include:
• Inherent risk assessment and gaining an understanding of the entity • Recording the entity's system of internal control • Evaluating the design of internal controls • Carrying out tests of control on the company's internal controls to ensure they are operating as expected • Performing substantive testing of transactions/balances to gain evidence that the books and records are a reliable basis for the preparation of financial statements • Identification of issues that may have an impact on work to take place at the final audit	• Substantive procedures involving verification of statement of financial position balances and amounts in the statement of profit or loss • Obtaining third-party confirmations • Analytical procedures relating to figures in the financial statements • Subsequent events review • Agreeing the financial statements to the accounting records • Examining adjustments made during the process of preparing the financial statements • Consideration of the going concern status of the entity • Performing tests to ensure that the conclusions formed at the interim audit are still valid • Obtaining written representations

1.3.2 Impact of interim audit work on the final audit in general

The benefit of spreading audit procedures over an interim and final audit is that it is possible to provide shareholders and other users of the financial statements with the audited accounts sooner than if all audit procedures were carried out at a final audit taking place after the year end.

Performing audit procedures before the period end can **assist in identifying significant matters at an early stage** of the audit and help resolve them with management's assistance or develop an effective audit approach to address them. This **reduces the time taken at the final audit** to gain the remaining sufficient appropriate audit evidence needed.

1.3.3 Impact of interim audit work relating to internal controls on the final audit

If the auditors are to place reliance on internal controls they must obtain evidence that **controls** have operated effectively **throughout the period**. If the auditor obtains audit evidence about the operating effectiveness of controls at the interim audit, when it comes to the final audit, instead of having to gain evidence over controls covering the whole year the auditor can focus on:

- Obtaining audit evidence about **significant changes to those controls** subsequent to the interim period

- Determining the **additional audit evidence** to be obtained for the remaining period

While at the final audit, the amount of work needed to gain additional audit evidence about controls that were operating during the period between the interim audit and the year end will depend on:

- The significance of the assessed risks of material misstatement at the assertion level

- The specific controls that were tested during the interim period, and significant changes to them since they were tested, including changes in the information system, processes and personnel

- The degree to which audit evidence about the operating effectiveness of those controls was obtained

- The length of the remaining period

- The extent to which the auditor intends to reduce further substantive procedures based on the reliance of controls

- The control environment

1.3.4 Impact of substantive procedures performed during the interim audit on the final audit

If substantive procedures are performed at an interim date, the auditor must cover the remaining period by performing substantive procedures, or substantive procedures combined with tests of controls for the intervening period.

Conclusions will have been reached on the testing carried out at the interim audit and the auditor essentially has to carry out any procedures necessary to provide a reasonable basis for extending the audit conclusions from the interim date to the period end.

One approach an auditor who has carried out an interim audit can take is to compare and reconcile information concerning the balance at the period end with the comparable information at the interim date. Essentially, because the interim balance has been audited, the auditor can focus on auditing the movements in the balance between the interim date and the year end.

A point to note is that when misstatements that the auditor did not expect when assessing the risks of material misstatement are detected at an interim date, the auditor many need to modify the planned nature, timing or extent of substantive procedures covering the remaining period. This may result in repeating the procedures in full that were performed at the interim date. Therefore part of the expected benefit of carrying out the interim audit will have been lost.

2 Audit documentation
Dec 10, June 12, June 14

It is important to document audit work performed in working papers to:

- Enable reporting partner to ensure all planned work has been completed adequately
- Provide details of work done for future reference
- Assist in planning and control of future audits
- Encourage a methodical approach

PER alert

Objective 17 of the PER performance objectives is to prepare for and collect evidence for audit. One of the ways to demonstrate PO 17 is through the preparation of working papers that document and evaluate audit tests. The knowledge you gain in this section will be a useful aid in preparing these sorts of working papers. An article published in the May 2010 edition of *Student Accountant* provides more detail on how you can achieve PO 17.

2.1 The objective of audit documentation

Key term

Audit documentation is the record of audit procedures performed, relevant audit evidence obtained, and conclusions the auditor reached (terms such as 'working papers' or 'work papers' are also sometimes used).

All audit work must be documented: the working papers are the tangible evidence of the work done in support of the audit opinion. ISA 230 *Audit documentation* states that the auditor shall prepare audit documentation on a **timely basis**.

Audit documentation is necessary for the following reasons:

(a) It provides evidence of the auditor's basis for a conclusion about the achievement of the overall objective.

(b) It provides evidence that the audit was planned and performed in accordance with ISAs and other legal and regulatory requirements.

(c) It assists the engagement team to plan and perform the audit.

(d) It assists team members responsible for supervision to direct, supervise and review audit work.

(e)   It enables the team to be accountable for its work.

(f)   It allows a record of matters of continuing significance to be retained.

(g)   It enables the conduct of quality control reviews and inspections (both internal and external).

2.2 Form and content of working papers

The ISA requires working papers to be sufficiently complete and detailed to provide an overall understanding of the audit. Auditors cannot record everything they consider. Therefore judgement must be used as to the extent of working papers, based on the following general rule.

> What would be necessary to provide an experienced auditor, with no previous connection to the audit, with an understanding of the work performed, the results of audit procedures, audit evidence obtained, significant matters arising during the audit and conclusions reached.

The form and content of working papers are affected by matters such as:

- The **size and complexity** of the entity
- The **nature** of the audit procedures to be performed
- The **identified risks** of material misstatement
- The **significance** of the audit evidence obtained
- The nature and extent of **exceptions** identified

2.2.1 Examples of working papers

(a)   Information obtained in understanding the entity and its environment, including its internal control, such as the following:

   (i)   Information concerning the legal documents, agreements and minutes

   (ii)   Extracts or copies of important legal documents, agreements and minutes

   (iii)   Information concerning the industry, economic environment and legislative environment within which the entity operates

   (iv)   Extracts from the entity's internal control manual

(b)   Evidence of the planning process including audit programmes and any changes thereto

(c)   Evidence of the auditor's consideration of the work of internal audit and conclusions reached

(d)   Analyses of transactions and balances

(e)   Analyses of significant ratios and trends

(f)   Identified and assessed risks of material misstatements

(g)   A record of the nature, timing, extent and results of audit procedures

(h)   Evidence that the work performed was supervised and reviewed

(i)   An indication as to who performed the audit procedures and when they were performed

(j)   Details of audit procedures applied regarding components whose financial statements are audited by another auditor

(k)   Copies of communications with other auditors, experts and other third parties

(l)   Copies of letters or notes concerning audit matters communicated to or discussed with management or those charged with governance, including the terms of the engagement and significant deficiencies in internal control

(m)   Written representations received from management of the entity

(n)   Conclusions reached by the auditor concerning significant aspects of the audit, including how exceptions and unusual matters, if any, disclosed by the auditor's procedures were resolved or treated

(o)   Copies of the financial statements and auditors' reports

(p)   Notes of discussions about significant matters with management and others

(q)   In exceptional circumstances, the reasons for departing from a basic principle or essential procedure of an ISA and how the alternative procedure performed achieved the audit objective

The following is an illustration of a typical audit working paper.

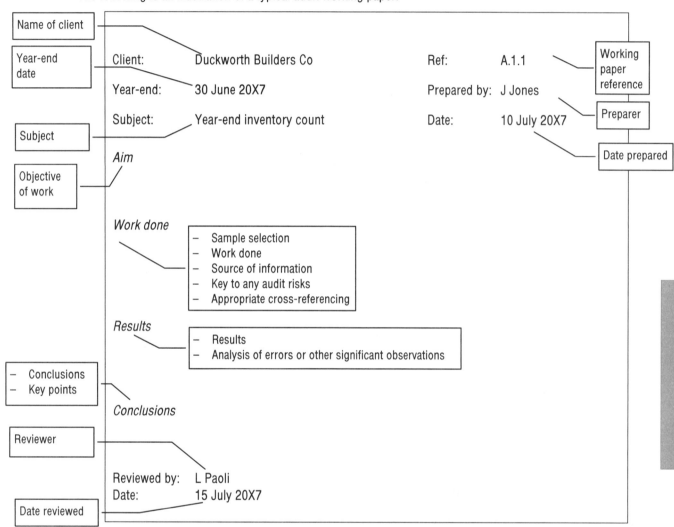

The auditor should record the identifying characteristics of specific items or matters being tested. Firms should have standard **referencing** and **filing** procedures for working papers, to facilitate their review.

2.2.2 Audit files

For recurring audits, working papers may be split between:

Permanent audit files (containing information of **continuing importance** to the audit). These contain:

- Engagement letters
- New client questionnaire
- The memorandum and articles
- Other legal documents such as prospectuses, leases, sales agreement
- Details of the history of the client's business
- Board minutes of continuing relevance
- Previous years' signed accounts, analytical review and reports to management
- Accounting systems notes, previous years' control questionnaires

Current audit files (containing information of relevance to the **current year's audit**). These should be compiled on a timely basis after the completion of the audit and should contain:

- Financial statements
- Accounts checklists
- Management accounts details
- Reconciliations of management and financial accounts
- A summary of unadjusted errors
- Report to partner including details of significant events and errors
- Review notes
- Audit planning memorandum
- Time budgets and summaries
- Written representations
- Report to management
- Notes of board minutes
- Communications with third parties such as experts or other auditors

They also contain working papers covering each audit area. These should include the following:

- A lead schedule including details of the figures to be included in the accounts
- Problems encountered and conclusions drawn
- Audit programmes
- Risk assessments
- Sampling plans
- Analytical review
- Details of substantive tests and tests of control

If it is necessary to modify/add new audit documentation to a file after it has been assembled, the auditor should document:

- Who made the changes, and when, and by whom they were reviewed
- The reasons for making changes
- The effect of changes on the auditors' conclusions

If, in exceptional circumstances, changes are made to an audit file after the audit report has been signed, the auditor should document:

- The circumstances
- The audit procedures performed, evidence obtained, conclusions drawn
- When and by whom changes to audit documents were made and reviewed

2.3 Standardised and automated working papers

The use of **standardised** working papers, for example, checklists and specimen letters, may improve the efficiency of audit work but they can be dangerous because they may lead to auditors' mechanically following an approach without using audit judgement.

Automated working paper packages have been developed which can make the documentation of audit work much easier. Such programs aid preparation of working papers, lead schedules, the trial balance and the financial statements themselves. These are automatically cross-referenced, adjusted and balanced by the computer.

The **advantages** of automated working papers are as follows.

- The risk of errors is reduced.

- The working papers will be neater and easier to review.

- The time saved will be substantial, as adjustments can easily be made to all working papers, including those summarising the key analytical information.

- Standard forms do not have to be carried to audit locations.

- Audit working papers can be transmitted for review via a modem or fax facilities.

2.4 Safe custody and retention of working papers

Judgement may have to be used in deciding the length of holding working papers, and further consideration should be given to the matter before their destruction. The ACCA recommends **seven years** as a minimum period.

Working papers are the property of the auditors. They are not a substitute for, nor part of, the entity's accounting records.

Auditors must follow ethical guidance on the confidentiality of audit working papers. They may, at their discretion, release parts of or whole working papers to the entity, as long as disclosure does not undermine 'the independence or validity of the audit process'. Information should not be made available to third parties without the permission of the entity.

Chapter Roundup

- The auditor formulates an **overall audit strategy** which is translated into a **detailed audit plan** for audit staff to follow.

- The overall audit strategy and audit plan shall be updated and changed as necessary during the course of the audit.

- It is important to document audit work performed in working papers to:
    - Enable reporting partner to ensure all planned work has been completed adequately
    - Provide details of work done for future reference
    - Assist in planning and control of future audits
    - Encourage a methodical approach

Quick Quiz

1   Complete the definitions.

An ……………… …….…….. ……………… is the formulation of a general strategy for the audit.

An ……………… ………..…... is a set of instructions to the audit team that sets out the further audit procedures to be carried out.

2   Changes to the overall audit strategy or audit plan do not need to be documented.

True ☐

False ☐

3   What is the general rule for audit documentation?

4   State two advantages of standardised working papers.

(1) …………………………………………

(2) …………………………………………

5   Complete the table, using the working papers given below.

Current audit file	Permanent audit file

Engagement letters	New client questionnaire
Financial statements	Report to management
Accounts checklists	Audit planning memorandum
Board minutes of continuing relevance	Accounting systems notes

1   Overall audit strategy, audit plan

2   False – any changes shall be fully documented in accordance with ISA 300 *Planning an audit of financial statements*.

3   What would be necessary to provide an experienced auditor, with no previous connection to the audit, with an understanding of the nature, timing and extent of the audit procedures performed, the results of audit procedures, audit evidence obtained, significant matters arising during the audit and conclusions reached.

4   Advantages of standardised working papers

    (1)   Facilitate the delegation of work
    (2)   Means of quality control

5

Current audit file	Permanent audit file
Financial statements	Engagement letters
Report to management	New client questionnaire
Accounts checklists	Board minutes of continuing relevance
Audit planning memorandum	Accounting systems notes

Now try the question below from the Practice Question Bank

Number	Level	Marks	Time
Q13	Examination	10	20 mins

7: Audit planning and documentation | Part B Planning and risk assessment

Introduction to audit evidence

Topic list	Syllabus reference
1 Audit evidence	D1
2 Financial statement assertions	D1

Introduction

In this chapter, we introduce the fundamental auditing concept of audit evidence. Audit evidence is required to enable the auditor to form an opinion on the financial statements. Therefore such evidence has to be sufficient and appropriate.

We also explain the financial statement assertions for which audit evidence is required. These will be particularly important when we consider detailed testing later in this Study Text, since audit tests are designed to obtain sufficient appropriate evidence about the assertions for each balance or transaction in the financial statements.

Study guide

		Intellectual level
D1	**Financial statement assertions and audit evidence**	
(a)	Explain the assertions contained in the financial statements about: classes of transactions and events and related disclosures; account balances and related disclosures at the period end.	2
(b)	Describe audit procedures to obtain audit evidence, including inspection, observation, external confirmation, recalculation, reperformance, analytical procedures and enquiry.	2
(c)	Discuss the quality and quantity of audit evidence.	2
(d)	Discuss the relevance and reliability of audit evidence.	2

Exam guide

The issues of audit evidence and financial statement assertions will underpin exam questions about detailed audit testing which we look at later in this Study Text. In addition, you could be asked a question on the theory of evidence, such as the different types of evidence that can be obtained by auditors.

(a) Defining substantive procedures and tests of control

(b) Explaining financial statement assertions relevant to transactions or account balances at the period end

(c) Explaining the factors that would influence the auditor's judgement regarding the sufficiency and reliability of audit evidence

(d) Explaining the audit procedures used in collecting audit evidence.

1 Audit evidence   Dec 07, June 08, Dec 09

FAST FORWARD

Auditors must design and perform audit procedures to obtain **sufficient appropriate** audit evidence.

1.1 The need for audit evidence

Remember that the objective of an audit of financial statements is to enable the auditor to express an opinion on whether the financial statements are prepared, in all material respects, in accordance with an identified financial reporting framework. In this section, we shall look at the **audit evidence** gathered, which enables the auditor to express the audit opinion.

Key term

> **Audit evidence** is all the information used by the auditor in arriving at the conclusions on which the auditor's opinion is based.

Audit evidence includes the information contained in the accounting records underlying the financial statements and other information gathered by the auditors, such as confirmations from third parties. Auditors are **not expected to look at all the information** that might exist. They will often select **samples** to test, as we shall see in Chapter 11.

1.2 Sufficient appropriate audit evidence   Dec 13

The **appropriateness** of audit evidence is the measure of the quality of audit evidence; that is, its relevance and its reliability in providing support for the conclusions on which the auditor's opinion is based.

The **sufficiency** of audit evidence is the measure of the quantity of audit evidence. The quantity of audit evidence needed is affected by the auditor's assessment of the risks of material misstatement and also by the quality of such audit evidence.

ISA 500 *Audit evidence* requires auditors to 'design and perform audit procedures that are appropriate in the circumstances for the purposes of obtaining **sufficient appropriate** audit evidence'. 'Sufficiency' and 'appropriateness' are interrelated and apply to both tests of controls and substantive procedures.

- **Sufficiency** is the measure of the **quantity** of audit evidence.
- **Appropriateness** is the measure of the **quality** or **reliability** of the audit evidence.

The **quantity** of audit evidence required is affected by the **level of risk** in the area being audited. It is also affected by the **quality** of evidence obtained. If the evidence is high quality, the auditor may need less than if it were poor quality. However, obtaining a high quantity of poor quality evidence will not cancel out its poor quality. The ISA requires auditors to consider the **relevance and reliability** of the information to be used as audit evidence when designing and performing audit procedures.

Relevance deals with the logical connection with the purpose of the audit procedure and the assertion under consideration (we look at assertions in the next section). The relevance of information may be affected by the direction of testing.

Reliability is influenced by the source and nature of the information, including the controls over its preparation and maintenance. The following generalisations may help in assessing the **reliability** of audit evidence.

QUALITY OF EVIDENCE	
External	Audit evidence from **external sources** is more reliable than that obtained from the entity's records because it is from an independent source.
Auditor	Evidence obtained **directly by auditors** is more reliable than that obtained indirectly or by inference.
Entity	Evidence obtained from the entity's records is more reliable when the related **control system operates effectively**.
Written	Evidence in the form of **documents (paper or electronic)** or **written representations** are more reliable than oral representations, since oral representations can be retracted.
Originals	**Original documents** are more reliable than photocopies or facsimiles, which can easily be altered by the client.

1.2.1 Management's expert

A **management's expert** is an individual or organisation possessing expertise in a field other than auditing or accounting, whose work in that field is used by the entity to assist the entity in preparing the financial statements.

ISA 500 considers the use of a management's expert by management and states that if information to be used as audit evidence has been prepared by a management's expert, the auditor must evaluate the competence, capabilities and objectivity of the expert, obtain an understanding of the work done, and evaluate the appropriateness of the work done as audit evidence.

1.2.2 Information produced by the entity

If information produced by the entity is to be used by the auditor, the auditor needs to evaluate whether it is sufficiently reliable for the auditor's purposes, including obtaining audit evidence regarding its accuracy and completeness, and evaluating whether it is sufficiently precise and detailed.

1.2.3 Selecting items to test

ISA 500 states that the auditor must determine the means of selecting items for testing that are effective in meeting the purpose of the audit procedure. The auditor could either select **all items**, select **specific items** or use **audit sampling**. We look at these in more detail in Chapter 11.

1.2.4 Inconsistencies and doubts over reliability

If audit evidence from one source is inconsistent with that from another, or the auditor has doubts over the reliability of information, the auditor must determine what modifications or additions to audit procedures are necessary to resolve the issues and must consider the effect on other aspects of the audit.

> Objective 17 of the PER performance objectives is to prepare for and collect evidence for audit. You can apply the knowledge you gain from this and subsequent chapters to assist in achieving this objective.

2 Financial statement assertions

June 08, Dec 08, June 09, June 11, June 12

FAST FORWARD

> Audit tests are designed to obtain evidence about the **financial statement assertions**. Assertions relate to **classes of transactions and events and related disclosures**, and **account balances at the period end and related disclosures**.

Key term

> **Financial statement assertions** are the representations by management, explicit or otherwise, that are embodied in the financial statements, as used by the auditor to consider the different types of potential misstatements that may occur.

ISA 315 states that the auditor must use assertions for **classes of transactions and related disclosures** (ie statement of profit or loss) and **account balances and related disclosures** (ie statement of financial position) in sufficient detail to form the basis for the assessment of risks of material misstatement and the design and performance of further audit procedures. It gives examples of assertions in these areas which are set out in the table that follows.

Assertions used by the auditor	
Assertions about **classes of transactions and events and related disclosures** for the period under audit	**Occurrence**: Transactions and events that have been recorded or disclosed have occurred, and such transactions and events pertain to the entity.
	Completeness: All transactions and events that should have been recorded have been recorded, and all related disclosures that should have been included in the financial statements have been included.
	Accuracy: Amounts and other data relating to recorded transactions and events have been recorded appropriately, and related disclosures have been appropriately measured and described.
	Cut-off: Transactions and events have been recorded in the correct reporting period.
	Classification: Transactions and events have been recorded in the proper accounts.
	Presentation: Transactions and events are appropriately aggregated or disaggregated and are clearly described, and related disclosures are relevant and understandable in the context of the requirements of the applicable financial reporting framework.

Assertions used by the auditor	
Assertions about **account balances and related disclosures** at the period end	**Existence**: Assets, liabilities and equity interests exist.
	Rights and obligations: The entity holds or controls the rights to assets, and liabilities are the obligations of the entity.
	Completeness: All assets, liabilities and equity interests that should have been recorded have been recorded, and all related disclosures that should have been included in the financial statements have been included.
	Accuracy, valuation and allocation: Assets, liabilities and equity interests have been included in the financial statements at appropriate amounts and any resulting valuation or allocation adjustments have been appropriately recorded, and related disclosures have been appropriately measured and described.
	Classification: Assets, liabilities and equity interests have been recorded in the proper accounts.
	Presentation: Assets, liabilities and equity interests are appropriately aggregated or disaggregated and clearly described, and related disclosures are relevant and understandable in the context of the requirements of the applicable financial reporting framework.

This is a key syllabus area and you **must** be very comfortable with the assertions that relate to each of the three areas, as the same assertions do not always apply to each of these areas. Exam questions are very likely to test this area in the context of audit procedures to test particular assertions so it's vital that you take the time to learn, understand and test your knowledge.

Exam focus point

When designing audit plans and procedures for specific areas, you must focus on the financial statement assertions that you are trying to find evidence to support. If a question asks for audit procedures relating to a particular assertion, make sure your answer addresses only the assertion required by the question.

2.1 Audit procedures to obtain audit evidence
Dec 08, June 10, June 11, June 13

FAST FORWARD

Audit evidence can be obtained by inspection, observation, enquiry and confirmation, recalculation, reperformance and analytical procedures.

The auditor obtains audit evidence by undertaking audit procedures to do the following.

- Obtain an understanding of the entity and its environment to assess the risks of material misstatement at the financial statement and assertion levels (**risk assessment procedures**)

- Test the operating effectiveness of controls in preventing, or detecting and correcting, material misstatements at the assertion level (**tests of controls**)

- Detect material misstatements at the assertion level (**substantive procedures**)

The auditor must **always** perform **risk assessment procedures** to provide a satisfactory assessment of risks.

Tests of controls are necessary to test the controls to support the risk assessment, and also when substantive procedures alone do not provide sufficient appropriate audit evidence. **Substantive procedures** must **always** be carried out for **material** classes of transactions, account balances and disclosures.

The audit procedures described in the table below can be used as risk assessment procedures, tests of controls and substantive procedures.

Tests of controls are an audit procedure designed to evaluate the operating effectiveness of controls in preventing, or detecting and correcting, material misstatements at the assertion level.

Substantive procedures are audit procedures designed to detect material misstatements at the assertion level. Substantive procedures comprise:

(a)   Tests of details (of classes of transactions, account balances, and disclosures); and

(b)   Substantive analytical procedures

It is essential that you know the difference between a test of control and a substantive procedure. In recent examiner reports, the examining team noted a number of candidates lost marks because they did not understand the difference between these two fundamental types of procedure.

Auditors obtain evidence by one or more of the following procedures.

PROCEDURES	
Inspection of tangible assets	Inspection of tangible assets that are recorded in the accounting records confirms existence, but does not necessarily confirm rights and obligations or valuation.
	Confirmation that assets seen are recorded in accounting records gives evidence of completeness.
Inspection of documentation or records	This is the examination of documents and records, both internal and external, in paper, electronic or other forms. This procedure provides evidence of varying reliability, depending on the nature, source and effectiveness of controls over production (if internal). Inspection can provide evidence of existence (eg a document constituting a financial instrument), but not necessarily about ownership or value.
Observation	This involves watching a procedure or process being performed (for example, post opening). It is of limited use, as it only confirms the procedure took place when the auditor was watching, and because the act of being observed could affect how the procedure or process was performed.
Enquiry	This involves seeking information from client staff or external sources.
	Strength of evidence depends on the knowledge and integrity of source of information. Enquiry alone does not provide sufficient audit evidence to detect a material misstatement at assertion level, nor is it sufficient to test the operating effectiveness of controls.
Confirmation	This is the process of obtaining a representation of information or of an existing condition directly from a third party eg confirmation from bank of bank balances.
Recalculation	This consists of checking the mathematical accuracy of documents or records and can be performed through the use of IT.
Reperformance	This is the auditor's independent execution of procedures or controls that were originally performed as part of the entity's internal control.
Analytical procedures	Evaluating and comparing financial and/or non-financial data for plausible relationships. Also include the investigation of identified fluctuations and relationships that are inconsistent with other relevant information or deviate significantly from predicted amounts.

Read the article 'Audit procedures' which was published in *Student Accountant*. This helpful article provides tips on how to approach questions which require you to identify audit procedures. The article can be found via the Technical Articles link on the ACCA's website: www.accaglobal.com/gb/en/student/acca-qual-student-journey/qual-resource/acca-qualification/f8/technical-articles.html

(a) Discuss the quality of the following types of audit evidence, giving two examples of each form of evidence.

(i) Evidence originated by the auditors
(ii) Evidence created by third parties
(iii) Evidence created by the management of the client

(b) Describe the general considerations which auditors must bear in mind when evaluating audit evidence.

Answer

(a) **Quality of audit evidence**

(i) *Evidence originated by the auditors*

This is in general the most reliable type of audit evidence because there is little risk that it can be manipulated by management.

Examples

(1) Analytical procedures, such as the calculation of ratios and trends in order to examine unusual variations

(2) Physical inspection or observation, such as attendance at inventory counts

(3) Reperformance of calculations making up figures in the accounts, such as the computation of total inventory values

(ii) *Evidence created by third parties*

Third-party evidence is more reliable than client-produced evidence to the extent that it is obtained from independent sources. Its reliability will be reduced if it is obtained from sources which are not independent, or if there is a risk that client personnel may be able to and have reason to suppress or manipulate it.

Examples

(1) Circularisation of trade receivables or payables, confirmation of bank balances

(2) Reports produced by experts, such as property valuations, actuarial valuations, legal opinions; in evaluating such evidence, the auditors need to take into account the expert's qualifications, independence and the terms of reference for the work

(3) Documents held by the client which were issued by third parties, such as invoices, price lists and statements; these may sometimes be manipulated by the client and so are less reliable than confirmations received directly

(iii) *Evidence created by management*

The auditors cannot place the same degree of reliance on evidence produced by client management as on that produced outside the company. However, it will often be necessary to place some reliance on such evidence. The auditors will need to obtain audit evidence that the information supplied is complete and accurate, and apply judgement in doing so, taking into account previous experience of the client's reliability and the extent to which the client's representations appear compatible with other audit findings, as well as the materiality of the item under discussion.

Examples

(1) The company's accounting records and supporting schedules. Although these are prepared by management, the auditors have a statutory right to examine such records in full: this right enhances the quality of this information.

(2) The client's explanations of, for instance, apparently unusual fluctuations in results. Such evidence requires interpretation by the auditors and, being oral evidence, only limited reliance can be placed on it.

(3) Information provided to the auditors about the internal control system. The auditors need to confirm that this information is accurate and up-to-date, and that it does not simply describe an idealised system which is not adhered to in practice.

(b) **General considerations in evaluating audit evidence**

Audit evidence will often not be wholly conclusive. The auditors must obtain evidence which is **sufficient and appropriate** to form the basis for their audit conclusions. The evidence gathered should also be **relevant** to those conclusions, and sufficiently **reliable** to form the basis for the audit opinion. The auditors must exercise skill and judgement to ensure that evidence is correctly interpreted and that only valid inferences are drawn from it.

Certain general principles can be stated. **Written evidence** is preferable to oral evidence; **independent evidence** obtained from outside the organisation is more reliable than that obtained internally; and **evidence generated by the auditors** is more reliable than that obtained from others.

Chapter Roundup

- Auditors must design and perform audit procedures to obtain **sufficient appropriate** audit evidence.

- Audit tests are designed to obtain evidence about the **financial statement assertions**. Assertions relate to **classes of transactions and events and related disclosures and account balances at the period end and related disclosures**.

- Audit evidence can be obtained by inspection, observation, enquiry and confirmation, recalculation, reperformance and analytical procedures.

Quick Quiz

1   Define sufficiency and appropriateness as they relate to audit evidence.

2   State the financial statement assertions.

3   Fill in the blanks.

    Audit evidence from external sources is .... than that obtained from the entity's records.

4   State five procedures which auditors can use to obtain audit evidence.

5   Explain what 'reperformance' is.

Answers to Quick Quiz

1   Sufficiency is the measure of the quantity of audit evidence.

     Appropriateness is the measure of the quality/reliability of audit evidence.

2   Existence, rights and obligations, occurrence, completeness, valuation, accuracy, classification and understandability, cut-off, allocation.

3   More reliable

4   Any five from:

     Inspection
     Observation
     Enquiry
     Confirmation
     Recalculation
     Reperformance
     Analytical procedures

5   'Reperformance' is the auditor's independent execution of procedures or controls that were originally performed as part of the entity's internal control.

Now try the question below from the Practice Question Bank

Number	Level	Marks	Time
Q14	Examination	10	20 mins

Internal control

Internal control

Topic list	Syllabus reference
1 Internal control systems	C1, D2
2 The use of internal control systems by auditors	C1, C2
3 The evaluation of internal control components	C2, C4
4 Internal controls in a computerised environment	C3

Introduction

The auditor generally seeks to rely on the internal controls within the entity in order to reduce the amount of substantive testing.

The initial evaluation of a client's system is essential as the auditor gains an understanding of the entity, as we outlined in Chapter 6. In this chapter, we shall look at some of the detailed requirements of ISA 315 with regard to internal controls, and shall also set out control issues the auditor may come across.

The auditor will assess the risks of material misstatement arising and, as we discussed in Chapter 6, may respond to those risks by carrying out tests of controls. If they conclude that they can rely on the controls in place, the level of substantive audit testing required can be reduced.

In this chapter we also look at the ways in which auditors can document the internal control systems using narrative notes, flowcharts, questionnaires and checklists, focusing particularly on the use of questionnaires.

We shall examine the detailed controls that businesses operate in Chapter 10 and the tests that the auditors may carry out in specific areas. You should bear in mind the principles discussed in this chapter when considering the controls needed over specific accounting areas.

Study guide

		Intellectual level
C1	**Internal control systems**	
(a)	Explain why an auditor needs to obtain an understanding of internal control relevant to the audit.	1
(b)	Describe and explain the five components of an internal control system: the control environment; the entity's risk assessment process; the information system, including related business processes relevant to financial reporting and communication; control activities relevant to the audit; and monitoring of controls.	2
C2	**The use and evaluation of internal control systems by auditors**	
(a)	Explain how auditors record internal control systems including the use of narrative notes, flowcharts, internal control questionnaires and internal control evaluation questionnaires.	2
(b)	Evaluate internal control components, including deficiencies and significant deficiencies in internal control.	2
(c)	Discuss the limitations of internal control components.	2
C3	**Tests of control**	
(a)	Describe computer system controls, including general IT controls and application controls.	2
C4	**Communication on internal control**	
(a)	Discuss the requirements and methods of how reporting significant deficiencies in internal control are provided to management and those charged with governance.	2
(b)	Explain, in a format suitable for inclusion in a report to management, significant deficiencies within an internal control system and provide recommendations for overcoming these deficiencies to management.	2
D2	**Audit procedures**	
(d)	Describe why smaller entities may have different control environments and describe the types of evidence likely to be available in smaller entities.	1
(e)	Discuss the difference between tests of control and substantive procedures.	2

Exam guide

Questions on internal control are highly likely to come up in a scenario-based setting focusing on control procedures in a given system or asking you to describe deficiencies in the system of internal control, together with recommendations of internal controls to mitigate those deficiencies.

Other topics likely to be examined include:

(a)   Explaining the components of an entity's system of internal control

(b)   Describing the methods for documenting and evaluating systems of internal control and discussing the advantages and disadvantages of each

(c)   Explaining the controls expected to be in place in a wages system / in respect of cash / in respect of purchases / in respect of non-current assets

(d)   Describing matters to consider in evaluating the control environment in different types of organisations (including charitable organisations)

The above can also be examined in the form of mini-case OTQs in Section A of the exam.

This Chapter also forms the foundation for tests of controls, which we will look at in Chapter 10 and which features in nearly every F8 exam.

1 Internal control systems

FAST FORWARD

> The auditors must **understand** the **accounting system** and **control environment** in order to determine their audit approach.

Key term

> **Internal control** is the process designed, implemented and maintained by those charged with governance, management, and other personnel to provide reasonable assurance about the achievement of the entity's objectives with regard to reliability of financial reporting, effectiveness and efficiency of operations, and compliance with applicable laws and regulations.

An understanding of internal control assists the auditor in identifying types of potential misstatements and factors that affect the risks of material misstatement, and in designing the **nature, timing and extent** of further audit procedures.

Initially, gaining an understanding of internal control helps auditors to determine which are **relevant to the audit**. ISA 315 (Revised) *Identifying and assessing the risks of material misstatement through understanding the entity and its environment* points out that there is a direct relationship between an entity's objectives and the controls it implements to provide reasonable assurance about their achievement. Many of these controls will relate to financial reporting, operations and compliance, but not all of the entity's objectives and controls will be relevant to the auditor's risk assessment.

Having determined which controls are relevant, and are adequately designed to aid in the prevention of material misstatements in the financial statements, the auditor can then decide whether it is more efficient to seek reliance on those controls and perform tests of controls in that area, or more efficient to perform substantive testing over that area.

If the controls are not adequately designed, the auditor needs to perform sufficient substantive testing over that financial statement area in light of the apparent lack of control and increased risk. Any deficiencies are noted and, where appropriate, these will be communicated to management (see Section 3.4).

ISA 315 (Revised) *Identifying and assessing the risks of material misstatement through understanding the entity and its environment* deals with the whole area of controls.

Internal control has **five components**:

- The control environment
- The entity's risk assessment process
- The information system relevant to financial reporting
- Control activities
- Monitoring of controls

Exam focus point

> *Student Accountant* published an article focusing on the components of internal control under ISA 315 (Revised). This article can be found via the Technical Articles link on the ACCA's website: www.accaglobal.com/gb/en/student/acca-qual-student-journey/qual-resource/acca-qualification/f8/technical-articles.html.

In obtaining an understanding of internal control, the auditor must understand the **design** of the internal control and the **implementation** of that control. In the following sub-sections, we look at each of the elements of internal control in turn.

1.1 Control environment

The control environment is the framework within which controls operate. The control environment is very much determined by the management of a business.

> **Control environment** includes the governance and management functions and the attitudes, awareness and actions of those charged with governance and management concerning the entity's internal control and its importance in the entity.

A strong control environment does not, by itself, ensure the effectiveness of the overall internal control system, but can be a positive factor when assessing the risks of material misstatement. A weak control environment can undermine the effectiveness of controls.

Aspects of the control environment (such as management attitudes towards control) will nevertheless be a significant factor in determining how controls operate. Controls are more likely to operate well in an environment where they are treated as being important. In addition, consideration of the control environment will mean determining whether certain controls (internal auditors, budgets) actually exist.

ISA 315 states that auditors shall have an understanding of the control environment. As part of this understanding, the auditor shall evaluate whether:

(a)   Management has created and maintained a culture of honesty and ethical behaviour.

(b)   The strengths in the control environment provide an appropriate foundation for the other components of internal control and whether those components are not undermined by deficiencies in the control environment.

The following table illustrates the elements of the control environment that may be relevant when obtaining an understanding of the control environment.

CONTROL ENVIRONMENT	
Communication and enforcement of integrity and ethical values	Essential elements which influence the effectiveness of the design, administration and monitoring of controls
Commitment to competence	Management's consideration of the competence levels for particular jobs and how those levels translate into requisite skills and knowledge
Participation by those charged with governance	• Independence from management • Experience and stature • Extent of involvement and scrutiny of activities • Appropriateness of actions and interaction with internal and external auditors
Management's philosophy and operating style	• Approach to taking and managing business risks • Attitudes and actions towards financial reporting • Attitudes towards information processing and accounting functions and personnel
Organisational structure	The framework within which an entity's activities for achieving its objectives are planned, executed, controlled and reviewed
Assignment of authority and responsibility	How authority and responsibility for operating activities are assigned and how reporting relationships and authorisation hierarchies are established
Human resource policies and practices	Recruitment, orientation, training, evaluating, counselling, promoting, compensation and remedial actions

The auditor shall assess whether these elements of the control environment have been implemented using a combination of **enquiries of management** and **observation** and **inspection**.

> The audit examining team has written an article entitled 'The Control Environment of a Company' in *Student Accountant*, focusing on the matters which auditors should consider when assessing the effectiveness of the control environment of a large limited liability company (UK – limited company). This article can be accessed via the Technical Articles link on the ACCA's website: www.accaglobal.com/gb/en/student/acca-qual-student-journey/qual-resource/acca-qualification/f8/technical-articles.html.

1.2 Entity's risk assessment process

ISA 315 says the auditor shall obtain an understanding of whether the entity has a process for:

- Identifying business risks relevant to financial reporting objectives
- Estimating the significance of the risks
- Assessing the likelihood of their occurrence
- Deciding on actions to address those risks

If the entity has established such a process, the auditor shall obtain an understanding of it. If there is not a process, the auditor shall discuss with management whether relevant business risks have been identified and how they have been addressed.

1.3 Information system relevant to financial reporting

> The **information system relevant to financial reporting** is a component of internal control that includes the financial reporting system, and consists of the procedures and records established to initiate, record, process and report entity transactions (as well as events and conditions) and to maintain accountability for the related assets, liabilities and equity.

The auditor shall obtain an understanding of the information system relevant to financial reporting objectives, including the following areas:

- The classes of transactions in the entity's operations that are significant to the financial statements

- The procedures, within both IT and manual systems, by which those transactions are initiated, recorded, processed, corrected, transferred to the general ledger and reported in the financial statements

- The related accounting records, supporting information and specific accounts in the financial statements, in respect of initiating, recording, processing and reporting transactions

- How the information system captures events and conditions, other than transactions, that are significant to the financial statements

- The financial reporting process used to prepare the entity's financial statements, including significant accounting estimates and disclosures

- Controls surrounding journal entries, including non-standard journal entries used to record non-recurring, unusual transactions or adjustments

The auditor shall obtain an understanding of how the entity **communicates** financial reporting roles and responsibilities and significant matters relating to financial reporting.

Conforming amendments to ISA 315 published in 2015 point out that as well as understanding how information is obtained from within the general and subsidiary ledgers, auditors must gain an understanding of the system relating to **information obtained outside of the ledgers**. Such information may include information disclosed in the financial statements, which has been derived from:

- Lease agreements disclosed in the financial statements

- The entity's risk management system

- Fair value reports produced by management's experts

- Calculations and models developed about accounting estimates, including internal assumptions about assets' useful lives and external interest rates

- Sensitivity analyses performed by management to consider alternative assumptions

- The entity's tax records

- Analyses to support management's assessment of the going concern assumption.

1.4 Control activities

> **Control activities** are those policies and procedures that help ensure that management directives are carried out.

ISA 315 states that the auditor shall obtain an understanding of control activities relevant to the audit and how the entity has responded to risks arising from IT.

Control activities include those activities designed to **prevent** or to **detect** and **correct errors**. Examples include activities relating to authorisation, performance reviews, information processing, physical controls and segregation of duties.

Examples of control activities

Example	Explanation	Category
Approval and control of documents	Transactions should be approved by an appropriate person. For example, overtime should be approved by departmental managers.	Authorisation
Controls over computerised applications	We shall look at computer controls later in this chapter.	Information processing
Checking the arithmetical accuracy of records	For example, checking to see if individual invoices have been added up correctly.	Information processing
Maintaining and reviewing control accounts and trial balances	Control accounts bring together transactions in individual ledgers. Trial balances bring together transactions for the organisation as a whole. Preparing these can highlight unusual transactions or accounts.	Performance review
Reconciliations	Reconciliations involve comparison of a specific balance in the accounting records with what another source says the balance should be; for example, a bank reconciliation. Differences between the two figures should only be reconciling items (resulting from eg timing differences).	Information processing
Comparing the results of cash, security and inventory counts with accounting records	For example, in a physical count of petty cash, the balance shown in the cash book should be the same as the amount held.	Performance review
Comparing internal data with external sources of information	For example, comparing records of goods despatched to customers with customers' acknowledgement of goods that have been received.	Performance review
Limiting physical access to assets and records	Only authorised personnel should have access to certain assets (particularly valuable or portable ones), eg ensuring that the inventory stores locked are unless store personnel are there.	Physical control
Segregation of duties	Assigning different people the responsibility of authorising transactions, recording transactions and maintaining custody of assets	Segregation of duties

1.4.1 Segregation of duties

Segregation implies a **number of people** being involved in the accounting process. This makes it more difficult for fraudulent transactions to be processed (since a number of people would have to collude in the fraud), and it is also more difficult for accidental errors to be processed (since the more people are involved, the more checking there can be). Segregation should take place in various ways:

(a) **Segregation of function.** The key functions that should be segregated are the **carrying out** of a transaction, **recording** that transaction in the accounting records and **maintaining custody** of assets that arise from the transaction.

(b) The various **steps** in carrying out the transaction should also be segregated. We shall see how this works in practice when we look at the major transaction cycles in Chapter 10.

(c) The **carrying out** of various **accounting operations** should be segregated. For example, the same staff should not record transactions and carry out the reconciliations at the period end.

1.5 Monitoring of controls

Key term

> **Monitoring of controls** is a process to assess the effectiveness of internal control performance over time. It includes assessing the design and operation of controls on a timely basis and taking necessary corrective actions modified for changes in conditions.

The auditor shall obtain an understanding of the major activities that the entity uses to monitor internal control over financial reporting, including those related to control activities relevant to the audit, and how the entity initiates corrective actions to deficiencies in its controls.

If the entity has an **internal audit function**, the auditor shall obtain an understanding of the **nature of its responsibilities**, its organisational status and the **activities** performed / to be performed.

The auditor shall also obtain an understanding of the **sources of the information** used in the monitoring activities and the **basis** on which management considers it reliable.

1.6 Small companies – the problem of control

Many of the controls which would be relevant to a large entity are neither practical nor appropriate for a small company which often have simple internal control systems. For a small company, the most important form of internal control is generally the **close involvement** of the **directors or proprietors**.

However, it is also important to note that close involvement by management will enable them to **override controls** and, if they wish, to **exclude transactions** from the records.

Auditors can also have difficulties, not because there is a general lack of controls but because the **evidence** available as to their operation and the completeness of the records is **insufficient**. For example, an owner-manager may well perform an independent review of payroll records, but will not sign and date to indicate the review has taken place, and may not document the investigation of anomalies or how problems were resolved. Therefore it is very difficult for the auditor to obtain evidence that a control is operating effectively, even if it is.

Segregation of duties will often appear inadequate in enterprises having a small number of staff. Similarly, because of the scale of the operation, organisation and management controls are likely to be rudimentary at best.

As discussed above, the onus is on the proprietor, by virtue of their day to day involvement, to compensate for this lack. This involvement should encompass physical, authorisation, arithmetical and accounting controls as well as supervision.

Where the manager of a small business is not the owner, the manager may not possess the same degree of commitment to the running of it as an owner-manager would. In such cases, the auditors will have to consider the adequacy of controls exercised by the shareholders over the manager in assessing internal control.

1.6.1 Evidence available in relation to internal control in small companies

We discussed above the fact that audit evidence for elements of the control environment in smaller entities may not be available in documentary form, in particular where communication between management and other personnel may be informal but effective. However, although not documented, small companies may develop a culture that emphasises the importance of integrity and ethical behaviour through verbal

communication and where management sets a good example. As a result, the attitudes, awareness and actions of management are very important to the auditor's understanding of a smaller entity's control environment.

Although size and economic considerations in smaller entities often reduce the opportunity for formal control activities, there is still likely to be some evidence available in relation to internal controls. Some basic control activities are likely to exist for the main transaction cycles, such as revenues, purchases and payroll costs.

In a small company, often management's sole authority for approval of, for example, purchases and payments can provide strong control over important account balances and the auditor can seek to test and rely on these controls. These key controls lessen or remove the need for more detailed control activities and if the auditor can gain enough evidence that these key controls are operating effectively substantive testing can be reduced.

However, because of the factors discussed in the preceding section, the auditor will often choose or be forced to turn to substantive procedures to gain sufficient appropriate audit evidence when auditing a smaller entity. This can often mean use of:

- Confirmations
- Agreeing samples related to different financial statement areas to source documents
- Analytical procedures where these are considered suitable

1.7 Limitations of accounting and control systems

Any internal control system can only provide the directors with **reasonable assurance** that their objectives are reached, because of **inherent limitations**. These include:

- The **costs** of control **not outweighing** their **benefits**
- The potential for **human error**
- **Collusion** between employees
- The possibility of **controls** being **bypassed** or **overridden** by management
- Controls being **designed to cope** with **routine** and **not non-routine transactions**

These factors demonstrate why auditors cannot obtain all their evidence from tests of the systems of internal control. The key factors in the limitations of control systems are **human error** and **potential for fraud**.

The safeguard of segregation of duties can help deter fraud. However, if employees decide to perpetrate frauds by collusion, or management commit fraud by overriding systems, the accounting system will not be able to prevent such frauds.

This is one of the reasons why auditors always need to be alert to the possibility of fraud, the subject of ISA 240, which was discussed in Chapter 6.

| Question | Internal control systems |

An internal control system has been described as comprising 'the control environment and control activities. It includes all the policies and procedures (internal controls) adopted by the directors and management of an entity to assist in achieving their objective of ensuring, as far as practicable, the orderly and efficient conduct of its business, including adherence to internal policies, the safeguarding of assets, the prevention and detection of fraud and error, the accuracy and completeness of the accounting records, and the timely preparation of reliable financial information'.

Explain the meaning and relevance to the auditors giving an opinion on financial statements of each of the management objectives above.

The auditors' objective in evaluating and testing internal controls is to determine the degree of reliance which they may place on the information contained in the accounting records. If they obtain reasonable assurance by means of tests of controls that the internal control system is effective in ensuring the completeness and accuracy of the accounting records, they may limit their substantive procedures.

(a)   *'The orderly and efficient conduct of its business'*

An organisation that is efficient and conducts its affairs in an orderly manner is much more likely to be able to supply the auditors with sufficient appropriate audit evidence on which to base their audit opinion. More importantly, the level of inherent and control risk will be lower, giving extra assurance that the financial statements do not contain material errors.

(b)   *'Adherence to internal policies'*

Management is responsible for setting up an effective system of internal control and management policy provides the broad framework within which internal controls have to operate. Unless management does have a pre-determined set of policies, then it is very difficult to imagine how the company could be expected to operate efficiently. Management policy will cover all aspects of the company's activities, ranging from broad corporate objectives to specific areas such as wage rates.

Given that the auditors must have a sound understanding of the company's affairs generally, and of specific areas of control in particular, then the fact that management policies are followed will make the task of the auditors easier in that they will be able to rely more readily on the information produced by the systems established by management.

(c)   *'Safeguarding of assets'*

This objective may relate to the physical protection of assets (for example locking cash in a safe at night) or to less direct safeguarding (for example ensuring that there is adequate insurance cover for all assets). It can also be seen as relating to the maintenance of proper records in respect of all assets.

The auditors will be concerned with ensuring that the company has properly safeguarded its assets so that they can form an opinion on the existence of specific assets and whether the company's records can be taken as a reliable basis for the preparation of financial statements. Reliance on the underlying records will be particularly significant where the figures in the financial statements are derived from such records rather than as the result of physical inspection.

(d)   *'Prevention and detection of fraud and error'*

The directors are responsible for taking reasonable steps to prevent and detect fraud. They are also responsible for preparing financial statements which give a true and fair view of the entity's affairs. However, the auditors must plan and perform their audit procedures and evaluate and report the results of these, recognising that fraud or error may materially affect the financial statements. A strong system of internal control will give the auditors some assurance that frauds and errors are not occurring, unless management are colluding to overcome that system.

(e)   *'Accuracy and completeness of the accounting records' / 'timely preparation of reliable financial information'*

This objective is most clearly related to statutory requirements relating to both management and auditors. The company generally has legal obligations to maintain proper accounting records. The auditors must form an opinion on whether the company has fulfilled these obligations and also conclude whether the financial statements agree with the underlying records.

2 The use of internal control systems by auditors   June 08

> The auditors shall assess the **adequacy** of the systems as a basis for the financial statements and shall identify **risks** of material misstatements to provide a basis for designing and performing further audit procedures.

Auditors are only concerned with assessing policies and procedures which are relevant to the financial statements. Auditors shall:

- **Assess the adequacy** of the accounting system as a basis for preparing the accounts
- **Identify** the types of **potential misstatements** that could occur in the accounts
- **Consider factors** that affect the **risk of misstatements**
- **Design appropriate audit procedures**

We have discussed the process of assessing the risks of material misstatement in Chapter 6. The assessment of the controls of an entity will have an impact on that risk assessment.

Risks arising from **poor control environments** are unlikely to be confined to particular assertions in the financial statements, and, if severe, may even raise questions about whether the financial statements are capable of being audited; that is, if control risk is so high that audit risk cannot be reduced to an acceptable level.

On the other hand, some **control procedures** may be closely connected to an assertion in financial statements; for example, controls over the inventory count are closely connected with the existence and completeness of inventory in the financial statements.

There may be occasions where substantive procedures alone are not sufficient to address the risks arising. Where such risks exist, auditors shall **evaluate the design** and **determine the implementation** of the controls; that is, by **controls testing**. This is most likely to be the case in a system which is highly computerised and which does not require much manual intervention.

2.1 Recording accounting and control systems   June 11, Dec 13

> The auditors must keep a record of the client's systems which must be updated each year. This can be done through the use of narrative notes, flowcharts, questionnaires or checklists.

There are several techniques for recording the assessment of control risk; that is, the system. One or more of the following may be used depending on the complexity of the system.

- Narrative notes   - Questionnaires
- Flowcharts   - Checklists

We look at each of these methods throughout the rest of Section 2, including the benefits and limitations of each.

In respect of questionnaires, you should note that there are two types, each with a different purpose.

(a)   **Internal Control Questionnaires (ICQs)** are used to ask whether controls exist which meet specific control objectives.

(b)   **Internal Control Evaluation Questionnaires (ICEQs)** are used to determine whether there are controls which prevent or detect specified errors or omissions.

The specific controls for each major transaction system (sales, purchases, inventory, cash, payroll, revenue and capital expenditure) are examined in detail in Chapter 10. However, some are also included in the examples included in Sections 2.1.3 and 2.1.4 for the purposes of illustrating how ICQs and ICEQs are used to record internal control systems. Whatever method of recording is used, the record will usually be retained on the permanent file and updated each year.

2.1.1 Narrative notes

The purpose of narrative notes is to **describe** and **explain** the **system**, at the same time as making any comments or criticisms which will help to demonstrate an intelligent understanding of the system.

Narrative notes	
Advantages	**Disadvantages**
They are relatively simple to record and can facilitate understanding by all audit team members.	Describing something in narrative notes can be a lot more time consuming than, say, representing it as a simple flowchart, particularly where the system follows a logical flow.
They can be used for any system due to the method's flexibility.	They are awkward to update if written manually.
Editing in future years can be relatively easy if they are computerised.	It can be difficult to identify missing internal controls because notes record the detail of systems but may not identify control exceptions clearly.

2.1.2 Flowcharts

Flowcharts can take many forms, but in general are graphic illustrations of the physical flow of information through the accounting system. Flowlines represent the sequences of processes, and other symbols represent the inputs and outputs to a process. An example of an accounts receivable flowchart follows.

Accounts Receivable

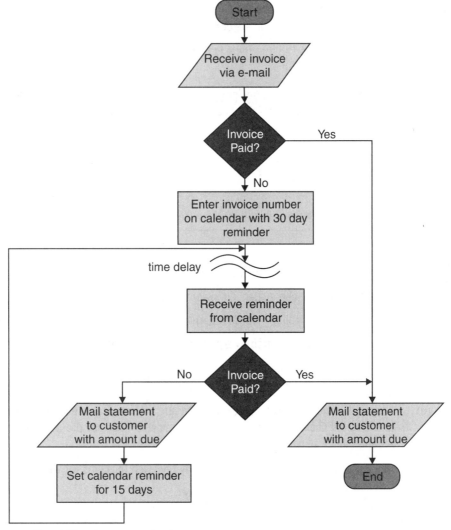

Source: www.rff.com/flowchart_samples.htm

Flowcharts have certain advantages and disadvantages.

Advantages
After a little experience they can be prepared quickly.
As the information is presented in a standard form, they are fairly easy to follow and review.
They generally ensure that the system is recorded in its entirety, as all document flows have to be traced from beginning to end. Any 'loose ends' will be apparent from a cursory examination.
They eliminate the need for extensive narrative and can be of considerable help in highlighting the salient points of control and any deficiencies in the system.

Disadvantages
They are most suitable for describing standard systems. Procedures for dealing with unusual transactions will normally have to be recorded using narrative notes.
Major amendment is difficult without redrawing.
Time can sometimes be wasted by charting areas that are of no audit significance.

2.1.3 Internal Control Questionnaires (ICQs)

The major question which ICQs are designed to answer is 'How good is the system of controls?'

Although there are many different forms of ICQ in practice, they all conform to the following basic principles.

(a) They **comprise a list of questions** designed to determine whether desirable controls are present (possible desirable controls are considered for each major transaction cycle in Chapter 10).

(b) They are formulated so that there is one list of questions to **cover each of the major transaction cycles**.

One of the most effective ways of designing the questionnaire is to phrase the questions so that all the answers can be given as 'YES' or 'NO' and a 'NO' answer indicates a deficiency in the system. An example would be:

Are purchase invoices checked to goods received notes before being passed for payment?	YES/NO/Comments

The ICQ questions below dealing with goods inward provide additional illustrations of the ICQ approach.

Goods inward

(a) Are supplies examined on arrival as to quantity and quality?

(b) Is such an examination evidenced in some way?

(c) Is the receipt of supplies recorded, perhaps by means of goods inward notes?

(d) Are receipt records prepared by a person independent of those responsible for:

    (i) Ordering functions?
    (ii) The processing and recording of invoices?

(e) Are goods inward records controlled to ensure that invoices are obtained for all goods received and to enable the liability for unbilled goods to be determined (by pre-numbering the records and accounting for all serial numbers)?

(f) (i) Are goods inward records regularly reviewed for items for which no invoices have been received?

    (ii) Are any such items investigated?

2.1.4 Internal Control Evaluation Questionnaires (ICEQs)

In recent years, many auditing firms have developed and implemented an evaluation technique more concerned with assessing whether specific errors (or frauds) are possible, rather than establishing whether certain desirable controls are present. This is achieved by reducing the control criteria for each transaction stream down to a handful of **key questions** (or control questions). The characteristic of these questions is that they concentrate on the significant errors or omissions that could occur at each phase of the appropriate cycle if controls are weak.

The nature of the key questions may best be understood by reference to the example below relating to the purchases (expenditure) cycle.

Internal control evaluation questionnaire: control questions

The purchases (expenditure) cycle

Is there reasonable assurance that:

(a)   Goods or services could not be received without a liability being recorded?

(b)   Receipt of goods or services is required in order to establish a liability?

(c)   A liability will be recorded:

    (i)   Only for authorised items?
    (ii)   At the proper amount?

(d)   All payments are properly authorised?

(e)   All credits due from suppliers are received?

(f)   All transactions are properly accounted for?

(g)   At the period end liabilities are neither overstated nor understated by the system?

(h)   The balance at the bank is properly recorded at all times?

(i)   Unauthorised cash payments could not be made and that the balance of petty cash is correctly stated at all times?

Each key control question is supported by detailed control points to be considered. For example, the detailed control points to be considered in relation to key control question (b) for the expenditure cycle (Is there reasonable assurance that receipt of goods or services is required to establish a liability?) are as follows.

---

(1)   Is segregation of duties satisfactory?

(2)   Are controls over relevant master files satisfactory?

(3)   Is there a record that all goods received have been checked for:

- Weight or number?
- Quality and damage?

(4)   Are all goods received taken on charge in the detailed inventory ledgers:

- By means of the goods received note (GRN)?
- Or by means of purchase invoices?
- Are there, in a computerised system, sensible control totals (hash totals, monetary values and so on) to reconcile the inventory system input with the payables system?

(5)   Are all invoices initialled to show that:

- Receipt of goods has been checked against the goods received records?
- Receipt of services has been verified by the person using it?
- Quality of goods has been checked against the inspection?

(6) In a computerised invoice approval system are there printouts (examined by a responsible person) of:

- Cases where order, GRN and invoice are present but they are not equal ('equal' within predetermined tolerances of minor discrepancies)?
- Cases where invoices have been input but there is no corresponding GRN?

(7) Is there adequate control over direct purchases?

(8) Are receiving documents effectively cancelled (for example cross-referenced) to prevent their supporting two invoices?

Alternatively, ICEQ questions can be phrased so that the deficiency which should be prevented by a key control is highlighted, such as the following.

Question	Answer	Comments or explanation of 'yes' answer
Can goods be sent to unauthorised suppliers?		

In these cases a 'yes' answer would require an explanation, rather than a 'no' answer.

2.1.5 Advantages and disadvantages of ICQs and ICEQs

ICQs and ICEQs	
Advantages	**Disadvantages**
If drafted thoroughly, they can ensure **all controls** are **considered**.	The principal disadvantage is that they can be **drafted vaguely**, hence **misunderstood** and important controls not identified.
They are **quick** to **prepare**.	They may contain a large number of **irrelevant controls**.
They are **easy** to **use** and **control**.	They may not include **unusual controls**, which are nevertheless effective in particular circumstances.
Because they are drafted in terms of **objectives** rather than specific controls, **ICEQs** are easier to apply to a variety of systems than **ICQs**.	They can give the impression that all controls are of **equal** weight. In many systems one NO answer (for example lack of segregation of duties) will cancel out a string of YES answers.
Answering ICEQs should enable auditors to **identify the key controls** which they are most likely to test during control testing.	The client may be able to **overstate controls**.
ICEQs can **highlight deficiencies** where extensive substantive testing will be required.	

2.1.6 Checklists

Checklists may be used instead of questionnaires to document and evaluate the internal control system. The subtle difference with these is that, instead of asking questions, statements are made to 'mark off' and tick boxes are used to indicate where the statement holds true. For example, a checklist may state 'Supplies are examined on arrival as to quantity and quality' which would be ticked if this does actually occur, or crossed if not. Checklists share many of the same advantages and disadvantages of ICQs and ICEQs.

3 The evaluation of internal control components June 10

If the auditors believe the system of controls is strong, they may choose to test controls to assess whether they can rely on the controls having operated effectively.

3.1 Confirming understanding

In order to confirm their understanding of the control systems, auditors will often carry out **walk-through tests**. This is where they pick up a transaction and follow it through the system to see whether all the controls they anticipate should be in existence were in operation with regard to that transaction.

3.2 Tests of control

Key term

Tests of control are tests performed to obtain audit evidence about the effectiveness of the:

- Design of the accounting and internal control systems, ie whether they are suitably designed to prevent, or detect and correct, material misstatement at the assertion level; and

- Operation of the internal controls throughout the period.

Tests of control are distinguished from substantive tests which are designed to detect material misstatements in the financial statements.

Tests of control may include the following.

(a) **Inspection of documents** supporting controls or events to gain audit evidence that internal controls have operated properly, eg verifying that a transaction has been authorised

(b) **Enquiries about internal controls** which leave no audit trail, eg determining who actually performs each function, not merely who is supposed to perform it

(c) **Reperformance of control procedures**, eg reconciliation of bank accounts, to ensure they were correctly performed by the entity

(d) **Examination of evidence of management views**, eg minutes of management meetings

(e) Testing of internal controls operating on **computerised systems** or over the overall IT function, eg access controls

(f) **Observation of controls** to consider the manner in which the control is being operated

Auditors should consider:

- **How** controls were applied
- The **consistency** with which they were applied during the period
- **By whom** they were applied

Deviations in the operation of controls (caused by change of staff etc) may increase control risk and tests of control may need to be modified to confirm effective operation during and after any change.

The use of **computer-assisted audit techniques** (CAATs) may be appropriate and these are discussed in detail in Chapter 11.

In a continuing engagement, the auditor will be aware of the accounting and internal control systems through work carried out previously but will need to update the knowledge gained and consider the need to obtain further audit evidence of any changes in control.

3.3 Revision of risk assessment, audit strategy and audit plan

The auditors may find that the evidence they obtain from controls testing indicates that controls did not operate as well as they expected. If the evidence contradicts the original risk assessment, the auditors will have to amend the further procedures they have planned to carry out.

In particular, if controls testing reveals that controls have not operated effectively throughout the year, the auditor may have to extend substantive testing.

Revising the risk assessment and audit procedures will necessitate an update of the audit strategy, which sets out the scope, timing and direction of the audit. For example, if tests of controls highlight that many controls are not operating as expected, this may lead to an increase in the strategy's emphasis on substantive procedures.

The new or changed procedures will need to be reflected on the audit plan, which, as we saw in Chapter 7, details the nature, timing and extent of audit procedures to be performed.

3.4 Communication of deficiencies in internal control   Dec 10

Significant deficiencies in internal controls shall be communicated in writing to those charged with governance in a **report to management** in accordance with ISA 265 *Communicating deficiencies in internal control to those charged with governance and management* which states that the objective of the auditor is to communicate appropriately to those charged with governance and management deficiencies in internal control identified during the audit which the auditor considers are of sufficient importance to warrant their attention.

We will look at an example report to management in more detail in Chapter 19, but in this section we will discuss the requirements of ISA 265.

Key terms

> A **deficiency in internal control** exists when:
>
> (a)   A control is designed, implemented or operated in such a way that it is unable to prevent, or detect and correct, misstatements in the financial statements on a timely basis; or
>
> (b)   A control necessary to prevent, or detect and correct, misstatements in the financial statements on a timely basis is missing.
>
> A **significant deficiency in internal control** is a deficiency or combination of deficiencies in internal control that, in the auditor's professional judgment, is of sufficient importance to merit the attention of those charged with governance.

ISA 265 requires the auditor to determine whether one or more deficiencies in internal control have been identified and, if so, whether these constitute significant deficiencies in internal control. The significance of a deficiency depends on whether a misstatement has occurred and also on the likelihood of a misstatement occurring and its potential magnitude. ISA 265 includes examples of matters to consider when determining whether a deficiency in internal control is a significant deficiency.

- The **likelihood** of the deficiencies resulting in material misstatements in the financial statements in the future

- The **susceptibility to loss or fraud** of the related asset or liability

- The **subjectivity and complexity** of determining estimated amounts

- The **amounts** exposed to the deficiencies

- The **volume of activity** that has occurred or could occur

- The **importance of the controls** to the financial reporting process

- The **cause and frequency** of the exceptions identified as a result of the deficiencies

- The **interaction** of the deficiency with other deficiencies in internal control

The ISA also lists examples of indicators of significant deficiencies in internal control, which include the following:

- Evidence of **ineffective aspects** of the control environment

- Absence of a **risk assessment process**

- Evidence of an **ineffective entity risk assessment process**

- Evidence of an **ineffective response to identified significant risks**

- **Misstatements** detected by the auditor's procedures that were not prevented, or detected and corrected, by the entity's internal control

- **Restatement** of previously issued financial statements that were corrected for a material misstatement due to fraud or error

- Evidence of **management's inability to oversee** the preparation of the financial statements.

The auditor shall communicate any significant deficiencies in internal control to **those charged with governance** on a timely basis. The auditor shall also communicate in writing to **management** on a timely basis significant deficiencies in internal control that the auditor has communicated or intends to communicate to those charged with governance and other deficiencies in internal control that have not been communicated to management by other parties and that the auditor considers are of sufficient importance to warrant management's attention. The communication to management of other deficiencies in internal control can be done orally.

The auditor shall include the following in the written communication:

(a)   A **description** of the deficiencies and an explanation of their **potential effects** (but there is no need to quantify the effects)

(b)   **Sufficient information** to enable those charged with governance and management to understand the context of the communication, in particular that:

  (i)   The purpose of the audit was for the auditor to express an opinion on the financial statements.

  (ii)   The audit included consideration of internal control relevant to the preparation of the financial statements in order to design audit procedures appropriate in the circumstances, but not to express an opinion on the effectiveness of internal control.

  (iii)   The matters being reported are limited to those deficiencies identified during the audit and which the auditor has concluded are sufficiently important to merit being reported to those charged with governance.

The auditor may also include suggestions for remedial action on the deficiencies, management's actual or proposed responses and a statement as to whether or not the auditor has undertaken any steps to verify whether management's responses have been implemented. In addition, the auditor may include the following information:

(a)   A statement that if the auditor had undertaken more extensive procedures on internal control, more deficiencies might have been identified or some of the reported deficiencies need not have been reported.

(b)   The written communication is for the purpose of those charged with governance and may not be suitable for other purposes.

3.4.1 Impact of deficiencies on the auditor's reliance on internal control

As we discussed in Section 1, if the controls are not adequately designed or not operating effectively, the auditor needs to revisit the risk assessment and design sufficient substantive testing over that financial statement area. Therefore, where significant deficiencies are identified, unless there are robust compensating controls, the auditor will have no choice but to use purely substantive procedures to obtain sufficient appropriate audit evidence. The auditor will not seek to place reliance on internal controls.

It may be that the deficiencies were not identified during planning and risk assessment, but only become apparent later in the audit process. If this is the case, and the original audit plan was based on a reliance on internal controls, that audit plan will need to be amended, with the likely result that further audit procedures will need to be performed.

4 Internal controls in a computerised environment

There are special considerations for auditors when a system is computerised. IT controls comprise **general** and **application** controls.

The internal controls in a computerised environment include both manual procedures and procedures designed into computer programs. Such control procedures comprise two types of control, **general controls** and **application controls**.

Key terms

General IT controls are policies and procedures that relate to many applications and support the effective functioning of application controls by helping to ensure the continued proper operation of information systems. General IT controls commonly include controls over data centre and network operations; system software acquisition, change and maintenance; access security; and application system acquisition, development and maintenance.

Application controls are manual or automated procedures that typically operate at a business process level. Application controls can be preventative or detective in nature and are designed to ensure the integrity of the accounting records. Accordingly, application controls relate to procedures used to initiate, record, process and report transactions or other financial data.

4.1 General controls

GENERAL CONTROLS	EXAMPLES
Development of computer applications	**Standards** over systems design, programming and documentation Full **testing procedures** using test data **Approval** by computer users and management **Segregation of duties** so that those responsible for design are not responsible for testing **Installation procedures** so that data is not corrupted in transition **Training** of staff in new procedures and availability of adequate **documentation**
Prevention or detection of unauthorised changes to programs	**Segregation of duties** **Full records** of program changes **Password protection** of programs so that access is limited to computer operations staff **Restricted access** to central computer by locked doors, keypads Maintenance of **programs logs** **Virus checks** on software: use of anti-virus software and policy prohibiting use of non-authorised programs or files **Back-up copies** of programs being taken and stored in other locations **Control copies** of programs being preserved and regularly compared with actual programs **Stricter controls** over certain programs (utility programs) by use of **read-only memory**
Testing and documentation of program changes	Complete **testing procedures** **Documentation standards** **Approval** of changes by computer users and management **Training** of staff using programs
Controls to prevent wrong programs or files being used	**Operation controls** over programs **Libraries** of programs **Proper job scheduling**

GENERAL CONTROLS	EXAMPLES
Controls to prevent unauthorised amendments to data files	**Password protection** **Restricted access** to authorised users only
Controls to ensure continuity of operation	Storing **extra copies** of programs and data files off-site **Protection of equipment** against fire and other hazards **Back-up power sources** **Disaster recovery procedures** eg availability of back-up computer facilities **Maintenance agreements** and **insurance**

The auditors will wish to test some or all of the above general IT controls, having considered how they affect the computer applications significant to the audit.

General IT controls that relate to some or all applications are usually interdependent controls, ie their operation is often essential to the effectiveness of application controls. As application controls may be useless when general controls are ineffective, it will be more efficient to review the design of general IT controls first, before reviewing the application controls.

4.2 Application controls

The purpose of application controls is to establish **specific control procedures** over the accounting applications in order to provide reasonable assurance that all transactions are authorised and recorded, and are processed completely, accurately and on a timely basis.

Application controls include the following.

APPLICATION CONTROLS	EXAMPLES
Controls over **input: completeness**	Manual or programmed agreement of **control totals** **Document counts** **One-for-one checking** of processed output to source documents **Programmed matching** of input to an expected input control file **Procedures** over resubmission of rejected controls
Controls over **input: accuracy**	**Programmes to check data** fields (for example value, reference number, date) on input transactions for plausibility: • Digit verification (eg reference numbers are as expected) • Reasonableness test (eg sales tax to total value) • Existence checks (eg customer name) • Character checks (no unexpected characters used in reference) • Necessary information (no transaction passed with gaps) • Permitted range (no transaction processed over a certain value) **Manual scrutiny** of output and reconciliation to source Agreement of **control totals** (manual/programmed)
Controls over **input: authorisation**	**Manual checks** to ensure information input was: • Authorised • Input by authorised personnel
Controls over **processing**	Similar controls to input must be in place when input is completed; for example, **batch reconciliations** **Screen warnings** can prevent people logging out before processing is complete

APPLICATION CONTROLS	EXAMPLES
Controls over **master files and standing data**	**One-for-one checking** **Cyclical reviews** of all master files and standing data **Record counts** (number of documents processed) and **hash totals** (for example, the total of all the payroll numbers) used when master files are used to ensure no deletions **Controls** over the deletion of accounts that have no current balance

Controls over input, processing, data files and output may be carried out by IT personnel, users of the system and a separate control group and may be programmed into application software. The auditors may wish to test the following application controls.

TESTING OF APPLICATION CONTROLS	
Manual controls exercised by the user	If manual controls exercised by the user of the application system are capable of providing reasonable assurance that the system's output is complete, accurate and authorised, the auditors may decide to limit tests of control to these manual controls.
Controls over system output	If, in addition to manual controls exercised by the user, the controls to be tested use information produced by the computer or are contained within computer programs, such controls may be tested by examining the system's output using either manual procedures or computers. Such output may be in the form of magnetic media, microfilm or printouts. Alternatively, the auditor may test the control by performing it with the use of computers.
Programmed control procedures	In the case of certain computer systems, the auditor may find that it is not possible or, in some cases, not practical to test controls by examining only user controls or the system's output. The auditor may consider performing tests of control by using computers, reprocessing transaction data or, in unusual situations, examining the coding of the application program.

As we have already noted, general IT controls may have a pervasive effect on the processing of transactions in application systems. If these general controls are not effective, there may be a risk that misstatements occur and go undetected in the application systems. Although weaknesses in general IT controls may preclude testing certain IT application controls, it is possible that manual procedures exercised by users may provide effective control at the **application level**.

Chapter Roundup

- The auditors must **understand** the **accounting system** and **control environment** in order to determine their audit approach.

- The auditors shall assess the **adequacy** of the systems as a basis for the financial statements and shall identify **risks** of material misstatements to provide a basis for designing and performing further audit procedures.

- The auditors must keep a record of the client's systems which must be updated each year. This can be done through the use of narrative notes, flowcharts, questionnaires or checklists.

- If the auditors believe the system of controls is strong, they may choose to test controls to assess whether they can rely on the controls having operated effectively.

- There are special considerations for auditors when a system is computerised. IT controls comprise **general** and **application** controls.

Quick Quiz

1   Complete the definition taking the words given below.

The .... includes the governance and management functions and
the..............., ... and .... of those charged with .... and management
concerning the entity's internal .... and its .... in the entity.

| attitudes | importance | control | environment | awareness | governance | actions | control |

2   Name two **key** inherent limitations of an internal control system.

1   ....

2   ....

3   Put the controls below in the correct category.

Application controls	General controls

One-for-one checking	Virus checks	Hash totals
Segregation of duties	Passwords	Program libraries
Review of master files	Training	Controls over account deletions
Back-up copies	Record counts	Back-up power source

4   Which of the following is not a test of control?

A   Inspection of documents
B   Reperformance of control procedures
C   Observation of controls
D   Verification of value to invoice

5   After the controls have been assessed, the audit plan may be modified.

True   ☐

False   ☐

1   Control environment, attitudes, awareness, actions, governance, control, importance

2   Human error

    Possibility of staff colluding in fraud

3

Application controls	General controls
One-for-one checking	Virus checks
Hash totals	Program libraries
Review of master files	Segregation of duties
Record counts	Passwords
	Controls over account deletion
	Training
	Back-up power source
	Back-up copies

4   D

5   True

Now try the question below from the Practice Question Bank

Number	Level	Marks	Time
Q15	Examination	10	20 mins

Tests of controls

Topic list	Syllabus reference
1 The sales system	C3
2 The purchases system	C3
3 The inventory system	C3
4 The bank and cash system	C3
5 The payroll system	C3
6 Revenue and capital expenditure	C3

Introduction

We discussed tests of controls in the last chapter. In this chapter we will look at how tests of controls might be applied in practice. We will examine each major component of a typical accounting system.

We have already stated that the auditors must establish what the accounting system and the system of internal control consist of. The auditors will then decide which controls, if any, they wish to rely on and plan tests of controls to obtain the audit evidence as to whether such reliance can be warranted. For each of the major transaction systems we will look at the system objectives the auditors will bear in mind while assessing the internal controls and give examples of common controls. We shall then go on to look at a 'standard' programme of tests of controls.

Study guide

		Intellectual level
C3	**Tests of control**	
(b)	Describe control objectives, control procedures, activities and tests of control in relation to: the sales system; the purchases system; the payroll system; the inventory system; the cash system; non-current assets.	2

Exam guide

Questions on tests of control are likely to come up in scenario-based situations, often in conjunction with the topics we discussed in Chapter 9. One typical question requirement would ask you to identify and explain internal control deficiencies, recommend suitable controls and describe the related tests of control.

You are likely to be asked to identify or describe controls that should be in place over a particular system or explain the control objectives for a given system. Questions on internal controls and tests of controls are very common and likely to come up, both in the form of written questions and in the form of OTQs in Section A. You need to be familiar with the major transaction cycles so that you can answer such questions competently.

1 The sales system   June 08, June 09, June 11, Dec 13, Dec 15, Specimen exam

FAST FORWARD

The tests of controls in the **sales system** will be based around:

- **Selling** (authorisation)
- **Goods outwards** (custody)
- **Accounting** (recording)

Exam focus point

The pages that follow contain control objectives, the controls themselves and possible tests of controls. It is very important to realise that the controls themselves should be thought of as distinct from the tests of controls. If you are asked for tests of controls in a scenario-based question, be careful not to just state control procedures managers should adopt. Instead you should focus on testing existing or potential controls. When formulating tests of controls based on information in a scenario, the best approach is to identify those controls present before considering how these controls can be confirmed. Make sure your explanations are not vague – **not** starting with the word 'check' should help you to avoid this.

The following diagram illustrates the sales system.

The sales system

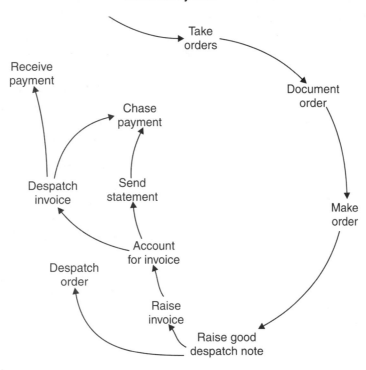

1.1 Sales system: Control objectives, controls and tests of controls

Assertion	Control objectives	Controls	Tests of controls
Occurrence and existence	• To ensure that recorded sales transactions represent goods or services provided.	• The tasks of taking orders, recording sales and receiving payment are allocated to three different staff members.	• Observe the processing of orders through the sales cycle and inspect sign-offs to evaluate whether proper segregation of duties is operating.
		• Sales are only recorded if there is an approved sales order form and shipping/despatch documentation.	• For a sample of sales invoices, ensure there is a related sales order form that has been authorised and shipping documentation. • Examine application controls for authorisation.
		• Accounting for numerical sequences of invoices.	• Inspect invoices to confirm whether they are sequentially numbered.
		• Monthly customer statements sent out and customer queries and complaints handled independently.	• Review entity's procedures for sending out monthly statements and dealing with customer queries and complaints.

BPP
LEARNING MEDIA

Assertion	Control objectives	Controls	Tests of controls
Occurrence and existence	• To ensure that goods and services are only supplied to customers with good credit ratings.	• Authorisation of credit terms to customers (senior staff authorisation, references/credit checks for new customers, regular review of credit limits).	• Review entity's procedures for granting credit to customers.
		• Authorisation by senior staff required for changes in other customer data such as address etc.	• Examine a sample of sales orders for evidence of proper credit approval by the appropriate senior staff member.
		• Orders not accepted unless credit limits reviewed first.	• Examine application controls for credit limits.
			• Review all new customer files to ensure satisfactory credit references have been obtained.
	• To ensure that goods and services are provided at authorised prices and on authorised terms. • To ensure that customers are encouraged to pay promptly.	• Authorised price lists and specified terms of trade in place.	• Verify that price lists and terms of trade are properly documented, authorised and communicated. • Examine application controls for authorised prices and terms.
Completeness	• To ensure that all revenue relating to goods despatched is recorded.	• Accounting for numerical sequences of invoices.	• Review and test entity's procedures for accounting for numerical sequences of invoices, and inspect invoices to confirm whether they are sequentially numbered.
	• To ensure that all goods and services sold are correctly invoiced.	• Shipping/despatch documentation is matched to sales invoices.	• For a sample of shipping/despatch documents, ensure each has been matched to a related sales invoice that was subsequently recorded.

Assertion	Control objectives	Controls	Tests of controls
Completeness		• Sales invoices are reconciled to the daily sales report.	• Review a sample of reconciliations performed. Reperform a sample of reconciliations.
		• An open-order file is maintained and reviewed regularly.	• Inspect the open-order file for unfilled orders.
Accuracy	• To ensure that all sales and adjustments are correctly journalised, summarised and posted to the correct accounts.	• Sales invoices and matching documents required for all entries and the date and reference of the entry are written on each document.	• Review supporting documents for a sample of sales entries to ensure they contain the written details that indicate they were referred to when entered.
Cut-off	• To ensure that transactions have been recorded in the correct period.	• All shipping documentation is forwarded to the invoicing section on a daily basis.	• Compare dates on sales invoices with dates of corresponding shipping documentation.
		• Daily invoicing of goods shipped.	• Compare dates on sales invoices with dates recorded in the sales ledger.
Classification	• To ensure that all transactions are properly classified in accounts.	• Chart of accounts (COA) in place and is regularly reviewed for appropriateness and updated where necessary.	• Inspect any documentary evidence of review (such as emails requesting update to COA as a result of review).
		• Codes in place for different types of products or services.	• Test application controls for proper codes.

 Question   Sales system

You are the auditor of Arcidiacono Stationery, and you have been asked to suggest how audit work should be carried out on the sales system.

Arcidiacono Stationery Ltd sells stationery to shops. Most sales are to small customers who do not have a sales ledger account. They can collect their purchases and pay by cash. For cash sales:

(i)   The customer orders the stationery from the sales department, which raises a pre-numbered multi-copy order form.

(ii)   The despatch department make up the order and give it to the customer with a copy of the order form.

(iii) The customer gives the order form to the cashier who prepares a handwritten sales invoice.

(iv)   The customer pays the cashier for the goods by cheque or in cash.

(v)   The cashier records and banks the cash.

Required

(a)   State the deficiencies in the cash sales system.
(b)   Describe the systems-based tests you would carry out to audit the controls over the system.

Answer

(a)   **Deficiencies in the cash sales system**

(i)   The physical location of the despatch department and the cashier are not mentioned here, but there is a risk of the customer taking the goods without paying. The customer should pay the cashier on the advice note and return for the goods, which should only be released on sight of the paid invoice.

(ii)   There is a failure in segregation of duties in allowing the cashier to both complete the sales invoice and receive the cash, as they could perpetrate a fraud by replacing the original invoice with one of lower value and keeping the difference.

(iii)   No one checks the invoices to make sure that the cashier has completed them correctly, for example by using the correct prices and performing calculations correctly.

(iv)   The completeness of the sequence of sales invoices cannot be checked unless they are pre-numbered sequentially and the presence of all the invoices is checked by another person. The order forms should also be pre-numbered sequentially.

(v)   There is no check that the cashier banks all cash received, and this is a further failure of segregation of duties.

If the sales department prepared and posted the invoices and also posted the cash for cash sales to a sundry sales account, this would solve some of the internal control problems mentioned above. In addition, the sales department could run a weekly check on the account to look for invoices for which no cash had been received. These could then be investigated.

All of these deficiencies, and possible remedies, should be reported to management.

(b)   **Tests**

(i)   Select a sample of order forms issued to customers during the year. Trace the related sales invoice and check that the details correlate (date, unit amounts etc). The customer should have signed for the goods and this copy should be retained by the despatch department.

(ii)   For the sales invoices discovered in the above test, I would check that the correct order form number is recorded on the invoice and that the prices used are correct (by reference to the prevailing price list).

(iii)   I would then trace the value of the sales invoices to the cash book and confirm from the cash book that the total receipts for the day have been banked and appear promptly on the bank statement.

(iv)   I would check that the sales invoices have been correctly posted to a cash or sundry sales account. For any sales invoices missing from this account (assuming they are sequentially numbered), I would trace the cancelled invoice and check that the cancelled invoice was initialled by the customer and replaced by the next invoice in sequence.

(v)   Because of the weaknesses in the system I would carry out the following sequence checks on large blocks of order forms/invoices, eg four blocks of 100 order forms/invoices.

(1)   Inspect all order forms to ensure all present; investigate those missing
(2)   Match sales invoices to order forms
(3)   Check all sales invoices in a sequence have been used; investigate any missing
(4)   Cash for each sales invoice has been entered into the cash book

Using the results of the above tests I would decide whether the system for cash sales has operated without material fraud or error. If I am not satisfied that it has then this may impact on the audit report.

2 The purchases system

Dec 10, June 13, June 14, Specimen Exam

FAST FORWARD

The tests of controls in the **purchases system** will be based around:

- **Buying** (authorisation)
- **Goods inwards** (custody)
- **Accounting** (recording)

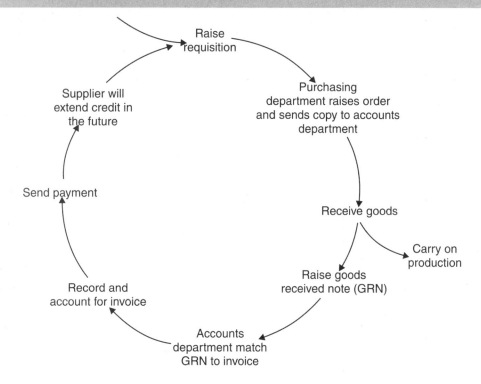

2.1 Control objectives, controls and tests of controls

Assertion	Control objectives	Controls	Tests of controls
Occurrence and existence	• To ensure that recorded purchases represent goods and services received.	• Authorisation procedures and policies in place for ordering goods and services.	• Inspect policies and procedures and enquire about them. • Observe the processing of purchase orders throughout the purchasing cycle and evaluate whether proper segregation of duties is operating.

Assertion	Control objectives	Controls	Tests of controls
Occurrence and existence		• The responsibility for placing the orders, recording the purchase order and making the payment is carried out by three different staff members.	
		• Purchase orders raised for each purchase and authorised by appropriate senior personnel.	• Examine a sample of purchase orders to ensure they have been appropriately authorised. • Review the delegated list of authority for purchases.
		• Approved purchase order for each receipt of goods.	• For a sample of goods received notes (GRNs), ensure there is a related purchase order that has been properly approved.
		• Staff receiving goods check them to the purchase order.	• Observe receipt of goods by staff to confirm whether the check is done. • Inspect a sample to confirm whether stores staff undertake this check.
		• Stores clerks sign for goods received.	
		• Purchase orders and GRNs are matched with the suppliers' invoices.	• Examine supporting documentation to ensure it has been matched for a sample of invoices.
		• Supplier statements independently reviewed and reconciled to trade payable records.	• Review procedures for reconciling supplier statements and reperform a sample of reconciliations.
Completeness	• To ensure that all purchase transactions that occurred have been recorded.	• Purchase orders and GRNs are matched with the suppliers' invoices.	• For a sample of purchase orders in the year ensure each has been matched to a related invoice that was subsequently recorded.

Assertion	Control objectives	Controls	Tests of controls
Completeness		• Periodic accounting for pre-numbered GRNs and purchase orders.	• Review entity's procedures for accounting for pre-numbered documents and inspect a sample of GRNs for sequential numbering.
		• Independent check of amount recorded in the purchase journal.	• Examine application controls. • Examine documentation for evidence of this check.
		• Supplier statements independently reviewed and reconciled to trade payable records.	• Review procedures for reconciling supplier statements and reperform a sample of reconciliations.
Rights and obligations	• To ensure that recorded purchases represent the liabilities of the entity.	• Purchase orders and GRNs are matched with the suppliers' invoices.	• Examine supporting documentation to ensure it has been matched for a sample of invoices.
Accuracy, valuation and allocation and classification	• To ensure that purchase transactions are correctly recorded in the accounting system.	• Purchase orders and GRNs are matched with the suppliers' invoices. • Mathematical accuracy of the supplier's invoice is verified.	• Examine supporting documentation for a sample of invoices. • Review a sample of invoices for evidence the accuracy has been verified (eg signature or initials) and reperform the check.
		• Amount posted to general ledger is reconciled to the purchases ledger.	• Review reconciliations for evidence of this check.
		• Chart of accounts in place.	• Review purchases journal and general ledger for reasonableness.

Assertion	Control objectives	Controls	Tests of controls
Cut-off	• To ensure that purchase transactions are recorded in the correct accounting period.	• All goods received reports forwarded to accounts payable department daily. • Procedures in place that require recording of purchases as soon as possible after goods/services received.	• Compare dates on reports to dates on relevant vouchers. • Compare dates on vouchers with dates they were recorded in the purchases journal.

Question

Purchase controls

Derek, a limited liability company, operates a computerised purchase system. Invoices and credit notes are posted to the purchases ledger by the purchases ledger department. The computer subsequently raises a cheque when the invoice has to be paid.

Required

List the controls that should be in operation:

(a)   Over the addition, amendment and deletion of suppliers, ensuring that the standing data only includes suppliers from the company's list of authorised suppliers

(b)   Over purchase invoices and credit notes, to ensure only authorised purchase invoices and credit notes are posted to the purchase ledger

Answer

(a)   Controls over the standing data file containing suppliers' details will include the following.

    (i)   All amendments/additions/deletions to the data should be authorised by a responsible official. A standard form should be used for such changes.

    (ii)   The amendment forms should be input in batches (with different types of change in different batches), sequentially numbered and recorded in a batch control book so that any gaps in the batch numbers can be investigated. The output produced by the computer should be checked to the input.

    (iii)   A listing of all such adjustments should automatically be produced by the computer and reviewed by a responsible official, who should also check authorisation.

    (iv)   A listing of suppliers' accounts on which there has been no movement for a specified period should be produced to allow decisions to be made about possible deletions, thus ensuring that the standing data is current. The buying department manager might also recommend account closures on a periodic basis.

    (v)   Users should be controlled by use of passwords. This can also be used as a method of controlling those who can amend data.

    (vi)   Periodic listings of standing data should be produced in order to verify details (for example addresses) with suppliers' documents (invoices/statements).

(b)   The input of authorised purchase invoices and credit notes should be controlled in the following ways.

    (i)   Authorisation should be evidenced by the signature of the responsible official, such as the Chief Accountant. In addition, the invoice or credit note should show initials to demonstrate

that the details have been agreed: to a signed GRN; to a purchase order; to a price list; for additions and extensions.

(ii)   There should be adequate segregation of responsibilities between the posting function, inventory custody and receipt, payment of suppliers and changes to standing data.

(iii)   Input should be restricted by use of passwords linked to the relevant site number.

(iv)   A batch control book should be maintained, recording batches in number sequence. Invoices should be input in batches using pre-numbered batch control sheets. The manually produced invoice total on the batch control sheet should be agreed to the computer generated total. Credit notes and invoices should be input in separate batches to avoid one being posted as the other.

(v)   A program should check calculation of sales tax at standard rate and total of invoice. Non-standard sales tax rates should be highlighted.

(vi)   The input of the supplier code should bring up the supplier name for checking against the invoice by the operator.

(vii)   Invoices for suppliers which do not have an account should be prevented from being input. Any sundry suppliers account should be very tightly controlled and all entries reviewed in full each month.

(viii) An exception report showing unusual expense allocation (by size or account) should be produced and reviewed by a responsible official. Expenses should be compared to budget and previous years.

(ix)   There should be monthly reconciliations of purchase ledger balances to suppliers' statements by someone outside the purchasing (accounting) function.

3 The inventory system

Dec 07, June 10

FAST FORWARD

Inventory controls are designed to ensure safe custody. Such controls include restriction of access, documentation and authorisation of movements, regular **independent inventory counting** and **review of inventory condition**.

3.1 Introduction

The inventory system can be very important in an audit because of the high value of inventory or the complexity of its audit. It is closely connected with the sales and purchases systems covered in the previous sections.

There are three possible approaches to the audit of inventory and the approach chosen depends on the control system in place over inventory.

(a)   If the entity has a perpetual inventory system in place where inventory is counted continuously throughout the year, and therefore a year-end count is not undertaken, a controls-based approach can be taken if control risk has been assessed as low.

(b)   If an inventory count is to be undertaken near the year end and adjusted by perpetual inventory records for the year-end value, this approach also requires control risk to be assessed as low.

(c)   If inventory quantities will be determined by an inventory count at the year-end date, a largely substantive approach is taken. This approach is covered in Chapter 13.

3.2 Control objectives, controls and tests of controls

Most of the controls testing relating to inventory has been covered in the purchase and sales testing outlined in Sections 1 and 2. Auditors will primarily be concerned at this stage with ensuring that the business keeps track of inventory. To confirm this, tests must be undertaken on how inventory **movements** are **recorded** and how **inventory** is **secured**. Auditors will carry out extensive tests on the **valuation** of inventory at the substantive testing stage (see Chapter 13).

Assertion	Control objectives	Controls	Tests of controls
Occurrence and existence	• To ensure that all inventory movements are authorised and recorded.	• Pre-numbered documentation such as GDNs and GRNs in use. • Reconciliations of inventory records with general ledger. • Separate responsibilities for maintenance of records and custodianship.	• Review documentation in use. • Review a sample of reconciliations to confirm they are performed and then reviewed by an independent person. • Observe the recording of inventory and discuss inventory procedures with relevant staff to ensure that proper segregation of duties is operating.
	• To ensure that inventory included on the statement of financial position physically exists.	• Physical safeguards in place to ensure inventory is not stolen. • Separate responsibilities for maintenance of records and custodianship. • Inventory counted regularly.	• Review security systems in place (eg locked warehouses, CCTV). • Review policies and procedures in place; discuss procedures with relevant staff. • Review procedures for counting inventory. • Attend inventory count.
Completeness	• To ensure that all purchases and sales of inventory have been recorded in the accounting system.	• Procedures in place to include inventory held at third parties and exclude inventory held on consignment for third parties. • Reconciliations of accounting records with physical inventory.	• Review entity's procedures relating to consignment inventory. • Review reconciliations performed and inspect them for evidence of review. Reperform a sample of reconciliations.

Assertion	Control objectives	Controls	Tests of controls
Rights and obligations	• To ensure that inventory records only include items that belong to the entity.	• Procedures in place to include inventory held at third parties and exclude inventory held on consignment for third parties.	• Review entity's procedures relating to consignment inventory.
Accuracy, valuation and allocation and classification	• To ensure that inventory quantities have been accurately determined.	• Periodic or annual comparison of inventory with amounts shown in continuous (perpetual) inventory records.	• Review and test entity's procedures for taking physical inventory.
	• To ensure that inventory is properly stated at the lower of cost and net realisable value.	• Standard costs reviewed by management. • Review of cost accumulation and variance reports. • Inventory managers review inventory regularly to identify slow-moving, obsolete and excess inventory.	• Review and test entity's procedures for developing standard costs. • Inspect variance reports produced. • Discuss with inventory managers how this is done. • Observe the procedure being performed.
Cut-off	• To ensure that all purchases and sales of inventory are recorded in the correct accounting period.	• All despatch documents processed daily to record the despatch of finished goods. • All goods inward reports processed daily to record the receipt of inventory. • Reconciliations of inventory records with general ledger.	• Inspect documentation to confirm daily processing. • Inspect documentation to confirm daily processing. • Review reconciliations performed.
Presentation	• To ensure that inventory transactions and balances are properly identified and classified in the financial statements.	• Orders for materials and production data forms used to process goods through manufacturing.	• Review entity's procedures and documentation used to classify inventory.
	• To ensure that disclosures relating to classification and valuation are sufficient.	• Approval by Finance Director.	• Review entity's working papers for evidence of review.

4 The bank and cash system

Dec 07, June 10

Controls over cash receipts and payments should prevent fraud or theft.

4.1 Control objectives, controls and tests of controls

The following table sets out the control objectives, controls and possible tests of controls over **cash payments**.

Assertion	Control objectives	Controls	Tests of controls
Occurrence	• To ensure that only valid cash payments are made.	• Separate responsibilities for the recording, payment and reconciliation of cash.	• Observe the processing of cash and review the entity's policies to evaluate whether proper segregation of duties is operating.
		• Supplier statements independently reviewed and reconciled to trade payable records.	• Review procedures for reconciling supplier statements.
		• Monthly bank reconciliations prepared and reviewed.	• Review reconciliations to confirm whether undertaken and reviewed.
		• Only authorised staff can make electronic cash payments and issue cheques.	• Review delegated list of authority for cash payments.
		• Electronic cash payments and cheques prepared only after all source documents have been independently approved.	• Inspect relevant documentation for evidence of approval by senior personnel.
Completeness	• To ensure that all cash payments that occurred are recorded.	• Separate responsibilities for the recording, handling and reconciliation of cash.	• Observe the processing of cash and review the entity's policies to evaluate whether proper segregation of duties is operating.

Assertion	Control objectives	Controls	Tests of controls
Completeness		• Supplier statements independently reviewed and reconciled to trade payable records.	• Review procedures for reconciling supplier statements.
		• Monthly bank reconciliations prepared and reviewed.	• Review reconciliations to confirm whether undertaken and independently reviewed.
		• Review of cash payments by manager before release.	• Inspect sample of listings for evidence of senior review.
		• Daily cash payments reconciled to posting to payable accounts.	• Review a sample of reconciliations for evidence that they have been done.
		• Use of pre-numbered cheques.	• Examine evidence of use of pre-numbered cheques.
Accuracy, valuation and allocation and classification	• To ensure that cash payments are recorded correctly in the ledger.	• Reconciliation of daily payments report to electronic cash payment transfers and cheques issued.	• Review reconciliation, to ensure performed, reviewed and any discrepancies followed up on a timely basis.
		• Supplier statements reconciled to payable accounts regularly.	• Review reconciliations for a sample of accounts.
		• Monthly bank reconciliations of bank statements to ledger account.	• Review bank reconciliation for evidence it was done and independently reviewed. Reperform a sample of bank reconciliations.
	• To ensure that cash payments are posted to the correct payable accounts and to the general ledger.	• Supplier statements reconciled to payable accounts regularly.	• Review reconciliations for a sample of accounts.
		• Agreement of monthly cash payments journal to general ledger posting.	• Review postings from journal to general ledger.

Assertion	Control objectives	Controls	Tests of controls
Accuracy, valuation and allocation and classification		• Payable accounts reconciled to general ledger control account.	• Review reconciliation, to ensure performed, reviewed and any discrepancies followed up on a timely basis.
Cut-off	• To ensure that cash payments are recorded in the correct accounting period.	• Reconciliation of electronic funds transfers and cheques issued with postings to cash payments journal and payable accounts.	• Review reconciliation and check it is carried out regularly.
Presentation	• To ensure that cash payments are charged to the correct accounts.	• Chart of accounts. • Independent approval and review of general ledger account assignment.	• Review cash payments journal to assess reasonableness of charging of accounts. • Review assignment of general ledger account.

The following table sets out the control objectives, controls and possible tests of controls over **cash receipts**.

Assertion	Control objectives	Controls	Tests of controls
Occurrence	• To ensure that all valid cash receipts are received and deposited.	• Separate responsibilities for the recording, receipt and reconciliation of cash. • Use of electronic cash receipts transfer not received or deposited. • Monthly bank reconciliations performed and independently reviewed. • Use of cash registers or point-of-sale devices.	• Observe the processing of cash and review the entity's policies to evaluate whether proper segregation of duties is operating. • Examine application controls for electronic cash receipts transfer. • Review monthly bank reconciliations to confirm performed and reviewed. • Observe cash sales procedures.

Assertion	Control objectives	Controls	Tests of controls
Occurrence		• Periodic inspections of cash sales procedures.	• Enquire of managers about results of inspections.
		• Restrictive endorsement of cheques immediately on receipt.	• Observe mail opening, including endorsement of cheques.
		• Mail opened by two staff members.	• Observe mail opening procedures.
		• Immediate preparation of cash book or list of mail receipts.	• Observe preparation of cash receipts' records.
		• Independent check of agreement of cash/cheques to be deposited at bank with register totals and receipts listing.	• Review documentation for evidence of independent check.
		• Independent check of agreement of bank deposit slip with daily cash summary.	• Review documentation for evidence of independent check.
Completeness	• To ensure that all cash receipts are recorded.	• Separate responsibilities for the recording, receipt and reconciliation of cash.	• Observe the processing of cash and review the entity's policies to evaluate whether proper segregation of duties is operating.
		• Use of electronic cash receipts transfer not received or deposited.	• Examine application controls for electronic cash receipts transfer.
		• Monthly bank reconciliations performed and independently reviewed.	• Review monthly bank reconciliations to confirm performed and reviewed. Reperform a sample of the reconciliations.
		• Daily cash receipts listing reconciled with posting to customer accounts.	• Review reconciliation.

Assertion	Control objectives	Controls	Tests of controls
Completeness		• Customer statements prepared and sent out on a regular basis.	• Enquire of management about handling of customer statements. • Examine a sample of customers and note frequency of statements.
Accuracy, valuation and allocation and classification	• To ensure that cash receipts are recorded at correct amounts.	• Daily remittance report reconciled to control listing of remittance advices. • Monthly bank statement performed and reviewed independently.	• Review reconciliations. • Review reconciliations for evidence they were performed and independently reviewed.
	• To ensure that cash receipts are posted to correct receivables accounts and to the general ledger.	• Daily remittance report reconciled daily with postings to cash receipts journal and customer accounts. • Monthly customer statements sent out. • Monthly cash receipts journal agreed to general ledger posting. • Receivables' ledger reconciled to control account.	• Review reconciliations. • Review entity's procedures for sending out statements. • Review journal and posting to general ledger. • Review reconciliations.
Cut-off	• To ensure that cash receipts are recorded in the correct accounting period.	• Bank reconciliation at period end.	• Review and test reconciliation.
Presentation	• To ensure that cash receipts are charged to the correct accounts.	• Chart of accounts (COA) in place and is regularly reviewed for appropriateness and updated where necessary. • Codes in place for different types of receipt.	• Inspect any documentary evidence of review (such as emails requesting update to COA as a result of review). • Test application controls for proper codes.

5 The payroll system

FAST FORWARD

Key controls over **payroll** cover:

- **Documentation** and **authorisation** of staff changes
- **Calculation** of wages and salaries
- **Payment** of wages
- **Authorisation** of **deductions**

5.1 Control objectives, controls and tests of controls

Assertion	Control objectives	Controls	Tests of controls
Occurrence and existence	• To ensure that payment is made only to *bona fide* employees of the entity.	• Segregation of duties between HR and payroll functions.	• Review payroll and HR job descriptions and company policies on payroll process, to evaluate whether proper segregation of duties is in place.
		• Personnel files held for all employees.	• Review a sample of starters and leavers in the year to ensure correct documentation is in place.
		• Authorisation procedures for hiring, terminating, time worked, wage rates, overtime, benefits etc.	• Review and test authorisation procedures in place.
		• Any changes in employment status of employees (eg maternity, special leave) informed to HR department.	• Review policies and procedures in place for changing status and consider whether adequate. • Review personnel files for a sample of employees whose status changed in the year.
		• Use of time clocks to record time worked.	• Observe employees' use of time clocks.
		• Clock cards approved by supervisor.	• Inspect a sample of clock cards for evidence of approval by appropriate level of management.

Assertion	Control objectives	Controls	Tests of controls
Occurrence and existence		• Employee numbers assigned to each employee in the payroll master file. Only employees with valid employee numbers are paid.	• Review and test procedures for entering and removing employee numbers from the payroll master file.
		• Payroll budgets in place and reviewed by management.	• Review budgeting procedures.
Completeness	• To ensure that all payroll costs are recorded for work done by employees.	• Pre-numbered clock cards in use.	• Review numerical sequence of clock cards.
		• Regular reconciliations carried out of payroll records and employee costs recorded in the general ledger.	• Review a sample of reconciliations to ensure they are properly carried out. Reperform a sample of reconciliations.
		• Comparison of cheques and bank transfer list with payroll to ensure all employees paid have been recorded via payroll.	• Enquire whether comparisons are being made between payment records and payroll and inspect any documentary evidence of the review.
		• Preparation and authorisation of cheques and bank transfer lists.	• Examine paid cheques or a certified copy of the bank list for employees paid by cheque or bank transfer to ensure proper authorisation.
Accuracy, valuation and allocation and classification	• To ensure that all benefits and deductions (tax, pension etc) are computed correctly.	• Reperformance of a sample of payroll benefit and deduction calculations.	• Review documentary evidence that recalculation occurred (eg spreadsheet printout).
		• Payroll budgets in place and reviewed by management.	• Review budgeting procedures.
		• Agreement of gross earnings and total tax deducted with taxation returns.	• Inspect documentation for evidence of management's review.

Assertion	Control objectives	Controls	Tests of controls
Accuracy, valuation and allocation and classification	• To ensure that payroll transactions are correctly recorded in the accounting system.	• Changes to master payroll file verified through 'before and after' reports. • Payroll master file reconciled to general ledger.	• Review reconciliation 'before and after' reports to payroll master file. • Review reconciliation payroll master file to general ledger. Confirm whether discrepancies are followed up promptly and resolved.
Cut-off	• To ensure that payroll transactions are recorded in the correct accounting period.	• All starters, leavers, changes to salaries and deductions are reported promptly to payroll department and changes are updated in the payroll master file promptly.	• Review entity's procedures for reporting changes to the payroll department. • Verify sample of starters and leavers.
Presentation	• To ensure that payroll transactions are properly classified in the financial statements.	• Chart of accounts. • Independent approval and review of accounts charged to payroll. • Payroll budgets in place and reviewed by management.	• Review chart of accounts. • Review procedures for classifying payroll costs. • Review budgeting procedures.

The following question aims to link the aspects we looked at in Chapter 9 with the control objectives and tests of control we have just looked at.

The audit of wages, particularly the internal controls around wages, is discussed in detail in an article in *Student Accountant* in August 2013 called 'The Audit of Wages'. This article can be accessed via the Technical Articles link on the ACCA website: www.accaglobal.com/gb/en/student/acca-qual-student-journey/qual-resource/acca-qualification/f8/technical-articles.html.

Question

Payroll controls

A good understanding of internal controls is essential to auditors. This helps them to understand the business and allows them to effectively plan and execute tests of controls together with an appropriate level of substantive procedures.

A small manufacturing company, Westfield, pays its staff in cash and by bank transfer, and the payroll department consists of a payroll clerk who maintains its payroll on a stand-alone laptop computer. The payroll clerk is supervised by the chief accountant, who in turn reports to the managing director. You are Westfield's auditor.

Required

(a) For the **payroll department** at Westfield, describe the internal control **objectives** that should be in place.

(b)   Describe the internal control **environment** and internal control **activities** that should be in place to achieve the internal control objectives in (a).

(c)   Using your answer above, suggest a control the auditor may seek to rely on when obtaining evidence over occurrence and existence in relation to payroll, and explain why. State **one** test of control the auditor might carry out to test the operating effectiveness of that control.

Answer

(a)   **Internal control objectives**

To ensure that:

- Only genuine staff are paid for work performed.
- Gross pay has been calculated correctly.
- Deductions from gross pay are calculated and recorded accurately.
- The correct employees are paid what they are entitled to.
- Wages and salaries paid are accurately recorded in the bank and cash records.
- The right amounts due in respect of tax and national insurance are paid to the relevant authority on a timely basis.

(b)   **Internal control environment and control activities**

Internal control environment

The control environment includes the governance and management functions and the attitudes, awareness and actions of management and those charged with governance in terms of the importance of internal control within the business. More specifically it would include the following.

(i)   The way in which management **communicate** to staff the need for integrity and enforce it.

(ii)   The consideration which management gives to ensure that the payroll staff have the **requisite skills** and **knowledge** through proper recruitment and training.

(iii)   Management's **philosophy** and **operating style**, including the way in which the importance of internal control in the processing of payroll is translated into positive action, for example providing sufficient resources to address security risks regarding access to the computer.

(iv)   The way that **authority** and **responsibility** is assigned. For example, the chief accountant might act in a supervisory role while the payroll clerk is responsible for the detailed calculations and processing.

Internal control activities

(i)   Responsibility for the preparation of the payroll should be delegated to a responsible, adequately trained member of staff.

(ii)   For hourly paid employees, the payroll should be prepared on the basis of timesheets / clock cards authorised by a factory supervisor.

(iii)   Standing data used by the computerised payroll system should be checked on a regular basis eg gross pay to personnel records.

(iv)   Any changes should be authorised by the chief accountant eg change in pay rates, overtime, joiners and leavers.

(v)   For a sample of employees, calculations for gross pay, net pay and deductions should be reperformed by the chief accountant.

(vi)   The payroll software should include computerised controls eg hierarchical password access and range checks. Exception reports should be produced and investigated.

(vii)   The managing director should review the payroll by comparing the total monthly cost with the budget and previous months' actual figures.

(viii) The bank transfer list and wage cheque should be authorised by the managing director.

(ix) Cash should be kept securely in the company safe until it is distributed.

(x) There should be segregation of duties between the member of staff responsible for processing the payroll and the individual handling the cash.

(xi) The chief accountant should maintain and reconcile a wages and salaries control account.

(c) **Occurrence and existence**

The segregation of duties between the member of staff responsible for processing the payroll and the individual making the bank transfers or cash payments is a key control in preventing the setting up of bogus employees and diverting funds to a private bank account.

This therefore helps fulfil the control objective that only genuine employees are paid and is one control the auditor may seek to test and rely on, to gain evidence in relation to 'occurrence and existence'.

The test of control would simply be to observe and evaluate proper segregation of duties.

6 Revenue and capital expenditure   June 15, Specimen Paper

FAST FORWARD

Most of the key controls over capital and revenue expenditure are the general purchase controls.

The nature of a statement of financial position and statement of profit or loss means that it is important to classify capital and revenue expenditure correctly, or profit will be over- or understated. You should know the distinction between them from your financial reporting studies.

The controls and tests outlined below are often considered and performed during the audit of non-current assets (see Chapter 12), as this is where the main issue of capitalisation occurs.

6.1 Controls and tests of controls

Assertion	Control objectives	Controls	Tests of control
Authorisation	• To ensure that expenditure is properly authorised.	• Orders for capital items should be authorised by appropriate levels of management.	• Review policies and procedures in place.
		• Orders should be requisitioned on appropriate (different to revenue) documentation.	• Examine a sample of orders for appropriate authorisation.
		• Invoices should be approved by the person who authorised the order.	• Inspect invoices to verify the invoice has been appropriately approved.
		• Invoices should be marked with the appropriate general ledger code.	• Inspect invoices to verify the invoice has the correct general ledger code marked on it.
Classification	• To ensure that expenditure is classified correctly in the financial statements as capital or revenue expenditure.	• All the standard controls over purchases are relevant here (see Section 2).	• See Section 2.

Assertion	Control objectives	Controls	Tests of control
Completeness	• To ensure that all non-current assets are correctly recorded in the accounting system.	• Capital items should be written up in the non-current asset register. • The non-current asset register should be reconciled regularly to the general ledger and any differences investigated and resolved promptly.	• Review reconciliation to ensure it is regularly carried out, reviewed by a more senior person, and that all discrepancies are followed up and resolved on a timely basis.

6.2 Tests of controls and substantive testing

If the ordering documentation is different for capital purchases, all the standard purchase control tests should be carried out. If the documentation is not different, the auditor should also enquire as to the client's system for recording and filing capital invoices.

It is likely that the number of capital purchases in the year will be less than the number of standard purchases in the year and if the invoices are not segregated it may not be cost-efficient to test the controls over this area, in which case substantive testing would have to be undertaken.

These substantive tests are often carried out as part of the substantive audit of non-current assets, which is covered in Chapter 12.

The auditor should be aware of the risks attaching to the audit of this area. As tests of controls might not be cost-effective, control risk in this area is higher than it would have been if they were tested.

Inherent risk can also be high in this area. Capital and revenue expenditure is treated differently for the purposes of tax, and, if the client is sensitive to the tax bill, there may be an incentive to account creatively.

Question	System control deficiencies

Jonathan is the sole shareholder of Furry Lion Stores, a company which owns five stores in the west of England. The stores sell mainly food and groceries.

Each store is run by a full-time manager and three or four part-time assistants. Jonathan spends on average half a day a week at each store, and spends the rest of his time at home, dealing with his other business interests.

All sales are for cash and are recorded on till rolls which the manager retains. Shop managers' wages are paid monthly by cheque by Jonathan. Wages of shop assistants are paid in cash out of the takings.

Most purchases are made from local wholesalers and are paid for in cash out of the takings. Large purchases (over $250) must be made by cheques signed by the shop manager and countersigned by Jonathan.

Shop managers bank surplus cash once a week, apart from a float in the till.

All accounting records, including the cash book, wages and sales tax records, are maintained by the manager. Jonathan reviews the weekly bank statements when he visits the shops. He also has a look at inventory to see if inventory levels appear to be about right. All invoices are also kept in a drawer by a manager and marked with a cash book reference, and where appropriate a cheque number when paid.

Required

Discuss the deficiencies in the control systems of Furry Lion Stores, and how the weaknesses can be remedied.

Deficiencies in the system, and their remedies, are as follows.

Inventory

The shops do not appear to have any inventory movement records. Jonathan has also only a very approximate indication of inventory levels, hence it will be difficult to detect whether inventory levels are too high, or too low with a risk of running out of inventory. Theft of inventory would also be difficult to detect. The company should therefore introduce inventory movement records, detailing values and volumes.

In addition, regular inventory counts should be made either by Jonathan or by staff from another shop. Discrepancies between the inventory records and the actual inventory counted should be investigated.

Cash controls

Too much cash appears to be held on site. In addition, the fact that most payments appear to be for cash may mean inadequate documentation is kept. The level of cash on site can be decreased by daily rather than weekly bankings. In addition, the need for cash on site can be decreased by paying wages by cheque, and by paying all but the smallest payments by cheque.

The cash book should obviously still be maintained but cheque stubs should also show details of amounts paid. The cash book should be supported by invoices and other supporting documentation, and should be cross-referenced to the general ledger (see below).

Cash reconciliations

There is no indication of the till rolls that are kept being reconciled to cash takings.

There should be a daily reconciliation of cash takings and till rolls; this should be reviewed if not performed by the shop manager.

Bank reconciliations

There is no mention of bank reconciliations taking place.

Bank reconciliations should be carried out at least monthly by the shop manager, and reviewed by the owner.

Purchases

There is no formal system for recording purchases. Invoices do not appear to be filed in any particular way. It would be difficult to see whether accounting records were complete, and therefore it would be difficult to prepare a set of accounts from the accounting records available.

In addition, the way records are maintained means that accounts would have to be prepared on a cash basis, and not on an accruals basis.

A purchase day book should be introduced. Invoices should be recorded in the purchase day book, and filed in a logical order, either by date received or by supplier.

General ledger

There is no general ledger, and again this means that annual accounts cannot easily be prepared (and also management accounts).

A general ledger should be maintained with entries made from the cash book, wages records and purchase day book. This will enable accounts to be prepared on an accruals basis.

Supervision

Jonathan does not play a very active part in the business, only signing cheques over $250, and visiting the shops for only half a day each week. This may mean that assets can easily go missing, and Jonathan cannot readily see whether the business is performing as he would wish.

Jonathan should review wage/sales tax/cash book reconciliations. Management accounts should also be prepared by shop managers for Jonathan.

Tutorial note. This question deals with controls that are possible given the circumstances of the business. Greater segregation of duties does not appear to be possible, as the shops are small, and Jonathan cannot spend more time at the shops (although he can use his time more productively by reviewing reconciliations).

<table>
<tr><td>

Exam focus point

</td><td>

In the exam you may be asked for deficiencies in a system, and the consequences of those deficiencies, or you could be asked for tests of controls.

If you are asked about appropriate controls or deficiencies, remember the **control objectives** for the accounting area. Controls should be in place to **fulfil** the **objectives** given; deficiencies will mean that the objectives are not fulfilled. You should give enough detail about the controls you suggest to enable a non-accountant to implement the controls.

You should use a similar thought process when deciding how to test the controls. Think of the **objectives** of the system; assess how the controls given **fulfil** those **objectives**; and set out tests which demonstrate whether the controls are working. Remember that different types of test can be used to test different controls. For example, inspection can be used to test whether different documents are being compared or documents are being properly authorised. Recalculation and reperformance can be used to test that invoices have been properly completed or reconciliations correctly performed.

The examining team noted, with regards to the June 2014 exam, that 'many candidates are still confusing substantive procedures and test of controls. A significant number of candidates suggested substantive procedures such as "recalculating gross and net pay calculations", rather than a test of control which might be to "review evidence of the recalculation of payroll".'

In addition, the examining team advised you to think about how to verify whether the test of control has **actually** operated, beyond ensuring that it is capable of functioning. 'In many instances candidates focused on reperforming the control rather than testing it had operated. Observation of a control was commonly suggested by candidates; however, in many cases this is not an effective way of testing that a control has operated throughout the year.'

</td></tr>
</table>

Chapter Roundup

- The tests of controls in the **sales system** will be based around:

    - **Selling** (authorisation)
    - **Goods outwards** (custody)
    - **Accounting** (recording)

- The tests of controls in the **purchases system** will be based around:

    - **Buying** (authorisation)
    - **Goods inwards** (custody)
    - **Accounting** (recording)

- **Inventory controls** are designed to ensure safe custody. Such controls include restriction of access, documentation and authorisation of movements, regular **independent inventory counting** and **review of inventory condition**.

- Controls over cash receipts and payments should prevent fraud or theft.

- Key controls over **payroll** cover:

    - **Documentation** and **authorisation** of staff changes
    - **Calculation** of wages and salaries
    - **Payment** of wages
    - **Authorisation** of **deductions**

- Most of the key controls over capital and revenue expenditure are the general purchase controls.

Quick Quiz

1 Complete the table, putting the sales system control considerations under the correct headings.

Ordering/credit approval	Despatch/invoicing	Recording/accounting

   (a) All sales that have been invoiced have been put in the general ledger.
   (b) Orders are fulfilled.
   (c) Cut-off is correct.
   (d) Goods are only supplied to good credit risks.
   (e) Goods are correctly invoiced.
   (f) Customers are encouraged to pay promptly.

2 State five controls relating to the ordering and granting of credit process.

   1 ....
   2 ....
   3 ....
   4 ....
   5 ....

3   Complete the table, putting the purchase system control considerations under the correct headings.

Ordering	Receipts/invoices	Accounting

(a)   Orders are only made to authorised suppliers.
(b)   Liabilities are recognised for all goods and services received.
(c)   Orders are made at competitive prices.
(d)   All expenditure is authorised.
(e)   Cut-off is correctly applied.
(f)   Goods and services are only accepted if there is an authorised order.

4   (a)   State four examples of purchase documentation on which numerical sequence should be checked.

1   ....

2   ....

3   ....

4   ....

(b)   Why is numerical sequence checked?

5   State five control objectives relating to inventory.

1   ....

2   ....

3   ....

4   ....

5   ....

6   List the five key aims of controls in the cash system.

1   ....

2   ....

3   ....

4   ....

5   ....

7   Give an example of a control which helps to ensure the completeness of non-current assets. Suggest how the auditor can test that the control is operating effectively.

1

Ordering/credit approval	Despatch/invoicing	Recording/accounting
(b) (d) (f)	(e)	(a) (c)

2   Any five of:

- Segregation of duties; credit control, invoicing and inventory despatch
- Authorisation of credit terms to customers
    - References/credit checks obtained
    - Authorisation by senior staff
    - Regular review
- Authorisation for changes in other customer data
    - Change of address supported by letterhead
    - Deletion requests supported by evidence balances cleared / customer in liquidation
- Orders only accepted from customers who have no credit problems
- Sequential numbering of blank pre-printed order documents
- Correct prices quoted to customers
- Matching of customer orders with production orders and despatch notes and querying of orders not matched
- Dealing with customer queries

3

Ordering	Receipts/invoices	Accounting
(a) (c)	(b) (f)	(d) (e)

4   (a)   Any four of:

   (1) purchase requisitions, (2) purchase orders, (3) goods received notes, (4) goods returned notes, (5) suppliers' invoices

   (b)   Sequence provides a control that sales are complete. Missing documents should be explained, or cancelled copies available.

5   Any five of:

- To ensure that all inventory movements are authorised and recorded
- To ensure that inventory records only include items that belong to the client
- To ensure that inventory records include inventory that exists and is held by the client
- To ensure that inventory quantities have been recorded correctly
- To ensure that cut-off procedures are properly applied to inventory
- To ensure that inventory is safeguarded against loss, pilferage or damage
- To ensure that the costing system values inventory correctly
- To ensure that allowance is made for slow-moving, obsolete or damaged inventory
- To ensure that levels of inventory held are reasonable

6
- All monies received are recorded.
- All monies received are banked.
- Cash and cheques are safeguarded against loss or theft.
- All payments are authorised, made to the correct payees and recorded.
- Payments are not made twice for the same liability.

7   You could have come up with a number of controls that help ensure completeness of non-current assets, but a common one is the regular reconciliation of the non-current asset register with the general ledger to ensure all items on the register have been recorded. The test of this control would be to obtain a copy of the reconciliation and ensure all discrepancies are followed up and resolved on a timely basis.

Now try the questions below from the Practice Question Bank

Number	Level	Marks	Time
Q17	Introductory	n/a	n/a
Q16a	Examination	6	12 mins

P
A
R
T

D

Audit evidence

223

Audit procedures and sampling

Topic list	Syllabus reference
1 Substantive procedures	D2
2 Accounting estimates	D2
3 Audit sampling	D3
4 Computer-assisted audit techniques	D5
5 Using the work of others	D6

Introduction

In this chapter we look at various audit procedures and the use of audit sampling.

First we consider substantive testing which encompasses tests of detail and the use of analytical procedures as substantive tests. These methods form the basis for the next five chapters which examine the detailed testing for various financial statement account areas, such as cash and inventory.

We also examine the audit of accounting estimates. We have mentioned in previous chapters that judgement has to be used in accounting for some of the figures in the accounts. Examples of accounting estimates include depreciation and provisions.

We will look in detail at audit sampling, which is an important aspect of the audit. We consider different types of audit sampling and the evaluation of errors.

Computer-assisted audit techniques (CAATs) are an important tool in the audit and we examine the two main types of CAATs, audit software and test data.

Finally in this chapter we will look at how the auditor can make use of the work of others as a source of audit evidence. We consider the use of auditor's experts, the work of internal audit and the use of service organisations in this regard.

Study guide

		Intellectual level
D2	**Audit procedures**	
(a)	Discuss the substantive procedures for obtaining audit evidence.	2
(b)	Discuss and provide examples of how analytical procedures are used as substantive procedures.	2
(c)	Discuss the problems associated with the audit and review of accounting estimates.	2
D3	**Audit sampling and other means of testing**	
(a)	Define audit sampling and explain the need for sampling.	1
(b)	Identify and discuss the differences between statistical and non-statistical sampling.	2
(c)	Discuss and provide relevant examples of the application of the basic principles of statistical sampling and other selective testing procedures.	2
(d)	Discuss the results of statistical sampling, including consideration of whether additional testing is required.	2
D5	**Computer-assisted audit techniques**	
(a)	Explain the use of computer-assisted audit techniques in the context of an audit.	1
(b)	Discuss and provide relevant examples of the use of test data and audit software.	2
D6	**The work of others**	
(a)	Discuss why auditors rely on the work of others.	2
(b)	Discuss the extent to which external auditors are able to rely on the work of experts, including the work of internal audit.	2
(c)	Discuss the audit considerations relating to entities using service organisations.	2
(d)	Explain the extent to which reference to the work of others can be made in audit reports.	1

Exam guide

This chapter forms a basis for the next five chapters in terms of substantive audit procedures to carry out during an audit.

This is a core part of the F8 syllabus. Substantive procedures requirements are likely to feature in the exam, including:

- Defining tests of control and substantive procedures
- Describing substantive audit procedures in respect of depreciation and a provision for legal claims
- Describing substantive audit procedures in respect of trade receivables
- Describing substantive audit procedures in respect of plant and equipment additions

You must make sure that you devote adequate exam preparation time to this critical area.

This chapter also covers analytical procedures, sampling and the use of computer-assisted audit techniques (CAATs) which, along with any of the requirements above, could come up in OTQs in Section A, or as part of Section B. Questions could require you to explain different sampling methods, for example.

The extent to which external auditors can place reliance on the work done by internal auditors could come up in a question on audit evidence or in one on internal audit. You could be asked to advise on the extent to which the external auditor could rely on a report prepared by the internal audit department, for example.

Sections of a scenario-based question may require you to explain the matters the external auditor should consider when using the work of an expert.

1 Substantive procedures
June 08, Dec 08, June 09, Dec 09, June 10, June 12, June 15

Auditors need to obtain **sufficient appropriate audit evidence** to support the financial statement assertions. Substantive procedures can be used to obtain that evidence.

1.1 Types of audit tests

To recap, **substantive procedures** are tests to obtain audit evidence to detect material misstatements in the financial statements. They are generally of two types:

- Analytical procedures
- Tests of detail of transactions, account balances and disclosures

The types of substantive tests carried out to obtain evidence about various financial statement assertions are outlined in the table below.

Audit assertion	Type of assertion	Typical audit tests
Completeness	Classes of transactions and related disclosures Account balances and related disclosures	(a) Review of post year end items (b) Cut-off testing (c) Analytical review (d) Confirmations (e) Reconciliations to control accounts
Rights and obligations	Account balances and related disclosures	(a) Reviewing invoices for proof that item belongs to the company (b) Confirmations with third parties
Accuracy, valuation and allocation	Account balances and related disclosures	(a) Matching amounts to invoices (b) Recalculation (c) Confirming accounting policy is consistent and reasonable (d) Review of post year end payments and invoices (e) Expert valuation
Existence	Account balances and related disclosures	(a) Physical verification (b) Third-party confirmations (c) Cut-off testing
Occurrence	Classes of transactions and related disclosures	(a) Inspection of supporting documentation (b) Confirmation from directors that transactions relate to business (c) Inspection of items purchased
Accuracy	Classes of transactions and related disclosures	(a) Recalculation of correct amounts (b) Third-party confirmation (c) Analytical review
Classification	Classes of transactions and related disclosures	(a) Confirming compliance with law and accounting standards (b) Reviewing notes for understandability

Audit assertion	Type of assertion	Typical audit tests
Cut-off	Classes of transactions and related disclosures	(a) Cut-off testing (b) Analytical review

Use the following model for drawing up an audit plan.

- **Agree opening balances** with **previous year's working papers**
- **Review general ledger** for unusual records
- **Agree client schedules to/from accounting records** to ensure completeness
- Carry out **analytical review**
- **Test transactions in detail**
- **Test balances in detail**
- **Review presentation** and **disclosure** in accounts

1.2 Directional testing

FAST FORWARD

Substantive tests are designed to discover errors or omissions.

Broadly speaking, substantive procedures can be said to fall into two categories.

- Tests to discover **errors** (resulting in over- or understatement)
- Tests to discover **omissions** (resulting in understatement)

1.2.1 Tests designed to discover errors

These tests will start with the **accounting records** in which the transactions are recorded to supporting documents or other evidence. Such tests should detect any overstatement and also any understatement through causes other than omission. For example, if a test is designed to ensure that sales are priced correctly, it would begin with a sales invoice selected from the sales ledger. Prices would then be checked to the official price list.

1.2.2 Tests designed to discover omissions

These tests must start from **outside the accounting records** and then matched back to those records. Understatements through omission will never be revealed by starting with the account itself, as there is clearly no chance of selecting items that have been omitted from the account. For example, if a test is designed to discover whether all raw material purchases have been properly processed, it would start with goods received notes to be agreed to the inventory records or purchase ledger.

1.2.3 Directional testing

For most systems, auditors would include tests designed to discover both errors and omissions. The type of test, and direction of the test, should be recognised before selecting the test sample. If the sample which tested the accuracy and validity of the sales ledger was chosen from a file of sales invoices then it would not substantiate the fact that there were no errors in the sales ledger.

Directional testing is particularly appropriate when testing the financial statement assertions of existence, completeness, rights and obligations, and valuation.

The concept of directional testing derives from the principle of double-entry bookkeeping, in that for every **debit** there should be a **corresponding credit**. Therefore, any **misstatement** of a **debit entry** will result in either a corresponding **misstatement** of a **credit entry** or a **misstatement** in the opposite direction, of **another debit entry**.

By designing audit tests carefully the auditors are able to use this principle in drawing audit conclusions, not only about the debit or credit entries that they have directly tested, but also about the corresponding credit or debit entries that are necessary to balance the books.

Tests are therefore designed in the following way.

Test item	Example
Test **debit items** (expenditure or assets) for overstatement by selecting debit entries recorded in the nominal ledger and checking value, existence and ownership	If a non-current asset entry in the nominal ledger of $1,000 is selected, it would be overstated if it should have been recorded at anything less than $1,000 or if the company did not own it, or indeed if it did not exist (eg it had been sold or the amount of $1,000 in fact represented a revenue expense).
Test **credit items** (income or liabilities) for understatement by selecting items from appropriate sources independent of the nominal ledger and ensuring that they result in the correct nominal ledger entry	Select a goods despatched note and agree that the resultant sale has been recorded in the nominal ledger sales account. Sales would be understated if the nominal ledger did not reflect the transaction at all (completeness) or reflected it at less than full value (say, if goods valued at $1,000 were recorded in the sales account at $900, there would be an understatement of $100).

A test for the overstatement of an asset simultaneously gives comfort on understatement of other assets, overstatement of liabilities, overstatement of income and understatement of expenses.

So, by performing the primary tests, the auditors obtain audit assurance in other audit areas. Successful completion of the primary tests will therefore result in them having tested all account areas for both overstatement and understatement.

1.3 Analytical procedures

Analytical procedures are used at all stages of the audit, including as substantive procedures. When using analytical procedures as **substantive tests**, auditors must consider the information available, assessing its **availability, relevance** and **comparability**.

We introduced analytical procedures in Chapter 6 where they were used at the planning stage of an audit. They can also be used as substantive procedures to obtain audit evidence directly. Remember, the use of analytical procedures at the substantive testing stage is optional, but auditors must perform analytical procedures at the planning and finalisation stages of the audit.

ISA 520 *Analytical procedures* provides guidance for auditors on the use of analytical procedures as substantive procedures. Remember from Chapter 6 that analytical procedures include:

(a)   The consideration of comparisons with:

- **Comparable information** for prior periods
- **Anticipated results** of the entity, from budgets or forecasts
- **Expectations** prepared by the auditors (eg estimation of depreciation)
- **Industry information**

(b) Those between elements of financial information that are expected to conform to a predicted pattern based on the entity's experience, such as the relationship of gross profit to sales

(c) Those between financial information and relevant non-financial information, such as the relationship of payroll costs to number of employees

ISA 520 states that when using analytical procedures as substantive tests, the auditor must:

(a) Determine the **suitability** of particular analytical procedures for given assertions.

(b) Evaluate the **reliability of data** from which the auditor's expectation of recorded amounts or ratios is developed.

(c) **Develop an expectation** of recorded amounts or ratios and evaluate whether this is **sufficiently precise** to identify a misstatement that may cause the financial statements to be materially misstated.

(d) Determine the amount of any difference that is **acceptable** without further investigation.

1.3.1 Suitability of analytical procedures

Substantive analytical procedures are usually more applicable to large volumes of transactions that tend to be predictable over time. The suitability of a particular analytical procedure will depend on the auditor's assessment of how effective it will be in detecting material misstatements. Determining the suitability will be influenced by the nature of the assertion and the auditor's assessment of the risk of material misstatement.

1.3.2 Reliability of data

The ISA sets out factors which influence the reliability of data. These are set out in the following table, with examples.

Reliability factors	Example
Source of the information	Information may be more reliable when obtained from independent sources outside the entity.
Comparability of information available	Broad industry data may need to be supplemented so it is comparable to that of an entity that produces and sells specialised products.
Nature and relevance of the information available	Whether budgets have been set up as results to be expected rather than goals to be achieved.
Controls over the preparation of the information to ensure its **completeness, accuracy and validity**	Controls over the preparation, review and maintenance of budgets.

The auditor will need to consider testing the controls, if any, over the **preparation** of **information** used in applying analytical procedures. When such controls are effective, the auditor will have greater confidence in the reliability of the information and therefore in the results of analytical procedures.

The **controls** over **non-financial information** can often be tested in conjunction with tests of **accounting-related controls**. For example, in establishing controls over the processing of sales invoices, a business may include controls over unit sales recording. The auditor could therefore test the controls over the recording of unit sales in conjunction with tests of controls over the processing of sales invoices.

Alternatively, the auditor may consider whether the information was subjected to audit testing. ISA 500 contains guidance in determining the audit procedures to be performed on information to be used for substantive analytical procedures.

1.3.3 Evaluation of whether the expectation is sufficiently precise

The factors to consider when evaluating whether the expectation can be developed sufficiently precisely to identify a misstatement that may cause the financial statements to be materially misstated are set out in the following table.

Factors to consider	Example
The **accuracy** with which the expected results of analytical procedures can be predicted	The auditor may expect greater consistency in comparing the relationship of gross profit to sales from one period to another than in comparing discretionary expenses, such as research and advertising.
The **degree to which information can be disaggregated**	Analytical procedures may be more effective when applied to financial information on individual sections of an operation or to the financial statements of components of a diversified entity than when applied to the financial statements as a whole.
The **availability** of the information	The auditor may consider whether financial information (eg budgets and forecasts) and non-financial information (eg number of units produced or sold) is available.

1.3.4 Acceptable differences

The amount of the difference of recorded amounts from the expected value that is acceptable depends on **materiality** and **consistency with the desired level of assurance**, having taken into account that a misstatement may cause the financial statements to be materially misstated. Therefore, as the **assessed risk increases**, the **amount of the difference that is acceptable** without further investigation **decreases**.

1.3.5 Practical techniques

Analytical procedures can be performed using various techniques, ranging from simple comparisons to complex analyses using advanced statistical techniques. In this section we look at some of the techniques that can be used to carry out analytical procedures.

Ratio analysis can be a useful technique. However, ratios mean very little when used in isolation. They should be calculated for previous periods and for comparable companies. This may involve a certain amount of initial research, but subsequently it is just a matter of adding new statistics to the existing information each year. The permanent file should contain a section with summarised accounts and the chosen ratios for prior years.

Exam focus point

It is important that you understand that an auditor needs to develop an expectation to compare results and ratios against. A useful article on the use of comparisons and ratios in auditing was published in the December 2009 edition of *Student Accountant*. Another article published in September 2010 outlined analytical procedures in general that are relevant to the ACCA's audit papers. You should read these.

In addition to looking at the more usual ratios, the auditors should consider examining other ratios that may be relevant to the particular client's business. Other analytical techniques include:

(a) **Examining related accounts** in conjunction with each other. Often revenue and expense accounts are related to accounts in the statement of financial position and comparisons should be made to ensure relationships are reasonable.

(b) **Trend analysis**. Sophisticated statistical techniques can be used to compare this period with previous periods.

(c) **Reasonableness test**. This involves calculating the **expected value** of an item and comparing it with its actual value; for example, for straight-line depreciation.

(Cost + Additions − Disposals) × Depreciation % = Charge in statement of comprehensive income

Important accounting ratios	<ul><li>Gross profit margins, in total and by product, area and months/quarter (if possible)</li><li>Operating profit margin</li><li>Receivables collection period (average collection period in days)</li><li>Payables payment period (average payment period in days)</li><li>Inventory holding period (average number of days' inventory is held)</li><li>Inventory revenue ratio (revenue divided into cost of sales)</li><li>Current ratio (current assets to current liabilities)</li><li>Quick or acid test ratio (liquid assets to current liabilities)</li><li>Gearing ratio (debt capital to equity capital)</li><li>Return on capital employed (profit before tax to total assets less current liabilities)</li></ul>

Related items	• Payables and purchases
	• Inventories and cost of sales
	• Non-current assets and depreciation, repairs and maintenance expense
	• Intangible assets and amortisation
	• Loans and interest expense
	• Investments and investment income
	• Receivables and bad debt expense
	• Receivables and sales

Other areas for consideration

- **Examine changes** in **products, customers and levels** of **returns**

- **Assess** the effect of **price and mix changes** on the cost of sales

- **Consider** the effect of **inflation, industrial disputes, changes in production methods** and **changes in activity** on the charge for wages

- **Obtain explanations** for all **major variances** analysed using a standard costing system. Particular attention should be paid to those relating to the over- or under-absorption of overheads since these may, *inter alia*, affect inventory valuations

- **Compare trends in production and sales** and assess the effect on any provisions for obsolete inventory

- **Ensure** that **changes in the percentage labour or overhead content** of production costs are also reflected in the inventory valuation

- **Review other expenditure**, comparing:

  - Rent with annual rent per rental agreement
  - Rates with previous year and known rates increases
  - Interest payable on loans with outstanding balance and interest rate per loan agreement
  - Hire or leasing charges with annual rate per agreements
  - Vehicle running expenses with those expected for the company's vehicles
  - Other items related to activity level with general price increase and change in relevant level of activity (for example telephone expenditure will increase disproportionately if export or import business increases)
  - Other items not related to activity level with general price increases (or specific increases if known)

- **Review** statement of comprehensive income for **items** which may have been **omitted** (eg scrap sales, training levy, special contributions to pension fund, provisions for dilapidation)

- **Ensure expected variations** arising from the following have occurred:

  - Industry or local trends
  - Known disturbances of the trading pattern (for example strikes, depot closures, failure of suppliers)

Some comparisons and ratios measuring liquidity and longer-term capital structure will assist in evaluating whether the company is a going concern, in addition to contributing to the overall view of the accounts. However, we shall see in Chapter 18 that there are factors other than declining ratios that may indicate going concern problems.

The working papers must contain the completed results of analytical procedures. They should include:

- The outline **programme** of the work
- The summary of **significant figures** and relationships for the period
- A summary of **comparisons** made with budgets and with previous years
- Details of all **significant fluctuations** or **unexpected relationships** considered
- Details of the **results of investigations** into such fluctuations/relationships
- The audit **conclusions** reached
- **Information considered** necessary for assisting in the **planning** of subsequent audits

1.3.6 Analytical procedures and financial statement assertions

Substantive analytical procedures help auditors to test for a wide range of financial statement assertions. Generally, analytical procedures can provide evidence on:

- all financial statement assertions relating to classes of transactions and related disclosures

- all financial statement assertions relating to account balances and related disclosures **except for** rights and obligations

Analytical procedures can be designed to test several assertions at the same time. The following tables give some practical examples.

Classes of transactions and related disclosures	
Analytical procedure	**Financial statement assertion tested**
Compare the current year gross profit margin with the prior year gross profit margin and with industry trends	<ul><li>Occurrence and completeness of revenue</li><li>Cut-off of revenue</li><li>Accuracy of revenue</li><li>Occurrence and completeness of cost of sales</li><li>Accuracy of cost of sales</li><li>Classification of cost of sales</li></ul>
Compare the current year effective tax charge with the applicable rate of corporation tax for the period	<ul><li>Accuracy of tax expense</li><li>Completeness of tax expense and disclosures</li></ul>
Perform a proof-in-total of payroll (based on number of employees multiplied by average wage)	<ul><li>Occurrence and completeness of payroll expenses</li><li>Accuracy of payroll expenses</li><li>Cut-off of payroll expenses</li></ul>

Account balances and related disclosures	
Analytical procedure	**Financial statement assertion tested**
Compare the current year receivables collection period to that of the prior year	<ul><li>Existence and completeness of trade receivables</li><li>Accuracy, valuation and allocation of trade receivables</li><li>Accuracy, valuation and allocation of provision for irrecoverable receivables</li></ul>
Calculate the current year current ratio and compare with that of the prior year	<ul><li>Existence and completeness of current assets</li><li>Accuracy, valuation and allocation of current assets</li><li>Existence and completeness of current liabilities</li><li>Accuracy, valuation and allocation of current assets</li><li>Presentation of going concern disclosures</li></ul>

Both classes of transactions and account balances	
Analytical procedure	**Financial statement assertion tested**
Calculate the effective rate of interest on borrowings and compare it to the applicable rate stated in the relevant loan agreements	• Accuracy of interest expense • Completeness of interest expense • Accuracy, valuation and allocation of borrowings
Proof in total of the depreciation charge	• Accuracy of depreciation expense • Accuracy, valuation and allocation of non-current assets

1.3.7 Investigating the results of analytical procedures

ISA 520 states that where analytical procedures identify fluctuations or relationships that are inconsistent with other relevant information or that differ significantly from the expected results, the auditor shall investigate by:

- **Enquiries of management** and obtaining appropriate audit evidence relevant to **management's responses**
- Performing **other audit procedures** if necessary (eg if management cannot provide an explanation or the explanation is not adequate)

Question	Analytical procedures

You are part of the audit team auditing the financial statements of Sweep Co, a small office supplies business, for the year ended 31 March 20X9. The company employed the following staff at the start of the financial year: 7 office and warehouse managers, 20 warehouse staff and 25 office staff.

The pay ranges for each category of staff is shown below.

Office and warehouse managers: $35-$50k per year
Warehouse and office staff: $18-$25k per year

You have been asked to audit the wages and salaries expense for the year. All staff were given a 4% pay rise in the year, backdated to the start of the year. One of the office managers left the company halfway through the year. Two new members of warehouse staff and three new members of office staff joined halfway through the year.

The expense for the year is shown in the draft statement of profit or loss as $1,249,450.

Required

Using analytical procedures, perform a proof in total on the wages and salaries expense for the year.

Answer

An expectation of the charge for the year can be developed using the information provided and compared to the charge in the draft statement of profit or loss to assess its reasonableness.

Managers	$
Based on salary range, average annual salary:	42,500
Applying the 4% rise:	44,200
Total average salary for year (ie × 7):	309,400
Leaver left halfway through year:	(22,100)
Total for managers:	**287,300**

Office and warehouse staff

Based on salary range, average annual salary:	21,500
Applying the 4% rise:	22,360
Total average salary for year (ie × 45, exclude starters):	1,006,200
Starters started halfway through year:	55,900
Total for office and warehouse staff:	**1,062,100**
Expected total expense for wages and salaries:	**$1,349,400**
Expense per draft statement of profit or loss:	**$1,249,450**
Difference:	**8%**

The difference between the expected total and the expense in the draft statement of profit or loss is 8%. The auditor needs to consider whether this is acceptable in light of materiality for the financial statements as a whole and performance materiality and the risk of material misstatement and whether further explanations from management may be necessary.

Exam focus point

Describing suitable analytical procedures will generally be worth a couple of marks in any question on substantive testing. However, you will not get any marks just for saying 'perform analytical procedures' – you will need to give details of the specific procedures that should be performed.

2 Accounting estimates   Dec 10

FAST FORWARD

When auditing **accounting estimates**, auditors must:

- Test the management process
- Use an independent estimate
- Review subsequent events

In order to assess whether the estimates are reasonable.

2.1 The nature of accounting estimates

ISA 540 *Auditing accounting estimates, including fair value accounting estimates, and related disclosures* provides guidance on the audit of accounting estimates contained in financial statements. The auditor's objective is to obtain sufficient appropriate audit evidence about whether accounting estimates are reasonable and related disclosures are adequate.

Key terms

An **accounting estimate** is an approximation of a monetary amount in the absence of a precise means of measurement.

Estimation uncertainty is the susceptibility of an accounting estimate and related disclosures to an inherent lack of precision in its measurement.

Management's point estimate is the amount selected by management for recognition or disclosure in the financial statements as an accounting estimate.

Auditor's point estimate or **auditor's range** is the amount, or range of amounts, respectively, derived from audit evidence for use in evaluating management's point estimate.

Examples of accounting estimates include:

- Allowance for doubtful accounts
- Inventory obsolescence
- Warranty obligations
- Depreciation method or asset useful life

- Outcome of long-term contracts

- Costs arising from litigation settlements and judgements

- Provision against the carrying amount of an investment where there is uncertainty regarding its recoverability

Some financial statement items cannot be measured precisely, only estimated. The **nature and reliability** of information available to management to support accounting estimates can vary enormously and this therefore affects the **degree of uncertainty** associated with accounting estimates, which in turn affects the **risk of material misstatement** of accounting estimates.

Management use their discretion when arriving at accounting estimates. Balances and transactions related to accounting estimates are therefore more susceptible to management bias, especially where management has an incentive to manipulate trading results (eg their remuneration is linked to the profit for the year).

Unless the actual outcome of an issue that has given rise to an accounting estimate is known at the time of the audit (eg settlement has occurred post year end), it is often difficult for auditors to obtain conclusive evidence over the reliability of estimates.

In particular, it may be difficult for an auditor to arrive at their own point estimate due to the uncertainties and assumptions involved. For example, there may be a warranty provision included in the financial statements relating to a relatively new product, for which there is little data available on the level of returns.

Even if the auditor can formulate a reasonable estimate, it will be difficult for auditors to challenge management's estimate on the basis that the auditor's point estimate is different. Management will often argue that they are better placed to make estimates due to their ongoing involvement with the business and its environment. However, despite any resistance from management, the auditor has a responsibility to assess and, if necessary, challenge management's estimates.

2.2 Risk assessment procedures

ISA 540 states that the auditor shall obtain an understanding of the following to provide a basis for the identification and assessment of the risks of material misstatement for accounting estimates:

- The requirements of the applicable financial reporting framework

- How management identifies those transactions, events and conditions that may give rise to the need for accounting estimates

- How management makes the accounting estimates and an understanding of the data on which they are based, including:
  - Method
  - Relevant controls
  - Assumptions
  - Whether change from prior period in method used
  - Whether management has assessed the effect of estimation uncertainty

The ISA also states that the auditor shall review the **outcome** of accounting estimates included in the **prior period**.

2.3 Risk identification and assessment

The auditor shall also evaluate the degree of **estimation uncertainty** associated with an accounting estimate. Where estimation uncertainty is assessed as high, the auditor shall determine whether this gives rise to **significant risks**.

2.4 Responding to the assessed risks

The ISA requires the auditor to perform one or more of the following:

(a) Determine whether events occurring up to the date of the auditor's report provide audit evidence regarding the accounting estimate.

(b)   Test how management made the accounting estimate and the data on which it is based.

(c)   Test the operating effectiveness of controls over how the accounting estimate was made.

(d)   Develop a point estimate or a range to evaluate management's point estimate.

2.5 Substantive procedures in response to significant risks

Where the auditor judges that the accounting estimate gives rise to a significant risk, they shall evaluate the following in accordance with ISA 540.

- How management has considered alternative assumptions and why these have been rejected
- Whether the assumptions used are reasonable
- Management's intent to carry out specific courses of action and its ability to do so

If the auditor considers that management has not adequately addressed the effects of estimation uncertainty on accounting estimates that give rise to significant risks, they shall, if necessary, develop a **range** with which to evaluate the reasonableness of the accounting estimate.

2.6 Other audit procedures

ISA 540 requires the auditor to do the following:

- Evaluate whether the accounting estimates are either **reasonable or misstated**

- Obtain sufficient appropriate audit evidence about whether **disclosures** are correct

- For accounting estimates that give rise to significant risks, evaluate the adequacy of **disclosure of their estimation uncertainty**

- Review the judgements and decisions of management in making the accounting estimates to identify if there are indications of **possible management bias**

- Obtain **written representations** from management as to whether management believes significant assumptions used are reasonable

3 Audit sampling   June 09, June 12, June 14

FAST FORWARD

Auditors usually seek evidence from less than 100% of items of the balance or transaction being tested by using **sampling techniques**.

3.1 Methods of selecting items for testing

Auditors do not normally examine all the information available to them, as it would be impractical to do so, particularly given that the alternative ofusing audit sampling will produce valid conclusions. The methods which auditors can use to select items for testing are covered in ISA 500 *Audit evidence*. ISA 530 *Audit sampling* then goes on to provide guidance specific to audit sampling.

ISA 500 introduces three methods of selecting items for testing:

- **Testing 100%** of items in a population
- Testing all items with a **certain characteristic**, as selection is not representative
- **Audit sampling**

Auditors are unlikely to test 100% of items when carrying out tests of controls, but 100% testing may be appropriate for certain substantive procedures. For example, if the population is made up of a small number of high value items, there is a high risk of material misstatement and other procedures do not provide sufficient appropriate audit evidence, then 100% examination may be appropriate.

Alternatively, auditors may select certain items from a population because of specific characteristics they possess. The results of items selected cannot be projected onto the whole population, but they may be used in conjunction with other audit evidence concerning the rest of the population. Auditors may focus on:

(a) **High value or key items**. The auditor may select high value items or items that appear suspicious, unusual or prone to error.

(b) **All items over a certain amount**. Selecting items this way may mean a large proportion of the population can be verified by testing a few items.

(c) **Items to obtain information**. This could be information about the client's business, the nature of transactions, or the client's accounting and control systems.

(d) **Items to test procedures**. This is to see whether particular procedures are being performed.

Because the results cannot be projected, and therefore cannot provide audit evidence on the population as a whole, **selecting specific items for testing does not constitute audit sampling**.

Now that we have considered the selection methods which do not constitute audit sampling, we will turn our attention to audit sampling techniques.

3.2 Introduction to audit sampling

Audit sampling is designed to enable the auditor to draw conclusions about an entire population, on the basis of testing a sample drawn from it.

Key terms

> **Audit sampling** is the application of audit procedures to less than 100% of items within a population of audit relevance such that all sampling units have a chance of selection in order to provide the auditor with a reasonable basis on which to draw conclusions about the entire population.
>
> The **population** is the entire set of data from which a sample is selected and about which the auditor wishes to draw conclusions.

Audit sampling can be done using either **statistical sampling** or **non-statistical sampling** methods.

Key terms

> **Statistical sampling** is an approach to sampling that has the following characteristics:
>
> (i) Random selection of the sample items; and
> (ii) The use of probability theory to evaluate sample results, including measurement of sampling risk.
>
> **Non-statistical sampling** is a sampling approach that does not have these characteristics.

So, bearing in mind the definitions above, sampling is non-statistical when it does not meet the criteria required of statistical sampling. If each item of the population does not have an equal chance of selection, the sampling technique is non-statistical.

The difference between the two types of sampling is that, with statistical sampling, the sampling risk can be measured and controlled (we look at sampling risk in Section 3.2). With non-statistical sampling it cannot be measured.

Although the audit procedures performed on the items in the sample will be the same whether a statistical or non-statistical approach is used, meaningful extrapolation can only occur from a statistical sample which has been selected randomly.

Exam focus point

> In September 2013, *Student Accountant* published an article by the F8 examining team on audit sampling which considers the various sampling methods in the context of Paper F8. You should read this as part of your studies. The article can be accessed via the Technical Articles link on the ACCA's website: www.accaglobal.com/gb/en/student/acca-qual-student-journey/qual-resource/acca-qualification/f8/technical-articles.html.
>
> Following the June 2014 exam, the examining team noted that many candidates struggled to define audit sampling.

3.3 Design of the sample

Sampling risk is the risk that the auditor's conclusion based on a sample may be different from the conclusion that would be reached if the entire population were subjected to the same audit procedure.

Non-sampling risk is the risk that the auditor reaches an erroneous conclusion for any reason not related to sampling risk; for example, the use of inappropriate audit procedures, or misinterpretation of audit evidence and failure to recognise a misstatement or deviation.

Sampling unit is the individual items constituting a population. It may be a physical item (eg credit entries on bank statements, sales invoices, receivables' balances) or a monetary unit.

Stratification is the process of dividing a population into sub-populations, each of which is a group of sampling units which have similar characteristics, often monetary value.

The auditor must consider the **purpose** of the audit procedure when designing an audit sample. The auditor must also consider the **characteristics of the population**. When considering the characteristics of the population, the auditor might determine that **stratification** or **value-weighted selection** is appropriate.

The auditor must design a sample size sufficient to reduce sampling risk to an **acceptably low level**. Sampling risk can lead to two types of erroneous conclusions: for tests of controls, that they are more effective than they actually are, or for tests of details, that a material misstatement does not exist when it actually does; and for tests of controls, that controls are less effective than they actually are, or for tests of details, that a material misstatement exists when it actually does not. The lower the risk the auditor is willing to accept, the greater the sample size will need to be. Sample size can be determined using a statistically-based formula or through the use of judgement.

ISA 530 also requires the auditor to select items for the sample in such a way that each sampling unit in the population has a chance of selection. When statistical sampling is used, each sampling unit has a **known probability** of being selected. When non-statistical sampling is used, judgement is applied. However, it is important that the auditor selects a **representative sample**, free from bias, by choosing sample items that have **characteristics typical** of the population. The main methods of selecting samples are **random selection, systematic selection** and **haphazard selection**. We discuss these and other methods below.

(a) **Random selection** ensures that all items in the population have an equal chance of selection, eg by use of random number tables or random number generators.

(b) **Systematic selection** involves selecting items using a constant interval between selections, the first interval having a random start. When using systematic selection auditors must ensure that the population is not structured in such a manner that the sampling interval corresponds with a particular pattern in the population.

(c) **Haphazard selection** may be an alternative to random selection provided auditors are satisfied that the sample is representative of the entire population. This method requires care to guard against making a selection which is biased, for example towards items which are easily located, as they may not be representative. It should not be used if auditors are carrying out statistical sampling.

(d) **Block selection** may be used to check whether certain items have particular characteristics. For example, an auditor may use a sample of 50 consecutive cheques to test whether cheques are signed by authorised signatories rather than picking 50 single cheques throughout the year. However, block sampling may produce samples that are not representative of the population as a whole, particularly if errors only occurred during a certain part of the period, and therefore the errors found cannot be projected onto the rest of the population.

(e) **Monetary unit sampling** is a type of value-weighted selection in which sample size, selection and evaluation results in a conclusion in monetary amounts.

3.4 Performing audit procedures

Once the sample has been selected, the auditor must perform **appropriate audit procedures** on each item in the sample. If the audit procedure is not applicable to the selected item, the test must be performed on a **replacement item**. This could happen if, for example, a voided check is selected when testing for evidence of authorisation of payment.

If the auditor cannot apply the designed audit procedures (eg if documentation relating to the item has been lost), or suitable alternative audit procedures to the selected item, that item must be treated as a **deviation** from the prescribed control (for tests of controls) or a **misstatement** (for tests of details).

3.5 Deviations and misstatements

An **anomaly** is a misstatement or deviation that is demonstrably not representative of misstatements or deviations in a population.

Once the sample has been tested, the auditor must investigate the nature and cause of any deviations or misstatements found and evaluate their possible effect on the purpose of the audit procedure and on other areas of the audit.

In rare cases, a deviation or misstatement may be considered an **anomaly**, in which case the auditor must obtain a high degree of certainty that this is not representative of the population, by carrying out additional audit procedures.

3.6 Projection of misstatements

For **tests of details**, the auditor shall **project** misstatements found in the sample onto the population to obtain a broad view of the scale of the misstatement but this may not be enough to determine an amount to be recorded.

Misstatements established as **anomalies** can be excluded when projecting sample errors to the population. However, note that the effect of any uncorrected anomalies still needs to be considered. Projected errors and anomalies are combined together when considering the possible effect of errors on the total class of transactions or account balance. Where the audited entity has corrected specific errors found in the sample, the projected error may be reduced by the amount of these corrections.

ISA 530 states that for **tests of controls**, no explicit projection of errors is necessary because the sample deviation rate is also the projected deviation rate for the population as a whole. So for example, if in a sample of 75, four errors are discovered, the projected deviation rate is 4/75, ie 5%.

3.7 Evaluating the results

Key terms

Tolerable misstatement is a monetary amount set by the auditor in respect of which the auditor seeks to obtain an appropriate level of assurance that the monetary amount set by the auditor is not exceeded by the actual misstatement in the population.

Tolerable rate of deviation is a rate of deviation from prescribed internal control procedures set by the auditor in respect of which the auditor seeks to obtain an appropriate level of assurance that the rate of deviation set by the auditor is not exceeded by the actual rate of deviation in the population.

ISA 530 requires the auditor to evaluate the results of the sample.

For tests of controls, an unexpectedly high deviation rate in the sample may result in an increase in the assessed risk of material misstatement, unless further audit evidence to substantiate the initial assessment of risk is obtained.

For tests of details, an unexpectedly high misstatement amount in the sample may lead the auditor to conclude that a class of transactions or account balance is materially misstated, in the absence of further audit evidence that no misstatement exists.

240 **11: Audit procedures and sampling** | Part D Audit evidence

BPP
LEARNING MEDIA

For tests of details, the total of the projected misstatement and anomalous misstatement is the auditor's best estimate of misstatement in the population. If the total exceeds tolerable misstatement, the sample does not provide a reasonable basis for conclusions about the population. The closer the total figure is to tolerable misstatement, the more likely it is that actual misstatement in the population could exceed tolerable misstatement. The auditor must therefore also consider the results of other audit procedures to assist in determining the risk that actual misstatement in the population exceeds tolerable misstatement. The risk may be reduced if additional audit evidence is obtained.

The auditor must also evaluate whether the use of sampling has provided a reasonable basis for conclusions about the population from which the sample was drawn. If the conclusion is that sampling has not provided this, the auditor may request management to investigate misstatements that have been identified and make any necessary adjustments, or tailor the nature, timing and extent of further audit procedures to best achieve the assurance required.

3.8 Summary

Key stages in the sampling process are as follows.

- Determining **objectives and characteristics of the population**
- Determining **sample size**
- Choosing method of **sample selection**
- **Projecting errors** and **evaluating** the **results**

Being able to apply the techniques of audit sampling discussed in this section will assist you in achieving PER Objective 17 on preparing for and collecting evidence for audit.

4 Computer-assisted audit techniques   Dec 07, June 09

FAST FORWARD

CAATs are the use of computers for audit work. The two most commonly used CAATs are **audit software** and **test data**.

Key term

Computer-assisted audit techniques (CAATs) are applications of auditing procedures using the computer as an audit tool.

The overall objectives and scope of an audit do not change when an audit is conducted in a computerised environment. However, the application of auditing procedures may require auditors to consider techniques that use the computer as an audit tool. These uses of the computer for audit work are known as **CAATs**.

CAATs may be used in performing various auditing procedures, including the following.

- **Tests of details** of transactions and balances
- **Analytical review procedures**
- **Tests of computer information system controls**

The advantages of using CAATs are:

(a)   Auditors can test program controls as well as general internal controls associated with computers.

(b)   Auditors can test a greater number of items more quickly and accurately than would be the case otherwise.

(c)   Auditors can test transactions rather than paper records of transactions that could be incorrect.

(d)   CAATs are cost effective in the long term if the client does not change its systems.

(e)   Results from CAATs can be compared with results from traditional testing – if the results correlate, overall confidence is increased.

The disadvantages associated with using CAATs include:

- Setting up the software needed for CAATs can be time consuming and expensive.
- Audit staff will need to be trained so they have a sufficient level of IT knowledge to apply CAATs.
- Not all client systems will be compatible with the software used with CAATs.
- There is a risk that live client data is corrupted and lost during the use of CAATs.

The major steps to be undertaken by the auditors in the application of a CAAT are as follows.

- **Set the objective** of the CAAT application
- **Determine** the **content** and **accessibility** of the entity's files
- **Define** the **transaction types** to be tested
- **Define** the **procedures** to be performed on the data
- **Define** the **output requirements**
- **Identify** the audit and computer **personnel** who may participate in the design and application of the CAAT
- **Refine** the estimates of **costs** and **benefits**
- Ensure that the **use of the CAAT is properly controlled** and **documented**
- Arrange the **administrative activities**, including the necessary skills and computer facilities
- Execute the **CAAT application**
- **Evaluate the results**

There are two particularly common types of CAAT, **audit software** and **test data**.

<table>
<tr><td>**Exam focus point**</td><td>Use of computers on audits is common practice. You should consider the computer aspects of auditing as a matter of course. In answering questions on obtaining evidence, remember to include reference to CAATs if they seem relevant. There are some useful articles on auditing in a computerised environment accessible on the ACCA's website, including one published in 2011 on specific aspects of auditing in a computer-based environment. You should read this as part of your study for F8.</td></tr>
</table>

4.1 Audit software

<table>
<tr><td>**Key term**</td><td>**Audit software** consists of computer programs used by the auditors, as part of their auditing procedures, to process data of audit significance from the entity's accounting system. It may consist of generalised audit software or custom audit software. Audit software is used for substantive procedures.</td></tr>
</table>

Generalised audit software allows auditors to perform tests on computer files and databases, such as reading and extracting data from a client's systems for further testing, selecting data that meets certain criteria, performing arithmetic calculations on data, facilitating audit sampling and producing documents and reports. Examples of generalised audit software are ACT and IDEA.

Custom audit software is written by auditors for specific tasks when generalised audit software cannot be used.

The following table provides some examples of the use of audit software in the course of an audit.

<table>
<tr><td>**Audit software: examples of use**</td></tr>
<tr><td>
- Perform calculations and comparisons in analytical procedures
- Sampling programs to extract data for audit testing, eg select a sample of receivables for confirmation
- Scan a file to ensure that all documents in a series have been accounted for or to search for large and unusual items
- Compare data elements in different files for agreement (eg prices on sales invoices to authorised prices in master file)
</td></tr>
</table>

- Reperform calculations eg totalling sales ledger
- Prepare documents and reports eg produce receivables' confirmation letters and monthly statements

Earlier we looked at the advantages and disadvantages of CAATs in general and, although some may be similar, we will now look specifically at the benefits of audit software along with the potential difficulties of using audit software.

Benefits of using audit software

(a) Audit software can perform calculations and comparisons more quickly than those done manually.

(b) Audit software makes it possible to test more transactions than when simply manually scanning printouts. For example, audit software may facilitate searches for exceptions, such as negative or very high quantities when auditing inventory listings. The additional information will give the auditor increased comfort that the figure being audited is reasonably stated.

(c) Audit software may allow the actual computer files (the source files) to be tested from the originating program, rather than printouts from spool or previewed files which are dependent on other software (and therefore could contain errors or could have been tampered with following export).

(d) Using audit software is likely to be **cost-effective in the long term** if the client does not change its systems.

Difficulties of using audit software

(a) The **costs** of designing tests using audit software can be substantial, as a great deal of planning time will be needed in order to gain an in-depth understanding of the client's systems so that appropriate software can be produced.

(b) The **audit costs in general may increase** because experienced and specially trained staff will be required to design the software, perform the testing and review the results of the testing.

(c) If errors are made in the design of the audit software, **audit time, and therefore costs, can be wasted** in investigating anomalies that have arisen because of flaws in how the software was put together rather than by errors in the client's processing.

(d) If audit software has been designed to carry out procedures during live running of the client's system, there is a risk that this **disrupts** the client's systems. If the procedures are to be run when the system is not live, extra costs will be incurred by carrying out procedures to verify that the version of the system being tested is identical to that used by the client in live situations.

4.2 Test data

Key term

> **Test data** techniques are used in conducting audit procedures by entering data (eg a sample of transactions) into an entity's computer system, and comparing the results obtained with pre-determined results. Test data is used for tests of controls.

Examples include:

(a) Test data used to test **specific controls** in computer programs, such as online password and data access controls.

(b) Test transactions selected from previously processed transactions or created by the auditors to test **specific processing characteristics** of an entity's computer system. Such transactions are generally processed separately from the entity's normal processing. Test data can for example be used to check the controls that prevent the processing of **invalid data** by entering data with, say, a non-existent customer code or worth an unreasonable amount, or a transaction which may if processed break customer credit limits.

(c) Test transactions used in an **integrated test facility**. This is where a 'dummy' unit (eg a department or employee) is established, and to which test transactions are posted during the normal processing cycle.

Bearing the examples above in mind, we can see that the main **benefits of using test data techniques** are:

(a) Test data provides evidence that the software or computer system used by the client are working effectively by testing the program controls and in some cases there may be no other way to test some program controls.

(b) Once the basic test data have been designed, the level of ongoing time needed and costs incurred is likely to be relatively low until the client's systems change.

However, there are some **problems with using test data**.

(a) A significant problem with test data is that any **resulting corruption of data files** has to be corrected. This is difficult with modern real-time systems, which often have built-in (and highly desirable) controls to ensure that data entered **cannot** be easily removed without leaving a mark.

(b) Test data only tests the operation of the system at a **single point of time** and therefore the results do not prove that the program was in use throughout the period under review.

(c) **Initial computer time and costs can be high** and the client may change its programs in subsequent years.

One of the PER performance objectives is to use information and communications technology (Objective 6). The use of CAATs by you during an audit assignment will help to achieve this objective.

5 Using the work of others
Dec 08, Dec 09, June 11, Dec 11, Dec 14, Specimen Exam

FAST FORWARD

External auditors may make use of the work of an **auditor's expert**, **internal auditors** and **service organisations** and their auditors when carrying out audit procedures.

5.1 Using the work of an expert

Key terms

An **auditor's expert** is an individual or organisation possessing expertise in a field other than auditing or accounting, whose work in that field is used by the auditor to assist the auditor in obtaining sufficient appropriate audit evidence. An auditor's expert may be either an auditor's internal expert (who is a partner or staff, including temporary staff, of the auditor's firm or a network firm) or an auditor's external expert.

Management's expert is an individual or organisation possessing expertise in a field other than accounting or auditing, whose work in that field is used by the entity to assist the entity in preparing the financial statements.

Professional audit staff are highly trained and educated, but their experience and training is limited to accountancy and audit matters. In certain situations it will therefore be necessary to employ an **auditor's expert**.

Examples of areas in which an auditor's expert may be needed to help gain audit evidence include:

• Valuations of land and buildings

• Valuation of inventory or work in progress, including the determination of the physical condition of inventory

• Legal opinions, including expert opinions on the possible outcomes of litigation or disputes

Guidance on this area is provided by ISA 620 *Using the work of an auditor's expert*. An auditor's expert could be employed by the auditor to assist in:

- Obtaining an understanding of the entity and its environment, including its internal control
- Identifying and assessing the risks of material misstatement
- Determining and implementing overall responses to assessed risks at the financial statement level
- Designing and performing further audit procedures to respond to assessed risks at the assertion level
- Evaluating the sufficiency and appropriateness of audit evidence obtained in forming an opinion on the financial statements

5.1.1 Competence, capabilities and objectivity of the auditor's expert

ISA 620 requires the auditor to evaluate whether the auditor's expert has the necessary competence, capabilities and objectivity. Where the auditor's expert is external, the evaluation of objectivity will include enquiry of interests and relationships that could create a threat to objectivity.

Information on these areas may come from the following sources:

- **Personal experience** with previous work done by the expert
- **Discussions with the expert**
- **Discussions with other people** who are familiar with the expert's work
- Knowledge of the expert's **qualifications, membership of a professional body or industry association, licence to practise** etc
- **Published papers or books** by the expert
- The auditor's firm's **quality control policies and procedures**

5.1.2 Obtaining an understanding of the field of expertise

The auditor shall obtain a sufficient understanding of the auditor's expert's field of expertise to allow the auditor to determine the nature, scope and objectives of the work and to evaluate the adequacy of the work done.

5.1.3 Agreement

ISA 620 requires the auditor to agree in writing the following with the auditor's expert.

- **Nature, scope and objectives** of the work
- Respective **roles and responsibilities** of the auditor and the auditor's expert
- **Nature, timing and extent of communication** between the auditor and the auditor's expert, including the **form of any report**
- **Confidentiality requirements**

The agreement between the auditor and the auditor's expert is often in the form of an engagement letter. The Appendix to ISA 620 lists matters to consider for inclusion in the engagement letter.

5.1.4 Evaluating the work of the auditor's expert

The auditor shall evaluate the adequacy of the auditor's expert's work, which will include the following:

- The **relevance and reasonableness** of the expert's work and **consistency** with other audit evidence
- The relevance and reasonableness of any **assumptions and methods** used
- The relevance, completeness and accuracy of any **source data** used

If the auditor's evaluation results in a conclusion that the expert's work is not adequate, the auditor must agree on the nature and extent of further work to be done by the expert, and perform additional audit procedures that may be necessary in the circumstances.

5.1.5 Reference to the auditor's expert in the auditor's report

The auditor must not refer to the work of an auditor's expert in the auditor's report containing an unmodified opinion (unless required by law or regulation). If the auditor makes reference to the work of an auditor's expert in the auditor's report because it is relevant to understanding a modification to the opinion, the auditor must state in the auditor's report that this reference does not reduce the auditor's responsibility for the opinion.

5.2 Using the work of internal audit

Exam focus point

> This is a topical issue that has prompted a recent revision of ISA 610 in 2013. You should make sure that you are familiar with the content in this section. In the past, those areas that have been recently revised or updated have often come up in the exam.

ISA 610 (Revised) *Using the work of internal auditors* provides guidance for the external auditor when the external auditor expects to use the work of the internal audit function to modify the nature or timing, or reduce the extent, of audit procedures to be performed directly by the external auditor.

The objectives of the auditor (as stated in ISA 610) are:

(a)   To determine whether the work of the internal audit function or direct assistance from internal auditors can be used and, if so, in which areas and to what extent

(b)   If using the work of the internal audit function, to determine whether that work is appropriate for the purposes of the audit

(c)   If using internal auditors to provide direct assistance, to appropriately direct, supervise and review their work

Key term

> **Internal audit function** is defined in the ISAs as a function of an entity that performs assurance and consulting activities designed to evaluate and improve the effectiveness of the entity's governance, risk management and internal control processes.
>
> **Direct assistance** refers to the use of internal auditors to perform audit procedures under the direction, supervision and review of the external auditor.

Although the work of internal audit may be used for the purposes of the external audit, it is important to note that the external auditor has **sole responsibility** for the audit opinion expressed on the financial statements.

The current ISA 610 was revised in March 2013 (effective for audits of financial statements for periods ending on or after 15 December 2014). In 2012, amendments were made to strengthen the framework for the evaluation and use of the internal audit function when obtaining audit evidence. The latest revision tackled the question of direct assistance, an ambiguous and contentious area on which the International Auditing and Assurance Standards Board (IAASB) felt it could no longer remain silent.

5.2.1 Scope and objectives of internal audit

As we discussed in Chapter 5, the scope and objectives of internal audit vary widely. Normally, however, internal audit operates in one or more of the following broad areas.

- Monitoring of internal control
- Examination of financial and operating information
- Review of operating activities
- Review of compliance with laws and regulations
- Risk management
- Governance

5.2.2 When can the work of the internal audit function be used?

An effective internal audit function may reduce, modify or alter the timing of external audit procedures, but it can **never** eliminate them entirely. Even where the internal audit function is deemed ineffective, it may still be useful to be aware of the conclusions formed. The effectiveness of internal audit will have a great impact on how the external auditors assess the whole control system and the assessment of audit risk.

The external auditor will need to determine whether the work of the internal audit function can be used for the audit and, if so, establish the **nature and extent** of work that can be used.

Determining whether the work of the internal audit function can be used

The following criteria must first be considered by the external auditors when determining **whether the work of the internal audit function can be used**.

EVALUATING THE INTERNAL AUDIT FUNCTION	
Criteria	**Relevant considerations**
The extent to which its **objectivity** is supported by its organisational status, relevant policies and procedures	Consider the **status** of the internal audit function, to whom it **reports**, any **conflicting responsibilities**, any **constraints or restrictions**, whether those charged with governance oversee **employment decisions** regarding internal auditors, whether management acts on **recommendations** made, whether internal auditors are members of professional bodies and obligated to comply with their requirements for objectivity.
The level of **competence** of the function	Consider whether the internal audit function is **adequately resourced**, whether internal auditors are **members of relevant professional bodies**, have adequate **technical training and proficiency**, whether there are **established policies for hiring and training**, whether internal auditors possess the **required knowledge** of financial reporting / the applicable financial reporting framework.
Whether the internal audit function applies a **systematic and disciplined approach** (including quality control)	Consider whether internal audit activities include a systematic and disciplined approach to **planning, supervising, reviewing and documenting** assignments, whether the function has **appropriate quality control procedures**, the **existence of audit manuals, work programmes** and **internal audit documentation.**

If the internal audit function is found to be lacking in **any** of the preceding areas, ISA 610 (Revised) states that the auditor shall **not** use the work of the internal auditor.

Determining the nature and extent of internal audit work that can be used

When determining the **areas and the extent** to which the work of the internal audit function can be used, the auditor must consider:

- The **nature and scope** of specific work performed or to be performed
- The **relevance** of that work to the audit strategy and audit plan
- The **degree of judgement** involved in evaluation of audit evidence gathered by internal auditors

The external auditor is responsible for the audit opinion and must make all significant judgements in the audit. Therefore, the external auditor must plan to use the work of the internal audit function less (and therefore perform more of the work directly) in any areas which might involve significant judgements being made. These will be areas where:

- More judgement is needed in planning/performing procedures and evaluating evidence

- The risk of material misstatement is high, including where risks are assessed as significant

- The internal audit function's organisational status and relevant policies/procedures are not as robust in supporting the internal audit function's objectivity

- The internal audit function is less competent

The external auditor must also take a 'step back' and consider whether the planned extent of internal auditors' involvement will still result in the external auditor being involved enough, in light of the fact that the external auditor is solely responsible for the audit opinion.

5.2.3 Communicating with those charged with governance and the internal audit function regarding the use of its work

If the auditor intends to use internal audit work to obtain evidence, then how the external auditor intends to use this work **must** be communicated to those charged with governance when the auditor communicates the planned scope and timing of the audit. It is therefore important that the auditor has made the above assessment before this communication takes place.

The auditor must also discuss the planned use of the work with the internal audit function so both parties' activities can be co-ordinated.

5.2.4 Using the work of internal audit

ISA 610 (Revised) requires the external auditor to read the reports of the internal audit function relating to the work the external auditor plans to use. This is to obtain an understanding of the nature and extent of audit procedures the internal audit function performed, as well as understanding the related findings.

Before using the work of internal audit, the external auditors need to **evaluate** and **perform audit procedures** on the entirety of the work that they plan to use, in order to determine its adequacy for the purposes of the audit.

The evaluation includes the following:

- Whether the work was **properly planned, performed, supervised, reviewed** and **documented**
- Whether **sufficient appropriate evidence** was obtained to allow the internal auditors to draw reasonable conclusions
- Whether the **conclusions** reached are **appropriate** in the circumstances and the reports prepared are **consistent** with the results of the work done

As we have already seen above, the **nature and extent** of the audit procedures performed on specific work of the internal auditors will depend on the external auditor's assessment of:

- The amount of **judgement involved**
- The assessed **risk** of material misstatement
- How well the audit function's organisational status and relevant policies and procedures support the **objectivity of the internal auditors**
- The level of **competence** of the function

Note that ISA 610 (Revised) requires the external auditor's procedures to include **reperformance** of some of the internal audit work used.

Audit procedures might include:

- Examination of items **already examined** by the internal auditors
- Examination of **other similar items**
- **Observation of procedures** performed by the internal auditors

As the work of internal audit is reviewed, the external auditor must consider whether the initial conclusions reached when deciding whether to use (and to what extent to use) internal audit work in the first place are still valid, and should tailor audit procedures accordingly.

5.2.5 Using direct assistance from internal auditors

Requirements relating to the use of direct assistance from internal auditors for the purposes of the external audit (ie external auditors assigning the performance of specific audit procedures to the entity's internal auditors) were introduced in the latest revision to ISA 610, in 2013.

Previously, the ISAs have remained silent on the subject of whether, and how, external auditors should involve the entity's internal auditors in obtaining and evaluating audit evidence. While some jurisdictions categorically prohibit direct assistance, the IAASB notes that the use of direct assistance, where it is allowed, does not appear to compromise audit quality. Given appropriate planning, direction, supervision and review from the external audit team, the use of internal auditors could lead to savings in terms of both time and cost for the audit client.

Exam focus point

As ISA 610 (Revised) is an examinable document, you should ensure that you familiarise yourself with the requirements around direct assistance. Recent changes to the ISAs are often examined.

5.2.6 When can direct assistance from internal auditors be used?

The approach for determining when, in which areas, and to what extent internal auditors can be used to provide direct assistance mirrors the requirements we have already seen in relation to using the work of the internal audit function. The external auditors must first consider **whether direct assistance can be obtained** at all, before **determining the nature and the extent of the work** that can be assigned to internal auditors.

Determining whether internal auditors can be used to provide direct assistance

If external auditors are prohibited by law or regulation from obtaining direct assistance from internal auditors then it should not be used.

If direct assistance is not prohibited by law, the external auditor should evaluate the following.

- The internal auditors' **objectivity** (existence and significance of any threats)
- The internal auditors' **competence**

If either of these are lacking, then the external auditor must **not** use direct assistance.

Determining the nature and extent of work that can be assigned to internal auditors

The external auditor will need to determine the nature and extent of the work that may be assigned to internal auditors. As part of this, it will be necessary to consider the direction, supervision and review that would be needed.

Three key areas must be considered.

(a) The amount of **judgement** involved in **planning** and **performing** the relevant audit procedures, and in **evaluating** the audit evidence gathered

(b) The assessed **risk** of material misstatement

(c) The external auditor's evaluation of the existence and significance of threats to the **objectivity** and the level of **competence** of the internal auditors

ISA 610 (Revised) **prohibits** the use of internal auditors to provide direct assistance to perform procedures that:

(a) Involve making **significant judgements** in the audit

(b) Relate to **higher assessed risks of material misstatement** where more than a limited degree of **judgement** is required: for example, in assessing the valuation of accounts receivable, internal auditors may be assigned to check the accuracy of receivables ageing, but they must not be involved in evaluating the adequacy of the provision for irrecoverable receivables

(c) Relate to work with which the **internal auditors have been involved**

(d) Relate to **decisions** the external auditor makes **regarding the internal audit function** and the use of its work or direct assistance

As we have already seen, ISA 610 (Revised) emphasises the fact that the sole responsibility for the audit opinion rests with the external auditors. The external auditor must therefore evaluate whether the combination of using the internal auditors to provide direct assistance, **and** the use of the work of the

internal audit function, will allow the external auditor to be sufficiently involved in the audit to express an audit opinion.

5.2.7 Communicating with those charged with governance regarding the use of direct assistance

Once the external auditors have evaluated the extent to which internal auditors can be used to provide direct assistance, they must **communicate the nature and extent of the planned use of direct assistance** to those charged with governance.

The external auditors and those charged with governance must reach a **mutual understanding** that the use of direct assistance is not excessive in the circumstances of the audit engagement.

5.2.8 Using internal auditors to provide direct assistance

Before using internal auditors to provide direct assistance, **written agreement must be obtained**:

(a) From an **authorised representative** of the entity (confirming that the internal auditors will be allowed to follow the external auditor's instructions, and that the entity will not intervene in the work that the internal auditor performs for the external auditor)

(b) From the **internal auditors** (confirming that they will keep specific matters confidential as instructed by the external auditor, and inform the external auditor of any threat to their objectivity)

It is especially important that the external auditor directs, supervises and reviews the work performed by the internal auditors, bearing in mind that the internal auditors are not independent of the entity.

ISA 610 (Revised) requires the external auditor to check back to the underlying audit evidence for at least some of the work performed by the internal auditors.

Throughout the process, the external auditor must consider the degree of judgement involved in, and the assessed risk of material misstatement associated with, the work assigned to the internal auditor, as we have already seen above. They should also remain alert for indications that the internal auditors lack the required **competence**, and **objectivity**, to perform the work.

5.2.9 Documentation

Where **the work of the internal audit function has been used**, ISA 610 (Revised) requires the external auditors to document:

(a) The evaluation of whether the function's organisational status and relevant policies/procedures support its independence adequately, the level of competence of the function and whether it is disciplined and systematic in its approach

(b) The nature and extent of the work used and the reasons for deciding on that approach

(c) The audit procedures performed by the external auditor to evaluate the adequacy of the internal audit function's work

Where the **external auditors have used direct assistance from the internal auditors**, ISA 610 (Revised) requires the following to be documented.

(a) The evaluation of the **existence** and **significance** of **threats to the objectivity** of the internal auditors, and the level of **competence** of the internal auditors used

(b) The **basis for the decision** regarding the **nature and extent** of the work performed by the internal auditors

(c) **Who reviewed** the work performed and the **date** and **extent** of that review

In addition, the written agreements obtained from the authorised representative of the entity and the internal auditors (see Section 5.2.8 above) should also be included in the audit documentation. The working papers prepared by the internal auditors who provided direct assistance should be filed.

5.3 Service organisations

FAST FORWARD

A **service organisation** provides services to user entities. There may be special considerations for the auditor of a user entity when that entity makes use of a service organisation.

Key terms

A **service organisation** is a third-party organisation that provides services to user entities that are part of those entities' information systems relevant to financial reporting.

A **user entity** is an entity that uses a service organisation and whose financial statements are being audited.

A **user auditor** is an auditor who audits and reports on the financial statements of a user entity.

A **service auditor** is an auditor who, at the request of the service organisation, provides an assurance report on the controls of a service organisation.

ISA 402 *Audit considerations relating to an entity using a service organisation* provides guidance to auditors whose clients use such an organisation. It expands on how the user auditor obtains an understanding of the user entity, including internal control sufficient to identify and assess the risks of material misstatement and in designing and performing further audit procedures responsive to those risks.

A client may use a service organisation, such as one that executes transactions and maintains related accountability or records transactions and processes related data. Many companies now outsource some aspects of their business activities to external service organisations. Examples relevant to the independent auditors include:

- Payroll processing
- Maintenance of accounting records

5.3.1 Understanding the services provided

User auditors must obtain an understanding of the services provided by the service organisation in accordance with ISA 315. This understanding must include the following:

- Nature of services provided and the significance of these to the user entity, including effect on user entity's internal control

- Nature and materiality of transactions processed or financial reporting processes affected

- Degree of interaction

- Nature of relationship including contractual terms

When obtaining an understanding of the internal control relevant to the audit, the user auditor must evaluate the design and implementation of relevant controls at the user entity that relate to the services provided by the service organisation.

The user auditor needs to determine whether a sufficient understanding of the nature and significance of the services provided and their effect on internal control has been obtained to allow for the identification and assessment of risks of material misstatement in the financial statements.

If the user auditor cannot get this understanding from the user entity, the understanding needs to be obtained from one or more of the following procedures:

- Obtaining a type 1 report (report on description and design of controls at a service organisation) or type 2 report (report on the description, design and operating effectiveness of controls at a service organisation) from a service auditor, if available

- Contacting the service organisation through the user entity

- Visiting the service organisation and performing necessary procedures

- Using another auditor to perform necessary procedures

If the user auditor uses a type 1 or type 2 report to obtain an understanding of the services, the auditor must be satisfied as to the service auditor's professional competence and independence, and the adequacy of standards used.

5.3.2 Responding to the assessed risks of material misstatement

In responding to the assessed risks in accordance with ISA 330, the user auditor must:

(a) Determine whether **sufficient appropriate audit evidence** concerning the relevant financial statement assertions is available from records held at the user entity; and if not

(b) Perform further audit procedures to obtain sufficient appropriate audit evidence or use another auditor to perform those procedures at the service organisation on the user auditor's behalf.

5.3.3 Reporting by the user auditor

The user auditor is always **solely responsible** for the auditor's opinion. (S)he must be assured that (s)he has gained sufficient appropriate audit evidence to form an opinion on the financial statements, and (s)he must then express the audit opinion in the auditor's report. The user auditor must therefore not refer to the work of a service auditor in the user auditor's report if it contains an unmodified opinion (unless required by law or regulation). If the user auditor makes reference to the work of a service auditor in the user auditor's report because it is relevant to understanding a modification to the opinion, the user auditor must state in the user auditor's report that this reference does not reduce the user auditor's responsibility for the opinion.

Chapter Roundup

- Auditors need to obtain **sufficient appropriate audit evidence** to support the financial statement assertions. Substantive procedures aim to obtain that evidence.

- Substantive tests are designed to discover errors or omissions.

- Analytical procedures are used at all stages of the audit, including as substantive procedures. When using analytical procedures as **substantive tests**, auditors must consider the information available, assessing its **availability, relevance** and **comparability.**

- When auditing **accounting estimates**, auditors must:

    - Test the management process
    - Use an independent estimate
    - Review subsequent events

  In order to assess whether the estimates are reasonable.

- Auditors usually seek evidence from less than 100% of items of the balance or transaction being tested by using **sampling techniques**.

- CAATs are the use of computers for audit work. The two most commonly used CAATs are **audit software** and **test data**.

- External auditors may make use of the work of an **auditor's expert**, **internal auditors** and **service organisations** and their auditors when carrying out audit procedures.

- A **service organisation** provides services to user entities. There may be special considerations for the auditor of a user entity when that entity makes use of a service organisation.

1   Link the type of account with the purpose of the primary test in directional testing.

(a)   Assets   (i)   Overstatement
(b)   Liabilities   (ii)   Overstatement
(c)   Income   (iii)   Understatement
(d)   Expense   (iv)   Understatement

2   State four issues auditors should consider when carrying out analytical procedures on wages and salaries.

(1)   ....

(2)   ....

(3)   ....

(4)   ....

3   Identify the significant relationships in the list of items below.

(a)   payables   (b)   interest   (c)   purchases   (d)   sales
(e)   amortisation   (f)   loans   (g)   receivables   (h)   intangibles

4   Complete the definition.

An accounting estimate is an .... of the .... of an item in the absence of a .... of measurement.

5   Give three examples of sample selection methods that can be used in audit sampling.

(1)   ....

(2)   ....

(3)   ....

6   Name two types of CAAT that are commonly used.

(1)   ....

(2)   ....

7   There are three criteria for evaluating whether the work of the internal audit function can be used. State these criteria.

(1)   ....

(2)   ....

(3)   ....

8   If the auditor relies on the work of an auditor's expert or service organisation, they may refer to that individual or organisation in the auditor's report and share responsibility with them.

True   ☐

False   ☐

1   (a)   (i)
    (b)   (iii)
    (c)   (ii)
    (d)   (iv)

2   (1)   Salary rate changes
    (2)   Average wage by month over the year
    (3)   Sale/employee
    (4)   Payroll proof in total

3   (a)   (c)
    (b)   (f)
    (d)   (g)
    (e)   (h)

4   Approximation, amount, precise means

5   Three from the following:

    • Random
    • Systematic
    • Haphazard
    • Block
    • Monetary unit sampling

6   (1)   Audit software

    (2)   Test data

7   (1)   The extent to which its objectivity is supported by its organisational status, relevant policies and procedures

    (2)   The level of competence of the function

    (3)   Whether the internal audit function applies a systematic and disciplined approach

8   False

> **Now try the questions below from the Practice Question Bank**

Number	Level	Marks	Time
Q11 parts (d) and (e)	Examination	10	20 mins
Q18	Examination	10	20 mins
Q19	Examination	20	39 mins
Q20	Examination	20	39 mins

Non-current assets

Topic list	Syllabus reference
1 Tangible non-current assets	D4
2 Intangible non-current assets	D4

Introduction

This chapter covers the audit of non-current assets, a key area of the statement of financial position.

It highlights the key objectives for each major component of non-current assets. You must understand what objectives the various audit tests are designed to achieve in relation to the financial statement assertions. Objectives of particular significance for tangible non-current assets are rights and obligations (ownership), existence and valuation.

Valuation is an important assertion. The auditors will concentrate on testing any external valuations made during the year, and also whether other values appear reasonable given asset usage and condition. An important aspect of testing valuation is reviewing depreciation rates. A topic we covered in Chapter 11, using the work of an expert, may well be important in the audit of non-current assets in respect of valuation.

Study guide

		Intellectual level
D4	The audit of specific items	
(e)	Tangible and intangible non-current assets	2
	(i) Evidence in relation to non-current assets, and	
	(ii) Depreciation	
	(iii) Profit/loss on disposal	
•	Explain the audit objectives and the audit procedures in relation to the balance.	

Exam guide

In the audit of non-current assets, if you are asked to identify and explain the audit procedures you would perform to confirm specific assertions, you must explain why you are carrying out that procedure.

Assertions could also be the focus of questions: you could be asked to describe audit procedures to test one particular assertion, or to identify the assertions relevant to the audit of tangible non-current assets, or indeed both.

Both audit procedures and assertions can be tested in the form of OTQs in Section A.

1 Tangible non-current assets
Dec 08, Dec 09, Dec 10, Jun 12, June 13, Dec 14, Specimen Exam

FAST FORWARD

Key areas when testing **tangible non-current assets** are:

- **Confirmation** of ownership
- **Inspection** of non-current assets
- **Valuation** by third parties
- **Adequacy** of **depreciation** rates

1.1 Audit objectives for tangible non-current assets

Financial statement assertion	Audit objective
Existence and occurrence	– Additions represent assets acquired in the year and disposal represents assets sold or scrapped in the year – Recorded assets represent those in use at the year end
Completeness	– All additions and disposals that occurred in the year have been recorded – Balances represent assets in use at the year end
Rights and obligations	– The entity has rights to the assets purchased and those recorded at the year end
Accuracy, valuation and allocation	– Non-current assets are correctly stated at cost less accumulated depreciation – Additions and disposals are correctly recorded
Classification	– Tangible assets have been recorded in the correct accounts, and expenses which are not of a capital nature are taken to profit or loss

Financial statement assertion	Audit objective
Presentation (occurrence and rights and obligations, completeness, Classification, accuracy, valuation and allocation)	– Disclosures relating to cost, additions and disposals, depreciation policies, useful lives and assets held under finance leases are adequate and in accordance with accounting standards

1.2 Internal control considerations

The **non-current asset register** is a very important aspect of the internal control system. It enables assets to be identified, and comparisons between the general ledger, non-current asset register and the assets themselves provide **evidence** that the assets are **completely recorded**.

Another significant control is procedures over acquisitions and disposals, that acquisitions are properly **authorised**, **disposals** are **authorised** and **proceeds accounted for**. The controls and tests outlined in Chapter 10 (Section 6) are often considered and performed during the audit of non-current assets, as this is where the main issue of capitalisation occurs.

Other significant aspects are whether:

- **Security arrangements** over non-current assets are **sufficient**.
- **Non-current assets** are **maintained properly**.
- **Depreciation** is **reviewed every year**.
- **All income** is **collected** from **income-yielding assets**.

1.3 Audit procedures for tangible non-current assets

The plan below contains procedures for non-current assets in the statement of financial position and the related statement of profit or loss and other comprehensive income items (such as the depreciation charge and profits or losses on disposals).

AUDIT PLAN: TANGIBLE NON-CURRENT ASSETS	
COMPLETENESS	• **Obtain** or **prepare** a **summary** of tangible non-current assets showing how the following **reconcile** with the **opening position**. – **Gross book value** – **Accumulated depreciation** – **Net book value** • **Compare non-current assets** in the general ledger with the **non-current assets register** and **obtain explanations** for **differences**. • For a sample of assets which physically exist, agree that they are **recorded** in the **non-current asset register**. • If a non-current asset register is not kept, **obtain** a **schedule** showing the original costs and present depreciated value of major non-current assets. • **Reconcile** the **schedule** of non-current assets with the **general ledger**.
EXISTENCE	• **Confirm** that the **company physically inspects** all items in the non-current asset register each year. • **Inspect assets**, concentrating on high value items and additions in-year. Confirm that items inspected: – Exist – Are in use – Are in good condition – Have correct serial numbers • **Review records** of **income-yielding assets**. • **Reconcile** opening and closing **vehicles** by numbers as well as amounts.
VALUATION	• **Verify valuation** to valuation certificate.

AUDIT PLAN: TANGIBLE NON-CURRENT ASSETS	

VALUATION	• **Consider reasonableness** of **valuation**, reviewing:
	  – Experience of valuer
	  – Scope of work
	  – Methods and assumptions used
	  – Valuation bases are in line with accounting standards

	• **Reperform** calculation of revaluation surplus. • Confirm whether valuations of all assets that have been revalued have been **updated regularly** (full valuation every five years and an interim valuation in year three generally) by asking the Finance Director and inspecting the previous financial statements. • **Inspect** draft accounts to check that client has recognised revaluation losses in the statement of profit or loss unless there is a credit balance in respect of that asset in equity, in which case it should be debited to equity to cancel the credit. All revaluation gains should be credited to equity. • **Review insurance policies** in force for all categories of tangible non-current assets and consider the adequacy of their insured values and check expiry dates.

VALUATION – DEPRECIATION	• **Review depreciation** rates applied in relation to:
	  – Asset lives
	  – Residual values
	  – Replacement policy
	  – Past experience of gains and losses on disposal
	  – Consistency with prior years and accounting policy
	  – Possible obsolescence
	
	• **Review** non-current assets register to ensure that **depreciation** has been **charged on all assets** with a limited useful life.
	
	• For **revalued assets**, ensure that the charge for **depreciation** is based on the revalued amount by recalculating it for a sample of revalued assets.
	
	• **Reperform calculation** of depreciation rates to ensure it is correct.
	
	• **Compare ratios** of depreciation to non-current assets (by category) with:
	  – Previous years
	  – Depreciation policy rates
	
	• **Scrutinise** draft accounts to ensure that **depreciation policies** and rates are **disclosed** in the accounts.

RIGHTS AND OBLIGATIONS	• **Verify title** to land and buildings by inspection of:
	  – Title deeds
	  – Land registry certificates
	  – Leases
	
	• Obtain a certificate from solicitors/bankers:
	  – **Stating purpose** for which the deeds are being held (custody only)
	  – **Stating deeds** are **free** from **mortgage** or **lien**
	
	• **Inspect registration documents** for vehicles held, confirming that they are in client's name.
	
	• **Confirm** all vehicles are used for the **client's business**.
	
	• **Examine documents** of **title** for other assets (including purchase invoices, architects' certificates, contracts, hire purchase or lease agreements).
	
	• **Review for evidence** of charges in statutory books and by company search.

AUDIT PLAN: TANGIBLE NON-CURRENT ASSETS	
RIGHTS AND OBLIGATIONS	• **Review leases** of leasehold properties to ensure that company has fulfilled covenants therein. • **Examine invoices received after year end, orders** and **minutes** for evidence of capital commitments.

ADDITIONS	These tests are to confirm **rights and obligations**, **valuation** and **completeness**.
	
	• Verify additions by inspection of architects' certificates, solicitors' completion statements, suppliers' invoices etc.
	
	• **Review** capitalisation of expenditure by examining for non-current assets additions and items in relevant expense categories (repairs, motor expenses, sundry expenses) to ensure that:
	  – Capital/revenue distinction is correctly drawn
	  – Capitalisation is in line with consistently applied company policy
	
	• **Inspect** non-current asset accounts for a sample of purchases to ensure they have been **properly allocated**.
	
	• Ensure that appropriate **claims** have been made for **grants**, and grants received and receivable have been received, by **inspecting** claims documentations and bank statements.
	
	• Verify that **additions** have been **recorded** by **scrutinising** the non-current asset register and general ledger.

SELF-CONSTRUCTED ASSETS	These tests are to confirm **valuation** and **completeness**.
	
	• **Verify material** and **labour** costs and **overheads** to invoices, wage records etc.
	
	• Ensure expenditure has been **analysed correctly** and **properly charged** to capital.
	
	• Expenditure should be capitalised if it:
	  – **Enhances** the **economic benefits** of the asset in excess of its previously assessed standard of performance
	  – **Replaces or restores a component** of the asset that has been treated separately for depreciation purposes, and depreciated over its useful economic life
	  – Relates to a **major inspection** or **overhaul** that restores the economic benefits of the asset that have been consumed by the entity, and have already been reflected in depreciation
	
	• **Review** costs to ensure that no profit element has been included.
	
	• **Review** accounts to ensure that **finance costs** have been **capitalised** or not capitalised on a consistent basis, and costs capitalised in period do not exceed total finance costs for period.

DISPOSALS	These tests are to confirm **rights and obligations**, **completeness**, **occurrence** and **accuracy**. • **Verify disposals** with supporting documentation, checking transfer of title, sales price and dates of completion and payment. • **Recalculate** profit or loss on disposal. • **Consider** whether **proceeds** are **reasonable**. • If the asset was **used as security**, ensure **release from security** has been correctly made.
CLASSIFICATION	• **Review** non-current asset disclosures in the financial statements to ensure they meet IAS 16 criteria. • For a sample of **fully depreciated assets**, inspect the register to ensure no further depreciation is charged.

Question

You are the manager in charge of the audit of Puppy, a building and construction company, and you are reviewing the non-current asset section of the current audit file for the year ended 30 September 20X5. You find the following five matters which the audit senior has identified as problem areas. He is reviewing the company's proposed treatment of the five transactions in the accounts and is not sure that he has yet carried out sufficient audit work.

(i)   During the year Puppy built a new canteen for its own staff at a cost of $450,000. This amount has been included in buildings as at 30 September 20X5.

(ii)   Loose tools included in the financial statements at a total cost of $166,000 are tools used on two of the construction sites on which Puppy operates. They are classified as non-current assets and depreciated over two years.

(iii)   A dumper truck, previously written-off in the company's accounting records, has been refurbished at a cost of $46,000 and this amount included in plant and machinery as at 30 September 20X5.

(iv)   The company's main office block has been revalued from $216,000 to $266,000 and this amount included in the statement of financial position as at 30 September 20X5.

(v)   A deposit of $20,000 for new equipment has been included under the heading 'plant and machinery' although the final instalment of $35,000 was not paid over until 31 October 20X5, which was the date of delivery of the plant.

You are required, for each of the above matters, to:

(a)   Comment on the acceptability of the accounting treatment and disclosure as indicated above.
(b)   Outline the audit work and evidence required to substantiate the assets.

Answer

(a)   *Acceptability of accounting treatment and disclosure*

(i)   **New staff canteen**. The costs of building a new staff canteen can quite properly be capitalised and treated as part of buildings in the statement of financial position, as work has produced future economic benefits (IAS 16). The company's normal depreciation policy should be applied, subject only to the canteen being completed and in use at the year end.

(ii)   **Loose tools**. Loose tools tend to have a very limited life and to be immaterial in value individually. For these reasons any capitalisation policy must be extremely prudent. The acceptability of this accounting treatment would depend on the policy in previous years and normal practice within the industry.

(iii)   **Dumper truck**. The refurbishment costs have obviously extended the useful life of this asset and it therefore seems reasonable to capitalise the expenditure. Depreciation should be charged on the refurbishment costs over the estimated remaining useful life.

(iv)   **Revaluation of office block**. The revaluation of property is acceptable, but the auditors will need to ensure that the company complies with a number of disclosure requirements. A note to the accounts should give details of the revaluation and the name of the valuer. The surplus on revaluation should be transferred to a separate non-distributable reserve in the statement of financial position as part of shareholders' funds. Furthermore, any other assets of a similar nature to this should also be revalued.

(v)   **Deposit for new equipment**. As the equipment was not actually in the company's possession and use at the year end, the deposit should not have been shown as plant and machinery, but rather as a payment on account. If the amount was considered to be material, a note to the accounts should give details of this prepayment.

(b)   The audit work and evidence required to substantiate each of the assets referred to in (a) above would be as follows.

(i) **New staff canteen**

(1) Physically confirm existence of the asset.

(2) Confirm title to building by reference to central registry certificate.

(3) Ascertain and confirm the details of any security granted over the asset, ensuring that this is properly recorded and disclosed.

(4) Review the detailed costings of the building and obtain explanations for any material variances from the original budget. Particular care should be taken in assessing the reasonableness of any overheads included as an element of cost.

(5) Review the depreciation policy for adequacy and consistency.

(ii) **Loose tools**

(1) Visit the two sites where the loose tools are used to confirm the existence and condition of a sample of them.

(2) Vouch the cost and ownership of the loose tools to purchase invoices and the company's asset register.

(3) Confirm the company's estimate of a two year life for these assets.

(4) Review control procedures for safe custody of the loose tools.

(5) Review the company's policy with regard to scrapping and/or sale of tools no longer required to ensure that any proceeds are properly recorded and the assets register appropriately updated and tools are completely recorded.

(iii) **Dumper truck**

(1) Inspect the truck to confirm its existence and to gain evidence of its valuation by reviewing its condition and the fact that it is still being used.

(2) If the vehicle is used at all on public roads then the vehicle registration document should be inspected as some evidence of title.

(3) Inspect the insurance policy for the truck as evidence of valuation.

(4) Vouch the expenditure on refurbishment to suppliers' invoices or company's payroll records where any of the work has been done by the client's own staff.

(5) Review the depreciation policy and assess for reasonableness by discussion with management and past experience of similar vehicles.

(iv) **Revaluation of office block**

(1) Inspect the building to confirm its existence and state of repair.

(2) Examine documents of title to confirm ownership.

(3) Enquire about any charges on the building and confirm that these have been properly recorded and disclosed.

(4) Review the valuer's certificate and agree to the amount used in the financial statements, with consideration also being given to their qualifications, experience and reputation.

(5) Assess the reasonableness of the valuation by comparison with any similar properties which may have recently changed hands on the open market.

(v) **Deposit for new equipment**

(1) Agree the payment of the deposit to the contract for purchase of the equipment.

(2) Confirm the existence of the plant following its delivery on 31 October 20X5, as it is unlikely that the audit work will have been completed by that date.

Exam focus point

Note that inspection of a building's title deeds does **not** give audit evidence about **existence** and if there is doubt that a building actually exists, the auditors should physically inspect it.

2 Intangible non-current assets

FAST FORWARD

Key assertions for intangible non-current assets are **existence** and **valuation**.

The key assertions relating to intangibles are **existence** (not so much 'do they exist?', but 'are they genuinely assets?') and **valuation**. They will therefore be audited with reference to criteria laid down in the financial reporting standards. As only purchased goodwill or intangibles with a readily ascertainable market value can be capitalised, **audit evidence should be available** (purchase invoices or specialist valuations). The audit of **amortisation** will be similar to the audit of depreciation.

AUDIT PLAN: OTHER NON-CURRENT ASSETS	
Goodwill	• Agree the consideration to sales agreement by **inspection**. • Consider whether asset valuation is reasonable. • Agree that the calculation is correct by **recalculation**. • **Review** the impairment review and **discuss** with management. • Ensure valuation of goodwill is reasonable / there has been no impairment not adjusted through **discussion** with management.
Research and development (R&D) costs	• Confirm that capitalised development costs conform to IAS 38 criteria by **inspecting** details of projects and **discussions** with technical managers. • Confirm feasibility and viability by **inspection** of budgets. • **Recalculate** amortisation calculation to ensure it commences with production / is reasonable. • **Inspect** invoices to verify expenditure incurred on R&D projects.
Other intangibles	• Agree purchased intangibles to purchase documentation agreement by **inspection**. • **Inspect** specialist valuation of intangibles and ensure it is reasonable. • Review amortisation calculations and ensure they are correct by **recalculation**.

Chapter Roundup

- Key areas when testing **tangible non-current assets** are:
    - **Confirmation** of ownership
    - **Inspection** of non-current assets
    - **Valuation** by third parties
    - **Adequacy** of **depreciation** rates

- Key assertions for intangible non-current assets are **existence** and **valuation**.

Quick Quiz

1   State the key financial statement assertions for tangible non-current assets.

2   Complete the table, showing which tests are designed to provide evidence over which financial statement assertion.

Completeness	Existence
Valuation	**Rights and obligations**

(a) Inspect assets.	(e) Review depreciation rates.
(b) Verify to valuation certificate.	(f) Verify material on self-constructed asset to invoices.
(c) Inspect title deeds.	
(d) Compare assets in ledger to non-current asset register.	(g) Examine invoices after the year end.
	(h) Review repairs in general ledger.

3   Which of the following tests would provide audit evidence as to the existence of a tangible non-current asset?

   (a)   Inspecting board minutes approving authorisation of the asset
   (b)   Physically inspecting the asset
   (c)   Reviewing the non-current asset register for inclusion of the asset
   (d)   Inspecting the invoice and purchase order documentation of the asset

4   Inspecting the title deeds of a building provides audit evidence concerning which one of the following financial statement assertions?

   (a)   Existence
   (b)   Valuation
   (c)   Rights and obligations
   (d)   Completeness

5   What are the key financial statement assertions for intangible non-current assets?

1   Rights and obligations, existence, valuation, completeness

2

Completeness		Existence	
(d)	Compare assets in ledger to register.	(a)	Inspect assets.
(h)	Review repairs in general ledger.		
Valuation		**Rights and obligations**	
(b)	Verify to valuation certificate .	(c)	Inspect title deeds.
(e)	Review valuation rates.	(g)	Examine invoices after the year end.
(f)	Verify material on self-constructed assets to invoice.		

3   (b)   Physically inspecting the asset

4   (c)   Rights and obligations

5   Existence, valuation

Now try the question below from the Practice Question Bank

Number	Level	Marks	Time
Q21	Examination	20	39 mins

13

Inventory

Topic list	Syllabus reference
1 Introduction to auditing inventory	D4
2 Accounting for inventory	D4
3 Audit procedures for inventory	D4
4 The physical inventory count	D4
5 Cut-off testing	D4
6 Valuation	D4

Introduction

No area of the statement of financial position creates more potential problems for the auditors than that of inventory.

Closing inventory does not normally form an integrated part of the double entry bookkeeping system and hence a misstatement (under- or overstatement) may not be detected from tests in other audit areas.

The key assertions relating to the substantive audit of inventory (completeness, existence, rights and obligations, cut-off and valuation) require careful consideration.

The auditor's attendance at the inventory count is a particularly important part of the audit of inventory. This is because the inventory count gives evidence about the existence and completeness of inventory, and a review of the condition of the inventory is an important part of assessing whether it has been correctly valued.

Study guide

		Intellectual level
D4	**The audit of specific items**	
(b)	Inventory	2
	(i) Inventory counting procedures in relation to year end and continuous inventory systems	
	(ii) Cut-off testing	
	(iii) Auditor's attendance at inventory counting	
	(iv) Direct confirmation of inventory held by third parties	
	(v) Valuation	
	(vi) Other evidence in relation to inventory	
•	Explain the audit objectives and the audit procedures in relation to the balance.	

Exam guide

You may be asked to list and explain audit procedures you would perform to confirm specific assertions relating to inventory. As inventory is often one of the most difficult areas in practice for auditors, it is also very important in the syllabus.

You could be asked to do the following, for example:

(a)   Describe the audit procedures to perform **before**, **during** and **after** attending the inventory count.

(b)   Describe the audit procedures to be applied in respect of specific financial statement assertions related to inventory (including work in progress).

The financial statement assertions and their related audit procedures could also constitute the subject of mini-case OTQs in Section A.

1 Introduction to auditing inventory

FAST FORWARD

The key assertions relating to inventory are:

- **Existence**
- **Completeness**
- **Rights and obligations**
- **Valuation**
- **Cut-off**

The audit of inventory can pose problems for auditors as a result of its nature and potential material value on the statement of financial position. The audit approach taken depends on the auditor's assessment of the controls in place. In this chapter we focus on the **substantive** audit of inventory.

The following table demonstrates the audit objectives for inventory and the related financial statement assertions. The audit procedures described in the remainder of this chapter are undertaken to provide audit evidence to support these assertions.

Financial statement assertion	Audit objective
Existence and occurrence	– Recorded purchases and sales represent inventories bought and sold. – Inventory on the statement of financial position physically exists.
Completeness	– All purchases and sales are recorded. – All inventory at year end is included on the statement of financial position.
Rights and obligations	– The entity has rights to inventory recorded in the period and at the year-end.
Accuracy, valuation and allocation	– Costs are accurately determined in accordance with accounting standards. – Inventory is recorded at year end at the lower of cost and net realisable value (NRV).
Classification	– Inventory is recorded in the proper accounts
Cut-off	– All purchases and sales of inventories are recorded in the correct period.
Presentation (classification and understandability, completeness, accuracy and valuation)	– Inventory is properly classified in the accounts. – Disclosures relating to classification and valuation are adequate and in accordance with accounting standards.

1.1 Internal control considerations

We saw in Chapter 10 that the approach taken to the audit of inventory depends on the control system in place over inventory.

Remember, if the entity has a perpetual inventory system in place (where inventory is counted continuously throughout the year) and a year-end count is not undertaken, a controls-based approach is feasible as long as the controls over the system are appropriately designed. In fact, a controls-based approach may actually be more efficient.

However, where inventory quantities will be determined by an inventory count at the year-end date, a largely substantive approach is taken. We look at both year-end inventory counts and periodic counts in support of perpetual inventory systems later in this chapter.

2 Accounting for inventory

FAST FORWARD

The **valuation** and **disclosure** rules for inventory are laid down in IAS 2 *Inventories*. Inventory should be valued at the **lower** of cost and net realisable value.

Key terms

Cost is defined by IAS 2 as comprising all costs of purchase and other costs incurred in bringing inventory to its present location and condition.

Net realisable value is the estimated selling price in the ordinary course of business, less the estimated cost of completion and the estimated costs necessary to make the sale.

Production costs (costs of conversion) include:

(a)   Costs specifically attributable to units of production
(b)   Production overheads
(c)   Other overheads attributable to bringing the product or service to its present location and condition

3 Audit procedures for inventory
Dec 09, June 10, Dec 11, June 12, Dec 13, June 14

The following table sets out audit procedures to test year-end inventory. The physical inventory count is discussed in detail in Section 4 of this chapter, and cut-off and valuation are expanded upon in Sections 5 and 6.

AUDIT PLAN: INVENTORY	
Completeness	<ul><li>Complete the **disclosure checklist** to ensure that all the disclosures relevant to inventory have been made.</li><li>**Trace** test counts to the detailed inventory listing.</li><li>Where inventory is held in **third-party locations**, **physically inspect** this inventory or **review confirmations** received from the third party and match to the general ledger.</li><li>**Compare** the gross profit percentage to the previous year or industry data.</li></ul>
Existence	<ul><li>Observe the **physical inventory count** (see Section 4 for details of attendance at the inventory count).</li></ul>
Rights and obligations	<ul><li>Verify that any **inventory held for third parties** is not included in the year-end inventory figure by being appropriately segregated during the inventory count.</li><li>For any **'bill and hold' inventory** (ie where the inventory has been sold but is being held by the entity until the customer requires it), identify such inventory and ensure that it is segregated during the inventory count so that it is not included in the year-end inventory figure.</li><li>Confirm that any inventory held at **third-party locations** is included in the year-end inventory figure by reviewing the inventory listing.</li></ul>
Accuracy, valuation and allocation	<ul><li>Obtain a copy of the inventory listing and **agree** the totals to the general ledger.</li><li>**Cast** the inventory listing to ensure it is mathematically correct.</li><li>**Vouch** a sample of inventory items to suppliers' invoices to ensure it is correctly valued.</li><li>Where **standard costing** is used, test a sample of inventory to ensure it is correctly valued.</li><li>For **materials**, agree the valuation of raw materials to invoices and price lists.</li><li>Confirm that an appropriate **basis of valuation** (eg FIFO) is being used by discussing with management.</li><li>For **labour** costs, agree costs to wage records.</li><li>**Review** standard labour costs in the light of actual costs and production.</li><li>**Reconcile** labour hours to time summaries.</li><li>Make **enquiries of management** to ascertain any slow-moving or obsolete inventory that should be written down.</li><li>**Examine prices** at which finished goods have been sold after the year end to ascertain whether any finished goods need to be written down.</li><li>If significant levels of finished goods remain unsold for an unusual period of time, **discuss** with management and consider the need to make allowance.</li><li>**Compare** the gross profit percentage to the previous year or industry data.</li><li>**Compare** raw material, finished goods and total inventory turnover to the previous year and industry averages.</li><li>**Compare** inventory days to the previous year and industry average.</li></ul>

AUDIT PLAN: INVENTORY	
Accuracy, valuation and allocation	• **Compare** the current year standard costs to the previous year after considering current conditions. • **Compare** actual manufacturing overhead costs with budgeted or standard manufacturing overhead costs. • Obtain a copy of the inventory listing and **cast** it, and test the mathematical extensions of quantity multiplied by price. • **Trace** test counts back to the inventory listing. • If the entity has adjusted the general ledger to agree with the physical inventory count amounts, **agree** the two amounts. • Where a **continuous (perpetual) inventory system** is maintained, agree the total on the inventory listing to the continuous inventory records, using CAATs.
Cut-off	• Note the numbers of the **last GDNs and GRNs** before the year end and the **first GDNs and GRNs** after the year end and check that these have been included in the correct financial year.
Occurrence and rights and obligations	• **Enquire** of management and **review** any loan agreements and board minutes for evidence that inventory has been pledged or assigned. • Enquire of management about warranty obligation issues.
Classification	• **Review** the inventory listing to ensure that inventory has been properly classified between raw materials, work-in-progress and finished goods. • **Read** the notes to the accounts relating to inventory to ensure they are understandable.
Presentation	• **Review** the financial statements to confirm whether the cost method used to value inventory is accurately disclosed. • **Read** the notes to the financial statements to ensure that the information is accurate and properly presented at the appropriate amounts.

4 The physical inventory count

Dec 07

Physical inventory count procedures are vital, as they provide evidence which cannot be obtained elsewhere or at any other time about the quantities and conditions of inventories and work-in-progress.

ISA 501 *Audit evidence – specific considerations for selected items* provides guidance for auditors on attending the physical inventory count to obtain evidence regarding the existence and condition of inventory.

It states that where inventory is **material**, auditors shall obtain sufficient appropriate audit evidence regarding its **existence** and **condition** by attending the physical inventory count (unless this is impracticable) to do the following:

- Evaluate management's instructions and procedures for recording and controlling the result of the physical inventory count

- Observe the performance of the count procedures

- Inspect the inventory

- Perform test counts

The auditor shall also perform audit procedures over the entity's final inventory records to determine whether they accurately reflect the count results.

Attendance at the inventory count can serve as either substantive procedures or tests of controls, depending on the auditor's risk assessment, planned approach and specific procedures carried out.

Factors to consider when planning attendance at the inventory count include the following:

- The **risks of material misstatement** of inventory
- **Internal controls** related to inventory
- Whether **adequate procedures** are expected to be established and **proper instructions** issued for counting
- The **timing** of the count
- Whether the entity maintains a **perpetual inventory system**
- **Locations** at which inventory is held (including materiality at different locations)
- Whether the assistance of an **auditor's expert** is required

4.1 The inventory count

A business may count inventory by one or a combination of the following methods.

(a) **Physical inventory counts** at the **year end**

From the viewpoint of the auditor, this is often the best method.

(b) **Physical inventory counts before** or **after** the **year end**

This will provide audit evidence of varying reliability depending on:

  (i) The **length of time** between the physical inventory count and the year-end (the greater the time period, the less the value of audit evidence)

  (ii) The business's system of internal controls

  (iii) The **quality of records** of **inventory movements** in the period between the physical inventory count and the year end

(c) **Continuous** (or **perpetual**) **inventory** where management has a programme of inventory counting throughout the year

If **continuous** inventory counting is used, auditors will verify that management:

(a) Ensures that all inventory lines are counted at least once a year

(b) Maintains **adequate inventory records** that are kept up to date. Auditors may compare sales and purchase transactions with inventory movements and carry out other tests on the inventory records, for example, checking casts and classification of inventory.

(c) Has **satisfactory procedures** for **inventory counts** and **test-counting**. Auditors should confirm the inventory count arrangements and instructions are as rigorous as those for a year-end inventory count by reviewing instructions and observing counts. Auditors will be particularly concerned with **cut-off**, that there are no inventory movements while the count is taking place and inventory records are updated up until the time of the inventory count.

(d) **Investigates** and **corrects** all **material differences**. Reasons for differences should be recorded and any necessary corrective action taken. All corrections to inventory movements should be **authorised** by a manager who has not been involved in the detailed work. These procedures are necessary to guard against the possibility that inventory records may be adjusted to conceal shortages. Auditors should check that the procedures are being operated.

- **Attend** one of the inventory counts (to observe and confirm that instructions are being adhered to).
- **Follow up** the **inventory counts attended** to compare quantities counted by the auditors with the inventory records, obtaining and verifying explanations for any differences, and checking that the client has reconciled count records with book inventory records.
- **Review** the **year's inventory counts** to confirm the extent of counting, the treatment of discrepancies and the overall accuracy of records (if matters are not satisfactory, auditors will only be able to gain sufficient assurance by a full count at the year end).
- Assuming a full count is not necessary at the year end, **compare** the **listing of inventory with the detailed inventory records**, and carry out other procedures (**cut-off, analytical review**) to gain further comfort.

The audit work when continuous inventory counting is used focuses on tests of controls rather than substantive audit work. Nevertheless, the auditor will also need to do some further substantive audit work on completeness and existence at the year end.

Attendance at an inventory count gives evidence of the **existence** and apparent **ownership** of inventory. It also gives evidence of the **completeness** of inventory, as do the follow-up tests to ensure all inventory sheets were included in the final count.

Exam focus point

In the June 2014 exam, it was identified that students did not really understand continuous inventory counts and the risks associated with them (ie that not all inventory items would be counted at least once a year).

4.2 Planning attendance at inventory count

Before the physical inventory count the auditors should ensure audit **coverage** of the **count** is **appropriate**, and that the client's **count instructions** have been reviewed.

AUDIT PLAN: PLANNING INVENTORY COUNT	
Gain knowledge	• **Review** previous year's **arrangements** • **Discuss with management** the inventory count arrangements and significant changes
Assess key factors	• The **nature** and **volume** of the **inventory** • **Risks** relating to inventory • **Identification** of **high value items** • **Method of accounting for inventory** • **Location** of inventory and how it affects inventory control and recording • **Internal control** and **accounting systems** to identify potential areas of difficulty
Plan procedures	• **Ensure** a **representative selection** of **locations, inventory** and **procedures** are covered • Ensure sufficient attention is given to **high value items** • **Arrange to obtain** from any **third parties confirmation** of inventory they hold • Consider the need for **expert help**
REVIEW OF INVENTORY COUNT INSTRUCTIONS	
Organisation of count	• **Supervision** by senior staff including senior staff not normally involved with inventory • **Tidying** and **marking** inventory to help counting • **Restriction** and **control** of the production process and inventory movements during the count • **Identification of damaged, obsolete, slow-moving, third-party** and **returnable** inventory
Counting	• **Systematic counting** to ensure all inventory is counted • Teams of **two counters**, with one counting and the other checking or **two independent counts**

AUDIT PLAN: PLANNING INVENTORY COUNT	
Recording	• **Serial numbering, control** and **return** of all inventory sheets • Inventory sheets being **completed** in **ink** and **signed** • **Information** to be recorded on the **count records** (location and identity, count units, quantity counted, conditions of items, stage reached in production process) • Recording of **quantity, conditions** and **stage of production** of **work-in-progress** • Recording of last numbers of **goods inwards** and **outwards** records and of internal transfer records • **Reconciliation** with **inventory records** and **investigation** and correction of any **differences**

4.3 Attendance at inventory count

During the count the auditors should **observe** whether the count is being carried out according to instructions, carry out **test counts**, and watch out for **third-party inventory** and **slow-moving inventory** and **cut-off problems.**

AUDIT PLAN: ATTENDANCE AT INVENTORY COUNT

- **Observe** whether the **client's staff** are following instructions, as this will help to ensure the count is complete and accurate.

- **Perform test counts** to ensure procedures and internal controls are working properly, and to gain evidence over existence and completeness of inventory.

- **Ensure** that the **procedures** for **identifying damaged, obsolete** and **slow-moving** inventory operate properly; the auditors should obtain information about the inventory's condition, age, usage and, in the case of work-in-progress, its stage of completion to ensure that it is later valued appropriately.

- **Confirm** that **inventory held** on behalf of **third parties** is separately identified and accounted for so that inventory is not overstated.

- **Conclude** whether the **count** has been **properly carried out** and is sufficiently reliable as a basis for determining the existence of inventories.

- **Consider** whether any **amendment** is necessary to subsequent **audit procedures**.

- **Gain** an **overall impression** of the levels and values of inventories held so that the auditors may, in due course, judge whether the figure for inventory appearing in the financial statements is reasonable.

When carrying out test counts the auditors should select items from the count records and from the physical inventory and check one to the other, to confirm the accuracy of the count records. These two-way tests provide evidence for completeness and existence. The auditors should concentrate on high value inventory. If the results of the test counts are not satisfactory, the auditors may request that inventory be recounted.

The auditors' working papers should include:

- Details of their **observations** and **tests**

- The manner in which **points** that are **relevant** and **material** to the inventory being counted or measured have been dealt with by the client

- Instances where the **client's procedures** have **not been satisfactorily carried out**

- **Items for subsequent testing**, such as photocopies of (or extracts from) rough inventory sheets

- **Details** of the **sequence** of **inventory sheets**

- The **auditors' conclusions**

4.4 After the inventory count

After the count the auditors should check that **final inventory sheets** have been **properly compiled** from count records and that **book inventory** has been **appropriately adjusted**.

After the count, the matters recorded in the auditors' working papers at the time of the count or measurement should be followed up. Key tests include the following.

AUDIT PLAN: FOLLOWING UP THE INVENTORY COUNT

- **Trace items** that were **test counted** to final inventory sheets.
- **Observe whether all count** records have been **included** in final inventory sheets.
- **Inspect final inventory sheets** to ensure they are **supported by** count records.
- **Ensure** that **continuous inventory records** have been **adjusted** to the amounts physically counted or measured, and that differences have been investigated.
- **Confirm cut-off** by using details of the last serial number of goods inward and outward notes and details of movements during the count.
- **Review replies** from **third parties** about inventory held by or for them.
- **Confirm** the client's final **valuation** of inventory has been calculated correctly.
- **Follow up queries** and **notify problems** to management.

4.5 Inventory held by third parties

Where the entity has inventory that is held by third parties and which is material to the financial statements, the auditor shall obtain sufficient appropriate audit evidence by performing one or both of the following:

- **Direct confirmation** from the third party regarding quantities and condition (in accordance with ISA 505 *External confirmations*)

- **Inspection** or other **appropriate audit procedures** (if third party's integrity and objectivity are doubtful, for example)

The other appropriate audit procedures referred to above could include the following:

- Attending, or arranging for another auditor to attend, the third party's inventory count

- Obtaining another auditor's report on the adequacy of the third party's internal control for ensuring that inventory is properly counted and adequately safeguarded

- Inspecting documentation in respect of third-party inventory (eg warehouse receipts)

- Requesting confirmation from other parties when inventory has been pledged as collateral

Question | Inventory count

In connection with your examination of the financial statements of Camry Products Co, a limited liability company, for the year ended 31 March 20X9, you are reviewing the plans for a physical inventory count at the company's warehouse on 31 March 20X9. The company assembles domestic appliances, and inventory of finished appliances, unassembled parts and sundry inventory are stored in the warehouse which is adjacent to the company's assembly plant. The plant will continue to produce goods during the inventory count until 5pm on 31 March 20X9. On 30 March 20X9, the warehouse staff will deliver the estimated quantities of unassembled parts and sundry inventory which will be required for production for 31 March 20X9; however, emergency requisitions by the factory will be filled on 31 March. During the inventory count, the warehouse staff will continue to receive parts and sundry inventory, and to despatch finished appliances. Appliances which are completed on 31 March 20X9 will remain in the assembly plant until after the count has been completed.

Required

(a) List the principal procedures which the auditors should carry out when planning attendance at a company's physical inventory count.

(b) Describe the procedures which Camry Products should establish in order to ensure that all inventory items are counted and that no item is counted twice.

Answer

(a) In planning attendance at a physical inventory count the auditors should:

(i) Review previous year's audit working papers and discuss any developments during the year with management.

(ii) Obtain and review a copy of the company's count instructions.

(iii) Arrange attendance at count planning meetings, with the consent of management.

(iv) Gain an understanding of the nature of the inventory and of any special problems this is likely to present, for example liquid in tanks, scrap in piles.

(v) Consider whether expert involvement is likely to be required as a result of any circumstances noted in (iv) above.

(vi) Obtain a full list of all locations at which inventories are held, including an estimate of the amount and value of inventories held at different locations.

(vii) Using the results of the above steps, plan for audit attendance by appropriately experienced audit staff at all locations where material inventories are held, subject to other factors (for example rotational auditing, reliance on internal controls).

(viii) Consider the impact of internal controls on the nature and timing of attendance at the count.

(ix) Ascertain whether inventories are held by third parties and if so make arrangements to obtain written confirmation of them or, if necessary, to attend the count.

(b) Procedures to ensure a complete count and to prevent double-counting are particularly important in this case because movements will continue throughout the count.

(i) Clear instructions should be given as to procedures, and an official, preferably not someone normally responsible for inventories, should be given responsibility for organising the count and dealing with queries.

(ii) Before the count, all locations should be tidied and inventory should be laid out in an orderly manner.

(iii) All inventory should be clearly identified and should be marked after being counted by a tag or indelible mark, so that it is evident that it has been counted.

(iv) Pre-numbered sheets should be issued to counters and should be accounted for at the end of the count.

(v) Counters should be given responsibility for specific areas of the warehouse. Each area should be subject to a recount.

(vi) A separate record should be kept of all goods received or issued during the day (for example by noting the GRN or GDN numbers involved).

(vii) Goods received on the day should be physically segregated until the count has been completed.

(viii) Similarly, goods due to be despatched on the day should be identified in advance and moved to a special area or clearly marked so that they are not inadvertently counted in inventory as well as being included in sales.

<table>
<tr><td>**Exam focus point**</td><td>You **must** have a thorough knowledge of audit procedures before, during and after the physical inventory count.</td></tr>
</table>

5 Cut-off testing

FAST FORWARD

Auditors should test **cut-off** by noting the **serial numbers** of GDNs and GRNs received and despatched just before and after the year end, and subsequently testing that they have been included in the **correct period**.

5.1 The importance of cut-off

Cut-off is most critical to the accurate recording of transactions in a manufacturing enterprise at particular points in the accounting cycle as follows.

- The **point** of **purchase** and **receipt** of **goods** and **services**
- The **requisitioning** of **raw materials** for production
- The **transfer** of **completed work-in-progress** to finished goods
- The **sale** and **despatch** of **finished goods**

While cut-off is a transaction assertion, it is important to note that it has a direct impact on the related statement of financial position balances. For example, a cut-off error in the recording of sales will result in misstatements in the inventory and receivables balances. A cut-off error in the recording of purchases of raw materials will have an equal knock-on effect on inventory and payables. Therefore, cut-off testing is often used to confirm the completeness of inventory, as well as the existence of receivables and payables.

5.2 Audit procedures

The auditors should consider whether management has implemented adequate cut-off procedures: procedures intended to ensure that movements into, within and out of inventories are properly identified and reflected in the accounting records.

Purchase invoices should be recorded as liabilities only if the goods were received prior to the count. A schedule of 'goods received not invoiced' should be prepared, and items on the list should be accrued for in the accounts.

Sales cut-off is generally more straightforward to achieve correctly than purchases cut-off. Invoices for goods despatched after the count should not appear in the income statement for the period.

Prior to the physical inventory count, management should make arrangements for cut-off to be properly applied.

(a) Appropriate systems of recording of receipts and despatches of goods are in place, and also a system for documenting materials requisitions. GRNs and GDNs should be sequentially pre-numbered.

(b) Final GRN and GDN and materials requisition numbers are noted. These numbers can then be used to subsequently check that purchases and sales have been recorded in the current period.

(c) Arrangements should be made to ensure that the cut-off arrangement for inventories held by third parties is satisfactory.

There should ideally be no movement of inventory during the count. Preferably, receipts and despatches should be suspended for the full period of the count. It may not be practicable to suspend all deliveries, in which case any deliveries which are received during the count should be segregated from other inventory and carefully documented.

6 Valuation   Specimen Exam

FAST FORWARD

Auditing the **valuation** of inventory includes:

- Testing the **allocation of overheads** is appropriate
- Confirming inventory is carried at the **lower** of **cost** and **net realisable value**

6.1 Assessment of cost and net realisable value

Auditors must understand how the company determines the cost of an item for inventory valuation purposes. Cost should include an appropriate proportion of overheads, in accordance with IAS 2.

There are several ways of determining cost. Auditors must ensure that the company is **applying** the method **consistently** and that each year the method used gives a **fair approximation** to cost. They may need to support this by additional procedures.

- **Reviewing price** changes near the year end
- **Ageing the inventory** held
- **Checking gross profit** margins to reliable management accounts

Exam focus point

> The requirement to consider valuation of inventory is a topic which is regularly examined. If asked for procedures in this area, then restrict your answer to only those procedures related to valuation. The examining team has noted that in previous exams, some candidates provided procedures related to other assertions, therefore wasting valuable time.

6.1.1 Valuation of raw materials and bought-in components

The auditors should perform work to test whether the correct prices have been used to value raw materials and bought-in components valued at actual costs by **referring** to **suppliers' invoices**. The valuation may include unrealised profit if inventory is valued at the latest invoice price. Reference to suppliers' invoices will also provide the auditors with assurance as regards ownership.

If standard costs are used, auditors should **check** the **basis** of the **standards**, **compare standard costs** with **actual costs** and **confirm** that **variances** are being **treated appropriately**.

6.1.2 Valuation of work-in-progress and finished goods

'Cost' comprises the cost of purchase plus the costs of conversion. The cost of conversion comprises:
- Costs specifically attributable to units of production
- Production overheads
- Other overheads attributable to bringing the product or service to its present location and condition

(Work-in-progress relating to construction contracts is outside the scope of the F8 syllabus.)

6.2 Audit procedures

The audit procedures will depend on the methods used by the client to value work-in-progress and finished goods, and on the adequacy of the system of internal control.

The auditors should consider what tests they can carry out to check the reasonableness of the valuation of finished goods and work-in-progress. **Analytical procedures** may assist comparisons being made with items and categories from the previous year's summaries. If the client has a computerised accounting system, the auditors may be able to request an exception report listing; for example, all items whose value has changed by more than a specified amount. A reasonableness check will also provide the auditors with assurance regarding completeness.

6.2.1 Cost

The auditors should ensure that the client includes a proportion of overheads **appropriate** to **bringing** the **inventory** to its **present location and condition**. The basis of overhead allocation should be:
- Consistent with prior years
- Calculated on the normal level of production activity

Thus, overheads arising from **reduced levels of activity**, **idle time** or **inefficient production** should be written-off to the income statement, rather than being included in inventory.

Difficulty may be experienced if the client operates a system of total overhead absorption. It will be necessary for those overheads that are of a general, non-productive nature to be identified and excluded from the valuation.

6.2.2 Cost vs NRV

Auditors should **compare cost and NRV** for each item of inventory. Where this is impracticable, the comparison may be done by group or category.

NRV is likely to be less than cost when there has been:

- An **increase in costs** or a fall in selling price
- **Physical deterioration**
- **Obsolescence** of products
- A **marketing decision** to manufacture and sell products at a loss
- Errors in production or purchasing

For work-in-progress, the **ultimate selling price** should be **compared** with the **carrying value** at the year end plus **costs** to be **incurred** after the year end to bring work-in-progress to a finished state.

Question | Cost vs NRV

Your firm is the auditor of Arnold Electrical, a limited liability company, and you have been asked to audit the valuation of the company's inventory at 31 May 20X1 in accordance with IAS 2. Arnold Electrical operates from a single store and purchases domestic electrical equipment from wholesalers and manufacturers and sells them to the general public. These products include video and audio equipment, washing machines, refrigerators and freezers. In addition, it sells small items, such as electrical plugs, tapes for video recorders, records and compact discs.

A full physical inventory count was carried out at the year end, and you are satisfied that the inventory was counted accurately and there are no cut-off errors. Because of the limited time available between the year end and the completion of the audit, the company has valued the inventory at cost by recording the selling price and deducting the normal gross profit margin.

Inventory which the company believes to be worth less than cost has been valued at NRV. The selling price used is that on the item in the store when it was counted.

The inventory has been divided into three categories.

(a) Video and audio equipment: televisions, video recorders, video cameras and audio equipment
(b) Domestic equipment: washing machines, refrigerators and freezers
(c) Sundry inventory: electrical plugs, magnetic tapes and compact discs

The normal gross profit margin for each of these categories has been determined and this figure has been used to calculate the cost of the inventory (by deducting the gross profit margin from the selling price). In answering the question you should assume there are no sales taxes.

Required

(a) List and describe the audit work you will carry out to check that inventory has been correctly valued at cost.

(b) List and describe the audit work you will carry out to:

(i) Find inventory which should be valued at NRV
(ii) Check that the NRV is correct

(c) List and describe the other work you will perform to check that the inventory value is accurate.

Note. In answering the question you are only required to check that the price per unit of the inventory is correct. You should assume that the inventory quantities are accurate and there are no purchases or sales cut-off errors.

(a)   This method of valuation at cost is permitted by IAS 2, but it is usually applied to large retail businesses which hold thousands of low value items in inventory, for example supermarket chains. This method is only permitted when it can be shown that it gives a reasonable approximation of the actual cost.

The following tests should be performed to ensure that the inventory is correctly valued at cost.

(i)   Obtain a schedule of the client's calculations of the gross profit margins. Check the mathematical accuracy and consider the reliability of all sources of information used in the calculation.

(ii)   Where the normal overall gross margin has been used, check the reasonableness of the figure by comparing it to the monthly management accounts for the year and last year's published accounts.

(iii)   Test a sample of items to make sure that gross profit does not vary too much across all items of inventory (which is unlikely for Arnold Electrical). The test will compare selling price to purchase price.

(iv)   If a weighted average gross margin has been used, check that the weighting is correct in terms of the proportion of each type of product in closing inventory.

(v)   Select a sample of high value lines and check the reasonableness of the gross profit estimate by calculating the gross profit for each of those lines. Sales price will be compared to inventory sheets and to sales prices in the shop at the year end. Cost will be checked by examining purchase invoices. The weighted average profit margin for the selected lines can then be calculated and compared to the gross margin applied to the whole inventory.

(vi)   Overvaluation of slow-moving inventory is possible when the prices of those items are affected by inflation. To check this, examine the inventory sheets for any slow-moving items (or ask the management of the company or use own observation). Compare the value of the inventory at the end of the accounting period to cost according to purchase invoices. If an overvaluation has occurred it should be quantified.

(vii)   Check whether any goods were being offered for sale at reduced prices at the year end. If the reduced price is greater than cost, the use of an average gross profit percentage will cause inventory to be undervalued. This undervaluation must be quantified. If full selling price was used in the calculation then the problem will not arise. Check a sample of inventory items to sales invoices issued around the year end to make sure that the correct price was used in the costing calculation.

(b)   (i)   Inventory which may be worth less than cost will include:

- Slow-moving inventory
- Obsolete or superseded inventory
- Seconds and items that have been damaged
- Inventories which are being, or are soon likely to be, sold at reduced prices
- Discontinued lines

Finished goods where the selling price is less than cost will be valued at NRV. This is defined as the actual or estimated selling price less costs to completion and marketing, selling and distribution expenses.

To identify inventories which may be worth less than cost, the following work will be carried out.

(1)   Examine the computerised inventory control system and list items showing an unacceptably low turnover rate. An unacceptable rate of turnover may be different for different items, but inventory representing more than six months' sales is likely to qualify.

(2) Review the inventory printout for items already described as seconds or recorded as damaged.

(3) Discuss with management the current position regarding slow-moving inventories and their plans and expectations in respect of products that may be discontinued. The standard system must be carefully considered and estimates obtained of the likely selling price of existing inventories. The most likely outcome regarding the use and value of discontinued components must be decided.

(4) At the physical inventory count, look for inventory which is dusty, inaccessible and in general not moving and mark on the inventory sheets.

(5) Find out whether any lines are unreliable and therefore frequently returned for repairs, as these may be unpopular.

(6) Review the trade press or other sources to see whether any of the equipment is out of date.

(ii) Determining the NRV of inventory involves management judging how much inventory can be sold and at what price, together with deciding whether to sell off raw materials and components separately or to assemble them into finished products. Each separate type of inventory item should be considered individually in deciding on the level of prudent provision.

The following tests should be carried out.

(1) Find the actual selling prices from the latest sales invoice. For items still selling, invoices will be very recent, but for slow-moving and obsolete items the invoiced prices will be out of date and allowance will have to be made for this.

(2) Estimate the value of marketing, selling and distribution expenses using past figures for the types of finished goods concerned as a base. Update and review for reasonableness against the most recent accounting records.

(3) Discuss with management what selling prices are likely to be where there is little past evidence. Costs to completion will be questioned where these are difficult to estimate and where there are any unusual assembly, selling or distribution problems.

(c) The following procedures would also be performed to check the value of inventory at the year end.

(i) Compare current results with the prior year(s). This would include gross profit margins, sales and turnover. Marked variations from the current year's results should be investigated.

(ii) Consider the effects of new technology and new fashions. The electrical appliance business will be exposed to obsolescence problems. Quantify any necessary write-down.

(iii) Compare selling prices with those charged elsewhere. If the prices elsewhere are lower, than the distortion in selling price might affect the value of the inventory of Arnold Electrical. Alternatively, if prices elsewhere are higher, then the company's prices may occasionally fall below cost. Again, any adjustment discovered to be necessary must be quantified.

(iv) Compare the valuation of inventory this year to that at the end of last year. This will be particularly useful for lines held at both dates. If the values are comparable, taking account of inflation, then the current valuation is more likely to be correct.

(v) Sale prices should be monitored as long after the year end as possible, to make sure that prices were not kept artificially high over the year end and then reduced at a later date. Inventory turnover should also be examined on the same basis.

Chapter Roundup

- The key assertions relating to inventory are:

    - **Existence**
    - **Completeness**
    - **Rights and obligations**
    - **Valuation**
    - **Cut-off**

- The **valuation** and **disclosure** rules for inventory are laid down in IAS 2 *Inventories*. Inventory should be valued at the **lower** of cost and net realisable value.

- Physical inventory count procedures are vital, as they provide evidence which cannot be obtained elsewhere or at any other time about the quantities and conditions of inventory and work-in-progress.

- Auditors should test **cut-off** by noting the **serial numbers** of GDNs and GRNs received and despatched just before and after the year end, and subsequently testing that they have been included in the **correct period**.

- Auditing the **valuation** of inventory includes:

    - Testing the **allocation of overheads** is appropriate
    - Confirming inventory is carried at the **lower** of **cost** and **net realisable value**

1   Complete the definition, using the words given below.

    .... is defined by IAS 2 as comprising all costs of .... and other costs incurred in bringing the inventory to its .... and ....

    | purchase | condition | present | cost | location |

2   List three methods of inventory counting.

    (1) ....   (2) ....   (3) ....

3   When should the following inventory counting tests take place – before, during or after the inventory count?

    (a)   Observe whether client staff are following instructions.
    (b)   Review previous year's inventory count arrangements.
    (c)   Assess method of accounting for inventories.
    (d)   Trace counted items to final inventory sheets.
    (e)   Review replies from third parties about inventory held for them.
    (f)   Conclude as to whether inventory count has been properly carried out.
    (g)   Gain an overall impression of levels and values of inventory.
    (h)   Consider the need for expert help.

    | BEFORE | DURING | AFTER |

4   State four points in the accounting cycle when cut-off is critical.

    (1) ....   (3) ....
    (2) ....   (4) ....

5   Give four occasions when the NRV of inventory is likely to fall below cost.

    (1) ....
    (2) ....
    (3) ....
    (4) ....

Answers to Quick Quiz

1   Cost, purchase, present location, condition

2   (1)   Year end   (2)   Pre/post year end   (3)   Continuous

3   (a)   DURING   (b)   BEFORE   (c)   BEFORE   (d)   AFTER
     (e)   AFTER   (f)   DURING   (g)   DURING   (h)   BEFORE

4   (1)   The point of purchase and receipt of goods and services
     (2)   The requisitioning of raw materials for production
     (3)   The transfer of completed work in progress to finished goods
     (4)   The sale and despatch of finished goods

5   Any four from:
     • An increase in costs or a fall in selling price
     • Physical deterioration
     • Obsolescence of products
     • A marketing decision to manufacture and sell products at a loss
     • Errors in production or purchasing

Now try the questions below from the Practice Question Bank

Number	Level	Marks	Time
Q22	Examination	20	39 mins
Q23	Examination	30	59 mins
Q24	Examination	20	39 mins

Receivables

14

Topic list	Syllabus reference
1 Introduction	D4
2 Audit procedures for receivables	D4
3 The receivables' confirmation	D4
4 Sales	D4

Introduction

Receivables will generally be a material figure on a company's statement of financial position. You must ensure that you are fully conversant with the 'standard' procedures, such as the confirmation of receivables. The receivables confirmation is primarily designed to test the client's entitlement to receive the debt, not the customer's ability to pay.

Auditors also need to consider cut-off for receivables. Sales testing is often carried out in conjunction with the audit of receivables, as the two are linked. We also briefly consider the audit of prepayments which is normally carried out using analytical procedures.

Study guide

		Intellectual level
D4	**The audit of specific items**	
(a)	Receivables	2
	(i) Direct confirmation of accounts receivable	
	(ii) Other evidence in relation to receivables and prepayments, and	
	(iii) Completeness and occurrence of revenue	
•	Explain the audit objectives and the audit procedures in relation to the balance.	

Exam guide

You may be asked to identify and explain audit procedures you would perform to confirm specific assertions relating to receivables: these can cover the receivables balance at the year end or allowances of receivables.

The requirement may extend to audit procedures in respect of revenue and sales invoicing. The receivables confirmation (or receivables circularisation) can also be tested.

1 Introduction

FAST FORWARD Receivables are usually audited using a combination of **tests of details** and **analytical procedures**.

The audit of receivables is important, as this is likely to be a material area. A combination of analytical procedures and tests of details are used, with sales also being tested in conjunction with trade receivables.

The following table sets out the assertions that apply to receivables. The audit procedures in the remainder of this chapter are used to provide evidence for these assertions.

Assertions about classes of transactions and related disclosures	
	– All sales transactions recorded have occurred and relate to the entity **(occurrence)**
	– All sales transactions that should have been recorded have been recorded **(completeness)**
	– Amounts relating to transactions have been recorded appropriately **(accuracy)**
	– All transactions have been recorded in the correct period **(cut-off)**
	– All transactions are recorded properly **(classification)**
	– All disclosed events and transactions relating to receivables have occurred and pertain to the entity **(occurrence, rights and obligations)**
	– All disclosures required have been included **(completeness)**
	– Financial information is appropriately presented and described and disclosures clearly expressed **(presentation)**
	– Financial and other information is disclosed fairly and at appropriate amounts **(presentation)**

Assertions about account balances at the period end and related disclosures	– Recorded receivables exist **(existence)**
	– The entity controls the rights to receivables and related accounts **(rights and obligations)**
	– All receivables that should have been recorded have been recorded **(completeness)**
	– Receivables are included in the accounts at the correct amounts **(accuracy, valuation and allocation)**
	– All disclosures required have been included **(presentation)**
	– Financial information is appropriately presented and described and disclosures clearly expressed **(presentation)**
	– Financial and other information is disclosed fairly and at appropriate amounts **(presentation)**

1.1 Internal control considerations

The audit of receivables and sales is closely linked to the objectives we looked at when we considered controls over the sales system in Chapter 10.

Segregating responsibilities in this area is a very important control. One person should not be responsible for taking orders, raising sales invoices and receiving and recording monies from customers. The failure to segregate these duties could lead to a fraud such as teeming and lading (explained in Chapter 10) which would overstate receivables balances.

From the company's point of view, the reconciliation of the aged receivables accounts with the receivables control account on a regular basis is a key control to highlight anomalies. However, as with a bank reconciliation, the auditor will usually only focus on the year-end reconciliation and listings, as this is often the most efficient way to obtain audit evidence.

As we saw in Chapter 10, a common control over the sales system is having numerically sequenced invoices which are matched to shipping documentation or goods despatched notes (GDNs).

One area in which the auditor may be able to make use of client controls is over the completeness of sales, where the client performs a reconciliation between sales records outside of the accounting system and the sales in the financial statements. However, if they are unable to test and rely on such controls, the auditor often uses samples of documents outside of the accounting system as a starting point for substantive tests of completeness. This might include testing completeness of sales by checking that there is an invoice for a sample of GDNs.

Note that the direction of testing is important, depending on what the auditor's objective is. For instance, starting with invoices and agreeing them to GDNs would not provide evidence of completeness.

2 Audit procedures for receivables   June 10, June 11, Dec 13

FAST FORWARD

Existence, completeness and **valuation** are key assertions relating to the audit of receivables.

Audit procedures for receivables are set out in the table below. This covers the audit of revenue and prepayments as well as trade receivables. Receivables are often tested in conjunction with revenue. The key assertions for sales are occurrence, completeness and accuracy. In the audit plan below, audit procedures related to revenue are shown in italics. It is worth noting that where an exam question asks specifically for audit procedures for receivables, no marks would be rewarded if you identify audit procedures relevant only for prepayments, for example.

The receivables confirmation is used as an audit procedure in the table below and is described in more detail in Section 3. Section 4 contains additional information on the audit of sales.

AUDIT PLAN: RECEIVABLES AND REVENUE

Completeness	• **Agree** the balance from the individual sales ledger accounts to the aged receivables' listing and vice versa. • **Match** the total of the aged receivables' listing to the sales ledger control account. • **Cast and cross-cast** the aged trial balance before selecting any samples to test. • **Trace** a sample of shipping documentation to sales invoices and into the sales and receivables ledger. • Complete the **disclosure checklist** to ensure that all the disclosures relevant to receivables have been made. • *Compare the gross profit percentage by product line with the previous year and industry data.* • *Compare the level of prepayments to the previous year to ensure the figure is materially correct and complete.* • *Review detailed statement of financial position to ensure all likely prepayments have been included.*

Existence	• Perform a **receivables circularisation** on a sample of year-end trade receivables (see Section 3 for details of how to undertake the receivables circularisation).
	
	• **Follow up** all balance disagreements and non-replies to the receivables confirmation.
	
	• **Perform alternative procedures** for any exceptions and non-replies to the receivables confirmation, such as:
	  – **Review after-date cash receipts** by inspecting bank statements and cash receipts documentation.
	  – Examine the **customer's account and customer correspondence** to assess whether the balance outstanding represents specific invoices and confirm their validity.
	  – Examine the **underlying documentation** (purchase order, despatch documentation, duplicate sales invoice etc).
	  – **Enquire from management** explanations for invoices remaining unpaid after subsequent ones have been paid.
	  – **Observe** whether the balance on the account is growing and, if so, find out why by discussing with management.

Rights and obligations	• Review **bank confirmation** for any liens on receivables. • Make **enquiries of management, review** loan agreements and review board minutes for any evidence of receivables being sold (eg to factors).

AUDIT PLAN: RECEIVABLES AND REVENUE

Accuracy, valuation and allocation	<ul><li>**Compare** receivables turnover and receivables days with the previous year and/or with industry data.</li><li>**Compare** the aged analysis of receivables from the aged trial balance with the previous year.</li><li>**Review** the adequacy of the allowance for uncollectable accounts through discussion with management.</li><li>**Compare** the irrecoverable debt expense as a percentage of sales with the previous year and/or with industry data.</li><li>**Compare** the allowance for irrecoverable debts as a percentage of receivables or credit sales with the previous year and/or with industry data.</li><li>Confirm adequacy of allowance by **reviewing correspondence** with customers and solicitors.</li><li>**Examine credit notes** issued after year end for allowances that should be made against current period balances.</li><li>**Examine** large customer accounts individually and compare with the previous year's balances.</li><li>For a sample of old debts on the aged trial balance, obtain further information regarding their recoverability by **discussions** with management and **review** of customer correspondence.</li><li>**Review after-date cash receipts** by inspecting bank statements and cash receipts documentation.</li><li>*For a sample of prepayments from the prepayments' listing, **recalculate** the amount prepaid to ensure that it has been accurately calculated.*</li></ul>
Cut-off	<ul><li>*For a sample of sales invoices around the year end, **inspect the dates** and compare with the dates of despatch and the dates recorded in the ledger for application of correct cut-off.*</li><li>*For **sales returns**, select a sample of returns documentation around the year end and trace to the related credit entries.*</li><li>*Perform **analytical procedures** on sales returns, comparing the ratio of sales returns to sales.*</li><li>***Review material** after-date invoices, credit notes and adjustments and ensure that they are recorded correctly in the relevant financial period.*</li><li>*For a sample of sales invoices, **compare** the prices and terms to the authorised price list and terms of trade documentation.*</li><li>*Test whether **discounts** have been properly applied by recalculating them for a sample of invoices.*</li><li>*Test the correct calculation of **tax** on a sample of invoices.*</li></ul>
Classification	<ul><li>*Take a sample of sales invoices and examine for proper **classification** into revenue accounts.*</li></ul>
Occurrence	<ul><li>*For a sample of sales transactions recorded in the ledger, **vouch** the sales invoice back to customer orders and despatch documentation.*</li></ul>
Occurrence and rights and obligations	<ul><li>Determine, through **discussion** with management, whether any receivables have been pledged, assigned or discounted and whether such items require disclosure in the financial statements.</li></ul>

AUDIT PLAN: RECEIVABLES AND REVENUE	
Classification	• **Review** the aged analysis of receivables for any large credits, non-trade receivables and long-term receivables and consider whether such items require separate disclosure. • **Read** the disclosure notes relevant to receivables in the draft financial statements and review for understandability.
Presentation	• **Read** the disclosure notes to ensure the information is accurate and properly presented at the appropriate amounts.

It is worth noting that some of the audit procedures above test for **more than one assertion**. For example,

- Reviewing after-date cash receipts is an excellent test for both valuation and existence

- Comparing the gross profit per product line with the previous year tests for the existence and completeness of receivables, as well as the occurrence and accuracy of sales and the completeness, occurrence, accuracy and classification of cost of sales

3 The receivables confirmation   June 08, Specimen Exam

A **confirmation of receivables** is a major procedure, usually achieved by **direct contact** with customers. There are two methods of confirmation: **positive** and **negative**.

3.1 Objectives of confirmation

Key term

External confirmations are audit evidence obtained as a direct written response to the auditor from a third party (the confirming party), in paper form, or by electronic or other medium.

ISA 505 *External confirmations* covers the confirmation of amounts by third parties, including the confirmation of amounts by receivables.

The verification of trade receivables by direct confirmation is the normal means of providing audit evidence to satisfy the objective of testing whether customers exist and owe *bona fide* amounts to the company (**existence** and **rights and obligations**).

Confirmation will produce for the current audit file a written statement from each respondent that the amount owed at the date of the confirmation is correct. This is, *prima facie*, reliable audit evidence, being from an **independent source** and in **documentary** form. The confirmation of receivables on a test basis should not be regarded as replacing other normal audit tests, such as the in-depth testing of sales transactions, but the results may influence the scope of such tests.

3.2 Client's mandate

Confirmation is essentially an act of the **client**, who alone can authorise third parties to divulge information to the auditors.

The ISA outlines what the auditors' response should be when management refuses permission for the auditors to contact third parties for evidence. If management asks the auditor not to seek the confirmation, the auditor shall enquire about management's reasons for the refusal and seek audit evidence regarding the validity and reasonableness of the reasons. They shall also evaluate the implications of the refusal on the assessment of the risk of material misstatement and on the nature, timing and extent of other audit procedures. The auditor shall perform alternative audit procedures to obtain relevant and reliable audit evidence. If the auditor concludes that the refusal is unreasonable, or the auditor cannot obtain relevant and reliable audit evidence elsewhere, the auditor shall communicate with those charged with governance in accordance with ISA 260 and consider the implications for the auditor's report.

3.3 Positive vs negative confirmation

A **positive confirmation request** is a request that the confirming party respond directly to the auditor indicating whether the confirming party agrees or disagrees with the information in the request, or providing the requested information.

A **negative confirmation request** is a request that the confirming party respond directly to the auditor only if the confirming party disagrees with the information provided in the request.

When confirmation is undertaken, the method of requesting information from the customer may be either **positive** or **negative**.

- Under the **positive** method, the customer is requested to confirm the accuracy of the balance shown or state in what respect they are in disagreement.

- Under the **negative** method, the customer is requested to reply only if the amount stated is disputed.

The positive method is generally preferable, as it is designed to encourage definite replies from those contacted.

The negative method provides less persuasive audit evidence and shall not be used as the sole substantive procedure to audit receivables unless all of the following are present:

(a)   The **risk** of material misstatement has been assessed as **low**.

(b)   The auditor has obtained sufficient appropriate audit evidence on the operating effectiveness of relevant **controls**.

(c)   The population consists of a **large number of small, homogeneous account balances**.

(d)   A **very low exception rate** is expected.

(e)   The auditor is not aware of circumstances or conditions that would cause customers to **disregard the requests**.

A specimen 'positive' confirmation letter is shown below.

The statements will normally be prepared by the client's staff, from which point the auditors, as a safeguard against the possibility of fraudulent manipulation, must maintain **strict control** over the preparation and despatch of the statements.

Precautions must also be taken to ensure that undelivered items are returned, not to the client, but to the auditors' own office for follow-up by them.

MANUFACTURING CO LIMITED
15 South Street
London

Date

Messrs   (customer)

In accordance with the request of our auditors, ABC Co, we ask that you kindly confirm to them directly your indebtedness to us at [insert date] which, according to our records, amounted to $.......... as shown by the enclosed statement.

If the above amount is in agreement with your records, please sign in the space provided below and return this letter direct to our auditors in the enclosed stamped addressed envelope.

If the amount is not in agreement with your records, please notify our auditors directly of the amount shown by your records, and if possible detail on the reverse of this letter full particulars of the difference.

Yours faithfully,

For Manufacturing Co Limited

```
┌────────────────────────────────────────────────────────────────────────┐
│                                                                          │
│  Reference No: ...........................                               │
│  .......................................................................│
│  (Tear-off slip)                                                         │
│  The amount shown above is/is not* in agreement with our records as at   │
│  Account No    ...........................   Signature       ............│
│  Date          ...........................   Title or position  .........│
│  * The position according to our records is shown overleaf.              │
│                                                                          │
└────────────────────────────────────────────────────────────────────────┘
```

Notes

- The letter is on the client's paper, signed by the client.
- A copy of the statement is attached.
- The reply is sent directly to the auditor in a prepaid envelope.

3.4 Sample selection

Auditors will normally only contact a **sample** of accounts receivable. If this sample is to yield a meaningful result it must be based on a **complete list** of all accounts receivable. In addition, when constructing the sample, the following classes of account should receive special attention:

- **Old, unpaid** accounts
- Accounts **written-off** during the period under review
- Accounts with **credit balances**
- Accounts settled by **round sum payments**
- Accounts with **large balances**
- Accounts with **nil balances**

3.5 Follow-up procedures

ISA 505 states that the auditor may send an additional confirmation request when a reply to a previous request has not been received within a **reasonable time**. For example, the auditor may send an additional or follow-up request having rechecked the accuracy of the original address. Also, with the client's permission, the auditor can phone the customer to request a reply to the original request.

3.5.1 Exceptions and non-responses

Key terms

┌──┐
│ An **exception** is a response that indicates a difference between information requested to be confirmed, or │
│ contained in the entity's records, and information provided by the confirming party. │
│   │
│ A **non-response** is a failure of the confirming party to respond, or fully respond, to a positive confirmation │
│ request, or a confirmation request returned undelivered. │
└──┘

Auditors will have to carry out further work in relation to those receivables who:

- **Disagree** with the **balance stated** (positive and negative confirmation), resulting in **exceptions**
- **Do not respond**, resulting in **non-responses**

In the case of disagreements, the customer response should have identified specific amounts which are disputed. These give rise to exceptions and may indicate misstatements or potential misstatements in the financial statements. When a misstatement is identified, the auditor must evaluate whether this is indicative of fraud (in accordance with ISA 240). Exceptions might also indicate a deficiency in internal control. Some exceptions of course do not represent misstatements, as they may be due to timing, measurement or clerical errors in the confirmation procedures. The table below outlines some reasons for exceptions occurring.

REASONS FOR EXCEPTIONS
There is a **dispute** between the client and the customer. The reasons for the dispute would have to be identified, and provision made if appropriate against the debt.
Cut-off problems exist, because the client records the following year's sales in the current year or because goods returned by the customer in the current year are not recorded in the current year. Cut-off testing may have to be extended (see below).
The customer may have sent the **monies before** the year end, but the monies were **not recorded** by the client as receipts until **after** the year end. Detailed cut-off work may be required on receipts.
Monies received may have been posted to the **wrong account** or a cash-in-transit account. Auditors should check if there is evidence of other mis-posting. If the monies have been posted to a cash-in-transit account, auditors should ensure this account has been cleared promptly.
Customers who are also suppliers may **net-off balances** owed and owing. Auditors should check that this is allowed.
Teeming and lading, stealing monies and **incorrectly posting** other receipts so that no particular customer is seriously in debt is a **fraud** that can arise in this area. Teeming and lading involves an employee first stealing the cash receipts from a receivable (receivable 1) and not recording the receipt against the customer account. Then the employee receives more cash from another receivable (receivable 2) and allocates it against receivable 1 in order to conceal the stolen funds. Similarly, they then allocate monies from receivable 3 against amounts owed from receivable 2, and so on. By allocating the funds in this way, there is only an apparent time lag on posting the receipt of cash, rather than an obvious uncollected debt. If auditors suspect teeming and lading has occurred, detailed testing will be required on cash receipts, particularly on prompt posting of cash receipts.

In the case of **non-responses**, the ISA states that the auditor shall perform **alternative audit procedures** to obtain relevant and reliable audit evidence. These could include reviewing subsequent cash receipts, shipping documentation and sales near the period end.

3.6 Reliability of responses

The ISA states that the auditor shall obtain further audit evidence to resolve any **doubts about the reliability** of a response to a confirmation request. This could include contacting the confirming party.

If the auditor concludes that a response to a request is **not reliable**, they shall evaluate the impact of this on the assessment of the risk of material misstatement (including the risk of fraud) and on the related nature, timing and extent of other audit procedures.

4 Sales

FAST FORWARD

Sales comprise a material figure in the statement of profit or loss that is often audited by analytical review, as it should have predictable relationships with other figures in the financial statements.

Accounts receivable will often be tested in conjunction with sales. Auditors are seeking to obtain evidence that sales pertain to the entity (occurrence), and are **completely** and **accurately recorded**. This will involve carrying out certain procedures to test for **completeness** of sales and also testing **cut-off**. We already looked at some audit procedures relating to sales earlier in this chapter (in the table in Section 2). However, we will now look in detail at some important procedures used when testing completeness and occurrence of sales.

4.1 Completeness and occurrence of sales

Analytical review is important when testing completeness. A client is likely to have a great deal of information about company sales and should be able to explain any fluctuations and variances. Auditors should consider the following.

- The **level of sales** over the year, compared on a month-by-month basis with the previous year
- The effect on sales value of **changes in quantities** sold
- The effect on sales value of **changes in products** or **prices**
- The level of **goods returned, sales allowances** and **discounts**
- The **efficiency of labour** as expressed in sales or profit per tax per employee

In addition, auditors must record reasons for changes in the **gross profit margin**. Analysis of the gross profit margin should be as detailed as possible, ideally broken down by **product area** and **month or quarter**.

As well as analytical review, auditors may feel that they need to carry out a directional test on **completeness of recording** of individual sales in the accounting records. To do this, auditors should start with the documents that first record sales (**GDNs** or **till rolls** for example) and trace sales recorded in these through intermediate documents such as sales summaries to the **sales ledger**.

Auditors must ensure that the population of documents from which the sample is originally taken is itself complete, by checking for example the **completeness** of the **sequence** of GDNs.

<table>
<tr><td>**Exam focus point**</td><td>You must remember the direction of this test. Since we are checking the completeness of recording of sales in the sales ledger, we cannot take a sample from the ledger because the sample would not include what has not been recorded.</td></tr>
</table>

Question

Receivables

Sherwood Textiles, a listed company, manufactures knitted clothes and dyes these clothes and other textiles. You are carrying out the audit of the accounts of the company for the year ended 30 September 20X6 which show a revenue of about $10 million and a profit before tax of about $800,000.

You are attending the final audit in December 20X6 and are commencing the audit of trade accounts receivable, which are shown in the draft accounts at $2,060,000.

The interim audit (tests of controls) was carried out in July 20X6 and it showed that there was a good system of internal control in the sales system and no serious errors were found in the audit tests. The company's sales ledger is maintained on a computer, which produces at the end of each month:

(i)   A list of transactions for the month

(ii)   An aged list of balances

(iii)   Open item statements which are sent to customers (open item statements show all items which are outstanding on each account, irrespective of their age)

Required

(a)   List and briefly describe the audit tests you would carry out to verify trade accounts receivable at the year end. You are not required to describe how you would carry out a direct confirmation of receivables.

(b)   Describe the audit work you would carry out on the following replies to a receivables circularisation:

(i)   Balance agreed by customer

(ii)   Balance not agreed by customer

(iii)   Customer is unable to confirm the balance because of the form of records kept by the customer

(iv)   Customer does not reply to the confirmation letter

(a)   The auditors will carry out the following tests on the list of balances.

  (i)   Agree the balances from the individual sales ledger accounts to the list of balances and vice versa.

  (ii)   Agree the total of the list to the sales ledger control account.

  (iii) Cast the list of balances and the sales ledger control account.

Other general tests auditors will carry out will be to:

  (i)   Agree the opening balance on the sales ledger control account to ensure that last year's audit adjustments were recorded.

  (ii)   Inspect ledger balances for unusual entries.

  (iii) Perform analytical procedures on trade receivables as follows:

    –   Compare receivables turnover and receivables days with the prior year and/or with industry data.

    –   Perform an age analysis on trade receivables and compare this with the prior year.

    –   Compare the bad debt expense as a percentage of sales with the prior year and/or with industry data.

    –   Examine large customer accounts individually and compare them with the prior year.

The determination of whether the company has made reasonable provision for bad and doubtful debts will be facilitated as the company produces an aged listing of balances.

Auditors will carry out the following procedures to audit the allowance for receivables.

  (i)   Debts against which specific allowance has been made (and debts written-off) should be examined in conjunction with correspondence, lawyers'/debt collection agencies' letters, liquidators' statements and so on, and their necessity or adequacy confirmed.

  (ii)   A general review of relevant correspondence may reveal debts where an allowance is warranted, but has not been made.

  (iii) Where specific and/or general allowances have been determined using the aged analysis, the auditors should ensure that the analysis has been properly prepared by comparing it with the dates on invoices and matching cash receipts against outstanding invoices. They should check the reasonableness and consistency of any formula used to calculate general allowances.

  (iv)   Additional tests that should be carried out on individual balances will include ascertaining the subsequent receipt of cash, paying particular attention to round sum payments on account, examination of specific invoices and, where appropriate, goods received notes, and enquiry into any invoices that have not been paid when subsequent invoices have been paid.

  (v)   Excessive discounts should be examined, as should journal entries transferring balances from one account to another and journal entries that clear customer balances after the year end.

  (vi)   Credit notes issued after the year end should be reviewed and allowances checked where they refer to current period sales.

In order to audit cut-off and hence completeness, the auditors should, during the physical inventory count, have obtained details of the last serial numbers of goods outwards issued before the commencement of the count. The following substantive procedures are designed to test that goods taken into inventory are not also treated as sales in the year under review and, conversely, goods despatched are treated as sales in the year under review and not also treated as inventory.

  (i)   Review goods outward and returns inward notes around year end to ensure that:

    (1)   Invoices and credit notes are dated in the correct period.

    (2)   Invoices and credit notes are posted to the sales ledger and nominal ledger in the correct period.

(ii) Reconcile entries in the sales ledger control around the year end to daily batch invoice totals, ensuring batches are posted in correct year.

(iii) Review sales ledger control account around year end for unusual items.

(iv) Review material after-date invoices and ensure that they are properly treated as following year's sales.

(b) The verification of trade receivables by direct confirmation is the normal means of providing audit evidence to prove that receivables represent *bona fide* amounts due to the company (existence and rights and obligations).

The audit work required on the various replies to a receivables circularisation would be as follows.

(i) *Balances agreed by customer*

All that is required would be to ensure that the debt does appear to be collectable, by reviewing cash received after-date or considering the adequacy of any allowance made for a long-outstanding amount.

(ii) *Balances not agreed by customer*

All balance disagreements must be followed up and their effect on total receivables evaluated. Differences arising that merely represent invoices or cash-in-transit generally do not require adjustment, but disputed amounts, and errors by the client, may indicate that further substantive work is necessary to determine whether material adjustments are required.

(iii) *Customer is unable to confirm the balance because of the form of records maintained*

Certain companies, often computerised, operate systems which make it impossible for them to confirm the balance on their account. Typically in these circumstances their purchase ledger is merely a list of unpaid invoices. However, with sufficient information the customer will be able to confirm that any given invoice is outstanding. Hence the auditors can circularise such enterprises successfully, but they will need to break down the total on the account into its constituent outstanding invoices.

(iv) *Customer does not reply to confirmation letter*

When the positive request method is used the auditors must follow up by all practicable means those customers who fail to respond. Second requests should be sent out in the event of no reply being received within two or three weeks and if necessary this may be followed by telephoning the customer with the client's permission.

After two or even three attempts to obtain confirmation, a list of the outstanding items will normally be passed to a responsible independent company official who will arrange for them to be investigated.

Alternative audit procedures might include the following.

(1) Check receipt of cash after-date by reviewing post year end bank statements.

(2) Verify valid purchase orders, if any.

(3) Examine the account to see if the balance represents specific outstanding invoices.

(4) Obtain explanations for invoices remaining unpaid after subsequent ones have been paid.

(5) Observe whether the balance on the account is growing, and, if so, find out why by discussions with management.

(6) Test the company's control over the issue of credit notes and the write-off of irrecoverable debts.

Exam focus point

The receivables confirmation provides good audit evidence of the existence of receivables, but not necessarily of their valuation. Therefore, in a question on the audit of receivables, remember to include other audit procedures, such as analytical procedures.

Chapter Roundup

- Receivables are usually audited using a combination of **tests of details** and **analytical procedures**.

- **Existence**, **completeness** and **valuation** are key assertions relating to the audit of receivables.

- A **confirmation of receivables** is a major procedure, usually achieved by **direct contact** with customers. There are two methods of confirmation: **positive** and **negative**.

- Sales comprise a material figure in the statement of profit or loss that is often audited by analytical review, as it should have predictable relationships with other figures in the financial statements.

Quick Quiz

1   The negative method of receivables confirmation should only be used if the client has good internal controls and a small number of large customer accounts.

   True ☐   False ☐

2   State four types of account which should receive special attention when picking a sample for a receivables confirmation.

   (1)   ....   (3)   ....

   (2)   ....   (4)   ....

3   Complete the following tests which aim to confirm the valuation of an allowance for receivables.

   (a)   Confirm adequacy of allowance by reviewing correspondence with the ....

   (b)   Examine .... issued after the year end for allowances that should be made against current period balances.

4   List three factors that should be considered when undertaking an analytical review on sales.

   (1)   ....

   (2)   ....

   (3)   ....

5   Give two examples of tests to verify prepayments.

   (1)   ....

   (2)   ....

1   False

2   Any four from:

- Old unpaid accounts
- Accounts written-off during the period under review
- Accounts with credit balances
- Accounts settled by round sum payments
- Accounts with nil balances
- Accounts which have been paid by the date of the examination

3   (a)   customers
    (b)   credit notes

4   (1)   Level of sales, month by month
    (2)   Price
    (3)   Goods returned

5   Any two from:

- Verify by reference to invoices, cash book, correspondence.
- Check calculations by reperformance.
- Review detailed statement of financial position to ensure all likely prepayments have been included.
- Use analytical procedures to review reasonableness.

Now try the question below from the Practice Question Bank

Number	Level	Marks	Time
Q25	Examination	20	39 mins

15

Cash and bank

Introduction

Work on cash and bank will concentrate on the completeness and valuation
using the bank reconciliation, bank confirmation letter and counting of cash as
key audit tests.

Study guide

		Intellectual level
D4	The audit of specific items:	
(d)	Bank and cash	2
	(i) Bank confirmation reports used in obtaining evidence in relation to bank and cash	
	(ii) Other evidence in relation to bank	
	(iii) Other evidence in relation to cash	
•	Explain the audit objectives and the audit procedures in relation to this balance.	

Exam guide

In the exam you may be asked to identify and explain audit procedures you would perform to confirm specific assertions relating to cash and bank. Shorter written question requirements and OTQs in Section A may also ask for audit procedures specifically used to obtain bank confirmation letters.

1 Introduction

'Cash' in the financial statements represents cash in-hand and cash on deposit in bank accounts. Most accounting transactions pass through the cash account so cash is affected by all of the entity's business processes, and is particularly impacted by the sales and purchases processes. We looked at the controls relating to cash in Chapter 10. In this chapter, we will consider the substantive audit testing applied to the year-end cash figure.

1.1 Audit objectives for cash

The following table demonstrates the audit objectives for cash balances and how these are related to the financial statement assertions relevant to this account area. The audit procedures described in the remainder of this chapter are undertaken to provide audit evidence to support these financial statement assertions.

Financial statement assertion	Audit objective
Existence	Recorded cash balances exist at the period end
Completeness	Recorded cash balances include the effects of all transactions that have occurred
Rights and obligations	The entity has legal title to all cash balances shown at the period end
Accuracy, valuation and allocation	Recorded cash balances are realisable at the amounts stated
Presentation	Disclosures relating to cash are adequate and in accordance with accounting standards and legislation

1.2 Internal control considerations

We covered internal control over the cash system in Section 4 of Chapter 10. The bank reconciliation is a key control for the company in this area and should be prepared frequently and routinely. However, the auditor is concerned with obtaining sufficient appropriate audit evidence on the year-end bank balance, so they will focus on the year end reconciliation (in conjunction with other substantive procedures set out in this chapter) when auditing the bank balance included on the statement of financial position.

2 Bank

Bank balances are usually **confirmed directly** with the bank in question.

2.1 Bank confirmation procedures

The audit of bank balances will need to cover **completeness**, **existence**, **rights and obligations and valuation**. All of these assertions can be audited directly by obtaining third-party confirmations from the client's banks and reconciling these with the accounting records, having regard to **cut-off**.

The audit objectives linking these assertions are as follows.

- Recorded cash balances exist at the year end **(existence)**.
- Recorded cash balances include the effects of all transactions that occurred **(completeness)**.
- Year-end transfers are recorded in the correct period **(cut-off)**.
- Recorded balances are realisable at the amounts stated **(accuracy, valuation and allocation)**.
- The entity has legal title to all cash balances shown at the year end **(rights and obligations)**.

This type of audit evidence is valuable because it comes directly from an **independent source** and, therefore, provides greater assurance of reliability than that obtained solely from the client's own records. The bank letter is mentioned as a source of external third-party evidence in ISA 505 *External confirmations*.

2.2 Confirmation requests

The **bank confirmation letter** can be used to ask a variety of questions, including queries about outstanding interests, contingent liabilities and guarantees.

The auditors should decide from which bank or banks to request confirmation, having regard to such matters as **size of balance**, **volume of activity**, **degree of reliance** on **internal control** and **materiality** within the context of the financial statements.

The auditors should determine which of the following approaches is the most appropriate in seeking confirmation of balances or other information from the bank:

- **Listing balances** and other information, and requesting confirmation of their accuracy and completeness, or

- **Requesting details of balances** and other information, which can then be compared with the requesting client's records

In determining which of the above approaches is the most appropriate, the auditors should weigh the **quality** of **audit evidence** they require in the particular circumstances against the **practicality** of obtaining a reply from the confirming bank.

Difficulty may be encountered in obtaining a satisfactory response even where the client company submits information for confirmation to the confirming bank. It is important that a response is sought for **all** confirmation requests. Auditors should not request a response only if the information submitted is incorrect or incomplete.

2.2.1 Preparation and despatch of requests and receipt of replies

Control over the content and dispatch of confirmation requests is the responsibility of the auditors. However, it will be necessary for the request to be **authorised** by the client entity. Replies should be returned directly to the auditors and to facilitate such a reply, a pre-addressed envelope should be enclosed with the request.

2.2.2 Content of confirmation requests

The form and content of a confirmation request letter will depend on the purpose for which it is required and on local practices.

The most commonly requested information is in respect of balances due to or from the client entity on **current, deposit, loan and other accounts**. The request letter should provide the account description number and the type of currency for the account.

It may also be advisable to request information about **nil balances** on accounts, and accounts which were **closed** in the 12 months prior to the chosen confirmation date. The client entity may ask for confirmation not only of the balances on accounts but also, where it may be helpful, of other information, such as the maturity and interest terms on loans and overdrafts, unused facilities, lines of credit/standby facilities, any offset or other rights or encumbrances, and details of any collateral given or received.

The client entity and its auditors are likely to request confirmation of **contingent liabilities**, such as those arising on guarantees, comfort letters and bills.

Banks often hold **securities** and other items in safe custody on behalf of customers. A request letter may therefore ask for confirmation of such items held by the bank.

The procedure is simple but important, and outlined below.

(a) The banks will require **explicit written authority** from their client to disclose the information requested.

(b) The **auditors' request** must **refer** to the **client's letter** of authority and the date thereof. Alternatively it may be countersigned by the client or it may be accompanied by a specific letter of authority.

(c) In the case of joint accounts, **letters of authority** signed by all **parties** will be necessary.

(d) Such **letters of authority** may either **give permission** to the bank to disclose information for a specific request or grant permission for an indeterminate length of time.

(e) The request should **reach** the **branch manager** at least **one month in advance** of the client's **year end** and should state both that year-end date and the previous year-end date.

(f) The **auditors** should themselves **check** that the bank response covers all the information in the standard and other responses.

2.3 Cut-off

Care must be taken to ensure that there is no **window dressing**, by auditing **cut-off** carefully. Window dressing in this context is usually manifested as an attempt to overstate the liquidity of the company by:

(a) Keeping the cash book open to take credit for **remittances actually received** after the year end, thus enhancing the balance at bank and reducing receivables

(b) **Recording cheques paid in** the period under review which are not actually despatched until after the year end, thus decreasing the balance at bank and reducing liabilities

A combination of (a) and (b) can contrive to present an artificially healthy looking current ratio.

With the possibility of (a) above in mind, where lodgements have not been cleared by the bank until the new period, the auditors should **examine the paying-in slip** to ensure that the amounts were actually paid into the bank on or before the period-end date.

As regards (b) above, where there appears to be a particularly **large number of outstanding cheques** at the year end, the auditors should check whether these were **cleared within a reasonable time** in the new period. If not, this may indicate that despatch occurred after the year end.

2.4 Audit plan for bank

AUDIT PLAN: BANK (to confirm completeness, valuation, existence, cut-off and presentation)
• **Obtain standard bank confirmations** from each bank with which the client conducted business during the audit period.
• **Reperform** arithmetic of bank reconciliation.
• **Trace cheques shown as outstanding** from the bank reconciliation to the cash book prior to the year end and to the **after-date bank statements** and **obtain explanations** for any **large or unusual items** not cleared at the time of the audit.
• **Compare cash book(s)** and **bank statements** in detail for the last month of the year, and **match items outstanding** at the reconciliation date to bank statements.
• **Review bank reconciliation** previous to the year-end bank reconciliation and test whether **all items** are **cleared** in the last period or **taken forward** to the year-end bank reconciliation.
• Obtain satisfactory explanations for **all items** in the **cash book** for which there are **no corresponding entries** in the **bank statement** and vice versa by **discussion** with finance staff.
• **Verify contra items** appearing in the cash books or bank statements with original entry.
• Verify by **inspecting** paying-in slips that **uncleared bankings** are **paid in** prior to the year end.
• **Examine all lodgements** in respect of which payment has been refused by the bank; ensure that they are cleared on representation or that other appropriate steps have been taken to effect recovery of the amount due.
• Verify balances per the cash book according to the bank reconciliation by **inspecting** cash book, bank statements and general ledger.
• **Verify** the **bank balances** with reply to **standard bank letter** and with the **bank statements**.
• **Inspect** the cash book and bank statements before and after the year end for **exceptional entries** or **transfers** which have a material effect on the balance shown to be in-hand.
• Identify whether any **accounts** are **secured** on the **assets** of the company by **discussion** with management.
• **Consider** whether there is a **legal right** of **set-off** of overdrafts against positive bank balances.
• Determine whether the bank accounts are **subject** to any **restrictions** by **enquiries** with management.
• **Review draft accounts** to ensure that disclosures for bank are complete and accurate and in accordance with accounting standards.

<table>
<tr><td>Exam focus point</td><td>Remember that the bank confirmation letter contains the balance held by the client at the bank **per the bank's records**. This must be **reconciled** to the balance held with the bank **per the client's records**. When suggesting audit procedures for verifying bank balances, although the bank confirmation letter is important, do **not forget to suggest other procedures** related to the year-end bank reconciliation. Previous candidates have lost out on marks for not focusing enough on these procedures.</td></tr>
</table>

Question

(a) Explain the importance of the bank letter and describe the procedures used to obtain confirmations from the bank.

(b) Describe how you would test the bank reconciliation shown below.

ANOTHER CO
BANK RECONCILIATION 31 DECEMBER 20X1

	$	$
Balance per bank statement 31 December 20X1		35,111.91
Add: deposits outstanding		
30 December (ref 1122)	10,222.00	
31 December (ref 1123)	25,000.00	35,222.00
		70,333.91
Less: outstanding cheques		
2411	10,250.00	
2721	2,300.40	
2722	5,000.00	
2723	1,345.25	
2724	1,900.00	
2726	2,200.00	
2728	1,005.50	
2729	1,576.75	
2730	1,255.65	26,833.55
Balance per bank in the general ledger 31 December 20X1		43,500.36

(c) Describe other procedures that should be carried out in respect of bank balances shown in the financial statements.

Answer

(a) The bank letter is important because it is independent confirmation of a number of significant matters in the client's financial statements. It confirms cash and bank balances which may well be a significant asset. It also provides confirmation of customers' assets held as security, customers' other assets held (as custodian) and contingent liabilities. Auditors also ask the bank to give details of other banks and branches that the respondent bank is aware of having a relationship with the client.

Audit procedures

(i) Obtain written authority from the client to the bank to disclose the necessary information.

(ii) Send a bank letter in standard form to the bank in sufficient time for it to arrive at least a month before the year end. The letter should state both the year-end date and the previous year-end date, and should refer to the client's granting of authority.

(iii) If additional information over and above what is in the standard letter is requested, send a separate letter requesting that information.

(iv) When confirmation is received from the bank, check that the bank has answered all the questions in the letter.

(v) Follow up all points disclosed in the bank letter.

(b) The following procedures should be carried out on the bank reconciliation.

    (i) Agree the balance per bank statement at 31 December 20X1 as shown on the reconciliation ($35,111.91) to the bank statement and to the amount for that account shown on the bank letter.

    (ii) Test arithmetic of bank reconciliation by recasting it.

    (iii) Review the bank reconciliation previous to the year-end bank reconciliation (30 November reconciliation if carried out monthly) and test whether items shown on it cleared in the last period or have been taken forward to the bank reconciliation at 31 December.

    (iv) Trace the cheques shown as outstanding on the bank reconciliation to the cash book prior to the year end and ensure they have cleared the bank by looking at the after-date bank statements. Obtain explanations for any that have not cleared at the time of the audit. In particular the outstanding cheque for $10,250 has a reference (2411) which appears to suggest it was raised much earlier in the year than the others and the fact it has not cleared is unusual. Enquiries should be made in respect of this outstanding cheque.

    (v) Verify by checking paying-in slips that the uncleared bankings (deposits outstanding – ref 1122 and 1123) were paid in prior to the year end, and review whether they cleared quickly after the year end. Any that have not cleared soon after the year end should be investigated.

    (vi) Verify that the year-end balance per the general ledger according to the reconciliation ($43,500.36) agrees with the general ledger account balance at 31 December 20X1 and that this has been properly reflected in the financial statements.

(c) (i) Obtain standard bank confirmations from each bank with which the client conducted business during the period.

    (ii) Verify the bank balances with reply to standard bank letter and with the bank statements.

    (iii) Scrutinise the cash book and bank statements before and after the period end for exceptional entries or transfers which have a material effect on the balance shown to be in hand.

    (iv) Identify whether any accounts are secured on the assets of the company.

    (v) Consider whether there is a legal right to set-off overdrafts against positive bank balances.

    (vi) Determine whether the bank accounts are subject to any restrictions.

    (vii) Review disclosures related to the cash at bank figure included in the financial statements and ensure they are in accordance with International Financial Reporting Standards.

3 Cash

June 13

Cash balances should be verified if they are **material** or **irregularities** are suspected.

Cash balances/floats are often individually immaterial but they may require some audit emphasis because of the opportunities for fraud that could exist where internal control is weak and because they may be material in total.

However, in enterprises such as hotels and retail organisations, the amount of cash-in-hand at the period end could be considerable. Cash counts may be important for internal auditors, who have a role in fraud prevention.

Auditors will be concerned that the cash **exists**, is **complete**, and belongs to the company (**rights and obligations**) and is stated at the correct **value**.

Where the auditors determine that cash balances are potentially material they may conduct a **cash count**, ideally at the period end. Rather like attendance at an inventory count, the conduct of the count falls into three phases: planning, the count itself, and follow-up procedures.

3.1 Planning the cash count

Planning is an essential element, as it is important that all cash balances are counted at the same time as far as possible. Cash in this context may include unbanked cheques received, IOUs and credit card slips, in addition to notes and coins.

As part of their planning procedures the auditors will need to determine the **locations** where cash is held and which of these locations warrant a count.

Planning decisions will need to be recorded on the current audit file, including:

- The **precise time** of the count(s) and location(s)
- The **names** of the **audit staff** conducting the counts
- The **names** of the **client staff** intending to be present at each location

Where a location is not visited it may be appropriate to obtain a letter from the client confirming the balance.

3.2 Cash count

The following matters apply to the count itself.

(a)   All cash/petty cash **books** should be **written up** to date in **ink** (or other permanent form) at the time of the count.

(b)   All **balances** must be **counted** at the **same time**.

(c)   All **negotiable securities** must be **available** and **counted** at the time the cash balances are counted.

(d)   At **no time** should the **auditors** be **left alone** with the cash and negotiable securities.

(e)   **All cash** and securities **counted** must be **recorded** on working papers subsequently filed on the current audit file. **Reconciliations** should be prepared where applicable (for example, imprest petty cash float).

AUDIT PLAN: CASH COUNT (to confirm completeness, valuation, existence and presentation)

- **Count cash balances** held and agree to petty cash book or other record:
  - Count all balances simultaneously
  - All counting to be done in the presence of the individuals responsible
  - Enquire into any IOUs or cashed cheques outstanding for a long period of time
- **Obtain certificates** of cash-in-hand from responsible officials.
- **Confirm** that bank and cash **balances** as reconciled above are **correctly stated** in the financial statements.

Follow up

- Obtain **certificates of cash-in-hand** as appropriate.
- Verify **unbanked cheques/cash receipts** have subsequently been **paid in** and agree to the bank reconciliation by **inspection** of the relevant documentation.
- Ensure **IOUs** and cheques cashed for employees have been **reimbursed**.
- Review whether **IOUs or cashed cheques outstanding** for **unreasonable periods** of time have been provided for.
- Verify the **balances** as counted are reflected in the accounts (subject to any agreed amendments because of shortages and so on) by **inspection** of draft financial statements.

Chapter Roundup

- **Bank balances** are usually **confirmed directly** with the bank in question.
- The **bank confirmation letter** can be used to ask a variety of questions, including queries about outstanding interests, contingent liabilities and guarantees.
- **Cash balances** should be verified if they are **material** or **irregularities** are suspected.

Quick Quiz

1   What are the relevant financial statement assertions for cash in the statement of financial position?

2   Summarise the procedure for obtaining confirmation from a client's bank of the year-end bank balance.

    (1)   ....

    (2)   ....

    (3)   ....

    (4)   ....

    (5)   ....

    (6)   ....

3   Complete the following two audit tests performed to verify the bank reconciliation.

    (a)   Trace cheques shown as outstanding on the .... to the ....
.... prior to the year end and ....
....

    (b)   Obtain satisfactory explanations for all items in the .... for which
there is no corresponding entry in the .... and ....
....

4   Give two examples of businesses where cash floats could be considerable.

    ....

    ....

5   What planning matters relating to a cash count should be recorded in the current audit file?

    ....

    ....

    ....

Answers to Quick Quiz

1   Existence, completeness, valuation and allocation

2   (1)   The banks will require **explicit written authority** from their client to disclose the information requested.

    (2)   The **auditors' request** must **refer** to the **client's letter** of authority and the date thereof. Alternatively it may be countersigned by the client or it may be accompanied by a specific letter of authority.

    (3)   In the case of joint accounts, **letters of authority** signed by all **parties** will be necessary.

    (4)   Such letters of authority may either give **permission** to the bank to disclose information for a **specific request** or grant permission for an **indeterminate length of time**.

    (5)   The request should **reach** the **branch manager** at least **one month in advance** of the client's **year end** and should state both that year-end date and the previous year-end date.

    (6)   The **auditors** should themselves **check** that the bank **answers all the questions** and, where the reply is not received direct from the bank, be responsible for establishing the authenticity of the reply.

3   (a)   bank reconciliations, cash book, after-date bank statements

    (b)   bank statements, cash book, bank reconciliation

4   Hotels
    Retail operations

5   Time of count
    Names of client staff attending
    Names of audit staff attending

Now try the question below from the Practice Question Bank

Number	Level	Marks	Time
Q26	Introductory	n/a	n/a

Liabilities, capital and directors' emoluments

Topic list	Syllabus reference
1 Introduction	D4
2 Procedures for trade payables, accruals and expenses	D4
3 Non-current liabilities	D4
4 Provisions and contingencies	D4
5 Capital and other issues	D4
6 Directors' emoluments	D4

Introduction

In this chapter, we examine the audit of liabilities, including payables and accruals, provisions and other long-term liabilities.

When auditing payables, the auditor must test for understatement (ie completeness). Rather than circularising payables, it is more common to obtain audit evidence from suppliers' statements.

The audit of provisions can be particularly complex due to the accounting treatment and the degree of judgement involved in calculating the provision.

This chapter ends with a look at the audit of share capital, reserves and directors' emoluments.

Study guide

		Intellectual level
D4	**The audit of specific items**	
(c)	Payables and accruals: (i) Supplier statement reconciliations and direct confirmation of accounts payable (ii) Obtain evidence in relation to payables and accruals, and (iii) Purchases and other expenses	2
(f)	Non-current liabilities, provisions and contingencies: (i) Evidence in relation to non-current liabilities (ii) Provisions and contingencies	2
(g)	Share capital, reserves and directors' emoluments: (i) Evidence in relation to share capital, reserves and directors' emoluments	2
•	Explain the audit objectives and the audit procedures in relation to each balance.	

Exam guide

You may be asked to identify and explain audit procedures you would perform to confirm specific assertions relating to liabilities. For example, you may be asked for the substantive audit procedures in respect of a provision for legal claims.

Every type of liability covered in this chapter can form the basis of a written question, or part of a question, in the exam. The audit procedures and financial statement assertions can also be tested in the form of OTQs in Section A.

1 Introduction

In this chapter we will examine the substantive audit of trade payables and accruals, long-term liabilities and provisions and end with a look at share capital, reserves and directors' emoluments. Purchases are often tested in conjunction with the audit of trade payables and so are included in the section on trade payables. The following table sets out the financial statement assertions to which audit testing is directed.

Assertions about classes of transactions and related disclosures	– All purchase transactions recorded have occurred and relate to the entity (**occurrence**). – All purchase transactions that should have been recorded have been recorded (**completeness**). – Amounts relating to transactions have been recorded appropriately (**accuracy**). – Purchase transactions have been recorded in the correct period (**cut-off**). – Purchase transactions are recorded properly in the accounts (**classification**). – All disclosed events and transactions relating to liabilities have occurred and relate to the entity (**presentation**). – All disclosures required have been included (**presentation**). – Financial information is appropriately presented and described and disclosures clearly expressed (**presentation**). – Financial information is disclosed fairly and at appropriate amounts (**presentation**).

Assertions about period-end account balances and related disclosures	– Trade payables and accrued expenses are valid liabilities (**existence**).
	– Trade payables and accrued expenses are the obligations of the entity (**rights and obligations**).
	– All liabilities have been recorded (**completeness**).
	– All liabilities are included in the accounts at appropriate amounts (**valuation and allocation**).
	– All disclosures required have been included (**presentation**).
	– Financial information is appropriately presented and described and disclosures clearly expressed (**presentation**).
	– Financial information is disclosed fairly and at appropriate amounts (**presentation**).

1.1 Internal control considerations for payables

The audit of payables is closely linked to the purchases system. We looked at controls over the purchases system in Section 2 of Chapter 10, where we saw that they were based around ensuring purchases were authorised, the segregation of duties, matching GRNs with invoices, and prompt recording to minimise cut-off issues.

A specific control often operated by clients over the completeness of trade payables balances is the reconciliation of month-end balances to supplier statements. If the client has carried out this reconciliation at the year end for all suppliers, the auditor can review these reconciliations.

However, if the client has not carried out these reconciliations, the auditor will need to compare supplier statements with year-end payables balances and investigate differences, so this becomes a substantive procedure that the auditor must undertake.

We look at supplier statement reconciliations and other substantive procedures in Section 2.

2 Procedures for trade payables, accruals and expenses
Dec 07, Dec 09, Dec 10, Dec 11, June 14

FAST FORWARD

The largest figure in **current liabilities** will normally be **trade accounts payable** which are generally audited by comparison of **suppliers' statements** with **purchase ledger accounts**.

2.1 Audit procedures

As with accounts receivable, accounts payable are likely to be a material figure in the statement of financial position of most enterprises. The tests of controls on the purchases cycle (Chapter 10) will have provided the auditors with some assurance as to the completeness of liabilities.

However, auditors should be particularly aware, when conducting their work on the statement of financial position, of the possibility of **understatement** of **liabilities** to improve liquidity and profits (by understating the corresponding purchases). The primary objective of their work will therefore be to ascertain whether **liabilities** existing at the year end have been **completely** and **accurately recorded**.

As regards **trade accounts payable**, this primary objective can be subdivided into two detailed objectives.

- Is there a **satisfactory cut-off** between goods received and invoices received, so that purchases and trade accounts payable are recognised in the correct year?

- Do trade accounts payable represent the *bona fide* amounts due by the company?

Before we ascertain how the auditors design and conduct their tests with these objectives in mind, we need to establish the importance of the list of balances.

The following table sets out audit procedures to test trade accounts payables and accruals. Many of the procedures in the table below are applicable to the **related statement of profit or loss items**, since the figures in that statement constitute the movement between the current and previous year's statement of financial position balances. Some are also procedures relating to statement of profit or loss figures which indirectly give evidence over the year-end balances. For example, the payroll proof in total is an estimate of the employee costs charge for the year but also provides evidence of the adequacy of any related accrual for payroll costs (eg for unpaid wages).

The audit procedures related to statement of profit or loss items are shown in italics.

AUDIT PLAN: ACCOUNTS PAYABLES AND ACCRUALS	
Completeness	• Obtain a listing of trade accounts payables and **agree** the total to the general ledger by casting and cross-casting.
	• Test for unrecorded liabilities by **enquiries of management** on how unrecorded liabilities and accruals are identified and examining post year end transactions.
	• Obtain selected suppliers' statements and **reconcile** these to the relevant suppliers' accounts (see Section 2.3 for details of suppliers' statements).
	• Examine files of unmatched purchase orders and supplier invoices for any **unrecorded liabilities**.
	• Perform a **confirmation of accounts payables** for a sample (see Section 2.2 for details of the accounts payables' confirmation).
	• Complete the **disclosure checklist** to ensure that all the disclosures relevant to liabilities have been made.
	• **Compare** the current year balances for trade accounts payables and accruals with the previous year.
	• **Compare** the amounts owed to a sample of individual suppliers in the trade accounts payables listing with amounts owed to these suppliers in the previous year.
	• **Compare** the payables turnover and payables days to the previous year and industry data.
	• *Reperform casts of payroll records to confirm completeness and accuracy.*
	• *Confirm payment of net pay per payroll records to cheque or bank transfer summary.*
	• *Agree net pay per cashbook to payroll.*
	• *Inspect payroll for unusual items and investigate them further by discussion with management.*
	• *Perform proof-in-total (analytical procedures) on payroll and compare to figure in draft financial statements to assess reasonableness.*
Existence	• **Vouch** selected amounts from the trade accounts payables listing and accruals listing to supporting documentation, such as purchase orders and suppliers' invoices.
	• Obtain selected suppliers' statements and **reconcile** these to the relevant suppliers' accounts.
	• Perform a **confirmation of accounts payables** for a sample.
	• Perform **analytical procedures** comparing current year balances with the previous year to confirm reasonableness, and also calculating payables' turnover and comparing with the previous year.
Rights and obligations	• **Vouch** a sample of balances to supporting documentation, such as purchase orders and suppliers' invoices, to obtain audit evidence regarding rights and obligations.

AUDIT PLAN: ACCOUNTS PAYABLES AND ACCRUALS	
Accuracy, valuation and allocation	• **Trace** selected samples from the trade accounts payables listing and accruals listing to the supporting documentation (purchase orders, minutes authorising expenditure, suppliers' invoices etc). • Obtain selected suppliers' statements and **reconcile** these to the relevant suppliers' accounts. • For a sample of **accruals, recalculate** the amount of the accrual to ensure the amount accrued is correct. • **Compare** the current year balances for trade accounts payables and accruals with the previous year. • **Compare** the amounts owed to a sample of individual suppliers in the trade accounts payables listing with amounts owed to these suppliers in the previous year. • **Compare** the payables turnover and payables days with the previous year and industry data. • *Recalculate the mathematical accuracy of a sample of suppliers' invoices to confirm the amounts are correct.* • *Recast calculation of **remuneration**.* • *Reperform calculation of **statutory deductions** to confirm whether correct.* • *Confirm validity of **other deductions** by **agreeing** to supporting documentation.* • *Recast calculation of **other deductions**.*
Cut-off	• *For a sample of vouchers, **compare the dates** with the dates they were recorded in the ledger for application of correct cut-off.* • *Test transactions around the year end to determine whether amounts have been recognised in the correct financial period.* • *Perform analytical procedures on purchase returns, comparing the purchase returns as a percentage of sales or cost of sales to the previous year.*
Occurrence	• *For a sample of vouchers, **inspect** supporting documentation, such as authorised purchase orders.* • *Agree individual remuneration per payroll to personnel records, records of hours worked, salary agreements etc.* • *Confirm **existence** of employees on payroll by meeting them, attending wages payout, inspecting personnel and tax records, and confirmation from managers.* • *Agree benefits on payroll to supporting correspondence.*
Classification	• **Review** the trade accounts payables listing to identify any large debits (which should be reclassified as receivables or deposits) or long-term liabilities which should be disclosed separately. • **Read** the disclosure notes relevant to liabilities in the draft financial statements and review for understandability.
Presentation	• **Read** the disclosure notes to ensure the information is accurate and properly presented at the appropriate amounts.

2.1.1 Audit procedures in relation to purchases, other expenses and wages costs

Dec 13

Although the table above includes details of some procedures which give evidence over items in the statement of profit or loss, the following are procedures specifically related to the audit of purchases and other expenses.

(a) Inspect a sample of purchase invoices to ensure they agree to the amount posted to the general ledger.

(b) Compare expenses making up administrative expenses to the prior year charge and to expectations on a line by line basis. Where differences from expectations are discovered they should be investigated.

(c) Enquire of management whether there are any unsettled claims or obligations arising before the year end and ensure these are provided for (to give evidence over the completeness of the charge in the related expense category in the statement of profit or loss)

(d) Recalculate accruals and prepayments to gain evidence that other expenses are not over- or understated.

(e) Compare gross profit margin with the previous year, the gross margin per the budget and expectations. Investigate any unexpected fluctuations.

One expense that may make up a significant proportion of expenses is the wages cost included in statement of profit or loss. It is important you know procedures that can be used when auditing this area. Although a number of these are included in the table on the previous page, as they are related to the statement of financial position balances, they are reproduced here for clarity along with other relevant procedures.

(a) Reconcile the gross costs on the payroll to the wages cost in the financial statements.

(b) Reperform casts of payroll records to confirm completeness and accuracy of costs used as a basis for the journals to the financial statements.

(c) Confirm payment of net pay per payroll records to cheque or bank transfer summary.

(d) Inspect payroll for unusual items and investigate them further by discussion with management.

(e) Perform proof-in-total (analytical procedures) on payroll by multiplying estimated average wage (using last year's figures plus expected increases) by average number of employees (therefore incorporating starters and leavers) and compare to figure in draft financial statements to assess reasonableness.

(f) Reperform calculations of statutory deductions to establish whether valid deductions have been included in the payroll expense.

2.2 Confirmation of trade payables

We have already discussed the receivables' confirmation procedure in Chapter 14. It is also possible to undertake confirmation of trade payables, although this is not used a great deal in practice because the auditor can test trade payables by examining **reliable, independent evidence** in the form of suppliers' invoices and suppliers' statements. However, where an entity's internal controls are weak, suppliers' statements may not be available, and, in this situation, it may be relevant to undertake confirmation procedures. Confirmation of trade payables provides evidence primarily for the **completeness** assertion.

Where the entity has **strong controls** in place to ensure that all liabilities are recorded, the confirmation will focus on **large balances**.

Where the auditor is **concerned** about the presence of **unrecorded liabilities**, regular suppliers with **small or zero balances** on their accounts and a sample of **other accounts** will be confirmed as well as **large balances**.

Auditors use a **positive confirmation** referred to as a **blank or zero-balance confirmation**. This confirmation **does not state** the balance owed but requires the supplier to declare the amount owed at the year end and to provide a detailed statement of the account. When the confirmation is received back, the amount must be **reconciled** with the entity's records.

The selection and sending out of accounts payables' confirmations should be controlled using the same procedures as for the receivables' confirmation that we discussed in Chapter 14.

2.3 Reconciliations of accounts payables with suppliers' statements

Many suppliers provide **monthly statements** to their customers. These may therefore be available in the entity for examination. Because they are a source of documentary evidence originating outside of the entity, they are a **reliable** source of evidence to support suppliers' balances and provide evidence as to the **existence, completeness** and **valuation** of balances.

Having said this, auditors do still need to be **cautious** when using them, as they may have been **tampered** with by the entity. The auditor should not rely on **photocopies or faxed statements**. If there is any doubt, the auditor should request a copy **directly** from the supplier or confirm the balance with the supplier (see above).

When selecting accounts for testing, the auditor should consider the **volume of business** during the year, not the balance outstanding at the year end, because the risk is understatement of balances. Most differences between balances on suppliers' statements and the year-end accounts payables' listing are likely to be due to goods and cash-in-transit and disputed amounts; however, all differences need to be investigated thoroughly.

Question	Trade payables and accruals

You have been assigned to the audit of Carter Brandon Co (CBC), and you are drafting the audit programme for payables and accruals for the year ended 31 December 20X7.

The company operates from a site in West Wendon. All raw materials are received in the stores and all deliveries are checked to the delivery note and purchase order. The stores supervisor raises a goods received note and is also responsible for raising credit requests if there are any problems with the raw materials delivered.

When the purchase ledger department staff receive the purchase invoices, they match them to the relevant goods received notes and purchase orders, and post them to the computerised purchase ledger. Suppliers are paid on the last day of each month.

Other payables and accruals consist of tax, wages and other statutory deductions, accruals and time-apportioned expenses such as electricity and telephone.

Required

Describe the audit work you will carry out:

(a)   To compare suppliers' statements with balances recorded on the purchase ledger
(b)   To check that purchases cut-off has been applied correctly
(c)   To confirm that other payables and accruals have been accurately stated

Answer

(a)   Comparing suppliers' statements with balances recorded:

     (i)   Select a sample of balances and **compare suppliers' statements with purchase ledger balances**. The extent of the sample will depend on the results of tests of controls and assessment of the effectiveness of controls within the purchases system.

     (ii)   **Select** the **sample on a random basis**. Selection of only large balances or those with many transactions will not yield an appropriate sample, as understatement of liabilities is being tested for. Nil and negative balances will also need to be included in the sample.

     (iii)   If **no statement** was **available** for the supplier, **confirmation** of the balance **from the supplier** should be requested.

        If the balance **agrees exactly**, no further work needs to be carried out.

        Where differences arise these need to be categorised as either in-transit items or other (including disputed) items. In-transit items will be either goods or cash.

(iv)   If the difference relates to goods-in-transit, **ascertain** whether the **goods** were **received** before the year end by reference to the GRN and that they are included in year-end inventory and purchase accruals. If not, a cut-off error has occurred and should be investigated. If the goods were received after the year end, the difference with the suppliers' accounts is correct.

(v)   Similarly, cash-in-transit would arise where the payment to the supplier was made by cheque before the year end but was not received by them until after the year end. The **date** the **cheque** was **raised** and its subsequent **clearing** through the bank account after the year end should be **verified by inspecting the cash book** and the post year end bank statements.

(vi)   However, if the cheque clears after the year-end date, it may indicate that the cheque, though raised before the year end, was not sent to the supplier until after the year end. The relevant amount should be added back to year-end accounts payable and to the end of year bank balance.

(vii)   Differences which do not arise from in-transit items need to be investigated and **appropriate adjustments** made where necessary.

These differences may have arisen due to **disputed invoices**, where for example the client is demanding credit against an invoice which the supplier is not willing to agree.

The client may decide not to post the invoice to the supplier account, as they do not consider it to be a liability of the company. However, differences may also arise because **invoices** have been **held back** in order to reduce the level of year-end accounts payable.

(viii)   If significant unexplained differences are discovered it may be necessary to **extend testing**. There may also be a problem if sufficient suppliers' statements are not available. Alternative procedures, eg a circularisation may then be required.

(b) Correct purchases cut-off:

(i)   From the inventory count working papers, the **number** of the **last GRN** that was issued before the year end will have been noted. **Select a sample** of GRNs issued in the period immediately before and immediately after the year end. The period to be covered would be at least two weeks either side of the year end.

(ii)   **Concentrate** the sample on **high value items**, and more on those GRNs from before the year end, as these represent the greatest risk of cut-off error.

(iii)   Check that the **GRNs** have a **correct number**, according to the last GRN issued in the year and whether the **goods** were **received before or after the year end**.

(iv)   For **GRNs** issued **before the year end**, check whether the **inventory** has been included in the year-end inventory total. Also check whether the **payable** is either **included** in **trade payables** or **purchase accruals** by **inspecting** the relevant documentation.

(v)   For **GRNs** issued **after the year end**, ensure that the **inventory** is **included** in the inventory records **after the year end**. In addition, review the **purchase ledger** to ensure that the relevant **invoice** has been **posted** to the supplier account after the year end.

(c) Other payables and accruals:

(i)   **Assess the system of control** instituted by management to identify and quantify accruals and accounts payable.

(ii)   From the client's sundry payables and accruals listing, check that **accruals** are **calculated correctly** and verify them by reference to subsequent payments. Check that **all time apportionments** have been made correctly (for example, for electricity) by **recalculation**.

(iii)   **Taxation balances**

(1)   Check the **amount paid to the tax authorities** by inspecting relevant documentation. The balance at the year end would normally represent one month's deductions and can be verified to the payroll records. The payment should be traced from the cash book to the payment book (if used) and subsequent bank statements.

(2)   For the sales tax balance, **review** for **reasonableness** to the **next return**. **Ensure** that the **payment** for the **previous return** was for the **correct** amount and has cleared through the bank.

(iv)   **Review the statement of financial position** and **prior year figures** (for any accruals which have not appeared this year or which did not appear last year) and consider liabilities inherent in the trade (eg weekly wages) to ensure that all likely accruals have been provided.

(v)   **Scrutinise payments** made after the year end to ascertain whether any payments made should be accrued. This will include consideration of any payments relating to the current year which are made a long time after the year end.

(vi)   **Consider and document** the basis for **round sum accruals** and ensure it is consistent with prior years.

(vii)   **Ascertain** why any **payments on account** are being made and **ensure** that the full **liability** is **provided**.

(viii)   **Accrued interest** and basic **charges on loans** or overdrafts can be **agreed** to the **bank letter** received for audit purposes.

3 Non-current liabilities

Non-current liabilities are usually authorised by the board and should be well documented.

We are concerned here with non-current liabilities comprising debentures, loan inventory and other loans **repayable** at a date **more than one year after the year end**.

Auditors will primarily try to determine:

- **Completeness**: whether all non-current liabilities have been disclosed
- **Accuracy**: whether interest payable has been calculated correctly and included in the correct accounting period
- **Classification**: whether long-term loans and interest have been correctly disclosed in the financial statements

The major complication for the auditors is that debenture and loan agreements frequently contain conditions with which the company must comply, including restrictions on the company's total borrowings and adherence to specific borrowing ratios.

The plan that follows contains procedures for non-current liabilities in the statement of financial position and the related interest charge in the statement of profit or loss.

AUDIT PLAN: NON-CURRENT LIABILITIES
• **Obtain/prepare schedule of loans** outstanding at the year-end date showing, for each loan: name of lender, date of loan, maturity date, interest date, interest rate, balance at the end of the period and security.
• **Compare opening balances** to previous year's papers.
• **Test the clerical accuracy** of the analysis.
• **Compare balances** to the **general ledger**.
• **Agree name** of **lender** to **register** of **debenture holders** or equivalent (if kept).
• **Trace additions** and **repayments** to **entries** in the **cash book**.
• **Confirm repayments** are in accordance with **loan agreement**.
• **Examine cancelled cheques** and **memoranda of satisfaction** for **loans repaid**.
• **Verify** that **borrowing limits** imposed by agreements are **not exceeded**.

- **Examine signed board minutes** relating to **new borrowings/repayments**.
- **Obtain direct confirmation** from **lenders** of the amounts outstanding, accrued interest and what security they hold.
- **Verify that interest charged** for the period is in accordance with statements and supporting agreements, and consistent with known interest rates. Consider the adequacy of accrued interest.
- **Confirm assets charged** have been **entered** in the **register of charges** and **notified** to the **Registrar**.
- **Review restrictive covenants** and provisions relating to default:
  - **Review** any **correspondence** relating to the loan
  - **Review confirmation** replies for non-compliance
  - If a **default** appears to exist, determine its **effect**, and schedule findings
- **Review minutes and cash book** to confirm that all **loans have been recorded**.
- **Review draft accounts** to ensure that **disclosures** for non-current liabilities are correct and in accordance with accounting standards. Any elements repayable within one year should be classified under current liabilities.

4 Provisions and contingencies

Dec 09, June 10, Dec 11, Specimen Exam

FAST FORWARD

The accounting treatments for provisions and contingencies are complex and involve judgement and this can make them difficult to audit.

4.1 Accounting issues

Key terms

A **provision** is a liability of uncertain timing or amount.

A **liability** is a present obligation of the entity arising from past events, the settlement of which is expected to result in an outflow from the entity of resources embodying economic benefits.

An **obligating event** is an event that creates a legal or constructive obligation that results in an entity having no realistic alternative to settling that obligation.

A **legal obligation** is an obligation that derives from:

(a) A contract (through its explicit or implicit terms);
(b) Legislation; or
(c) Other operation of law.

A **constructive obligation** is an obligation that derives from an entity's actions where:

(a) By an established pattern of past practice, published policies or a sufficiently specific current statement, the entity has indicated to other parties that it will accept certain responsibilities; and

(b) As a result, the entity has created a valid expectation on the part of those other parties that it will discharge those responsibilities.

A **contingent liability** is:

(a) A possible obligation that arises from past events and whose existence will be confirmed only by the occurrence or non-occurrence of one or more uncertain future events not wholly within the control of the entity; or

(b) A present obligation that arises from past events but is not recognised because:

(i) It is not probable that an outflow of resources embodying economic benefits will be required to settle the obligation; or

(ii)   The amount of the obligation cannot be measured with sufficient reliability.

A **contingent asset** is a possible asset that arises from past events and whose existence will be confirmed only by the occurrence or non-occurrence of one or more uncertain future events not wholly within the control of the entity.

Under IAS 37 *Provisions, contingent liabilities and contingent assets*, an entity should not recognise a contingent asset or a contingent liability. However, if it becomes probable that an outflow of future economic benefits will be required for a previous contingent liability, a provision should be recognised. A contingent asset should not be accounted for unless its realisation is virtually certain; if an inflow of economic benefits has become probable, the asset should be disclosed.

Examples of the principal types of contingencies disclosed by companies are:

- **Guarantees** (for group companies, of staff pension schemes, of completion of contracts)
- **Discounted bills of exchange**
- **Uncalled liabilities** on shares or loan inventory
- **Lawsuits** or claims pending
- **Options** to purchase assets

4.2 Obtaining audit evidence of contingencies

Part of ISA 501 *Audit evidence – specific considerations for selected items* covers contingencies relating to litigation and legal claims, which will represent the major part of audit work on contingencies. Litigation and claims involving the entity may have a material effect on the financial statements, and so will require adjustment to/disclosure in those financial statements.

The auditor shall design and perform procedures in order to identify any litigation and claims involving the entity which may give rise to a risk of material misstatement. Such procedures would include the following.

- **Make appropriate enquiries of management** and others including in-house legal advisers.

- **Review minutes of meetings** of those charged with governance and **correspondence** between the entity and its external legal advisers.

- **Review legal expense** accounts.

- **Use any information** obtained regarding the entity's business, including information obtained from discussions with any in-house legal department.

When litigation or claims have been identified or when the auditor believes they may exist, the auditor shall seek **direct communication** with the entity's external legal advisers through a **letter of inquiry** that is prepared by management and sent by the auditor, requesting the legal adviser to communicate directly with the auditor. This assists the auditor in obtaining sufficient appropriate audit evidence as to whether potentially material litigation and claims are known and management's estimates of the financial implications, including costs, are reasonable.

The letter may be one of **general inquiry** or one of **specific inquiry**.

A letter of **general inquiry** requests the entity's external legal advisers to inform the auditor of any litigation and claims that they are aware of, together with an assessment of the outcome of the litigation and claims, and an estimate of the financial implications, including costs involved.

However, if it is considered **unlikely** that the entity's external legal advisers will respond appropriately to a letter of general inquiry, the auditor may seek direct communication through a letter of **specific inquiry**. This will include:

- A **list** of litigation and claims

- Where available, **management's assessment** of the outcome of each of the identified litigation and claims and its **estimate** of the financial implications, including costs involved

- A request that the entity's external legal advisers **confirm the reasonableness** of management's assessments and provide the auditor with **further information** if they consider the list to be incomplete or incorrect

In certain circumstances (the matter is a significant risk, the matter is complex, there is disagreement between management and legal advisers), the auditor also may judge it necessary to **meet** with the entity's external legal advisers to discuss the likely outcome of the litigation or claims. These meetings require management's permission and a member of management will be present at the meeting.

If management **refuses** to give the auditor permission to communicate or meet with the entity's external legal advisers, or the entity's external legal advisers refuse to respond appropriately to the letter of inquiry, or are prohibited from responding, and the auditor is unable to obtain sufficient appropriate audit evidence by performing alternative audit procedures, the auditor shall modify the opinion in the auditor's report in accordance with ISA 705 *Modifications to the opinion in the independent auditor's report.*

The auditor shall request management and, where appropriate, those charged with governance to provide **written representations** that all known actual or possible litigation and claims whose effects should be considered when preparing the financial statements have been disclosed to the auditor and accounted for and disclosed in accordance with the applicable financial reporting framework.

4.3 The audit of provisions

The following audit plan can be used in the audit of provisions.

AUDIT PLAN: PROVISIONS/CONTINGENCIES

- **Obtain details** of all **provisions** which have been included in the **accounts** and all **contingencies** that have been disclosed.
- **Obtain** a **detailed analysis** of all **provisions** showing opening balances, movements and closing balances.
- **Determine** for each material provision whether the company has a **present obligation** as a result of past events by:
  - **Review** of **correspondence** relating to the item
  - **Discussion** with the **directors**. Have they created a valid expectation in other parties that they will discharge the obligation?
- **Determine** for each material provision **whether** it is **probable** that a **transfer of economic benefits** will be required to settle the obligation by:
  - Checking whether any **payments** have been made in the post year end period in respect of the item by reviewing after-date cash
  - **Review of correspondence** with solicitors, banks, customers, insurance company and suppliers both pre and post year end
  - **Sending** a **letter** to the **solicitor** to obtain their views (where relevant)
  - **Discussing** the **position** of similar **past provisions** with the directors. Were these provisions eventually settled?
  - **Considering** the **likelihood** of **reimbursement**
- **Recalculate** all provisions made.
- **Compare** the **amount provided** with any post year end payments and with any amount paid in the past for similar items.
- In the event that it is not possible to estimate the amount of the provision, check that a **contingent liability** is **disclosed** in the accounts.
- **Consider** the **nature** of the **client's business**. Would you expect to see any other provisions eg warranties?
- Consider the adequacy of **disclosure** of provisions, contingent assets and contingent liabilities in accordance with IAS 37.

The audit of provisions is notoriously complex because of the degree of judgement used and the availability of sufficient appropriate audit evidence. This is likely to be tested in a mini scenario type question so you must be able to apply your knowledge to the circumstances in the question.

5 Capital and other issues

FAST FORWARD

The main concern with **share capital and reserves** is that the company has complied with the law.

The issued share capital as stated in the accounts must be **agreed** in total with the **share register**. An examination of transfers on a test basis should be made in those cases where a company handles its own registration work. Where the registration work is dealt with by independent registrars, auditors will normally examine the reports submitted by them to the company, and obtain from them at the year end a certificate of the share capital in issue.

Auditors should check carefully whether clients have complied with local legislation about share issues or purchase of own shares. Auditors should take particular care if there are any movements in reserves that cannot be distributed, and should confirm that these movements are **valid**.

AUDIT PLAN: CAPITAL AND RELATED ISSUES	
SHARE EQUITY CAPITAL	• **Agree** the **authorised share capital** with the statutory documents governing the company's constitution.
	• **Agree changes** to **authorised share capital** with **properly authorised resolutions**.
ISSUE OF SHARES	• **Verify any issue** of share capital or other changes during the year with general and **board minutes**.
	• **Ensure issue or change** is within the **terms** of the **constitution**, and directors possess appropriate **authority** to issue shares.
	• **Confirm** that **cash** or **other consideration** has been **received** or **receivable(s) is included** as called-up share capital not paid.
TRANSFER OF SHARES	• **Verify transfers of shares** by reference to:
	– Correspondence
	– Completed and stamped transfer forms
	– Cancelled share certificates
	– Minutes of directors' meeting
	• **Review the balances** on **shareholders' accounts** in the register of members and the total list with the amount of issued share capital in the general ledger.
DIVIDENDS	• **Agree dividends** paid and declared pre year end to **authority** in minute books and **reperform calculation** with **total share capital** issued to ascertain whether there are any outstanding or unclaimed dividends.
	• **Agree dividend payments** to **documentary evidence** (say, the returned dividend warrants).
	• Test that **dividends do not contravene** distribution provisions by reviewing the legislation.
RESERVES	• Agree **movements on reserves** to supporting authority.
	• **Ensure that movements on reserves do not contravene** the **legislation** and the company's constitution by reviewing the legislation.
	• **Confirm** that the **company** can **distinguish distributable** reserves from those that are **non-distributable**.
	• **Ensure that appropriate disclosures** of movements on reserves are made in the company's accounts by **inspection** of the financial statements.

6 Directors' emoluments

FAST FORWARD

> The auditor will need to make sure the disclosure of **directors' emoluments** is complete, accurate and compliant with both applicable accounting standards and local legislation.

The term 'directors' emoluments' is most likely to appear in local legislation. For example, under UK legislation director's emoluments must be disclosed in the financial statements. Emoluments include salaries, fees, bonuses, pension contributions and retirement benefits, non-cash benefits and any compensation for loss of office.

The shareholders and other users of the financial statements will be very interested in how much of the company's wealth is being paid out to the directors and this area will always be a material one. The area of directors' emoluments is said to be **material by nature**.

Companies listed in the UK have to disclose details of directors' emoluments as part of their Directors' Remuneration report. The part of this report which discloses directors' emoluments must be audited and, if the disclosure is inadequate (in the auditor's opinion), the auditor is required by UK law to highlight this in their auditor's report.

The requirement to disclose directors' emoluments can also be linked to International Financial Reporting Standards because they require compensation payments to **key management personnel** to be disclosed. Although IAS 24 *Related party disclosures* is outside of the syllabus, it is useful to look at its requirements here to illustrate the sorts of payments and benefits a company needs to disclose in respect of management and the board.

IAS 24 requires that the financial statements of a company disclose **key management personnel** compensation details in total. Key management will include the board of directors and compensation will include:

(a) Short-term employee benefits, such as wages, salaries and social security contributions, paid annual leave and paid sick leave, profit-sharing and bonuses and non-monetary benefits for current employees

(b) Post-employment benefits, such as pensions, other retirement benefits, post-employment life insurance and post-employment medical care

(c) Other long-term employee benefits, including long-service benefits and deferred compensation

(d) Termination benefits

(e) Share-based payments

Auditors must therefore ensure that they are comfortable with the requirements of International accounting standards **and** any local legislation. Then procedures adopted must ensure that related disclosure is accurate, complete and covers all areas required by local legislation.

Exam focus point

> Candidates in the June 2014 exam struggled to suggest appropriate audit procedures in respect of directors' bonus payments. Many focused erroneously on the authorisation of the bonuses.

The table below lists some valid audit procedures when auditing directors' emoluments.

AUDIT PLAN: DIRECTORS' EMOLUMENTS
• For each director, obtain a schedule of emoluments for the year, split between wages, bonuses, benefits, pension contributions and other emoluments.
• Check the addition of the schedule and ensure the totals are in agreement with the disclosure in the financial statements.
• Ask each individual director to confirm the emoluments listed are complete and in line with their expectations.
• Compare the emoluments with both the previous year's emoluments and with expectations, taking into account the knowledge obtained during the audit (for example, if you know a director has left during the year, is there any compensation for loss of office expected?).
• Agree salaries, fees, bonuses and pension contributions **to payroll records** for the individual directors and check the amounts paid on the bank statements agree with the payroll records.
• Review the **directors' contracts** and ensure emoluments are consistent with the terms of these contracts.
• Review **board meeting minutes** and meetings of any remuneration committee for evidence of any bonuses, fees or other emoluments not disclosed.
• Review the cash book for any unusual transactions which suggest undisclosed directors' emoluments.
• Obtain and review **returns to tax authorities** made by the company on behalf of the directors which detail non-cash benefits. Ensure these are consistent with the benefits disclosed in the financial statements.
• Consider the adequacy of **disclosure** of directors' emoluments in accordance with applicable accounting standards and local legislation, including the separate disclosure of amounts due to or from directors in respect of directors' emoluments.

Chapter Roundup

- The largest figure in **current liabilities** will normally be **trade accounts payable** which are generally audited by comparison of **suppliers' statements** with **purchase ledger accounts.**

- Non-current liabilities are usually authorised by the board and should be well documented.

- The accounting treatments for provisions and contingencies are complex and involve judgement and this can make them difficult to audit.

- The main concern with **share capital and reserves** is that the company has complied with the law.

- The auditor will need to make sure the disclosure of **directors' emoluments** is complete, accurate and compliant with both applicable accounting standards and local legislation.

Quick Quiz

1   What are the two primary objectives of year-end work on liabilities?

　　(1)   ....

　　(2)   ....

2   Give two instances where trade accounts payables' confirmation is required.

　　(1)   ....

　　(2)   ....

3   Link the following assertion names (1-3) in respect of non-current liabilities with the appropriate description (a-c).

　　(1)   Completeness
　　(2)   Accuracy
　　(3)   Classification and understandability

　　(a)   Whether long-term loans and interest have been correctly disclosed in the financial statements
　　(b)   Whether interest payable has been calculated correctly and included in the correct period
　　(c)   Whether all non-current liabilities have been disclosed

4   Complete the definition

　　Non-current liabilities comprise ...., ... at a date .... a year .... the year end.

5   What two matters should auditors consider in auditing dividends paid?

　　(1)   ....

　　(2)   ....

Answers to Quick Quiz

1   To ensure (1) completely and (2) accurately recorded.

2   (1)   Supplier statements are unavailable
    (2)   Weak internal controls

3   (1) (c)
    (2) (b)
    (3) (a)

4   Debentures, repayable, more than, after.

5   (1)   Have the dividends paid been authorised?
    (2)   Are the dividends distributed legal? Do they contravene distribution provisions?

Now try the question below from the Practice Question Bank

Number	Level	Marks	Time
Q27	Examination	30	59 mins

17

Not-for-profit organisations

Topic list	Syllabus reference
1 Objectives of not-for-profit organisations	D7
2 Audit planning	D7
3 Audit evidence	D7
4 Audit reporting	D7

Introduction

This chapter looks at the audit of not-for-profit organisations. Such entities may or may not be required to have a statutory audit under legislation. They may choose to have a non-statutory audit under the terms of a charitable deed or as part of good practice.

The points made in this chapter about the issues inherent in these entities are relevant for any kind of assurance work in not-for-profit organisations. These entities will have particular features, the most obvious being the difference in objectives of the entity, which will affect the way the work is carried out.

In this chapter we look specifically at the aspects of audit planning, evidence and reporting in not-for-profit organisations and how these differ from for-profit organisations.

Study guide

		Intellectual level
D7	**Not-for-profit organisations**	
(a)	Apply audit techniques to not-for-profit organisations.	2

Exam guide

An exam question on not-for-profit organisations may come up as a scenario-based question on audit planning or evidence. In this case, use your knowledge of not-for-profit organisations as well as the clues given in the scenario to generate ideas for your answer.

Previous exams have included written requirements relating to audit planning and the system of internal control (such as the control environment) relating specifically to not-for-profit organisations. This topic can equally be examined in the form of OTQs in Section A.

1 Objectives of not-for-profit organisations

There are various types of organisations such as charities which do not exist for the purpose of maximising shareholder wealth but which may still require an audit.

1.1 Not-for-profit organisations

Before considering what a not-for-profit organisation's audit will entail, it will be helpful to consider the types of entities that might exist with objectives other than to make a profit and their objectives, as these will impact on the way that they report and the audit that is carried out.

1.2 Objectives of not-for-profit organisations

A hospital could operate at a profit by not spending all the money it receives in its budget. However, the key objective of a hospital is to provide health services to the public, not to make a profit. As its income is fixed, it is more likely to focus on **cost saving** so that it can operate within its budget.

Question · Objectives

Identify the key objectives and focus of the types of association listed above.

Charities and friendly societies	To carry out the charitable purpose. May involve fundraising, receiving donations, managing invested funds, controlling costs.
Schools	To provide education. Likely to involve managing a tight budget (either from fees or government funds).
Clubs, associations, societies, unions	To further the aims of the club, provide a service for members. May include managing subscriptions paid and keeping costs of running the club down.
Housing associations	Managing the related houses and providing facilities for residents. May involve rent collection and maintenance costs or even building costs of future developments.
Local councils, public services	To provide local services to a budget based on public money. Likely to be focused on value for money, as they are in the public eye.

This section can be linked back to the performance measures we covered in Chapter 5 when we looked at Value for Money audits in the context of internal audit. The performance measures were **economy**, **effectiveness** and **efficiency**.

Exam focus point

> Many organisations which are focused on service use VFM indicators that can be used to assess the entity's performance against objectives. Where the organisation has public accountability (for example, they are funded by taxpayers) performance measures are often required to be reported to the public to demonstrate that funds have been used in the most cost-effective manner.
>
> In written scenario-based questions, it is vital that you spot clues given in the scenario indicating what is important to the organisation. Particularly on the 20-mark questions, you need to be able to link different areas of the syllabus, for instance applying your knowledge of VFM and internal control in the context of a not-for-profit entity funded by taxpayers.

1.3 Financial reporting

We noted in Chapter 1 that many not-for-profit organisations are legislated for and the acts which relate to them may specify how they are to report their results.

Many of the organisations mentioned above may be companies (often companies limited by guarantee) and so are required to prepare financial statements and have them audited under companies' legislation. For example, some public sector bodies are established as private companies limited by guarantee (eg industry regulators).

However, they may exist as other types of entity. Other business forms include the following.

(a) Private sector not-for-profit entities may be established as co-operatives, industrial or provident societies (mutual organisations, owned by it members), by trust or as clubs or associations.

(b) In the public sector not-for-profit functions may be government departments, schools or hospitals.

In the UK, some entities have **statements of recommended practice** (SORP). SORPs are recommendations on accounting practices for specialised industries or sectors (please note that SORPs are not examinable for F8). They supplement accounting standards and other legal and regulatory requirements. Similar local guidance exists in other countries.

One example is a SORP for charities entitled *Accounting and reporting by charities* issued by the Charity Commission for England and Wales. It suggests:

(a) A **statement of financial activities** (SOFA) that shows all resources made available to the charity and all expenditure incurred, and reconciles all changes in its funds

(b)   Where the charity is required to prepare accounts in accordance with the Companies Act, or similar legislation, or where the governing instrument so requires, a **summary income and expenditure account** (in addition to the SOFA) in certain circumstances

(c)   A **balance sheet** (the equivalent of a statement of financial position) that shows the assets, liabilities and funds of the charity

(d)   A **cash flow statement**, where required by accounting standards

(e)   **Notes**.

1.4 Audit

Where a statutory audit is required, the auditors will be required to produce the statutory audit opinion concerning the truth and fairness of financial statements.

Where a statutory audit is not required, it is possible that the organisation might have one anyway for the benefit of interested stakeholders, such as the public if the entity is funded by taxpayers (eg transport services and hospitals in some countries) and, if the not-for-profit entity is a charity, people who donate to the charity.

It is also possible that such entities will have special, additional requirements of an audit. These may be required by a regulator, or by the constitution of the organisation. For example, a charity's constitution may require an audit of whether the charity is operating in accordance with its charitable purpose. The Charity Commission for England and Wales was established by law as the regulator and registrar for charities in England and Wales and requires that certain charities are subject to an annual statutory audit.

If the not-for-profit organisation receives government funding (for example a school or an academy) then the Government may ask for the auditor to provide assurance on additional specific areas in addition to the statutory audit (although the Government may well carry out its own procedures instead to ensure that funds are being used as they should be).

1.5 Conclusion

An audit of a not-for-profit organisation may vary from a 'for profit audit' due to:

●   Its objectives and the impact on operations and reporting
●   The purpose for which an audit is required

When carrying out an audit of a not-for-profit organisation, it is vital that the auditor establishes:

●   Whether a statutory audit is required
●   If a statutory audit is not required, what the objectives of the engagement are
●   What the engagement is to report on
●   To whom the report should be addressed
●   What form the report should take

Exam focus point

> You should think around the issues raised for the audit in relation to all the following entities, and be able to apply similar facts and reasoning to any not-for-profit organisation which comes up in the exam. Remember, the issues relating to small companies that we have discussed in this Study Text may also apply to small not-for-profit organisations as well. There are two useful articles on not-for-profit organisations in the September 2009 and October 2009 editions of *Student Accountant*, which you can also access on the ACCA's website.

2 Audit planning

The audit risks associated with not-for-profit organisations may well be different from other entities.

2.1 Auditing not-for-profit organisations

When planning the audit of a not-for-profit organisation, the auditors should particularly consider the following:

- The **scope** of the audit
- Recent **recommendations** of the regulatory bodies
- The **acceptability of accounting policies** adopted
- **Changes in circumstances** in the sector in which the organisation operates
- **Past experience** of the effectiveness of the organisation's accounting system
- **Key audit areas**
- The **amount of detail included** in the financial statements on which the auditors are required to report

The scope of the audit is twofold. The auditors have to report on the truth and fairness of the financial statements for the benefit of the trustees and also on whether the not-for-profit organisation is meeting its objectives. The auditors should therefore establish what the objectives are and consider how they can identify whether the objectives are being met. In order to identify the key audit areas, the auditors will have to consider **audit risk**.

2.1.1 Audit risk

Cash may be significant in not-for-profit organisations and **controls** may be **limited**. Income may well be a risk area, particularly where money is donated or raised informally.

There are certain risks applicable to not-for-profit organisations that might not necessarily be applicable to other small companies. The auditors should consider the following.

Issue	Key factors
Inherent risk	• The complexity and extent of regulation (particularly in relation to public sector not-for-profit organisations) • The significance of donations and cash receipts • Difficulties of the organisation in establishing ownership and timing of voluntary income where funds are raised by non-controlled bodies • Lack of predictable income or precisely identifiable relationship between expenditure and income • Uncertainty of future income For charities in particular: • Restrictions imposed by the objectives and powers given by charities' governing documents • The importance of restricted funds • The extent and nature of trading activities must be compatible with the entity's charitable status • The complexity of tax rules (whether income, capital, sales or local rates) relating to charities • The sensitivity of certain key statistics, such as the proportion of resources used in administration • The need to maintain adequate resources for future expenditure while avoiding the build-up of reserves which could appear excessive

Issue	Key factors
Control risk	• The amount of time committed by directors/trustees to the organisation's affairs
	• The skills and qualifications of individual directors/trustees
	• The frequency and regularity of board/trustee meetings
	• The form and content of board/trustee meetings
	• The independence of trustees from each other
	• The division of duties between management/trustees
	• The degree of involvement in, or supervision of, the organisation's transactions on the part of individual directors/trustees
Control environment	• A recognised plan of the organisation's structure clearly showing the areas of responsibility and lines of authority and reporting
	• Segregation of duties
	• Supervision by management/trustees of the activities of staff where segregation of duties is not practical
	• Competence, training and qualification of paid staff and any volunteers appropriate to the tasks they have to perform
	• Involvement of the board/trustees in the recruitment, appointment and supervision of senior executives
	• Access of trustees to independent professional advice where necessary
	• Budgetary controls in the form of estimates of income and expenditure for each financial year and comparison of actual results with the estimates on a regular basis
	• Communication of results of such reviews to the board/trustees on a regular basis

2.1.2 Internal controls

Small not-for-profit organisations will generally suffer from internal control deficiencies common to small enterprises, such as **lack of segregation of duties** and the use of **unqualified staff**. Shortcomings may arise from the staff's lack of training and also, if they are volunteers, from their attitude, in that they may resent formal procedures.

The auditors will have to consider particularly carefully whether they will be able to obtain adequate assurance that the accounting records do reflect all the transactions of the enterprise and bear in mind whether there are any related statutory reporting requirements.

Using **charities as an example**, the following types of internal control might be typical.

Cash donations	
Source	**Examples of controls**
Collecting boxes and tins	Numerical control over boxes and tins
	Satisfactory sealing of boxes and tins so that any opening prior to recording cash is apparent
	Regular collection and recording of proceeds from collecting boxes
	Dual control over counting and recording of proceeds
Postal receipts	Unopened mail kept securely
	Dual control over mail opening
	Immediate recording of donations on opening of mail or receipt
	Agreement of bank paying-in slips to record of receipts by an independent person
Deeds of covenant	Regular checks and follow-up procedures to ensure due amounts are received
	Regular checks to ensure all tax repayments have been obtained

Cash donations	
Legacies	Comprehensive correspondence files maintained in respect of each legacy
	Regular reports and follow-up procedures undertaken in respect of outstanding legacies
Donations in kind	In case of charity shops, separation of recording, storage and sale of inventory

Other income	
Source	**Examples of controls**
Fundraising activities	Records maintained for each fundraising event
	Other appropriate controls maintained over receipts
	Controls maintained over expenses as for administrative expenses
Central and local government grants and loans	Regular checks that all sources of income or funds are fully utilised and appropriate claims made
	Ensuring income or funds are correctly applied by adequate monitoring

Use of resources	
Resource	**Examples of controls**
Restricted funds	Separate records maintained of relevant income, expenditure and assets
	Terms controlling application of funds
	Oversight of application of fund monies by independent personnel or trustees
Grants to beneficiaries	Records maintained, as appropriate, of requests for material grants received and their treatment
	Appropriate checks made on applications and applicants for grants, and that amounts paid are in accordance with legislation
	Records maintained of all grant decisions, checking that proper authority exists, that adequate documentation is presented to decision-making meetings, and that any conflicts of interest are recorded
	Controls to ensure grants made are properly spent by the recipient for the specified purpose

Of course, the examples of controls over some areas, such as fundraising activities and central and local government grants, can be applied to other not-for-profit organisations and not just charities. In the following question we look at another type of not-for-profit organisation – an 'association' run for the benefit of the members.

Question

Audit risks

The Midvale League is a small association. It runs several local football leagues for various ages and stages. It employs a general administrator and some casual staff to man the bar. Any player who appears in more than 30% of a team's games for the season is required to pay a subscription to the association. The subscriptions pay for the administrator's wages, the referee's fees, team coaches' expenses and a lease on a sports club comprising a clubhouse, changing facilities and three football pitches. The administrator also acts as groundsman. There is a bar in the clubhouse which is run for the benefit of members at a profit which covers bar staff wages and contributes to other expenses of the club. The association pays a local firm of accountants to prepare management accounts every quarter and to produce annual financial statements which it then audits for the benefit of members of the club.

Required

Identify any audit risks arising from The Midvale League.

The classification of the sport's club **lease** may be problematic. It is certainly likely to be their biggest financial commitment. The auditor will need to determine whether the terms of the lease mean that it should be included on the statement of financial position as an asset, showing the corresponding liability or whether it does not qualify. If the terms of the lease agreement imply that the lease is merely an operating lease, the auditors should consider whether this has implications for the **going concern** of the association, as, if it obtains no long-term benefit from the lease, it might be faced with the situation where it has nowhere to operate in the foreseeable future, in which case the purpose of the association is gone.

The auditors will also have to consider the role of the general administrator, who fulfils a number of roles. General administrators are clearly **key** to the association, and it might have difficulties if they were incapacitated, not least perhaps in affording a replacement and any sickness benefit it was required to pay by law.

It is unclear what degree of financial record-keeping the administrator takes on. The audit firm is hired to produce **quarterly management accounts**. It will gain some assurance from the fact that it prepares the accounts, but there is also a risk that day to day transactions are not **properly recorded**, as there appears to be nobody with financial expertise 'at the coal face'. Given that the administrator will record or maintain the relevant records to be passed on to the accountancy firm, there is also an issue of **segregation of duties** here.

The auditors should be aware of any legal issues relating to the bearing of a licence for the bar, particularly perhaps the danger that the licence might be jeopardised by the sale of liquor to underage drinkers. The loss of the licence to serve alcohol could severely diminish the income of the club to the point where it could no longer function.

The auditors will also need to pay attention to the membership of the association from the point of view of completeness of income.

2.2 Auditing not-for-profit organisations in the public sector

As we pointed out at the start of the Chapter, some not-for-profit organisations are public sector organisations. These can include hospitals, schools and local government.

Because these organisations are government funded and receive taxpayers' money, they are obliged to deliver **value for money**. We looked at the concept of value for money in Chapter 5 when we considered internal audit assignments in the context of a not-for-profit entity. However, to recap, not-for-profit organisations in the public sector will rely on measures that estimate the performance of the organisation in relation to the three Es, **economy, efficiency and effectiveness**. As a result, many of the internal controls in such entities will be focused on providing the best service possible at the lowest price. For example, a government-funded hospital may implement the following controls.

- Requirements to compare prices of two or more suppliers before raising a purchase order; this helps with economy of the process, attaining resources at the lowest cost

- Capital expenditure committees put in place to authorise significant capital expenditure items

- Time card clocking in to ensure employees are only paid for those hours worked

- Strict controls over the authorisation of overtime to ensure it is only worked where really needed

Although they are aimed at providing value for money they also serve to provide control over the financial statement areas over which the auditor needs to gain evidence and the auditor may be able to test and rely on some of these controls.

Auditors of not-for-profit public sector entities will need to take into account the specific requirements of any other **relevant regulations** which affect the audit mandate and any special auditing requirements. These special requirements will often relate to verifying that government funding is used for its intended purpose.

Often the audit mandate will be more specific than those in the private sector and encompass a wider range of objectives and a broader scope than is ordinarily applicable for the audit of private sector financial statements.

However, it is important to note that the ISAs are applicable to public sector entities and additional considerations specific to public sector entities are included within the ISAs.

2.2.1 Risk assessment and materiality

When carrying out risk assessment and obtaining an understanding of the entity's objectives and strategies that may result in material misstatement the auditor must take into account that 'management objectives' for public sector entities may be influenced by concerns regarding **public accountability** and may include objectives which have their source in law, regulation or other authority.

Due to the high degree of regulation in the public sector there are increased risks of non-compliance with laws and regulations and the auditor must formulate procedures to respond to those risks.

When considering assertions about the financial statements of public sector not-for-profit entities, in addition to the assertions we looked at in earlier chapters, management may often assert that transactions and events have been carried out in accordance with law, regulation or other authority. These assertions may fall within the scope of the financial statement audit.

It is also important to note that materiality levels for not-for-profit entities in the public sector are likely to be influenced by law, the needs of legislators and the public. Due to the focus on obtaining value for money and keeping costs down, percentages applied to benchmarks linked to costs (rather than profit) may be used to set materiality.

3 Audit evidence

FAST FORWARD

Obtaining audit evidence may be a problem, particularly where organisations have informal arrangements and this may impact on the auditor's report.

3.1 Designing procedures for not-for-profit entities

When designing substantive procedures for not-for-profit entities the auditors should give special attention to the possibility of:

- **Understatement or incompleteness** of the **recording of all income**, including gifts in kind, cash donations and legacies

- **Overstatement of cash grants or expenses**

- **Misanalysis** or misuse in the application of funds, including the misuse of taxpayers' funds if the entity is government funded

- **Misstatement** or omission of **assets**, including donated properties and investments

- The existence of **restricted or uncontrollable funds** in foreign or independent branches

Completeness of income can be a particularly problematic area. Areas auditors may check include:
- Loss of income through fraud
- Recognition of government funding
- Recognition of income from professional fundraisers
- Recognition of income from branches, associates or subsidiaries
- Income from informal fundraising groups
- Income from grants

3.1.1 Overall review of financial statements

The auditors must consider carefully whether the **accounting policies** adopted are **appropriate** to the activities, constitution and objectives of the not-for-profit entity, and are consistently applied, and whether the financial statements adequately disclose these policies and present fairly the state of affairs and the results for the accounting period.

In particular, the auditors should consider the basis of disclosing income from fundraising activities (for example, net or gross), accounting for income and expenses (accruals or cash), the capitalising of expenditure on non-current assets, apportioning administrative expenditure and recognising income from donations and legacies.

Charities without significant endowments or accumulated funds will often be dependent on future income from voluntary sources. In these circumstances auditors may question whether a going concern basis of accounting is appropriate.

Question	Charity audit

You have recently been appointed auditor of Links Famine Relief, a registered charity which receives donations from individuals to provide food in famine areas around the world.

The charity is run by a voluntary management committee, which has monthly meetings and employs the following full-time staff:

(a)   A director, Mr Roberts, who suggests fundraising activities and payments for relief of famine, and implements the policies adopted by the management committee

(b)   A secretary and bookkeeper, Mrs Beech, who deals with correspondence and keeps the accounting records

You are planning the audit of income of the charity for the year ended 5 April 20X7 and are considering the controls which should be exercised over this area.

The previous year's financial statements to 5 April 20X6 (which have been audited by another firm) show the following income.

	$	$
Gifts under non-taxing arrangements		14,745
Tax reclaimed on gifts under non-taxing arrangements		4,915
		19,660
Donations through the post		63,452
Autumn Fair		2,671
Other income		
Legacies	7,538	
Bank deposit account interest	2,774	
		10,312
		96,095

Notes

1   Income from gifts under non-taxing arrangements is stated net. Each person who pays by deed of covenant has filled in a special tax form, which is kept by the full-time secretary, Mrs Beech.

2   All gifts under non-taxing arrangements are paid by banker's order – they are credited directly to the charity's bank account from the donor's bank. Donors make their payments by deed of covenant either monthly or annually.

3   The tax reclaimed on these gifts is one-third of the net value of the gifts, and relates to income received during the year – as the tax is received after the year end, an appropriate amount recoverable is included in the statement of financial position. The treasurer, who is a voluntary (unpaid) member of the management committee, completes the form for reclaiming the income tax, using the special tax forms (in Note 1 above) and checks to the secretary's records that each donor has made the full payment in the year required by the arrangement.

4   Donations received through the post are dealt with by Mrs Beech. These donations are either cheques or cash (bank notes and coins). Mrs Beech prepares a daily list of donations received, which lists the cheques received and total cash (divided between the different denominations of bank notes and coins). The total on this form is recorded in the cash book. She then prepares a paying-in slip and banks these donations daily. When there is a special fundraising campaign, Mrs Beech receives help in dealing with these donations from voluntary members of the management committee.

5   The Autumn Fair takes place every year on a Saturday in October – members of the management committee and other supporters of the charity give items to sell (for example food, garden plants, clothing). A charge is made for entrance to the fair and coffee and biscuits are available at a small charge. At the end of the fair, Mrs Beech collects the takings from each of the stalls and she banks them the following Monday.

6   Legacies are received irregularly, and are usually sent direct to the director of the charity, who gives them to Mrs Beech for banking – they are stated separately on the daily bankings form (in Note 4 above).

7   Bank deposit account interest is paid gross of income tax by the bank, as the Links Famine Relief is a charity.

Required

List and briefly describe the work you would carry out on the audit of income of the charity, the controls you would expect to see in operation and the problems you may experience for the following sources of income, as detailed in the statement above.

(a)   Gifts under non-taxing arrangements
(b)   Tax reclaimed on gifts made under non-taxing arrangements
(c)   Donations received through the post
(d)   Autumn Fair

Answer

The audit consideration in relation to the various sources of income of the Links Famine Relief charity would be as follows.

(a)   *Gifts made under non-taxing arrangements*

This type of income should not present any particular audit problem, as the donations are made by banker's order direct to the charity's bank account and so it would be difficult for such income to be 'intercepted' and misappropriated.

Specific tests required would be as follows.

(i)   Agree a sample of receipts from the bank statements to the cash book to ensure that the income has been properly recorded.

(ii)   Agree a sample of the receipts to the special tax forms to ensure that the full amount due has been received.

Any discrepancies revealed by either of the above tests should be followed up with Mrs Beech.

(b)   *Tax reclaimed on gifts made under non-taxing arrangements*

Once again, this income should not pose any particular audit problems. The auditors should inspect the claim form submitted to the tax authorities and calculate whether the amount of the claim represents $^1/_3$ of the net value of the covenants recorded as having been received.

(c)   *Donations received through the post*

There is a serious problem here, as the nature of this income is not predictable and also because of the lack of internal checks, with Mrs Beech being almost entirely responsible for the receipt of these monies, the recording of the income and the banking of the cash and cheques received. The auditors may ultimately have to express a qualified opinion in this area.

Notwithstanding the above reservations, specific audit tests required would be as follows.

(i) Agree the details on the daily listings of donations received to the cash book, bank statements and paying-in slips, observing whether the details agree in all respects and confirming that there is no evidence of any delay in the banking of this income.

(ii) Agree the donations received by reference to any correspondence which may have been received with the cheques or cash.

(iii) Consider whether the level of income appears reasonable by performing analytical procedures to make comparison with previous years and in light of any special appeals that the charity is known to have made during the course of the year.

(iv) Carry out, with permission from the management committee, surprise checks to vouch the completeness and accuracy of the procedures relating to this source of income.

(d) *Autumn Fair*

Once again, there is a potential problem here because of the level of responsibility vested in one person, namely Mrs Beech.

Specific work required would be as follows.

(i) Attend the event to observe the proper application of procedures laid down and count the cash at the end of the day.

(ii) Agree any records maintained by individual stallholders to the summary prepared by Mrs Beech.

(iii) Inspect the vouchers supporting any expenditure deducted from the proceeds in order to arrive at the net bankings.

(iv) Agree the summary prepared by Mrs Beech to the entry in the cash book and on the bank statement.

4 Audit reporting

The nature of the report will depend on statutory and entity requirements, but it should conform to the criteria in ISA 700 *Forming an opinion and reporting on financial statements*.

For not-for-profit audits where a statutory audit report is required, the auditors should issue the same report that we have considered briefly in Chapter 1. They should also consider whether any additional statutory requirements fall on the audit report.

Where an association or charity is having an audit for the benefit of its members or trustees, or if the entity is government funded and highly regulated, the standard audit report may not be required or appropriate. The auditor should bear in mind the objectives of the audit and make suitable references in the audit report. However, the ISA 700 format will still be relevant.

The auditor should ensure that they make the following matters clear:

- The addressees of the report
- What the report relates to
- The scope of the engagement
- The respective responsibilities of auditors and management/trustees/directors
- The work done
- The opinion drawn

Chapter Roundup

- There are various types of organisations such as charities which do not exist for the purpose of maximising shareholder wealth but which may still require an audit.

- The audit risks associated with not-for-profit organisations may well be different from other entities.

- **Cash** may be significant in not-for-profit organisations and **controls** may be **limited**. Income may well be a risk area, particularly where money is donated or raised informally.

- Obtaining audit evidence may be a problem, particularly where organisations have informal arrangements and this may impact on the auditor's report.

- The nature of the report will depend on statutory and entity requirements, but it should conform to the criteria in ISA 700 *Forming an opinion and reporting on financial statements*.

Quick Quiz

1   List five examples of not-for-profit organisations.

2   All not-for-profit organisations must have a statutory audit.

     True   ☐   False   ☐

3   Explain why income can be a problem when auditing charities.

4   Complete the table, giving two examples of controls in each area.

Cash donations	Other donations	Other income

5   Explain why the control environment in a small not-for-profit entity might be weak.

6   Explain why the materiality figure when auditing local government may not be based on a benchmark linked to percentage profit.

1 Any five from charities, hospitals, schools, clubs, associations, friendly societies, local councils, public services, trade unions, societies, housing associations

2 False

3
- Loss of income through fraud
- Recognition of income from professional fundraisers
- Recognition of income from branches, associates or subsidiaries
- Income from informal fundraising groups
- Income from grants

4

Cash donations	Other donations	Other income
Numerical control over boxes and tins	Regular checks and follow-up procedures to ensure due amounts are received	Records maintained for each fundraising event
Satisfactory sealing of boxes and tins so that any opening prior to recording cash is apparent	Regular checks to ensure all tax repayments have been obtained	Other appropriate controls maintained over receipts
Regular collection and recording of proceeds from collecting boxes	Comprehensive correspondence files maintained in respect of each legacy	Controls maintained over expenses as for administrative expenses
Dual control over counting and recording of proceeds	Regular reports and follow-up procedures undertaken in respect of outstanding legacies	Regular monitoring that all sources of income or funds are fully utilised and appropriate claims made
Unopened mail kept securely	In case of charity shops, separation of recording, storage and sale of inventory	
Dual control over the opening of mail		
Immediate recording of donations on opening of mail or receipt		
Agreement of bank paying-in slips to record of receipts by an independent person		

5
- Lack of segregation of duties
- Lack of staff training
- High staff turnover
- Unqualified staff
- Voluntary staff so unclear responsibilities
- Lack of internal audit department

6 Local government will need to focus on obtaining value for money and keeping costs down. Therefore percentages applied to benchmarks linked to costs are more likely to be used to set materiality.

Now try the questions below from the Practice Question Bank

Number	Level	Marks	Time
Q30	Examination	20	39 mins

Review and reporting

Audit review and finalisation

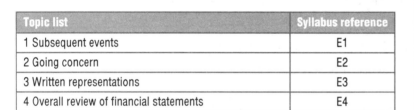

Topic list	Syllabus reference
1 Subsequent events	E1
2 Going concern	E2
3 Written representations	E3
4 Overall review of financial statements	E4

Introduction

This chapter will consider the reviews that take place during the completion stage of the audit, which include subsequent events and going concern. These are both important disclosure issues in the financial statements because, if the disclosures are not correct, this will impact on the auditor's report.

In this chapter, we also consider the use and reliability of written representations from management as audit evidence.

Financial reporting knowledge is particularly important at the review stage of the audit. Auditors need to be able to interpret accounts and understand the requirements of specific accounting standards. Analytical procedures must be used when undertaking the final review of the financial statements.

Study guide

		Intellectual level
E1	**Subsequent events**	
(a)	Explain the purpose of a subsequent events review.	1
(b)	Explain the responsibilities of auditors regarding subsequent events.	1
(c)	Discuss the procedures to be undertaken in performing a subsequent events review.	2
E2	**Going concern**	
(a)	Define and discuss the significance of the concept of going concern.	2
(b)	Explain the importance of and the need for going concern reviews.	2
(c)	Explain the respective responsibilities of auditors and management regarding going concern.	1
(d)	Identify and explain potential indicators that an entity is not a going concern.	2
(e)	Discuss the procedures to be applied in performing going concern reviews.	2
(f)	Discuss the disclosure requirements in relation to going concern issues.	2
(g)	Discuss the reporting implications of the findings of going concern reviews.	2
E3	**Written representations**	
(a)	Explain the purpose of and procedure for obtaining written representations.	2
(b)	Discuss the quality and reliability of written representations as audit evidence.	2
(c)	Discuss the circumstances where written representations are necessary and the matters on which representations are commonly obtained.	2
E4	**Audit finalisation and the final review**	
(a)	Discuss the importance of the overall review in ensuring that sufficient, appropriate evidence has been obtained.	2
(b)	Describe the procedures an auditor should perform in conducting their overall review of financial statements.	2
(c)	Explain the significance of uncorrected misstatements.	1
(d)	Evaluate the effect of dealing with uncorrected misstatements.	2

Exam guide

The review stage of the audit is very important and likely to come up in the exam, both in Section A and in Section B. It is very important that you understand the difference between the review stage of the audit and the earlier testing stage and are able to describe auditor's responsibility in respect of misstatements.

Other topics likely to be examined include:

- Matters requiring written representations
- Going concern indicators, and audit procedures to test the going concern assumption
- The effect of subsequent events on the auditor's report

1 Subsequent events

FAST FORWARD

Subsequent events are events occurring between the period end and the date of the auditor's report and also include facts discovered after the auditor's report has been issued. Auditors shall consider the effect of such events on the financial statements and on their audit opinion.

Key term

Subsequent events are events occurring between the date of the financial statements and the date of the auditor's report, and facts that become known to the auditor after the date of the auditor's report.

IAS 10 *Events after the reporting period* deals with the treatment in the financial statements of events, both favourable and unfavourable, occurring after the period end. There are two types of event defined by IAS 10.

- Those that provide evidence of conditions that existed at the year-end date (**adjusting events**)
- Those that are indicative of conditions that arose after the year-end date (**non-adjusting events**)

You should be familiar with adjusting and non-adjusting events from your financial reporting studies. Here are some examples.

Adjusting events	Non-adjusting events
Settlement of a court case	Dividends declared after the year end
Sale of inventory after year end providing evidence of its net realisable value at year end	Fire causing destruction of major plant
Fraud or error showing the accounts are incorrect	Announcement of a major restructuring

ISA 560 *Subsequent events* provides guidance to auditors in this area. The objectives of the auditor are:

(a) To obtain sufficient appropriate audit evidence about whether events occurring between the date of the financial statements and the date of the auditor's report that need adjustment or disclosure in the financial statements are properly reflected in the financial statements

(b) To respond appropriately to facts that become known to the auditor after the date of the auditor's report which may have caused the auditor to amend the auditor's report if they were known to the auditor at the date of the report

Exam focus point

An article published in April 2011 considers how subsequent events can affect an entity's financial statements, and discusses the auditing requirements Paper F8 candidates need to know. You should read this as part of your F8 study, as it makes some very important observations, such as stressing the importance of being able to differentiate between an adjusting and a non-adjusting event.

The F8 assessor has also written an article in September 2013 entitled 'Subsequent Events'. This article considers the financial reporting aspects of subsequent events using a case study scenario, and discusses in concrete detail how you should approach a scenario-based question on subsequent events in the exam. Please make sure that you read this article.

Both articles can be found on the ACCA's website: http://www.accaglobal.com/gb/en/student/exam-support-resources/fundamentals-exams-study-resources/f8/technical-articles.html.

1.1 Procedures

FAST FORWARD

Auditors have a **responsibility** to **review subsequent events** before they sign the auditor's report, and may have to take action if they become aware of subsequent events between the date they sign the auditor's report and the date the financial statements are issued.

The following timeline is helpful when considering subsequent events and the auditor's responsibilities concerning them.

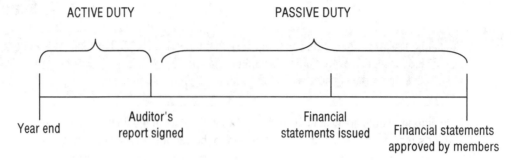

1.1.1 Events occurring up to the date of the auditor's report

The auditor shall perform procedures designed to obtain sufficient appropriate audit evidence that all events up to the date of the auditor's report that may require adjustment of, or disclosure in, the financial statements have been identified.

These procedures should be applied to any matters examined during the audit which may be susceptible to change after the year end. They are in addition to tests on specific transactions after the period end, eg cut-off tests.

ISA 560 lists procedures to identify subsequent events which may require adjustment or disclosure. They should be performed as near as possible to the date of the auditor's report.

AUDIT PROCEDURES TO TEST SUBSEQUENT EVENTS	
Enquiries of management	Status of items involving **subjective judgement**
	Status of items accounted for using **preliminary or inconclusive** data
	Whether there are any new **commitments, borrowings or guarantees**
	Whether there have been any:
	• **Sales** or destruction of **assets**
	• **Issues** of **shares/debentures** or changes in business structure
	• **Developments** involving **risk areas, provisions** and **contingencies**
	• **Unusual accounting adjustments**
	• **Major events** (eg going concern problems) affecting appropriateness of accounting policies for estimates
	• Litigations or claims
Other procedures	**Review** management procedures for identifying subsequent events to ensure that such events are identified.
	Read minutes of general board/committee meetings and enquire about unusual items.
	Review latest available interim financial statements and budgets, cash flow forecasts and other management reports.
	Obtain evidence concerning any litigation or claims from the company's solicitors (only with client permission).
	Obtain **written representation** that all events occurring subsequent to the period end which need adjustment or disclosure have been adjusted or disclosed.

1.1.2 Facts discovered after the date of the auditor's report but before the financial statements are issued

The financial statements are the management's responsibility. They should therefore inform the auditors of any material subsequent events between the date of the auditor's report and the date the financial statements are issued. The auditor does **not** have any obligation to perform procedures, or make enquiries regarding the financial statements, **after** the date of the report.

However, if the auditor becomes aware of a fact that, had it been known to the auditor at the date of the auditor's report, may have caused the auditor to amend the auditor's report, the auditor shall:

- **Discuss** the matter with management and those charged with governance.

- **Determine** whether the financial statements need amendment.

- If amendment is required, **enquire** how management intends to address the matter in the financial statements

If amendment is required to the financial statements and management makes the necessary changes, the auditor must carry out a number of procedures:

- Undertake any **necessary audit procedures** on the changes made.

- **Extend audit procedures** for identifying subsequent events that may require adjustment of or disclosure in the financial statements to the date of the new auditor's report.

- Provide a **new auditor's report** on the amended financial statements.

If management does not amend the financial statements:

- If the auditor's report has not yet been provided to the entity, the auditor shall **modify the opinion** and then provide the auditor's report.

- If the auditor's report has already been provided to the entity, the auditor shall notify management and those charged with governance **not to issue** the financial statements before the amendments are made; but if the financial statements are issued anyway, the auditor shall take action to seek to **prevent reliance** on the auditor's report.

1.1.3 Facts discovered after the financial statements have been issued

Auditors have **no obligations** to perform procedures or make enquiries regarding the financial statements **after** they have been issued.

However, if the auditor becomes aware of a fact that, had it been known to the auditor at the date of the auditor's report, may have caused the auditor to amend the auditor's report, the auditor shall:

- **Discuss** the matter with management and those charged with governance

- **Determine** whether the financial statements need amendment

- If amendment is required, **enquire** how management intends to address the matter in the financial statements

If management amends the financial statements, the auditor shall carry out any necessary procedures on the amendment and review the steps taken by management to ensure that anyone in receipt of the previously issued financial statements is **informed**.

The auditor shall also issue a **new or amended auditor's report,** which will include an **explanatory paragraph** (known as an **emphasis of matter paragraph** or **other matter paragraph** – we discuss these further in Chapter 19) that refers to a note in the financial statements that discusses the reason for the amendment. Audit procedures will be extended up to the date of the new report.

If management does not take the necessary steps, the auditor shall **notify** management and those charged with governance that the auditor will **seek to prevent future reliance** on the report. If management still does not act, the auditor shall take appropriate action to **seek to prevent reliance** on the auditor's report.

2 Going concern

FAST FORWARD

> If the entity has inappropriately used the going concern assumption or a material uncertainty exists, this may impact on the auditor's report.

Key term

> Under the **going concern assumption**, an entity is viewed as continuing in business for the foreseeable future. When the use of the going concern assumption is appropriate, assets and liabilities are recorded on the basis that the entity will be able to realise its assets and discharge its liabilities in the normal course of business.

The financial statements should be prepared on the going concern basis unless management either intends to liquidate the entity or has no realistic alternative but to do so. Therefore, as we discuss in Section 2.1, the going concern assumption is a fundamental principle in the preparation of the financial statements and IAS 1 *Presentation of financial statements* therefore requires management to assess whether the entity is a going concern.

It is vital that the going concern assumption is considered since it affects the value of many areas of the financial statements, how account balances are presented and the financial statement disclosures.

If the going concern basis is not appropriate, the financial statements are prepared on a **break-up basis**.

Using the break-up basis is likely to result in non-current assets and liabilities being reclassified as current. Asset values will need to be stated at their realisable value, as they are no longer to be used in an ongoing business. More liabilities may also arise as a result of closing down operations, and extra provisions may be necessary (for example, over inventories to be sold at a reduced price). Management will also need to disclose the fact the going concern assumption has not been used and explain why.

Since the going concern assumption has such significance in the preparation of the financial statements, the going concern review is a very important part of the audit. As we will see in Section 2.5, the outcome of this review can have a direct impact on the auditor's report. Its importance means it is allocated its own ISA, ISA 570 *Going concern*.

ISA 570 *Going concern* provides guidance to auditors in this area. The objectives of the auditor are:

(a) To obtain sufficient appropriate audit evidence regarding the **appropriateness** of management's use of the going concern assumption

(b) To conclude whether a **material uncertainty** exists related to events or conditions that may cast significant doubt on the entity's ability to continue as a going concern

(c) To report in accordance with ISA 570.

ISA 570 includes examples of events or conditions that may cast doubt about the going concern assumption. These are sometimes referred to as **going concern indicators** and fall under three headings: 'financial', 'operating' and 'other', and are shown in the table below.

Events or conditions that may cast doubt about the going concern assumption (potential indicators that an entity is not a going concern).	
Financial	• Net liability or net current liability position
	• Fixed-term borrowings approaching maturity without realistic prospects of renewal or repayment
	• Indications of withdrawal of financial support by creditors
	• Negative operating cash flows (historical or prospective)
	• Adverse key financial ratios
	• Substantial operating losses or significant deterioration in the value of assets used to generate cash flows
	• Arrears or discontinuance of dividends

Events or conditions that may cast doubt about the going concern assumption (potential indicators that an entity is not a going concern).	
Financial (continued)	• Inability to pay creditors on due dates • Inability to comply with terms of loan agreements • Change from credit to cash-on-delivery transactions with suppliers • Inability to obtain financing for essential new product development or other essential investments
Operating	• Management intentions to liquidate or cease operations • Loss of key management without replacement • Loss of a major market, key customers, licence, or principal suppliers • Labour difficulties • Shortages of important supplies • Emergence of a highly successful competitor
Other	• Non-compliance with capital or other statutory requirements • Pending legal or regulatory proceedings against the entity that may, if successful, result in claims that the entity is unlikely to be able to satisfy • Changes in laws/regulations/government policy expected to adversely affect the entity • Uninsured or underinsured catastrophes when they occur

Exam focus point

'Identify and explain potential indicators that an entity is not a going concern' was an addition to the syllabus for exams in 2012. You should make sure you study the above indicators carefully and bear them in mind when you are faced with identifying going concern problems from scenarios in the F8 exam.

The F8 examining team has written an article, 'Going Concern', discussing the respective responsibilities of auditors and management regarding going concern. This is an important topic for the paper. Please read the article by accessing the Technical Articles link on the ACCA's website:
http://www.accaglobal.com/gb/en/student/exam-support-resources/fundamentals-exams-study-resources/f8/technical-articles.html.

2.1 Management's responsibilities for going concern

Management has specific responsibilities relating to going concern that may be set out in law or regulation and in the financial reporting framework. IAS 1 *Presentation of financial statements* contains a specific requirement that management makes an assessment of an entity's ability to continue as a going concern.

Because general purpose financial statements are prepared on a going concern basis, the going concern assumption is a **fundamental principle** in the preparation of financial statements. Therefore management's responsibility for the preparation and presentation of the financial statements also encompasses a responsibility to assess the entity's ability to continue as a going concern even if there is no explicit requirement to do so in the financial reporting framework.

Management's assessment involves making a **judgement** about inherently uncertain future outcomes of events or conditions. This judgement is affected by the following:

- **Degree of uncertainty** which increases the further into the future an event/condition/outcome occurs

- **Size and complexity** of the entity

- **Nature and condition** of the business

- Judgement about the future is based on **information available** at the time the judgement is made but **subsequent events** may result in **inconsistent outcomes**

If, during their assessment, management become aware of material uncertainties related to events or conditions that may cast significant doubt on the entity's ability to continue as a going concern, then those **uncertainties must be disclosed** in the financial statements.

As discussed earlier in the chapter, if management conclude the going concern assumption is not appropriate they will need to prepare the accounts on a different basis. When this happens they must disclose the fact the going concern assumption has not been used and explain why.

This section highlights why audit work on going concern is crucial – because of the **judgements** used by management in making its assessment of going concern.

2.2 Management's assessment

Management may have performed a **preliminary assessment** of whether the entity can continue as a going concern. If it has, the auditor shall discuss it with management. If the assessment has not been performed, the auditor shall discuss with management the basis for the intended use of the going concern assumption.

2.2.1 Auditors' responsibilities in relation to management's assessment

Exam focus point

> Don't get these responsibilities mixed up with the auditors' reporting responsibilities in relation to going concern (which we look at later). It is important you look at what is being asked for in questions on going concern. In a previous exam, the examining team noted that when asked for auditor's **reporting** responsibilities in relation to going concern issues, students often focused on general responsibilities or directors' responsibilites. They therefore wasted time writing on a subject there were no marks available for.

The auditor must **remain alert** throughout the audit for evidence of events or conditions that may cast significant doubt on the entity's ability to continue as a going concern. However, the auditor also has specific responsibilities in relation to management's assessment.

The auditor shall **evaluate** management's assessment of the entity's ability to continue as a going concern. However, if this assessment covers less than 12 months from the date of the financial statements, the auditor shall ask management to extend its assessment period to **at least 12 months** from that date. The auditor shall also enquire of management its knowledge of events or conditions beyond the period of the assessment that may cast significant doubt on the entity's ability to continue as a going concern.

2.3 Events or conditions identified

If events or conditions are identified that may cast significant doubt on the entity's ability to continue as a going concern, the auditor shall obtain sufficient appropriate audit evidence to determine whether a material uncertainty exists by:

- Requesting management to make its **assessment** where this has not been done

- Evaluating management's **plans for future action**

- Evaluating the **reliability of underlying data** used to prepare a cash flow forecast and considering the **assumptions** used to make the forecast

- Considering whether any **additional facts or information** have become available since the date management made its assessment

- Requesting **written representations** from management and those charged with governance about plans for future action and the feasibility of these plans

2.4 Audit procedures applied in performing going concern reviews

Specific audit procedures the auditor might carry out could include the following.:

- **Analyse and discuss cash flow**, profit and other relevant forecasts with management
- **Analyse and discuss** the entity's latest available **interim financial statements** (or management accounts)
- **Review the terms of debentures and loan agreements** and determine whether they have been breached
- **Read minutes** of the meetings of shareholders, the board of directors and important committees for reference to financing difficulties
- **Enquire** of the entity's lawyer regarding **litigation and claims**
- **Confirm the existence, legality and enforceability** of arrangements to provide or maintain financial support with related and third parties
- **Assess** the **financial ability** of such parties to **provide additional funds**
- **Consider the entity's position** concerning unfulfilled customer orders
- **Review events after the period end** for items affecting the entity's ability to continue as a going concern
- Confirm the existence, terms and **adequacy of borrowing facilities**
- Obtaining and **reviewing reports of regulatory actions**
- Determining the **adequacy of support for any planned disposals** of assets

2.5 Audit reporting

Exam focus point

It is very important that you are aware of the reporting implications when faced with scenarios in which a company has going concern problems. This is an area where students have struggled in the past and this has been highlighted in recent examiner's reports. Don't forget to take into account any information you are given in the scenario. For example, if you know a material uncertainty exists and management has provided disclosures, the audit report issued will depend on the adequacy of those disclosures.

ISA 570 (Revised) extends the auditor's reporting responsibilities in relation to going concern. Make sure that your knowledge is brought up to date in this area.

The auditor shall consider whether a **material uncertainty** exists related to events or conditions which may cast doubt on the entity's ability to continue as a going concern, as this will have an impact on the opinion issued in the auditor's report because the uncertainty must be disclosed.

The following table summarises the possible scenarios that could arise following the auditor's review of going concern. We discuss audit reporting in detail in Chapter 19, so you may wish to revisit this section again after having studied Chapter 19. ISA 570 does provide example extracts in respect of the scenarios presented in the following table.

Scenario	Impact on auditor's report
1 Going concern assumption appropriate but material uncertainty which is adequately disclosed	Unmodified opinion Section headed 'Material Uncertainty Related to Going Concern'
2 Going concern assumption appropriate but material uncertainty which is not adequately disclosed	Qualified or adverse opinion (ie modified opinion)
3 Use of going concern assumption inappropriate	Adverse opinion (ie modified opinion)
4 Management unwilling to make or extend its assessment	Qualified or disclaimer of opinion (ie modified opinion)

Scenario 1: Going concern assumption appropriate but material uncertainty which is adequately disclosed

In this situation, the opinion on the financial statements will be **unmodified** but the auditor's report will include a Material Uncertainty Related to Going Concern paragraph which explains the uncertainty.

Here is an example of an auditor's report where there is a **material uncertainty**, with **adequate disclosure**. The report is standard/unmodified, except for this new paragraph, placed straight after the 'Basis for Opinion':

Material Uncertainty Related to Going Concern

We draw attention to Note 6 in the financial statements, which indicates that the Company incurred a net loss of ZZZ during the year ended December 31, 20X1 and, as of that date, the Company's current liabilities exceeded its total assets by YYY. As stated in Note 6, these events or conditions, along with other matters as set forth in Note 6, indicate that a material uncertainty exists that may cast significant doubt on the Company's ability to continue as a going concern. Our opinion is not modified in respect of this matter.

Scenario 2: Going concern assumption appropriate but material uncertainty which is not adequately disclosed

In this situation, as inadequate disclosure has been made of the material uncertainty, the auditor's opinion will be modified – either a qualified or adverse opinion will be issued depending on the magnitude of the uncertainty. An extract from the auditor's report where a qualified opinion is issued is provided by the ISA follows.

Qualified Opinion

In our opinion, except for the incomplete disclosure of the information referred to in the Basis for Qualified Opinion paragraph, the financial statements present fairly, in all material respects (or 'give a true and fair view of') the financial position of the Company as at December 31, 20X0, and of its financial performance and its cash flows for the year then ended in accordance with International Financial Reporting Standards (IFRSs).

Basis for Qualified Opinion

The Company's financing arrangements expire and amounts outstanding are payable on 19 March 20X1. The Company has been unable to conclude re-negotiations or obtain replacement financing. This situation indicates that a material uncertainty exists that may cast significant doubt on the Company's ability to continue as a going concern. The financial statements do not fully disclose this matter.

Scenario 3: Use of going concern assumption inappropriate

When the going concern assumption has been used but this is considered inappropriate by the auditor, an adverse opinion must be issued, regardless of whether or not the financial statements include disclosure of the inappropriateness of management's use of the going concern assumption.

Adverse Opinion

In our opinion, because of the omission of the information mentioned in the Basis for Adverse Opinion section of our report, the accompanying financial statements do not present fairly (or do not give a true and fair view of), the financial position of the Company as at December 31, 20X1, and of its financial performance and its cash flows for the year then ended in accordance with International Financial Reporting Standards (IFRSs).

Basis for Adverse Opinion

The Company's financing arrangements expired and the amount outstanding was payable on December 31, 20X1. The Company has been unable to conclude re-negotiations or obtain replacement financing and is considering filing for bankruptcy. This situation indicates that a material uncertainty exists that may cast significant doubt on the Company's ability to continue as a going concern. The financial statements do not adequately disclose this fact.

Scenario 4: Management unwilling to make or extend its assessment

In some circumstances, the auditor may ask management to make or extend its assessment. If management does not do this, a qualified opinion or a disclaimer of opinion may be appropriate, because it may not be possible for the auditor to obtain **sufficient appropriate audit evidence** regarding the use of the going concern assumption in the preparation of the financial statements. Examples of auditor's reports with a disclaimer of opinion are provided in Chapter 19 which looks at modifications to the auditor's opinion in detail.

2.6 Communicating to those charged with governance

The auditor shall **communicate with those charged with governance** events or conditions that may cast doubt on the entity's ability to continue as a going concern. This will include:

- Whether the events or conditions constitute a material uncertainty

- Whether the use of the going concern assumption is appropriate in the preparation and presentation of the financial statements

- The adequacy of related disclosures

3 Written representations   June 08, Dec 10

FAST FORWARD

The auditor obtains **written representations** from management concerning its responsibilities and to support other audit evidence where necessary.

Key term

> **Written representations** are written statements by management provided to the auditor to confirm certain matters or to support other audit evidence. They do not include the financial statements, assertions or supporting books and records.

ISA 580 *Written representations* provides guidance to auditors in this area. The objectives of the auditor are:

- To obtain written representations that management believes that it has fulfilled the fundamental responsibilities that constitute the premise on which an audit is conducted

- To support other audit evidence relevant to the financial statements if determined by the auditor or required by other ISAs

- To respond appropriately to written representations or if management does not provide written representations requested by the auditor

There are three areas in which written representations are necessary – to **confirm management's responsibilities**, where they are **required by other ISAs** and to **support other audit evidence**. We discuss these below in more detail.

3.1 Written representations about management's responsibilities

The auditor shall request management to provide written representations on the following matters.

(a)   That management has fulfilled its responsibility for the **preparation and presentation of the financial statements** as set out in the terms of the audit engagement and whether the financial statements are prepared and presented in accordance with the applicable financial reporting framework

(b)   That management has provided the auditor with all **relevant information** agreed in the terms of the audit engagement and that all transactions have been recorded and are reflected in the financial statements

3.2 Other written representations

Other ISAs require written representations on specific issues but if the auditor considers it necessary to obtain representations in addition to these to support other audit evidence, the auditor shall request these other written representations.

The following table includes examples of other written representations.

Other written representations
Whether the selection and application of accounting policies are appropriate
Plans or intentions that may affect the carrying value or classification of assets and liabilities
Liabilities, both actual and contingent
Title to, or control over, assets, liens or encumbrances on assets and assets pledged as collateral
Aspects of laws, regulations and contractual agreements that may affect the financial statements, including non-compliance
All deficiencies in internal control that management is aware of have been communicated to the auditor
Written representations about specific assertions in the financial statements
Significant assumptions used in making accounting estimates are reasonable
All subsequent events requiring adjustment or disclosure have been adjusted or disclosed
The effects of uncorrected misstatements are immaterial, both individually and in aggregate
Management has disclosed the results of its assessment of the risk that the financial statements may be materially misstated as a result of fraud
Management has disclosed all information in relation to fraud or suspected fraud involving management, employees with significant roles in internal control, and others where fraud could have a material effect on the financial statements
Management has disclosed all information in relation to allegations of fraud or suspected fraud communicated by employees, former employees, analysts, regulators or others
Management has disclosed all instances of non-compliance or suspected non-compliance with laws or regulations

3.3 Quality and reliability of written representations as audit evidence

In Chapter 8 we looked at the quality of audit evidence and pointed out that **written representations** are more reliable than oral representations, since oral representations can be retracted.

However, although written representations are a form of audit evidence, they are from an internal source and **on their own** they **do not provide sufficient appropriate audit evidence** about the issues they relate to.

In addition, the fact that management has provided reliable written representations does not affect the nature or extent of other audit evidence obtained by the auditor regarding the fulfilment of management's responsibilities, or about specific assertions in the financial statements.

You will have noted at the start of Section 3 on the objectives of the auditor regarding written representations that the second objective is 'To **support** other audit evidence ...' This is because although written representations are necessary, they cannot provide sufficient appropriate audit evidence when they stand alone.

3.4 Obtaining written representations

The written representations are usually obtained in the form of a **letter** addressed to the auditor.

Throughout the course of the audit, the auditors will determine those items on which written representations are required and should inform management of those areas on which they will be seeking written representations.

At the finalisation and review stage the auditors will provide management with a draft written representation containing the necessary representations. The auditors will then ask management to print the letter on their headed paper, review the representations, and sign the document to confirm them.

ISA 580 includes an example written representation in an appendix. The date of the written representation must be as near as practicable to, **but not after**, the date of the auditor's report on the financial statements and must be for all the financial statements and period(s) referred to in the auditor's report.

Written representations are requested from those responsible for the preparation of the financial statements – **management** is usually the responsible party. These representations can therefore be requested from the chief executive officer and chief financial officer, or equivalent. In some cases, though, it may be that those charged with governance are also responsible for the preparation of the financial statements.

3.5 Doubt about the reliability of written representations

If written representations are **inconsistent** with other audit evidence, the auditor shall perform audit procedures to try to resolve the matter. If the matter cannot be resolved, the auditor shall reconsider the assessment of the competence, integrity and ethical values of management, and the effect this may have on the reliability of representations and audit evidence in general.

If the auditor concludes that written representations are not reliable, the auditor shall take appropriate actions, including determining the impact on the auditor's report.

3.6 Written representations not provided

If management does not provide one or more requested written representations, the auditor shall:

- **Discuss** the matter with management

- **Re-evaluate** the integrity of management and evaluate the effect this may have on the reliability of representations and audit evidence in general

- Take **appropriate actions**, including determining the **impact** on the auditor's report

4 Overall review of financial statements

Dec 13, June 14, June 15, Specimen Exam

FAST FORWARD

The auditors must perform and document an **overall review** of the financial statements by undertaking **analytical procedures** before they can reach an opinion.

Once most of the substantive audit procedures have been carried out, the auditors will have a draft set of financial statements which should be supported by appropriate and sufficient audit evidence. At the beginning of the end of the audit process, it is usual for the auditors to undertake an **overall review** of the financial statements.

This review of the financial statements, in conjunction with the conclusions drawn from the other audit evidence obtained, gives the auditors a reasonable basis for their opinion on the financial statements. It should be carried out by a senior member of the audit team, with appropriate skills and experience.

4.1 Compliance with accounting regulations

The auditors should consider whether:

(a) The information presented in the financial statements is in accordance with local/national statutory requirements.

(b) The accounting policies employed are in accordance with accounting standards, properly disclosed, consistently applied and appropriate to the entity.

When examining the **accounting policies**, auditors should consider:

(a) Policies **commonly adopted in particular industries**

(b) Policies for which there is **substantial authoritative support**

(c) Whether any **departures from applicable accounting standards** are necessary for the financial statements to give a true and fair view

(d) Whether the **financial statements reflect the substance** of the underlying transactions and not merely their form

When compliance with local/national statutory requirements and accounting standards is considered, the auditors may find it useful to use a **checklist**.

4.2 Review for consistency and reasonableness

The auditors should consider whether the financial statements are **consistent** with their knowledge of the entity's business and with the results of other audit procedures, and the manner of disclosure is fair.

This can be done by applying **analytical procedures** at or near the end of the audit in accordance with ISA 520 *Analytical procedures* which states that the auditor shall design and perform analytical procedures near the end of the audit that assist in forming an overall conclusion as to whether the financial statements are consistent with the auditor's understanding of the entity.

The principal considerations are as follows.

(a) Whether the financial statements adequately reflect the **information** and **explanations** previously obtained and conclusions previously reached during the course of the audit

(b) Whether it reveals any **new factors** which may affect the presentation of, or disclosure in, the financial statements

(c) Whether **analytical procedures** applied when completing the audit, such as comparing the information in the financial statements with other pertinent data, **produce results** which assist in arriving at the overall conclusion as to whether the financial statements as a whole are consistent with their knowledge of the entity's business

(d) Whether the **presentation** adopted in the financial statements may have been unduly influenced by the **directors' desire** to present matters in a favourable or unfavourable light

(e) The potential impact on the financial statements of the **aggregate of uncorrected misstatements** (including those arising from bias in making accounting estimates) identified during the course of the audit and the preceding period's audit, if any

The analytical review at the final stage should cover the following:

- Important accounting ratios
- Related items
- Changes in products/customers
- Price and mix changes
- Wages changes
- Variances
- Trends in production and sales
- Changes in material and labour content of production
- Other expenditure in the statement of profit or loss
- Variations caused by industry or economy factors

As at other stages of the audit process, significant fluctuations and unexpected relationships must be investigated by **enquiries of management** and obtaining appropriate audit evidence relevant to **management's responses**, and **performing other audit procedures** considered necessary.

4.3 Accounting treatment issues

As noted in the previous section, auditors review the financial statements to assess whether the **accounting policies are consistently applied**. Auditors should therefore consider whether new accounting policies are appropriate, whether matters in financial statements are consistent with each other, and whether the financial statements give a true and fair view.

4.4 Treatment of misstatements   June 11

Key terms

> A **misstatement** is a difference between the amount, classification, presentation, or disclosure of a reported financial statement item and the amount, classification, presentation, or disclosure that is required for the item to be in accordance with the applicable financial reporting framework. Misstatements can arise from error or fraud.
>
> An **uncorrected misstatement** is a misstatement that the auditor has accumulated during the audit and that have not been corrected.

ISA 450 *Evaluation of misstatements identified during the audit* requires the auditor to accumulate misstatements identified during the audit, other than those that are clearly trivial. The ISA distinguishes between **factual misstatements** (misstatements about which there is no doubt), **judgemental misstatements** (misstatements arising from management's judgement concerning accounting estimates or accounting policies) and **projected misstatements** (the auditor's best estimate of misstatements arising from sampling populations).

ISA 450 requires the auditor to communicate all misstatements accumulated during the audit with the appropriate level of management on a timely basis and to request management to correct those misstatements. If management refuses, the auditor must establish the reasons why and consider this when evaluating whether the financial statements as a whole are free from material misstatement.

As part of their completion procedures, auditors shall consider whether the **aggregate of uncorrected misstatements** in the financial statements is **material**, having first reassessed materiality in accordance with ISA 320 *Materiality in planning and performing an audit* to confirm that it is still appropriate. When determining whether uncorrected misstatements are material (individually or in aggregate), the auditor shall consider the size and nature of the misstatements and the effect of uncorrected misstatements related to prior periods on the financial statements as a whole.

4.4.1 Communication of uncorrected misstatements

ISA 450 requires the auditor to **communicate uncorrected misstatements** and their effect to those charged with governance, with material uncorrected misstatements being identified individually. The auditor shall request uncorrected misstatements to be corrected. The auditor shall also communicate the effect of uncorrected misstatements relating to prior periods.

The auditor shall request a **written representation** from management and those charged with governance whether they believe the effects of uncorrected misstatements are immaterial (individually and in aggregate) to the financial statements as a whole. A summary of these items shall be included in or attached to the representation.

4.4.2 Misstatements in disclosures

Conforming amendments to ISA 450, published in 2015 as part of IAASB's project on 'Addressing Disclosures in the Audit of Financial Statements', require auditors to consider misstatements in disclosures as well as those relating to transactions and account balances.

Professional judgement is required in determining whether a misstatement in a qualitative disclosure is material or not. ISA 450 gives some examples of misstatements which may be material.

- For insurance or banking companies, inaccurate or incomplete descriptions of information about the objectives, policies and processes for managing capital

- The omission of information about the events which have led to an impairment loss (for example, in a mining company, this may be a significant long-term decline in the demand for a metal)

- The incorrect description of an accounting policy relating to a significant item in the statement of financial position, the statement of comprehensive income, the statement of changes in equity or the statement of cash flows

- For an entity trading internationally, the inadequate description of the sensitivity of an exchange rate

Depending on the circumstances, misstatements in disclosures could also indicate fraud – for example, where they result from management bias, or where the disclosures are intended to obscure a proper understanding of the financial statements. Professional scepticism is therefore required in considering misstatements in disclosures.

4.4.3 Documentation

ISA 450 requires the auditor to document the following information:

- The amount below which misstatements would be regarded as clearly trivial

- All misstatements accumulated during the audit and whether they have been corrected

- The auditor's conclusion as to whether uncorrected misstatements are material and the basis for that conclusion

Exam focus point

> The audit review and finalisation stage of the external audit is very important. It is vital that you are completely comfortable with this stage of the audit process and can distinguish it from the audit testing stage.
>
> The June 2014 exam included a scenario with an uncorrected inventory misstatement. Instead of determining whether the misstatement was material, and suggesting further substantive audit procedures to confirm the size of the misstatement, many candidates focused wrongly on subsequent events. The examining team noted that 'it was apparent that there were significant gaps in candidates' technical knowledge in this area'.

Chapter Roundup

- **Subsequent events** are events occurring between the period end and the date of the auditor's report and also include facts discovered after the auditor's report has been issued. Auditors shall consider the effect of such events on the financial statements and on their audit opinion.

- Auditors have a **responsibility** to **review subsequent events** before they sign the auditor's report, and may have to take action if they become aware of subsequent events between the date they sign the auditor's report and the date the financial statements are issued.

- If the entity has inappropriately used the going concern assumption or a material uncertainty exists, this may impact on the auditor's report.

- The auditor obtains **written representations** from management concerning its responsibilities and to support other audit evidence where necessary.

- The auditors must perform and document an **overall review** of the financial statements by undertaking **analytical procedures** before they can reach an opinion.

Quick Quiz

1   State three enquiries that should be made of management to test subsequent events.

    1   ....

    2   ....

    3   ....

2   Complete the definition, using the words given below.

    Under the .... assumption, an entity is viewed as ....
in business for the ....

future	going	continuing	foreseeable	concern

3   The auditors must satisfy themselves that the use of the going concern basis in the financial statements is appropriate.

    True   ☐

    False   ☐

4   List four examples of areas that analytical review at the final stage should cover.

    1   ....

    2   ....

    3   ....

    4   ....

5   In evaluating whether the financial statements give a true and fair view, auditors shall assess the materiality of uncorrected misstatements.

    True   ☐

    False   ☐

Answers to Quick Quiz

1   Any three from:

- What the status is of items involving subjective judgement
- Whether there are any new commitments, borrowings or guarantees
- Whether any assets have been sold or destroyed
- Whether any new shares/debentures have been issued
- Whether there have been any developments in risk areas
- Any unusual accounting adjustments
- Any major events

2   Going concern, continuing, foreseeable future

3   True

4   Any four from:

- Important accounting ratios
- Related items
- Changes in products/customers
- Price and mix changes
- Wages changes
- Variances
- Trends in production and sales
- Changes in material and labour content of production
- Other income statement expenditure
- Variations caused by industry or economy factors

5   True

Now try the questions below from the Practice Question Bank

Number	Level	Marks	Time
Q10 part (b) (ii)	Examination	6	12 mins
Q31	Examination	20	39 mins

Reports

Introduction

The auditor's report is the means by which the external auditors express their opinion on the truth and fairness of a company's financial statements. It is for the benefit of the shareholders principally, but also for other users, as the audit report is usually kept on public record with the filed financial statements.

Many of the contents of the auditor's report are prescribed by statute. They are also subject to professional requirements in the form of ISA 700 *Forming an opinion and reporting on financial statements.* The auditor's report may contain an unmodified or a modified opinion. The different types of modified opinion are considered in detail in this chapter. Sometimes it is necessary to bring matters to the user's attention without modifying the audit opinion. We will see how emphasis of matter and other matter paragraphs can be used to do just that.

We also look at the auditor's responsibilities and procedures to be applied in other areas which may impact on the auditor's report. These areas include other information in documents containing audited financial statements, and opening balances and comparatives.

We end this chapter by looking at the report to management submitted to the directors and management of a company. This is also known as a letter of weakness or report to management or letter on internal control and is submitted at the end of the audit as a by-product of the audit.

Study guide

		Intellectual level
E5	**Audit reports**	
(a)	Identify and describe the basic elements contained in the independent auditor's report.	1
(b)	Explain unmodified audit opinions in the auditor's report.	2
(c)	Explain modified audit opinions in the audit report.	2
(d)	Describe the format and content of emphasis of matter and other matter paragraphs.	2
C4	**Communication on internal control**	
(a)	Discuss the requirements and methods of reporting significant deficiencies in internal control to management and those charged with governance.	2
(b)	Explain, in a format suitable for inclusion in a report to management, significant deficiencies within an internal control system and provide recommendations for overcoming these deficiencies to management.	2

Exam guide

You will not be expected to reproduce a full auditor's report in the exam; however, you may be required to describe different types of modification to the audit opinion, either in a knowledge-based part of a question or in a scenario-based situation. In the exam, you could be provided with extracts from an auditor's report and asked to identify where ISAs have not been followed. You could also be asked to explain the meaning of phrases in an auditor's report.

Questions on the report to management setting out deficiencies in internal control are highly likely to come up in a scenario-based context.

The elements of an unmodified auditor's report have been tested previously. The impact on the auditor's report of specific issues arising during the audit is also a common angle in a scenario-based question, both in Section A and Section B of the exam. Key Audit Matters is a topical area and is likely to be tested. You should be able to identify the issues which need to be reported in the Key Audit Matters section of the auditor's report. You should also ensure that you know the difference between the Key Audit Matters section and the Emphasis of Matter and Other Matter paragraphs.

1 The auditor's report on financial statements
June 09, Dec 09, June 10, June 11, Dec 11, June 12, Dec 13, June 13, Dec 14

FAST FORWARD

> The auditor is required to produce an **auditor's report** at the end of the audit which sets out their **opinion** on the truth and fairness of the financial statements. The report contains a number of **consistent elements** so that users know the audit has been conducted according to **recognised standards**.

PER alert

Objective 20 of the PER performance objectives is to evaluate and report on audit. The knowledge you gain in this key chapter will assist you in demonstrating the achievement of this objective in practice.

Point to note

This is a **topical** area. The ISAs in this area have been revised, so you probably won't have studied them before. There is also a new ISA (701) which requires auditors to report on 'key audit matters'.

Auditor's reports are covered by the following ISAs.

- ISA 700 *Forming an opinion and reporting on financial statements*
- ISA 701 *Communicating key audit matters in the independent auditor's report*
- ISA 705 *Modifications to the opinion in the independent auditor's report*
- ISA 706 *Emphasis of matter paragraphs and other matter paragraphs in the independent auditor's report*

These ISAs were revised in 2015. The IAASB believes that the revisions are 'essential to the continued relevance of the audit profession globally' – so quite important then! The aims of the revisions are to respond to users, who said that:

- The audit opinion is valued, but could be more informative
- More relevant information is needed about the entity and the audit

The main response has been to include **Key audit matters** in the middle of the auditor's report. The audit opinion is placed at the start of the report, and there is a more detailed description of the auditor's responsibilities and the key features of an audit.

ISA 700 *Forming an opinion and reporting on financial statements* establishes standards and provides guidance on the form and content of the auditor's report issued as a result of an audit performed by an independent auditor on the financial statements of an entity. It states that the auditor shall form an opinion on whether the financial statements are prepared, in all material respects, in accordance with the **applicable financial reporting framework**.

In order to form the opinion, the auditor needs to conclude whether reasonable assurance has been obtained that the financial statements are free from material misstatement. The auditor's conclusion needs to consider the following.

- Whether **sufficient appropriate audit evidence** has been obtained (ISA 330)
- Whether **uncorrected misstatements are material** (ISA 450)
- **Qualitative aspects of the entity's accounting practices**, including indicators of **possible bias** in management's judgements – this includes considering whether the accounting policies disclosed are relevant to the entity, and whether they have been presented in an understandable manner
- Whether the financial statements **adequately disclose the significant accounting policies selected and applied**
- Whether the accounting policies selected and applied are **consistent** with the applicable financial reporting framework and are **appropriate**
- Whether **accounting estimates** made by management are **reasonable**
- Whether **the information** in the financial statements is **relevant, reliable, comparable and understandable**
- Whether the financial statements provide **adequate disclosures** to allow users to understand the effect of material transactions and events on the information presented in the financial statements
- Whether the **terminology** used in the financial statements is **appropriate**
- The **overall presentation, structure and content** of the financial statements
- Whether the financial statements represent the underlying transactions and events so as to achieve **fair presentation**
- Whether the financial statements **adequately refer to or describe the applicable financial reporting framework**

1.1 Unmodified opinions in the auditor's report

Key term

An **unmodified opinion** is the opinion expressed by the auditor when the auditor concludes that the financial statements are prepared, in all material respects, in accordance with the applicable financial reporting framework.

ISA 700 states that the auditor shall express an unmodified opinion when the auditor concludes that the financial statements are prepared, in all material respects, in accordance with the applicable financial reporting framework.

If the auditor concludes that the financial statements as a whole are not free from material misstatement or cannot obtain sufficient appropriate audit evidence to make this conclusion, the auditor must modify the opinion in accordance with ISA 705 *Modifications to the opinion in the independent auditor's report*. We discuss modifications to the opinion later in this chapter.

The following extract from an auditor's report shows an example of the opinion paragraph for an unmodified report, in accordance with ISA 700, which contains illustrations of unmodified auditors' reports in its appendix. The full unmodified report was also set out in Chapter 1 of this Study Text.

In our opinion, the financial statements present fairly, in all material respects, *(or give a true and fair view of)* the financial position of ABC Company as of December 31, 20X1, and (*of*) its financial performance and its cash flows for the year then ended in accordance with International Financial Reporting Standards.

1.2 Basic elements of the auditor's report

A measure of **consistency** in the form and content of the auditor's report is desirable because it **promotes credibility** in the global marketplace and also helps to promote the **reader's understanding** of the report and to **identify unusual circumstances** when they occur.

The auditor's report must be **in writing** and includes the following basic elements, usually in the following layout.

Basic elements of audit report	Explanation
Title	The auditor's report must have a title that clearly indicates that it is the report of the independent auditor. This signifies that the auditor has met all the ethical requirements concerning independence and therefore distinguishes the auditor's report from other reports.
Addressee	The addressee will be determined by law or regulation, but is likely to be the shareholders or those charged with governance.
Opinion paragraph	The opinion paragraph must identify the entity being audited, state that the financial statements have been audited, identify the title of each statement that comprises the financial statements being audited, refer to the summary of significant accounting policies and other explanatory notes, and specify the date or period covered by each statement comprising the financial statements.
	If the auditor expresses an unmodified opinion on financial statements prepared in accordance with a fair presentation framework, the opinion shall use one of the following equivalent phrases:
	• The financial statements present fairly, in all material respects, ...in accordance with [the applicable financial reporting framework]; or
	• The financial statements give a true and fair view of ... in accordance with [the applicable financial reporting framework].

Basic elements of audit report	Explanation
Basis for opinion	The basis for opinion paragraph must state that the audit was conducted in accordance with the ISAs, and refer to the 'Auditor's responsibilities for the audit of the financial statements' section which describes the auditor's responsibilities under the ISAs. The auditor must also state that they are independent of the audited entity, in accordance with the relevant ethical requirements relating to the audit. Finally, the auditor must state that they believe the audit evidence obtained is sufficient and appropriate to provide a basis for the audit opinion.
Going concern	Where the auditor considers a material uncertainty related to going concern exists, this should be described in a separate paragraph headed 'Material uncertainty related to going concern'.
Key audit matters	For the audit of listed entities, or where required by law or regulation, the auditor should include a 'Key audit matters' section. This section describes the matters that, in the auditor's professional judgement, are most significant to the audit. (See section below.)
Other information	For the audit of listed entities or any other entity where the auditor has obtained other information, an 'Other information' section should be included in the auditor's report. This section should include: • a statement that management is responsible for the other information • an identification of the other information obtained before the date of the auditor's report (for listed entities, also the other information expected to be obtained after the date of the auditor's report) • a statement that the auditor's opinion does not cover the other information • a description of the auditor's responsibilities for reading, considering and reporting on other information, and • where other information has been obtained, either a statement that the auditor has nothing to report, or a description of any uncorrected material misstatement
Responsibilities for the financial statements	This part of the report describes the responsibilities of those who are responsible for the preparation of the financial statements. This section should describe management's responsibility including the following: • The preparation of the financial statements in accordance with the applicable financial reporting framework; • The implementation of such internal control as are necessary to enable the preparation of financial statements that are free from material misstatement, whether due to error or fraud. • The assessment of the entity's ability to continue as a going concern, the appropriateness of the going concern basis of accounting and adequacy of related disclosures; Reference shall be made to 'the preparation and fair presentation of these financial statements' (or 'the preparation of financial statements that give a true and fair view') where the financial statements are prepared in accordance with a fair presentation framework.

Basic elements of audit report	Explanation
Auditor's responsibilities for the audit of the financial statements	The report must state that: • the auditor's objectives are to obtain **reasonable assurance** whether the financial statements as a whole are free from material misstatement, and to **issue an auditor's report** that includes the auditor's opinion; and • reasonable assurance is a high level of assurance, but is not a guarantee that an audit conducted in accordance with the ISAs will always detect a material misstatement when it exists. The report must also: • explain that misstatements can arise from fraud or error • describe the meaning of materiality • explain that the auditor exercises professional judgement and maintains professional scepticism throughout the audit • describe the auditor's responsibilities in an audit. The description of the auditor's responsibilities must either be set out in the body of the auditor's report, in an appendix to the auditor's report or by including a specific reference in the body of the auditor's report to such a description on the website of an appropriate authority, where this is permitted by law and regulation.
Other reporting responsibilities	If the auditor is required by law to report on any other matters, this must be done in an additional paragraph titled 'Report on other legal and regulatory requirements' or otherwise as appropriate.
Name of the engagement partner	The name of the engagement partner should be identified, unless such a disclosure is reasonably expected to lead to a significant personal security threat.
Auditor's signature	The report must contain the auditor's signature, whether this is the auditor's own name or the audit firm's name or both.
Auditor's address	The location where the auditor practises must be included.
Date of the report	The report must be dated no earlier than the date on which the auditor has obtained sufficient appropriate audit evidence on which to base the auditor's opinion on the financial statements.

1.3 Key audit matters

FAST FORWARD Listed company auditor's reports include a description of the key audit matters.

ISA 701 *Communicating key audit matters in the independent auditor's report* sets out the auditor's responsibility to communicate KAMs. Let's start with the definition:

Key terms

Key audit matters. Those matters that, in the auditor's professional judgment, were of most significance in the audit of the financial statements of the current period. Key audit matters are selected from matters communicated with those charged with governance.

Reporting on KAMs aims to improve **transparency** by helping users to understand the most significant issues the auditor faced. This should enhance the **communicative value** of the auditor's report.

KAMs are part of every listed company auditor's report, and can be included by other auditors if needed. **KAMs do not constitute a modification of the report** or of the opinion. They are a part of the standard report which must be tailored to each company's circumstances. KAMs are not a substitute for disclosures, for EoM/OM paragraphs, nor for modified opinions. KAMs must always relate to matters already included within the financial statements.

Matters which the auditor may determine to be KAMs include:

- Areas of **higher risk** of material misstatement, or 'significant risks' identified in line with ISA 315 (eg at the planning stage)

- **Significant judgements** in relation to areas where management made judgements

- The effect of **significant events or transactions**

The key part of the definition of KAMs above is that these are the **most significant matters**. Identifying the most significant matters involves using the auditor's **professional judgement**.

Other factors to consider when determining KAMs include:

- The importance of the matter to intended **users' understanding**, including **materiality**

- The nature of the underlying accounting policy relating to the matter or the **complexity** or **subjectivity** involved

- Any **misstatements** related to the matter

- The nature and extent of **audit effort** needed to address the matter

- The nature and severity of **difficulties** in applying audit procedures, obtaining evidence or forming conclusions, including **more subjective judgements**

- The severity of any **control deficiencies**

- Whether **several separate issues** interacted, eg if a long-term contract had repercussions in several areas (revenue recognition, litigation or contingencies).

KAMs are communicated in a separate subsection of the auditor's report. The description of each KAM says **two main things**:

ISA 701.13

The description of each key audit matter in the Key Audit Matters section of the auditor's report shall include a reference to the related disclosure(s), if any, in the financial statements and shall address:

(a)   Why the matter was considered to be one of most significance in the audit and therefore determined to be a key audit matter; and

(b)   How the matter was addressed in the audit.

Here is an example of how KAMs could appear, taken from the IAASB's guidance publication *Auditor reporting – illustrative key audit matters*:

Key Audit Matters

Key audit matters are those matters that, in our professional judgment, were of most significance in our audit of the financial statements of the current period. These matters were addressed in the context of our audit of the financial statements as a whole, and in forming our opinion thereon, and we do not provide a separate opinion on these matters.

Goodwill

Under IFRSs, the Group is required to annually test the amount of goodwill for impairment. This annual impairment test was significant to our audit because the balance of XX as of December 31, 20X1 is material to the financial statements. In addition, management's assessment process is complex and highly judgmental and is based on assumptions, specifically [describe certain assumptions], which are affected by expected future market or economic conditions, particularly those in [name of country or geographic area].

Our audit procedures included, among others, using a valuation expert to assist us in evaluating the assumptions and methodologies used by the Group, in particular those relating to the forecasted revenue growth and profit margins for [name of business line]. We also focused on the adequacy of the Group's disclosures about those assumptions to which the outcome of the impairment test is most sensitive, that is, those that have the most significant effect on the determination of the recoverable amount of goodwill.

The Company's disclosures about goodwill are included in Note 3, which specifically explains that small changes in the key assumptions used could give rise to an impairment of the goodwill balance in the future.

Revenue Recognition

The amount of revenue and profit recognised in the year on the sale of [name of product] and aftermarket services is dependent on the appropriate assessment of whether or not each long-term aftermarket contract for services is linked to or separate from the contract for sale of [name of product]. As the commercial arrangements can be complex, significant judgment is applied in selecting the accounting basis in each case. In our view, revenue recognition is significant to our audit as the Group might inappropriately account for sales of [name of product] and long-term service agreements as a single arrangement for accounting purposes and this would usually lead to revenue and profit being recognised too early because the margin in the long-term service agreement is usually higher than the margin in the [name of product] sale agreement.

Our audit procedures to address the risk of material misstatement relating to revenue recognition, which was considered to be a significant risk, included:

- Testing of controls, assisted by our own IT specialists, including, among others, those over: input of individual advertising campaigns' terms and pricing; comparison of those terms and pricing data against the related overarching contracts with advertising agencies; and linkage to viewer data; and

- Detailed analysis of revenue and the timing of its recognition based on expectations derived from our industry knowledge and external market data, following up variances from our expectations.

1.3.1 Relationship with the auditor's opinion

The KAMs are the key matters for the audit of the whole financial statements. They are **not** separate auditor's opinions for each part of the financial statements, but merely further information on the process that led up to the opinion on the financial statements as a whole. Likewise, the auditor's opinion refers to the financial statements as a whole: as a whole they might give a true and fair view, or as a whole they might be true and fair 'except for' one area (and so on).

If a **modified opinion** is expressed, the matter that gives rise to the modified opinion will be described in the 'basis for modified opinion' paragraph, so it **must not be included as a KAM**. ISA 701 emphasises this:

> *The auditor shall not communicate a matter in the Key Audit Matters section of the auditor's report when the auditor would be required to modify the opinion in accordance with ISA 705 (Revised) as a result of the matter.* (ISA 701 paragraph 12)

Note that where the auditor **disclaims an opinion** on the financial statements, a Key Audit Matters section must not be included in the auditor's report.

ISA 701 also makes special mention of **going concern** problems, which we have covered in Chapter 18. Where there is a material uncertainty in relation to going concern, this is described in the 'Material uncertainty in relation to going concern' paragraph. **Going concern issues should not be included as a KAM**.

1.3.2 Relationship with Emphasis of Matter and Other Matter paragraphs

The Key Audit Matters section does not overlap with Other Matter paragraphs because KAMs must refer to issues present in the financial statements, whereas Other Matter paragraphs do not by definition.

There is some degree of overlap with EoM paragraphs. The difference is that **KAMs do not modify the report**, and are included as standard in every listed company auditor's report. An EoM, on the other hand, does modify the report – although neither modifies the opinion. You could think of the issues giving rise to an EoM as being like KAMs but just more extreme: the EoM is for a 'matter of such importance that it is fundamental for users' understanding', whereas KAMs are merely 'most significant matters', ie less than fundamental.

1.4 Emphasis of matter paragraphs and other matter paragraphs in the auditor's report

FAST FORWARD

Emphasis of matter paragraphs and **other matter paragraphs** can be included in the auditor's report under certain circumstances. Their use does not modify the auditor's opinion on the financial statements.

ISA 706 *Emphasis of matter paragraphs and other matter paragraphs in the independent auditor's report* provides guidance to auditors on the inclusion of paragraphs in the auditor's report that either draw users' attention to a matter that is of such importance that it is **fundamental** to their understanding or that is **relevant** to their understanding of the audit, the auditor's responsibilities or the auditor's report.

1.4.1 Emphasis of matter paragraphs

Key term

An **emphasis of matter paragraph** is a paragraph included in the auditor's report that refers to a matter appropriately presented or disclosed in the financial statements that, in the auditor's judgement, is of such importance that it is fundamental to users' understanding of the financial statements.

Emphasis of matter paragraphs are used to draw readers' attention to a matter **already presented or disclosed** in the financial statements that the auditor feels is **fundamental** to their understanding, provided that the auditor has obtained sufficient appropriate audit evidence that the matter is **not materially misstated**.

Note that an emphasis of matter paragraph is **not used** when the issue has been covered as a **key audit matter**. The auditor must choose whether a matter is simply a key audit matter, or whether it needs an emphasis of matter paragraph.

Point to note

A change was recently made to ISA 706 in relation to going concern. Emphasis of matter paragraphs are **not used in relation to going concern**. They used to be used where there was a 'materiality uncertainty' that was appropriately disclosed, but now the auditor uses a 'Material uncertainty' paragraph instead.

ISA 706 (Revised) calls on the auditor to exercise judgement in deciding where to place the emphasis of matter paragraph in the auditor's report. This decision depends on the nature of the information to be communicated in the emphasis of matter paragraph, and the relative significance of this information to the intended users of the financial statements.

Where there is a Key Audit Matters section, the emphasis of matter paragraph can come either before or after the KAMs, depending on how significant the matters discussed is.

The paragraph must contain a **clear reference** to the matter being emphasised and to where relevant disclosures that fully describe it can be found in the financial statements. The paragraph must state that **the auditor's opinion is not modified** in respect of the matter emphasised.

In addition, the paragraph must clearly state that the audit opinion is not modified.

The following are examples of situations in which the auditor might include an emphasis of matter paragraph in the auditor's report.

- An uncertainty relating to the future outcome of **exceptional litigation or regulatory action**

- **Early application of a new accounting standard** that has a **pervasive effect** on the financial statements

- A **major catastrophe** that has had, or continues to have, **a significant effect** on the entity's financial position

ISA 706 contains an example auditor's report that contains an emphasis of matter paragraph, relevant extracts of which are shown below.

Emphasis of Matter

We draw attention to Note X of the financial statements, which describes the effects of a fire in the Company's production facilities. Our opinion is not modified in respect of this matter.

Exam focus point

The examining team noted following the June 2014 exam that many candidates failed to distinguish between a modified audit opinion and a modified auditor's report. It is crucial to understand that where an Emphasis of Matter paragraph is included, the report is modified, but the audit opinion remains unmodified.

1.4.2 Other matter paragraphs

Key term

An **other matter paragraph** is a paragraph included in the auditor's report that refers to a matter other than those presented or disclosed in the financial statements that, in the auditor's judgement, is relevant to users' understanding of the audit, the auditor's responsibilities or the auditor's report.

Other matter paragraphs are used where the auditor considers it necessary to draw readers' attention to a matter that is relevant to their understanding of the audit, the auditor's responsibilities or the auditor's report.

The other matter paragraph can be used whenever the auditor judges the matter to be relevant to users' understanding of the audit. Examples include:

- The auditor is unable to withdraw from the engagement and yet is unable to obtain sufficient appropriate audit evidence;
- The auditor has been requested to report on other matters or to provide more clarifications in line with the legal jurisdiction of the country.

An other matter paragraph must not refer to something that has been included as a key audit matter.

The following is an example of an Other Matter paragraph, taken from the appendix to ISA 710.

Other Matter

The financial statements of ABC Company for the year ended December 31, 20X0, were audited by another auditor who expressed an unmodified opinion on those statements on March 31, 20X1.

Again, the auditor must exercise judgement in deciding where to place the other matter paragraph. ISA 706 (Revised) states:

- When an Other Matter paragraph is included to draw users' attention to a matter relating to Other Reporting Responsibilities addressed in the auditor's report, the paragraph may be included in the Report on Other Legal and Regulatory Requirements section.
- When relevant to all the auditor's responsibilities or users' understanding of the auditor's report, the Other Matter paragraph may be included as a separate section following the Report on the Audit of the Financial Statements and the Report on Other Legal and Regulatory Requirements.

The content of the other matter paragraph must reflect clearly that the other matter is not required to be presented and disclosed in the financial statements, and does not include information that the auditor is prohibited from providing by law and regulations or other standards, or information that is required to be provided by management.

1.4.3 Communication with those charged with governance

ISA 706 states that when the auditor expects to include an emphasis of matter paragraph or an other matter paragraph, the auditor must communicate with those charged with governance the circumstances and the proposed wording of the paragraph in the auditor's report.

1.5 Modified opinions in auditors' reports   June 15, Specimen Exam

FAST FORWARD

> There are three types of **modified opinion**: a **qualified opinion**, an **adverse opinion** and a **disclaimer of opinion**.

Exam focus point

As the examining team has pointed out in recent exams, audit reports are the only output of a statutory audit and hence an understanding of how an audit report can be modified, and in which circumstances, is very important for this exam.

ISA 705 *Modifications to the opinion in the independent auditor's report* sets out the different types of modified opinions that can result. It identifies three possible types of modification.

- A **qualified** opinion
- An **adverse** opinion
- A **disclaimer** of opinion

1.5.1 Types of modification

Key term

Pervasiveness is a term used to describe the effects or possible effects on the financial statements of misstatements or undetected misstatements (due to an inability to obtain sufficient appropriate audit evidence). There are three types of pervasive effect:

- Those that are not confined to specific elements, accounts or items in the financial statements
- Those that are confined to specific elements, accounts or items in the financial statements and represent or could represent a substantial portion of the financial statements
- Those that relate to disclosures which are fundamental to users' understanding of the financial statements

The type of modification issued depends on the following.

- The **nature of the matter** giving rise to the modifications (ie whether the financial statements **are materially misstated** or whether they **may be misstated** when the auditor cannot obtain sufficient appropriate audit evidence)
- The auditor's judgement about the **pervasiveness** of the effects/possible effects of the matter on the financial statements

A modified opinion is required in either of the following situations.

(a)   The auditor concludes that the financial statements as a whole are not free from material misstatements.

(b)   The auditor cannot obtain sufficient appropriate audit evidence to conclude that the financial statements as a whole are free from material misstatement.

1.5.2 Qualified opinions

A qualified opinion must be expressed in the auditor's report in the following two situations.

(1)   **The auditor concludes that misstatements are material, but not pervasive, to the financial statements.**

Material misstatements could arise in respect of:

- The appropriateness of selected accounting policies

- The application of selected accounting policies
- The appropriateness or adequacy of disclosures in the financial statements

(2) **The auditor cannot obtain sufficient appropriate audit evidence on which to base the opinion but concludes that the possible effects of undetected misstatements, if any, could be material but not pervasive.**

The auditor's inability to obtain sufficient appropriate audit evidence is also referred to as a limitation on the scope of the audit and could arise from:

- Circumstances beyond the entity's control (eg accounting records destroyed)
- Circumstances relating to the nature or timing of the auditor's work (eg the timing of the auditor's appointment prevents the observation of the physical inventory count)
- Limitations imposed by management (eg management prevents the auditor from requesting external confirmation of specific account balances)

1.5.3 Adverse opinions

An adverse opinion is expressed when the auditor, having obtained sufficient appropriate audit evidence, concludes that misstatements are both **material and pervasive** to the financial statements. The table below gives one example of why an adverse opinion might be expressed for each of the three possible reasons for misstatements being determined as pervasive (as stated in the Key term box in Section 1.3.1).

Reason deemed pervasive	Example
Misstatements are not confined to specific elements, accounts or items in the financial statements	No depreciation has been provided on plant and equipment, a receivable balance consisting half of total receivables is irrecoverable and has not been provided and trade payables have been significantly understated. All misstatements are material and these balances are significant on the statement of financial position (SOFP).
Misstatements are confined to specific elements, accounts or items in the financial statements and represent a substantial portion of the financial statements	A house building company has included all the houses it has constructed in the year as non-current assets rather than inventory. The value of these houses constitutes 90% of the total asset value on the SOFP.
Misstatements relate to disclosures which are fundamental to users' understanding of the financial statements	There is a material uncertainty in respect of going concern which has not been adequately disclosed.

Sometimes it is easier to think in more general terms when deciding whether an adverse opinion is warranted (apart from specific instances where reasons for adverse opinions are specified by ISAs, such as in relation to going concern).

The question to ask yourself is this: Am I significantly diverted from the real financial position of the company as a result of the misstatement(s)?

In the house builder example above, the accounts presented would suggest that the company was holding no property for sale but had significant company property that was being utilised by the business. The effects of the misstatement are clearly pervasive.

1.5.4 Disclaimers of opinion

An opinion must be disclaimed when the auditor **cannot obtain sufficient appropriate audit evidence** on which to base the opinion and concludes that the **possible effects** on the financial statements of undetected misstatements, if any, **could be both material and pervasive**.

The opinion must also be disclaimed in situations involving **multiple uncertainties** when the auditor concludes that, despite having obtained sufficient appropriate audit evidence for the individual uncertainties, it is not possible to form an opinion on the financial statements due to the **potential interaction of the uncertainties and their possible cumulative effect** on the financial statements.

One example of when a disclaimer of opinion is used was given in Chapter 18 where, in relation to going concern, management is unwilling to make or extend its assessment. Another example might be where the auditor is unable to attend the inventory count and unable to request receivable confirmations, and there is no other realistic means of gathering evidence on these two areas. If these two areas form a significant element of the total assets value, a disclaimer may be appropriate.

1.5.5 Impact on the auditor's report

When the auditor has had to modify the auditor's opinion, the auditor's report must include a paragraph before the opinion paragraph, which provides a description of the matter giving rise to the modification. This paragraph will be entitled 'Basis for qualified opinion' or 'Basis for adverse opinion' or 'Basis for disclaimer of opinion' depending on the type of modification.

The section of the auditor's report containing the opinion will be headed either 'Qualified opinion', 'Adverse opinion' or 'Disclaimer of opinion', again depending on the type of modification.

When the auditor expresses a qualified or adverse opinion, the section of the report on the auditor's responsibilities must be amended to state that the auditor believes that the audit evidence obtained is sufficient and appropriate to provide a basis for the auditor's modified audit opinion.

When the auditor disclaims an opinion due to being unable to obtain sufficient appropriate audit evidence, the section on the auditor's responsibilities must be amended to include the following: 'Because of the matter(s) described in the Basis for Disclaimer of Opinion paragraph, however, we were not able to obtain sufficient appropriate audit evidence to provide a basis for an audit opinion.'

We will now look at some examples of extracts from auditors' reports with modified opinions for each of the situations we have discussed above.

Example 1: Qualified opinion due to material misstatement

In this example, inventories are materially misstated but the effect is not pervasive.

Qualified Opinion

We have audited the financial statements of ABC Company (the Company), which comprise the statement of financial position as at December 31, 20X1, and the statement of comprehensive income, statement of changes in equity and statement of cash flows for the year then ended, and notes to the financial statements, including a summary of significant accounting policies.

In our opinion, except for the effects of the matter described in the Basis for Qualified Opinion paragraph, the financial statements present fairly, in all material respects, (or *give a true and fair view of*) the financial position of ABC Company as at December 31, 20X1, and (*of*) its financial performance and its cash flows for the year then ended in accordance with International Financial Reporting Standards.

Basis for qualified opinion

The company's inventories are carried in the statement of financial position at xxx. Management has not stated inventories at the lower of cost and net realisable value but has stated them solely at cost, which constitutes a departure from International Financial Reporting Standards. The company's records indicate that, had management stated the inventories at the lower of cost and net realisable value, an amount of xxx would have been required to write the inventories down to their net realisable value. Accordingly, cost of sales would have been increased by xxx, and income tax, net income and shareholders' equity would have been reduced by xxx, xxx and xxx, respectively.

We conducted our audit in accordance with International Standards on Auditing (ISAs). Our responsibilities under those standards are further described in the Auditor's Responsibilities for the Audit of the Financial Statements section of our report. We are independent of the Company in accordance with the ethical requirements that are relevant to our audit of the financial statements in [jurisdiction], and we have fulfilled our other ethical responsibilities in accordance with these requirements. We believe that the audit evidence we have obtained is sufficient and appropriate to provide a basis for our qualified opinion.

Example 2: Adverse opinion due to material misstatement with a pervasive effect

This example is an adverse opinion due to a pervasive material misstatement in the consolidated financial statements..

Adverse Opinion

We have audited the consolidated financial statements of ABC Company and its subsidiaries (the Group), which comprise the consolidated statement of financial position as at December 31, 20X1, and the consolidated statement of comprehensive income, consolidated statement of changes in equity and consolidated statement of cash flows for the year then ended, and notes to the consolidated financial statements, including a summary of significant accounting policies.

In our opinion, because of the significance of the matter discussed in the Basis for Adverse Opinion paragraph, the financial statements do not present fairly (or *do not give a true and fair view of*) the financial position of ABC Company as at December 31, 20X1, and (*of*) its financial performance and its cash flows for the year then ended in accordance with International Financial Reporting Standards.

Basis for adverse opinion

As explained in Note X, the Group has not consolidated subsidiary XYZ Company that the Group acquired

during 20X1 because it has not yet been able to determine the fair values of certain of the subsidiary's material assets and liabilities at the acquisition date. This investment is therefore accounted for on a cost basis. Under IFRSs, the Company should have consolidated this subsidiary and accounted for the acquisition based on provisional amounts. Had XYZ Company been consolidated, many elements in the accompanying consolidated financial statements would have been materially affected. The effects on the consolidated financial statements of the failure to consolidate have not been determined.

We conducted our audit in accordance with International Standards on Auditing (ISAs). Our responsibilities under those standards are further described in the Auditor's Responsibilities for the Audit of the Consolidated Financial Statements section of our report. We are independent of the Group in accordance with the ethical requirements that are relevant to our audit of the consolidated financial statements in [jurisdiction], and we have fulfilled our other ethical responsibilities in accordance with these requirements. We believe that the audit evidence we have obtained is sufficient and appropriate to provide a basis for our adverse opinion.

Example 3: Qualified opinion due to inability to obtain sufficient appropriate audit evidence

In this example, the inventory count was not attended by the auditor, but, in the context of the financial statements, even though inventory could be materially misstated (which the auditor can not conclude on – so the phrase 'possible effects' is used), the effects would not be pervasive.

Qualified Opinion

We have audited the consolidated financial statements of ABC Company and its subsidiaries (the Group), which comprise the consolidated statement of financial position as at December 31, 20X1, and the consolidated statement of comprehensive income, consolidated statement of changes in equity and consolidated statement of cash flows for the year then ended, and notes to the consolidated financial statements, including a summary of significant accounting policies.

In our opinion, except for the possible effects of the matter described in the Basis for Qualified Opinion paragraph, the financial statements present fairly, in all material respects, (or *give a true and fair view of*) the financial position of ABC Company as at December 31, 20X1, and (*of*) its financial performance and its cash flows for the year then ended in accordance with International Financial Reporting Standards.

Basis for qualified opinion

With respect to inventory having a carrying amount of $X the audit evidence available to us was limited because we did not observe the counting of the physical inventory as at 31 December 20X1, since that date was prior to our appointment as auditor of the company. Owing to the nature of the company's records, we were unable to obtain sufficient appropriate audit evidence regarding the inventory quantities by using other audit procedures.

We conducted our audit in accordance with International Standards on Auditing (ISAs). Our responsibilities under those standards are further described in the Auditor's Responsibilities for the Audit of the Consolidated Financial Statements section of our report. We are independent of the Group in accordance with the ethical requirements that are relevant to our audit of the consolidated financial statements in [jurisdiction], and we have fulfilled our other ethical responsibilities in accordance with these requirements. We believe that the audit evidence we have obtained is sufficient and appropriate to provide a basis for our qualified opinion.

Example 4: Disclaimer of opinion due to inability to obtain sufficient appropriate audit evidence about multiple elements of the financial statements

In this example, the auditor has not only been unable to attend the inventory count, but has also been unable to gain evidence over other areas. As a result, the auditor has concluded that the effects of the possible misstatements could be material and pervasive.

Disclaimer of Opinion

We were engaged to audit the consolidated financial statements of ABC Company and its subsidiaries (the Group), which comprise the consolidated statement of financial position as at December 31, 20X1, and the consolidated statement of comprehensive income, consolidated statement of changes in equity and consolidated statement of cash flows for the year then ended, and notes to the consolidated financial statements, including a summary of significant accounting policies.

Because of the significance of the matters described in the Basis for Disclaimer of Opinion paragraph, we have not been able to obtain sufficient appropriate audit evidence to provide a basis for an audit opinion. Accordingly, we do not express an opinion on the financial statements.

Basis for disclaimer of opinion

We were not appointed as auditors of the company until after December 31, 20X1 and thus did not observe the counting of physical inventories at the beginning and end of the year. We were unable to satisfy ourselves by alternative means concerning the inventory quantities held at December 31, 20X0 and 20X1 which are stated in the statement of financial position at xxx and xxx, respectively. In addition, the introduction of a new computerised accounts receivable system in September 20X1 resulted in numerous errors in accounts receivable. As of the date of our audit report, management was still in the process of rectifying the system deficiencies and correcting the errors. We were unable to confirm or verify by alternative means accounts receivable included in the statement of financial position at a total amount of xxx as at December 31, 20X1. As a result of these matters, we were unable to determine whether any adjustments might have been found necessary in respect of recorded or unrecorded inventories and accounts receivable, and the elements making up the statement of profit or loss, statement of changes in equity and cash flow statement.

1.5.6 Communication with those charged with governance

ISA 705 states that when the auditor expects to express a modified opinion, the auditor must **communicate with those charged with governance** the circumstances leading to the expected modification and the proposed wording of the modification in the auditor's report.

This allows the auditor to give **notice** to those charged with governance of the intended modification and the reasons for it, to **seek agreement or confirm disagreement** with those charged with governance with respect to the modification, and to give those charged with governance an **opportunity to provide further information and explanations** on the matter giving rise to the expected modification.

1.5.7 Summary of modifications and impact on the auditor's report

The following table summarises the different types of modified opinion that can arise.

Nature of circumstances	Material but not pervasive	Material and pervasive
Financial statements are materially misstated	QUALIFIED OPINION	ADVERSE OPINION
Auditor unable to obtain sufficient appropriate audit evidence	QUALIFIED OPINION	DISCLAIMER OF OPINION

Question

Modified reports

During the course of your audit of the non-current assets of Eastern Engineering Inc at 31 March 20X4, two problems have arisen.

(a)   The calculations of the cost of direct labour incurred on assets in the course of construction by the company's employees have been accidentally destroyed for the early part of the year. The direct labour cost involved is $10,000.

(b)   The company incurred development expenditure of $25,000 spent on a viable new product which will go into production next year and which is expected to last for ten years. These costs have been expensed in full to the statement of profit or loss.

(c)   Other relevant financial information is as follows.

	$
Profit before tax	100,000
Non-current asset additions (excluding constructed assets)	133,000
Assets constructed by company	34,000
Non-current asset at net book value	666,667

Required

(a)   List the general forms of modification available to auditors in drafting their report and state the circumstances in which each is appropriate.

(b)   State whether you feel that a modified audit opinion would be necessary for each of the two circumstances outlined above, giving reasons in each case.

(c)   On the assumption that you decide that a modified audit opinion is necessary with respect to the treatment of the development expenditure, draft the section of the report describing the matter (the whole report is not required).

Answer

(a)   ISA 705 *Modifications to the opinion in the independent auditor's report* suggests that the auditor may need to modify the opinion under one of two main circumstances:

- The auditor concludes that the financial statements as a whole are not free from material misstatements, or

- The auditor cannot obtain sufficient appropriate audit evidence to conclude that the financial statements as a whole are free from material misstatement.

For both circumstances there can be two 'levels' of modified opinion.

(i)   **Material but not pervasive**, where the circumstances prompting the misstatement or possible misstatement are material. These circumstances will result in a qualified opinion.

(ii)   **Material and pervasive** to the overall view shown by the financial statements, ie the financial statements are or could be misleading. These will result in an adverse opinion

(financial statements are misstated) or a disclaimer of opinion (the auditor is unable to obtain sufficient appropriate audit evidence).

(b) Whether a modification of the audit opinion would be required in the circumstances described would depend on whether or not the auditors considered either of them to be material to the financial statements as a whole. An item is likely to be considered material in the context of a company's financial statements if its omission, misstatement or non-disclosure would prevent a proper understanding of those statements on the part of a potential user.

(i) *Loss of records relating to direct labour costs for assets in the course of construction*

The loss of records supporting one of the asset figures in the statement of financial position would cause a limitation in scope of the auditor's work because the auditor would be unable to obtain sufficient appropriate audit evidence. The $10,000 represents 29.4% of the expenditure incurred during the year on assets in course of construction but only 6% of total additions to non-current assets during the year and 1.5% of the year-end net book value for non-current assets. The total amount of $10,000 represents 10% of pre-tax profit but, the real consideration by the auditor should be the materiality of any over- or understatement of assets resulting from error in arriving at the $10,000 rather than the total figure itself.

Provided there are no suspicious circumstances surrounding the loss of these records and the total figure for additions to assets in the course of construction seems reasonable in the light of other audit evidence obtained, then it is unlikely that this matter would be seen as sufficiently material to merit any modification of the audit opinion. If other records have been lost as well, however, it may be necessary for the auditor to comment on the directors' failure to maintain proper books and records.

(ii) *Development cost debited to the statement of profit or loss*

The situation here is one of misstatement in the financial statements, since best accounting practice as laid down by IAS 38 requires that development costs should be taken to the statement of comprehensive income over the useful life of the product to which they relate.

This departure from IAS 38 does not seem to be justifiable and would be material to the reported pre-tax profits for the year, representing 25% of that figure.

While this understatement of profit would be material to the financial statements, it is not likely to been seen as pervasive and therefore a qualified opinion would be appropriate.

(c) *Qualified audit opinion extract*

Qualified opinion

We have audited the consolidated financial statements of ABC Company and its subsidiaries (the Group), which comprise the consolidated statement of financial position as at December 31, 20X1, and the consolidated statement of comprehensive income, consolidated statement of changes in equity and consolidated statement of cash flows for the year then ended, and notes to the consolidated financial statements, including a summary of significant accounting policies.

In our opinion, except for the effects of the matter described in the Basis for Qualified Opinion paragraph, the financial statements present fairly, in all material respects, *(or give a true and fair view of)* the financial position of Eastern Engineering Inc as at March 31, 20X4, and *(of)* its financial performance and its cash flows for the year then ended in accordance with International Financial Reporting Standards.

Basis for qualified opinion

As explained in note ... development costs in respect of a potential new product have been deducted in full against profit instead of being spread over the life of the relevant product as required by IAS 38; the effect of so doing has been to decrease profits before and after tax for the year by $25,000.

We conducted our audit in accordance with International Standards on Auditing (ISAs). Our responsibilities under those standards are further described in the Auditor's Responsibilities for the Audit of the Financial Statements section of our report. We are independent of the Company in accordance with the ethical requirements that are relevant to our audit of the financial statements in [jurisdiction], and we have fulfilled our other ethical responsibilities in accordance with these requirements. We believe that the audit evidence we have obtained is sufficient and appropriate to provide a basis for our qualified opinion.

1.6 Reporting on Compliance with International Financial Reporting Standards

As we have discussed above, the objective of an audit is to enable the auditor to express an opinion on whether the financial statements are prepared, in all material respects, in accordance with an **applicable financial reporting framework**. The auditor's report must indicate the financial reporting framework that has been used to prepare the financial statements.

1.7 Other information in documents containing audited financial statements

FAST FORWARD

Auditors shall review the **other information** in documents containing audited financial statements for material inconsistencies and misstatements of fact.

ISA 720 (Revised) *The auditor's responsibilities relating to other information in documents containing audited financial statements* provides guidance to auditors in this area. The objective of the auditor is to respond appropriately when documents containing audited financial statements include other information that could **undermine the credibility** of the financial statements and the auditor's report.

Key terms

Other information is financial and non-financial information (other than the financial statements and the auditor's report thereon) included in an entity's annual report

An **annual report** is a document, or combination of documents, prepared typically on an annual basis by management or those charged with governance in accordance with law, regulation or custom.

Its purposes is to provide owners (or similar stakeholders) with information on the entity's operations and the entity's financial results and financial position as set out in the financial statements.

A **misstatement of the other information** exists when the other information is incorrectly stated or otherwise misleading (including because it omits or obscures information necessary for a proper understanding of a matter disclosed in the other information).

Examples of other information include the following:

- A report by management or those charged with governance on operations
- Financial summaries or highlights
- Employment data
- Planned capital expenditures
- Financial ratios
- Names of officers and directors
- Selected quarterly data

1.7.1 Material misstatements of the other information

ISA 720 states that the auditor shall **read** the other information to identity **material inconsistencies** with the audited financial statements. If a material inconsistency is identified, the auditor shall determine whether the audited financial statements or other information is **misstated**.

If the **financial statements** is materially misstated but management refuses to correct the misstatement, the auditor shall **modify** the audit opinion.

If the **other information** is materially misstated and needs to be revised but management refuses, the auditor shall **communicate** this matter to those charged with governance and:

- Include an **Other information** section in the auditor's report that describes the material inconsistency, or

- **Withdraw** from the engagement (where this is legally permitted).

In reading and considering the other information, the auditor should also consider whether the auditor's understanding of the entity and its environment needs to be updated.

1.8 The audit report as a means of communication

1.8.1 Implied information

Audit reports with unmodified opinions may not appear to give a great deal of information. However, the report says much by implication. Remember that the auditors report **by exception**, so a standard report tells the user that, for example:

- **Adequate accounting** records have been **kept**.
- The **accounts agree** with the **records**.
- The **auditors** have **received** all **necessary information**.
- All **directors' transactions** have been **disclosed**.
- The **directors' report** is consistent with the **accounts**.

The real problem here is that, unfortunately, most users do not know that this is what an auditor's report tells them. This issue is also confused by the fact that many users do not understand the responsibilities of either the auditors or the directors in relation to the financial statements.

1.8.2 Expectations gap

This difference between the actual and the public perception is part of what is called the '**expectations gap**', defined as the difference between the apparent public perceptions of the responsibilities of auditors on the one hand (and therefore the assurance that their involvement provides) and the legal and professional reality on the other. The question remains: how can we make the **meaning** of an unmodified auditor's report clear to the user?

The above definition of the expectations gap is not definitive but we can highlight some specific issues.

(a) **Misunderstandings of the nature of audited financial statements**, for example that:

- The statement of financial position provides a fair valuation of the reporting entity.

- The amounts in the financial statements are stated precisely.

- The audited financial statements will guarantee that the entity concerned will continue to exist.

(b) **Misunderstanding as to the type and extent of work undertaken by auditors**

(c) **Misunderstanding about the level of assurance provided by auditors**, for example that:

- An unmodified auditor's opinion means that no frauds have occurred in the period.

- The auditors provide absolute assurance that the figures in the financial statements are correct (ignoring the concept of materiality and the problems of estimation).

Different countries have tackled this problem in different ways. The role of auditors has been included in the debate on corporate governance in many countries, leading to further rules which are nevertheless voluntary, not mandatory, as we discussed in Chapter 3.

2 Reports to management

FAST FORWARD

Reports to management can be sent by external auditors after both the interim and final audits. They set out deficiencies in internal control, the implications of those deficiencies on the business and suggested recommendations to mitigate them.

ISA 265 *Communicating deficiencies in internal control to those charged with governance and management* sets out guidance on internal control deficiencies. We covered the requirements of this standard in detail in Chapter 9 of this Study Text. Many external auditors produce a **report to management** as a by-product of an external audit, listing any deficiencies they have found in systems and making recommendations for improvements. The report to management may also be referred to as the report to management, letter of weakness or letter on internal control.

One of the PER performance objectives is to 'communicate effectively'. Examples of this in practice would be to compile written reports for management or clients. This would therefore include a report to management. The knowledge you attain in this section of the Study Text will help you in situations where you are asked to draft a report to management and, therefore, assist you in achieving this particular PER objective. At the same time it also applies to Objective 18 ('evaluate and report on audit') – examples under this objective include drafting and presenting reports to management.

2.1 The report to management

Recommendations regarding internal control are a by-product of the audit of the financial statements, not a primary objective, but nonetheless are frequently of great value to a client. The auditors shall communicate with those charged with governance any material deficiencies in the design, implementation or operating effectiveness of internal control which have come to their attention during the course of the audit. This shall be done on a **timely basis**.

When auditors prepare a written communication on internal control matters, the following points should be considered:

(a)   It should not **include language** that **conflicts** with the **opinion** expressed in the auditor's report.

(b)   It should state that the **accounting and internal control** system were **considered only** to the **extent necessary** to **determine** the **auditing procedures** to report on the financial statements and not to determine the adequacy of internal control for management purposes or to provide assurances on the accounting and internal control systems.

(c)   It will state that it **discusses only deficiencies** in internal control which have **come to the auditors' attention** as a result of the **audit** and that other deficiencies in internal control may exist.

(d)   It should also include a statement that the **communication is provided for use only by management** (or another specific named party).

After the above items and the auditors' suggestions for corrective action are communicated to management, the auditors will usually ascertain the actions taken, including the reasons for those suggestions rejected. The auditors may encourage management to respond to the auditors' comments, in which case any response can be included in the report.

The significance of findings relating to the accounting and internal control systems may change with the passage of time. Suggestions from previous years' audits which have not been adopted, if any, should normally be repeated or referred to.

2.1.1 Example report to management

This is an example of a report to management with a covering letter which demonstrates how the principles described above might be put into practice.

> ABC & Co
Certified Accountants
29 High Street
>
> The Board of Directors
> Manufacturing Ltd
> 15 South Street
>
> 1 April 20X8
>
> Members of the board,
>
> *Financial statements for the year ended 31 May 20X8*
>
> Please find below the report to management which includes sets out deficiencies in internal control we identified as a result of our review of the accounting systems and procedures operated by your company during our recent audit. The matters dealt with in the report came to our notice during the conduct of our normal audit procedures which are designed primarily for the purpose of expressing our opinion on the financial statements.
>
> ### Purchases: ordering procedures
>
> *Deficiency*
> During the course of our work we discovered that it was the practice of the stores to order certain goods from X Co orally without preparing either a purchase requisition or purchase order.
>
> *Implication*
> There is therefore the possibility of liabilities being set up for unauthorised items and at a non-competitive price.
>
> *Recommendation*
> We recommend that the buying department should be responsible for such orders and, if they are placed orally, an official order should be raised as confirmation.
>
> ### Payables ledger reconciliation
>
> *Deficiency*
> Although your procedures require that the payables ledger is reconciled against the control account on the nominal ledger at the end of every month, this was not done in December or January.
> *Implication*
> The balance on the payables ledger was short by some $2,120 of the nominal ledger control account at 31 January 20X8 for which no explanation could be offered. This implies a serious breakdown in the purchase invoice and/or cash payment batching and posting procedures.
>
> *Recommendation*
> It is important in future that this reconciliation is performed regularly by a responsible official independent of the day to day payables ledger, cashier and nominal ledger functions.
>
> ### Receivables ledger: credit control
>
> *Deficiency*
> As at 28 February 20X8 trade receivables accounted for approximately 12 weeks of sales, although your standard credit terms are cash within 30 days of statement, equivalent to an average of about 40 days (6 weeks) of sales.
>
> *Implication*
> This has resulted in increased overdraft usage and difficulty in settling some key suppliers' accounts on time.

Recommendation

We recommend that a more structured system of debt collection be considered using standard letters and that statements should be sent out a week earlier if possible.

Preparation of payroll and maintenance of personnel records

Deficiency

Under your present system, just two members of staff are entirely and equally responsible for the maintenance of personnel records and preparation of the payroll. Furthermore, the only independent check of any nature on the payroll is that the chief accountant confirms that the amount of the wages cheque presented to him for signature agrees with the total of the net wages column in the payroll. This latter check does not involve any consideration of the reasonableness of the amount of the total net wages cheque or the monies being shown as due to individual employees.

Implication

It is a serious weakness of your present system that so much responsibility is vested in the hands of just two people. This situation is made worse by the fact that there is no clearly defined division of duties between the two of them. In our opinion, it would be far too easy for fraud to take place in this area (eg by inserting the names of 'dummy workmen' into the personnel records and hence on to the payroll) and/or for clerical errors to go undetected.

Recommendations

(i)   Some person other than the two wages clerks be made responsible for maintaining the personnel records and for periodically (but on a surprise basis) checking them against the details on the payroll.

(ii)   The two wages clerks be allocated specific duties in relation to the preparation of the payroll, with each clerk independently reviewing the work of the other.

(iii)   When the payroll is presented in support of the cheque for signature to the chief accountant, he should be responsible for assessing the reasonableness of the overall charge for wages that week.

Please note that this report only sets out those significant deficiencies identified during our audit. If more extensive procedures on internal control had been carried out, we may have identified and reported more deficiencies.

This letter has been produced for the sole use of your company. It must not be disclosed to a third party, or quoted or referred to, without our written consent. No responsibility is assumed by us to any other person.

We should like to take this opportunity of thanking your staff for their co-operation and assistance during the course of our audit.

Yours faithfully

ABC & Co

Exam focus point

If you are answering a question which requires you to prepare a report to management you should **only include a covering letter if you are asked to** provide one.

A question in the December 2010 exam asked for a report to management and included a requirement which asked candidates to include a covering letter. Two marks were available for presentation.

If you are asked for a covering letter, in addition to including the report to management, you should make sure your letter includes:

- An address and the date
- A short introduction explaining the purpose and content of the report to management
- A closing paragraph that states the report only sets out those significant deficiencies identified during the audit and more extensive procedures on internal control may have resulted in more deficiencies being identified. It should also state that the report is solely for management's use

Chapter Roundup

- The auditor is required to produce an **auditor's report** at the end of the audit which sets out their **opinion** on the truth and fairness of the financial statements. The report contains a number of **consistent elements** so that users know the audit has been conducted according to **recognised standards**.

- Listed company auditor's reports include a description of the key audit matters.

- **Emphasis of matter paragraphs** and **other matter paragraphs** can be included in the auditor's report under certain circumstances. Their use does not modify the auditor's opinion on the financial statements.

- There are three types of **modified opinion**: a **qualified opinion**, an **adverse opinion** and a **disclaimer of opinion**.

- Auditors shall review the **other information** in documents containing audited financial statements for material inconsistencies and misstatements of fact.

- **Reports to management** can be sent by external auditors after both the interim and final audits. They set out deficiencies in internal control, the implications of those deficiencies on the business and suggested recommendations to mitigate them.

Quick Quiz

1 The statement of management's responsibilities is always included in the auditors' report.

   True ☐

   False ☐

2 Draw a table that summarises the different modified opinions that can arise in the auditor's report.

3 The inclusion of an emphasis of matter paragraph in the auditor's report does not affect the auditor's opinion on the financial statements.

   True ☐

   False ☐

4 Give three examples of misunderstandings which contribute to the expectations gap.

   (1) ....

   (2) ....

   (3) ....

5 Which of the following are examples of other information in documents containing audited financial statements?

   - Employment data
   - Information contained on the entity's website
   - Written representations
   - Financial ratios
   - Names of officers and directors

1   False

2   Modification table

Nature of circumstances	Material but not pervasive	Material and pervasive
Financial statements are materially misstated	QUALIFIED OPINION	ADVERSE OPINION
Auditor unable to obtain sufficient appropriate audit evidence	QUALIFIED OPINION	DISCLAIMER OF OPINION

3   True

4   (1)   The nature of the financial statements
      (2)   The type and extent of work undertaken by auditors
      (3)   The level of assurance given by auditors

5   Employment data, financial ratios and the names of officers and directors are all examples of other information in documents containing audited financial statements.

Now try the questions below from the Practice Question Bank

Number	Level	Marks	Time
Q32	Examination	10	20 mins
Q33	Examination	n/a	n/a
Q34	Examination	20	39 mins

Practice question and answer bank

The questions in this Practice Question Bank are not in the current exam format, but are intended as useful practice for the material in the chapters. The Practice & Revision Kit provides a large number of exam format questions.

Section A

Multiple choice questions

1   Which of the following statements is correct in relation to external statutory audits?

    A   External audits give absolute assurance that the financial statements are free from all misstatement.

    B   External audits give limited assurance that the financial statements are free from material misstatement.

    C   External audits give reasonable assurance that the financial statements are free from material misstatement.   **(1 mark)**

2   Is the following statement regarding stewardship true or false?

Directors are stewards of the investment made by shareholders in a company.

    A   True

    B   False   **(1 mark)**

3   The International Standards on Auditing are issued by which of the following bodies?

    A   IAESB

    B   IAASB

    C   IASB

    D   FRC   **(2 marks)**

4   Which TWO of the following statements are correct with regards to the International Standards on Auditing (ISA)?

    (1)   The ISAs aim to ensure that audits performed on different companies, in different jurisdictions, adhere to common standards.

    (2)   Where it is not possible to comply with one or several of the ISAs in an audit, the auditor should explain the reason for the non-compliance in the auditor's report.

    (3)   The ISAs apply to the audit of smaller entities.

    A   (1) and (2)

    B   (1) and (3)

    C   (2) and (3)   **(2 marks)**

5   To ensure transparency, the internal audit team should report to:

    A   The company's directors

    B   The audit committee

    C   Both the directors and the audit committee

    D   The shareholders   **(2 marks)**

6   Is the following statement true or false?

In an effective system of corporate governance the directors take responsibility for risk management strategies within the business.

A   True
B   False   **(1 mark)**

7   AB & Co audits DEF Co. In accordance with ACCA *Code of Ethics and Conduct* which **two** of the following circumstances would constitute a threat to objectivity?

(1)   An employee of AB & Co owns shares in DEF Co but is not part of the audit team

(2)   The best friend of the engagement partner owns a significant indirect financial interest in DEF Co

(3)   The audit manager of DEF Co owns a small number of shares in DEF Co

(4)   The husband of the audit partner owns shares in DEF Co

A   (1) and (2)
B   (1) and (4)
C   (2) and (3)
D   (3) and (4)   **(2 marks)**

8   AAB & Co is the statutory auditor of Y Co, a public interest entity.

Which of the following services is AAB & Co prohibited from providing to Y Co under any circumstances?

A   Provision of bookkeeping services
B   Assistance in the resolution of tax disputes
C   Internal audit services
D   Valuation services where the valuation will have a material effect on the financial statements   **(2 marks)**

9   Which of the following internal audit assignments is described below?

The examination of the economy, efficiency and effectiveness of activities and processes.

A   Regulatory compliance audit
B   Value for money audit
C   Financial audit
D   IT audit   **(2 marks)**

10   What are the two elements of the risk of material misstatement at the assertion level?

A   Inherent risk and detection risk
B   Audit risk and detection risk
C   Inherent risk and control risk
D   Detection risk and control risk   **(2 marks)**

11   Is the following statement true or false?

The audit engagement partner must review all audit documentation before the date of the auditor's report, in order to ensure that sufficient and appropriate audit evidence has been obtained to support the audit opinion.

A   True
B   False   **(1 mark)**

12   F Co is an oil and gas company mining for crude oil reserves in sub-Saharan Africa. In the external audit of F Co, to which of the following might specific performance materiality levels apply?

(1)   Directors' remuneration

(2)   Exploration and development costs

(3)   The financial statements as a whole – to reduce to an appropriately low level the probability that the aggregate of uncorrected and undetected misstatements exceeds materiality for the financial statements as a whole

(4)   The financial statements as a whole – to determine whether misstatements identified during the audit should be accumulated and communicated to management

A   (1), (2) and (3)
B   (1), (2) and (4)
C   (1) and (2)
D   (2) and (4)   (2 marks)

13   Which of the following matters would the overall audit strategy include?

A   The applicable financial reporting framework
B   The nature, timing and extent of audit procedures at the assertion level
C   The timetable of planned audit work   (1 mark)

14   'Existence is an assertion about account balances at the period end.'

Is this statement true or false?

A   True
B   False   (1 mark)

15   The auditor of A Co wishes to reduce audit risk. Which of the following actions could the auditor take to achieve this?

(1)   Increase sample sizes
(2)   Reduce control risk
(3)   Assign more experienced staff to the engagement team

A   (1) only
B   (2) only
C   (1) and (3)
D   (2) and (3)   (2 marks)

16   When gaining an understanding of the specific business operations of an audit client which of the following matters would an auditor need to consider?

A   Accounting principles and industry specific practices relevant to the client's business
B   Acquisitions or disposals of the client's business activities
C   Leasing of property, plant or equipment for use in the client's business
D   Products or services and markets of the client's business   (2 marks)

17   Is the following statement true or false regarding the retention of working papers?

ACCA recommends that working papers should be retained for a minimum period of five years.

A   True
B   False   (1 mark)

18   The audit team of which you are a member is in the process of documenting the audit client's system of internal controls. You wish to assess what specific errors or frauds may occur, in order to identify the key controls that the team will then need to test during control testing.

Which of the following methods for recording control systems should you use?

A   ICQ
B   ICEQ
C   Narrative notes
D   Flowcharts   **(2 marks)**

19   Application controls relate to procedures used to initiate, record, process and report transactions and other financial data.

Which **two** of the following are application controls?

(1)   Records of program changes
(2)   Virus checks
(3)   Batch reconciliations
(4)   Document counts

A   (1) and (2)
B   (1) and (4)
C   (2) and (3)
D   (3) and (4)   **(2 marks)**

20   One of the control objectives of the sales system of B Co is to ensure that goods and services are sold to credit-worthy customers.

Which of the following control activities would assist B Co in achieving this objective?

A   All sales orders are based on authorised price lists.
B   Credit limits are checked before sales orders are accepted.
C   Overdue debts are chased each month by the credit controller.
D   The aged-debt listing is reviewed by the finance director on a monthly basis.   **(2 marks)**

21   The auditor of Q Co has identified that Q Co does not match dispatch notes to sales invoices as part of the controls in the sales system.

What is the potential consequence of this deficiency?

A   Customer orders may not be fulfilled accurately.
B   Sales and trade receivables may be overstated.
C   Sales and trade receivables may be understated.
D   Sales invoices may be posted inaccurately in the receivables control account.   **(2 marks)**

22   The external auditor has identified a deficiency in the internal controls of S Co.

Which of the following factors would indicate that the deficiency is a significant deficiency in accordance with ISA 265 *Communicating deficiencies in internal control to those charged with governance and management*?

(1)   The likelihood of the deficiency leading to material misstatement is low
(2)   There is a risk of fraud
(3)   The number of transactions affected by the deficiency is low
(4)   The deficiency interacts with other deficiencies identified

A   (1) and (2)
B   (1) and (3)
C   (2) and (4)
D   (3) and (4)   **(2 marks)**

23 The sales invoices of Z Co are matched to dispatch notes with any mismatched items investigated before they are recorded in the sales day book.

Which of the following control objectives does this help to achieve?

A   It ensures that sales and receivables are valid and accurate.
B   It ensures that all goods dispatched are recognised as sales and receivables.
C   It ensures that all goods ordered by customers are dispatched.
D   It ensures that customers do not exceed their credit limits.   **(2 marks)**

24 To ensure that the recorded sales transactions represent goods that have actually been despatched, D Co's sales system only records sales if there is matching despatch documentation.

Which of the following would be an appropriate test of control to confirm that the control is operating effectively?

A   For a sample of sales invoices, verify that there are matching goods despatched notes.
B   For a sample of goods despatched notes, verify that there are matching sales invoices.
C   Verify that the numerical sequence of sales invoices is complete.
D   Inspect the open-order file for unfulfilled orders.   **(2 marks)**

25 As the external auditor of G Co, you have performed analytical procedures which have highlighted a 40% increase in revenue compared to the previous period.

Which further audit procedures would you perform in response to this?

(1)   For a sample of sales invoices around the period end, inspect the dates and compare with the dates of goods despatch and the dates recorded in the sales and receivables ledger to confirm the application of correct cut-off.

(2)   Trace a sample of shipping documentation to sales invoices and into the sales and receivables ledger.

(3)   For a sample of sales transactions recorded in the ledger, vouch the sales invoice back to customer orders and shipping documentation.

(4)   For a sample of sales invoices, examine for proper classification into revenue accounts.

A   (1) and (2)
B   (1) and (3)
C   (2) and (4)
D   (3) and (4)   **(2 marks)**

26 The draft financial statements of T Co show the following information:

	$'000
Revenue	420
Cost of sales	270
Gross profit	150
Trade receivables	160
Trade payables	130

What is the receivables collection period?

A   139 days
B   175 days
C   758 days
D   958 days   **(2 marks)**

27 Is the following statement regarding audit sampling true or false?

Audit sampling is the application of audit procedures to less than 100% of items within a population of audit relevance such that all sampling units have a chance of selection.

A True

B False (1 mark)

28 The auditor of P Co is planning the audit work on trade receivables.

Which of the following procedures could **not** be performed by using computer-assisted audit techniques?

A Selection of a sample of receivables for confirmation

B Calculation of receivables days

C Production of receivables' confirmation letters

D Evaluation of the adequacy of the allowance for irrecoverable receivables (2 marks)

29 X Co has an internal audit function. The external auditor has concluded that the internal audit function does not apply a systematic and disciplined approach to its work.

How does this affect the extent to which the external auditor can rely on the work of the internal audit function?

A The external auditor must not use the work of the internal audit function.

B The external auditor can use the work of the internal audit function provided the individuals have been assessed as competent.

C The external auditor can use the work of the internal audit function provided the organisational status of the function supports its objectivity.

D The external auditor can use work performed by the internal audit function which relates to low risk areas of the external audit only. (2 marks)

30 The auditor of G Co is performing audit procedures to confirm the company's ownership of motor vehicles.

Which of the following would provide the most persuasive evidence of this?

A Physical inspection of the motor vehicles

B Inspection of vehicle registration documents

C Checking that the motor vehicles are recorded in the non-current asset register

D Review of vehicle insurance documentation (2 marks)

31 The auditor of Q Co has performed purchases cut-off procedures and has identified that in two material instances goods received prior to the inventory count have not been included on the schedule of 'goods received not invoiced'. At the period end purchase invoices have not been received. What is the auditor's conclusion based on this evidence?

A Inventory is overstated and liabilities are understated.

B Inventory is understated and liabilities are understated.

C Inventory is overstated and liabilities are overstated.

D Inventory is understated and liabilities are overstated. (2 marks)

32 'Auditors have no obligations to perform procedures or make enquiries regarding the financial statements after they have been issued.'

Is this statement true or false?

A True

B False (1 mark)

33   M Co has a year end of 31 December 20X4. The auditor has identified that management's assessment of M Co's ability to continue as a going concern covers the period to 30 June 20X5.

What action should the auditor take?

A   Request that management extends the assessment period to 30 September 20X5

B   Request that management extends the assessment period to 31 December 20X5

C   Request that management extends the assessment period to 31 December 20X6

D   No action is required provided the auditor is satisfied with management's assessment to 30 June 20X5   **(2 marks)**

34   Is the following statement regarding written representations true or false?

Written representations by management regarding specific assertions in the financial statements provide sufficient appropriate audit evidence in their own right.

A   True

B   False   **(1 mark)**

35   Misstatements can arise from error or fraud.

Which of the following statements is correct regarding the auditor's accumulation of identified misstatements?

A   The auditor must accumulate all misstatements identified during the audit.

B   The auditor must only accumulate individually material misstatements identified during the audit.

C   The auditor must accumulate misstatements identified during the audit, other than those that are clearly trivial.   **(1 mark)**

36   ISA 700 *Forming an opinion and reporting on financial statements* sets out the basic elements of an auditor's report.

Which of the following is **not** included in an unmodified auditor's report?

A   Management's responsibility for the financial statements
B   Auditors' responsibilities
C   Audit opinion
D   Deficiencies of internal controls   **(2 marks)**

37   The statement of financial position of R Co includes a material amount of $200,000 in respect of costs capitalised in the year as development expenditure. The auditor has concluded that these costs are research expenditure.

If the auditor is to issue an unmodified opinion which financial statements will require adjustment?

A   Statement of financial position only
B   Statement of profit or loss only
C   Statement of financial position and statement of profit or loss
D   Neither the statement of financial position nor the statement of profit or loss   **(2 marks)**

38   Due to disruptions caused by the recent transition to a new accounting system, one month of H Co's inventory records have been lost. The auditors performing the statutory audit for the twelve-month period have determined that the possible effects of undetected misstatements could be material, but not pervasive.

What form of audit opinion would the auditor give?

A   Unmodified opinion with an emphasis of matter paragraph
B   Qualified opinion
C   Adverse opinion
D   Disclaimer of opinion   (2 marks)

39   C Co has a substantial bank loan which is due to mature in 20X7, and the company plans to negotiate for a new loan in March 20X7. The auditors concluded that the company's use of the going concern assumption in the financial statements for the year ended 31 December 20X6 is appropriate. However, they believe there is a material uncertainty related to going concern, which has been appropriately disclosed in the financial statements.

What action should the auditor take with regards to going concern in the auditor's report?

A   Express an unmodified opinion and describe the material uncertainty in the other matter paragraph

B   Express an unmodified opinion and describe the material uncertainty in the material uncertainty related to going concern paragraph

C   Express a modified opinion and describe the material uncertainty in the emphasis of matter paragraph

D   Express a qualified opinion and describe the material uncertainty in the basis for qualified opinion paragraph   (2 marks)

40   Is the following statement regarding key audit matters true or false?

Where the auditor disclaims an opinion on the financial statements, the auditor's report must not include a key audit matters section.

A   True
B   False   (1 mark)

41   Which of the following is likely to be carried out as part of an engagement quality control review for a listed entity?

(1)   Review of audit working paper files to ensure that the audit has been performed in accordance with professional standards and regulatory and legal requirements

(2)   Review of selected audit documentation relating to significant audit judgements

(3)   Review of the engagement team's evaluation of the firm's independence towards the audit

(4)   Consideration of whether appropriate consultations have taken place on differences of opinion/contentious matters

A   (1) and (3)
B   (2) and (4)
C   (1), (2) and (4)
D   (2), (3) and (4)   (2 marks)

Section B

Written questions

1 Objectives, characteristics and responsibilities

Your client, Mr Neville, has written to you saying he has been considering setting up an internal audit department but has heard from his brother that he would be better off abandoning this idea and getting the external auditor to do some assurance work instead. His brother also claimed that if the external auditor does some work for the company, there would be no need to have an external audit.

Required

Write a letter to Mr Neville explaining the objectives, characteristics and responsibilities of internal audit, external audit and assurance.

2 Audit and assurance engagements   20 mins

(a)   Explain the difference between negative and positive assurance in the context of the external audit and review engagements. State some of the limitations of the external audit.   **(4 marks)**

(b)   The audit opinion sets out explicit opinions which must be stated in the audit report. State what these are and outline the possible implied opinions, which are only reported on by exception.

(3 marks)

(c)   Auditors have certain rights to allow them to carry out their duties. State and explain what these rights are, using the UK as an example.   **(3 marks)**

(Total = 10 marks)

3 Standards

Discuss the advantages and disadvantages of auditing standards to auditors and the consequences of them being enforceable by statute.

4 Corporate governance

The objective of a system of corporate governance is to secure the effective, sound and efficient operation of companies. This objective transcends any legislation or voluntary code. Good corporate governance embraces not only making the company prosper but also doing business in a legal and ethical manner. A key element of corporate governance is the audit committee. The audit committee is a committee of the board of directors and is of a voluntary nature regulated by voluntary codes.

Required

(a)   Explain how an audit committee could improve the effectiveness of the external auditor's work.

(b)   Discuss the problems of ensuring the 'independence' of the members of the audit committee.

(c)   Discuss the view that the role of the audit committee should not be left to voluntary codes of practice but should be regulated by statute.

5 Independence

It has been suggested that the most important matter affecting the credibility of the auditor is that of 'independence'.

Required

(a)   Discuss, giving examples, matters other than independence, which might be relevant in relation to the credibility of the auditor and steps that the accounting profession has taken or might take in relation to them.

(b)   Discuss the following situations in the context of the independence of the auditor, showing clearly the principles involved.

   (i)   The audit manager in charge of the audit assignment of Andrew Co holds 1,000 $1 ordinary shares in the company (total shares in issue – 100,000). The audit partner holds no shares.

   (ii)   The recurring audit fee receivable from Janet Co, a private company, is $100,000. The total fee income of the audit firm is $700,000.

   (iii) The audit senior in charge of the audit of Margot Bank Co has a personal loan from the bank of $2,000 on which she is currently paying 12% interest.

   (iv)   The audit partner is responsible for two audit assignments, Harry Co and Jean Co. Harry Co has recently tendered for a contract with Jean Co for the supply of material quantities of goods over a number of years. Jean Co has asked the audit partner to advise on the matter.

6 Confidentiality and independence   39 mins

(a)   Explain the situations where an auditor may disclose confidential information about a client.

(8 marks)

(b)   You are an audit manager in McKay & Co, a firm of Chartered Certified Accountants. You are preparing the engagement letter for the audit of Ancients, a public limited liability company, for the year ending 30 June 20X6.

Ancients has grown rapidly over the past few years, and is now one of your firm's most important clients. Ancients has been an audit client for eight years and McKay & Co has provided audit, taxation and management consultancy advice during this time. The client has been satisfied with the services provided, although the taxation fee for the period to 31 December 20X5 remains unpaid.

Audit personnel available for this year's audit are most of the staff from last year, including Mr Grace, an audit partner, and Mr Jones, an audit senior. Mr Grace has been the audit partner since Ancients became an audit client. You are aware that Allyson Grace, the daughter of Mr Grace, has recently been appointed the financial director at Ancients.

To celebrate her new appointment, Allyson has suggested taking all the audit staff out to an expensive restaurant prior to the start of the audit work for this year.

Required

Identify and explain the risks to independence arising in carrying out your audit of Ancients for the year ending 30 June 20X6, and suggest ways of mitigating each of the risks you identify.

(12 marks)

(Total = 20 marks)

7 ZX

39 mins

You are a recently qualified Chartered Certified Accountant in charge of the internal audit department of ZX, a rapidly expanding company. Revenue has increased by about 20% p.a. for the last five years, to the current level of $50 million. Net profits are also high, with an acceptable return being provided for the four shareholders.

The internal audit department was established last year to assist the board of directors in their control of the company and to prepare for a possible listing on the stock exchange. The Managing Director is keen to follow the principles of good corporate governance with respect to internal audit. However, he is also aware that the other board members do not have complete knowledge of corporate governance or detailed knowledge of International Auditing Standards.

Required

Write a memo to the board of ZX that:

(a) Explains how the internal audit department can assist the board of directors in fulfilling their obligations under the principles of good corporate governance. **(10 marks)**

(b) Explains the advantages and disadvantages to ZX of an audit committee. **(10 marks)**
(Total = 20 marks)

8 Glo

39 mins

Glo-Warm Co, a limited liability company, manufactures various heating products which it sells to both high street and catalogue retailers.

The statement of financial position for the years ended 20X7 and 20X6 are set out below. Last year, materiality for the financial statements as a whole was set at $10,000.

	20X7		20X6	
	$'000	$'000	$'000	$'000
Non-current assets				
Tangible non-current assets		20		21
Investments		2		2
Current assets				
Inventory	52		179	
Receivables	78		136	
Cash at bank	12		34	
Cash in hand	1		1	
	143		350	
Total assets		165		373
Current liabilities				
Trade payables	121		133	
Bank loan	5		5	
	126		138	
Long-term liabilities				
Bank loan		20		25
Provision*		20		–
Capital and reserves				
Share capital		2		2
Reserves		(3)		208
Total liabilities		165		373

* The provision of $20,000 consists entirely of a warranty provision.

Required

(a) Discuss whether the materiality level for the financial statements as a whole used in 20X6 will be appropriate for this year's audit, giving reasons for your answer. **(3 marks)**

(b) Explain audit risk. **(3 marks)**

(c) Review the statement of financial position given above and state the areas in which audit work should be concentrated, giving reasons in each case. **(14 marks)**

(Total = 20 marks)

9 Stone Holidays   39 mins

Fraud and error present risks to an entity. Both internal and external auditors are required to deal with risks to the entity. However, the responsibilities of internal and external auditors in relation to the risk of fraud and error differ.

Required

(a) Explain how the internal audit function helps an entity deal with the risk of fraud and error.

(5 marks)

(b) Explain the responsibilities of external auditors in respect of the risk of fraud and error in an audit of financial statements. **(9 marks)**

(c) Stone Holidays is an independent travel agency. It does not operate holidays itself. It takes commission on holidays sold to customers through its chain of high street shops. Staff are partly paid on a commission basis. Well-established tour operators run the holidays that Stone Holidays sells. The networked reservations system through which holidays are booked and the computerised accounting system are both well-established systems used by many independent travel agencies.

Payments by customers, including deposits, are accepted in cash and by debit and credit card. Stone Holidays is legally required to pay an amount of money (based on its total sales for the year) into a central fund maintained to compensate customers if the agency should cease operations.

Describe the nature of the risks to which Stone Holidays is subject arising from fraud and error.

(6 marks)

(Total = 20 marks)

10 Parker

39 mins

(a) Explain the term 'audit risk' and describe the components of audit risk. **(4 marks)**

(b) You are the audit manager for Parker, a limited liability company which sells books, CDs, DVDs and similar items via two divisions: mail order and online ordering on the internet. Parker is a new audit client. You are commencing the planning of the audit for the year ended 31 May 20X7. An initial meeting with the directors has provided the information below.

The company's revenue is in excess of $85 million with net profits of $4 million. All profits are currently earned in the mail order division, although the Internet division is expected to return a small net profit next year. Revenue is growing at the rate of 20% p.a. Net profit has remained almost the same for the last four years.

In the next year, the directors plan to expand the range of goods sold through the Internet division to include toys, garden furniture and fashion clothes. The directors believe that when one product has been sold on the internet, then any other product can be as well.

The accounting system to record sales by the mail order division is relatively old. It relies on extensive manual input to transfer orders received in the post onto Parker's computer systems. Recently errors have been known to occur, in the input of orders and in the invoicing of goods following despatch. The directors maintain that the accounting system produces materially correct figures and they cannot waste time in identifying relatively minor errors. The company accountant, who is not qualified and was appointed because he is a personal friend of the directors, agrees with this view.

The directors estimate that their expansion plans will require a bank loan of approximately $30 million, partly to finance the enhanced website but also to provide working capital to increase inventory levels. A meeting with the bank has been scheduled for three months after the year end. The directors expect an auditor's report with an unmodified audit opinion to be signed prior to this time.

Required

(i) Identify and describe the matters that give rise to audit risks associated with Parker.

(10 marks)

(ii) Explain the enquiries you will make, and the audit procedures you will perform to assist you in making a decision regarding the going concern status of Parker in reaching your audit opinion on the financial statements. **(6 marks)**

(Total = 20 marks)

11 Heels

59 mins

ISA 315 (Revised) *Identifying and assessing the risks of material misstatement through understanding the entity and its environment* says that the auditor shall identify and assess the risks of material misstatement at the financial statement level and at the assertion level for classes of transactions, account balances and disclosures. As part of the risk assessment, the auditor shall determine whether any of the risks are 'significant risks'.

Required

(a)   (i)   Explain the steps the auditor must take when identifying and assessing the risks of material misstatement.   **(4 marks)**

(ii)   Define a 'significant risk' and list six factors which could indicate that a risk might be significant.   **(4 marks)**

Heels Co, a limited liability company, has traditionally specialised in the manufacture and wholesaling of ladies' shoes to retailers. The shoes are manufactured for ladies' fashion retailers, who generally also sell luxury ladies' clothes and accessories. You have been assigned as audit senior for the year ended 31 December 20X1 and have established the following at a recent planning visit.

In January 20X1, the company expanded into retailing and opened a shop selling shoes to the general public. The store was an instant success and the company rushed through the purchase of three additional stores before the end of May 20X1. These opened in June 20X1 and have also been well received. Customers can pay by cash, debit card or credit card in all stores.

In order to accommodate the retailing activities, Heels recently upgraded its computerised accounting system. The new system uses a central computer at the company's head office which is linked to computers at its warehouses and retail outlets. The software includes a bespoke inventory control system.

The new retail operations are expected to account for 15% of revenue for the year to 31 December 20X1 despite only being open for part of the year. However, as a result of the expansion, the company took out a significant loan secured against two of the stores and funded the remainder of the expansion out of working capital and by extending its overdraft facility.

Due to the increased volume of business and additional interest payments, the company is now trading at its overdraft limit. The board are seeking to increase the overdraft facility further.

Required

(b)   Describe SIX audit risks arising at the planning stage of the Heels Co audit.   **(6 marks)**

(c)   For the risks identified above, describe possible audit work that could be performed in response to those risks.   **(6 marks)**

On a later visit to Heels, you discover that the retail stores have been offering a three-month return period on all shoes. Customers are entitled to a refund or can exchange the shoes. Management at Heels have said they will estimate the figure for the returns relating to 20X1 sales expected between 1 January 20X2 and 31 March 20X2 (inclusive). They will then make a provision for it in the financial statements for the year ended 31 December 20X1. The provision is likely to be material.

There is expected to be considerable time pressure on the audit this year because the board want to get it 'out of the way' by the middle of February 20X2 so they can focus on operational issues.

Required

(d)   Define an 'auditor's point estimate' and explain how the auditors of Heels could formulate and use a point estimate to gain evidence over the provision for shoe returns.   **(5 marks)**

(e)   Describe FIVE other possible audit procedures you could carry out in respect of the provision.   **(5 marks)**

(Total = 30 marks)

12 Turbo   59 mins

(a) ISA 320 *Materiality in planning and performing an audit* deals with the auditor's responsibility to apply the concept of materiality in planning and performing an audit of financial statements. Materiality has both qualitative and quantitative aspects.

Required

(i) Explain what is meant by 'performance materiality' and contrast it with materiality for the financial statements as a whole. Give two examples of qualitative factors which may cause misstatements of quantitatively small amounts to be material. **(6 marks)**

(ii) State what the auditor must document in relation to materiality. **(2 marks)**

(b) You are the audit senior for Purnell & Co and Turbo Co is a longstanding audit client of your firm. You have started the planning for the audit of Turbo Co for the year ended 31 May 20X1. You have obtained the following information from the previous year's file and from preliminary discussions with management.

Background and revenue sources

Turbo is a magazine publisher. It publishes a number of titles, all of which are weekly or monthly car and motorcycle magazines. The magazines are sold to supermarkets and newsagents who then sell them to the general public. Turbo generates its income in two ways; from the sale of the magazines themselves and from selling advertising space in the magazines to companies who want to promote their cars or motorcycles. The revenue split has typically been around 50% in total for each sale type.

The key advertisers are large household names in the car and motorcycle industry. Turbo has to negotiate contracts with these advertisers for the provision of advertising space. These contracts can vary in length and can range from between one month and six months. The contract will set out all details of the arrangement, including the price of the adverts, the number or size of the adverts and how often the advertisements will appear.

An invoice is raised on the date of the first advertisement and the advertisers pay within ten days of this for shorter contracts. For six-month contracts the advertising fees are paid for by Turbo's customers in two instalments (half of the fee on the first date of advertising and the rest after three months). If recurring contracts have not been re-signed by the date advertising is meant to start Turbo raises an invoice based on the last contract and the paperwork is sorted out later. A few of the larger contracts run up to 31 May 20X1.

In respect of the magazine sales Turbo offers the supermarkets and newsagents up to 45 days' credit but many of the newsagents are struggling financially and tend to take longer than this to pay their invoices.

Trading conditions

In the last ten years the market for the magazines has become more and more competitive, resulting in Turbo needing to discount magazine prices. There is also increasing pressure from online competition and Turbo's revenue has been gradually decreasing over the last few years. This year has been a particularly bad year because difficult economic conditions have resulted in reductions in advertising revenue, as many of the car and motorcycle manufacturers that advertise in the magazines have seen their marketing budgets slashed and have renegotiated their contract terms.

Other relevant information

Turbo does not employ journalists or photographers for its magazines. Instead, it uses the best self-employed journalists, commentators and photographers in the industry. However, due to their numerous commitments these freelancers often get behind on their paperwork and don't get around to sending in their invoices to Turbo until a month or more after they have written their article or provided the photos requested.

Turbo prints its own magazines and as a result has a significant amount of plant and equipment. Turbo has been around for a number of years now and the equipment had become quite old and inefficient compared to that used by newly formed competitors. As a result, in December 20X0 extensive refurbishment of the printing equipment took place and this expenditure will be material to the financial statements. The heavy investment in refurbishment and declining revenues has seen Turbo operate close to its overdraft limit during the last six months. Although there is likely to be a small profit for the year, the management accounts for last six months show an operating loss.

The company would like to apply for a bank loan to ease cash flow concerns and has discussed this with its bank. However, the initial response from the bank was not overwhelmingly positive due to the competitive market Turbo operates in. As a result, Turbo needs to produce a cash flow forecast for the bank showing where the cash will be generated to pay back any loan. The bank also wants to see audited financial statements for the year to 31 May 20X1 before the end of June 20X1.

The forecasts currently being put together will include Turbo's plan to make popular titles available to the public online in exchange for a subscription fee. Online advertising fees will also be included in the forecast. However, the website will need to be quite complex and the investment in it will be significant.

Required

Using the information provided, describe **nine** audit risks and explain the auditor's response to each risk in planning the audit of Turbo Co. **(18 marks)**

(c)   Turbo's bank has said it would like a report from the external auditors to confirm the accuracy of the forecast. Following this request, Turbo has asked if you will examine the cash flow forecast when it has been prepared and then provide a report for the bank.

Required

Explain the type of assurance you could give in the context of the request by the bank and contrast this with the level of assurance given in the statutory audit of the financial statements.   **(4 marks)**

(Total = 30 marks)

Approaching the answer to part (b)

Question requirements which ask students to identify audit risks and suggest suitable responses to those risks are common in the F8 exam. Therefore we will take a look at how you should approach part (b) of the question above. The requirement is part of a 30-mark question so if you were in the exam you would want to use some time to familiarise yourself with the lengthy scenario.

(1)   Read the requirement carefully!

First of all you should read the requirement carefully. Note that you are being asked to describe the **audit** risks and then come up with responses. A good way to structure your answer therefore may be to set up two columns with headings of 'Audit risk' and 'Response to Risk'.

(2)   Identify your audit risks

Then, bearing this requirement in mind, you should actively read the scenario picking out the audit risks as you go. You might want to underline key points and make notes on the question paper as you go and we look at this technique in more detail in our approach to question 28 later in this question bank.

(3) **Describe your audit risks and make sure they are audit risks!**

You may choose to plan your answer. Alternatively, you could enter the risks straight into your 'Audit risk' column of your answer as you progress though the scenario but be careful that bits of the scenario may need linking together to form a risk. It is very important to remember that for a risk to be an audit risk rather than just a general business risk it needs to have an impact on the financial statements being audited.

You should therefore include the relevant assertion or area of the financial statements affected. If you do this you can be sure you have come up with a valid audit risk. For example, you may have identified it is a problem that journalists and photographers send in their invoices late – but you need to follow this through to the impact on the financial statements. Your audit risk is that liabilities and expenses in the financial statements are incomplete (understated) because purchase invoices are received late and not recorded until after the year end.

(4) **Use your risks to formulate responses**

When you have listed your risks you can then set about coming up with a relevant response for each.

Make sure your responses to risks in a question like this are responses of the auditor, not of management. This is where the approach you took before in relating your risks to financial statement areas will help you come up with responses more quickly. You now know there is a risk of incomplete or unrecorded liabilities in respect of the freelance invoices, so your response will be an audit procedure that tests for understatement of liabilities, such as reviewing payments after the year end and ensuring they were recorded as liabilities at the year end where the invoices related to work pre year end.

(5) **Keep to time**

You were asked for nine risks and there are 18 marks available so you can work out that you also need nine valid responses to get to the full 18 marks. Don't provide more than needed and stick to your time allowance for each requirement and the question as a whole. 18 marks for part (b) means 35 minutes – get into the habit now of not overrunning on your allotted question time.

13 Audit planning and documentation   20 mins

(a)   Explain the difference between the overall audit strategy and the audit plan and state the key contents of the overall audit strategy document.   **(4 marks)**

(b)   Briefly explain the reasons for auditors documenting their work.   **(3 marks)**

(c)   Many audit firms use standardised working papers. List the advantages and disadvantages of audit firms using standardised working papers to document their audit work.   **(3 marks)**

(Total = 10 marks)

14 Audit evidence considerations   20 mins

(a)   Discuss how analytical procedures can be used as substantive audit procedures to provide audit evidence. Illustrate your answer with an example.   **(5 marks)**

(b)   ISA 500 *Audit evidence* requires auditors to obtain sufficient appropriate audit evidence to be able to draw reasonable conclusions on which to base their audit opinion. Discuss the different sources of evidence available to auditors and assess their relative appropriateness.   **(5 marks)**

(Total = 10 marks)

15 Internal control systems

20 mins

An understanding of internal control assists the auditor in identifying potential misstatements and factors that affect the risks of material misstatement, and in designing the nature, timing and extent of further audit procedures.

(a)   Explain the limitations of internal control systems.   **(4 marks)**

One method of recording an audit client's accounting and internal control system is using narrative notes.

(b)   (i)   Describe two advantages and two disadvantages of using narrative notes to document accounting and control systems.   **(4 marks)**

        (ii)   Briefly describe two alternative methods of documenting accounting and control systems.
                                                                                            (2 marks)

                                                                            (Total = 10 marks)

16 Fenton Distributors

51 mins

Fenton Distributors Co is a small company which maintains its sales, purchase and nominal ledgers on a small PC, using a standard computerised accounting package. The company buys products from large manufacturers and sells them to shops which either sell or hire them to the general public. The products include drain clearing machines, portable generators, garden cultivators and wallpaper strippers.

You have been asked to carry out an audit of the nominal ledger system to verify that items are accurately recorded in the year. At the end of the year, the nominal ledger produces a trial balance, which is used to prepare the annual accounts.

The company employs a bookkeeper, who is responsible for posting the sales and purchase ledgers, and maintaining the nominal ledger. Data is posted to the nominal ledger as follows.

(1)   At the start of the financial year, all the balances on the nominal ledger accounts are set to zero (using the standard year-end procedure of the computer package).

(2)   The following procedures relate to purchase transactions.

        (i)   When invoices are posted to the purchase ledger, the purchase analysis code (for the nominal ledger), the purchases value and the sales tax value are entered. The total invoice value is posted to the purchase ledger.

        (ii)   At the end of the month, the computer posts the following items to the nominal ledger.

                 –   The total of each category of invoice expense and sales tax for purchase invoices and credit notes posted in the month (at the same time the computer prints details of the individual invoices making up the total of each invoice expense and sales tax for the month).

                 –   The total of purchase ledger cash payments, discount received and adjustments posted to the purchase ledger in the month (the computer prints details of the individual items comprising the total cash discount and adjustments for the month).

                 –   Where there is no account in the nominal ledger relating to the items being posted, the computer posts the items to a payables suspense account. Also, all adjustments are posted to the suspense account.

(3)   Sales ledger data is posted to the nominal ledger in a similar way to purchase ledger data.

(4)   Journals are posted manually to the nominal ledger for:

        (i)   The opening balances at the start of the year

        (ii)   Other cash book items (other than sales and purchase ledger cash)

        (iii)   Petty cash payments

        (iv)   Wages analysis (details are obtained from the computerised payroll system)

(v) Adjustments, which include:

- Correction of errors
- Dealing with items in the sale and purchase ledger suspense accounts (adjustments posted to the ledger, and items where there is no account in the nominal ledger)

All these journals are written manually in an accounts journal book, and they must be authorised by the managing director before posting. The opening balances are posted to the nominal ledger when the previous year's accounts have been approved by the auditors. Although the employee wages are calculated using another computer package, the total wages expense is posted to the nominal ledger manually. The wages expense is calculated from the payroll's monthly summary, using a spreadsheet package, and the wages expense is analysed into directors, sales, warehouse and office wages (or salaries).

Required

(a) List three control objectives of a sales system and three control objectives of a purchases system.

(6 marks)

(b) List and describe the audit work you would perform on the computerised nominal ledger system, and in particular:

(i) The audit procedures you would perform to verify the accuracy of purchases transactions which are posted to the nominal ledger. **(5 marks)**

(ii) The audit procedures you would perform to verify the validity and accuracy of journals posted to the nominal ledger. Also, you should briefly describe any other tests you would perform to verify the accuracy of the year-end balances on the nominal ledger. **(15 marks)**

(**Note**. You should assume that sales transactions are accurately recorded and correctly posted to the nominal ledger.)

(Total = 26 marks)

17 Cheque payments and petty cash

Mr A Black has recently acquired the controlling interest in Quicksand Co, which is an importer of sportswear. In his review of the organisational structure of the company Mr Black became aware of weaknesses in the procedures for the signing of cheques and the operation of the petty cash system. Mr Black engages you as the company's auditor and requests that you review the controls over cheque payments and petty cash. He does not wish to be a cheque signatory himself because he feels that such a procedure is an inefficient use of his time. In addition to Mr Black, who is the managing director, the company employs 20 personnel including four other directors, and approximately 300 cheques are drawn each month. The petty cash account normally has a working balance of about $300, and $600 is expended from the fund each month. Mr Black has again indicated that he is unwilling to participate in any internal control procedures which would ensure the efficient operation of the petty cash fund.

Required

(a) Prepare a letter to Mr Black containing your recommendations for good internal control procedures for:

(i) Cheque payments
(ii) Petty cash

(b) Discuss the audit implications, if any, of the unwillingness of Mr Black to participate in the cheque signing procedures and petty cash function.

18 Using the work of others

20 mins

(a) ISA 402 *Audit considerations relating to an entity using a service organisation* provides guidance to auditors whose clients use service organisations.

Required

In the context of an audit, explain what a service organisation is and explain what the auditor's responsibilities are in relation to gaining an understanding of a service organisation used by an audit client. **(4 marks)**

(b) ISA 620 *Using the work of an auditor's expert* provides guidance to auditors on relying on work carried out by an auditor's expert.

Required

(i) List four examples of audit evidence that might be obtained from the use of an auditor's expert. **(2 marks)**

(ii) Describe the factors that should be considered by the auditor when evaluating the work carried out by the expert. **(2 marks)**

(iii) Explain the actions the auditor should take if they conclude that the results of the expert's work do not provide sufficient appropriate audit evidence or if the results are inconsistent with other audit evidence. **(2 marks)**

(Total = 10 marks)

19 Elsams

39 mins

You are the auditor of Elsams Co which operates a chain of retail shops throughout the country selling a wide range of electrical goods. Each branch has computerised cash registers linked into the central computerised sales, receivables and inventory records. At the point of sale, the information keyed in includes the following: branch reference, product number, inventory location, unit selling price and date of sale.

The file of inventory records is updated daily for sales and receipts. It contains both cost (on a FIFO basis) and selling price information. The only regular printed output is sales summaries analysed by value, product and branch.

Required

(a) Explain the ways in which you, as the auditor of Elsams Co, could use computer programs to assist in the verification of inventory at the year end, and explain their limitations. **(8 marks)**

(b) Without particular reference to Elsams Co, describe the objectives and principles of using test data and comment on the areas where it can be of most use in an audit, and on the difficulties of this technique. **(5 marks)**

(c) Describe the following different methods of sample selection:

(i) Random selection
(ii) Systematic selection
(iii) Haphazard selection
(iv) Block selection **(7 marks)**

(Total = 20 marks)

20 ZPM

ISA 610 (Revised) *Using the work of internal auditors* provides guidance to the external auditor when the external auditor expects to use the work of the internal audit function in order to modify the nature or timing, or reduce the extent, of audit procedures to be performed directly by the external auditor.

Required

(a)   Explain the factors the external auditor will consider when:

    (i)   Determining whether the work of the internal audit function can be used for the audit

    (ii)   Determining the nature and extent of work of the internal audit function that can be used

(5 marks)

(b)   ZPM is a listed limited liability company with a year end of 30 June. ZPM's main activity is selling home improvement or 'Do-It-Yourself' (DIY) products to the public. Products sold range from nails, paint and tools to doors and showers; some stores also sell garden tools and furniture. Products are purchased from approximately 200 different suppliers. ZPM has 103 stores in eight different countries.

ZPM has a well-staffed internal audit department, which reports on a regular basis to the audit committee. Areas where the internal and external auditors may carry out work include:

    (i)   Attending the year-end inventory count in 30 stores annually. All stores are visited rotationally.

    (ii)   Checking the internal controls over the procurement systems (eg ensuring a liability is only recorded when the inventory has been received).

Required

For each of the above two areas, discuss:

    (i)   The objectives of the internal auditor   **(4 marks)**

    (ii)   The objectives of the external auditor   **(4 marks)**

    (iii)   Whether the external auditor will rely on the internal auditor and, if reliance is required, the extent of that reliance   **(4 marks)**

(c)   Although an internal audit function may undertake a number of assignments and provide useful information for the organisation, it does have limitations.

Required

Explain THREE limitations of the internal audit function.   **(3 marks)**

(Total = 20 marks)

21 Boston Manufacturing

39 mins

You are the audit assistant assigned to the audit of Boston Manufacturing. The audit senior has asked you to plan the audit of non-current assets. He has provisionally assessed materiality at $72,000.

Boston Manufacturing maintains a register of non-current assets. The management accountant reconciles a sample of entries to physical assets and *vice versa* on a three-monthly basis. Authorisation is required for all capital purchases. Items valued at less than $10,000 can be authorised by the production manager; items costing more than $10,000 must be authorised by the Managing Director. The purchasing department will not place an order for capital goods unless it has been duly signed.

The company has invested in a large amount of new plant this year in connection with an eight-year project for a government department.

The management accountant has provided you with the following schedule of non-current assets.

	Land and buildings $	Plant and equipment $	Computers $	Motor vehicles $	Total $
Cost					
At 31 March 20X6	500,000*	75,034	30,207	54,723	659,964
Additions		250,729	1,154		251,883
At 31 March 20X7	500,000	325,763	31,361	54,723	911,847
Accumulated depreciation					
At 31 March 20X6	128,000	45,354	21,893	25,937	221,184
Charge for the year	8,000	28,340	2,367	13,081	51,788
At 31 March 20X7	136,000	73,694	24,260	39,018	272,972
Carrying amount					
At 31 March 20X7	364,000	252,069	7,101	15,705	638,875
At 31 March 20X6	372,000	29,680	8,314	28,786	438,780

*Of which $100,000 relates to land.

Required

(a) Without undertaking any calculations, assess the risk of the tangible non-current assets audit, drawing reasoned conclusions. **(6 marks)**

(b) State the audit procedures you would undertake on non-current assets in respect of the following assertions:

    (i)   Existence   **(3 marks)**
    (ii)   Valuation (excluding depreciation)   **(4 marks)**
    (iii) Completeness   **(3 marks)**

(c) Describe how you would assess the appropriateness of the depreciation rates. **(4 marks)**

(Total = 20 marks)

22 Wandsworth Wholesalers

39 mins

Your firm is the auditor of Wandsworth Wholesalers Co, and you have been asked to carry out audit checks on cut-off and verifying inventory quantities at the year end.

The company maintains details of inventory quantities on its computer. These inventory quantities are updated from goods received notes and sales invoices. The company carries out inventory counts each month, when all the fast-moving and high value inventory is counted, and a third of the remaining inventory is counted in rotation so that all items are counted at least four times a year.

You attend the inventory count on Sunday 13 October, and a further inventory count was carried out on Sunday 10 November. The company's year end was Thursday 31 October 20X1, and the inventory quantities at that date, as shown by the computer, have been used in the valuation of the inventory. No inventory was counted at the year end.

Required

List and describe:

(a) The principal matters you should have checked and the matters you should have recorded when you attended the company's inventory count on Sunday 13 October. **(8 marks)**

(b) The tests you will perform in ensuring that sales and purchases cut-off has been correctly carried out:
(i) At the date of inventory count on 13 October 20X1
(ii) At the year end. **(4 marks)**

(c) The work you will carry out to test whether the book inventory records have been correctly updated from the counts at the inventory count. **(4 marks)**

(d) The work you will carry out to satisfy yourself that the inventory quantities used in the valuation of the inventory at the year end are correct. **(4 marks)**

(Total = 20 marks)

(**Note**. You should assume that the price per unit of inventory is correct.)

23 Snu

59 mins

Some organisations conduct inventory counts once a year and external auditors attend those counts. Other organisations have perpetual systems (continuous inventory counting) and do not conduct a year-end count.

Snu is a family-owned company which retails beds, mattresses and other bedroom furniture items. The company's year end is 31 December 20X3. The only full inventory count takes place at the year end. The company maintains up-to-date computerised inventory records.

Where the company delivers goods to customers, a deposit is taken from the customer and customers are invoiced for the balance after the delivery. Some goods that are in inventory at the year end have already been paid for in full – customers who collect goods themselves pay by cash or credit card.

Staff at the company's warehouse and shop will conduct the year-end count. The shop and warehouse are open seven days a week except for two important public holidays during the year, one of which is 1 January. The company is very busy in the week prior to the inventory count but the shops will close at 15.00 hours on 31 December and staff will work until 17.00 hours to prepare the inventory for counting. The company has a high turnover of staff. The following inventory counting instructions have been provided to staff at Snu.

(i) The inventory count will take place on 1 January 20X4 commencing at 09.00 hours. No movement of inventory will take place on that day.

(ii) The count will be supervised by Mr Sneg, the inventory controller. All staff will be provided with pre-printed, pre-numbered inventory counting sheets that are produced by the computerised system. Mr Sneg will ensure that all sheets are issued, and that all are collected at the end of the count.

(iii) Counters will work on their own, because there are insufficient staff for them to work in pairs, but they will be supervised by Mr Sneg and Mrs Zapad, an experienced shop manager who will make checks on the work performed by counters. Staff will count inventory with which they are most familiar in order to ensure that the count is completed as quickly and efficiently as possible.

(iv) Any inventory that is known to be old, slow-moving or already sold will be highlighted on the sheets. Staff are required to highlight any inventory that appears to be soiled or damaged.

(v) All inventory items counted will have a piece of paper attached to them that will show that they have been counted.

(vi) All inventory that has been delivered to customers but that has not yet been paid for in full will be added back to the inventory quantities by Mr Sneg.

Required

(a) Explain why year-end inventory counting is important to the auditors of organisations that do not have perpetual inventory systems. **(5 marks)**

(b) Describe audit procedures you would perform in order to rely on a perpetual inventory system in a large, dispersed organisation. **(6 marks)**

(c) Briefly describe the principal risks associated with the financial statements' assertions relating to inventory. **(4 marks)**

(d) Describe the deficiencies in Snu's inventory counting instructions and explain why these deficiencies are difficult to overcome. **(15 marks)**

(Total = 30 marks)

24 Sitting Pretty   39 mins

Sitting Pretty Co is a small, family-run company that makes plastic chairs in a variety of shapes and colours for children and 'fun at heart' adults. It buys in sheets of plastic which can be cut and bent into the correct shape and a plastic leg that is custom made by another company to Sitting Pretty's requirements. All off-cut plastic is sent back to the supplier who melts it down and reuses it, for which Sitting Pretty receives a 10% discount off its purchase price.

For the inventory count, the factory manager ensures that no work in progress is outstanding and closes down production for the day. The factory workers come in early on the day of the inventory count to count the inventory, and they are entitled to go home as soon as inventory is counted. Good controls have always been maintained over the inventory count in previous years. There are no perpetual inventory records. Raw materials are all kept in the stores and are only taken out when they are required for production. Finished goods are kept at the end of the factory, near the delivery exit.

You are the audit assistant assigned to attend the inventory count. You have just rung the factory manager and he has mentioned that on the day of the inventory count a large consignment of plastic is going to be delivered. It is the only day that his supplier can make the delivery, and he needs the material to continue with production on the day after the count.

The audit engagement partner has told you that he is aware that Sitting Pretty changed the specification of their customised leg recently, after a series of complaints over the stability of their chairs. Last year's inventory was valued at $200,000 in the statement of financial position, of which $30,000 related to raw material inventory.

Finished goods are all carried at the same valuation as each other, as there is very little difference between the inventory ranges. Planning materiality for this year has been set at $5,000 on the grounds, at this stage, that the figures are expected to be similar to last year.

Required

(a) Explain the importance of the inventory count in this situation. **(3 marks)**

(b) Prepare notes for your audit supervisor detailing the procedures you propose to undertake in relation to your inventory count attendance. **(7 marks)**

(c) State the procedures which should be taken in relation to cut-off at the final audit. **(5 marks)**

(d) Describe the audit procedures you would carry out on the valuation of inventory at the final audit. **(5 marks)**

(Total = 20 marks)

25 Bright Sparks   39 mins

Bright Sparks, a limited liability company, distributes domestic electrical equipment from one warehouse. Customers are mainly installers of such equipment, but there is a 'cash and carry' counter in the warehouse for retail customers. The warehousemen are responsible for raising invoices and credit notes relating to credit sales, as well as handling cash sales.

You have carried out your interim audit in respect of the year ending 31 December 20X0 which included a circularisation of 80 trade accounts receivable as at 30 September 20X0 selected from a total credit customer list of 1,000. Replies were received from all customers circularised. The interim audit work disclosed the following.

(a) Of the 80 customers' accounts circularised, 8 disagreed but could be reconciled by bringing into account payments stated by the customers concerned to have been made before 30 September 20X0 but which in each case were recorded in Bright Sparks's books between 14 and 18 days after the dates stated by the customers as the date of payment.

(b) Your tests suggested that some 25% of credit customers were allowed settlement discounts of 2.5% although payments were consistently received after the latest date eligible for discount.

(c) A large number of credit notes were raised representing approximately 12% of the total number of invoices raised. A review of the copy credit notes indicated that they usually arose from arithmetical and pricing errors on invoices raised.

Required

Explain the conclusions you would draw as a result of the interim audit and, based on those conclusions, describe the work you would plan to carry out at the final audit on trade receivables at 31 December 20X0.

(20 marks)

26 Audit of cash and bank

(a) State the characteristics of a bank confirmation letter.
(b) List six examples of items requested in the bank confirmation letter.
(c) Explain the purpose and importance of the bank reconciliation.

27 Understatement

59 mins

Research into the distribution of errors in accounts has shown that for most items on the statement of financial position the errors are normally distributed. However, with payables the distribution is skewed, and there is a greater risk that payables will be understated than overstated. Understatement of payables will lead to overstatement of profit, so auditors must design their tests to ensure that payables are not understated.

You have been asked by the manager in charge of the audit of Heanor Wholesale Co to verify trade payables and accruals at the company's year end of 30 April 20X2. The company maintains its purchase ledger on a microcomputer, using a standard purchase ledger accounting package. Purchase invoices are posted to the purchase ledger after they have been checked to the delivery note and the purchase order and have been authorised by either the financial director or the managing director.

The purchase ledger can show for each purchase ledger account:

(a)   The unpaid invoices and credit notes
(b)   An ageing of the balance into current month, one month, two months and three or more months
(c)   The total balance on the account

Also, the system is able to provide the total of the balances of all the accounts on the purchase ledger.

Your audit of the purchases system has revealed that the system for recording receipt of goods is relatively weak. The company does not use goods received notes, but the supplier's delivery note should be dated by the goods received department when the goods are received. Your audit tests have revealed that some delivery notes are not dated by the goods received department. The delivery note is filed with the purchase invoice in alphabetical order (by supplier).

A full inventory count was carried out at the company's year end and you are satisfied that it was counted accurately.

In the company's draft financial statements the value of trade payables and accruals at 30 April 20X2 are as follows.

	$
Trade payables	509,200
Purchase accruals	27,050
	536,250
Sundry payables and accruals	59,480
Current liabilities	595,730

Heanor's annual revenue figure is about $3.5 million and its profit before tax is $190,000. The age of payables at 30 April 20X2 is 3.4 months, which is similar to the previous year. Sundry payables and accruals comprise mainly wages accruals (including income tax and other deductions) and a sales tax liability of $20,000.

Required

(a)   Consider and discuss the reasons why:

    (i)   It is more likely that payables will be understated than overstated.

    (ii)   It is difficult for auditors to ensure that payables are not understated.   **(6 marks)**

(b)   Describe the audit work you will perform to verify trade payables and purchase accruals. Your answer should include consideration of:

    (i)   Tests using suppliers' statements

    (ii)   Why most auditors do not carry out a payables circularisation, and the circumstances when a payables circularisation should be carried out

    (iii)   Audit tests which are designed to detect understatement of payables   **(14 marks)**

(c)   Describe the audit procedures you will perform to verify sundry payables and accruals, including the sales tax liability.   **(10 marks)**

                                         (Total = 30 marks)

28 'Tap!'

You are an audit assistant in the firm Rogers and Smith. You have been asked to plan the audit of 'Tap!' for the year ended 30 June 20X4. It is the first time your audit firm has audited the charity, which has not been audited previously. The trustees have expressed interest in receiving a 'value added' audit and are particularly interested in business advice, especially in the area of systems controls.

'Tap!' is a registered charity that raises money for projects building wells in Africa through musical entertainment. The group consists of volunteers who travel around the country, putting on variety shows of music and dance, the proceeds of which are put towards building the wells. The main show is a tap dance production, acting out the difficulties many people face when they are not near a clean water supply.

The administrative offices of 'Tap!' are located in a large provincial town. It owns a house, donated by legacy in the past, where the administration is carried out and where the volunteers stay during off periods.

A large proportion of 'Tap!'s income comes from box office receipts which are taken by the theatre at which they are performing. The theatres usually waive their standard terms for use of the premises and merely take a 10% commission on ticket receipts to cover light and heat and other such expenses. Income usually comes in after every booking in the form of a lump sum cheque from the theatre, together with a breakdown of takings and commission.

'Tap!' also receives donations towards the work. These come from a variety of sources:

- Cash donations from buckets passed around at the interval of each performance
- Cash donations on the (rare) occasion that the team does street performances
- Cash donations made over the phone or by post by interested donors

The troupe consists largely of volunteers so they are only paid expenses for their work. The cost of housing the group while they are on the road is borne by the charity. The charity employs an administrator who organises bookings, handles publicity and co-ordinates all the finances.

Required

(a) Discuss the risks arising for the audit of the year ending 30 June 20X4. **(8 marks)**

(b) State the audit procedures you would undertake in respect of cash income in the financial statements. **(6 marks)**

(c) List some controls over cash which the charity should implement. **(6 marks)**

(Total = 20 marks)

Approaching the answer

You should read through the requirement before working through and annotating the question as we have so that you are aware of what things you are looking for.

You are an audit assistant in the firm Rogers and Smith. You have been asked to plan the audit of 'Tap!' for the year ended 30 June 20X4. It is the first time your audit firm has

> **First time audit for firm so little cumulated knowledge and experience.**

> **Impact on opening balances and comparatives.**

audited the charity, which has not been audited previously. The trustees have expressed interest in receiving a 'value added' audit and are particularly interested in business advice, especially in the area of systems controls.

> **High degree of regulation. Do we have any experience in this field?**

> **Not just a simple audit. This may make the engagement too risky – given the potential bad publicity that could result if there were problems with the audit.**

'Tap!' is a registered charity that raises money for projects building wells in Africa through

> **Where is the audit evidence? Also, is expenditure in line with the Trust Deed?**

musical entertainment. The group consists of volunteers who travel around the country, putting on variety shows of music and dance, the proceeds of which are put towards building the wells. The main show is a tap dance production, acting out the difficulties many people face when they are not near a clean water supply.

The administrative offices of 'Tap!' are located in a large provincial town. It

> **Is this common? Are there restrictions on expenditure? Also, ensure accounts are correct for disclosures.**

owns a house, donated by legacy in the past, where the administration is carried out and where the volunteers stay during off periods.

> **Trust?**

A large proportion of 'Tap!'s income comes from box office receipts which are taken by the theatre at which they are performing. The theatres usually waive their standard terms for use of the premises and merely take a 10% commission on ticket receipts to cover light and heat and other such expenses. Income usually comes in after every booking in the form of a lump sum cheque from the theatre, together with a breakdown of takings and commission.

> **Cash income – risky.**

> **How is this accounted for?**

> **Trust for completeness?**

'Tap!' also receives donations towards the work. These come from a variety of sources:

> **Again, cash. Also, poor in future years for analytical evidence. Lack of good evidence available.**

> **Again, cash. Also, what are the controls here? Completeness may be a problem.**

- Cash donations from buckets passed around at the interval of each performance

- Cash donations on the (rare) occasion that the team does street performances

- Cash donations made over the phone or by post by interested donors

The troupe consists largely of volunteers so they are only paid expenses for

No salaries.

their work. The cost of housing the group while they are on the road is borne by the charity. The charity employs an administrator who organises

Expenditure issues again.

Not a specialist? But drafting complex accounts.

bookings, handles publicity and co-ordinates all the finances.

Required

You should have been noticing and annotating risks as you have worked through the scenario. Try and categorise them in your mind (inherent, control, detection).

(a)   Discuss the risks arising for the audit of the year ending 30 June 20X4.

(8 marks)

Note that you are looking specifically for **audit** risks.

You must tailor your answer to the scenario.

(b)   State the audit procedures you would undertake in respect of cash income in the financial statements.

(6 marks)

Only cash income!!

(c)   List some controls over cash which the charity should implement.

(6 marks)

Think of control objectives and then design reasonable controls that meet the objective. There are more control problems in the scenario than you need to identify/solve for the marks.

Answer plan

(a)   Audit risks

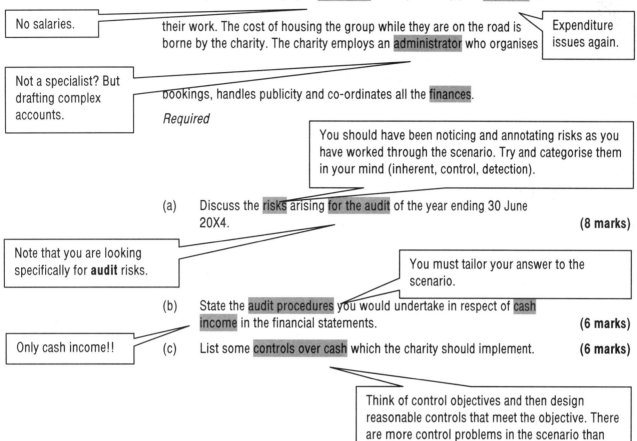

(b)   Audit procedures

- Income from box office
- Income from buckets
- Income from other donations

(c)   Controls

- Schedule of seats
- Two people to collect
- Pre-numbered forms

Security of cash during collection and between banking?

Other income

Use pre-numbered forms

Periodic reviews of work by trustees

29 Namul

29 mins

Namul Co is a retailer of mid- to low-range children's clothing. It operates in many countries around the world and has expanded steadily from its base in Asia. Its main market is aimed at 4 to 14 year olds. The company's year end was 31 March 20X0.

In the past, the company has bulk ordered its stock of children's clothing twice a year. However, if their goods failed to meet the key fashion trends then this resulted in significant inventory write-downs. As a result of this, the company has recently introduced a Just-in-Time ordering system. The fashion buyers make an assessment nine months in advance as to what the key trends are likely to be; these goods are sourced from their suppliers but only limited numbers are initially ordered.

Ordering process

Each country has a purchasing manager who decides on the initial inventory levels for each store. This is not done in conjunction with store or sales managers. These quantities are communicated to the central buying department at the head office in Asia. An ordering clerk amalgamates all country orders by specified regions of countries, such as South East Asia, Central Europe and North America, and passes them to the purchasing director to review and authorise.

As the goods are sold, it is the store manager's responsibility to reorder the goods through the purchasing manager; they are prompted weekly to review inventory levels as, although the goods are just in time, it can still take up to four weeks for goods to be received in store.

It is not possible to order goods from other branches of stores, as all ordering must be undertaken through the purchasing manager. If a customer requests an item of clothing which is unavailable in a particular store, then the customer is provided with other branch telephone numbers or recommended to try the company website.

Goods received and invoicing

To speed up the ordering to receipt of goods cycle, the goods are delivered directly from the suppliers to the individual stores. On receipt of goods the quantities received are checked by a sales assistant against the supplier's delivery note, and then the assistant produces a goods received note (GRN). This is done at quiet times of the day so as to maximise sales. The checked GRNs are sent to head office for matching with purchase invoices.

As purchase invoices are received they are manually matched to GRNs from the stores. This can be a very time-consuming process, as some suppliers may have delivered to over 500 stores. Once the invoice has been agreed then it is sent to the purchasing director for authorisation. It is at this stage that the invoice is entered onto the purchase ledger.

Required

As the external auditors of Namul Co:

(i)   Identify and explain FIVE deficiencies in the company's purchasing system.

(ii)   Explain the possible implication of each deficiency.

(iii)   Provide a recommendation to address each deficiency.

(15 marks

30 Ajio

39 mins

Ajio is a charity whose constitution requires that it raises funds for educational projects. These projects seek to educate children and support teachers in certain countries. Charities in the country from which Ajio operates have recently become subject to new audit and accounting regulations. Charity income consists of cash collections at fundraising events, telephone appeals and bequests (money left to the charity by deceased persons). The charity is small and the trustees do not consider the charity able to afford to employ a qualified accountant. The charity employs a part-time bookkeeper and relies on volunteers for fundraising. Your firm has been appointed as accountants and auditors to this charity because of the new regulations. Accounts have been prepared (but not audited) in the past by a volunteer who is a recently retired Chartered Certified Accountant.

Required

(a) Describe the risks associated with the audit of Ajio under the headings inherent risk, control risk and detection risk and explain the implications of these risks for overall audit risk. **(10 marks)**

(b) Identify and explain the audit tests to be performed on income and expenditure from fundraising events. **(10 marks)**

Note. In part (a) you may deal with inherent risk and control risk together. You are not required to deal with the detail of accounting for charities in either part of the question.

(Total = 20 marks)

31 Going concern

39 mins

Carrington Joinery, a private company, owned by its directors, manufactures wooden window frames, doors and staircases for domestic houses. It has prepared draft accounts for the year ended 30 September 20X6 and you are concerned that they indicate serious going concern problems. The statements of profit or loss and statements of financial position for the last five years (each ended 30 September) are given below.

STATEMENT OF PROFIT OR LOSS

	20X2	20X3	20X4	20X5	20X6
	$'000	$'000	$'000	$'000	$'000
Sales	625	787	1,121	1,661	1,881
Cost of sales	(478)	(701)	(962)	(1,326)	(1,510)
Gross profit	147	86	159	335	371
Other expenses	(88)	(86)	(161)	(240)	(288)
Interest	(6)	(9)	(58)	(90)	(117)
Net profit/(loss)	53	(9)	(60)	5	(34)

STATEMENT OF FINANCIAL POSITION

	20X2 $'000	20X3 $'000	20X4 $'000	20X5 $'000	20X6 $'000
Assets					
Current assets					
Inventory	67	133	181	307	449
Trade accounts receivable	91	240	303	313	364
	158	373	484	620	813
Net current assets	89	161	544	600	587
Total assets	247	534	1,028	1,220	1,400
Liabilities and shareholders' funds					
Current liabilities					
Trade accounts payable	90	317	355	490	641
Bank overdraft	10	65	211	269	365
Lease creditor	14	28	98	92	59
	114	410	664	851	1,065
Non-current loan	–	–	300	300	300
	114	410	964	1,151	1,365
Shareholders' funds					
Share capital	17	17	17	17	17
Reserves	116	107	47	52	18
	133	124	64	69	35
Total liabilities and shareholders' funds	247	534	1,028	1,220	1,400

The company has been in business for about fifteen years. In January 20X3 it decided to build a new factory on a site leased from the local authority which would allow a major increase in sales. This new factory with new equipment was completed a year later. The factory was financed by a non-current loan of $300,000 from a merchant bank and an increase in the bank overdraft.

The loan from the merchant bank is secured by a fixed charge on the leasehold factory and the bank overdraft is secured by a second charge on the leasehold factory, a fixed charge on the other non-current assets and a floating charge on the current assets.

The company purchases its main raw material, wood, from timber wholesalers. It sells around 75% of its production to about 12 local and national builders of new domestic houses. The remaining sales are mainly to smaller builders with very few sales to local builders merchants.

Required

(a)   In relation to the financial statements above, list and briefly describe the factors which indicate that the company may not be a going concern. You should also highlight certain figures and calculate relevant ratios in the accounts.   **(13 marks)**

(**Note**. You will only be given credit for going concern problems which can be determined from the accounts above.)

(b)   Describe the investigations and tests you would carry out, in addition to those described in part (a) above, to determine whether the company is a going concern.   **(7 marks)**

(Total = 20 marks)

32 Audit review and finalisation

20 mins

(a) ISA 560 *Subsequent events* provides guidance on the responsibilities of auditors regarding subsequent events. Briefly explain the responsibilities of auditors for facts discovered up to the date of the auditor's report, facts discovered after the date of the auditor's report but before the accounts are issued and for facts discovered after the financial statements have been issued.

(4 marks)

(b) ISA 580 *Written representations* explains the purpose and use of written representations as audit evidence. State six items that could be included in a written representation. **(3 marks)**

(c) Briefly discuss the use of analytical procedures at the review stage of the audit. **(3 marks)**

(Total = 10 marks)

33 Wiseguys National Bakeries

Your firm acts as auditor of Wiseguys National Bakeries Co. The finance director has prepared financial statements of the company for the year to 31 December 20X9 which show a pre-tax profit of $450,000. You have been advised that the board of directors has approved the financial statements and decided that no amendments should be made thereto.

As partner responsible for the audit you have noted the following matters during your review of the financial statements and the audit working papers:

(i) The freehold property which was included at cost in previous years' statement of financial position has now been restated at a professional valuation of $1,250,000 carried out during the year. You are satisfied with the valuation and that the relevant figures have been correctly adjusted and the necessary information disclosed in the notes to the financial statements.

(ii) An amount of $45,000 due from a customer in respect of sales during the year is included in receivables but, from information made available to you, you conclude that no part of this debt will be recovered. No allowance has been made against this amount.

(iii) The financial statements do not disclose the existence of a loan of $36,000 made by the company to a director, which remains outstanding from 1 February 20X9.

Required

Explain how each of the above will impact on the auditor's report.

34 Homes'r'Us

Homes'r'Us is a large listed construction company based in the north of the country, whose activities encompass house building and development. Its annual revenue is $550 million and profit before tax is $70 million.

You are the audit senior involved with the audit of Homes'r'Us for the year ended 31 December 20X7. The following matters have come to your attention during the review stage of the audit in April 20X8.

(i)   Customer going into liquidation

One of Homes'r'Us's major commercial customers has gone into liquidation shortly after the year end. As at the year end, the customer owed the company $7.5 million.   **(7 marks)**

(ii) Claim for unfair dismissal

One of the company's construction workers, Basil Evans, was dismissed in November 20X7 after turning up to work under the influence of alcohol. In December 20X7, Mr Evans began a case against the company for unfair dismissal. Lawyers for the company have advised that it will be highly unlikely that he will be successful in his claim.   **(7 marks)**

(iii) In March 20X8 a fire was started by vandals at one of the company's ten storage depots, destroying $1 million worth of building materials.   **(6 marks)**

Required

For each of the three events at Homes'r'Us mentioned above:

(a)   Describe the additional audit procedures you will carry out.
(b)   State whether the financial statements will need to be amended and explain your reasoning.
(c)   Discuss the potential impact on the auditor's report, fully explaining your answers.

Note. The mark allocation is shown against each of the three events.   **(Total = 20 marks)**

35 Builders Merchants

39 mins

You are the auditor of Builders Merchants, a listed company which distributes materials to the construction industry from eight depots in the south of the country, and you are currently finalising the audit for the year ended 31 March 20X1. Your audit procedures have proved satisfactory with the exception of the following four matters.

(i)   The physical inventory count sheets for one of the depots were lost before they were made available to you, and you have not been able to confirm the inventory quantities and values for this depot by alternative methods. The directors have valued this part of the inventory at $75,000 and this figure is included in the overall inventory valuation of $640,000.

(ii)   Included in trade receivables, which total $580,000, is a debt amounting to $45,000 from a customer which went into liquidation on 15 June 20X1. You have ascertained from the liquidator that your client is unlikely to receive a distribution. The statement of comprehensive income for the year shows a pre-tax profit of $100,000 but the directors are not prepared to provide for this debt.

(iii)   The financial statements of Builders Merchants do not contain a statement of cash flows.

(iv)   A substantial claim has been lodged against the company by a major customer. The matter is fully explained in the notes to the financial statements, but no provision has been made for legal costs or compensation payable, as it is not possible to determine with reasonable accuracy the amounts, if any, which may become payable. The directors have received legal advice which appears to be reliable in indicating that the claim can be successfully defended.

Required

Explain the individual and cumulative impact of the above issues on the auditor's report.   **(20 marks)**

Section A
Multiple choice answers

1   C   Statutory audits give reasonable assurance. It is not possible to give absolute assurance, given the inherent limitations of audit. Limited assurance is given in review engagements, where the audit opinion is expressed in a negative form.

2   A   Directors are stewards of the shareholders' investment.

3   B   The ISAs are issued by the International Auditing and Assurance Standards Board (IAASB), a technical standing committee of the IFAC. The International Accounting Education Standards Board (IAESB), also part of the IFAC, publishes the International Education Standards aiming to increase the competence of the global accountancy profession. The International Accounting Standards Board (IASB) issues the International Financial Reporting Standards. The Financial Reporting Council (FRC) issues ISAs (UK & Ireland), not the international standards.

4   B   All of the ISAs must be complied with in an audit of historical financial information. A 'comply or explain' approach is not possible here. The ISAs also apply to smaller entities, although specific guidance is given on how certain requirements may be met in this case.

5   C   Best practice indicates that the internal audit function should have a dual reporting relationship, reporting both to management and the audit committee. If the internal audit function does not report to the audit committee, management may be able to unduly influence the internal audit plan and scope, thus compromising the effectiveness of internal audit. The external auditors, not the internal auditors, report to the shareholders.

6   A   Risk management is a key feature of effective corporate governance.

7   D   The ACCA Code does not allow the following to have a direct or indirect material financial interest in a client: the audit firm, a member of the audit team and an immediate family member of a member of the audit team.

8   D   Bookkeeping services can be provided in an emergency. Assistance can be given in tax disputes provided the firm is not acting as an advocate of the client and the effect of the matter is material to the financial statements. Internal audit services can be provided except where this would result in the audit firm's personnel assuming management responsibility.

9   B   Economy, efficiency and effectiveness are sometimes referred to as the '3E's' of VFM audits.

10   C   The risk of material misstatement at the assertion level is made up of inherent risk and control risk. Detection risk is the risk that the auditor's procedures will not detect a misstatement that exists in an assertion that could be material. Audit risk is the risk that the auditor gives an inappropriate audit opinion when the financial statements are materially misstated. Audit risk is made up of inherent risk, control risk and detection risk ($AR = IR \times CR \times DR$)

11   B   The audit engagement partner is not required to review all audit documentation. However, ISA 220 requires reviews to be performed to ensure that any significant issues are addressed on a timely basis and sufficient and appropriate audit evidence is obtained to support the audit opinion.

12   A   Performance materiality may be set for particular classes of transactions, account balances or disclosures. Directors' remuneration is an account where law and regulation affect users' expectations regarding disclosure. A lower level of performance materiality therefore should be applied. Exploration and development costs are material due to the industry in which the company operates, and therefore merits a lower performance materiality level.

ISA 320 requires performance materiality to be set to reduce to an appropriately low level the probability that the aggregate of uncorrected and undetected misstatements exceeds materiality for the financial statements as a whole. All uncorrected misstatements should be cumulated and communicated to management, unless they are clearly trivial.

13	A	The applicable financial reporting framework would be expected to be covered in an overall audit strategy document. The nature, timing and extent of audit procedures at the assertion level should be included in the more detailed audit plan, as should the timetable for audit work.
14	A	The statement is true. Existence asserts that asset, liabilities and equity interests exist.
15	C	The auditor cannot affect control risk or inherent risk. The auditor can reduce audit risk by manipulating detection risk. Increasing sample sizes and assigning more experienced staff to the audit will both reduce detection risk and therefore audit risk.
16	D	The matters mentioned in option D relate specifically to business operations. The matters mentioned in the other options relate specifically to financial reporting A, investments B and financing C.
17	B	ACCA recommends a minimum retention period of seven years.
18	B	ICEQs would be best suited to help auditors identify the key controls for controls testing. ICQs focus on whether the desirable controls are present, and so would not identify the areas at risk of specific errors or frauds. Narrative notes describe and explain the system, but their detailed nature makes it difficult to identify control exceptions at a glance. Flowcharts also describe the system but do not highlight exceptions.
19	D	Records of program changes and virus checks are general IT controls.
20	B	This means that customers are not able to exceed their credit limits and are therefore more likely to be able to pay. A helps to ensure that goods are sold at the right price. C & D are effective controls regarding the recovery of debts but do not prevent sales being made to customers who are unlikely to pay as the sale has already been made by this stage.
21	C	The matching of dispatch notes to an invoice ensures that for all goods dispatched an invoice has been raised. If this is not the case sales and trade receivables may be understated. For answer B an appropriate control would be to match dispatch notes to invoices. Matching dispatch notes and invoices would not prevent orders being dispatched incorrectly (A) or prevent invoices being input incorrectly (D).
22	C	This is in accordance with guidance given in ISA 265.
23	A	The control helps to ensure sales are valid as sales are only recognised for goods which have been dispatched.
24	A	The direction of the test is important here. The sample is taken from sales invoices, as this tests whether each sales order has been fulfilled (the assertion of occurrence). If the sample is taken from goods despatched notes, this would instead confirm whether the goods sold had been correctly invoiced (the assertion of completeness). C and D both test for completeness.
25	B	The risk here is the overstatement of sales revenue. Audit procedure 1 tests for cut-off, where potential errors may cause revenue to be overstated. Audit procedure 3 is a test of occurrence, also focusing on the overstatement of revenue. Audit procedure 2 tests for completeness, so therefore identifies the understatement of revenue instead. Audit procedure 4 relates to classification – this assertion has no impact on the overall revenue balance.
26	A	$(160/420) \times 365$
27	A	As set out in ISA 530 Audit sampling.

28	D	Computer-assisted audit techniques cannot replace the skill of judgement used by the auditor.
29	A	In accordance with ISA 610 *Using the work of internal auditors* the external auditor is prohibited from using the work of internal audit in this situation as the risks to the quality of the evidence provided are too great.
30	B	The vehicle registration document records the details of the legal registered owner of the vehicle.
31	B	As the goods have been received, the goods must be recognised as an asset and the liability for the goods must be recognised at the period end. As a purchase invoice has not been received and the invoice amount has not been accrued for, liabilities are understated. This implies that the corresponding asset (inventory) is also understated.
32	A	This statement is true. However, if the auditor does become aware of a fact that, had it been known at the date of the auditor's report, may have caused the auditor to amend the auditor's report, the auditor shall discuss the matter with management and determine whether the financial statements need amendment.
33	B	Where the period used by management to determine whether the entity is a going concern is less than 12 months from the period end, the auditor should request that management extends the assessment period to at least 12 months from the period end.
34	B	In accordance with ISA 580 *Written representations*, written representations support other evidence relevant to financial statements, ie they are not sufficient appropriate evidence on their own.
35	C	This is in accordance with ISA 450 *Evaluation of misstatements* identified during the audit.
36	D	The basic elements of the auditor's report are title, addressee, introductory paragraph, management's responsibility for financial statements, auditor's responsibility, opinion paragraph, other reporting responsibilities, auditor's signature, date of the report and auditor's address.
37	C	Both statements are materially misstated as the asset must be written off reducing the profit for the year. An unmodified opinion can only be issued if both statements are adjusted.
38	B	A qualified opinion is appropriate, because the matter is considered to be material, but not pervasive. An unmodified opinion with an emphasis of matter paragraph is not relevant: it serves to draw the attention of users to a matter appropriately presented or disclosed in the financial statements, which is fundamental to the users' understanding of the financial statements.
39	B	The matter should be described in a material uncertainty related to going concern paragraph, in accordance with ISA 570 (Revised) *Going concern*. The other matter paragraph is used to refer to a matter that is not presented or disclosed in the financial statements: the material uncertainty is disclosed in this case, so that would not be appropriate. The emphasis of matter paragraph does not modify the audit opinion. As the going concern assumption is appropriate and there is adequate disclosure, the audit opinion should not be modified.
40	A	ISA 701 states that the auditor must not include a key audit matters section in the auditor's report where a disclaimer of opinion is expressed.
41	D	The review of audit working paper files to ensure that the audit has been performed in accordance with professional standards and regulatory and legal requirements is carried out by the audit engagement partner.

Section B

1 Objectives, characteristics and responsibilities

Bird & Co
1 Old Street
New Town
M1 3WQ

1 January 20X1
Mr G Neville
1 Any Street
New Town
M2 5LM

Dear Mr Neville

In response to your queries I have produced some information on the difference between statutory audit, assurance work and internal audit. I have included this information in an appendix. However, it is important to note that the external audit is a legal requirement for many companies and cannot be avoided by employing the auditor to do other work.

If you require any further details please do not hesitate to contact me.

Yours sincerely

A N Accountant

Enclosure: Appendix

External audit	Assurance work	Internal audit
Characteristics and objectives		
The external audit is a legal requirement for limited liability companies above a certain size. Partnerships and sole traders do not normally need to have any audit, though some may opt to do so to give independent credibility to their financial statements.	Assurance work is voluntary for companies. Management can employ the external auditor to report on any specific areas. Directors may employ the external auditor when they feel a specific investigation or some specific work needs to be done, eg in support of an insurance claim or loan application.	Internal audit departments are not a legal requirement, though the *UK Corporate Governance Code* recommends them as best practice for listed companies in the UK and other countries are following this model.
In an external audit the auditor gives an independent opinion on whether the financial statements are presented fairly, in all material respects (or give a true and fair view), in accordance with the applicable financial reporting framework. Implied opinions may also be given on such issues as whether the financial statements agree with the underlying records and all information and explanations which are relevant to the audit have been received.	The scope of assurance work is determined by management.	Internal auditors are employees of the company. They report on the internal controls, identifying problems and suggesting improvements. They may also report on the effectiveness of efficiency of operations.

External audit	Assurance work	Internal audit
External audits are performed annually, and the auditor is paid based on hours worked. The audit fee is normally disclosed in a set of financial statements.	Assurance work is a one-off specific assignment; fees are normally agreed with management and based on hours worked.	Internal auditors are full-time employees, and as such there are ongoing costs involved with setting up an internal audit department.
The auditor's report is a formal report with standard wording, prepared for shareholders. An auditor's report with an unmodified audit opinion indicates that the auditor believes the financial statements are presented fairly, in all material respects (or give a true and fair view).	Reports are tailored to the scope of work, and addressed to management.	Reports are prepared for management. There is no guidance governing the wording of reports, though companies may have their own internal guidelines.
Responsibilities		
Work and procedures are governed by International Standards on Auditing, produced by the International Auditing and Assurance Standards Board of IFAC. Compliance with these standards is a good defence should the auditor end up in court.	The *International Framework for Assurance Engagements* provides guidance on the nature of assurance engagements. ISAE 3000 *Assurance engagements other than audits or reviews of historical financial information* provides standards for assurance engagements other than audits or reviews of historical financial information. Auditors are expected to comply with this standard for both reasonable and limited assurance engagements.	There are no ISAs to govern internal audit work.

2 Audit and assurance engagements

(a)   Assurance engagements are engagements in which a professional accountant expresses a conclusion which provides the intended user with a level of assurance about a particular subject matter. External audits and review engagements are examples of assurance engagements.

An external audit provides only reasonable assurance because of the inherent limitations of the audit, such as the fact that not all the transactions in the accounts can be tested and that judgement is required in the audit of provisions.

Review engagements only provide negative assurance. This means that nothing has come to the attention of the auditor which indicates that the accounts have not been prepared according to the applicable framework.

Limitations of the external audit:

- Not all items in the financial statements are tested.
- Judgement is required.
- There are limitations in the accounting and control systems.
- The audit report is often issued a while after the statement of financial position date.

(b) The explicit opinions stated in the audit report:

    (i) The state of the company's affairs at the end of the financial year in the statement of financial position

    (ii) The company's profit or loss for the financial year in the statement of profit or loss and other comprehensive income

Implied opinions are reported on in the audit report only by exception and could include the following:

    (i) Adequate accounting records have been kept.

    (ii) Returns adequate for the audit have been received from branches not visited.

    (iii) The accounts are in agreement with the accounting records and returns.

    (iv) All information and explanations have been received by the auditors and they have had access at all times to the company's books, accounts and records.

    (v) Details of directors' emoluments and other benefits have been correctly disclosed in the accounts.

    (vi) Particulars of loans and other transactions in favour of directors and others have been correctly disclosed in the accounts.

(c) Using the UK as an example, auditors have the following rights:

    (i) Access to records: Auditors have a right to access at all times, the books, accounts and vouchers of the company.

    (ii) Information and explanations: Auditors have a right to require from the company's officers any information and explanations that they consider necessary for the performance of their duties.

    (iii) Attendance at and notices of general meetings: Auditors have a right to attend any general meetings of the company and to receive all notices of and communications relating to such meetings which any member of the company is entitled to receive.

    (iv) Right to speak at general meetings: Auditors have a right to be heard at general meetings which they attend on any part of the business that concerns them as auditors.

    (v) Rights in relation to written resolutions: Auditors have a right to receive a copy of any written resolution proposed.

    (vi) Right to require laying of accounts: Auditors have a right to give notice in writing that a general meeting is held for the purpose of the laying of accounts and reports before the company.

3 Standards

The major advantages and disadvantages of auditing standards can be summarised as follows.

Advantages
They give a framework for all audits around which a particular audit can be developed.
They help to standardise the approach of all auditors to the common objective of producing an opinion.
They assist the court in interpretation of the concept of 'due professional care' and may assist auditors when defending their work.
They increase public awareness of what an audit comprises and the work behind the production of an audit report.
They provide support for auditors in potential disputes with clients regarding the audit work necessary.

Disadvantages
It may appear that they impinge on, rather than assist, professional judgement.
They are considered by some to stifle initiative and development of new auditing methods.
They may create additional and unnecessary work and thus raise fees, particularly in the audit of small companies.

If auditing standards were to be enforceable by statute it would mean that there would be government intervention in areas currently controlled solely by the profession itself. This might ultimately lead to a diminished role of self-regulation. To be enforceable by statute the standards would have to be applicable to all circumstances and thus need to be very general and broad in their instructions. This might reduce their usefulness to the auditors. Auditors might spend unnecessary time ensuring that they have complied with the law rather than considering the quality of service to their clients.

Finally, it should be considered whether full statutory backing for standards would force auditors into narrow views and approaches which might gradually impair the quality of accounting and auditing practices.

4 Corporate governance

(a) **Improving the effectiveness of audit**

- Increasing assurance from stronger corporate governance and internal controls

- Providing an opportunity to discuss the terms and scope of external audit in an impartial way

- Strengthening the ability of the external auditor to request changes in control systems

- Ensuring that there is minimal duplication of work where internal auditors are involved, by discussing the audit plan with the external auditors via the audit committee

- Ensuring that directors' statements on internal control are reviewed by the audit committee

- Reviewing going concern issues and ensuring that appropriate disclosures are made

- Acting as a forum for resolving problems between the directors and the external auditors

- Resolving difficulties over the availability of information and key client personnel

- Reviewing draft financial statements before presentation to the auditors and the executive board

(b) **Independence of audit committees**

- The members should be **independent** and declare any interests in the company.

- Non-executive directors often sit on several boards, so **conflicts of interest** can easily arise.

- Salaries are paid by the company so **financial independence** can be compromised.

- Members of the audit committee tend to have **other roles** at the client, eg personnel. They act in several capacities and **independence may be impaired**.

- Members may have had **previous involvement** in executive positions and could have share options or pension schemes, again **compromising independence**.

(c) **Statutory regulation**

Statutory regulation could impose additional costs and regulatory burdens, which might not justify the end in all cases and could sometimes be detrimental to shareholders.

However, an argument in favour of statutory regulation is that **voluntary codes of practice** may not be applied consistently by companies. Another is that the non-executive audit committee may not feel able to criticise management unless they have **statutory backing**.

Shareholders do not readily understand the role of the audit committee. If it was appointed by statute and governed this role might be better understood, but this is not necessarily the case. There is no evidence that shareholders understand legal regulations any better than voluntary ones in many cases. It is difficult to arrive at a **'model' audit committee** suitable for all entities, as would be required if statutory regulation were introduced. Companies are unique and have unique requirements.

A **statutory monitoring report** on the audit committee would be required. This would further increase costs for the company. It would be very difficult to set **standards for non-executive directors** on audit committees.

5 Independence

(a)   If auditors are to have credibility, then it is vital that they should be seen to be independent of any concern on which they are required to report. However, independence is but one of a number of qualities which the modern auditor must possess if they are to be accepted as suitable for their role.

Outside of independence, perhaps the two most important qualities required of an auditor are:

(i)   *Integrity*

Auditors must be seen as honest. Having formed their opinion, based on the audit evidence they have collected, they will not allow others to sway their judgement to suit their own ends. It is the auditor's integrity which will allow interested parties to place reliance on their reports.

IFAC (through the IESBA) and national supervisory bodies do a great deal to try to ensure that the integrity of the profession as a whole, as well as that of individual members, is maintained. This is done by laying down ethical guidelines which all members are required to follow (disciplinary proceedings are taken against any member known to have breached such guidelines). The accounting bodies also assist in this area by providing a broad framework for the training and examination of prospective new members, such as the ACCA's *Code of Ethics and Conduct*.

(ii)   *Professional competence*

Clearly the auditor must be in possession of certain technical skills. This fact is clearly recognised so far as statutory audits are concerned, as only suitable qualified accountants are recognised as being competent to hold office as auditor. Examples of some of the skills required of modern auditors are that they must be:

- Aware of and understand audit objectives

- Able to interpret systems

- Able to communicate well with others

- Conversant with required techniques such as sampling

- Able to cope with the impact of modern technology on accounting and internal control systems

The accounting profession is only too well aware of the need to maintain and improve standards of professional competence and for this reason has issued and recently revised a number of International Standards on Auditing. In addition, the accounting bodies are heavily involved in running courses to assist members in maintaining and improving their technical skills.

(b)   Independence on the part of the auditor as a reporting accountant is seen by many to be a fundamental concept of auditing. It has been said that it would never be sufficient for auditors to claim that they were independent. In fact, they must always be clearly seen to be independent in practice. Given this situation, it would be almost impossible to draw up a set of rules to cover every conceivable situation where an auditor's independence might be called into question.

While not able to provide an exhaustive list of recommendations, the main principles which should be applied when considering the question of independence may be found in the relevant section of the ACCA's *Code of Ethics and Conduct*. With this in mind, the following comments could be made in relation to the situations specified in the question.

(i) The audit partner has no shareholdings in the client company and so, all other things being equal, they could be seen as giving an objective audit opinion. However, the audit manager does have a shareholding in the client company which, while not material to the company (at 1% of issued share capital), could be material to the audit manager and certainly might be seen to influence their ability to give an impartial opinion in relation to the company's affairs. In fact, the ACCA Code does not permit a member of the audit team to have a direct financial interest in an audit client. As the partner will inevitably have to rely on the work completed and controlled by the audit manager, it is clearly undesirable for the manager to have such a financial involvement in the client's affairs. The audit manager should either be excluded from the audit team or requested to dispose of their shares.

(ii) The Code states that when a firm receives a high proportion of its fee income from just one audit client, a self-interest or intimidation threat. The reason for this is that the fear of losing a major client, and thus a substantial proportion of fee income, could prejudice the auditor's objectivity and make them more likely to bow to pressures from the client.

The Code does not set out specific guidelines in relation to percentages of total fees except for in relation to public interest clients, where the Code requires communication of the situation to those charged with governance and an independent review if total fees from a client are more than 15% of the firm's total fees for two consecutive years. Auditors of private companies could adopt the same approach as best practice.

The audit fee from Janet Co contributes some 14.3% of the total fees income of the practice, which is a significant proportion. It would be necessary to consider whether any other fee income was received from this client, as this could result in a proportion well in excess of 15%. Depending on the other fees the firm would need to assess the threats to independence taking into account the operating structure of the firm and the significance of the client to the firm both qualitatively and quantitatively. The firm should consider what safeguards are necessary; these may include reducing the dependency on the client, arranging independent quality control reviews or consulting a third party on key judgements. The firm would need to keep this situation under constant review.

(iii) As another instance of where financial involvement in a client's affairs could be seen to impair an auditor's objectivity, the code recommends that between an auditor and a client there should be no loans or guarantees in respect of loans either way. Any such financial involvement could be seen to impair the auditor's judgement either because of a client putting pressure on the auditor or because of the auditor's own fear of suffering some financial loss.

However, the code does allow for one exception in making the above recommendation and that is where the loan is in the normal course of business and on normal commercial terms. It is part of a bank's normal business to make personal loans, and, if the rate of interest being paid by the audit senior appears to be a commercial rate of interest, this transaction is unlikely to be seen as impairing the auditor's independence.

(iv) The Code also considers the problems that can be created when conflicts of interest arise between different clients and between clients and the auditor's own business interests. It concludes that every effort should be made to avoid conflicts of interest arising and that it would be unethical for accountants to act in a situation where they knew that a conflict of interest existed.

The situation described in the question is a good example of the type of conflict of interest with which the code is concerned. The audit partner should not advise Jean Co with regard to the contract tender received from Harry Co. The auditor should explain the professional reasons why he is unable to act on this occasion and suggest that Jean Co seek advice from another firm of accountants.

6 Confidentiality and independence

(a) **Situations where an auditor may disclose confidential information about a client**

Auditors have a professional duty of confidentiality and this is an implied term of the agreement made between the auditor and the client.

However, there may be a legal right or duty to disclose confidential information or it may be in the public interest to disclose details of clients' affairs to third parties.

Also, the client may have given the auditor consent to disclose confidential information. These are general principles only and there is more specific guidance, which is discussed below.

Obligatory disclosure

If the auditor knows or suspects that their client has committed money-laundering, treason, drug-trafficking or terrorist offences then they are obliged to disclose all the information they have to a competent authority.

Under ISA 250 *Consideration of laws and regulations in an audit of financial statements* auditors must also consider whether non-compliance with laws and regulations may affect the accounts. They might have to include in the audit report a statement that non-compliance with laws and regulations has led to significant uncertainties (in an emphasis of matter paragraph), or may consider modifying the audit opinion if there is a disagreement over the way specific items have been treated in the accounts.

Voluntary disclosure

Voluntary disclosure may be applicable in the following situations.

- Disclosure is reasonably necessary to protect the auditor's interests, for example to enable them to sue for fees or defend an action for, say, negligence.

- Disclosure is authorised by statute.

- It is in the public interest to disclose, say, where an offence has been committed which is contrary to the public interest.

- Disclosure is to non-governmental bodies which have statutory powers to compel disclosure.

If an auditor is requested to assist the police, the taxation or other authorities by providing information about a client's affairs in connection with enquiries being made, they should first enquire under what statutory authority the information is demanded.

Unless the auditor is satisfied that such statutory authority exists they should decline to give any information until they have obtained their client's authority. If the client's authority is not forthcoming and the demand for information is pressed, the auditor should not accede unless advised to do so by their legal adviser.

If an auditor knows or suspects that a client has committed a wrongful act they must give careful thought to their own position. The auditor must ensure that they have not prejudiced themselves by, for example, relying on information given by the client which subsequently proves to be incorrect or unreliable.

However, it would be a criminal offence for a member to act positively, without lawful authority or reasonable excuse, in such a manner as to impede with intent the arrest or prosecution of a client whom they know or believe to have committed an 'arrestable offence'.

(b) **Risks to independence**

Audit partner

Mr Grace has been the audit partner on the audit of Ancients for the last eight years. His independence and objectivity are likely to be impaired as a result of this close relationship with a

key client and its senior management. The *ACCA Code of Ethics and Conduct* requires key audit partners to be rotated after seven years and Mr Grace's involvement for eight years already contravenes this rule.

This threat could (and should) be addressed by appointing another audit partner to the audit of Ancients and rotating partners at suitable intervals thereafter.

Tax fees outstanding

There are taxation fees outstanding from Ancients for work that was done six months previously. In effect, McKay & Co are providing an interest-free loan to Ancients. This can threaten independence and objectivity of the audit firm, as it may not want to modify the audit opinion in case the outstanding fees are not paid.

This can be addressed by discussing the issue with the directors of Ancients and finding out why the fees have not been paid. If the fee is still not paid the firm should consider delaying the start of the audit work or even the possibility of resigning.

Fee dependence

Ancients is one of McKay & Co's most important clients and the firm provides other services to this client as well as audit, including taxation services. Also, the company is growing rapidly. Objectivity and independence are considered to be threatened to the degree that an independent engagement review is needed by an external firm or regulator (and disclosure to those charged with governance) if the fees for audit and recurring work exceed 15% of the firm's total fees for a listed client such as Ancients.

This threat could be mitigated by reviewing the total of the audit and recurring fee income from Ancients as a percentage of McKay & Co's total fee income on a regular basis and possibly limiting the provision of the other services if deemed necessary to maintain independence.

Relationship to Financial Director of Ancients plc

Allyson Grace, the daughter of Mr Grace, has recently been appointed the Financial Director of Ancients. The independence of Mr Grace could be threatened because of their close family relationship. The extent of the threat depends on the position the immediate family member holds with the client and the role of the professional on the assurance team.

As Financial Director, Allyson has direct influence over the financial statements and as engagement partner, Mr Grace has ultimate responsibility for the audit opinion, so there is a clear threat to objectivity and independence.

This threat to independence could (and should) be mitigated by the appointment of another audit partner to this client.

Meal

The fact that Allyson Grace wants to take the audit team out for an expensive meal before the audit commences could be considered a threat to independence, as it might influence the audit team's decisions once they start the audit of the financial statements. The ethics rules state that gifts or hospitality from the client should not be accepted unless the value is trivial and inconsequential.

This threat could be mitigated by declining the invitation.

7 ZX

From: Chief Internal Auditor
To: Board of ZX Co
Subject: Role of Internal Audit and Audit Committee
Date: Today

(a)   Areas where the internal audit department can assist the directors with the implementation of good corporate governance include:

(i) Internal controls

The directors are responsible for assessing the risks faced by the company, implementing appropriate controls and monitoring the effectiveness of those controls.

The internal audit department could assist the board in a number of ways:

- They could review the directors' risk assessment and report on its adequacy.
- In certain areas (perhaps in respect of the accounting system) they could actually carry out the risk assessment.
- They could review and report on the adequacy of the controls that are to be implemented.
- They could carry out annual audits of the effectiveness of controls (performing tests of the controls), identifying weaknesses and making recommendations for improvements.

It would be inappropriate for them to be involved at every stage, ie assessing risks, designing controls and reviewing their effectiveness, as this would mean that they are checking their own work. This would undermine the credibility of their reports.

In a sense, the existence of an internal audit serves as a control procedure in its own right. An example would be that the existence of an internal audit department is likely to act as a deterrent against fraud, and so helps the directors meet their responsibilities to implement appropriate controls to prevent and detect fraud.

(ii) Financial statements

Good corporate governance requires the directors to prepare financial statements that give a balanced and understandable view. As the internal audit department has experience in accounting and auditing and is led by a qualified Chartered Certified Accountant it can assist the directors in applying accounting standards and meeting the expectations of readers of the accounts (particularly as these expectations will greatly increase if ZX proceeds with the possible listing).

(iii) Board reports

A principle of good corporate governance is that the board should be properly briefed. The internal audit department can review the reports that are presented to the board to ensure that they are properly prepared and presented in a way that can be easily understood.

(iv) Communication with external auditors

Although it is mainly the audit committee (if one has been established) that will act as a channel of communication between the external auditors and the board, it will often be the case that the external and internal auditors will work together on some areas. This could be the case if the external auditor found it appropriate to rely on internal audit reports on some areas (for example, on periodic inventory counting procedures) or where the external auditor wants to extend computer-assisted testing over the whole year under the supervision of the internal auditors. This could add value to information available to the board where areas have been considered by both groups of auditors.

(v) **Knowledge of corporate governance and auditing standards**

As qualified professionals the internal audit department will have up to date knowledge of corporate governance requirements and of developments in auditing standards. They will be able to help the board keep up to date with what is expected of them under the codes of corporate governance and with what will be expected of them from the external auditors.

(b) **Advantages and disadvantages of an audit committee**

(i) *Advantages*

Proposed listing

If ZX is listed it will in all probability have to follow tighter requirements, such as the UK Corporate Governance Code. The establishment of an audit committee is considered good practice under this code. If ZX did not establish one it would have to disclose the non-compliance with the code in that respect and this might affect shareholder confidence in respect of the accounting and auditing functions within the company.

'Critical friend' of the board

An effective audit committee will be made up of individuals with relevant knowledge and experience, who are independent of the day-to-day running of the company. This will give the shareholders confidence that there is some independent oversight of the board which should help ensure that the company is being run in the best interests of the shareholders. They should also be able to advise the executive directors on areas such as corporate governance where their own knowledge may be incomplete.

Communication

The existence of an audit committee gives an effective channel of communication for the external auditors. It means there is a quasi-independent body with whom the external auditor can discuss contentious audit issues, such as disagreements over accounting treatments, rather than going directly to the board who have made the decisions on those matters.

This may increase stakeholders' confidence in the financial statements and the audit process.

Financial reporting

The non-executive directors are expected to have a good knowledge of financial reporting. In the case of ZX, this should prove a useful source of advice to the board. Also, externally, it should increase confidence in the financial reporting processes and reports of ZX.

Appointment of external auditors

The audit committee, rather than the board, would recommend which auditors should be appointed. They would also review annually any circumstances, such as provision of other services, which might threaten the perceived independence of the external auditor. This should again increase the confidence that readers of the financial statements have in the objectivity of the opinion given by the external auditors, and, therefore, the credibility of the financial statements.

(ii) *Disadvantages*

Cost

Although the non-executive directors will not require full-time salaries, the level of fees that will be required to attract suitably experienced individuals may be significant but must be weighed against the benefits which will be derived, especially in view of the planned listing.

Knowledge and experience

The board may question whether individuals from outside ZX will have adequate experience of the business to make a useful contribution to the board. As explained above, it is their very independence that adds value to their role as well as their particular experience in respect of financial accounting and corporate governance issues.

Responsibilities

The current board may be concerned that the establishment of an audit committee of non-executive directors may diminish their powers in running the company. It could be seen as another tier of management. They should be assured that the audit committee would act in support of the board, not as an alternative to it.

8 Glo

(a) **Materiality for the financial statements as a whole**

It is **never appropriate** to apply the prior year's materiality figure to the current year figures. Materiality should be assessed in each year.

If the financial position has not changed much and the results are comparable with the prior year, it is possible that the materiality assessed year on year is very similar, but this does not mean that the auditors should not assess it for each audit. When assessing materiality, the auditor must consider **all known factors at the current date**. In this case, the position has changed considerably, increasing the risk of the audit, which may lower materiality itself.

As the **position** on the statement of financial position has **changed considerably**, when materiality is assessed, it is unlikely that it will be similar to the prior year. Using the information available, **materiality is likely to be assessed extremely low** in monetary terms, due to the overall decrease in assets and the loss that appears to have been made in the year. It is also possible that, given the current position, the figures on the statement of financial position will not be used to assess materiality in this year.

(b) **Audit risk**

Audit risk is the risk that the auditor will give an inappropriate opinion on financial statements. It is made up of three different elements of risk:

- **Inherent risk**: the risks arising naturally in the business and specific accounts/transactions
- **Control risk**: the risk that the accounting system will fail to detect and prevent errors
- **Detection risk**: the risk that the auditors will not detect material misstatements

Detection risk comprises **sampling risk** (the risk that the auditors' conclusion drawn from a sample is different to what it would have been, had the whole population been tested) and **non-sampling risk** (the risk that auditors may use inappropriate procedures or misinterpret evidence).

Inherent and control risk are assessed by the auditors. Detection risk is then set at a level which makes overall audit risk acceptable to them.

(c) **Specific audit areas of risk**

A review of this statement of financial position suggests that audit work should be directed to the following areas:

Going concern

Total assets have fallen from $373,000 to $165,000. Although the statement of profit or loss has not been reviewed, the statement of financial position shows a **retained loss** for the year of $211,000.

Net assets show a **reduction in both inventory and receivables**, which **suggests a decrease in activity**, although trade payables do not seem to have fallen so considerably. However, this could be accounted for by Glo-Warm not paying its suppliers in a similar fashion to the previous year. It will be **necessary to review** the **statement of profit or loss** to substantiate whether activity has reduced.

The **cash position has also worsened**, with cash falling by $22,000. The statement of cash flows should reveal more detail about this fall. However, the company has paid off $5,000 of its bank loan, reducing overall net debt.

In summary, audit work should be directed at going concern, as **several indicators of going concern problems** exist on the statement of financial position. This will be further amplified when the statement of profit or loss is available.

Inventory

Inventory has been mentioned above in the context of going concern. Audit work should be directed at inventory specifically, as this **balance has fallen significantly** from the previous year, which seems **odd in a manufacturing company**. There is no suggestion on the statement of financial position for why this should be so (for example, receivables are not correspondingly high, suggesting high pre-year-end sales, and payables are not correspondingly low, suggesting low pre-year-end purchases). It may be that the inventory count did not include every item of inventory. Alternatively it could simply point to a fall in activity (discussed above).

Warranty provision

A provision of $20,000 has been included in 20X6 for warranties. The reasons for this must be investigated and the auditors must check that it has been accounted for correctly.

It seems **odd that a warranty provision should suddenly appear on a statement of financial position**. It suggests a change in the terms of contracts given to customers, or a change in the customers themselves (with different terms then applying). Alternatively it suggests that **IAS 37** has been **wrongly applied in the current year, or should have been applied in the previous year**, and was not.

Other material items

As stated above, given the indications of loss and the reduction in total asset value, it is likely that materiality will be assessed low in monetary terms. In this case, most balances on the statement of financial position are likely to be material (excluding investments and cash-in-hand which appear to be very low risk).

However, as the bank loan is likely to be substantiated by good audit evidence, the most risky of the other balances are **trade receivables** and **trade payables**, for reasons discussed above in going concern. More detail is required to make a judgement about the risk of tangible non-current assets.

9 Stone Holidays

(a) **Internal audit and the risk of fraud and error**

(i)   The management of an entity have the primary responsibility of preventing and detecting fraud and error. An internal audit function may assist them in this responsibility. This is encouraged under the UK Corporate Governance Code. The role of the internal audit function in respect of fraud and error will be decided by the entity's management but is likely to include some of the following:

- **Risk assessment** – The internal audit function may carry out risk assessments identifying the main risks of fraud and error or may review that process if it is carried out by management.

- **Control recommendations** – Internal audit reports may recommend controls to address the risks of fraud and error identified by management.

- **Control procedures** – The internal audit function may be involved in carrying out certain control functions, such as counting cash or inventories and comparing to book records. It may be management's objective to detect even low-value frauds and misappropriations.

- **Monitoring controls** – The internal audit function may perform procedures to monitor whether the control procedures implemented by management are operating effectively. This could involve inspecting documents for evidence of appropriate authorisation or using test data to check the operation of computerised controls.

(ii) It would not be appropriate for the internal audit function to be involved in all of these areas in a particular entity, as they would effectively be checking their own work thus undermining their credibility.

(iii) The existence of an internal audit function within an entity is likely to act as a deterrent against fraud and error.

(b) **External audit and the risk of fraud and error**

(i) The ultimate responsibility of external auditors is to give an opinion on the **truth and fairness** of the financial statements. This means that the auditors give **reasonable assurance** that the financial statements are free from **material misstatement**.

(ii) **Professional scepticism**. The auditor is responsible for maintaining professional scepticism throughout the audit, considering the possibility of management override of controls, and recognising that audit procedures effective for detecting errors may not be effective for detecting fraud.

(iii) **Discussion**. The members of the audit team must also discuss the possibility of the entity's financial statements containing material misstatements resulting from fraud or error.

(iv) **Risk assessment**. When obtaining an understanding of the entity, the external auditor will consider any indications of frauds that may lead to material misstatements. This would involve enquiries of management, internal audit (if applicable) and analytical procedures. Any risks of material misstatement due to fraud will be treated as significant risks.

(v) **Responses to assessed risk**. The auditor must determine **overall responses** to address the assessed risks of material misstatement due to fraud at the financial statement level. This will involve:

- **Assigning and supervising** staff responsible taking into account their knowledge, skill and ability
- Evaluating whether the **accounting policies** may be indicative of fraudulent financial reporting
- Incorporating **unpredictability** in the selection of the nature, timing and extent of audit procedures

(vi) **Specific audit procedures**. Irrespective of the auditor's assessment of the risks of management override, audit procedures must be performed which test the appropriateness of journals and other adjustments. Accounting estimates must be reviewed for bias and, where significant transactions appear to be outside the normal course of business, the auditor must consider if they are concealing a fraud or are themselves fraudulent entries.

(vii) **Written representations**. The external auditor must obtain written representations from management:

- Acknowledging their responsibility for the design, implementation and maintenance of internal control to prevent and detect fraud
- That they have disclosed to the auditor management's assessment of the risk of fraud in the financial statements

- That they have disclosed to the auditor their knowledge of fraud/suspected fraud involving management, employees with significant roles in internal control, and others where fraud could have a material effect on the financial statements
- They have disclosed to the auditor their knowledge of any allegations of fraud/suspected fraud

(viii) **Limitations**. It is not reasonable to expect external auditors to identify all instances of material misstatements where fraud is involved even when the audit is properly planned and performed in accordance with the ISAs. Where a fraud has been perpetrated, particularly if it is at management level, it is likely to be carefully concealed and collusion may be involved.

(ix) **Reporting**. Where the external auditor detects or suspects that a fraud has occurred, this should be reported to the appropriate level of management. In certain circumstances, for example in matters subject to legislation such as money laundering, the auditor may have to report to external bodies.

(c) **Risks arising from fraud and error**

(i) Staff are paid on a **commission basis**. This may result in deliberate overstatement of sales figures as individuals try to inflate their own income.

(ii) The use of the networked reservations system introduces the risk that information may be lost or corrupted in transmission.

(iii) Errors may occur in the computerised accounting system if the controls within that system are not operating effectively. It may also be the case that certain employees have discovered how to circumvent the controls and are able to amend records perhaps to hide misappropriations of assets.

(iv) Some payments are received in **cash**. This introduces the risk that cash may be misappropriated and the records falsified to conceal this.

(v) The amount that the entity is required to pay into the central compensation fund is based on the sales figure for the year. There may be management bias towards understating sales to reduce the amounts payable or delaying revenue recognition thus deferring the due date of the payment.

(vi) Customers may attempt to defraud Stone Holidays by using stolen credit or debit cards.

10 Parker

(a) The term 'audit risk' literally means the risk that the auditor will give an incorrect opinion. The concern for the auditor is that an unmodified opinion may be issued in circumstances where there are material misstatements in the financial statements.

It can be analysed into three separate components.

(i) **Inherent risk**

This arises from factors specific to the business or its operating environment and which make errors more likely to occur. It could result from complex transactions, such as leases, or from pressures on management to achieve particular targets.

(ii) **Control risk**

This is the risk that the audit client's internal control does not prevent errors occurring or detect them after the event so that they may be corrected. This could be due to failures in the control environment, such as management allowing a culture of carelessness towards control procedures to develop or to failures of specific control procedures; for example, a lack of proper reconciliation of payables ledger balances to supplier statements could allow misstatements in trade payables to go undetected.

(iii)   **Detection risk**

This is the risk that the auditor's substantive procedures do not detect material errors that exist. One component of this is sampling risk. Many audit procedures are performed using samples so introducing the possibility that while the sample may have been free from errors, there could be material misstatements elsewhere in the population.

There are a variety of other reasons why the auditor may fail to detect errors. These include lack of experience and time pressure.

(b)   (i)   **Audit risks**

Nature of goods

The company sells books, CDs, DVDs and similar items. These goods are subject to fashions and trends, and this is a very competitive business where undercutting of sales prices is common. As a result, inventory values could be overstated if some lines cannot be sold or have to be sold at substantially discounted prices.

New audit client

Parker is a new audit client and this increases the detection risk for the auditor, as the firm has no previous experience of the company. This makes it harder to establish which areas of Parker's accounting systems are most susceptible to errors and also means that less reliance can be placed on analytical procedures.

Controls over online ordering

Online ordering over the internet may increase the control risk, as the ordering and sales system is reliant on the security and procedures of not only Parker itself but also its counter-parties and service provider etc.

Expansion of product range

The directors plan to expand the range of goods to include toys, garden furniture and fashion clothes.

The directors are moving into areas of business where they have less experience. In particular, furniture is very different from the CDs and books – the furniture being bulky and likely to incur high delivery and storage costs. Also, the level of clothes sales will be susceptible to swift changes in taste.

There is a risk that new systems are not properly set up to deal with the new products and inventory may be overvalued if clothes go out of fashion. If the expansion is unsuccessful, the company's going concern status may be threatened.

Mail ordering accounting system

The high level of manual input into the mail ordering accounting system appears to introduce many errors into the records. This could lead to errors in sales and receivables in the financial statements. The related invoicing errors may destroy customer goodwill and in the longer term may add to the threats to the company's going concern status.

The directors appear to disregard the importance of internal control, meaning that no efforts are being made to detect and correct the errors mentioned above.

Unqualified company accountant

The accountant seems to have been appointed solely because he is a friend of the directors rather than for his skill and experience. Also, as he is not a member of a reputable professional body, he is under no ethical obligations if he does have any doubts about the integrity of management.

Over-trading

There must be doubts over whether a business, which is suffering so much pressure on its margins and is moving into new areas of activity, is going to be able to generate sufficient cash to repay loans required to fund the expansions. This will raise the question of whether the company can continue as a going concern.

Meeting with bank after the year end

The directors will want to present a healthy set of financial statements to the bank manager so there will be a risk that figures may have been manipulated. There will be an increased risk of error throughout the financial statements, particularly in areas that are at all subjective.

Additionally, the directors expect an audit report with an unmodified audit opinion to be signed before the meeting with the bank. This increases detection risk, as the auditor is under time pressure and also will lack evidence of events after the reporting period. If the new loan is essential to the company's going concern status it may be difficult for the auditor to reach an opinion before the completion of the loan negotiations.

(ii) **Enquiries**

(1) Enquire about management's views on the prospects for profitability of the planned new lines of business.

(2) Enquire into any planned cost cutting to improve the company's profit margins.

(3) Enquire into whether there have been any problems with the operation of the online ordering system.

Procedures

(1) Obtain management's forecasts and projections and:

- Assess reasonableness of assumptions (for example, compare projected margins with those achieved by similar businesses)

- Review projections to verify that they have been based on these assumptions

- Review projections to check that all the information is consistent; for example, as the directors are planning to increase the inventory levels, check that allowance has been made for related increases in inventory holding costs.

- Calculate ratios, eg receivables days, to check reasonableness

(2) Review loan agreements for terms and conditions of existing borrowings and consider whether it appears likely that interest and capital payments can be met.

(3) Review minutes of board and committee meetings to assess management's views of the proposed new lines of business.

(4) Review correspondence with bank for any indications of the current relationship between Parker and its bankers and the likelihood of the bank providing more finance.

(5) These reviews should all be continued in the period after the year-end date right up to the date of the auditor's report.

(6) Obtain written representations from management acknowledging their responsibility for:

- Assessing the going concern status of the company
- Making reasonable assumptions in preparing forecasts and projections
- Deciding on the appropriate basis of preparation of the financial statements

11 Heels

(a)　(i)　**Steps to identify and assess risks of material misstatement**

The auditor must take the following steps to identify and assess risks of material misstatement.

- Identify risks throughout the process of obtaining an understanding of the entity and its environment.
- Assess the identified risks and evaluate whether they relate more pervasively to the financial statements as a whole.
- Relate the risks to what can go wrong at the assertion level.
- Consider the likelihood of the risks causing a material misstatement.

(ii)　**Significant risks**

A significant risk is an identified and assessed risk of material misstatement that, in the auditor's judgement, requires special audit consideration.

The following factors indicate that a risk might be significant.

- It is a risk of fraud.
- Its relationship with recent economic, accounting or other developments.
- There is a high degree of subjectivity in the related financial information.
- It results from an unusual transaction.
- It results from a significant transaction with a related party.
- The related transaction is very complex.

(b) and (c)

Risk (b)	Responses to risks (c)
The company sells fashion shoes. These are desirable items susceptible to theft. Also, they may not be saleable, as fashion tastes change. Therefore Inventory may be misstated because it is stated at a value in excess of the net realisable value (NRV) or actual quantities are below those recorded.	At the physical inventory count particular attention needs to be paid to the instructions to identify slow-moving lines. Increased emphasis on reviewing the year-end aged inventory analysis for evidence of slow-moving inventory. Physical controls over shoes at stores and warehouses will need to be observed. Extension of the review of post year end sales values for items in inventory at 31 December 20X1 to assess their NRV.
The company has rushed through the purchase of new stores. These are significant purchases and there is a risk they have not been adequately recorded in non-current assets. In particular, some of the shop fittings and the new systems may not have been correctly allocated between capital and revenue expenditure.	Specific tests to be undertaken to inspect documentation relating to property purchases. Detailed review of repairs accounts to take place for any items which should be included in non-current assets. Review of asset register to ensure only capital items have been included.
The retail stores have resulted in cash income, increasing the risk of incomplete or unrecorded income due to fraud or theft.	Analytical procedures specified where monthly takings from each store are compared with those of other stores to identify anomalies. Reconcile a sample of till records to actual bankings.

Risk (b)	Responses to risks (c)
The company's rapid expansion has meant significantly extending its borrowing as well as needing to operate close to its overdraft facility. There is a risk the bank could withdraw the facility and the company may not be able to pay its debts as they fall due (a going concern risk).	Correspondence with the bank will need to be reviewed for any evidence of withdrawal/extension of the facility. Post year end results and cash flow forecasts will need to be reviewed if prepared.
Although management are experienced in selling shoes, they are inexperienced in the retail market. Although the stores have been initially successful, in the long term the lack of experience may result in poor results and threaten the going concern of the company.	Review or discuss management's long-term plans and consider their viability.
Heels has opened new stores and implemented a new bespoke system. Staff might not be fully trained on the system and controls might not be suitably designed or may not be operating effectively. This increases the risk of errors flowing through to the financial statements.	Store visits will be needed to assess the effectiveness of controls operating at the stores. Extra work will be needed to document and assess the controls over the new accounting system, performing tests of controls where necessary.

> **Top tips.** There are other risks you could have identified and explained for (b), such as the risk of the new loans not being properly accounted for and disclosed, but only six are needed for full marks.
>
> There are a number of procedures listed for (c) and you may have thought of other valid ones, but only six were needed for full marks.

(d) **Auditor's point estimate**

An auditor's point estimate is the amount derived from audit evidence for use in evaluating management's point estimate.

Management at Heels have indicated that they will provide a point estimate. The auditors could formulate their own point estimate by establishing what proportion of, say, July, August and September 20X1 sales were returned in October, November and December 20X1.

This percentage could be applied to the sales made in the period from 1 October to 31 December 20X1 to arrive at an estimate of returns expected in the first three months of 20X2 which related to pre year end sales.

The auditor's point estimate could be adjusted for any known returns in January 20X2, as the audit report is not expected to be signed off until February.

This estimate could then be compared with management's estimate to assess whether management's estimate is reasonable.

(e) **Audit procedures**

Enquire of management how their point estimate is made and the data on which it is based.

Review the method of measurement used by management in respect of their estimate and assess the reasonableness of assumptions made.

Review the January 20X1 period to compare the level of returns actually made against the amounts provided.

Review board minutes to assess whether any changes are required to the level of the provision as a result of an increased or decreased level of returns by customers.

Request written representations from management on the level of the provision.

Test the operating effectiveness of the controls over how management made their point estimate.

> **Note**. Only five procedures were required in (e).

12 Turbo

(a) (i) **Performance materiality**

Performance materiality is the amount or amounts set by the auditor at less than materiality for the financial statements as a whole (see below) to reduce to an appropriately low level the probability that the aggregate of uncorrected and undetected misstatements exceeds materiality for the financial statements as a whole.

It also refers to the amount or amounts set by the auditor at less than the materiality level or levels for particular classes of transactions, account balances or disclosures.

Materiality for the financial statements as a whole

The materiality level for the financial statements as a whole is set for the purposes of evaluating the effect of misstatements on the financial statements and will generally exceed performance materiality levels used while carrying out audit procedures.

Misstatements are considered material to the financial statements as a whole if they, individually or in aggregate, could reasonably be expected to influence the economic decisions of users. Therefore a misstatement in isolation that exceeds performance materiality may not necessarily be considered material to the financial statements as a whole.

Determining materiality for the financial statements as a whole involves the exercise of professional judgement but generally a percentage is applied to a chosen benchmark as a starting point for determining materiality for the financial statements as a whole (eg 5% of profit before tax).

When setting all materiality levels and judging the materiality of misstatements, the auditor will consider both qualitative and quantitative effects.

Qualitative factors

Examples of qualitative factors which may cause misstatements of quantitatively small amounts to be material include:

- Laws or regulations that affect users' expectations regarding the measurement or disclosure of certain items (for example, related party transactions, and the remuneration of management and those charged with governance).

- Disclosures that are key disclosures in relation to the industry in which the entity operates (for example, research and development costs for a pharmaceutical company).

(ii) **Documentation of materiality**

The auditor must document the following in relation to materiality:

- Materiality for the financial statements as a whole

- Materiality level or levels for particular classes of transactions, account balances or disclosures if applicable

- Performance materiality

- Any revision of the above as the audit progresses

(b)　**Risks and responses**

Risk	Response(s) to risk
Contracts for adverts may span year end and the timing of invoicing does not necessarily reflect the timing of adverts. Invoicing for half or the whole contract coincides with the advert start date. Therefore there is a risk that sales are recognised early and not matched appropriately to costs, overstating revenue in the financial statements.	In relation to a sample of contracts in place at the year end or commencing near to the year end – it should be checked that revenue is recognised in the financial statements according to the timing of the adverts. Any deferred or accrued income should be recalculated and traced to the financial statements.
If recurring contracts have not been re-signed by the date advertising is meant to start an invoice is raised for the same amount as before but it is known that key customers are renegotiating contracts. Key contracts are to be renewed on 25 May and invoiced amounts for these may not reflect the revenue due if contracts are still being negotiated.	Procedures planned for the audit should include a review of renewal invoices close to the year end and these should be traced to contracts to ensure the correct amount and proportion of revenue has been included in respect of these.
Receivables may be overvalued, as newsagents are taking credit beyond the agreed 45 day limit. This could indicate poor credit control which could result in uncollectable receivable balances.	The auditors should undertake external confirmation of receivables balance to ensure they exist and extend cash-after-date testing to test recoverability of receivables. Customer correspondence files should be reviewed for evidence of any disputes.
Journalist and photographer invoices are often received after their services have been provided. As a result, liabilities and related costs may be incomplete, understating the amounts included in the financial statements.	Review payments made to journalists or photographers after the year end to identify any payments which relate to pre-year-end articles/pictures.
There is a risk that Turbo may not be a going concern due to falling revenues, losses and poor cash flow.	Ask management for their assessment as to whether Turbo is a going concern and how they arrived at their conclusions and obtain written representation on their conclusion. Review any contracts that have recently been renegotiated and compare to previous contract to ascertain the extent to which revenues are falling.
There is increased competition from new entrants and online publications. Unless the bank provides additional finance the business may struggle to continue for the foreseeable future. Whether finance is obtained is dependent on the forecasts being prepared.	When available, review the forecasts prepared by management, paying particular attention to the appropriateness of the assumptions made and the sensitivity of forecasts to changes in variable factors. Review post-year-end management accounts to identify any significant changes in the performance of the business and compare with the forecast to assess the accuracy of them.

Risk	Response(s) to risk
Turbo's bank intends to rely on the audited financial statements when making a decision to provide loan finance. As a result, management have an incentive to overstate profits by manipulating balances which are reliant on an element of judgement.	Particular attention should be directed to judgemental areas in the financial statements (eg any provisions reversed and revenue recognition policies). An independent partner review should be undertaken for judgemental areas of the financial statements.
Material refurbishment of printing equipment has taken place and there is a risk some repair costs have been included as non-current assets and *vice versa*. Non-current assets and repair costs could be misstated.	An analysis of the refurbishment costs should be reviewed and traced to invoices. The invoice descriptions and supporting documents should be reviewed to assess the nature of the expenditure. Once established as either capital or revenue it should be traced to the general ledger and the financial statements to ensure it has been classified correctly as an asset or repairs.
The company plans to embark on a costly project in an area it has no experience of – online publishing for subscriptions. This may add to its going concern problems by putting additional strain on cash flows without generating adequate returns, given that Turbo seems to be later to market with this than competitors.	Discuss the project with management including their assumptions for growth and returns and compare with the forecasts when available. Review any formal planning documents and quotes from businesses bidding for the website construction to assess the level of expenditure likely to be needed.

> **Top tips.** There are other risks you could have identified and explained for (b) but only nine were asked for.
>
> In the answer above there is often more than one response listed for each risk to demonstrate that there are different valid responses you could use. However, one well-explained response for each of the nine risks would have been sufficient.

(c)   **Level of assurance over accuracy of forecasts**

Purnell & Co will be unable to confirm the accuracy of the forecast as requested by the bank. The forecast will be based on assumptions made by management at Turbo and it will not be possible to gain enough evidence to confirm that these are completely accurate.

Due to the uncertainties of the future cash flows included in the forecast, the bank should be informed that only a limited level of assurance can be provided in any report, expressed in the form of negative assurance. The report will set out the types of procedures undertaken and the assumptions made by management. If no irregularities were found during the work performed, the report will state that nothing had come to the attention of Purnell & Co that would cause them to believe that management's assumptions do not provide a reasonable basis for the cash forecast.

The negative assurance expressed is a lower level of assurance than the reasonable assurance provided in the statutory audit of financial statements. In the auditor's report on financial statements, a positive form of expression of the practitioner's conclusion is given rather than a negative one. The auditor expresses an opinion on whether the financial statements are prepared, in all material respects, in accordance with the applicable financial reporting framework.

13 Audit planning and documentation

(a) The overall audit strategy is a document that outlines the general strategy of the audit. It sets the direction of the audit, describes the expected scope and conduct of the audit and provides guidance for the development of the audit plan.

The audit plan is a more detailed document than the overall audit strategy and includes instructions to the audit team that set out the audit procedures the auditors intend to adopt. The audit plan may also contain references to other matters, such as audit objectives, timing, sample sizes and the basis of selection for each account area. It also serves as a means to control and record the proper execution of the audit work.

Key contents of an overall audit strategy:

- Section on understanding the company's environment
- Section on understanding the company's accounting and internal control system
- Risk and materiality considerations
- Nature, timing and extent of audit procedures
- Section on co-ordination, direction, supervision and review
- Any other matters

(b) ISA 230 *Audit documentation* requires auditors to document their audit work. Audit work needs to be documented for a number of reasons which are outlined below.

Audit documentation provides evidence of the auditor's basis for a conclusion about the achievement of the auditor's objectives and evidence that the audit was planned and performed in accordance with ISAs and other applicable legal and regulatory requirements.

It also assists the engagement team to plan and perform the audit; it assists team members responsible for supervision to direct and supervise the audit work; it enables the team to be accountable for its work; it allows a record of matters of continuing significance to be retained; and it allows for the conduct of quality control reviews and inspections (both internal and external).

(c) Standardised audit working papers

Advantages

- May improve efficiency of audit work, through the use of checklists and specimen letters, for example
- Automated working paper packages may make documenting audit work easier, because they include features such as automatic cross-referencing
- Facilitate review
- Can lead to time saving

Disadvantages

- May lead to a mechanical approach without applying audit judgement
- May not be applicable to all clients
- New audit staff will require training to use the audit documentation system used by the audit firm

14 Audit evidence considerations

(a) Analytical procedures can be used at the planning stage, as substantive procedures, and at the review stage of the audit. Analytical procedures consist of the analysis of significant ratios and trends including the resulting investigations of fluctuations and relationships that are inconsistent with other relevant information or which deviate from predictable amounts. Analytical procedures include comparisons with similar information from prior periods, comparisons to budgets and forecasts, comparisons with predictions prepared by auditors, and comparisons with industry information.

When using analytical procedures as substantive tests, auditors need to consider the information available in terms of its availability, relevance and comparability. They also need to consider the plausibility and predictability of the relationships they are testing. Other factors to consider include materiality, other audit procedures, the accuracy with which the expected results can be predicted, the frequency with which a relationship is observed and the assessments of inherent and control risks.

An example of an analytical procedure that can be used as a substantive test is a proof in total test on depreciation and amortisation. In this test, the auditor predicts the expected charge for the year for depreciation and amortisation by using the client's accounting policy for depreciation and applying this to the brought forward figures for non-current assets from the prior year's audited financial statements, factoring in additions and disposals for the year. The figure obtained can be compared to the charge in the draft financial statements to assess its reasonableness and accuracy.

(b)   Audit evidence is available to auditors in a variety of forms. These include auditor-generated evidence (eg analytical procedures), external sources of evidence from third parties (eg solicitors' correspondence, valuation reports from surveyors for land and buildings), internal sources of evidence from within the entity being audited (eg minutes of meetings from the Board of Directors, reports generated from the accounting system), and oral or written evidence. Another factor to consider is whether the evidence, if written, is from an original document or a copy.

Audit evidence from external sources to the entity is more reliable than that obtained from the entity's records. Evidence from the entity's records is more reliable when the related internal control system is operating effectively. Auditor-generated evidence is more reliable than that obtained indirectly or by inference. Evidence in the form of documents or written representations is more reliable than oral representations. Where evidence is written, original documents are more reliable than photocopies, which can be altered by the client relatively easily.

15 Internal control systems

(a)   *Limitations of accounting and control systems*

Management can only obtain a certain level of assurance (reasonable assurance) that internal control objectives have been achieved because of certain inherent limitations of accounting and control systems. These limitations include the following.

(i)   Control systems still rely on human input and compliance. Therefore there is always a possibility of human error rendering the control ineffective.

(ii)   Employees can collude to bypass controls. For example, one employee may 'sign in' or 'clock in' another employee to bypass controls designed to monitor hours worked.

(iii)   Management can use their authority to override controls.

(iv)   Controls are usually designed to cope with routine transactions. When a non-routine or unusual transaction occurs, the system may not be adequately designed to ensure it is properly recorded.

(v)   The costs of implementing controls should not outweigh the benefits. This means that controls are not always implemented where management has taken the view they would rather accept the risk of certain errors occurring than incur the cost of implementing a preventative control.

(b)   (i)   Narrative notes

Advantages

Narrative notes are relatively simple to record and can facilitate understanding by all audit team members.

They can be applied to any system and are therefore a flexible method of documenting systems.

Updating narrative notes in future years can be relatively easy if they are computerised notes.

Disadvantages

Narrative notes can be time consuming to prepare compared to alternative methods.

When using narrative notes it can be difficult to identify missing internal controls because notes record the detail of systems but may not identify control exceptions clearly.

They are difficult to update if prepared manually.

Note. Only two advantages and two disadvantages were needed.

(ii) Alternative methods of documenting accounting and control systems include:

Flowcharts

Flowcharts are graphic illustrations of the physical flow of information through the accounting system. Flowlines represent the sequences of processes, and other symbols represent the inputs and outputs to a process.

Internal control questionnaires (ICQs)

ICQs comprise a list of questions designed to determine whether desirable controls are present. Often the questions are phrased to ask whether the desirable control is present, so the user can answer 'yes' or 'no'. A 'no' answer will then indicate a potential deficiency. There is usually a list of questions to cover each of the major transaction cycles.

Internal control evaluation questionnaires (ICEQs)

This is a questionnaire designed to assess (evaluate) whether specific errors (or frauds) are possible, rather than establishing whether certain desirable controls are present. This is achieved by reducing the control criteria for each transaction stream down to a handful of key questions (or control questions). These questions concentrate on the significant errors or omissions that could occur at each phase of the appropriate cycle if controls are weak.

Checklists

Checklists may be used to document and evaluate the internal control system. They include statements (rather than questions) to 'mark off' and tick boxes are used to indicate where the statement holds true. Those statements not marked off will indicate potential deficiencies.

Note. Only two alternative methods were needed.

16 Fenton Distributors

(a) Control objectives

Sales system

- Goods and services are only supplied to customers with good credit ratings.
- Customers are encouraged to pay promptly.
- Orders are recorded correctly.
- Orders are fulfilled.
- All despatches are recorded.
- All goods and services sold are correctly invoiced.
- All invoices raised relate to goods and services supplied by the business.
- Credit notes are only issued for valid reasons.
- All sales that have been invoiced are recorded in the accounting system.
- All entries in the sales ledger are made to the correct accounts.
- Potentially doubtful debts have been identified.

Purchases system

- All orders for goods and services are properly authorised and are for goods and services that are actually received and are for the company.

- Orders are only made to authorised suppliers and at competitive prices.

- Goods and services are only accepted if they have been ordered and the order has been authorised.

- All goods and services received are accurately recorded.

- Liabilities are recorded for all goods and services that have been received.

- All credit notes received are recorded in the nominal and purchase ledger.

(**Note**. Only three were required for each.)

(b)   (i)   To verify the accuracy of the purchases transactions posted to the nominal ledger I would perform the following tests.

- I would verify that the bookkeeper was up to date with the monthly posting of all purchases transactions to the nominal ledger.

- Specific tests on purchase transactions will include the following.

  - Purchase transactions will be traced from the invoice to the nominal ledger and the analysis and analysis code will be checked.

  - The total invoice value will be traced to the nominal ledger.

  - The category of invoice expense and the expense amount will be examined to confirm that it appears correctly on the detailed computer list for the month concerned.

  - The total of the items on the detailed list will be matched to the nominal ledger.

  - Transactions will also be traced backwards from the entries in the nominal ledger making up the monthly total posted to the purchase ledger back to both the detailed analysis and the individual invoice.

  - The amount of the invoice expense will be agreed with the amount posted to the nominal ledger.

  The tests above check accounting entries forwards and backwards within the system and any errors would be fully investigated as to their type, cause, materiality and pattern.

- The tests on the detailed list and total postings of cash payments, discounts received and adjustments will follow the same procedure as for invoices and credit notes. The monthly cash book total will be agreed to the total posted from the purchase ledger to the nominal ledger.

- An examination of the analysis and coding of purchase invoices will be carried out to establish the level of accuracy achieved. Particular care will be taken to see that the expense category 'purchases' is correctly identified and coded from invoices and is not confused with other categories, for example stationery, rates, gas and telephone. Incorrect analysis and/or coding may be indicated where the expense category is high or low in comparison with its budget to date.

  Large variations between actual and budget on expense categories should be examined further to verify that they are not due to errors in analysis, coding or posting.

(ii)   To verify the validity and accuracy of the journals posted to the nominal ledger I would carry out the following tests.

- Firstly, I would check the opening balances at the start of the financial year from the opening trial balance back to the closing entries on the previous year's accounts. After this, each item would be agreed to the nominal ledger ensuring that both the value and analysis are correct. These opening postings should be the first entries in the new year, as all nominal ledger balances should have been set to zero, and this should be confirmed.

- Other cash book items would be agreed to the nominal ledger to confirm that postings are correct as to value and expense category. Large items would require a larger sample size and large, unusual or suspicious items should all be checked and evidenced by supporting documentation or Board approval.

- The year-end balances of cash and bank on the nominal ledger should be agreed with the year-end balances in the cash book. This would require the last month to be scrutinised, as the closing balances at all previous month ends will have been agreed already.

- The tests on petty cash payments transactions would include the following.

    - Check that transactions are supported by vouchers and correctly posted to the right nominal ledger account. This would include checking that transactions are valid and coded to the correct expense category.
    - Check that petty cash transactions are within any limits, regarding the type of expenditure or maximum value, established by management.
    - Agree that the petty cash balance in the nominal ledger at the end of each month and at the financial year end matches with the balance in the petty cash book.

- The wages expense is posted manually to the nominal ledger from the monthly payroll summaries by means of a journal. To verify that the journals are correctly posted I would select several journals and check the following matters.

    - The totals of the analysis columns on the monthly summary shown on the spreadsheet should be posted to the journal, and forwarded to the nominal ledger.
    - The breakdown of wages expense into directors and the several departmental categories will be checked. The correct identification of directors' pay is important, as this requires statutory disclosure. I would obtain the current list of directors. I would add up the totals in the analysis columns to confirm the summary total and consider its reasonableness.
    - Amounts owing at the year end for income tax, accrued pay and other deductions will be verified and any reconciliation drawn up by the bookkeeper agreed.
    - Any additions to, or amendments of, weekly wages records posted to the nominal ledger through the adjustments journal will be fully investigated and their validity established.
    - The analysis of wages expense for the year will be compared with the budget and an explanation will be sought for any significant variances.

- Adjustment journals are potentially a high-risk area and any tests would include the following.

    - Check that all the manually written adjustment journals were authorised by the managing director and supported by documentation and proper narratives.
    - Check journals are posted in numerical order and that there are no missing numbers gaps in the postings.

–   Examine all large adjustments and the reasons given for the errors. These will be traced to the nominal ledger to ensure that postings do correct the errors.

–   Closely investigate recurring errors to establish their cause and whether these can be avoided in future by management action.

–   Examine the purchase ledger suspense account (payables suspense) and trace all postings in and out.

–   Where there was no account in the nominal ledger, agree back to the purchase invoice, establish the account number and verify that the item has been posted from the suspense account to the correct account.

–   Where the adjustment is due to the wrong account number being used, agree that the journal correctly transfers the item to the right account.

–   Where the bookkeeper has created contra entries between the purchase ledger and the sales ledger, check that the supplier/customer company concerned is posted with a purchase ledger and sales ledger contra of the same value.

–   All other adjustments will be checked for validity and supporting documentation.

Reasons will be established for postings that increase or reduce purchase ledger balances.

- Year-end balances on the nominal ledger would be further tested as follows.

  –   Any balances remaining on the purchase ledger and sales ledger suspense accounts should be itemised on a supporting schedule and the existence of each item justified.

  –   Nominal ledger balances for the cash book, petty cash book, sales ledger and purchase ledger should agree to, or be reconciled to, the cash book, petty cash book, total sales ledger and total purchase ledger balances at the year end. I will investigate further to confirm that any difference is reconciled and explained. It may be that further adjustments are required to reduce or eliminate a difference.

  –   All non-current asset movements should be checked, including purchases, sales, revaluations and depreciation.

  –   All outstanding liabilities should be verified and their size reviewed for reasonableness.

  –   The bank reconciliation should establish the correctness of balances on all types of bank account, ie loan, current, deposit and special transactions.

  –   A review of the financial statements would be carried out to ensure that material changes in assets, expenses, revenues, liabilities and share capital are justified and explained. Justification would be sought in both relative and absolute terms.

17 Cheque payments and petty cash

(a)

A Black	MNO & Co
Managing Director	3 Green Street
Quicksand Co	Anytown
12 Kelvin Street	
Anytown	Date

Dear Mr Black

You recently requested that we should advise you on good internal controls over cheque payments and petty cash.

The main objectives of control over payments are to ensure that payments are made only in respect of valid transactions and that they are suitably authorised. The following control procedures will contribute towards attaining these objectives.

(i) *Cheque payments*

(1) Cheques should be raised only on the basis of authorisation, for example a purchase invoice which has been suitably authorised.

(2) Cheques should be signed by people other than those who approve invoices.

(3) There should be two independent signatories for each cheque; for instance, two directors might act as signatories. Signatories should inspect the documents supporting the cheque to ensure that the details agree. They should also mark the document so that it cannot be reused.

(4) Cheques should be restrictively crossed.

(5) Unused cheques should be kept in a secure place. Blank cheques should never be signed.

(6) Cheques should be under sequential control and all numbers should be accounted for. Spoilt cheques should therefore be retained.

(7) When cheques have been signed, they should be despatched immediately.

(ii) *Petty cash*

(1) Petty cash payments should be made only on the basis of suitably authorised vouchers, which should be under sequential control. Vouchers should be retained for subsequent references. Where independent evidence is also available, for example invoices and receipts, this should be retained.

(2) An imprest system should be used to control petty cash. This means that the petty cash float is maintained at a specific amount and is reimbursed at regular intervals on the basis of vouchers showing the payments which have been made. It is suggested that the float should be kept at a level of $300 and be reimbursed on a weekly basis.

(3) The petty cash float should be subject to periodic surprise counts by a responsible person not involved with the petty cash system. The balance in-hand should be reconciled to the imprest account by reference to the vouchers not yet reimbursed.

(4) The size of individual payments out of petty cash should be subject to a maximum to be agreed by the directors.

(5) Staff should not be allowed to cash personal cheques or borrow from petty cash.

I hope that the above information is useful to you in designing your systems of internal control. If you require any more information, please let me know.

Yours sincerely,

A Smith

(b)   Mr Black presumably feels that involvement in cash and cheque controls will be time-consuming, and that he is too busy to be involved in it. He may feel that he does not want to play a direct part in the petty cash function. Because of the small amounts involved, he may wish to delegate this function to another director. He should appreciate, however, that involvement at least in the authorisation of cheque payments would help to ensure that he is aware of major transactions in his business. He might consider the possibility of authorising cheques in excess of a given amount; this would minimise the demands on his time, while exercising control and keeping him informed of significant outgoings from the business.

Auditors may wish to consider whether Mr Black's lack of involvement may be symptomatic of insufficient attention being given to financial matters by the board.

18 Using the work of others

(a)   **Service organisations**

A service organisation is a third-party organisation that provides services to user entities that are part of those entities' information systems relevant to financial reporting. A user entity is an entity that uses a service organisation and whose financial statements are being audited.

An auditor who audits and reports on the financial statements of a user entity is known as a 'user auditor' and a user auditor must obtain an understanding of the services provided by the service organisation that are relevant to the audit. A relevant example is where the audit client outsources its payroll processes to an external organisation.

This understanding obtained by the user auditor must include the following.

*   The nature of services provided and the significance of these to the user entity, including effect on user entity's internal control

*   The nature and materiality of transactions processed or financial reporting processes affected

*   The degree of interaction

*   The nature of relationship including contractual terms

When obtaining an understanding of the internal control relevant to the audit, the user auditor must also evaluate the design and implementation of relevant controls at the user entity that relate to the services provided by the service organisation.

(b)   (i)   **Audit evidence that could be obtained from an expert**

*   Valuations of assets, such as land and buildings, plant and machinery, works of art, precious stones

*   Determination of quantities or physical condition of assets

*   Determination of amounts using specialised techniques or methods, such as an actuarial valuation

*   Measurement of work completed and to be completed on contracts in progress

*   Legal opinions concerning interpretations of agreements, statutes and regulations

(**Note**. Only four were required.)

(ii)   **Factors to consider when evaluating the work carried out by an auditor's expert**

When evaluating the expert's work the auditor should consider how relevant the work is, the standard of the work and its consistency with other audit evidence.

The auditor should also consider the relevance and reasonableness of any assumptions and methods used, along with the relevance, completeness and accuracy of any source data used.

(iii) **Actions to take if evidence is not sufficient or results are inconsistent**

If the results of the expert's work do not provide sufficient appropriate audit evidence or are inconsistent with other audit evidence, the auditor needs to resolve the matter.

This could be done through discussions with the entity and the expert or applying additional audit procedures, including engaging another expert.

The auditor must consider the need to modify the auditor's opinion in the auditor's report (this is a last resort if the issues are still unresolved after all the other avenues have been explored).

19 Elsams

(a) *Use of computer programs to verify inventory*

If physical inventory counting takes place at the year end, it may be assumed that the results of the physical inventory count are entered into, and valued by, the computer. If so, then it is important to compare the results of the physical count with the book quantities. The client may have a computer program to make this comparison. It would be possible for the auditor to check this comparison by reperformance using their own specially written computer audit program or a computer audit package. The auditor's computer audit program or package, when run against the file of book inventory, might also be used to carry out the following tasks.

- Select a monetary unit or random sample of book inventory items for the auditor to check the physical count quantities.

- Select items with specific characteristics, eg no sale since a specific date, unit selling price over a specified figure for further testing (test counts or obsolescence enquiries).

- Prepare an aged analysis of inventory items.

- Re-perform calculation of the FIFO cost of each inventory item, compare with the book inventory figure and print details if there is a discrepancy.

- Cast the file of book inventory and print the total.

- Print details (product number, supplier, quantity, cost, date of supply) for a sample of recent inventory receipts contained in the file of book inventory for substantiation against suppliers' invoices.

- Prepare summaries of inventory by branch, product number and location to assist in analytical procedures on the inventory figure, especially when comparing with previous years.

- Compare the unit FIFO cost of each inventory item with the unit selling price and print details of all inventory items where unit selling price is the lower to assist in evaluating net realisable value.

Limitations

Computer audit programs specific to the client are expensive to write. Computer audit packages that are tailored to the client's computer and file structure are less expensive. However, packages are often only compatible with certain makes of computer. The audit software can work only with the information contained in the computer files. For example, an inventory ageing cannot be produced if the dates of inventory movements are not available. Clearly audit software cannot perform audit tests where an element of judgement is involved. For example, it can produce an inventory ageing analysis but the auditor must decide, on the basis of all available evidence, what level of obsolescence provision is reasonable. Audit software requires the auditor to have a detailed knowledge of the software and of the computer files to be used.

(b)   *Test data*

Audit test data consists of data submitted by the auditor for processing by the enterprise's computer-based accounting system. It may be processed during a normal production run (live test data) or during a special run separate from the normal cycle (dead test data). The auditor predicts the results of processing the data and compares the prediction with the actual results. The primary objective of test data is to test programmed controls. For example, if the program contains a control which rejects overtime hours greater than 20 per week, then the test data might include the case of 21 hours' overtime to see if it is rejected. The basic principle of using test data is that if the program processes the test data correctly, then the logic of the program and the program coding works and will process the actual data correctly.

Difficulties

(i)   When live test data is used there is difficulty in ensuring that the dummy data does not become included in the actual data.

(ii)   When dead test data is used it may be difficult to ensure that the program tested is identical with that used for the actual data.

(iii)   The initial time spent designing the test data is excessive in relation to the benefit it brings – many auditors would rather devote that time to substantive audit work.

(c)   *Audit sampling*

(i)   Random selection ensures that all items in the population have an equal chance of selection, eg by use of random number tables or computerised generator.

(ii)   Systematic selection involves selecting items using a constant interval, the first interval having a random start. When using this method, the auditor must be sure that the population is not structured in such a way that the sampling interval corresponds with a particular pattern in the population.

(iii)   Haphazard selection is an alternative to random selection, as long as the auditor is satisfied that the sample is representative of the whole population. This method requires care to guard against making a selection that is biased. It should not be used if statistical sampling is being carried out.

(iv)   Block selection can be used to check whether certain items have particular characteristics. However, it may produce samples that are not representative of the population as a whole, especially if errors only occurred during a certain part of the period and therefore the errors found cannot be projected onto the rest of the population.

20 ZPM

(a)   (i)   **Factors to consider when determining whether the work of the internal audit function can be used**

- The extent to which its objectivity is supported by its organisational status, relevant policies and procedures

- The level of competence of the function

- Whether the internal audit function applies a systematic and disciplined approach (including quality control)

(ii)   **Factors to consider when determining the nature and extent of work of the internal audit function that can be used**

- The nature and scope of specific work performed or to be performed

- The relevance of that work to the audit strategy and audit plan

- The degree of judgement involved in evaluation of audit evidence gathered by the internal audit function

(b)   (i)   **Objectives of the internal auditor**

Year-end inventory count

The objective of the year-end inventory count is to ensure that the figure for inventories in the financial statements is materially correct. The internal auditors will review the control system over inventory counting and ensure that all inventory is counted as well as performing test counts themselves to check the accuracy of the counting.

Procurement system

The objective of the internal auditor is to ensure that the procurement system is operating in accordance with company guidelines. For example, they will undertake work to ensure that all purchases are authorised, quantity discounts are received and goods received are documented and recorded appropriately.

(ii)   **Objectives of the external auditor**

Year-end inventory count

The objective of the external auditor is to determine whether inventory is materially correct in the year-end financial statements. Inventory should be valued appropriately at the lower of cost and net realisable value in accordance with accounting standards and legislation. In the case of ZPM, the main risk appears to be inaccurate counting of inventory, as some of it consists of lots of small items. The external auditor will attend the inventory count to check whether the quantities and condition of inventory are correctly recorded.

Procurement system

The objective of the external auditor is to determine whether payables and purchases in the financial statements are materially correct. If the testing allows the external auditor to conclude that the controls over procurement are operating effectively, this will form part of the evidence that purchases and payables are recorded completely and accurately, eg in the correct year of account.

(iii)   **Extent of reliance**

Year-end inventory count

The company has over a hundred stores in various countries, making it impossible for the external auditors to attend the inventory count in every one of these. The external auditors can place reliance on the work of the internal auditors, in addition to their own attendance at a small sample of inventory counts. The external auditors will still have to review the work of internal audit to ensure that they can rely on the work undertaken. They should also compare their own results with those obtained by internal audit.

Procurement system

The external auditors may be able to rely on the work performed by internal audit on the controls over the procurement system, as these are relevant to financial statement assertions such as completeness of liabilities. The external auditors will still have to carry out their own work on the system, although it will be reduced if they can place reliance on any of the work done by the internal auditors.

(c)   **Limitations of the internal audit function**

(i)   Internal auditors are employed by the organisation and this can impair their independence and objectivity. They may be reluctant to report fraud/error to senior management because of perceived threats to their continued employment within the company.

(ii)   Internal auditors are not required to be professionally qualified and so there may be limitations in their knowledge and technical expertise.

(iii)   If internal audit only reports to one level of management, management may be able to unduly influence the internal audit plan, scope, and whether issues are reported appropriately. This results in a serious conflict, limits the scope and compromises the effectiveness of the internal audit function.

21 Boston Manufacturing

(a)   **Risk in the tangible non-current asset audit**

Control risk

The controls over non-current assets at Boston Manufacturing appear to be strong. The company maintains and reconciles a non-current asset register and there are authorisation procedures in operation. These controls should be tested and, if they prove effective, control risk could be assessed as low.

Inherent risk

The tangible non-current assets are material on the basis of the proposed materiality level. There has been a substantial movement on the plant and equipment account this year, but this appears to be supported by the information given by the management accountant. There appear to be no disposals in the year, which may indicate that they have been omitted, or that obsolete items are included in the register. It is also unclear whether land is being depreciated. It would be inappropriate if it was being depreciated. Overall, the inherent risk seems to be medium.

Detection risk

Given that inherent risk has been assessed as moderate and control risk has been assessed as low, detection risk will be assessed as higher. However, there is usually good evidence in relation to the existence and valuation of non-current assets and these are the key assertions which the auditors are interested in. There will also be scope to carry out good analytical procedures, such as proof in total of depreciation.

Conclusion

The audit of non-current assets appears to be medium to low risk.

(b)   **Audit procedures**

(i)   **Existence**

In many cases it is self-evident that land and buildings exist. However, it is important for the auditors to verify all components of land and buildings contained within the statement of financial position if, for example, they are on a site different to the one which the auditors are primarily attending. Land and buildings should also be verified to **title deeds** to ensure **not only** that they **exist** but also that **they are owned** by the client.

The other classes of asset should be **inspected**. A sample of assets from the **register should be agreed to the physical asset**. There may be scope to rely on the work that the management accountant has undertaken here. The auditor should check a reconciliation which the accountant has performed. The auditors should make use of any identification marks on assets recorded in the register, for example security tags or bar codes which are kept on assets to distinguish them. The auditor should inspect the **condition** of the assets and ensure that they are **in use**.

The motor vehicles should be **reconciled in terms of number of vehicles existing at the opening and closing positions**. Again, to ensure not only that they exist, but also that they are owned by the company, the auditors should check the **registration documents** to ensure that the company is the registered owner.

For all the above assets, the external auditor should also review the insurance provision for the assets. This gives **third-party evidence** of the existence of assets, as the insurer would not insure an asset which did not exist.

(ii) **Valuation (excluding depreciation)**

Land and buildings appear to be stated at historical **cost**, as the schedule does not contain the words 'at valuation'. The auditors should **confirm** that this is the case with the management accountant. The cost can then be **agreed to brought forward figures**, as there have been no additions in the year. These figures will have been audited in the previous year. If the assets are held at valuation, the auditors must ensure that the requirements of IAS 16 in relation to revaluations are being complied with.

Similarly, as there have been no movements in the year, **motor vehicles** can be agreed to the **opening position**.

To audit the valuation of **plant and computers**, the auditors should **agree the opening position**. They should then **obtain a schedule of additions** to non-current assets, which can be **agreed to purchase invoices** to verify valuation.

Lastly, the auditors should investigate whether the cost figures include any **fully written down assets**. This is implied by the fact that the depreciation charge on plant, excluding additions, is low. If so, the auditor should find out whether these assets **are still in use** and, if not, consider whether they **should be excluded** from the cost and accumulated depreciation figures contained within the notes to the accounts. Excluding them would have a net effect on the reported figure of $0.

(iii) **Completeness**

The schedule of non-current assets prepared should be reconciled to:

- The **opening position** (that is, the previous statement of financial position)
- The **closing position** (what is disclosed in the financial statements)
- The **underlying records** (the nominal ledger)

If the non-current asset register contains details of the cost and accumulated depreciation of each asset, the **register should also be reconciled to the schedule**. Explanations should be sought for any differences.

The additions of the schedule should also be checked to ensure that the opening and closing positions reconcile within the schedule.

The auditors should also carry out a test on some of the **individual additions**, tracing the transaction through the system, from purchase orders to delivery notes and invoices and through the ledgers to the financial statements to ensure that additions have been included completely.

(c) **Depreciation**

(i) **Appropriateness**

The appropriateness of the rates should be considered and discussed with management. **Relevant factors** to consider are matters such as:

- The **replacement policy** for the asset
- The pattern of **usage** in the business
- The **purpose of the asset** being owned

In this instance, the auditors should establish the rationale behind the depreciation rates applied, particularly in the case of plant. In the case of the plant purchased this year, the depreciation rate applied is 10%. However, the assets have been purchased in relation to an 8-year project, so 12.5% might be a more appropriate rate.

(ii) **Audit procedures**

Depreciation on **buildings** can be verified by agreeing the purchase date of the buildings to last year's file or historical invoices / purchase documents and the valuation applied to the building portion.

For the other classes of asset, depreciation should be agreed for individual assets, as it is not possible to agree them in total. The auditors should obtain a **breakdown of the charges** for the year. They should be able to **recalculate the depreciation** from details in the non-current asset register and compare the results.

22 Wandsworth Wholesalers

(a) I would have checked the following matters at the pre-year-end inventory count.

(i) Counting staff, although not the usual custodians of the inventory, were competent. They were briefed before the count and given sufficiently detailed written instructions. They were assigned marked areas to count.

(ii) No inventory was moved during the count. If inventory had to be moved, then the count supervisor would make a detailed note of quantities, inventory numbers and goods despatched notes (GDNs).

(iii) The inventory was clearly identified and well laid out. The counters should work in an organised way, with one counting and one checking. Each inventory line or area should be marked or tagged when counted to avoid any double counting.

(iv) Count sheets should be pre-numbered if possible, to ensure that they are all returned. Numbers should be in ink, not pencil.

(v) Management (or internal audit) should perform test counts throughout the inventory count. Any discrepancies should be investigated and resolved, usually by a recount.

(vi) Slow-moving, obsolete and damaged inventory should be marked as such on the inventory count sheets in as much detail as possible to highlight inventory which possibly should be valued at net realisable value.

(vii) The management present should initial all the inventory sheets after performing random tests to check that all items of inventory have been counted.

I should record the following matters during my attendance at the inventory count.

(i) Perform test counts, selecting items from the floor to check to the sheets and vice versa. I would record all these tests (including inventory numbers and inventory sheets) and any discrepancies I find should be investigated by the count staff and management present at the time.

(ii) Record all the inventory sheet numbers used in the count.

(iii) Record the last goods received note (GRN) number received and the last GDN number issued prior to the inventory count.

(iv) Complete an inventory count checklist.

(v) Record any problems or unresolved discrepancies. This would include obsolete, slow-moving or damaged inventory and any inventory movements during the inventory count.

(b) (i) To test cut-off at the inventory count on 13 October I would perform the following procedures.

(1) **Sales cut-off**. Select a few GDNs from immediately both before and after the inventory count. Check that they have been recorded in the book inventory records in the appropriate period as being despatched before or after the inventory count date.

(2) **Purchases cut-off**. Select a few GRNs from immediately both before and after the inventory count. Check that they have been recorded as received in the appropriate period, either before or after the inventory count date.

(ii) At the year end it will be necessary to perform full **cut-off** tests, rather than just a check on the computerised book records as in (b)(i) above. After performing these tests for transactions about the year end, the following additional tests will be carried out.

   (1) **Sales cut-off**. Trace the goods from the GDNs to the relevant sales invoices and check that those invoices were posted to the sales ledger either before or after the year end, as appropriate.

   (2) **Purchases cut-off**. Trace the goods from the GRNs to the relevant purchase invoices and check that the invoices have been recorded in the purchase ledger in the correct period, as appropriate. Invoices which relate to the period prior to the year end may not have been received in time to be posted in the ledger. In these cases, such invoices should be included in the purchase accruals at the year end.

(c) The following procedures are relevant.

   (i) Trace the check counts I performed at the inventory count to the inventory sheets, and from there to the book records. Some small adjustments may have been made to the book inventory. These discrepancies, if not material, may be explained by small differences found at the inventory count.

   (ii) Investigate any material discrepancies between the inventory-sheet quantities counted at the inventory count and the book inventory records. Adjustments between the inventory count date and the year end should also be investigated.

   Large differences should be explained by the results of the inventory count. Evidence should be seen that further check counts were performed to ensure the inventory counts were correct. There should also be evidence that the management of the company have investigated large differences.

(d) As well as the tests detailed above in relation to the inventory count and cut-off, I would perform the following procedures.

   (i) Vouch the quantities used in the year and valuation to the book inventory records. This test should also be performed in reverse.

   (ii) An overall check of complete book inventory against the amounts used in the valuation might be attempted using a computer program if the book inventory records are held on file. The program might produce all material discrepancies.

   (iii) Investigate all material adjustments to the book inventory records at the year end.

   (iv) Investigate the level of adjustments made to book inventory records throughout the year. Consider whether the adjustments are small enough to give comfort that the book inventory records are reasonably accurate.

   (v) Review the inventory counts from throughout the year to ensure that all inventory lines have been counted at least once during the year.

   (vi) Review the book inventory records at the year end and check for any negative inventory quantities. Where such negative figures have occurred, there should be evidence that the managers of the company have investigated the reasons for them, and that the figures have been adjusted to the actual physical amount.

23 Snu

(a) Importance of year-end inventory counts

Auditors are required to obtain **sufficient appropriate** evidence to support the inventory figure stated in the accounts. This is particularly relevant where inventories are material to the financial statements. Where perpetual inventory systems are not maintained, the year-end count is the most reliable means by which the auditor can obtain the following audit evidence:

- **Quantity and existence** of inventory
- An indication of the **value** of inventory and the means by which management identify slow and obsolete items
- **Cut-off** details
- The overall **control environment** in which the inventory system operates
- Evidence of **fraud or misappropriation**

(b) Audit procedures

The following procedures would be performed in order to rely on a perpetual inventory system.

- **Check management procedures** to ensure that all inventory lines are counted at least once a year.
- Confirm that **adequate inventory records** are maintained and that they are kept up-to-date. Tests would include a comparison of sales and purchase transactions with inventory movements. Inventory records would also be checked for correct casting and classification of inventory.
- For a sample of counts at a number of locations the inventory count **instructions should be reviewed**.
- **Attend and observe** the counts at a sample of locations. (As the organisation is dispersed, this may involve the use of staff from other offices.) Those visited should be chosen on the basis of the materiality of the inventory balance and whether the site is identified as high risk eg where controls have historically been weak. The remainder could then be visited on a rotational basis.
- Assess the extent to which the results of **internal audit work** can be relied on. As the organisation is large, it is likely to have an internal audit function. Results of test counts performed by internal audit may reduce the extent of external audit test counts.
- Check that procedures are in place to **correct book inventories** for discrepancies identified at the inventory counts. Changes should be **authorised** and made accurately and on a timely basis.

(c) Principal risks associated with the financial statement assertions for inventory

One of the risks associated with inventory is its appropriate valuation. Inventory should be valued at the lower of cost and net realisable value per IAS 2 *Inventories*. Inventory can be a material figure in the financial statements of many entities, particularly manufacturing companies, and therefore appropriate valuation of inventory is very important, particularly for obsolete and slow-moving items. The valuation can also be a matter of judgement and this increases the risk associated with inventory.

Inventory in the statement of financial position must **exist** – this is another key assertion. Inventory can be subject to theft and misappropriation, and is often held at more than one location, and so controls to safeguard it are very important.

Cut-off is another key issue for inventory. All purchases, transfers and sales of inventory must be recorded in the correct accounting period, as again inventory can be a material figure for many companies. Incorrect cut-off can result in misstatements in the financial statements at the year end and this can be of particular concern where inventory is material. Auditors therefore need to consider whether the management of the entity being audited have implemented adequate cut-off procedures to ensure that movements into and out of inventory are properly identified and reflected in the accounting records and ultimately in the financial statements.

(d)

Deficiency	Explanation
Timing of the inventory count The count is due to take place on New Year's Day. This is unlikely to be popular with staff. Resentment and a desire to get the job done as quickly as possible may mean that the counts are not done thoroughly. There is also little time given to preparation before the count, a problem exacerbated by the fact that both the shops and warehouse are very busy in the period leading up to the count.	As the company operates seven days a week it would be difficult to find an alternative date for the inventory count. In addition, it is at this time of year to coincide with the company's December year end. It would be expensive and difficult to find alternative staff to perform the task and it is unlikely that the business will change its year end simply because the inventory count is inconvenient. It may be possible to perform the count a week before or a week after the year end and roll forward/back the inventory calculation. This would involve closing the business for an extra day and would also involve a degree of reliance on inventory records.
There is a **lack of segregation of duties**. Mr Sneg is the inventory controller as well as being the count supervisor and count checker. This means that he is responsible for the physical assets as well as maintaining the book records. It would therefore be possible for Mr Sneg to cover up theft of inventory or mistakes made by himself. This situation affects the control environment of the overall performance of the inventory count.	In some respects this situation could be resolved if an alternative senior member of staff were made the inventory supervisor. However, in family businesses it is common for a small number of loyal and trusted staff to bear the majority of the responsibility. There is likely to be strong resistance from Mr Sneg himself who would feel that his good character was being questioned. Other senior members of staff are also likely to be reluctant to take on a role for which they may feel they have little experience and understanding.
Counters will work on their **own**. Normally counts should be performed by pairs of counters, as this reduces the risk of error.	Where there is a limited number of staff it may be difficult to work in pairs and get the count completed in the available timescale. Due to the timing of the count it will not be easy to get staff from other areas of the business to volunteer to take part.
This is of particular concern in this case as the company has a high turnover of staff. Counters are likely to be **inexperienced** and may not be motivated to do a good job.	Where staff turnover is high it is difficult to resolve the problem of inexperience in the short term. Management could consider the factors which contribute to staff leaving eg poor pay to determine whether these can be addressed in the medium term. However, warehouse work is often unskilled and therefore an element of staff turnover is inevitable.
The treatment of inventory delivered to customers that has not yet been paid for is **incorrect**. The inventory should not be added back and the unpaid balances should be included as receivables.	There is no reason why this matter cannot be dealt with. The treatment of inventory not paid for should be corrected.

24 Sitting Pretty

(a)   **Importance of the inventory count**

The inventory count provides important **audit evidence** as to the **existence** and **completeness** of inventory included in the financial statements.

In this case, the inventory count is particularly important because the **company does not maintain perpetual inventory records**. As no perpetual records are maintained, the only basis for the inventory entries in the financial statements is the result of this inventory count.

Inventory is **generally material** to the statement of financial position of a manufacturing company and is also one of the **higher risk areas** on the statement of financial position. The inventory count provides important audit evidence, reducing the risk of material misstatement in relation to inventory.

(b)   **Planning for attendance**

Gain knowledge. I must review the notes of last year's inventory count and I must contact the factory manager to obtain details of this year's. I must review this year's details to ensure that the inventory count appears to be planned efficiently and effectively.

Assess key factors. There are various key factors given in the scenario.

(i)   **Nature and volume of the inventory**. There should be no WIP, so I will count raw materials (approximately 10% of the inventory) and finished goods. However, raw material plastic should be low because a delivery is required to continue with production.

(ii)   **Possible obsolescence**. I must make a note of the number of old chair legs maintained in raw materials, as these are now obsolete, a new specification having been agreed.

(iii)   **Cut-off issues**. I need to ensure that the delivery on the day is isolated and that I obtain details of the delivery made during the inventory count. I need to determine whether this should be included as deliveries for the year, but most of all ensure that it does not get counted twice (as it arrives, and if it is put into stores). I should also obtain copies of the relevant documents, for example, the last invoices in the year and the last goods received and despatched notes.

(iv)   **Off-cuts**. I need to consider whether any off-cuts are maintained on site and whether these are being included in the inventory count. As the company receives a discount relating to them, they are unlikely to be considered Sitting Pretty's legally and so should not be included.

(v)   **Staff issues**. It appears that the inventory count is undertaken by the people who work in the factory and handle the inventory on a daily basis. This is not best practice, although in practical terms it is difficult to avoid. However, I should discuss this with the factory manager to assess whether staff can be allocated to counting inventory they have not produced. Also, as the staff are allowed to go home as soon as the inventory count is completed, there is a risk that the inventory count will be rushed and mistakes will be made.

Plan procedures. I need to determine my sample sizes and whether there is a need for expert assistance at this inventory count.

(i)   **Procedures**. I will carry out test counts, checking from a sample of physical items to the count sheets and a sample of count sheet items to the physical items.

(ii)   **Samples**. There are no higher value items that I should concentrate particularly on. Materiality for the year has been set at $5,000 currently. Dividing last year's figures for inventory by this materiality level would give a sample size of six items for raw materials and 34 items for finished goods. I need to determine the batches in which inventory is valued to ensure that I count the correct items. I need to assess the levels of inventory when I arrive to ascertain whether this remains appropriate.

(c) **Cut-off at final audit**

General procedures

The audit team should take a **sample of delivery notes** for sales and purchases on either side of the year end and **trace** these to **invoices** and **ledgers** and **inventory** records to ensure that **sales and purchases have been included in the correct period** and that **inventory is accounted for where appropriate** (that is, sales have not been counted twice and purchases have been included in inventory). As the factory has been shut down, there is a lower risk that sales cut-off is inappropriate than purchases cut-off.

Inventory count delivery

Once it is determined whether this delivery should count as this year's inventory (which it should if the inventory count was the year-end date), the delivery information should be traced to purchase invoices and ledgers to ensure that the purchase is recorded in the year and that the creditor is accounted for in the year. The inventory should then also be included.

Other matters

If **inventory returns** are material, the returns after the year end should be reviewed to ensure that items are not included as sales in the year and that the inventory is added to the inventory figure unless it is now obsolete, whereupon it should be written-off.

(d) **Valuation of inventory**

The auditors should obtain the client's working papers relating to the valuation of inventory. Items which the auditor sampled at the inventory count should already have been verified to the inventory count records as part of the verification of existence.

Cost

The auditors should then **trace a sample of items to purchase invoices** to ensure that **cost has been correctly applied**. Cost of purchase excludes trade discounts and rebates, so the auditors should ensure that the valuation **cost excludes the 10% discount** received for returning the off-cuts of plastic.

The auditors should then ensure that for a sample of finished goods items, **costs of conversion** (comprising costs of labour and overheads) have been included. This should be on a comparable basis to the previous year and therefore can be audited by analytical review.

Net realisable value

The auditors should ensure that **cost is lower than net realisable value** by tracing their sample to **after-date sales**. If no invoices are yet available, the auditors can make confirmations by reviewing sales orders and price lists.

Obsolete

Lastly, the auditors should ensure by review and by discussion with management that inventory which has been identified as **obsolete** at the inventory count has **not been attributed value** and has been **scrapped**.

Analytical procedures

The auditors will undertake general analytical procedures to ensure that the inventory figure stacks up. This could include calculating ratios such as inventory turnover and ensuring that they tally with the facts that have been presented to them in the course of the inventory audit.

25 Bright Sparks

(a)   *Conclusions to be drawn as a result of the interim audit*

The following deficiencies exist in the company's systems.

(i)   In any system of internal control, one person should not be able to process a whole transaction from start to finish:

    (1)   Authorisation
    (2)   Execution
    (3)   Recording

The most serious deficiency in the company's system is that warehousemen can:

    (1)   Sell goods
    (2)   Receive cash from cash sales
    (3)   Raise sales invoices for credit sales
    (4)   Raise credit notes

Moreover, there appears to be no procedures in place for checking any of their work. Since the accounting records are written up on the evidence of these invoices and credit notes, any errors made by the warehousemen will be carried into the records. It may also be the case that the issue of credit notes is not authorised by a senior member of staff.

Possible consequences

    (1)   Errors on invoices may not be detected except by customers

    (2)   Risk of unauthorised or fraudulent invoices or credit notes being raised without detection

    (3)   Risk of goods leaving the premises without being invoiced, whether through error or fraud (this is particularly dangerous in a business such as this, with a variety of high-value items)

    (4)   Time wasted by needless disagreements with customers about amounts owing

(ii)   There appears to be a weakness in the recording of cash received by the company. The dates recorded in the books are presumably the dates when the entries were written up. If so, there is clearly an excessive delay in recording cash received, and possibly also in banking it. There may also be no record of cash received made when incoming mail is opened.

Possible consequences

    (1)   Errors and defalcations can arise where a cash received system is weak.

    (2)   The longer the gap between receipt and recording, the more likely it is that discrepancies can occur.

    (3)   Specific possibilities:

       •   Falsification of records leading to misappropriation of cash (teeming and lading)

       •   Mislaying of cheques if not banked promptly

       •   Errors in the records, especially concerning dates

(iii) Stricter control is needed over the granting of cash discounts (assuming that it is the actual receipt of cash which is later than the due date, not merely the late recording of same).

Possible consequence

Discounts given to a standard list of customers who may be friends of staff or regular customers, not necessarily prompt payers.

(b)   *Audit work on trade accounts receivable at the final audit*

    (i)   Second circularisation

        (1)   Consider circularising all trade receivables accounts, or at least a larger sample than before of accounts not circularised at 30 September.

        (2)   Circularise and investigate disagreeing replies. Discover if reasons are similar to those given at 30 September circularisation.

    (ii)   To gain further evidence about the rights and obligations and existence of receivables:

        (1)   Check the sales invoices which make up the balances with backing documentation, for example purchase orders and despatch notes (if the latter exist).

        (2)   Ascertain extent of cash received from customers after the year end; reconcile the individual invoices to ensure that no discrepancies exist.

        (3)   Obtain explanations for invoices remaining unpaid after subsequent invoices have been paid.

To gain evidence about the valuation of receivables, I would review the cash received after-date and would also carry out the following tests.

        (1)   Check calculation of outstanding invoices.

        (2)   Carry out further tests on settlement discounts and ascertain whether the position has improved or deteriorated since the time of the interim audit.

        (3)   Confirm necessity/adequacy of provision against write-off of specific debts by review of correspondence, solicitors' debt collection, agencies' letters, liquidation statements.

        (4)   Consider whether amounts owed may be not recovered where there have been round sum payments on account or invoices unpaid after subsequent invoices paid.

        (5)   Review customer files/correspondence from solicitors and circularisation results for evidence of potential bad debts.

        (6)   Confirm any general provisions for uncollectable (bad) debts, considering how well previous year's provisions predicted actual bad debts and whether the formula used is reasonable and consistent with previous years.

I would check the completeness of receivables by carrying out cut-off tests at 31 December to ensure that all goods leaving the premises by that date (and only those) have been included in sales. I would also check that all returns of goods after the year end relating to 20X0 sales have been correctly recorded.

Other general tests include:

        (1)   Agree the opening balance on the sales ledger control account with the previous year's working papers to ensure all the necessary adjustments were put through last year.

        (2)   Scrutinise sales ledger control for unusual entries.

        (3)   Check list of trade account receivables balances to and from sales ledger, and reconcile with sales ledger control account.

        (4)   Carry out analytical procedures, particularly reviewing changes in the receivables turnover period, and changes in the age profile of receivables.

        (5)   Check that trade receivables have been separately disclosed in the notes to the accounts.

26 Audit of cash and bank

(a)   Characteristics of bank confirmation letter

*   The client must give its permission in writing to the bank for disclosure of information to the auditors.
*   The bank letter must refer to the client's letter of authority and the date of that letter.
*   The bank letter should reach the bank at least one month before the year-end date and should state the year-end date and the previous year-end date.

(b)   Items requested in the bank confirmation letter

*   Balances due to or from the client on current, deposit and loan accounts
*   Nil balances on accounts
*   Accounts closed during the year
*   Maturity and interest terms on loans and overdrafts
*   Confirmation of contingent liabilities on guarantees etc
*   Confirmation of securities and other items in safe custody
*   Any offset or other rights or encumbrances
*   Collateral given or received

(**Note**. Only six were required.)

(c)   The bank reconciliation is carried out because the balance on a company's general ledger cash account is unlikely to match the figure in the year-end bank statement because of timing differences for cheques and other payments and receipts clearing. The bank reconciliation is an exercise to compare the balance per the ledger and the balance per the bank statement and therefore to confirm the accuracy of the figure on the company's statement of financial position.

27 Understatement

(a)   (i)   It is more likely that payables will be understated than overstated because of the nature of the evidence available to indicate that liabilities exist.

It is relatively simple to ensure whether a recorded liability has been correctly accrued at the year end. However, it is more difficult to identify liabilities which have been omitted from payables.

(ii)   The auditor's difficulty in ensuring that payables are not understated arises precisely because of the circumstances described above. The auditor can test accrued invoices to ensure that they are a valid liability of the company at the year-end date. However, identifying liabilities which have been omitted at the year end presents a more difficult problem. As there may be no direct evidence of the liability (say, an invoice) understatement may have to be identified using indirect evidence, such as unmatched pre-year-end goods received notes or post-year-end cash book entries.

(b)   Audit work to verify trade payables and purchase accruals would be as follows.

(i)   *Purchases cut-off*

As goods received notes are not used, the normal procedures for auditing cut-off will need to be adapted.

(1)   Examine purchase invoices on either side of the year end to dated supplier's delivery note to ensure invoices have been correctly accrued. (Where the Goods Received department has not date-stamped the delivery date it will be necessary to use the supplier's despatch date.)

(2)   Enquire if the goods received department or bought ledger department are holding any unmatched delivery notes (those without an invoice) relating to the period before the year end.

(ii) *Completeness, existence and ownership*

   (1) Select invoices from the trade payables listing and trace to supporting documentation to ensure that the purchase was for the purpose of the business.

   (2) Reconcile a sample of suppliers' statements with purchase ledger balances. This will highlight any purchases that have been omitted. Where there are major accruals for which statements are not available it may be necessary to carry out a payables circularisation. (A circularisation is not normally the primary procedure to be selected, as the supplier's statement provides more effective evidence and a reconciliation is simpler to carry out than a circularisation.)

   (3) Review balances for unusually low balances with major suppliers.

   (4) Compare the ratio of trade payables to purchases and inventory with the previous year's figures.

   (5) Match cash payments posted in purchase ledger accounts before and after the year end to cash records to ensure they were posted in the right period.

(iii) *Trade payables listing*

   (1) Agree the total unpaid invoices and credit notes to balances on the aged payables listing.

   (2) Agree the total of balances on the aged payables listing to the purchase ledger control account.

   (3) Agree the list of balances to individual ledger accounts and *vice versa*.

   (4) Review the listing for large payable balances and enquire into reasons for them and action being taken.

   (5) Review the control account around the year end for unusual items.

(c) Sundry payables and accruals is an area that lends itself to analytical review and reconciliation techniques, except for liabilities such as income tax and sales tax, which should be checked in detail.

   (i) From the sundry payables and accruals listing confirm that the calculation of accruals is reasonable and verify to subsequent payments. Income tax and related deductions liabilities should also be verified to payroll.

   (ii) Scrutinise post year end payments/invoices received to check for understatement of sundry payables and accruals.

   (iii) Ascertain whether any expenditure is likely to be invoiced a long time after the goods or services are received.

   (iv) Compare sundry payable and accruals with prior year balances and enquire into significant variations.

   (v) Check that the sales tax accrual is disclosed at correct amount by vouching to returns and accounting records.

   (vi) Ensure that no non-deductible tax is reclaimed on the return by scrutinising it.

   (vii) Vouch payments or refunds of sales tax to cash book from sales tax returns.

   (viii) Obtain sales tax returns for the period and check that they have been properly prepared and filed promptly.

   (ix) Test sales tax totals from prime records to monthly/quarterly summaries and test cast summaries and scrutinise for unusual items.

   (x) Review correspondence with taxation authority and results of any recent control visits.

28 'Tap!'

(a) **Audit risks**

There is a higher audit risk associated with a charity as, in the event of problems arising and litigation taking place, the audit firm could experience a significant amount of bad publicity.

Inherent risks

(i) **Cash**. The charity operates with a high number of cash and cheque transactions. A substantial part of its **income** comes from cash donations. Put another way, it is likely that very little of its income comes from direct bank transfers. Also, it is likely that many of the **expenses** which 'Tap!' incurs are also cash expenses. Cash is **risky for audit purposes** because it is **susceptible to loss, miscounting or misappropriation**.

(ii) **Charity**. The theatre company is a charity, and is therefore subject to a high degree of **regulation**. This raises the risk for our audit.

(iii) **Accounting specialist**. The charity employs an administrator, but there is no mention of an accountant. It is **unclear who is going to draft the charity accounts** (which must comply with specialist requirements) but it does not appear that a specialist exists to undertake this job. This increases the risk of errors existing in the accounts.

(iv) **Completeness of income**. As the charity appears to have **no control** over the primary collection of income from box office receipts, there is a significant **risk that income is understated** and that the theatres have not accounted properly to the charity.

(v) **Disclosure of income**. The disclosure of income must be considered. It is unlikely to be appropriate to show the 'net income from theatres' figure. Rather, the gross income less commission should probably be disclosed.

(vi) **Expenditure**. The charity expenses may be well-recorded, or they may be **difficult to substantiate** – this is not clear. It may also be difficult to substantiate payments made to build wells in Africa. We currently have no knowledge about how that aspect of the charity operates. It will be important to check that expenditure is made in accordance with the trust deed. Some essential administrative expense will not necessarily be conducive to the aims of the charity. We must ensure that it is all analysed correctly.

Control

There currently appear to be **no controls over cash** in the charity.

Detection

This is a **first year audit**, so there is little knowledge of the business at present. It is also the **first ever audit** of the charity, so the comparatives are unaudited. We must make this clear in our report, and we will need to undertake more detailed work on the **opening balances**. As the charity is to a large degree **peripatetic**, we may find audit evidence difficult to obtain, if it has not been properly returned to the administrative offices.

Conclusion

This appears to be a high-risk first year audit. It is likely to result in a modified audit opinion.

(b) **Audit procedures**

Income from box office takings

Income from box office takings can be **verified to the statement from the theatre** and the **bank statements** to ensure that it is complete. The **commission** can be agreed by **recalculation**.

It might be necessary to **circularise** a number of the theatres and request **confirmation of the seats sold** for each performance to ensure that income is completely stated on the return from the theatre. (However, if theatres have been defrauding the charity, they are unlikely to confirm this to the auditors. This may have to be an area which is aided by stronger controls over income.)

Income from buckets (theatres and streets)

We must discover whether the charity fills out 'counting sheets' when the buckets of money are originally counted. If so, the **money in buckets can be verified from the original sheet to the banking documentation**.

However, in the **absence of strong controls** over the counting, it will be **impossible to conclude that this income is complete**.

Income from other donations

Donations made over the phone should have been noted on documents and then retained at the administrative offices. Donations made by post should have **original documents**. A sample of these should be **traced to banking documentation** and bank statements.

Again, in the **absence of originating documentation**, it will be **difficult to conclude that income is fairly stated**.

(c) **Controls over cash**

Income from box office takings

It would be a good control over completeness of income to request a **schedule of seats sold** from the theatres for every night a performance is given. This is likely to be information that theatres can print off their systems with no trouble. This will lead to the theatre company having more assurance as to the completeness of income.

Income from buckets

As this income is highly susceptible to loss or misappropriation, strong controls should be put in place.

(i) **Number of people**. If possible, the charity should assign **two people** to each bucket during the collection phase and two people should count the money in the bucket at the end of the day. These people will act as a **check on each other** to ensure that cash is kept more secure.

(ii) **Security**. The security arrangements for buckets should be strong. The charity could invest in a **transportable safe** in which to store the money between collection and banking. It might also be wise to use **collecting tins** rather than buckets, as this simple measure would ensure that the cash was less open to the public. The cash should also be **banked frequently**. It should not be kept unbanked for longer than 24 hours after collection.

(iii) **Recording**. A record should be made of cash counts and it should be signed by both the people that undertook the count. This can provide an initial record of the cash takings.

Other income

The controls over other income will be restricted by the number of staff at the provincial office. It appears that only the administrator may work there regularly. If this is the case, it is going to be difficult to introduce supervision into the cash operations.

All phone donations should be **recorded on pre-numbered documentation** so as to give evidence of completeness.

As the administrator largely works alone, it would be a good idea for the Board of Trustees to carry out a cyclical review of the work of the administrator. This would provide useful protection from problems for both the charity and the administrator.

29 Namul

Determination of inventory levels

(i)   *Deficiency*

        The purchasing manager determines store inventory levels without consulting those who are best placed to judge the local market; the store or sales managers.

(ii)   *Implication*

        Certain clothes and accessories may be initially over-ordered and may need to be sold at reduced prices. This may also result in overvalued inventory (if held at cost) in the management accounts and ultimately the financial statements. Also, some inventory may not be ordered in enough volume to meet demand and the reputation of Greystone may suffer.

(iii)   *Recommendation*

        The purchasing manager should consult (in a meeting or by conference call) the store managers and a joint decision should be made on the initial inventory levels to be ordered for clothes/accessories.

Reordering

(i)   *Deficiency*

        Store managers are responsible for reordering through the purchases manager and it can take four weeks for goods to be received.

(ii)   *Implication*

        The reliance is on store managers to be proactive and order four weeks before a potential stock-out. Without prompting they may order too late and inventory may run out for a period of up to four weeks, resulting in lost revenue.

(iii)   *Recommendation*

        Realistic reorder levels should be established in the inventory system. When inventory is down to the predetermined level, the purchasing manager should be prompted to raise a purchase order (for example, the system may generate an automatic reorder request which is emailed to the purchasing manager).

Internal ordering

(i)   *Deficiency*

        Stores can not transfer goods between each other to meet demand. Customers are directed to try other stores/the website when an item of clothing is sold out.

(ii)   *Implication*

        Revenue is lost because the system is inconvenient for the customer, who may not follow up at other stores, but may have purchased if the goods were transferred to their local store. Additionally, the perceived lack of customer service may damage the store's reputation.

(iii)   *Recommendation*

        An internal ordering system should be set up which allows for the transfer of goods between stores. In particular, stores with very low inventory levels should be able to obtain excess inventories from those with high levels to meet demand while goods are reordered.

Checking of goods received

(i)   *Deficiency*

        Goods received are not checked against purchase orders.

(ii)   *Implication*

Goods which were not ordered in the first place could be received. Once received, it may be difficult to return these goods and they may need to be paid for. In any case, there is a potential unnecessary administrative cost. Additionally, some goods ordered may not be received, leading to insufficient inventory levels and potential lost revenue.

(iii)   *Recommendation*

A copy of authorised orders should be kept at the relevant store and checked against GRNs. If all details are correct, the order should be marked completed and sent to head office. The purchasing clerk should review the purchase orders at regular intervals for incomplete items and investigate why these are not completed.

Review of purchase orders

(i)   *Deficiency*

The purchase orders reviewed and authorised by the purchasing director are aggregated by region.

(ii)   *Implication*

The lack of detail does not allow the purchasing director to make an informed assessment of the buying policies and they may be unsuitable for specific markets within regions.

(iii)   *Recommendation*

A country by country review of orders should be carried out by the purchasing director. Where appropriate, discussions should take place between the purchasing director and local purchasing managers before authorisation of orders.

This letter has been produced for the sole use of your company. It must not be disclosed to a third party, or quoted or referred to, without our written consent. No responsibility is assumed by us to any other person.

We should like to take this opportunity of thanking your staff for their co-operation and assistance during the course of our audit.

Yours faithfully

ABC & Co

Top tips. The answer to (a) includes four well-explained deficiencies, implications and recommendations as four were needed to gain 12 marks. Together with the 2 marks available for presentation, this would be enough for the full 14 marks.

Please note, however, there were a number of alternative deficiencies/implications/recommendations you may have identified, including those shown in the table below.

(i) Deficiency	(ii) Implication	(iii) Recommendation
Quality of goods is not checked by sales assistants, only quantity.	Poor quality clothes are accepted and may not be saleable (also inventory may be temporarily overvalued).	Goods should be checked on arrival for quantity and quality prior to acceptance.
Purchase invoices and GRNs are manually matched, which is time consuming.	The manual process of such a high volume of documents is prone to human error. Invalid invoices may be processed as a result.	A purchasing system should be adopted which allows for logging of GRNs against original invoices, and then electronic/automatic matching of invoices against GRNs. A regular review by the purchasing clerk should then be focused on unmatched items.
A purchase invoice is not put on the system until it is ready for authorisation by the purchasing director.	The purchase ledger will not have all invoices posted, understating liabilities. Also, payables may be paid late.	Invoices not matched should be filed separately, as should those not posted. These should be reviewed at period ends and accrued for to ensure completeness of payables.

30 Ajio

(a) **Risks**

Inherent and control risks (risk of material misstatement)

The complexity and extent of regulations

There is a risk that the charity will **fail to comply** with new and existing regulations. It may also be involved in activities which are not compatible with its charitable status. This is particularly the case where small charities like Ajio are involved, as they may not be run by individuals with the required expertise. However, the fact that the accounts are prepared by a recently retired accountant should reduce the auditor's assessment of this risk.

Completeness of income

There is a risk that **income may be misstated**. This risk is increased by the high levels of cash donations made, as these are not supported by any documentary evidence. Cash may be misappropriated or errors could be made in counting and recording. Completeness of income from bequests would also be difficult to confirm, as there is no predictable pattern in terms of their receipt. This risk is likely to be increased by the fact that Ajio is unlikely to have sophisticated controls in place.

Uncertainty of future income

Due to the **unpredictable nature of income** there is a risk that the charity will undertake projects which it subsequently finds it is unable to finance. This factor will also make it more difficult for the auditor to assess whether the charity is viable on an ongoing basis.

Skills and qualifications of trustees

Control risk is increased if the trustees do not have the skills required to manage the affairs of the charity. It will also be affected by the extent to which they are involved and the amount of time which they are able to devote to its affairs.

Use of volunteers

Control risk is increased by the use of volunteers. The charity is dependent on their integrity and commitment. Shortcomings may arise from a lack of training and from their attitude in that they may resent formal procedures. Bogus volunteers may commit fraud.

Quality of paid staff

Lack of resources may result in staff being employed who are not sufficiently qualified. In the case of Ajio, a part-time bookkeeper has been employed instead of a full-time accountant. If this individual is under constant time pressure the **risk of errors** in the accounts is increased.

Lack of formal procedures

There is a risk that the charity may be run in an informal manner which will result in a **poor control environment**. This problem is likely to be accentuated by a lack of segregation of duties due to the small number of staff involved.

Detection risk

Recent appointment

Detection risk is increased by the fact that the firm has only recently been appointed. The audit team will not be able to rely on their experience of this audit from previous years. In addition, the regulations are new. There is a risk that the auditors will fail to perform specific procedures required by the regulations due to a lack of familiarity with them. Adequate planning will reduce this risk.

Reduced reliance on analytical procedures

Due to the unpredictable nature of income it may be more difficult to rely on the results of analytical procedures to assess the **completeness of income**. This increases detection risk, as analytical procedures are one of the key tests in this area. The results of alternative procedures will reduce this risk.

Implications for overall audit risk

The aim of the auditor is to reduce overall audit risk (the risk of issuing an inappropriate opinion) to a reasonable level. Audit risk is a function of the risk of material misstatement (inherent risk and control risk) and detection risk. As inherent risk and control risk in Ajio appear to be high/medium, **detection risk will need to be low**. This will be achieved by increasing audit work eg increasing sample sizes. Risk areas will also be targeted, in this case income and cash being key balances.

(b) **Audit tests**

Income

- Attend a fundraising event and observe procedures to confirm that they are in accordance with the guidance set down by the charity eg use of sealed collection boxes.
- Count cash at the end of the day and agree to returns submitted by volunteers.
- Match returns submitted with amounts on the bank paying-in slips.
- Trace entry of cash received to cash book and bank statements.
- Review the preparation of monthly bank reconciliations.
- Compare amounts received by cash collections with previous years' balances and forecasts. Discuss major fluctuations with trustees.
- Obtain representations from the trustees regarding the completeness of income.

Expenditure

- Obtain a breakdown of expenditure relating to fundraising events and check that the nature of the cost is reasonable.
- For a sample of expenses trace the cost to a supporting invoice or other documentation.
- Compare the overall level of expenditure with previous years and with budgets. Discuss any major fluctuations with management.
- For a sample of major expenses confirm that the expenditure has been authorised by the trustees.

31 Going concern

Workings

The following significant accounting ratios are based on the accounts provided in the question.

	20X2	20X3	20X4	20X5	20X6
Gross profit (%)	23.50	10.90	14.20	20.20	19.70
Other expenses: sales (%)	14.10	10.90	14.40	14.40	15.30
Interest: sales (%)	0.90	1.10	5.20	5.50	6.20
Net profit (%)	8.50	(1.10)	(5.40)	0.30	(1.80)
Current ratio	1.39	0.91	0.73	0.73	0.76
Liquidity ratio	0.80	0.59	0.46	0.37	0.34
Leverage (%)	84.71	57.14	9.52	9.45	4.83
Inventory (months)	1.68	2.28	2.26	2.77	3.57
Receivables (months)	1.75	3.66	3.24	2.26	2.32
Payables (months)	2.26	5.43	4.43	4.43	5.09

Notes

$$\text{Inventory age} = \frac{\text{Year-end inventory}}{\text{Cost of sales}} \times 12$$

$$\text{Receivables' age} = \frac{\text{Year-end receivables}}{\text{Sales}} \times 12$$

$$\text{Payables' age} = \frac{\text{Year-end payables}}{\text{Sales}} \times 12$$

$$\text{Leverage} = \frac{\text{Shareholders' equity} + \text{Long-term loans} + \text{Bank overdraft} + \text{Lease}}{\text{Shareholders' equity}}$$

(a) The various factors in the accounts which may be indicative of going concern problems are as follows.

   (i) Only losses or low profits are being made and the company is not generating sufficient funds to finance the expansion required.

   (ii) There has been a dramatic increase in the level of overdraft over the last year, and there seems to be little prospect of the borrowing being reduced and the security is threatened.

   (iii) There are signs of overtrading, as the expansion has been financed by borrowings and the increase in current assets is being financed by trade accounts payable.

   (iv) The leverage is low and decreasing, with very little security being available for the loans.

   (v) There is a low current ratio and short-term funds are being used to finance long-term assets.

   (vi) The liquidity ratio is low and decreasing and the company's ability to meet its liabilities on demand must be very questionable.

   (vii) Inventory levels are increasing, suggesting that one or more of the following problems may exist: deteriorating sales, poor inventory control, obsolete or slow-moving inventories.

   (viii) The value and age of trade accounts payable are increasing: some suppliers are probably having to wait a considerable time before being paid and it can only be a matter of time before pressure is put on the company by one or more of its creditors.

   (ix) High and increasing interest charges make the company very vulnerable, especially in a period of recession and high interest rates.

   (x) The fluctuating gross profit would suggest that the company's profit margins are under pressure. The present level of gross profit does not seem sufficient given the company's high level of expenses.

(b) The other important steps to be taken by the auditors in determining whether or not the company may be properly regarded as a going concern at the year end would include:

   (i) Review carefully the cash and profit forecasts for the next year to see if they suggest any improvement in the company's position.

   (ii) Seek some evidence that the company's bank is prepared to continue supporting the company.

   (iii) Review the level of post year end trading to see if this supports the forecasts and shows any signs of improvement in the company's position.

   (iv) Examine correspondence files for any evidence that suppliers might be putting pressure on the company for repayment of monies owing.

   (v) Consider how the company's position compares with similar companies in the same business.

   (vi) Discuss generally the situation with management and review any recovery plans which they may have in mind.

32 Audit review and finalisation

(a) The auditor shall perform audit procedures designed to obtain sufficient appropriate audit evidence that all events up to the date of their report that may require adjustment or disclosure in the financial statements have been identified. These procedures should take place as near as possible to the date of the auditor's report. They would include, for example, reading minutes of meetings with shareholders and audit committee meetings, reviewing the entity's latest interim accounts, and reviewing procedures that management have for identifying subsequent events. The auditor shall request that management and those charged with governance provide a written representation that all subsequent events requiring adjustment or disclosure have been adjusted or disclosed.

The auditor has no obligation to undertake audit procedures or make enquiries regarding the financial statements after the date of the auditor's report. Between this date and the date of issue of the financial statements, it is the management's responsibility to inform the auditors of any facts that might affect the financial statements. If such facts do arise which the auditor becomes aware of, they shall consider whether the financial statements need amending, discuss the matter with management and take appropriate action. If the financial statements are amended, a new audit report must be issued. If management refuses to make any amendments required, the auditor shall modify the audit opinion.

After the financial statements have been issued, the auditor has no obligation to make any enquiry regarding the financial statements. Where the auditor becomes aware of facts that may affect the financial statements after they have been issued, they shall consider whether they need to be revised and shall discuss with management and take appropriate action. If amendments are made to the financial statements, the auditor shall issue a new audit report which shall include an emphasis of matter paragraph referring to a note in the financial statements that discusses the reason for the revised financial statements in more detail.

(b) Written representation:

(i) Addressed to the auditor

(ii) Signed and dated, normally the date of the auditor's report

(iii) Acknowledgement from management for the design and implementation of internal control to prevent and detect error

(iv) A statement that management believes that the effects of uncorrected misstatements are immaterial, both individually and in aggregate; the letter should contain a summary of these items

(v) A statement confirming the completeness of information provided regarding the identification of related parties

(vi) A statement that the financial statements are free from material misstatements, including omissions

(vii) A statement that the management have made available to the auditors all books of account and supporting documentation and all minutes of meetings of shareholders and the board of directors

(viii) A statement that the entity has satisfactory title to all assets and there are no liens or encumbrances on the entity's assets, except where disclosed in the notes to the accounts

(ix) A statement that all liabilities, both actual and contingent, have been disclosed in the accounts, as well as any guarantees to third parties

(x) A statement that there have been no events subsequent to the year end which require adjustment or disclosure in the accounts, other than where specifically disclosed in the accounts

(c)   The auditors must perform and document an overall review of the financial statements before they can reach an opinion. This review gives the auditors a reasonable basis for their opinion on the financial statements. At the review stage, the auditors consider compliance with accounting regulations, consistency and reasonableness and application of accounting policies.

Analytical procedures are a very useful tool at this stage of the audit. They can be used to calculate important accounting ratios, changes in products or customers, price and mix changes, variances, trends in production and sales and variations caused by industry or economic factors. Any significant fluctuations and unexpected relationships must be investigated through enquiries with management and obtaining appropriate audit evidence relevant to **management's responses**, and **performing other audit procedures** considered necessary in the circumstances.

33 Wiseguys National Bakeries

(i)   *Freehold property*

In past years this property has been shown in the statement at its original cost, whereas it is now restated at $1,250,000 as professionally valued during the year. The auditor is satisfied as to the basis of the revaluation, adjustment to and disclosure made in the financial statements. As a result of the audit evidence obtained, no further reference to the property revaluation will be required in the auditor's report.

(ii)   *Allowance for doubtful debts*

No part of the debt of $45,000 due from XYZ Co will be recovered by the company. Since the financial statements which the directors have approved include no allowance for this debt, a qualified opinion should be issued.

It will be necessary for the auditor's report to state that in the auditor's opinion, except for the failure to make such allowance, the financial statements present fairly, in all material respects (or give a true and fair view of), the state of the company's affairs and its results.

The Basis for Opinion paragraph should explain that no allowance has been made against an amount of $45,000 owing by the customer, while the auditor believes such amount to be irrecoverable.

(iii)   *Loan to a director*

The outstanding loan of $22,000 constitutes a related party transaction, and disclosure is required under IAS 24. Since no disclosures have been made in the financial statements, and the amount is material ($36k/$450k = 8% of profit before tax), the auditors should issue a qualified opinion.

The opinion paragraph in the auditor's report should state that in the auditor's opinion, except for the failure to make such a disclosure, the financial statements present fairly, in all material respects (or give a true and fair view of), the state of the company's affairs and its results.

The Basis for Opinion paragraph should describe the outstanding loan to the director, including:

–   The amount of the loan and any interest
–   The zero outstanding balance at the year end
–   Terms and conditions

34 Homes'r'Us

(i) **Customer going into liquidation**

Audit procedures

- Assess the likelihood of recovery of this amount by discussion with the directors of Homes'r'Us.

- Confirm the amount of the amount outstanding as at the year end by inspection of the receivables ledger and correspondence with the customer.

- Review any correspondence between the company and the customer to assess the likelihood of recovery of any amounts.

- Obtain a written representation point regarding the amount outstanding from the customer from the directors of Homes'r'Us.

- Confirm the details of the bankruptcy to documents received by Homes'r'Us from the liquidator.

Impact on financial statements

The financial statements will need to be amended, as this is an example of an adjusting event after the reporting period. It provides additional information concerning the recoverability of the debt at the reporting date.

Revenue, profit and net assets will all be overstated by $7.5 million if the accounts are not adjusted. The amount represents 10.7% of profit before tax and 1.4% of revenue so is clearly material.

An adjustment is required in the financial statements to reduce the receivables balance and profits.

Effect on auditor's report

The effect of the matter on the financial statements is clearly material. If the adjustments required are made, then there would be no effect on the audit report.

If the directors refused to make the adjustment required, the audit opinion would be modified on the basis that the accounts are not free from material misstatement and a qualified 'except for' opinion would be issued, as the matter is material but not pervasive.

(ii) **Claim for unfair dismissal**

Audit procedures

- Discuss the case for unfair dismissal with the directors of Homes'r'Us to find out background of case, date when claim was lodged and assessment of success.

- Review lawyer's correspondence regarding this case, as it may have an impact for next year's audit.

- Review any press reports in the local or national papers about this claim against the company.

- Review minutes of board meetings regarding this case and any other claim cases against the company.

- Obtain written representations on this matter from the directors of Homes'r'Us.

Impact on financial statements

A provision for this claim is not required since the requirements for recognising a provision under IAS 37 *Provisions, contingent liabilities and contingent assets* are not met. Under IAS 37, a provision should be recognised when there is a present obligation as a result of a past event, it is probable that a transfer of economic benefits will be required to settle it and a reliable estimate can be made.

In this case, it appears unlikely that Mr Evans will be successful in his claim and so no provision should be recognised in the financial statements for the year ended 31 December 20X7.

Disclosure of a contingent liability is also unlikely to be required since the possibility of any transfer in settlement appears to be remote.

Effect on auditor's report

There would be no effect on the audit report as a result of this matter, as no amendment would be required to the financial statements. An unmodified report on the financial statements could therefore be issued.

(iii)   **Fire**

Audit procedures

- Discuss fire with management of Homes'r'Us to clarify facts of the situation.
- Read minutes of board meetings and any reports submitted by insurers.
- Review insurance documents to confirm that damage cause by the fire is covered.

Impact on financial statements

The fire at the storage depot is a non-adjusting event after the reporting period – it does not relate to conditions which existed at the year end. It is unlikely that the fire is significant enough to impact on the going concern of the company. Disclosure of the event surrounding the fire should be made, together with an estimate of the financial effect.

Effect on auditor's report

Provided that adequate disclosure has been made of the event and its financial impact, there would be no need to modify the audit opinion as a result of this incident. An emphasis of matter paragraph drawing attention to this issue is probably not likely to be required, provided adequate disclosure has been made in the notes to the financial statements.

35 Builders Merchants

(i)   This represents a potential material limitation on scope because the 'missing' inventory represents 12% of the total value of the inventory. The auditor would expect all inventory counting sheets to be available. The auditor's opinion would be modified.

The opinion paragraph would state that 'except for' adjustments that may have been necessary in relation to this inventory, the financial statements present fairly, in all material respects (or give a true and fair view).

The auditor's report would include a basis of opinion paragraph after the opinion paragraph, which would refer to the fact that the inventory counting sheets for this depot were lost. The same paragraph would explain, in relation to inventory quantities:

- All information and explanations considered necessary were not obtained.
- The auditor was unable to determine whether proper accounting records were kept.

(ii)   This represents a material misstatement. The debt represents 8% of the total receivables balance and 45% of the profit for the year.

The auditor's opinion would be modified. A qualified opinion would be issued.

The qualified opinion paragraph would state that 'except for' the absence of this allowance the financial statements are presented fairly, in all material respects (or give a true and fair view), in accordance with the applicable financial reporting framework.

The basis of opinion paragraph would refer to the fact that the customer is in liquidation and there is little prospect of payment. It would also state that net assets and profits are overstated by $45,000.

(iii)   As the client is listed, its financial statements should include a statement of cash flows.

The auditor's opinion should therefore be qualified, as the financial statements are materially misstated. This misstatement is not pervasive to the financial statements; it is limited to the statement of cash flows, so this would be a qualified opinion.

The Qualified Opinion paragraph will state that the financial statements give a true and fair view and have been prepared, in all material respects, in accordance with an applicable financial reporting framework except for the omission of a statement of cash flows.

The Basis for Opinion paragraph will refer to the fact that the financial statements do not contain a statement of cash flows and include the figures required.

(iv)   It appears that the disclosure in the financial statements is adequate and there appears to be no basis on which to make a provision in the financial statements.

However, the auditor's report will be affected by the fact that there is an uncertainty affecting the business. The auditor will have to decide whether the matter is fundamental to users' understanding. If so, the auditor's report should include an emphasis of matter paragraph beneath the opinion paragraph describing this matter. It should also state that the auditor's opinion on the financial statements is not modified in relation to this matter.

If the auditor does not consider the matter to be fundamental, the substantial nature of the claim may still warrant its inclusion as a 'matter of most significance' within the Key Audit Matters section.

The auditor may also need to consider the effect of the claim on the company's ability to continue as a going concern. For example, an adverse outcome could mean that the going concern assumption may no longer be appropriate. If this is the case, the auditor should include a separate 'Material uncertainty related to going concern' paragraph.

Index

Note. **Key Terms** and their references are given in **bold**.

Review Form – Paper F8 Audit and Assurance (02/16)

Please help us to ensure that the ACCA learning materials we produce remain as accurate and user-friendly as possible. We cannot promise to answer every submission we receive, but we do promise that it will be read and taken into account when we update this Study Text.

Name: _____

Address: _____

_____

_____

How have you used this Study Text?
(Tick one box only)

☐ On its own (book only)

☐ On a BPP in-centre course _____

☐ On a BPP online course

☐ On a course with another college

☐ Other _____

Why did you decide to purchase this Study Text? *(Tick one box only)*

☐ Have used BPP Study Texts in the past

☐ Recommendation by friend/colleague

☐ Recommendation by a lecturer at college

☐ Saw information on BPP website

☐ Saw advertising

☐ Other _____

During the past six months do you recall seeing/receiving any of the following?
(Tick as many boxes as are relevant)

☐ Our advertisement in *ACCA Student Accountant*

☐ Our advertisement in *Pass*

☐ Our advertisement in *PQ*

☐ Our brochure with a letter through the post

☐ Our website www.bpp.com

Which (if any) aspects of our advertising do you find useful?
(Tick as many boxes as are relevant)

☐ Prices and publication dates of new editions

☐ Information on Study Text content

☐ Facility to order books

☐ None of the above

Which BPP products have you used?

Study Text ☑   Passcards ☐   Other ☐

Kit ☐   i-Pass ☐

Your ratings, comments and suggestions would be appreciated on the following areas.

	Very useful	Useful	Not useful
Introductory section	☐	☐	☐
Chapter introductions	☐	☐	☐
Key terms	☐	☐	☐
Quality of explanations	☐	☐	☐
Case studies and other examples	☐	☐	☐
Exam focus points	☐	☐	☐
Questions and answers in each chapter	☐	☐	☐
Fast forwards and chapter roundups	☐	☐	☐
Quick quizzes	☐	☐	☐
Question Bank	☐	☐	☐
Answer Bank	☐	☐	☐
Index	☐	☐	☐

Overall opinion of this Study Text	Excellent ☐	Good ☐	Adeqate ☐	Poor ☐

Do you intend to continue using BPP products?   Yes ☐   No ☐

On the reverse of this page is space for you to write your comments about our Study Text We welcome your feedback.

The author of this edition can be emailed at: accaqueries@bpp.com

Please return this form to: Head of ACCA & FIA Programmes, BPP Learning Media Ltd, FREEPOST, London, W12 8AA

TELL US WHAT YOU THINK

Please note any further comments and suggestions/errors below. For example, was the text accurate, readable, concise, user-friendly and comprehensive?